PATERNOSTER BIBLICAL MONOGRAPHS

Lukan Theology in the Light of the Gospel's Literary Structure

PATERNOSTER BIBLICAL MONOGRAPHS

A full listing of titles in both this series and
Paternoster Theological Monographs
appears at the end of this book

PATERNOSTER BIBLICAL MONOGRAPHS

Lukan Theology in the Light of the Gospel's Literary Structure

Douglas S. McComiskey

Eugene, Oregon

Wipf and Stock Publishers
199 W 8th Ave, Suite 3
Eugene, OR 97401

Lukan Theology in the Light of the Gospel's Literary Structure
By McComiskey, Douglas S.
Copyright©2004 Paternoster
ISBN: 1-59752-786-6
Publication date 6/22/2006
Previously published by Paternoster, 2004

This Edition Published by Wipf and Stock Publishers
by arrangement with Paternoster

Paternoster
9 Holdom Avenue
Bletchley
Milton Keyes, MK1 1QR
Great Britain

Unless otherwise stated, Scripture quotations are taken from the
NEW AMERICAN STANDARD BIBLE
Copyright © 1960, 1962, 1963, 1968, 1971, 1972, 1973, 1975, 1977 1995
by the Lockman Foundation. Used by permission.
Also Nestle-Aland 26th ed. of the Greek NT.

l scholarship by
nographs of high
angelical tradition
ns who recognise
sage and assent to
ersity within this
freedom for frank
y and sometimes
est of writing by
founded biblical

I. Howard M
Aberdeen, Sc

Richard J. B
Professor, Un

Craig Blomb
Colorado, US

Robert P. Gor

Tremper Lon
Biblical Studi

To my wife, Robin, with deepest affection and love

and

*to my father (1928–1996)
for his faithful love,
his warm friendship,
his eminent scholarship,
and his example of devotion to Christ*

Contents

	Preface	xv
	Introduction	**1**
1	Lukan Correspondences and Structure: Previous Work and a New Contribution	1
2	The Analysis of Structure in Narrative	6
3	Eleven Tests for Intentionality	8
3.1	*General Presentation of the Tests*	12
3.2	*Validation of the Tests: Luke 1:5–38 as a Test Case for the Tests for Intentionality*	14
4	A New Proposal for the Structure of Luke	27
5	The Need for this Study	31

	Chapter 1 **Lukan Correspondences from the Literary Perspective of Robert C. Tannehill**	**33**
1	Previews, Reviews, Echoes, Parallels, and Type-scene in Luke: Theory and Evaluation of Selected Examples	37
1.1	*Preview and Review*	37
1.2	*Echo and Parallel*	44
1.3	*Type-scene*	55
2	Correspondences between Luke and Acts	58
2.1	*Preview and Review*	60
2.1.1	PREVIEW OF ACTS IN LUKE	60
2.1.2	REVIEW OF LUKE IN ACTS	67
2.2	*Echo and Parallel*	72

	Chapter 2 **Lukan Correspondences Observed by Charles H. Talbert**	**76**
1	Talbert's Theoretical Basis for the Existence of Architectonic Patterns	78
1.1	*Interplay between Art and Literature*	79
1.2	*Literary Precedent*	79
1.3	*The Nature of Talbert's Architectonic Correspondences and How He Supports Them*	81

2	Evaluation of Talbert's Patterns Using the Tests for Intentionality	89
2.1	*General Correspondences between Luke and Acts and Their Analysis*	90
2.2	*Focus on Specific General Correspondences between Luke and Acts and Their Analysis*	103
2.2.1	DEVELOPMENT OF GENERAL PARALLEL 5	104
2.2.2	DEVELOPMENT OF GENERAL PARALLEL 12	108
2.2.3	DEVELOPMENT OF GENERAL PARALLEL 26	111
2.3	*Correspondence between Luke 9 and Acts 1*	115
2.4	*Correspondences between Luke 24 and Acts 1*	119
2.5	*Correspondences between Luke 1:57–80 and Luke 2:1–52*	121
2.6	*Correspondences between Luke 3:1–20 and Luke 3:21–4:15*	123
2.7	*Correspondences between Luke 4:16–7:17 and Luke 7:18–8:56*	126
2.8	*Correspondences between Luke 9:1–48 and Luke 22:7–23:16*	135
2.9	*Chiastic Correspondence between Luke 10:21–13:30 and Luke 14:1–18:30*	147
3	Evaluation of Talbert's Understanding of the Significance behind the Correspondences	157

Chapter 3
Analysis of Ancient Literature Relevant to the Structure of Luke — 163

1	Examples of Literature Preceding and Contemporary with Luke and Bearing Similar Structure	163
1.1	*Old Testament Precedent Structures*	164
1.1.1	ELIJAH-ELISHA CYCLES	164
1.1.2	1 SAMUEL 9–31	166
1.1.3	2 SAMUEL 11–20	167
1.1.4	2 CHRONICLES 14–35	168
1.1.5	JUDGES	170
1.1.6	JOB	171
1.1.7	DANIEL	172
1.2	*Similar Structure in New Testament Writings*	173
1.2.1	JOHN 2:1–12:50	173
1.2.2	MATTHEW	177

1.2.3	ACTS	179
1.2.4	REVELATION	182
1.2.5	1 JOHN	183
1.3	*Precedent Structures from Greco-Roman Literature*	184
1.3.1	HERODOTUS' HISTORIES	185
1.3.2	THUCYDIDES' HISTORY OF THE PELOPONNESIAN WAR	186
1.3.3	PLUTARCH'S LIVES	187
1.3.4	PLUTARCH'S ALCIBIADES	188
1.3.5	LIVY'S HISTORY	188
1.3.6	VERGIL'S AENEID	188
2	Basis for Structural Correspondence: An Analysis of the Above Precedent and Contemporary Cases	192
3	Thomas L. Brodie's Greco-Roman *Imitatio* as a Possible Lukan Compositional Mechanism	194
	Excursus: The Deuteronomy Hypothesis	200

Chapter 4
A New Proposal for the Structure and Composition of Luke 4:14–24:53 — 204

1	The Cyclical Narrative Structure of Luke 4:14–24:53	204
1.1	*Presentation of the Narrative Structure*	204
1.1.1	PARALLEL NARRATIVE FEATURES THAT ESTABLISH THE STRATA	207
1.1.2	DISCUSSION OF THE NARRATIVE STRATA ACROSS THE FOUR CYCLES	210
1.2	*Domain and Size of the Units that Comprise the Narrative Strata*	214
1.3	*Reasonableness of the Narrative Bases for the Correspondences*	227
1.4	*Application of the Tests for Intentionality to the Cyclical Narrative Structure of Luke 4:14–24:53*	228
2	Lukan Introductions to Episodes: An Argument for Markan Priority in Lukan Composition	269
2.1	*The Need for Another Argument*	270
2.2	*A New and Irreversible Argument*	273
2.3	*Introductions to Episodes with a Change of Scene*	273
2.4	*Introductions with Minimal Change in Scene*	278
2.5	*Analysis of Introductions in Markan Sections of Luke*	279
2.6	*Markan Redaction of Lukan Episodic Order, Assuming Lukan Priority*	281

Chapter 5
Literary and Theological Purposes and Implications of the Proposed Narrative Structure of Luke — 285

1	Literary Purposes and Implications of the Structure	286
1.1	*Reader Oriented Purposes*	286
1.2	*Lukan Interpretation of Passages*	293
1.3	*Contribution to Redaction Criticism*	294
1.4	*The Composition of the Gospel of Luke and the Proto-Luke Hypothesis*	295
2	Theological Purposes and Implications of the Structure	302
2.1	*Christology Communicated through the Structure (Strata 1–3 and 11)*	302
2.1.1	DEATH AND RESURRECTION AS THE GOAL OF JESUS' INCARNATE MINISTRY (STRATA 1 AND 11)	303
2.1.2	PROPHETIC STATUS OF JESUS (STRATUM 2)	303
2.1.3	AUTHORITY (STRATUM 3)	305
2.1.3.1	Authority Displayed through Conflict	305
2.1.3.2	Authority Displayed through Healing	307
2.1.3.3	Authority Displayed over Disciples	308
2.2	*Salvation and the Crowds/People (Stratum 4)*	309
2.3	*Discipleship (Strata 6–9)*	309
2.3.1	THREAT AGAINST DISCIPLES FROM MISGUIDED RELIGIOUS LEADERS (STRATUM 6)	310
2.3.2	CHALLENGE TO GROW IN FAITH (STRATUM 7)	311
2.3.3	RETURN OF CHRIST AS MOTIVATION FOR GREATER FAITH AND MINISTRY (STRATA 7 AND 8)	312
2.3.4	ROLE OF THE DISCIPLES AS APPRENTICES AND PERPETUATORS OF CHRIST'S MINISTRY (STRATUM 9)	316
2.4	*Ecclesiology*	317
3	Conclusion	318

Chapter 6
Conclusion — 320

Appendix A
Evaluation of Talbert's Correspondences within Acts — 327

1	Correspondences between Acts 1–12 and 13–28	327
2	Additional Correspondences between Acts 1–12 and 13–28	331
3	Correspondences between Acts 1:12–4:23 and 4:24–5:42	338

Appendix B
The Preface to Luke as a Possible Indication of the Gospel's Structural Nature — 341

Appendix C
The Relationship between Intertextuality and the Theory Espoused in This Book — 345

1	The Problem of the Author in the Theory of Intertextuality	346
1.1	*The Intertextualists' Tendency to Deny the Author's Importance*	346
1.2	*The Debate among Literary Theorists: Arguments in Favor of the Author's Importance*	348
2	The Form of Intertextuality Exhibited in this Book	352

Bibliography — 356

Index of Scripture and Ancient Texts — 369

Author Index — 385

Preface

This work began as a Ph.D. thesis, submitted to the University of Aberdeen in 1997, and I am delighted that it will now reach a much broader readership. I am deeply grateful to Paternoster Press for their willingness to publish it and for their cheerful assistance at every stage in its preparation for publication. The focus of the work is on the literary structure of the Gospel of Luke and ultimately on theology that may be derived from its structure.

The Gospel of Luke exhibits numerous correspondences between pericopes. These take various forms and work at differing levels. For example, previews guide the reader by pointing forward in the narrative to other material that Luke considered relevant to the pericope at hand. Correspondence in such cases is often somewhat subtle. There are however sets of correspondences between broad sections of material that constitute the very structure of the Gospel. The various correspondences intentionally constructed by Luke, at whatever level, reflect how he understood the individual units of tradition that he incorporated into Luke-Acts. They reflect an interrelationship he perceived between the corresponding pericopes. Accordingly, in the process of composing his volumes, Luke read the individual units of tradition in the light of each other. In this study, the intent of Luke is frequently sought through the evidence of the correspondences.

In the first chapter, the work of Robert C. Tannehill on Luke-Acts is evaluated. He is representative of scholars who study correspondences that are not strictly structural in nature. In the Introduction, we formulate eleven tests that evaluate the likelihood of authorial intent behind proposed correspondences and apply them to Tannehill's work in the first chapter. Many of his proposals are demonstrated to be very likely intentional. One great benefit of his work is the exploration of how Luke encourages the reader to read passages in the light of other passages within the Gospel. Aspects of his theory will serve us well in chapters four and five.

The second chapter applies the same eleven tests mentioned above to the correspondences suggested by Charles H. Talbert. His observations cover often extensive sets of correspondences between different blocks of material in Luke-Acts and are representative of other such scholarly proposals. He considers these correspondences to be the architecture, the very framework of Luke-Acts. Under scrutiny of our eleven tests, authorial intent is proven probable in many of his proposed sets of correspondences. Talbert's analysis of literary structure in Luke-Acts and other Greco-Roman literature provides a strong theoretical foundation for our own proposal in chapter four.

Chapter three establishes the literary precedent for the multi-fold parallel cyclical structure of Luke to be proposed in chapter four (e.g. ABC... A'B'C'...A''B''C''...). Numerous examples are presented of OT, Greco-Roman and NT texts that bear a similar patterned architecture, including Acts.

The new proposal for the cyclical structure of Luke 4:14–24:53 is developed in chapter four. The eleven tests for authorial intent are applied and the results strongly favor its intentional construction. Additionally, a viable method of Lucan composition, consistent with the proposed structure, is suggested.

Chapter five discusses the many implications of the structure, both literary and theological. New ground is broken in several areas. Importantly, we shed fresh light on numerous commonly noted Lukan themes and bring to light some themes rarely if ever noted.

The concluding chapter highlights the more important contributions of the thesis. It sketches out how these integrate into a cohesive body that suggests further exploration and benefit to Lucan scholarship beyond the scope of the book.

Appendix A offers an analysis of correspondences within Acts proposed by Talbert. Appendix B investigates whether Luke's prologue provides any indication of the Gospel's literary structure. Finally, Appendix C discusses how our thesis is consistent with a form of the literary theory called "intertextuality," namely the form that studies the interrelationships between various sub-texts within a single text and that accepts the importance of the author for interpretation of a text.

For the reader who finds the detailed analysis of chapters one and two a bit heavy going, a phenomenon that sometimes happens with works that were theses in a previous life, I recommend moving to chapters three through five and the Conclusion. These are certainly the heart and soul of the book.

Sincerest appreciation is expressed to the supervisor of my doctoral study, Professor I. Howard Marshall, for his keen insights, wise guidance, persistent cheerfulness and warm godliness. His contribution served only to strengthen the work. All weaknesses are entirely my responsibility. Thanks to the Committee of Vice-Chancellors and Principals is owed for their provision of an Overseas Research Studentship award, which greatly diminished the financial pressures of study abroad. To my wife, Robin, who regularly served as a capable sounding board and who, with remarkable generosity, kindly earned our keep while I studied, my deepest gratitude is offered.

Douglas S. McComiskey
Ridley Theological College and Seminary
Melbourne, Australia

Introduction

Throughout the years, Lukan scholars have detected elements of structure, even patterned structure, in the gospel of Luke ranging from a few verses to many pericopes. Often a broad consensus is achieved over the basic thrust of a proposal, such as the parallelism between John the Baptist and Jesus in the infancy narrative. Often there is little agreement, especially over finer details. Underneath all this, there is common recognition that there is more to the structure of the Third Gospel than is immediately obvious and than has been unearthed to the present. As the title of this work indicates, Luke will be analyzed for literary structure, structural features and theology that may be derived from its structure. A structure for the entire Gospel will be presented and defended. Related to this, a possible process of composition will be explored in conjunction with the study of structure. Ultimately, our focus will be the unique theological perspective yielded by an awareness of the above. Several areas of study are involved and these are outlined below.

1 Lukan Correspondences and Structure: Previous Work and a New Contribution

Luke's arrangement of material and his variety of compositional techniques often reveal his perception of interrelatedness between pericopes. As he considered where to place various accounts in his Gospel, or how to interconnect them through previews and the like, the decisions were greatly affected by similarities (or interrelatedness) he observed between them. Our interest is in this sense, perhaps, as much in the Lukan compositional process as in the final product. We will study the pervasive Lukan technique of linking units of tradition for the reader using various types of correspondences. By this method, the Evangelist communicates how he has interpreted the linked passages in light of each other. He reveals the interrelatedness he discerns. The phenomenon ranges from the subtle use of a brief preview or review to bold structural interconnection between extensive blocks of material. Thus, our study covers correspondences that are *not* structural, but guide the reading process by pointing ahead or behind to material that Luke considered relevant for interpreting the passage at hand. It also covers correspondences that *are* structural. These too guide the reading process in similar fashion, but they additionally reflect the intended organization of material from the level of a section to that of the whole Gospel. Our proposal contributes to the work of scholars on non-structural correspondences and especially on correspondences that shape entire sections of the Gospel. It furthermore develops a detailed parallel structure that organizes all of Luke 4:14–24:53, and therefore, coupled with the generally accepted parallel structure of 1:1–4:13, covers the entire Gospel.

The phenomenon of Lukan correlations has been observed and studied by numerous scholars at its various levels. Robert Tannehill[1] for instance probes into how Luke links passages through such techniques as echoes and previews where limited numbers of pericopes, two or so, are involved. Charles Talbert[2] considers the interrelatedness that spans larger blocks of Lukan material and accordingly focuses on the broader structural level of Luke-Acts.[3]

Chapter 1 – Tannehill's two-volume work, *The Narrative Unity of Luke-Acts*, is the most thorough analysis available of non-structural Lukan correspondences such as previews, reviews, echoes, parallels and type-scenes. One of his primary purposes is to demonstrate that the Evangelist joins Luke and Acts together. Previews, reviews and other literary devices span the two books and thereby directly show their narrative unity. Further evidence of unity is found in that the same devices employed in Luke, and the manner in which they are used, are also evident in Acts.

A summary and evaluation of Tannehill's study of the Gospel and its links to Acts are valuable to us in three ways. First, he has effectively

---

1   Robert C. Tannehill, *The Narrative Unity of Luke-Acts: A Literary Interpretation, Vol. 1: The Gospel According to Luke* (Philadelphia: Fortress Press, 1986); and *The Narrative Unity of Luke-Acts: A Literary Interpretation, Vol. 2: The Acts of the Apostles* (Philadelphia: Fortress Press, 1990).
2   Charles H. Talbert, *Literary Patterns, Theological Themes and the Genre of Luke-Acts* (Missoula: Scholars Press, 1974).
3   Of course, Luke is not the only Synoptic Gospel to receive attention regarding its narrative structures and interrelatedness. Among many works are David Rhoads, and Donald Michie, *Mark as Story: An Introduction to the Narrative of a Gospel* (Philadelphia: Fortress Press, 1982) 45–55; John Paul Heil, "The Progressive Narrative Pattern of Mark 14,53–16,8," *Bib* 73 (1992) 331–58; Joanna Dewey, "Mark as Interwoven Tapestry: Forecasts and Echoes for a Listening Audience," *CBQ* 53 (1991) 221–36; Warren Carter, "Kernels and Narrative Blocks: The Structure of Matthew's Gospel," *CBQ* 54 (1992) 463–81; and David R. Bauer, *The Structure of Matthew's Gospel: A Study in Literary Design*, JSNT Supplement Series 31 (Sheffield: Sheffield Academic Press, 1988).

demonstrated that Luke used a wide variety of correspondences and constituents to these correspondences. Our evaluation will confirm this. Second, he reveals Luke's strong predisposition to interconnect passages in various ways and often with fine detail. This is evident within Luke and between Luke and Acts.[4] Third, he investigates the functions and purposes of Lukan previews, reviews, echoes, parallels and type-scenes. Tannehill shows concern for the interpretative impact of correlations, the effect that they have on the interpretation and theology of the individual passages involved. This draws out Lukan interpretation of the material. These three points provide solid groundwork for chapters 4 and 5. In chapter 4, a structure for Luke is offered that is founded on interconnections of the kind and of the level of detail observed by Tannehill. Indeed, some of Tannehill's observed correspondences find representation in it. In chapter 5, the theological and interpretative implications of our proposal are developed. The strengths and weaknesses of Tannehill's method are instructive here.

The main weakness of Tannehill's contribution is that he has insufficient controls to evaluate whether his observed interconnections are indeed of Lukan intent. This is the thrust of our evaluation of his work in chapter 1. Eleven tests for authorial intent are proposed and defended below (see pages 8ff.). These are applied to selected correspondences offered by Tannehill to evaluate the strength of his conclusions.

Chapter 1 is divided into two main parts. The first discusses the theory behind Tannehill's correspondences (previews, reviews, echoes, parallels, and type-scenes) and evaluates selected examples that exist within Luke. The second part, founded on the theory of the first, evaluates major interconnections between Luke and Acts.

Chapter 2 – Of all scholars who have written on the subject of structured parallels in Luke-Acts, Talbert offers the most numerous and rigorously supported collection in his book, *Literary Patterns, Theological Themes and the Genre of Luke-Acts*. Quite intentionally, he includes an impressive proportion of other such scholarly observations within his own proposal.[5] These correspondences are more extensive, detailed and struc-

---

4 Tannehill explores interconnections between pericopes within Acts in volume 2 of *Narrative Unity*, but our concern is specifically with the Gospel. Correspondences within Acts are considerably less relevant to the nature of Luke than are those between Luke and Acts.
5 See for example F.C. Baur, *Paul: the Apostle of Jesus Christ* (London: Williams & Norgate, 1875) 6, 81, 87, 95, 96, 98, 104, 145, 150, 165, 174, 191, 196, 198, 202, 227, 229, 231, 237, 240, 250; Matthias Schneckenburger, *Über den Zweck der Apostelgeschichte: Zugleich eine Ergänzung der neueren Commentare* (Bern: Christian Fischer, 1841) 52–6; Reni Laurentin, *Structure et théologie de Luc I–II*, E. Bib (Paris: Gabalda, 1964) 32–3; M.D. Goulder, "The Chiastic Structure of the Lucan Journey," in F.L. Cross (ed.), *Studia Evangelica, II*, Texte und Untersuchungen 87,

tural than Tannehill's, so the term that he uses for it, "architecture," is quite appropriate.

A review of the theory behind Talbert's contribution and an evaluation of his results provide additional valuable groundwork for us. As will be seen, he demonstrates that detailed, patterned structure was normative in the ancient world and that Luke constructed such correspondence sets in Luke-Acts. This is the nature of our proposal in chapter 4 for Luke's compositional method and for the structure of Luke. Occasionally, individual parallels observed by Talbert appear in the proposed structure. Additional understanding of Lukan composition is gained thorough Talbert's redactional study of the parallels he proposes. Redaction closely relates to how the Evangelist constructed his patterns. Naturally, this meshes with our interest in Luke's method of composition. Finally, Talbert develops the theology that may be derived from the observed correspondences. The task of our chapter 5 is similar, to explore Lukan theology behind the formation of the proposed structure. Therefore, an analysis of Talbert's method informs our own.

Although Talbert is very concerned about proving that his correspondences are of Lukan intent, it is not within the scope of his work to develop their impact on the individual interpretation of pericopes. He is concerned with the larger picture of structure and genre. Chapter 2 will suggest that, although many of his proposed Lukan correspondences appear correct, he could be more rigorous in testing them. The methodology we will apply to our own proposed correspondences will involve rigorous testing and a development of the ways that Lukan interpretation of individual pericopes is different from the standard interpretations that do not demonstrate an awareness of or concern for these correspondences.

Chapter 2 is divided into three parts. The first discusses the theoretical basis behind Talbert's architectonic patterns. The second applies the eleven tests for intentionality below (see pages 8ff.) to his patterns to evaluate the probability of Lukan intent behind each, and the third examines the significance he attributes to his understanding of Lukan architecture.

Chapter 3 – All too often proposals of specific types of correspondences

---

(Berlin: Akademie-Verlag, 1964) 195–202; *Type and History in Acts* (London: SPCK, 1964) 138–39; J.G. Davies, "The Prefigurement of the Ascension in the Third Gospel," *JTS* n.s., 6 (1955) 229–33; Paul S. Minear, "Luke's Use of the Birth Stories," in L.E. Keck, and J.L. Martyn (eds.), *Studies in Luke-Acts* (Nashville: Abingdon, 1966) 111–30; R. Morgenthaler, *Die lukanische Geschichtsschreibung als Zeugnis: Gestalt und Gehalt der Kunst des Lukas*, ATANT 14, vol. 1 (Zurich: Zwingli, 1949); Helmut Flender, *St. Luke: Theologian of Redemptive History* (Philadelphia: Fortress, 1967) ch. 1; W.C. van Unnik, "Éléments artistique dans l'Évangile de Luc," *ETL* 46 (1970) 401–12; and Eckhard Plümacher, *Lukas als hellenistischer Schriftsteller* (Göttingen: Vandenhoeck & Ruprecht, 1972).

Introduction 5

and structure in Luke fail to demonstrate that such composition was actually known and practiced in Luke's day.[6] Chapter 3 presents and evaluates representative examples from Old Testament, New Testament and relevant Greco-Roman literature of the same type of structure that we propose for Luke, cyclical parallelism (sometimes called step-parallelism or regular parallelism; e.g., A B C A' B' C'...). These examples show that our proposal for Luke is reasonable. Greco-Roman *imitatio* (imitation) is suggested as a viable compositional method that could achieve the observed structure. A method must not only be "possible," but it must also be consonant with the intentions of an intelligent first-century Christian author. Source-critical matters apply. Apparently Luke employed the pervasive ancient literary practice of *imitatio* whereby he could choose to copy simply the patterned structure of a normative document (e.g., A B C A' B' C'), without necessary reference to its content, by placing pericopes from his sources in the appropriate positions. This need not have been a sterile procedure without regard for flow of thought because it seems that his structure is based on the narrative flow of Jesus' climactic Jerusalem ministry in the gospel of Mark, one of his normative documents.[7] This will be clarified later.

Chapter 4 – Chapters 4 and 5 constitute the core of this book, our proposal for the structure of Luke and its theological and interpretational implications. Chapter 4 posits a structure for the entire Gospel that meshes with the most probably correct elements of Tannehill's and Talbert's correspondences and other similar previous works.[8] The eleven tests for

---

6 See for example Wilhelm Wilkens' article, "Die theologische Struktur der Komposition des Lukasevangeliums," *TZ* 34 (1978) 1–13.

7 Our proposal of patterned structure for Luke does not require Markan priority, nor do virtually all of our observations derived from the structure. An argument for Markan priority however will be delineated later, and some discussion throughout the thesis will be tailored to the presumption that Luke used Mark even though this relationship is not logically essential to the discussion.

8 Talbert notes an assumption of classical literature scholars that is pertinent to our study. They presume that if a work employs patterns for the arrangement of small units of text, then there is probably a pattern for the arrangement of the larger units (Talbert, *Literary Patterns*, 8).

As to why the structure has not been identified before, G.N. Stanton's observation, in his chapter on literary theory, regarding the broad structure of Matthew, applies. He considers that there is little consensus because the Gospel is intended to be read aloud and probably in its entirety, something modern readers do not do. Reading shorter sections at a time fosters awareness virtually only of structural indicators for smaller units, and there is fair consensus on these. Reading through the whole Gospel makes more accessible structural markers that indicate broader structure. See G.N. Stanton, *A Gospel for a New People: Studies in* Matthew (Edinburgh:

intentionality below are rigorously applied to the structure to evaluate the probability of Lukan intent. The apparent patterned arrangement of material in Luke does not require Markan priority, but dependence on Mark, it will be shown, offers a feasible mechanism for the composition of the proposed structure. I introduce a new argument for Markan priority at the end of the chapter as part of our exploration of the Lukan compositional process.

Chapter 5 – Naturally, if Luke composed his Gospel by arranging material according to a detailed pattern, there would probably be more than aesthetic purposes behind it. The parallelism between Jesus and John is a prime example. Accordingly, chapter five, informed by the many strengths (and occasional weaknesses) of Tannehill's and Talbert's approaches, develops reasonable literary and theological purposes and implications from the proposed structure in chapter 4.

For readers who are interested in modern literary theory, our proposal for the structure and composition of the Gospel reveals Luke's intertextual reading of the pericopes incorporated in the Gospel. By studying his intertextual reading, we practice a form of the literary theory *intertextuality*. For a definition of this literary theory and a discussion of how it relates to our discussion, see Appendix C. Clearly, we speak frequently in this book of the Third Gospel's author. This may be objectionable to those who espouse certain principles of modern literary theory. Be aware, then, that if you remove the author concept wherever it is mentioned, this does not substantially diminish the value of our results. Appendix C, however, does offer a defense of the author concept in literary theory.

2 The Analysis of Structure in Narrative

Obviously, this book concentrates heavily on the analysis of structure in Luke, especially since a patterned structure is proposed for Luke 4:14–24:53. Many of the correspondences between pericopes that we may attribute to Lukan intent are building blocks of the Gospel's patterned architecture. Shimon Bar-Efrat offers some pertinent guidelines and cautions for such an enterprise in his article "Some Observations on the Analysis of Structure in Biblical Narrative".[9] We believe that the common errors and pitfalls he describes are successfully avoided in our proposal. One guideline offered is that if "the analysis evinces an indiscriminate use of heterogeneous elements,... [it is] of course detrimental to the quality of

---

T. & T. Clark, 1992). Ancient readers were far more attuned to this and therefore far more likely to notice Luke's cues.

9 Shimon Bar-Efrat, "Some Observations on the Analysis of Structure in Biblical Narrative," *VT* 30 (1980) 154–173.

the structural analysis and may impair its validity".[10] Of course, if an author chooses to form a structure from heterogeneous elements, that is his prerogative; but biblical authors do not generally appear to do so, according to his observation. The elements of our proposed structure are all narrative features possessing a degree of similarity that lies well within the bounds illustrated by Bar-Efrat.

Four levels of structural elements may be employed, and these constitute another of his guidelines: "(1) the verbal level; (2) the level of narrative technique; (3) the level of the narrative world; (4) the level of the conceptual content".[11] The *verbal level* obviously refers to correspondence between words and phrases. This is the easiest to recognize in a text. The level of *narrative technique* "is based on variations in narrative method, such as narrator's account as opposed to character's speech (dialogue), scenic presentation versus summary, narration as against description, explanation, comment, etc".[12] Even the handling of time may play a structural role.[13] One illustration he offers of patterned structure on this level is 1 Samuel 29.[14]

> Narrator's account (verses 1–2)
> Dialogue (verses 3–5)
> Dialogue (verses 6–10)
> Narrator's account (verse 11)

The level of the *narrative world* includes primarily characters (identity, nature, function, etc.) and events, but also such things as setting, clothes and arms.[15] One example provided for this level is 2 Samuel 13 (italics and underline mine, to demonstrate additional pattern described by Bar-Efrat).[16]

> Jonadab-*Amnon* (verses 3–5)
> Amnon-David (verse 6)
> David-Tamar (verse 7)
> Tamar-*Amnon* (verses 8–16)
> Amnon-servant (verse 17)
> servant-Tamar (verse 18)
> Tamar-Absalom (verses 19–20)

---

10 Bar-Efrat, "Observations," 155.
11 Bar-Efrat, "Observations," 157.
12 Bar-Efrat, "Observations," 158.
13 Bar-Efrat, "Observations," 159–160.
14 Bar-Efrat, "Observations," 159.
15 Bar-Efrat, "Observations," 161.
16 Bar-Efrat, "Observations," 163.

He cautions that, concerning structure involving events (specifically, resemblance in plot between simple unit narratives), similar content may coincidentally create a degree of resemblance in structure. Therefore "it is essential not to describe the plots in too abstract and general terms, because obviously the more abstract and general the formulations, the greater the number of narratives that will fit the given plot outline".[17] His examples include basic events, tension versus relaxation, reversal, climax, location and time references. Our structural proposal is worded in extremely specific terms, such that the occurrence of an element apart from its position in the structure is rare to non-existent. The level of *conceptual content* "is based on the themes of the narrative units or the ideas contained therein".[18] Bar-Efrat notes that a major danger here is the identification of a structure composed of elements that "are themselves the product of the rather subjective process of interpretation. So in order to steer clear of undue arbitrariness, themes and ideas should be borne out by the facts of the narrative as clearly and unambiguously as possible".[19] Although our proposal for Luke's structure is essentially on the level of the narrative world, whenever themes are involved they are tied directly and unambiguously to the facts of the narrative.

A final word of advice from Bar-Efrat is that structures are more plausible if they are reinforced by the presence of more than one type of element, but less plausible if there is a "mixing of miscellaneous elements".[20] As will be seen, our proposal seeks to satisfy both criteria.

Bar-Efrat's observations are empirically reasonable and helpful for determining the probability that an observed structure is intended by the author. The eleven tests mentioned above that will be applied to the proposals of Tannehill, Talbert and this work incorporate all of his guidelines and cautions, and much more, and will therefore serve well to evaluate the probability of authorial intent behind suggested correspondences.

3 Eleven Tests for Intentionality

An important aspect of our study is the establishment and use of objective tests for evaluating the *probability* of authorial intent behind proposed correspondences between passages at whatever level. Below, eleven specific tests are developed for this task and later applied to the proposals of Tannehill (chapter 1), Talbert (chapter 2) and this book (chapter 4).

---

17 Bar-Efrat, "Observations," 164–165.
18 Bar-Efrat, "Observations," 168.
19 Bar-Efrat, "Observations," 170.
20 Bar-Efrat, "Observations," 172.

Obviously, correspondences that accidentally result from Luke's[21] complex process of compilation may not have been noticed by him, but the concern of our investigation is the evaluation of the probability of intent. When intentional parallels are convincingly identified, one may assume underlying theological and/or literary purposes behind their construction and attempt to identify those purposes. If this aim is satisfactorily achieved, then greater confidence is justified for theological statements flowing from the parallels.

The need for such tests has in part arisen due to the increasing numbers of scholars employing modern literary theories to Luke and other biblical texts, theories that were formulated based on modern compositional methodology that is vastly different from that of the biblical periods. Interestingly, most of the Lukan literary devices or techniques proposed by these scholars are founded on some form of parallelism or correspondence. This is certainly true for the literary analysis (narrative criticism) of Tannehill in both volumes of *The Narrative Unity of Luke-Acts: A Literary Interpretation*.[22] Any theory that involves works constructed from a variety of sources with a considerable amount of verbatim transcription and imitation, must account for the inevitable parallels that will result from similarities between different units of traditional material prior to incorporation into the text. The tests presented below are pertinent to conscious interconnection between traditional units both within the Gospel and between Luke and Acts. They also account for parallels that are coincidentally the result of Lukan style or other unintentional causes.

The inconsistency between scholars in the criteria used to evaluate correspondences between biblical texts is great, as is the number used. Often the criteria applied are unrealistic against actual practice in the ancient world. For instance, perfect symmetry may be demanded of chiastic proposals for the central section of Luke.[23] Yet, as will be seen in chapters 2 and 3, ancient writers preferred to violate symmetry to some degree. Another problem, identified in nearly all the cases I have examined, occurs when scholars apply a criterion only when it supports their proposed correspondence and not when it works against it. Obviously, it would be impossible to comment on the criteria of every scholar who suggests or criticizes corre-

---

21 We will assume throughout that the author of the Third Gospel is Luke, the traveling companion of Paul. This assumption however does not affect any argumentation or conclusions drawn throughout the entire work. Consequently, those of differing opinion will not find the discussions irrelevant.
22 For references, see page 2, note 1.
23 See Craig L. Blomberg, "Midrash, Chiasmus, and the Outline of Luke's Central Section," in R.T. France and David Wenham (eds.), *Gospel Perspectives, Studies in Midrash and Historiography* (Sheffield: JSOT Press, 1983) 3:236.

spondences in Luke-Acts. A large portion of commentaries would contain at least several instances. Therefore, comment will be restricted to a few representative scholars who devote substantial effort to the subject.

The criteria used by scholars to demonstrate the existence of a correspondence or, negatively, to invalidate one, may be summarized under nine headings. The first seven relate to basic constituents of parallelism; and the issues are whether the constituents actually exist as identified in the passages and, if they do, whether they correspond enough to be parallel. These seven are parallelism of language (identical or similar wording), content, form (form-critical), theme, structure (surface structure of passages), function (of a pericope in its context), and sequence (of parallel features or passages). The remaining two are, of course, not constituents of parallelism. Redaction-criticism determines whether there is evidence that any constituents of a parallel were incorporated by the redactor possibly to form the correspondence. The final criterion logically assumes that the greater the number of parallels between texts, the less chance there is for the observer to have read parallelism into the text. These nine criteria are distributed in the table below by the scholars who employ them in their proposals of Lukan correspondences.[24]

---

24 In the table, scholars are listed by number of criteria employed. When the same number are used two or more scholars, they are listed by date from the most recent to the earliest. The table is constructed on the basis of the following works: Talbert, *Literary Patterns*; Tannehill, *Narrative Unity*, vol. 1; Goulder, "Chiastic Structure," 195–202; *Type and History*; Walter Radl, *Paulus und Jesus im lukanischen Doppelwerk: Untersuchungen zu Parallelmotiven im Lukasevangelium und in der Apostelgeschichte*, Europäische Hochschulschriften (Bern: Herbert Lang, 1975); Schneckenburger, *Über den Zweck*; A.J. Mattil, Jr., "The Jesus-Paul Parallels and the Purpose of Luke-Acts: H.H. Evans Reconsidered," *NovT* 17 (1975) 15–46; A. Schwegler, *Das nachapostolische Zeitalter in den Hauptmomenten seiner Entwicklung*, vols. 1 and 2 (Tübingen: Fues, 1846); Laurentin, *Structure et théologie*; R.F. O'Toole, "Parallels Between Jesus and His Disciples in Luke-Acts: A Further Study," *BZ* 27 (1983) 195–212; F.C. Baur, *Paulus, der Apostel Jesu Christi: Sein Leben und Wirken, seine Briefe und seine Lehre: Ein Beitrag zu einer kritischen Geschichte des Urchristentums* (Leipzig: Fues, 1866); E. Zeller, *Die Apostelgeschichte nach ihrem Inhalt und Ursprung kritisch untersucht* (Stuttgard: Mäcken, 1854); B. Bauer, *Die Apostelgeschichte des Paulinismus und des Judentums innerhalb der christlichen Kirche* (Berlin: Hempel, 1850); G. Muhlack, *Die Parallelen von Lukas-Evangelium und Apostelgeschichte*, Theologie und Wirklichkeit 8 (Frankfurt: Lang, 1979); J.G. Davies, "Prefigurement," 229–33; Helmut Flender, *St. Luke*; and Morgenthaler, *Die lukanische Geschichtsschreibung*. I became aware of Susan Marie Praeder's article, "Jesus-Paul, Peter-Paul, and Jesus-Peter Parallelisms in Luke-Acts: A History of Reader Response," in Kent Harold Richards (ed.), *SBL Seminar Papers* 23 (Chico: Scholars Press, 1984) 23–39, after an initial review of most of the works in the table. My analysis was quite similar and has been supplemented by hers.

	language	content	form	theme	structure	function	sequence	redaction	no. of parallels
Talbert (1974)	x	x	x	x	x		x	x	
Tannehill (1986)	x	x	x	x	x		x		
Radl (1975)	x	x				x	x	x	x
Goulder (1964)	x	x	x	x	x		x		
Mattill (1975)	x	x		x				x	
Schwegler (1846)	x	x	x				x		
Schneckenburger (1841)	x	x	x				x		
O'Toole (1983)	x	x			x				
Muhlack (1979)	x					x	x		
Laurentin (1964)	x	x					x		
Baur (1850)	x	x					x		
Zeller (1854)	x	x					x		
Bauer (1850)	x	x					x		
Flender (1967)	x	x							
Davies (1955)	x	x							
Morgenthaler (1949)	x	x							

Susan Marie Praeder correctly observes that rarely among the proposals of these scholars are their stated criteria applied rigorously beyond merely offering the parallels to the reader.[25] Not only that, but the mere existence of what might constitute a parallel is not evidence that a parallel is intentional. Similar language or content for example may exist due to other causes than the formation of a correspondence. Criteria must be defined more rigorously than is generally the case. They must also preferably be applied as a set and not just individually whenever they support a proposal.

Andrew C. Clark suggests the criterion, "disruption of the text," in *Parallel Lives: The Relation of Paul to the Apostles in the Lukan Perspective* (Carlisle, Cumbria, UK: Paternoster, 2001) 77–79. He states, "If Luke is willing to create a pericope which is tortuous, either within itself, or in relation to its context, then this strongly suggests that the parallel is not just a question of style or partly unconscious literary shaping, but a deliberate creation in line with his overall purpose," p. 77. This appears to be a useful criterion, but it proves to be highly subjective. Clark's examples of disruption (e.g. pp. 77–79) may readily be viewed as non-tortuous and even integral to their contexts. He admits as well that instances of disruption are rare. My attempts to find clear disruption in the proposals of parallelism by Talbert and Tannehill have borne little fruit, so this criterion, though potentially usefull, is not incorporated into our eleven tests for intentionality.

25 Praeder, "Jesus-Paul, Peter-Paul," 29–34.

The eleven tests below were devised logically and experimentally through the study of universally accepted correspondence patterns, some of which are presented in chapter 3. They reflect qualities typically inherent in these correspondences and patterns. Their similarity to the above criteria is mostly incidental since they were developed before I performed that review, and they were developed as a set. Another distinction from the criteria above as generally applied by other scholars is the more realistic assumption that an individual criterion by itself cannot establish or rule out authorial intent. It can only speak to the probability of intent.

3.1 General Presentation of the Tests

The eleven tests for intentionality are as follows:

1. The greater the restriction of elements of correspondence to the relevant passages, the greater is the probability of authorial intent.

2. The greater the number of reasonable parallel features between parallel passages, the greater is the probability of intent.

3. Similarly, the greater the number of parallel passages (or panels) that match a proposed pattern or grouping of features, the greater is the case for intent.[26]

4. An element of correspondence that attracts the reader's attention contributes to the probability of intent.

5. Parallelism between complex units, such as combined pericopes, that appears constructive rather than random or coincidental increases the probability of intent.

6. If redaction critical observations yield evidence of Lukan adjustment to include or create the elements that constitute the literary device, the probability of intent is greater insofar as there are no superior reasons for the observed redaction.

7. If the elements of correspondence that constitute the literary device are related to important Lukan themes, the probability of intent is enhanced.

8. Intent is more certain if there is no clear historical or genre expectation for the inclusion of the features in question and their sequence, if parallelism of sequence is observed.

---

26 Tannehill states this principle and applies it to a series of three pericope groups fitting a basic pattern; *Narrative Unity*, 2:50–52 (especially 52).

Introduction 13

9. If a sequence or grouping of features in parallel is uncommon in other relevant literature, then the likelihood of coincidence due to common expression is diminished.

10. If the passages that constitute parallel groupings of passages are contiguous within the groupings, and not distributed broadly throughout the text, then selectivity on the part of the reader is diminished.

11. The probability of intent increases as more of the above tests are passed.

The purpose of the tests is to make more certain which literary devices are more probably intentional. They impose stringent demands on the features that constitute the literary device and thereby filter out accidental or subconscious constructions that could be perceived as devices. A consequence of this function is that subtle constructions intended by Luke may not be labeled "probable" since they are often indistinguishable from coincidental phenomena. Still, an "uncertain" or "improbable" device, whether intended or not, should be treated with caution for the attribution of purpose or theology to the Lukan message. Undoubtedly, the reader will occasionally observe unintentional textual features that resemble devices used elsewhere by the author, for example an apparent echo. Although the reader is impacted as though the literary devices were intended, the impact may be divergent from or superfluous to the author's purpose. Reader-response critics note the legitimate intrinsic value of such impact, but the interpreter interested in authorial communication must attempt to filter out the uncertain, or at least label it as such in his argumentation. Too often, we make a tentative assertion and later treat it as established evidence in our argument.

A word is in order on the basic philosophy behind the application of a set of tests such as these. Applying a set of tests where each one looks for a different characteristic that a correspondence might or might not have will almost always result in certain tests that run counter to the final conclusion. This is inherent in the scientific method too. It must be borne in mind that the tests are not *determiners* of authorial intent. If they were, then having some tests favor intent and others not would be problematical. A correspondence cannot be both intentional and accidental. The tests individually and collectively speak only to probability of intent and primarily indicate likelihood rather than unlikelihood. They are like trying to find a tree by testing whether the object has a woody trunk, branches and leaves. In wintertime, most trees will fail the leaf test, but they are nonetheless trees. Therefore, the occurrence of varying results does not weaken the value of the tests for their stated purpose; rather, it should usually be expected. Occasionally, for the sake of perspective, a comment will be made under one test about the results of another or others. This may appear to violate the objectivity generally claimed for the tests individually. In other words, if an individual test is to be an objective indicator of probability, then its result must not be influenced positively or negatively by the results of other tests. The problem is easily avoided by ensuring that the conclusion of each test is derived solely from the application of that test. I have rigorously guarded against conclusions on any one test being influenced by the results of others even when an integrating comment is made.

3.2 Validation of the Tests: Luke 1:5–38 as a Test Case for the Tests for Intentionality

Intentional Lukan parallelism is universally recognized in Luke 1:5–2:52.[27] Below is a variety of representative schemes that illustrate the sections that are generally accepted as parallel, namely 1:5–25 with 1:26–38 and 1:57–80 with 2:1–40.[28] The strength of this pattern presents a rigorous proving ground for the validity of our eleven indicators of authorial intent behind correspondences in Lukan writings. Throughout the course of this book, correspondence and parallelism will be demonstrated as fundamental to Lukan composition. Therefore, if the eleven indicators correctly judge the parallelism in 1:5–38, then they will serve as objective tools for the evaluation of actual Lukan intent behind the proposals of such scholars as Robert Tannehill, and Charles Talbert, as well as the proposal of this work. Our interest at this point is only in whether Luke intended this detailed parallelism observed by scholars. For a reasonable development of the theology communicated by it, see Augustin George's brief discussion.[29]

---

[27] One conclusion of Talbert's study of patterned literature and the ancient reader is that the parallelism in Lk. 1–2 would lead the Evangelist's readers to expect more pattern throughout the Gospel (Talbert, *Literary Patterns*, 80).

[28] See also Raymond E. Brown's selection in *The Birth of the Messiah: A Commentary on the Infancy Narratives in the Gospels of Matthew and Luke* (London: Geoffrey Chapman, 1993) 248–249.

[29] Augustin George, *Études sur l'oeuvre de Luc*, Sources Bibliques (Paris: Gabalda, 1978) 62–65.

Introduction

John Nolland[30] and François Bovon[31]

1:5–25	1:26–38	
	1:39–56	
1:57–66	2:1–21	
1:67–80	2:22–40	
	2:41–52	

Charles Talbert[33]

1:5–7	1:26–27
1:8–11	1:28
1:12	1:29
1:13–17	1:30–33
1:18	1:34
1:19–23	1:35–37
1:24–25	1:38
1:57	2:1–7
1:58	2:8–20 [16]
1:65–66	2:17–18
1:59–64	2:21
1:67–79	2:22–38
1:80a	2:39–40
1:80b	2:41–52

René Laurentin[32]

1:5–25	1:26–38
	1:39–56
1:57–58	2:1–20
1:59–80	2:21–40
	2:41–52

Raymond Brown[34]

1:5–23	1:26–38
1:24–25	1:39–45, 56
	(1:46–55 added later)
1:57–66	2:1–27, 34–39
(1:67–79 and 2:28–33 added later)	
1:80	2:40

Joel Green[35]

1:5–7	1:26–27
1:8–23	1:28–38
1:24–25	1:39–56
1:57–58	2:1–20
1:59–66	2:21–24
1:67–79	2:25–39
1:80	2:40–52

---

30 Nolland, *Luke 1–9:20*, Word Biblical Commentary 35a (Dallas: Word Books, 1989) 34–35.
31 François Bovon, *Das Evangelium nach Lukas: 1 Teilband Lk 1,1–9,50* (Zürich: Benziger Verlag, 1989) 45–48.
32 René Laurentin, *Structure et théologie*, 32–33.
33 Talbert, *Literary Patterns*, 44.
34 R. Brown, *Birth of the Messiah*, 251–252.
35 Joel B. Green, *The Gospel of Luke*, New International Commentary on the New Testament (Grand Rapids: Eerdmans, 1997) 50.

Joseph Fitzmyer[36]

I. The Angelic Announcements of the Births (1:5–56)

1:5–25 About John	1:26–38 About Jesus
(5–10) The parents introduced, expecting no child (because barren)	(26–27) The parents introduced, expecting no child (because unmarried)
(11) Appearance of the angel	(28) Entrance of the angel
(12) Zechariah is troubled (ἐταράχθη)	(29) Mary is troubled (διεταράχθη)
(13) "Do not fear…" (Μὴ φοβοῦ)	(30) "Do not fear…" (Μὴ φοβοῦ)
(13) Your wife will bear a son	(31) You will bear a son
(13) You shall call him John	(31) You shall call him Jesus
(15) He shall be great before the Lord	(32) He shall be Great
(18) Zechariah's question: "How shall I know?"	(34) Mary's question: "How shall this be?"
(19) Angel's answer: I have been sent to announce this to you	(35) Angel's answer: The Holy Spirit will come upon you
(20) Sign given: You shall become mute	(36) Sign given: Your aged cousin Elizabeth has conceived
(22) Zechariah's forced silence	(38) Mary's spontaneous answer
(23) Refrain A: Zechariah "went back" (ἀπῆλθεν)	(38) Refrain A: The angel "went away" (ἀπῆλθεν)

1:39–45
1:46–55 Canticle
1:56 Refrain A

---

[36] Joseph A. Fitzmyer, *The Gospel According to Luke I–IX*, Anchor Bible 28 (Garden City, N.Y.: Doubleday, 1981) 313–314.

Introduction   17

II. The Birth, Circumcision, and Manifestation
of the Children (1:57–2:52)

1:57–58   The birth of John   2:1–20   The birth of Jesus
  (57)   (1–12)
                                        (13–14) Canticle
  (58)   (15–18)
                                        (19) Refrain B
                                        (20) Refrain A

1:59–80   2:21–40
  (59–64)   (21)
  (65–66)   (25–38)
  (68–79) Canticle   (29–32) Canticle
                                        (39) Refrain A
  (80) Refrain C   (40) Refrain C

                   2:41–52
                     (51) Refrain A
                     (51) Refrain B
                     (52) Refrain C

Aside from 1:5–25 with 1:26–38, John Nolland poses some serious questions about Lukan intent behind these proposed detailed parallelisms. He notes the presence of three growth statements, one of which must not correspond, and notes that agreement about section boundaries has not been achieved. "Indeed, the difficulties with the structure point more than anything to a significant Lucan use of sources: only the two annunciations are closely parallel in form."[37] With this caution in mind, the annunciation parallel of 1:5–25 with 1:26–38 may be selected as a test case with overwhelming acceptance that it was intended in detail by Luke. Tannehill concurs that the parallels of chapters one and two are strongest right here.[38] The tests for intentionality should provide strong signals of Lukan intent if they are valid indicators.

Tannehill's scheme for this parallel pattern is representative and is depicted in the table below.[39] References in italic represent parallels described in the book where he does not provide reference to chapter and verse. This addition simplifies an accurate analysis of sequence. Bold case indicates a

---

37 Nolland, *Luke 1–9:20*, 19–21.
38 Tannehill, *Narrative Unity*, 1:15.
39 See his presentation of this parallelism; Tannehill, *Narrative Unity*, 1:15. A careful comparison of Tannehill's and Fitzmyer's schemes shows that they are virtually identical.

violation of sequence as compared with Luke 1:5–25. The Old Testament passages in the table are noted in *Narrative Unity* as "type-scenes" of the Lukan accounts,[40] but are not evaluated in detail by Tannehill. They are presented here merely for the sake of interest.

	John, Lk. 1:5–25	Jesus, Lk. 1:26–38	OT Type-Scenes		
			Ishmael, Gn. 16:1–13	Isaac, Gn. 17:1–3, 15–21; 18:1–2, 10–15	Samson, Jdg. 13:2–23
1. "The same angel, Gabriel, appears to John's father and to Jesus' mother, followed by a similar sequence of events."	*1:5–11*	*1:26–28*	16:1–8 Angel of the Lord to Hagar	17:1–3 The Lord to Abram	13:2–3 Angel of the Lord to wife of Manoah
2. "Both parents are 'troubled' by the encounter with the angel."	1:12 ἐταράχθη	1:29 διεταράχθη			
3. "The angel responds, 'Do not fear,'" [Μὴ φοβοῦ]	*1:13*	*1:30*			
4. "announces the unexpected birth of a son,"	*1:13*	*1:31*	*16:9–11*	*17:15–16*	*13:3–5*
5. "determines the child's name,"	*1:13*	*1:31*	*16:11*	**17:19**	
6. "indicates that he 'will be great,'"	*1:14–15*	*1:32*		17:16?	
7. "connects the child's conception or fetal life with the Holy Spirit,"	*1:15*	**1:35**			
8. "and announces the child's future role in God's saving purpose."	1:13–17 *1:16–17*	1:30–35 *1:32–33*	16:12 character, not role	**17:19, 21**	*13:5*

---

40 Tannehill, *Narrative Unity*, 1:18.

9. "Both Zechariah and Mary respond with a question which emphasizes that this birth is not possible by normal human power,"	*1:18*	*1:34*	*16:13* Response is a statement of faith, not a question.	*17:17;* *18:10–15*	***13:3??***
10. "and the angel gives each an additional sign, which in Zechariah's case involves temporary punishment for his unbelief."	1:18–22	1:34–38 1:35–38		*18:1–2,* *10, 14*	*13:15–23*

The eleven tests for intentionality will now be applied to the certain parallelism between Luke 1:5–25 and 1:26–38. The theory behind each criterion will be discussed in conjunction with its application to the parallelism. This helps to clarify the theory by way of immediate illustration.

Test 1: *The greater the restriction of elements of correspondence to the relevant passages, the greater is the probability of authorial intent.*

This test has two valuable sides.[41] First, it evaluates the possibility that the reader has read parallelism into the text. If the elements that form the correspondence are found all throughout the text outside of the corresponding passages, then the reader has had ample opportunity to find a parallel through that element. Conversely, when the elements are well restricted to the parallel passages, that opportunity is restricted. Second, if a writer would like a correspondence to be observable by the reader, he would need to ensure that the elements that form it are not too common in the text. This would cloud the parallelism. Test 1 is one of the more important of the eleven because it covers both the writer and the reader, and because the identification of elements in the text is objective. (The issue of whether an element of correspondence is significant will be covered later.)

Parallel 1 – Only in Luke 1:19 and 26 does the angel Gabriel make an appearance, and in each instance to a parent of the one to be born. *Parallel 2* – Luke uses two verbal forms of the same root (ἐταράχθη and διεταράχθη respectively) to indicate the response to the angel. He uses the root once more (Lk. 24:38) to express the reaction of the disciples to the post-resurrection appearance of Jesus in their midst. The only other appearances of angels (to the shepherds and to the women at the tomb)

---

41 Praeder uses restriction in this sense in criticism of the way criteria are employed by other scholars in defending their correspondences; "Jesus-Paul, Peter-Paul," 37.

elicit fear not trouble. *Parallel 3* – Of the four angelic appearances, three describe the angel comforting with similar words (Lk. 1:13, 30; 2:10). *Parallels 4–8* – Obviously, the angelic announcements of the birth of a son, the namings, the indications of greatness, the linkings of the child with the Holy Spirit, and the announcements of the child's future role are absolutely restricted to their locations in Luke 1. *Parallel 9* – Likewise, the response to the angel with a question is strictly limited to this parallel. *Parallel 10* – Beyond parallel 10, one other location narrates angelic provision of an additional sign, Luke 2:12, where the sign is the baby in a manger.

Within the whole of Luke, each parallel element in this pattern is absolutely or highly restricted to its location in the pattern. Therefore, test 1 correctly indicates a strong probability of Lukan intent. The Evangelist apparently resisted the repetition of elements chosen for the creation of his structure, possibly to avoid clouding the parallelism and/or diminishing its special nature in comparison with the rest of the narrative. Consistent with this, the other two angelic encounters are distinctly different from those involving the parents. Similarly, one would expect that whenever Luke wanted to create a parallel to impact the reader, whether subtly or plainly, he would restrict the essential elements to keep them more obvious and effective.

Test 2: *The greater the number of reasonable parallel features between parallel passages, the greater is the probability of intent.*

This test is the same as the criterion, "number of parallels," in the table on page 11. The term "reasonable parallel feature" involves the determination of whether the proposed elements of correspondence actually fit the assigned texts. There is a greater chance that parallelism is incidental if there is only one feature shared by two or more passages than if several are shared. Probability would suggest that a grouping of features in a passages is more rare the greater the number of features. A value of this test is that it assesses the possible involvement of the reader in forcing the text. It is much harder to find passages that share several features than those that share only one. In practice, test 2 is one of the more important of the eleven when the number of proposed parallel features in a correspondence is three or more.

Tannehill enumerates ten parallel units,[42] which is a substantial number for parallel passages. The features are clearly valid in content and often show strong verbal similarity. Consequently, this test strongly favors the

---

[42] Notice that Fitzmyer proposes twelve units. Several of these are equivalent to Tannehill's, but a few are less convincing. "Angel's answer…" (1:19 ‖ 1:35) is weak since an answer is expected when a question is asked, and the content is not demonstrated to correspond. Furthermore, the parallel element of the final refrain (1:23 ‖ 1:38) seems trivial.

Introduction 21

parallelism. Ten is well beyond what would be expected both from coincidental similarity between units of tradition and through the manner in which Luke tells stories. A comparison of the three Old Testament parallel passages in the table above exemplifies the number of correspondences typical of stories with formal literary dependence, apparently only four or five.[43] The validity of the test is supported because this overwhelmingly accepted parallelism is strongly indicated as intentional.

---

43 Useful to our investigation is an awareness of how detailed the subconscious similarities between stories of a single genre/form may be. Since most of the passages in the above table (page 18) are essentially simple stories, they are suitable for structural analysis, which examines such subconscious similarities. It is reasonable to infer from the contribution of structuralism that three (or a similarly small number) basic constituents in a story may be expected to follow a conventional or even subconscious sequence, a pattern that is a consequence of how people think and relate stories. These constituents are reflected on the level of plot (e.g., violation of social norm or order → attempt at restoration → restored social norm or order) and could result in various coincidental parallels between separate stories. Daniel Patte exemplifies this in *What is Structural Exegesis?* (Philadelphia: Fortress Press, 1976) 16–69. For a structural analysis of Gn. 32:23–33 that illustrates the common structural identification of three parts to a story, see Roland Barthes' "The Struggle with the Angel; Textual Analysis of Gn. 32:23–33," in R. Barthes, F. Bovon, F.-J. Leenhardt, R. Martin-Archard, and J. Starobinski, *Structural Analysis and Biblical Exegesis: Interpretational Essays* (Pittsburgh, Pickwick Press, 1974) 21–33. N.T. Wright also advocates the three-part plot analysis of a simple story in *The New Testament and the People of God* (London: SPCK, 1992) 71–7. The work of Propp and Greimas are seminal to this aspect of structural theory – see Corina Galland, "An Introduction to the Method of A.J. Greimas," in Alfred M. Johnson, Jr. (ed. and tr.), *The New Testament and Structuralism* (Pittsburgh: Pickwick Press, 1976) 5–7. For a brief discussion of the theory that predisposes the typical identification of three parts in plot, see Daniel Patte and Aline Patte, *Structural Exegesis: From Theory to Practice* (Philadelphia: Fortress Press, 1978) 23–4. The more that three parallel constituents between stories are exceeded, the greater is the likelihood of the author's conscious awareness of the parallelism. The implication for our purposes is that a grouping of parallel elements greater than three in number *may* indicate conscious construction when one or more stories are in parallel, especially if a sequence is maintained.

The limited number of expected constituents per form identified in Form-Criticism confirms the findings of structuralism regarding the likely number of incidental parallel components between passages of the same form. Rudolf Bultmann, for example, lists many *common* inclusions for each form but rarely does he explicate essential components; *The History of the Synoptic Tradition*, John Marsh (tr.), (Oxford: Basil Blackwell, 1968). (Vincent Taylor is certainly more helpful regarding the explication of essential components; *The Formation of the Gospel Tradition* [London: Macmillan, 1949]). This results in overlap of just a few components between any two instances of a particular form. In summary then, three correspondences or less seems a reasonable general expectation for incidental parallel elements related to basic form-critical or plot constituents. When details of correspondence exceed this, then there is valid ground to suspect authorial intent.

Test 3: *The greater the number of parallel passages (or panels) that match a proposed pattern or grouping of features, the greater is the case for intent.*

I have not found this test used elsewhere. The logic is similar to the one above. It is less likely that three passages in a text share a certain set of features than for two to share them. The validity of this test is self-evident in that the role of the observer's subjectivity is diminished inversely according to the number of corroborative panels.

Two passages match the proposed pattern in this instance in 1:5–38. This is naturally the minimum possible for parallelism. Inherently, test 3 is valid as a restriction to the observer's subjectivity.

Test 4: *An element of correspondence that attracts the reader's attention contributes to the probability of intent.*

This test is not clearly utilized by other scholars, but Praeder seems to approximate the idea.[44] One expects that a writer, trying to establish complex parallelism that will somehow impact the reader, would employ elements that would be noticed. This test naturally involves some subjectivity. Nevertheless, in practice the decisions are usually obvious (for instance, between the dramatic and the drab), so the test retains substantial value.

Only elements two and three of the parallelism between John and Jesus might be considered insignificant, yet they are aspects of the plot with which the reader easily identifies. The remaining elements are striking, so the validity of the test is supported.

Test 5: *Parallelism between complex units, such as combined pericopes, that appears constructive rather than random or coincidental increases the probability of intent.*

Corroborative parallelism reduces the apparent influence of the observer's subjectivity. For example, imagine two adjacent passages bearing the features 1, 2, 3, 4, 5 in these groupings: (1, 2, 3)(4, 5). It is less likely that another pair of adjacent passages in the same text would have the groupings (1, 2, 3)(4, 5) than a random arrangement, e.g. (4, 2)(3, 1, 5). Although such correspondence between pericope complexes is not required for intentional parallelism to exist, it makes the observation and validation more certain. This test is not found among scholars dealing with Lukan correspondences.

If the general pattern represented by Bovon, Nolland, Talbert and Fitzmyer, above – a pair of parallel passages followed by a convergence, then two more pairs of parallel passages – is accepted, then the combination of 1:5–25 with 1:57–80 parallel to 1:26–38 with 2:1–40 is highly constructive.

---

44 Praeder, "Jesus-Paul, Peter-Paul," 37.

Test 5 is confirmed as a useful indicator of intended parallelism.

Test 6: *If redaction critical observations yield evidence of Lukan adjustment to include or create the elements that constitute the device, the probability of intent is greater insofar as there are no superior reasons for the observed redaction.*

Redactional observations are obscured by the absence of Markan and Matthean parallels to Luke 1:5–38. Still, the validity of this test is self-evident. If a feature in parallel exists due to Lukan redaction, then the probability is greater that Luke intended it than if there is no redactional support. Redaction of sources is not always necessary, though, to construct parallelism; but locations where Luke actually did such work should be identifiable when there is a Markan parallel (assuming Markan priority). Any instances where parallelism identified in Luke is imported in its entirety from Mark will be noted under this test. In such circumstances, Luke's awareness of the parallelism becomes an issue. The direct relationship of redaction to Lukan composition makes this test perhaps the strongest of the eleven.

Test 7: *If the elements of correspondence that constitute the device are related to important Lukan themes, the probability of intent is enhanced.*

The formation of patterned correspondences is a means of highlighting particular themes or events. It is probable then that Luke would have emphasized through corresponding passages mainly themes he personally considered important. This poses a potential difficulty. If certain themes are important to Luke and are used in correspondences, would they not by virtue of being important be found elsewhere in the work outside the corresponding passages? If so, then there is an apparent conflict with test 1, which looks for restriction of the elements of correspondence to the passages of the correspondence set. This conflict is avoided in two ways, both distinguishing between "element of correspondence" and "important theme". First, the "elements of correspondence" are often not themes in themselves, but are related to them. For example, Jesus warning the disciples (an element of correspondence in our proposal for Luke's structure) is more an action or motif than a theme, yet it is closely related to the important Lukan theme of the disciples' preparation for ministry. Therefore, although the related theme may be important and common, the *element* of correspondence may be absolutely restricted to the correspondence. Second, if the element of correspondence happens to be a theme, then test 7 only looks for it to be *related* to an important theme and not necessarily to be one. Test 1 does not contradict this. If a thematic element of correspondence is merely related to an important theme, then the element may certainly be well restricted to the relevant passages. For instance, Peter verbalizing faith and commitment toward Christ (an element of correspondence in our proposal for Luke's structure) is a subset of the motif of *professing* faith in Christ. This is a rare Lukan theme in the Gospel, but it is closely related to one that is common, the identity of Christ. So a thematic element of correspondence may be both restricted to its correspondence and be related to an important and common theme. Test 7 is therefore consistent with test 1 and is an effective indication of authorial intent.

In that Luke 1:5–25 and 1:26–38 ultimately serve to characterize the origin, identity and significance of Jesus, they necessarily relate to important Lukan themes. John the Baptist is used by Luke to develop the Messianic identity of Jesus, among other things. Therefore, the existence of such important themes concerning Jesus in this clearly intentional pattern supports the validity of this test.

Test 8: *Intent is more certain if there is no clear historical or genre[45] expectation for the inclusion of the features in question and their sequence, if parallelism of sequence is observed.*

Incidental parallelism is probable in texts where two events are recorded that were inherently similar to each other in the way they occurred. Furthermore, if a particular genre suggests a specific format, then incidental parallelism may result. For example, if Luke knew of a "miracle story" genre, he may have been disposed to follow it regularly. If so, his miracle accounts would be inclined toward uniformity that would result in similarities perhaps not intended as literary parallels.

A comparison with the other Gospels confirms that there is no genre expectation for the observed features and sequence in the parallelism between John and Jesus in Luke 1:5–38. Some involvement of John the Baptist appears normal, but nothing of Luke's structure. The form, presumably taken from the Old Testament, may itself be considered a genre and thereby predispose unintentional parallels. Yet this does not appear to be the case in this instance since Luke's accounts have four additional parallel features to the basic OT pattern. This implies further conscious development of the overall parallelism. There is no reason to believe that Luke felt *compelled* by the fact that he was writing annunciations to follow therefore the OT "annunciation genre". There appears to be no expectation (cultural or otherwise), just choice. Coats examines the Old Testament annunciation genre and the sub-genre in which many annunciations are

---

45 Throughout this work, our analysis treats individual pericopes as complete texts manipulated by Luke according to his understanding of them. In other words, his location of a pericope in the Gospel and his alterations of it were often substantially influenced by the literary quality and/or theology of other material within the Gospel or without, such as the Old Testament. Therefore, when features that constitute a proposed parallel between pericopes are basic to its form-critical shape, the particular form should be treated cautiously as a genre.

found, the annunciation to a barren woman. The first consists of the announcement of the birth of a son, the name of the child, and a "definition of his destiny".[46] The second consists of "(1) recognition of the problem, (2) annunciation (birth, name, destiny, although the series may not be stated in full), (3) expression of doubt, and (4) fulfillment of the annunciation".[47] Elizabeth's story basically conforms to the barren woman genre, which accounts for parallels 1, 4, 5, 8 and 9. Recognition of the problem and fulfillment are located at Luke 1:5 and 1:57–80. The annunciation to Mary follows the expected sequence, parallels 1, 4, 5 and 8, but quite unexpectedly she is also treated as a barren woman. Her "problem," the obstacle to conception, is that she is a virgin (Lk. 1:27). Her expression of faith substitutes for an "expression of doubt". Of course, the fulfillment takes place in 2:1–52. This unexpected conformity of Mary's story points toward Lukan intent, especially with his addition of parallels 2, 3, 6 and 7 to the Old Testament pattern and their verbal similarity to each other. His misuse of the barren woman genre demonstrates that he felt no compulsion by genre and that he was exercising free choice. The genre did not make him think, "This is how it is supposed to be done". Undoubtedly, the actual events could have generated the observed features; but the similarity of wording between the two accounts in Luke and the lack of a parallel to the infancy narrative of the Baptist in the other Gospels diminish any apparent historical demand and highlight the structural interest. If history or genre had proven strongly to predispose the accounts toward the observed inclusion of features (or, additionally, their sequence), then the parallelism would be less motivated by structural concerns and more likely coincidental. The Lukan infancy narrative supports the validity of test 8.

Test 9: *If a sequence or grouping of features in parallel is uncommon in other relevant literature, then the likelihood of coincidence due to common expression is diminished.*

Under this test, we are assuming that texts may exert an influence on Luke regardless of what genre they are. The influence is through the sheer number of instances available to Luke in which the sequence or grouping of features is found. In other words, Luke may not be compelled by or even recognize a particular genre, yet the frequency of the sequence or grouping of features may impress them upon his thinking. They may even originate from a genre different from what Luke is employing. This test is of lesser value than many of the other tests due to the difficulty in identifying the features in other literature and in determining what relevant literature is.

---

46 George W. Coats, *Genesis: With an Introduction to Narrative Literature*, vol. 1 of *The Forms of the Old Testament Literature* (Grand Rapids: Eerdmans, 1983) 131, 135.
47 Coats, *Genesis*, 138.

Tannehill has done the difficult work of locating other relevant literature that incorporates the features in Luke 1:5–38 and their sequence. The examples are few and are presented in the final three columns in the above table. The Old Testament obviously had a powerful literary influence on Luke, so it is reasonable to assume that these birth announcements could have formed the basis for his accounts. However, the infrequency of annunciation texts means that Luke was not subtly influenced by the sheer number of them. This militates against mere common expression.

Had the Lukan features and pattern of the annunciations been frequent in literature available to Luke, then the parallelism might be explained as coincidence due to influence by a frequent pattern. Identification of a pattern that is occasional in the relevant literature (as here, the OT) is not as potent a case as a unique Lukan construction would be, but it is not weak. This test correctly indicates authorial intent.

Test 10: *If the passages that constitute parallel groupings of passages are contiguous within the groupings, and not distributed broadly throughout the text, then selectivity on the part of the reader is diminished.*

In complex narrative, there are usually key themes that recur periodically. Therefore, it is sometimes possible to "find" parallel patterns in a lengthy text through a process of selective identification of instances.[48] If you roll a die a hundred times and record the results, you will find several cycles of the sequence 1, 2, 3, 4, 5, 6 spread throughout noncontiguously. You would very rarely find a single contiguous example. However, we are dealing with a product of the human mind, not a random number generator, so incidental patterns are more likely. Nevertheless, contiguity greatly restricts the subjectivity of the observer and decreases the chance of the "pattern" being unintentional. This is a less important test due to the freedom ancient writers apparently felt to have gaps between parallel material.

If a pattern for Luke 1:5–2:40 similar to those proposed by Nolland, Bovon, Fitzmyer and Talbert is accepted – a pair of parallel passages followed by a convergence, then two more pairs of parallel passages – then only 1:39–56 appears to break the contiguity of the parallelism. Yet, even this section is clearly an integral element of the overall structure. The mothers-to-be of both John and Jesus meet together. Therefore, actually, there is unbroken contiguity in terms of the defined pattern. Test 10 correctly looks for this, so Luke 1:5–2:40 is evidence in favor of its value as an indicator of authorial intent.

Test 11: *The probability of intent increases as more of the above tests*

---

48 This is the thrust of Praeder's criticism of various proposed Lukan correspondences in "Jesus-Paul, Peter-Paul," 23–39.

are passed.

Each of the above tests only indicates probability of authorial intent. Individually they have little determinative power. One might ask why test 11 is considered another test and not simply a tallying up of the results. When one examines texts that exhibit broadly accepted patterned structure, like several of the examples in chapter 3, they tend to satisfy most of the above ten tests. Dubious correspondences satisfy few. Consequently, general performance under the above tests is a separate indicator of probable authorial intent. This is one of the less important tests since any subjectivity in the others is complexly accumulated in this one.

The intentional pattern of Luke 1:5–2:40 is strongly indicated as a conscious construction by all the tests but number 6, which did not apply due to lack of redactional evidence. Had only a portion of them pointed to intent, then the set of tests would not be supported as a cumulative indication of the degree of certainty regarding its conscious design. A pattern universally recognized as planned by Luke must be identified as such by a set of indicators, if indeed they are valuable. These eleven indicators of authorial intent are confirmed by this analysis.

Of course, one could say that the entire structure was incorporated wholesale by Luke from a source, in which case the source author would have designed the pattern. With the permeation of Lukanisms throughout the section, however, few deny at least a major Lukan influence. Whoever was primarily responsible for the presence of the features that are in parallel is naturally the one who intentionally constructed the pattern.

4 A New Proposal for the Structure of Luke

Beyond the parallelism of Luke 1:5–38 there is scholarly recognition of a parallel structure incorporating 1:39–4:13. These in conjunction with our proposal for 4:14–24:53 offer a structure that covers the entire Gospel. See the table below. Our proposal for the structure of Luke 4:14–24:53 is developed fully in chapter 4, so at this point only a brief introduction will be provided.

	1:1–4	
	John the Baptist	Jesus
	1:5–25	1:26–38
	1:39–56	
	1:57–66	2:1–21
	1:67–80	2:22–40
	2:41–52	
	3:1–20	3:21–4:13

	Cycle 1		Cycle 2		Cycle 3		Cycle 4	
	passage	feature	passage	feature	passage	feature	passage	feature
Stratum 1	4:14–15	to Galilee	9:51	1	13:22	1	19:28	1
Stratum 2	4:16–30	2	9:52–56	2	13:23–30	2	19:29–40	2
			9:57–62	2	13:31–35	2	19:41–44	2
Stratum 3	4:31–37	3a, b	10:1–24	3a, b	14:1–14	3a, f	19:45–20:8	3b, e
	4:38–39	3a						
	4:40–44	3a						
	5:1–11	3c						
	5:12–16	3a						
	5:17–26	3a, b, d	10:25–37	~3f				
	5:27–32	3c	10:38–42	3g				
	5:33–39	3e	11:1–13	3e				
	6:1–5	3f						
	6:6–11	3a, f						
	6:12–16	3c						
	6:17–49	3a, g	11:14–26	3a				
	7:1–10	3a,b						
	7:11–17	3a						
	7:18–35	3e; 4a						
	7:36–50	3d						
Stratum 4	8:1–21	4a, b	11:27–36	4a, b	14:15–24	4b	20:9–18	4a, b
					14:25–35	4a, b		
Stratum 5			11:37–54	5	15:1–16:31	5	20:19–44	5
Stratum 6			12:1–21	6	17:1–4	6	20:45–47	6
Stratum 7	8:22–25	7	12:22–34	7	17:5–10	7	21:1–4	7
					17:11–19	7; 3a		
Stratum 8	8:26–39	~8; 3a;	12:35–40	8	17:20–37	8	21:5–38	8
	8:40–56	~8; 3a			18:1–8	8		
Stratum 9	9:1–17	9; 3a, b	12:41–48	9	18:9–17	9	22:1–30	9
Stratum 10	9:18–21	10			18:18–28	10	22:31–34	10; 3a
Stratum 11	9:22–27	11	12:49–53	11	18:29–34	11	22:35–24:53	11
Stratum 12[49]	9:28–36	–*	12:54–59	4a*	18:35–43	3a		
	9:37–45	3a	13:1–9	–*	19:1–10	–		
	9:46–50	–	13:10–17	3a	19:11–27	3b		
			13:18–21	–*				

Reference Table Indicating Cycles and Parallel Strata Along with Corresponding Features[50]

---

49 Stratum 12 is considered an interlude in the structure. See the first paragraph of the section "Discussion of the Narrative Strata Across the Four Cycles" below, 210.

50 For a discussion of how the passages in a stratum fit that stratum, see the pages in columns A and B for that stratum in the table below. For why certain passages outside a stratum do not fit that stratum, see the page in column C for that stratum.

I propose that Luke 4:14–24:53 is arranged in four cycles where a sequence of twelve strata is successively repeated, as displayed in the table above. The text begins at cycle 1, stratum 1 and progresses down the first cycle to stratum 12. It continues at stratum 1 of cycle 2 and moves down that cycle, and so on. Each stratum is formed by the presence in the text of a consistent narrative feature (or features) characteristic of that stratum. The features are represented in the gray columns of the table. They are described in detail below, and only their numerical designations are included in the structure table. Beside each pericope, in the gray column, is the feature(s) that is present in that pericope. Therefore, Luke 21:5–38 exhibits feature #8, "Jesus delivers an eschatological discourse to his disciples". A dash (–) indicates a pericope in that location that does not show any of the specific narrative features in the list below. It will be seen that that does not imply it is a misfit. A tilde (~) notes a passage that exhibits the feature in modified form.

Doubtless, many questions arise even at this early stage. The reader is referred to chapter 4 for a detailed explanation of the structure and an application to it of the eleven tests for intentionality.

Below are the observed narrative features that form the strata of the structure.

Stratum 1:

Feature #1: The key phrase, "to Jerusalem" (εἰς Ἱεροσόλυμα or εἰς Ἱερουσαλήμ), is found in an introductory section to a pericope (narrator's voice) where the context highlights this destination as the driving purpose of Jesus' journey.

Stratum 2:

Feature #2: The prophetic status of Jesus is conveyed, involving direct reference and/or allusion to the Elijah-Elisha cycle in 1 and 2 Kings, and is accompanied by the theme of divine rejection of those who reject Jesus/God. This immediately follows a reference to the journey to Jerusalem.

Stratum	A	B	C	Stratum	A	B	C
1	215	234	228	7	220	250	232
2	216	235	231	8	221	251	232
3	216	240	230	9	223	255	232
4	217	244	231	10	225	259	232
5	218	246	231	11	225	260	232
6	219	249	231				

Stratum 3:

    Feature #3a: An account or summary of healing is related (validation of authority).

    Feature #3b: Ἐξουσία is attributed to Jesus.

    Feature #3c: Jesus chooses disciples or designates apostles (exercise of authority).

    Feature #3d: Jesus forgives sins (expression of authority).

    Feature #3e: The ministry of Jesus is likened to or related to that of John the Baptist (a recognized authority), but not equated.

    Feature #3f: Jesus asks, "Is it lawful?" (assertion of authority to interpret the law).

    Feature #3g: The priority of hearing (ἀκούω) the word (λόγος) of Jesus.

Stratum 4:

    Feature #4a: Jesus directly teaches a crowd (ὄχλος or λαός) of non-disciples (content of teaching included).

    Feature #4b: A parable representing Jesus as bearer of a message from God is related, concluding with parables that convey the importance of responding to Jesus' message.

Stratum 5:

    Feature #5:   Jesus personally confronts Jewish leaders, exposing their typical spiritual, moral and religious depravity and therefore implying a lost state.

Stratum 6:

    Feature #6:   Jesus warns (προσέχετε) the disciples or others against being like the religious leaders.

Stratum 7:

    Feature #7:   Jesus encourages the disciples to have greater faith.

Stratum 8:

    Feature #8:   Jesus delivers an eschatological discourse to his disciples.

Stratum 9:

    Feature #9:   Jesus addresses the twelve regarding their role.

Stratum 10:

> Feature #10: Peter verbalizes faith and commitment toward Christ.

Stratum 11:

> Feature #11: Jesus predicts his passion (and resurrection) in the context of the cost of discipleship.

Stratum 12:

> Apparently, no well-restricted features link these passages. The timing of the Kingdom seems to be a common thread, however, and the reappearance of feature 3a, a healing account, establishes tentative parallelism.

According to Bar-Efrat's analysis, as presented above, our "narrative feature" generally equates with his "narrative world," as will be explained in chapter 4. For any questions regarding these features, see that chapter. When the eleven tests are applied there to the proposed structure, they indicate high probability of Lukan intent.

5 The Need for this Study

There is a great need for what is attempted here. Confusion has always existed over the structure of Luke 4:14–24:53.[51] The many proposals of chiasm for the central section add more to this confusion than they do clarity because there is little consensus achieved.[52] Scholars who *evaluate* proposals of structure often use unrealistic criteria, such as the requirement of perfect pattern, and thereby exclude what is probably valid. They also tend to apply criteria with insufficient rigor to rule out the improbable. Scholars who *propose* structure for the Gospel, or even just occasional interrelatedness between passages that is supposedly intended by the Evangelist, often fail to test their proposals with sufficient rigor.[53] In the historical-critical realm, redaction critics take insufficient account of Luke's efforts to build structure. This is demonstrated through a detailed compari-

---

51 To my knowledge there is only one structural proposal that encompasses the entire Gospel, that of Wilkens. He detects a multi-layered, highly complex combination of the sequence "announcement," "manifestation/ revelation," "mission." The complexity itself seems absurd. Furthermore, his categories are broad enough to describe most any Gospel material, which enables him to achieve such complexity. Finally, he has not provided any evidence that such structuring he proposes was employed by another ancient writer ("theologische Struktur," 1–13).
52 This point is well noted by John Nolland, *Luke 9:21–18:34*, Word Biblical Commentary 35b (Dallas: Word Books, 1993) 525–531.
53 See the discussion above, page 9.

son of redaction-critical suggestions for various instances of apparent editorial work that relate to our proposed structure. A surprising number of these instances favor the formation of the structure and have no other substantial scholarly explanation. Finally, an awareness of correspondences actually intended by Luke provides significant clues to how Luke, an early Christian, interpreted gospel material, clues not obtainable through any other approach. There are many other needs and benefits not mentioned here but that will manifest themselves throughout the course of the book.

CHAPTER 1

Lukan Correspondences from the Literary Perspective of Robert C. Tannehill

Robert C. Tannehill, in his book *The Narrative Unity of Luke-Acts*,[1] volume 1, is particularly concerned about Lukan interrelationships, correspondences, between pericopes within Luke and between the Gospel and Acts. Occasionally, however, the literary dependence of Luke on the Old Testament is developed both through the device of the "type-scene" and the broader use of Septuagintal language in Luke 1–2. In addition to "type-scene," he approaches the interrelationship between pericopes through other such literary devices as *preview, review, echo, parallelism,* and *repetition*. It is profitable to examine each device to gain a systematic understanding of the Lukan methodology behind his interrelating of texts as Tannehill perceives it. "Repetition" will be adequately treated as an integral part of the other devices.

This study of Tannehill's work will be of particular benefit to us. Our structure for the gospel of Luke, presented in table form and briefly described in the introduction (see pages 28ff.), is the core of this book and will be developed in chapter 4. It posits many Lukan correspondences similar to those suggested by Tannehill in *The Narrative Unity of Luke-Acts*. Chapters 2 and 3 will demonstrate that ancient writers commonly

---

1 Stephen D. Moore attacks Tannehill's very attempt to find unity in the Gospel of Luke. He presupposes a poststructural philosophy toward text where unity is essentially *defined* as an impossibility. Naturally he will disagree with Tannehill's effort because of his own presupposition. The difficulty with Moore's position is that, although the majority of literary critics espouse his philosophy, they have far from proven that it is correct. Actually, it is beginning to show the faltering that structuralism did before its demise. Furthermore, in a broader assault on narrative criticism as practiced by biblical scholars he defines the discipline in restricted literary-critical terms and implies that no non-expert may define its method differently from his description. Such exclusive claims must not be accepted without careful evaluation since in the literary-critical realm theory is extremely varied and variable, and sometimes even overlaps with aspects of Tannehill's method which he opposes. See Moore's article "Are the Gospels Unified Narratives?", in Kent Harold Richards (ed.), *SBL Seminar Papers* 26 (Atlanta: Scholars Press, 1987) 443–458.

composed using such correspondences. As will be seen in this chapter, Tannehill successfully demonstrates that Luke composed in this manner too. He presents an impressive number of correspondences within Luke, between Luke and Acts, and within Acts. His primary purposes are to show the narrative unity of Luke with Acts through intentional correspondences and to draw theological and interpretational implications from these correspondences. *The Narrative Unity of Luke-Acts*, volumes one and two, is the most thorough treatment available of the broad range of Lukan correlations and their implications. A summary and evaluation of Tannehill's contribution provides valuable groundwork for our proposal of Lukan structure in at least three areas. First, he demonstrates the large variety of types of correspondences and their constituents employed by Luke. It will be evident in chapter 4 that our structure for the Gospel is built on correspondences within the range of these types and constituents. Second, he establishes the strong predisposition in Luke's method of composition to link passages in various ways even to the level of fine detail. Our structure of course reflects this penchant. Third, Tannehill explores the purposes and functions of Lukan previews, reviews, echoes, parallels, and type-scenes, deriving theological and literary implications for interpretation. An evaluation of his methods and conclusions will allow us to utilize and build on the most certain and profitable of these purposes and functions. Chapter 5 investigates the apparent purposes and functions of many correspondences defined by our structure. The goal there is to determine the underlying theology and to suggest Luke's interpretation of certain passages as revealed by the structure. Tannehill's contribution is excellent groundwork for these three aspects of our study.

This chapter is divided into two major sections. The first section discusses the theory behind the types of correspondences Tannehill identifies in Luke-Acts (previews, reviews, echoes, parallels, and type-scenes) and evaluates key examples within Luke. Founded on this discussion of theory in the first section, the second section evaluates Tannehill's major previews, reviews, echoes and parallels that join the Gospel to Acts, probably his primary concern. Naturally, the correspondences within the Gospel are relevant to our proposal of structure for Luke. The links between Luke and Acts are valuable also since they are more related to structure (they join two volumes) than Tannehill's other examples, and they add to the evidence that Luke composed his gospel using detailed correspondences. Most of the previews, reviews, echoes and parallels identified in *The Narrative Unity of Luke-Acts*, vol. 1 (Luke), will appear in this chapter.

One matter that must be kept in mind throughout this study is whether Tannehill's observations reflect what Luke intended or reflect merely coincidental similarities inherent in his source material or even in the underlying tradition or events. Regarding intentionality Tannehill states,

> Some connections are emphasized strongly and are supported by clear literary signals, such as repetition of key words and phrases, indicating either that the author consciously intended the connection or that the author's message was bound to certain controlling images which repeatedly asserted themselves in the process of writing. These connections can contribute to our understanding of a narrative's message at a primary level.[2]

Perhaps this statement does not adequately account for coincidental connections that may well appear intentional. A number of his observed connections involve merely two or three instances within the entire Gospel and do not therefore appear to be "repeated assertions". In such cases, redaction criticism may provide additional support. However, abiding by standard text linguistic theory, he deemphasizes the usefulness of redaction criticism and depends primarily on the final form of the text.

> I am concerned with Luke-Acts in its finished form, not with pre-Lukan tradition. Furthermore, I do not engage in elaborate arguments to distinguish tradition from Lukan redaction of that tradition. Brief comparisons of Luke with Matthew and Mark are useful where there are parallel texts, for these comparisons help us to recognize the distinctiveness of the Lukan version. But detailed analysis of the changes and additions introduced in Luke would lead me away from my main task. Moreover, all material in Luke-Acts, whether it originated as tradition or redaction, is potentially important for my task. The decision to include a unit of tradition in the work is a choice which affects the total work. Even if the wording of the traditional unit is unchanged, it has been redacted by inclusion in a new writing.[3]

However, is the "distinctiveness" of Luke the only significant contribution of redaction criticism to Tannehill's task? Consider the fact that there are scores of distinct interpretations of Melville's *Moby Dick*, only a few of which could have been intentional or even subconscious factors in its composition. At least with the Third Gospel, unlike *Moby Dick*, redactional considerations provide a substantial reference-point for the determination of why Luke included a particular unit.

For example, Tannehill views the repetition of, "What do you have to do with me?" (4:34; 8:28), as "verbal indication that a basic situation – a

---

2 Tannehill, *Narrative Unity*, 1:3.
3 Tannehill, *Narrative Unity*, 1:6.

demon sensing the threatening presence of Jesus – has returned".[4] Yet, assuming Markan priority, each question came directly from this source. Certainly, Luke *could* have intended that the reader relate the two, but it is equally possible that the accounts suited his purpose for different reasons, regardless of the particular wording in question. Although readers can and do remember 4:34 when they encounter 8:28, to press the point and build a case on such an uncertainty may put word's into Luke's mouth. There may be value in how the reader understands Luke apart from his intent, but the "message" must be more closely bound to purpose than to coincidence even if there is a subconscious influence. A heavier dependence on redaction criticism at least provides additional data regarding intent.

Clearly, when considering what was intended by the author, the application of literary-critical methods must treat the Synoptic Gospels – or any literature that involves extensive copying or imitation of source material – differently from that which entails greater creativity of composition, as found in most modern works. Western literature, today, is legally restricted from the compositional methodology evident in the Gospels. Thus, the likelihood of incidental verbal and structural parallelisms that resemble literary devices is abated. Once again, the question arises of whether modern literary theories that are founded on the observation of modern literature and composition may be applied readily to ancient texts.

Part of our analysis involves the determination of whether certain key correspondences suggested by Tannehill are likely to have been intended by Luke. Having demonstrated in the introduction the objective and practical value of our eleven tests for authorial intent, they may now be applied to selected proposals by Tannehill of substantial links within the Gospel and also between Luke and Acts. He shows that much of this interplay between texts is facilitated by various literary devices that depend on correspondence and parallelism. Accordingly, the eleven tests will be valuable for determining the degree of certainty behind his suggestions. Due to the number of correspondences offered by Tannehill, only selected instances will be evaluated for the sake of brevity. The eleven tests are reiterated below for convenience.

1. The greater the restriction of elements of correspondence to the relevant passages, the greater is the probability of authorial intent.
2. The greater the number of reasonable parallel features between parallel passages, the greater is the probability of intent.
3. Similarly, the greater the number of parallel passages (or panels) that

---

4 Tannehill, *Narrative Unity*, 1:94.

match a proposed pattern or grouping of features, the greater is the case for intent.

4. An element of correspondence that attracts the reader's attention contributes to the probability of intent.

5. Parallelism between complex units, such as combined pericopes, that appears constructive rather than random or coincidental increases the probability of intent.

6. If redaction critical observations yield evidence of Lukan adjustment to include or create the elements that constitute the literary device, the probability of intent is greater insofar as there are no superior reasons for the observed redaction.

7. If the elements of correspondence that constitute the literary device are related to important Lukan themes, the probability of intent is enhanced.

8. Intent is more certain if there is no clear historical or genre expectation for the inclusion of the features in question and their sequence, if parallelism of sequence is observed.

9. If a sequence or grouping of features in parallel is uncommon in other relevant literature, then the likelihood of coincidence due to common expression is diminished.

10. If the passages that constitute parallel groupings of passages are contiguous within the groupings, and not distributed broadly throughout the text, then selectivity on the part of the reader is diminished.

11. The probability of intent increases as more of the above tests are passed.

1 Previews, Reviews, Echoes, Parallels, and Type-scene in Luke: Theory and Evaluation of Selected Examples

Treatment of the literary devices in this section is broken into "definition" and "function". The eleven tests for authorial intent are applied to selected instances in the "function" portions.

1.1 Preview and Review

Initially it is most helpful to discuss the function Tannehill attributes to previews and reviews before examining the definitions applied and the means of identifying them. This is because the definition and identifying features are founded on the function they perform. Only the most relevant tests of the eleven above will be applied to the selected instances for the sake of brevity.

Function: According to Tannehill, the purposes or functions of previews and reviews are manifold. They tie narrative together, aid in the comprehension of plot, interpret events, create expectations, and indicate what is central to the message or story.[5]

1. Tie narrative together. Perhaps his most representative example of the function of tying narrative together is Luke 24, which also happens to illustrate the others exceptionally well. This chapter serves to join the Gospel to Acts through the review of important aspects of Luke and the preview of what the reader will encounter in the second volume. One key instance of review is the direct reference to passion predictions earlier in Luke as well as in the Old Testament (Lk. 24:6–7, 25–26, 44, 46).[6] Therefore, a review can even cover relevant material chronologically prior to the events of the text. Furthermore, within three short scenes in Luke 24, a broad span of the Gospel is encompassed. The passion announcements in the Galilean ministry (9:22, 44) are to be remembered, as the angel indicates to the women at the tomb, "Remember (μνήσθητε) how He spoke to you while He was still in Galilee…" (24:6). The remaining announcements spread throughout the Gospel are referred to by Jesus (24:44–46), "These are my words which I spoke to you while I was still with you…" (24:44). This, among other reviews in this chapter, freshens in the reader's mind the key events in the whole of Luke and links them with previews of Acts. The probability of Lukan intent is high, obviously; and the relevant tests bear this out. **Test 1:** *Restriction to passages* – Naturally the restriction is absolute since Luke 24 refers to all passion predictions earlier in Luke and in the OT. **Test 3:** *Number of panels/passages* – There are several passion predictions in Luke and several prophesies in the OT that are reviewed. In addition, there are four reviews in Luke 24. **Test 4:** *Attracts attention* – Passion predictions clearly attract attention. **Test 6:** *Redaction criticism* – Each review in Luke 24 (6–7, 25–26, 44, 46) is found only in Luke, so redaction criticism provides no assistance here. **Test 7:** *Important themes* – The passion of Christ is an important Lukan theme. **Test 8:** *Historical/genre expectation* – The other Gospels suggest that there is no strong historical or genre expectation of such a review (only Mt. 28:6). **Test 9:** *Common expression* – Clearly reviews of Christ's passion predictions are

---

5 Tannehill, *Narrative Unity*, 1:2, 21, 61, 162.
6 See Tannehill's discussion of this "review" of prior passion predictions, *Narrative Unity*, 1:277–278.

not common in relevant literature.

In conjunction with his review of the passion predictions, Jesus provides a sweeping preview of volume two (24:44–49).[7] Major themes central to the Acts of the Apostles are clustered: the name of Jesus, repentance for the forgiveness of sins, mission to all nations, the apostles as witnesses, and "power from on high". This preview will be examined in detail later (see pages 60ff.). As Tannehill demonstrates clearly, Luke employs previews and reviews to tie Acts to Luke.

2. Aid in the comprehension of plot. Previews and reviews enhance comprehension of plot in a somewhat less obvious and more intuitive manner. An excellent example Tannehill develops is the account of the large catch of fish (Lk. 5:1–11).[8] Whether or not the reader knows the coming events that will contribute toward Peter's preparation for catching people, Jesus' words suggest the direction in which the plot might head, and in fact does. Eventually, when Acts 2 is reached, the interplay between the response to Peter's sermon and the implication behind the large catch of fish enables us to make a connection that otherwise might have been obscured by the length and detail of Luke's story. Thus, the plot, as it pertains to Peter, is made more comprehensible.

3. Interpret events. Previews and reviews often play an interpretative role in Lukan writings, as Tannehill reveals. Such a function is evident within the transfiguration account where the tenor is set for the entire travel narrative. Jesus, Moses and Elijah

> were speaking of 'his departure, which he was going to fulfill in Jerusalem' (9:31). Here we find an explicit reference to future events which integrates the transfiguration scene into the larger narrative and enables it to serve as a preview for the reader and as preparation for Jesus. For the reader, 9:31 reemphasizes the importance of the announcement of Jesus' death in 9:22 and interprets that event as part of the divine purpose.[9]

The reader is encouraged to interpret progress toward Jerusalem and the crucifixion as within God's plan. Reinforcing this is the use of ἔξοδος, which adds Old Testament salvific flavor. So with this framework, all the events that transpire up to and including Christ's death are understood as within the bounds of God's overarching plan of salvation.

4. Create expectations. The creation of expectation is demonstrated in a series of three previews (19:11–27; 19:41–44 and 20:9–19) that, as Tanne-

---

[7] For a detailed presentation of this and several other previews of Acts, including verbal similarities, see Tannehill, *Narrative Unity*, 1:294–296.
[8] Tannehill, *Narrative Unity*, 1:204–205.
[9] Tannehill, *Narrative Unity*, 1:223.

hill explains, lead the reader to expect the rejection of Jesus in Jerusalem.[10] When Jesus laments over Jerusalem, 19:41–44, he indicates that the people will not recognize him and that the city will consequently be destroyed at some future time. The parable of the tenants, 20:9–19, teaches again that Jesus will be rejected and adds the fact of his death; but Tannehill steps on uncertain ground when he suggests that, in light of 19:41–44, 20:16 likely alludes to the destruction of Jerusalem. It is the Jewish leaders who are specified, 20:19; but in Tannehill's favor, most of these resided in Jerusalem, so the brunt of any divine action would strike the city. In keeping with the theme of immediate rejection in Jerusalem, Tannehill proposes this as the primary referent of the rebellion against the king described in the parable of the ten minas (19:11–27). He supports the argument with references to the kingship of Jesus at the triumphal entry (19:38) and at the trial (23:2, 37). More likely, the primary referent is rebellion occurring between the ascension and Parousia that, to a degree, is reflected in the rejection in Jerusalem.[11] Several factors point to this conclusion. (1) Luke consistently links the departure of Jesus, portrayed here in 19:12, with his death. If such a link were intended in this parable, then the appointment as king would likely be post-resurrection. (2) When the king returns, he carries out judgment that entails capital punishment of the irresponsible, and no such action was taken by Jesus in the city. If the departure occurred some time before his entry into Jerusalem and the return is other than to the city, as Tannehill suggests, then the origin and destination of the journey are obscured and it is difficult to see in what sense he was in a "distant country" for the duration. (3) Apparently Luke considered the appointment of Jesus as king to have occurred in conjunction with his exaltation to the right hand of the Father (Acts 1:29–36). Still, the parable of the ten minas, as well as the other two passages, do foster the definite expectation that the Jewish leaders will not accept Jesus when he arrives at his destination.

A fascinating instance of the creation of expectation is found in the Benedictus (Lk. 1:68–79) where joy and redemption for God's people, implying the Jews, are exclaimed; but the expectation this creates would have been known by most readers to be false within the time frame of the Gospel. If not, the remainder of the narrative would drive it home. Jesus was heading to the cross. Certainly, joy and redemption would result; but the Jews had largely rejected Jesus from before the crucifixion through to the readers' day, and only after the resurrection was joy the most appropriate emotional response to the plot. The mix of joy and anticipation with the

---

10 Tannehill, *Narrative Unity*, 1:159–162.
11 See I. Howard Marshall's helpful discussion of the time-frame of this parable in *The Gospel of Luke, A Commentary on the Greek Text*, New International Greek Testament Commentary (Exeter: The Paternoster Press, 1978) 700–704.

supposed success of Jesus' opponents' murderous plans creates a powerful tragedy due to the emotional contradiction.[12]

5. Indicate what is central to the message or story. Tannehill also demonstrates that previews and reviews are one of four types of material that provide "important clues to what is central in the narrative".[13] Jesus' reading from Isaiah at the synagogue in Nazareth (Lk. 4:18–19; cf. Is. 61:1–2) constitutes a preview of his ministry and, as such, highlights its essential nature.[14] It is a commission from God that involves the Holy Spirit and Jesus' Messianic identity. Its goal is release, which is accomplished primarily through proclamation, and benefits those who suffer from various physical and spiritual needs. Unambiguously, the Gospel fleshes out this theoretical statement. A case can be made that this essential nature of Jesus' ministry is carried as a central theme even throughout the Acts of the Apostles.[15]

It is likely that Luke intended this quotation from Isaiah to preview the ministry of Jesus as Tannehill suggests. **Test 1:** *Restriction to passages* – Instances where Jesus quotes Isaiah to proclaim his ministry a fulfillment are rare (see also Lk. 7:22). **Test 2:** *Number of features* – Tannehill identifies many features in the Isaiah quotation that are paralleled throughout the rest of Luke.[16] **Test 4:** *Attracts attention* – The Isaiah passage describes miraculous events. **Test 6:** *Redaction criticism* – Luke 4:16–30 evidences "a considerable use of source materials as opposed to free composition,"[17] so Luke is probably responsible for the specific inclusion of the quotation. **Test 7:** *Important themes* – Fulfillment of prophecy and the specific elements of the Isaiah quotation are common in Luke. **Test 8:** *Historical/genre expectation* – This quotation is not expected by genre or history, as the other Gospels show.

Tannehill admits this passage to be remarkable in terms of its function in the narrative, which opens the question of whether many previews and reviews identified in his book – and virtually every conceivable instance is treated – would designate what Luke considered central. Obviously, not every example proposed in *Narrative Unity* functions in this manner or

---

12 Tannehill, *Narrative Unity*, 1:34–37.
13 These types are "major Old Testament quotations, statements of commission which an important character has received from God, previews and reviews of the course of the narrative, and disclosures of God's purpose by characters presented as reliable." See Tannehill, *Narrative Unity*, 1:61.
14 For a more detailed account of the specific elements of preview, see Tannehill, *Narrative Unity*, 1:61–68.
15 Tannehill cites several passages in Acts which characterize the ministry of Jesus in similar terms. See particularly, *Narrative Unity*, 1:63–68.
16 See Tannehill, *Narrative Unity*, 1:61–68.
17 Nolland, *Luke 9:21–18:34*, 192–193.

there would be an unacceptable number of "central" elements. On the other hand, every instance specified as a preview or review does spring from material where the topic is *important* to the work. The preview that John the Baptist would turn people to God (Lk. 3:3, 7–14),[18] for instance, is important but not central to the plot. The suggested previews of the destruction of Jerusalem (Lk. 19:41–44; 20:9–19)[19] are important but, again, not central to Luke-Acts.

Definition: The examples of previews and reviews Tannehill presents create the impression that such phenomena are easily identifiable. Scanning all the instances Tannehill cites, however, may leave the impression that any passage which has as its referent an event or account further on in the text, or even beyond the chronology of events in the text, is a preview; and the reverse applies to reviews. Regarding these two related narrative techniques he writes, "Recent theoretical discussions of narrative have noted that the sequential experience of events in the story may be controlled by disclosing information out of chronological order. There may be previews of coming events and reviews of past events, often in a way that interprets these events from some perspective."[20] An inherent aspect of this definition, then, is that a preview may not be recognized as such until the referent is reached in the reading process or unless the referent is already familiar to the reader. For example, someone unfamiliar with the historical Peter and the events to come in Luke and Acts might not initially perceive the great catch of fish (Lk. 5:1–11) as a preview.[21] This is because that reader might not know that the words of Jesus, "from now on you will be catching men" (v. 10), actually come true. Despite this, when coupled with its referent, the preview is enabled to function as described above. Caution must be exercised in the attribution of intent to text events that qualify as a preview or review by Tannehill's definition since they are numerous and may occasionally be coincidental to material incorporated by Luke for different reasons. This caution is practiced admirably in *Narrative Unity*, but could easily be neglected by those following the methodology with less skill or care. The skill he exhibits yields convincing results.

An obvious note that aids in the identification of previews and reviews is that the perspective of previews is to the future and that of reviews is to the past. This is not to say that all allusions to the future or to the past qualify. Less obviously, either technique may be employed through the narrator's

---

18 Tannehill, *Narrative Unity*, 1:23.
19 Tannehill, *Narrative Unity*, 1:159–161.
20 Tannehill, *Narrative Unity*, 1:21.
21 Luke 5:1–11 is noted by Tannehill as a prefiguration of future events. See *Narrative Unity*, 1:203–206.

voice, as in the reference to Christ's ἔξοδος (Lk. 9:31),[22] or through the voice of a character, as in the great catch of fish (Lk. 5:10b).[23] Accordingly, the type of narrative is not a factor in locating previews and reviews.

The above definition and means of identifying previews and reviews is subject to the criticism that it is overly inclusive. On one or two occasions, Tannehill seems drawn to a questionable conclusion. Specifically, he considers Luke 14:26–27, 33 (teaching on the requirements of discipleship) to be a review of 9:57–62 (rejection of three people interested in discipleship).[24] True, 9:57 is earlier in time and contains similar material, but the pair lacks other features of reviews that he has utilized outside this instance. The second passage does not look to the past, and no information seems to be disclosed out of chronological order. Perhaps the denial of family and possessions may point to this aspect of the disciples' experience in the past, but this is not made explicit. Not every passage on discipleship reviews or previews the others.

Overall, however, Tannehill's identification of previews and reviews is remarkably sensitive and cautious. In virtually every instance, the devices are shown to relate to important matters of plot and theology. Yet, one question remains, as mentioned above. Are these previews and reviews the product of Luke's intent or are they a by-product of the inclusion of varied source material? It is not enough to hold that observations regarding the final form reflect the author's intent merely because the author chose to include a unit,[25] especially when it is well founded that Luke incorporated, wholesale, large amounts of detailed narrative from Mark. It is inconceivable that Luke had a handle on and employed all the details contained in this material. Furthermore, there is a lack in the examples of previews and reviews of "repetition of key words and phrases" that Tannehill accepts as indication of authorial intent or awareness.[26]

To illustrate the problem of intent, notice that Luke 20:9–19 (parable of the tenants) is located in the middle of a block of four pericopes extracted from Mark. It is proposed, as discussed earlier, that this parable constitutes an intentional preview of the rejection of Jesus in Jerusalem,[27] which is reasonable. However, can we be certain that it was not simply included because it was part of a Markan block that Luke deemed suitable to this narrative section, and no reason of incompatibility was found to excise it? This would result in an unintentional "preview". Admittedly, there is value

---

22 For Tannehill's treatment of this preview, see *Narrative Unity*, 1:223.
23 Tannehill discusses this preview in *Narrative Unity*, 1:204.
24 Tannehill, *Narrative Unity*, 1:231–232.
25 As cited earlier, Tannehill, *Narrative Unity*, 1:6.
26 As cited previously, Tannehill, *Narrative Unity*, 1:3.
27 Tannehill, *Narrative Unity*, 1:161.

in the identification of unintentional text phenomena that impact the reader similarly to corresponding intentional techniques, but the determination of Lukan purpose is not productively served.

Although there is uncertainty regarding the foundation of intentionality behind Tannehill's individual examples of previews and reviews, the impression created is that the majority must have been intended. None is trivial and most are in Lukan material. The uncertainty could be diminished with a greater dependence on redaction criticism than his text linguistic presuppositions allowed.

1.2 Echo and Parallel

The remaining narrative devices (echoes and parallels, type-scenes, and repetition) have a great deal of overlap with each other, yet each makes its own distinct contribution to the interrelationship between pericopes in Luke-Acts. For example, echoes and parallels exhibit repetition or similar themes with their referents. In fact, repetition will surface in each of the others, especially type-scene, which owes its existence to a form of repetition. In the following discussion, an attempt will be made to distinguish between the essential attributes of these techniques. Only the relevant tests from the "tests for intentionality" will be employed in the discussion below for brevity.

Definition: The closest to a definition that Tannehill offers for "echo" is that "characters and actions may echo characters and actions in another part of the story, as well as characters and action of the scriptural story which preceded Luke-Acts".[28] Throughout *The Narrative Unity of Luke-Acts*, "echo" and "parallel" are used somewhat interchangeably and will therefore be treated together.[29] A number of narrative features are considered by Tannehill at least partially to constitute an echo or parallel, and these assist in pinpointing a definition. Luke's presentation of the annunciation to Mary parallels the annunciation to Zechariah through repetition in identical order of, among other things, events, words, and character responses: Gabriel is the messenger, both Zechariah and Mary are troubled and are instructed by the angel not to be afraid, then follows the birth announcement. Each announcement conforms to a pattern: birth of the child, his name, his greatness, involvement of the Holy Spirit, and future role of the son. Then Zechariah and Mary ask a question and receive a sign.[30] Although Luke provides no indication that such a structure underlies each account, the echo or parallel is intricately formed.

---

28 Tannehill, *Narrative Unity*, 1:3.
29 See *Narrative Unity*, 2:50, where Tannehill equates the two terms.
30 Tannehill, *Narrative Unity*, 1:15.

A less complex example illustrates how simply an echo may be formed. Tannehill proposes that the repetition of four words between the Benedictus (Lk. 1:67–79) and Jesus' lament over Jerusalem at the triumphal entry (Lk. 19:40–44) comprises an echo.[31] Each employs ἐπισκέπτομαι/ἐπισκοπή (1:68, 78 and 19:44 respectively), the root of which occurs elsewhere in the Gospel only at 7:16; each mentions the enemies (ἐχθροί) of Israel (1:71, 74 and 19:43), and peace (εἰρήνη, 1:79 and 19:42). Finally, knowledge (γνῶσις/γινώσκω) is repeated (1:77 and 19:42 respectively). Similarly, he proposes that Lk. 19:38 echoes 2:14,[32] obviously because of the repetition of δόξα ἐν ὑψίστοις and εἰρήνη.

More subtly, the teaching of John the Baptist in Luke 3:11, "Let the man who has two tunics share with him who has none; and let him who has food do likewise," is said to be echoed in the teaching of Jesus (Lk. 6:30; 12:33; 14:12–14; 16:9; 18:22)[33] despite the lack of consistent verbal repetition. In this instance, the echo or parallel is based on the concept of giving to the poor. Again, we must ask whether such a phenomenon may be considered a literary device, which implies authorial intent, or whether it is a mere product of the frequency of this topic in the actual teaching of John and of Jesus. All instances of Jesus' and John's teaching on the subject are included, so restriction of the features to the passages in parallel is naturally strong (**test 1:** *restriction to passages*) and several passages are involved (**test 3:** *number of panels/passages*). The topic of giving to the poor is related to the prominent Lukan theme of possessions (**test 7:** *important themes*).[34] However, these are the only tests under which this set of echoes performs well. Redactionally, although Luke 3:10–14 is found only in Luke, it is likely that it comes from Q (compare Lk. 3:7–14 with Mt. 3:7–10).[35] If so, the Evangelist probably included 3:7–14 for a general example of the teaching of John rather than for the specific teaching on giving to the poor. Therefore, no clear support is gained from redaction criticism (**test 6:** *redaction criticism*).

---

31 See Tannehill's discussion, *Narrative Unity*, 1:36.
32 Tannehill, *Narrative Unity*, 1:36.
33 Tannehill, *Narrative Unity*, 1:51.
34 Luke Timothy Johnson, *The Literary Function of Possessions in Luke-Acts*, Howard C. Kee, and Douglas A. Knight (eds.), SBL Dissertation Series 39, (Atlanta: Scholars Press, 1977).
35 Heinz Schürmann, *Das Lukasevangelium: Erster Teil: Kommentar zu Kap. 1, 1–9, 50*, HTKNT 3/1 (Freiburg: Herder, 1969) 169. Joachim Jeremias believes portions of 3:10–14 are from the Lukan *Sondergut*. See *Die Sprache des Lukasevangeliums: Redaktion und Tradition im Nicht-Markusstoff des dritten Evangeliums*, Kritisch-exegetischer Kommentar über das Neue Testament (Göttingen: Vandenhoeck & Ruprecht, 1980) 106–109.

Another means whereby Luke establishes parallels within the Gospel is the formation of parallels with Old Testament passages. These OT passages may bear relation to one another and thus link the Lukan pericopes, or the Lukan pericopes may parallel a single OT account by means of echoes. Tannehill suggests a possible "series of parallels" between Luke 4:14–30 (Jesus' visit to Nazareth) and Luke 7:2–23 (a complex of three pericopes) established through links with the Elijah-Elisha cycle and quotation from Is. 61.[36] In Luke 4:14–30 Jesus reads from Is. 61 and then refers to Elijah with the widow of Zarephath and Elisha with Naaman the Syrian. Regarding Luke 7:2–23, he cites Larrimore Crockett's proposition that the healing of the centurion's servant is parallel to Elisha's healing of Naaman the Syrian.[37] Furthermore, Jesus' raising of the widow's son is parallel to the revivification performed by Elijah on the son of the widow of Zarephath. Finally, in response to the disciples of John the Baptist, Jesus quotes Is. 61. It will be shown shortly that there is high probability that this is intentional parallelism.

In summary, Tannehill proposes several means by which Luke created echoes or parallels between characters and actions in separate pericopes, means that define the identifying features of these phenomena. A plurality of repeated words may suffice, or merely a repeated motif. The duplication of a pattern of events, words and character behavior suggests such a link. Finally, an echo or parallel between passages within Lukan material may be formed through any clear mutual link with distinct but related material from another significant text (such as the Elijah-Elisha cycle).

Function: Tannehill discerns a variety of functions performed by echoes and parallels within Luke-Acts. These, briefly, include commentary, theological attribution, reminder, comparison, engagement of the imagination, highlight, and thematic unification.[38] There is often a combination of functions evidenced by a single echo or parallel, and no function appears to be restricted by the type of echo or parallel. Each of these functions will be exemplified, several of them using the passages discussed above.

1. Commentary. Compared with the other functions, "commentary" suggests that Luke is not simply enabling the reader to perform an evaluation or analysis, but that he is actually informing the reader of his own evaluation. This need not be identical to the function of the attribution of theological significance, since commentary may lack theological emphasis. Certainly, theological significance forms a subset of commentary and non-

---

36 See his discussion in *Narrative Unity*, 1:72.
37 As cited, Larrimore Crockett, *The Old Testament in the Gospel of Luke, with Emphasis on the Interpretation of Isaiah 61:1–2*, Ph.D. diss. (Brown University, 1966) 138–40.
38 See Tannehill, *Narrative Unity*, 1:3, 15–6, 9, 15–6, 20, 66, 108, respectively.

theological commentary may cumulatively constitute theological attribution, but we shall examine the less theological first.

Luke appears to create a tragic atmosphere surrounding the ministry of Jesus through a variety of echoes at the end of Jesus' ministry that have their referents in the first two chapters. The formation of the echo in Luke 19:38 (the praise of the multitude at the triumphal entry) by repetition of key words, for instance, dashes the expectations of the reader that were raised by its parallel passage (2:14).[39] Initially the reader is excited by the high praise of the multitude of angels in response to the birth of the Savior, "*Glory to God in the highest*, and on earth *peace* among men with whom He is pleased" (italics mine). Without previous knowledge of the life and death of Jesus, one would expect at this point a career virtually devoid of what could be perceived as failure. Naturally, a familiarity with Jewish hopes would foster the anticipation, additionally, of a nationalistic victory within the lifetime of Jesus. Even Luke 19:38 sustains a positive note, "...*peace* in heaven and *glory in the highest*" (italics mine – note the repetition of words from Lk. 2:14). Yet, the context of this echo clarifies the tragedy. Jesus had not brought peace, but division (see Lk. 12:51–53). The Jews had not responded to their Messiah, (see Lk. 20:1–19). Even his life would be terminated before any success of the type expected was achieved. "The approaching tragic turn in the narrative is forcefully expressed through repeating the language of the birth story while Jesus makes clear that the salvation anticipated at the beginning will not be realized now for Jerusalem."[40] I would add to this that closure of the earthly ministry is also achieved by this form of inclusio, with Jesus' heavenly accomplishment anticipated. Through such echoes, therefore, Luke has stamped his comment on the story of Jesus, interpreting it as a tragedy (a tragedy need not finish in disaster; obviously, neither does Luke's Gospel).

In the case of the above echo, Tannehill has redactional support that substantiates the probability of Lukan intent (**test 6:** *redaction criticism*). Note that Luke 2:14 is within a large block of L material, chapters 1–2. Luke 19:38, although within a pericope of triple tradition, has been edited in a manner that establishes repetition of key words from Luke 2:14; εἰρήνη and δόξα are added to the ἐν ὑψίστοις present in Mark and Matthew.[41] Based on a few repeated words, however, it is difficult to claim authorial intent; yet, Tannehill has the additional support of both the angels and the disciples described as a multitude (πλῆθος, 8x in Luke) praising (αἰνέω, 3x in Luke) God (**test 2:** *number of features*). Again, we may only speak in

---

39 Tannehill, *Narrative Unity*, 1:36.
40 Tannehill, *Narrative Unity*, 1:36.
41 Tannehill makes a subtle appeal to this redactional evidence, *Narrative Unity*, 1:36.

terms of probability due to the complexity of the Gospel and the uncertainty of Luke's sources, but the present redactional evidence suggests high probability when coupled with the key locations of the two passages (**test 5:** *constructive complexity*) and the restricted employment of the above terms by Luke (**test 1:** *restriction to passages*).

2. Theological Attribution. As stated above, the function of theological attribution is authorial commentary with a theological emphasis. An excellent example Robert Tannehill proposes is the parallelism between the ministries of Jesus and Elijah-Elisha evident in Luke 4:14–30 and 7:2–23. The first explicitly refers to two accounts in the Elijah-Elisha cycle and the second contains the story of Jesus raising the widow's son (Lk. 7:11–17), which has verbal and formal parallels with the account of Elijah raising a widow's son. Regarding theological attribution to Jesus by this echo he states, "The narrator is apparently interested in Jesus as a prophet on the model of Elijah-Elisha both because he is a great miracle-working prophet (see 7:16) and because of the ministry to outsiders suggested by the incidents cited in 4:25–27." Furthermore, such "…allusions to events and person's of Israel's story…provide precedents and interpretive models for understanding Jesus' mighty acts".[42] This establishment of Jesus as a prophet enhances the readers understanding of the people's rejection of Jesus since this was the common reception experienced by the Old Testament prophets.[43]

Certainly the echo of the Elijah-Elisha cycle in Luke 4:14–30 was intended by Luke, as evidenced by its very inclusion and the prominence of the explicit citations in the pericope. Redactionally (**test 6:** *redaction criticism*), it is Lukan regardless of whether one considers the account in Luke to be modeled after the Markan version (Mk. 6:1–6a). In addition, it would be no surprise if Luke 7:11–17 was intended as an echo of Elijah's miracle, due to the frequency of allusions to Elijah in the Gospel (**test 7:** *important themes*).[44] The fact that it is L material removes the possibility that it was merely one of a block of Markan accounts incorporated wholesale by Luke without literary consideration of this element of content. Its validity as an echo must stand on the points of similarity between the two stories. The response of the people in the Lukan story suggests they had made the connection to Elijah. Marshall points out that Jesus exhibited "the kind of powers similar to those of Elijah and Elisha (1 Ki. 17:17–24; 2 Ki. 4:18–37) which led the people to conclude that he was a prophet and that

---

42 Tannehill, *Narrative Unity*, 1:87.
43 Tannehill, *Narrative Unity*, 1:72–73.
44 For a discussion of the details regarding the relation between Jesus and Elijah/Elisha and the attribution of prophet status to Jesus throughout Luke, see Tannehill, *Narrative Unity*, 1:72, 88 n.25, 96–9, 230–231.

through his activity God was visiting his people".[45] Such links between Jesus and such an important and fascinating OT character would probably attract the attention of a reader familiar with the OT (**test 4:** *attracts attention*). Fitzmyer and Evans contribute several additional points of parallel including a widow, a town, meeting at a gate, a son restored to life, the child is given back to his mother, and the miracle-worker is declared a "man of God" (**test 2:** *number of features*).[46] Jesus' prophetic status and his relationship to Elijah are relatively important Lukan themes (**test 7:** *important themes*).

3. Reminder. Tannehill demonstrates well the function of echoes as reminders in his treatment of the series of pericopes that picture Jesus "releasing sins" (Lk. 5:17–32; 7:31–50; 15:1–32; 18:9–14; 19:1–10). He understands these scenes to be intentionally connected to cumulatively characterize Jesus in the reader's mind.[47]

> Beginning in 5:17 the narrator demonstrates special interest in Jesus as the proclaimer of the release of sins by taking a diverse group of stories related to this theme and artfully connecting them, even though they are separated by other material. The stories are connected because later stories repeatedly remind the reader of earlier, related stories. This contributes to the unity of the narrative. It also encourages a reading process of recall and comparison so that as each new episode is sounded, the related episodes resound with enriching harmonies.[48]

Luke appears to have repeated particular themes, words and characters from one story to another to form these connections, as the following table illustrates.[49]

---

45 Marshall, *Gospel of Luke*, 283.
46 Fitzmyer, *Luke I–IX*, 656; C.F. Evans, *Saint Luke*, TPI New Testament Commentaries (London: SCM, 1990) 346–347.
47 Tannehill, *Narrative Unity*, 1:9, 103–109.
48 Tannehill, *Narrative Unity*, 1:103–104.
49 The data for this table is extracted from Tannehill's *Narrative Unit*, 1:103–109.

Connection	5:17–32	7:31–50	15:1–32	19:1–10
Scribes and/or Pharisees	x	x	x	
Declaration that Jesus forgives sins	x	x		
Son of Man	x	x		x
Fellowship with tax collectors and/or sinners	x	x	x	x
Jesus' critics grumble (γογγύζω or διαγογγύζω)	x		x	x
Statement of Jesus' mission.[50]	x			x
Contrast between the righteous and sinners	x		x	
Jesus seeks the lost			x	x

The first passage (Lk. 5:17–32), incorporating the healing of the paralytic, the call of Levi and the meal at his house, establishes the foundation for the connections to follow. Tannehill notes that this is the first instance where Jesus forgives sins and where he encounters the scribes and Pharisees. He considers the three scenes to function as one, in this instance, because they each carry the theme of official opposition to Jesus' fellowship with sinners, and since Luke has drawn them closer than Mark through the deletion of the reference to Jesus' teaching by the sea. In addition, the Lukan account specifies the location of the meal as Levi's house, while the location is unclear in Mark. Seven of the eight features enumerated in the table are contained in this complex. As mentioned above, Tannehill interprets the sequence of four connected passages as a portrayal of Jesus forgiving sins, which raises the question of how the story of the meal at Levi's house bears this weight. It is precisely due to the thematic continuity with the preceding account where Jesus is explicitly attributed as having authority to forgive sins. The Levi account serves to confirm the extension of this forgiveness even to those considered unworthy by the scribes and

---

50 The fact that the two summaries of Jesus' mission lie at the beginning and end of his ministry suggests an inclusion, "That is, we have similar general statements about Jesus' mission early and late in his ministry, statements which serve to interpret the whole ministry which lies between them. Through repetition and significant placement the narrator emphasizes that these are important and comprehensive interpretations of the purpose of Jesus in God's plan." Tannehill, *Narrative Unity*, 1:107–108.

Pharisees.

When Luke 7:31–50 is examined, again two separate scenes are related, as in Luke 5:17–32.[51] Reference to Jesus as a friend to tax-gatherers and sinners reminds the reader of Levi (compare 5:30 with 7:34), and the next scene focuses on Jesus as the mediator of divine forgiveness, a ministry exemplified through his response to an unworthy woman. This forgiveness, linked to faith, reminds the reader of the paralytic forgiven through his faith (compare 5:20–21 with 7:48–50).

An appeal to the literary device of echo relates the otherwise problematic Luke 15:1–32 into the web of connected units.[52] Verses one and two set the scene with three key constituents repeated from Luke 5:29–32. Jesus associates with tax-gatherers and sinners, the Pharisees and their scribes are present, and they grumble about this association. The three parables that follow, function as an explanation of this fellowship with sinners. They are joined by the common picture of the finding of something that was lost, a clear allusion to the ministry of Jesus to the outcasts. A more direct link between the parables and Luke 5:29–32 is the contrast between the righteous and sinners (cf. 5:32 with 15:7,10). Forgiveness of sins is not expressly mentioned in chapter fifteen, but Tannehill believes the demonstrated connections to Luke 5:17–32 import the theme into this chapter in the reading process, a suggestion certainly consistent with the father's reception of the prodigal son.

Jesus' encounter with Zacchaeus (Lk. 19:1–10) also contains a number of connections with the earlier material and, thus, reiterates the topic of forgiveness, according to Tannehill.[53] There is grumbling over Jesus' fraternization with this tax collector. There is a statement of Jesus' mission (Lk. 19:10), as in Luke 5:32. "Furthermore, the use of 'Son of Man' in 19:10 may relate this statement to the general statement about Jesus' authority to forgive in 5:24, where this title was also used."[54] This last argument, however, depends heavily on the other connections since the term "Son of Man" is common in Luke (24x). Finally, the reference to the lost in the mission statement recalls the parables in chapter fifteen. Again, forgiveness of sin is not expressly mentioned here, so reliance on the connections is substantial; yet, forgiveness is undoubtedly implied in the salvation of Zacchaeus (Lk. 19:9).

There is no doubt that Luke portrays Jesus as one with authority to forgive sins; but we must ask whether the suggested connections between passages, two of the four with no explicit reference to the forgiveness of

---

51 For a more detailed discussion, see Tannehill, *Narrative Unity*, 1:105–106.
52 Tannehill, *Narrative Unity*, 1:106–107.
53 Tannehill, *Narrative Unity*, 1:107–108.
54 Tannehill, *Narrative Unity*, 1:107.

sins, were intended by Luke. This is not to question whether Luke constructed various echoes and parallels as reminders, but rather whether the methodology used to identify them adequately tests for authorial intent.

Notice, first, the complexity of Luke 5:17–32 in terms of corresponding elements. There is risk that a complex passage may appear related to a number of others simply by virtue of the number of possible combinations of connections inherent in its complexity. Additional controls are necessary to strengthen the case for intent. This is particularly the case when the elements of proposed correspondence are common in Luke. As indicated earlier, "Son of Man" is quite common, as is the presence of scribes and Pharisees. Furthermore, the combination of two or more scenes increases the likelihood of correspondence by enlarging the pool of features from which to draw parallels. This applies to Luke 5:17–32 and 7:31–50. Account must also be taken that traditional material may have contained stock features prior to Luke's incorporation of it, which could coincidentally produce correspondences.

The above series of echoes proposed by Tannehill demonstrates clear signs of Luke's literary hand. With the exception of the presence of the scribes and Pharisees and the title, "Son of Man," the connecting features are restricted almost exclusively to these passages (**test 1:** *restriction to passages*). Each passage incorporates two or more of these restricted features (**test 2:** *number of features*), which all attract attention (**test 4:** *attracts attention*). No additional support for intentional parallelism is gained through the complex combination of the four pericopes since the parallelism between the last three passages (7:31–50; 15:1–32; and 19:1–10) is minimal (**test 5:** *constructive complexity*). Only a little support is found in redactional observations due to the non-Markan nature of the last three passages. Note, however, that the grumbling of Jesus' critics is inserted into Luke 5:17–32 (**test 6:** *redaction criticism*). Several features are related to different important Lukan themes (**test 7:** *important themes*). There is no historical or genre demand for the specific groupings of features (**test 8:** *historical/genre expectation*). It is impossible to prove absolutely that any one of these echoes is not the product of coincidence. We may only speak in terms of probability, and Tannehill has presented a strong case with this particular series.

4. Highlight. The above series of connected passages that relate to Jesus' authority to release sins, Tannehill explains, also *highlights* this authority, another function of parallels and echoes. Obviously, concepts that recur frequently are understood as important to a literary work and stand out by virtue of that frequency.

It is possible, however, that a recurrent concept or feature is a coincidental consequence of a separate concern and thus not an intentional highlight. Two good tests would be the centrality of the concept to the plot, message or theology of Luke and the accompaniment of supporting parallel features. For example, reference to mountain(s) is recurrent (ὄρος, 12 x), but does not create the impression of being highlighted. Rather, it serves as a support feature to such scenes as the selection of the twelve (Lk. 6:12–19) and the transfiguration (Lk. 9:28–37). Jesus' authority to forgive sins, however, is both central to Lukan theology and supported by the subordinate connections listed in the table above (page 50).

5. Thematic Unity. Again, concerning the series of echoes relating to the forgiveness of sins, Tannehill illustrates the function of the creation of "thematic unity out of separate scenes, suggesting relationships among scenes through repeated reminiscences of previous episodes".[55] Attendant with this is the unification of the larger narrative framework.[56] We saw earlier that Luke 15:1–32 and 19:1–10 have no explicit mention of Jesus' authority to forgive sins; yet, through various connections to Luke 5:17–32 this message is imported to these suitable locations. A passage that thus receives an imported concept may thereby be adjusted in theme, producing thematic unity with the other connected passages. When Luke 15 is read separately from its associations with the series, the theme could be stated as God's joyful reception of the lost who repent. Jesus' involvement, then, is as one consistent with the Father's attitude toward sinners, and not necessarily as the seeker or the one who bestows forgiveness. Through the thematic unity established through the series of echoes, Jesus may appropriately be regarded as the "seeking shepherd of 15:4–7,"[57] a shift to a more involved and central role.

6. Comparison. Tannehill points out another function of echoes and parallels: the enabling of comparison.[58] He illustrates it through the Lukan parallel between Jesus and John in the birth narrative.

> ...the comparisons between John and Jesus suggested by the parallels will show the superiority of Jesus over John...Repetitive pattern heightens awareness of both similarities and differences, for it guides the reader in making comparisons. The multiple possibilities of comparison suggested by the pattern of repetition promote a complex interaction of narrative elements with an enriching background. This interaction reaches beyond the single episode and awakens echoes from more distant parts of the nar-

---

55 Tannehill, *Narrative Unity*, 1:108.
56 Tannehill, *Narrative Unity*, 1:108.
57 Tannehill, *Narrative Unity*, 1:107.
58 Tannehill, *Narrative Unity*, 1:15–6,19–20.

rative, or from other stories.[59]

The parallelism between Jesus and John in chapter one exemplifies the assertion of Jesus' superiority to John by comparison.[60] John "will be called the prophet of the Most High" (Lk. 1:76), but Jesus "will be called the Son of the Most High" (Lk. 1:32). Further, the Holy Spirit would fill John while still in the womb, but even the conception of Jesus would be the work of the Holy Spirit.

There is no doubt that Luke intended the parallelism between John and Jesus to foster comparison of the two (see the application of the eleven tests to this parallelism on pages 14–27). Debate only surrounds what particular comparisons were to imply, but this is beyond the present concern. Naturally, any intentional parallelism may only be identified when the reader makes at least a rudimentary comparison, whether it is of verbal, structural or descriptive similarities. Again, the crux of the matter is whether the proposed parallelism or echo is reasonable and bears marks of authorial intent of the kind discussed above under the function, "reminder".

7. Engagement of the Imagination. Repetition inherent in echoes and parallels, when perceived, not only invites comparison, but also engages the imagination "…in the exploration of the narrative's symbolic world…. Repetitive pattern can contribute to deepening disclosure as new associations are suggested, guiding readers in the discovery of expanding symbols with hidden residues of meaning."[61]

As with comparison, this function is integral to every intentional parallel. The writer would naturally be concerned with the extent to which the reader's imagination strayed from the literal word. Genre, chosen by the author, provides a suitable guideline. Tannehill's sensitive and productive interpretation of the Gospel through its parallels is largely a product of this function. Deconstructionists would say entirely a product, but this goes too far because clear boundaries to the imagination are provided by the author so that a reader's interpretation is not completely individual. Some such boundaries are genre, explicit statement, reference to a specific pool of common knowledge, and contextual qualification. Regarding genre, for example, an historical work naturally presupposes greater restriction of the imagination than fiction. Explicit statements such as "Prophet of the Most High" and "Son of the Most High", in the system of echoes we have been discussing, define the nature of the association between John and Jesus. Pools of common knowledge, like Old Testament stories and their standard interpretations, provide predictable fields for the imagination, exploited by

---

59 Tannehill, *Narrative Unity*, 1:20.
60 Tannehill, *Narrative Unity*, 1:25.
61 Tannehill, *Narrative Unity*, 1:20.

Luke in his use of type-scene. Even the context of a parallel unit limits the imaginative range. If the surrounding passages depict conflict, then the imagination will likely be influenced accordingly. Such guidelines for the imagination reflect authorial intent in the instance of an actual parallel or echo.

Tannehill successfully identifies intentional narrative phenomena in Luke that may be defined as echoes or parallels. Some phenomena so defined, however, are not clearly intentional. The teaching of Jesus has similarities to that of John the Baptist in topic and occasionally in wording, but it is difficult to demonstrate that they are not a coincidence of teaching style between the two, or a subconscious adaptation reflecting Luke's interests or style. One must consider that the reader will discover unintentional textual features that resemble devices employed elsewhere by the author. In these instances the reader is impacted as though the device were intended, yet the impact may be divergent from or superfluous to the author's purpose. Similar phenomena to what Tannehill has developed may be found in the *Gospel of Thomas*, which is more a collection of sayings than a typical narrative. When he presents a plurality of parallels highly restricted to the relevant passages, Tannehill's case for intentionality is much stronger since coincidence is less likely.

The several functions of echoes and parallels operate as authorial guidance for the reading process. They are in essence a subtle form of communication directly linked to the message of Luke and, therefore, important to the discernment of that message.

1.3 Type-scene

As observed earlier, the use of type-scenes may produce echoes and, by definition, involves parallels. Yet, due to their unusually strict structural relationship, the unique phenomenon of a series of passages so joined deserves individual attention. Our discussion will include only the relevant tests for intentionality.

Definition and function: Tannehill defines type-scene and its function thus,

> A type-scene is a basic situation which recurs several times within a narrative. Each occurrence has a recognizably similar set of characteristics, sometimes highlighted by the repetition of key phrases, but this similarity permits – even requires, if boredom is to be avoided – new variations in the development of the scene. Therefore, comparison of all the instances of the type-scene will present a richer picture of the possibilities of human response within that situation and (if the same character appears in all the instances) of the characteristics and capabilities of the leading character.

The repeated use of a basic situation suggests that it held special interest for the narrator.[62]

Elsewhere, he describes the use of type-scenes in the Lukan birth narrative as free imitation of the Old Testament texts, or where a character "resembles" an Old Testament character.[63] A review of his examples in Luke reveals that type-scenes may also be developed on the foundation of a scene within the Gospel rather than from the Old Testament or another external text.

In the instance of a prototype passage external to the Lukan narrative, such as from the Old Testament, knowledge of that passage is assumed for the identification of the parallel and for the function to be realized in the reading process. A partial exception exists when two or more Lukan scenes stem from the same external text and have sufficient similarities with each other to be related by the reader; still, the external flavor is lost.

Not surprisingly, Tannehill does not develop the more mundane side of Robert Alter's treatment of type-scene, the work upon which his own is based. Alter explains that the device could be employed because it was expected by the reader;[64] therefore, it could have diminished authorial purpose in terms of impact on the reader. Yet, Tannehill's examples in the gospel of Luke are never that insignificant, which would reflect Luke's respect for the device.

Commenting further on the function of type-scenes, Tannehill speaks of the enrichment of the story of Jesus through the inclusions of additional familiar concepts from other accounts, and of the highlight created by the inherent repetition of ideas and situations.[65] He helpfully examines Luke's use of type-scene in his treatment of religious leaders. Several stories are bound together by similar circumstances and responses so that the role of these leaders in the narrative is intensified.[66] One grouping (Lk. 6:6–11; 13:10–17; 14:1–6) shares such common elements as Jesus healing on the Sabbath, the presence of Jewish leaders who oppose Jesus' actions, and an unanswered question posed by Jesus in defense of his healing. Tannehill enumerates other similarities between pairs of these three scenes. This grouping of passages demonstrates evidence of authorial intent. There are several reasonable parallel features between the accounts (**test 2:** *number of*

---

62 Tannehill, *Narrative Unity*, 1:170–71, cites as the foundation for his definition Robert Alter's discussion of type-scene in *The Art of Biblical Narrative* (New York: Basic Books, 1981) 47–62.
63 Tannehill, *Narrative Unity*, 1:18.
64 Alter, *Art of Biblical Narrative*, 50–51.
65 Tannehill, *Narrative Unity*, 1:4.
66 Tannehill, *Narrative Unity*, 1:172.

features); two features are restricted primarily to the relevant passages (**test 1:** *restriction to passages*); the features are important to the Gospel (**test 7:** *important themes*); and each feature attracts the readers attention (**test 4:** *attracts attention*). Strength is also found in the number of accounts bearing the parallel features (**test 3:** *number of panels/passages*). Luke adds explicit reference to the presence of scribes and Pharisees in Luke 6:7 (par. Mk. 3:2 and Mt. 12:10) which lends minor support (**test 6:** *redaction criticism*).

Tannehill's type-scene that consists of the two "What shall I do to inherit eternal life?" passages (Lk. 10:25–37; 18:18–23),[67] however, lacks strength in the number of accounts (**test 3:** *number of panels/passages*) and the number of reasonable parallel features (**test 2:** *number of features*). Also, three of the four features are hardly restricted to these locations (**test 1:** *restriction to passages*); rather, they are quite typical and common in Jesus' interaction with religious leaders. The four features are: (1) a Jewish leader who asks Jesus, "Teacher, what shall I do to inherit eternal life?"; (2) Jesus' response immediately cites the law; (3) the answer lies in an interpretation of that law; and (4) this interpretation challenges the leader's prior understanding of that section of the Old Testament. Certainly, the identical wording of the questions put to Jesus is striking. The question is restricted to only these two passages, and the topic is central to the Gospel. Still, the other three features are typical of Luke's portrayal of Jesus' interaction with Jewish leaders who meet him with a challenge or request. In addition to the above two passages, there are at least six others with the three features (Lk. 6:1–5; 11:37–44, 45–52; 14:1–14; 16:14–18; 20:27–44). In other words, the validity of an intentional type-scene formed by these two passages depends almost entirely on the first feature.

Is the first feature sufficiently strong to have likely been intended by Luke to link the two passages and encourage comparison of the leaders' human responses and the behavior of Jesus? Many factors argue against this. No weight may be placed on the term "teacher" since, in Luke, Jesus is commonly so addressed by non-disciples.[68] Furthermore, the question may have been in both primary sources that Luke employed (**test 6:** *redaction criticism*). In Luke 18:18–23 the question is taken verbatim from Mark 10:17. The source behind Luke 10:25–37 is uncertain. Although Luke evidences awareness of Mark 12:28–34, where the question is different, the differences outweigh the similarities. Marshall and Fitzmyer convincingly argue for a non-Markan origin.[69] This allows the possibility that the

---

67 For Tannehill's discussion of this type-scene, see *Narrative Unity*, 1:171.
68 Nolland, *Luke 1–9:20*, 355.
69 Marshall, *Gospel of Luke*, 440–41; Joseph A. Fitzmyer, *The Gospel According to Luke X–XXIV*, Anchor Bible 28a (Garden City, N.Y.: Doubleday, 1985) 877–78. For

question is derived from an unknown source. Even if one assumes that Luke inserted it into the pericope, the conclusion that Luke's intent was the formation of a parallel scene is not required. Indeed, similar wording is attested to in Rabbinic writings, which suggests it might have been a common question even in the time of Jesus (**test 8:** *historical/genre expectation*).[70] Marshall cites Manson's suggestion that the lawyer could have asked a question that he heard Jesus had asked before, in order to open the topic of neighborliness, which was inherent in the expected answer.[71] In the light of the above discussion, appropriate uncertainty must be maintained when theological statements are synthesized based on this parallel.

A consistent question that arises in the consideration of Lukan literary devices is the possibility that parallel features noted by Tannehill as the foundation of a device may be a product of the similarity in form between traditional units developed prior to Luke's incorporation. They might even be due to Lukan style in some instances, or to some other coincidence.

2 Correspondences between Luke and Acts

On the foundation of the above discussion of Tannehill's Lukan literary devices, we may approach his treatment of the interplay between the Gospel and Acts. As the title of his two-volume work, *The Narrative Unity of Luke-Acts*, suggests, he endeavors to demonstrate the unity between the two books.

> Despite the episodic style of large portions of Luke, it traces the unfolding of a single dominant purpose. This unifies the gospel story and unites Luke with Acts, for this purpose is not only at work in the ministry of Jesus but also in the ministries of Jesus' witnesses. Luke-Acts is a unified narrative because the chief human characters (John the Baptist, Jesus, the apostles, Paul) share in a mission which expresses a single controlling purpose – the purpose of God.[72]

Not surprisingly, in addition to discussing this unity in terms of plot, he discloses literary devices of the sort observed in the Gospel that bridge the gap between the two books. Naturally, the ultimate function of these new instances is to support the overarching unity he finds in "the purpose of

---

a defense of Markan origin, see Gerhard Schneider, *Das Evangelium nach Lukas*, Ökumenischer Taschenbuchkommentar zum Neuen Testament 3/1, 2 (Würzburg: Echter, 1977) 247.
70 Marshall, *Gospel of Luke*, 442; Fitzmyer, *Luke X–XXIV*, 1198–1199.
71 Marshall, *Gospel of Luke*, 441.
72 Tannehill, *Narrative Unity*, 1:xiii.

God". One might justifiably question the simplicity of this unifying theme because of its breadth. Most or all of the books of the Bible could fit under this umbrella. Nevertheless, the issue at hand is the validity of the devices he presents that tie Luke to Acts. Are they demonstrably intentional?[73]

Tannehill's correspondences between Luke and Acts are more directly related to structure than his other correspondences because they serve the structural role of linking two volumes. Clearly, they are of greater importance to his argument for the narrative unity of Luke-Acts. Furthermore, our primary concern is with the structure of Luke (see chapter 4). Therefore, it is appropriate that our evaluation of selected examples from his correspondences between Luke and Acts be a bit more rigorously presented. The results of all eleven tests for intentionality will be provided.

No chronological priority between Luke and Acts need be assumed in an evaluation of apparent literary connections. Devices that tie them together could have been constructed at any stage of composition, from the planning stage to the final touches. Tannehill and this writer, however, presume with the scholarly consensus that Acts followed the Gospel. Application of the criteria for intentionality employed above affirms authorial knowledge of the chronologically prior book if a substantial number of parallels are validated. The assumption is that the existence of several distinct instances of detailed parallelism between such different works, in terms of their content, is beyond the scope of coincidence. The presence of intentional connections, though, does not demand identical authorship; that must be developed by other means, such as grammar, style and vocabulary.[74] Although it is not his stated purpose, Tannehill effectively demonstrates that the similarity between kinds and functions of literary techniques in Luke and Acts suggests identical authorship, since it would take exceptional skill to notice and imitate such depth of variety and detail.

The present concern, however, is simply to test Tannehill's literary-critical observations of Lukan correspondences for authorial intent. Again, the analysis will concentrate on his devices of *preview* and *review*, *echo* and *parallel*, and *type-scene* as identifiable reflections of conscious linking of passages in the literary method of the author; but note at the outset that no instances of type-scene between Luke and Acts were found in Tannehill's two volumes. It should not necessarily be expected. Type-scene exists within Acts,[75] so the narrative shows consistency with Luke in this regard. Still, Luke may have found no suitable application for the function of the device, as he understood it, within his overall purpose for the two volumes.

---

73 At this point, Tannehill's second volume becomes relevant to the discussion with its specific treatment of literary features in Acts; *Narrative Unity*, 2.
74 Tannehill makes a similar point, *Narrative Unity*, 2:6–7.
75 Tannehill, *Narrative Unity*, 2:201–203, 208–209, 221–24, 226.

Certainly he comes close with such scenes as Peter's healing of a lame man, compared with Jesus' healing of a paralytic (Acts 3:1–10 and Lk. 5:17–26).[76] Tannehill does however explore several examples of the other techniques.

2.1 Preview and Review

2.1.1 PREVIEW OF ACTS IN LUKE

Perhaps the most significant preview of Acts in Luke is Luke 24:45–9, mentioned earlier (page 39). Coupled with the first chapter of Acts, there is apparently an intentional literary bond established.[77] Rolloff considers Acts 1:1–12 and Luke 24:33–53 to be free composition,[78] which if true would allow Luke ample opportunity to create connections. Tannehill suggests several elements in the Gospel passage that are paralleled in Acts 1–5 and through which the basic plot of the second volume is anticipated.[79]

Jesus emphasizes that preaching will be in his *name* (Lk. 24:47);
    which is borne out in the apostolic preaching (Acts 2:21, 38; 3:6, 16; 4:7, 10, 12).

The content of proclamation was to be "repentance and forgiveness of sins" (Lk. 24:47),
    which is carried out in Acts 2:38; 3:19 and 5:31.

The range of this proclamation was "to all the nations" (Lk. 24:47),
    a fact reiterated in Acts 1:8.

Commencement of the mission was to be at Jerusalem (Lk. 24:47),
    as Acts 1:4 and 8 remind the reader.

Jesus designates the apostles "witnesses" (Lk. 24:48),
    a term repeatedly used of the apostles in Acts (1:8, 22; 2:32; 3:15; 4:33; 5:32).

The Spirit will be sent (Lk. 24:49),
    which is attested to in Acts 1:4, 8 and 2:23.

---

76 Refer to Tannehill's comments on their relationship as to why this does not constitute a type-scene, *Narrative Unity*, 2:51–52.
77 Tannehill believes the shared group of themes between Lk. 24:47–49 and Acts 1:4–5, 8 indicates the Acts passage to be a repetition of the other; *Narrative Unity*, 1:296.
78 Jürgen Roloff, *Die Apostelgeschichte*, Das Neue Testament Deutsch 5 (Göttingen: Vandenhoeck und Ruprecht, 1981) 17.
79 Tannehill, *Narrative Unity*, 1:292, 294–296.

The above Acts references may be grouped by pericope/scene:

	Name	Repentance	All Nations	Jerusalem	Witness	Spirit
1.			1:8	1:4	1:8	1:4, 8
2.					1:22	
3.	2:21, 38	2:3, 8			2:32	2:23
4.	3:6, 16	3:19			3:15	
5.	4:7, 10, 12					
6.					4:33	
7.		5:31			5:32	

Obviously, this preview is different from those encountered to this point in that its referents are numerous, dispersed, and contain fewer elements of correspondence with their preview. It is a complex preview that plays the greater role of linking two major texts that were expected to be read at separate sittings, Luke and Acts. The existence of an apparent function, however, does not verify authorial intent, especially when the elements of correspondences seem so common and theologically and historically expected. The matter is clarified when the tests for intentionality are applied.

Test 1: *The greater the restriction of elements of correspondence to the relevant passages, the greater is the probability of authorial intent.* Since Tannehill has defined this preview to incorporate virtually all instances of these individual connections in Acts 1–5, naturally the restriction to the relevant passages is strict. This definition is certainly possible – Luke could well have consciously constructed all these links – but this test is neutralized by this inclusiveness. Unfortunately, a definition of this sort allows virtually any frequent repetition of themes or words to be labeled a literary device. A further factor that diminishes any support from this test is the frequency of references to Jesus' name, to apostolic witness, and to the Holy Spirit beyond chapter five (at least 24x, 5x, and 46x respectively). If the referent of Luke 24:47–49 is considered the entirety of Acts, then the definition is all inclusive and a study of how common the concepts are in contemporary relevant literature would be required to gauge restriction. This will be discussed shortly.

Test 2: *The greater the number of reasonable parallel features between parallel passages, the greater is the probability of intent.* Taken by pericope, some of these correspondences lack support from his test. Pericope number 2, Acts 1:22, is indeed a distinct pericope from number 1 because it is separated from Acts 1:1–11 by a change in scene; so its one feature stands alone as a tie to Luke 24:47–49. Two others, pericopes 5 (Acts 4:7, 10, 12) and 6 (4:33), also each have a stand-alone feature without the support of additional features. Pericope 7 (Acts 5:31, and 32) is stronger, with two elements of correspondence; but two elements could easily be coincidental. The remainder (pericopes 1, 3 and 4) have three or four elements, which makes coincidence a bit less probable. On the strength of these three passages, the preview gains support from this test.

Test 3: *The greater the number of parallel passages (or panels) that match a proposed pattern or grouping of features, the greater is the case for intent.* There are two proposed passages in Acts that include four elements from the Lukan passage (pericopes 1 and 3), and one with three (pericope 4 – see the table above). The instance of only two elements in chapter five has a substantially greater chance of coincidence, so one or two parallel features will not be considered significant. This is because many single statements, themes or scenes that bear accidental similarity to another may be dissected sufficiently to produce two elements that correspond. Finding three is much more difficult if the elements are to remain reasonable. Intent is mildly favored by this test, especially for pericopes 1, 3 and 4.

Test 4: *An element of correspondence that attracts the reader's attention contributes to the probability of intent.* Manifestly, each of the proposed elements is striking, so they are realistic features for Luke to employ; but this must be tempered if they are common expressions evidenced in other contemporary Christian writings, such as those found in the New Testament. This will be examined shortly. Certainly, the themes of Jesus' name, apostolic witness, and the Holy Spirit are very common throughout the remainder of Acts. Nevertheless, with the number of striking elements, this test enhances the case for conscious Lukan construction.

Test 5: *Parallelism between complex units, such as combined pericopes, that appears constructive rather than random or coincidental increases the probability of intent.* Naturally, Acts 1–5 is a complex unit when taken as the parallel referent to Luke 24:47–49. The sequence of elements in Luke 24 is not distinctly maintained in Acts, so the proposed parallelism does not appear constructive. However, when the first three chapters are understood as the critical location for the establishment of a literary bond, the cluster of these elements here is somewhat constructive. Detracting from this, however, are the frequencies of the "name," apostolic witness, and Holy Spirit themes throughout the rest of Acts. Therefore, the verdict of this test is "inconclusive".

Test 6: *If redaction critical observations yield evidence of Lukan adjustment to include or create the elements that constitute the literary device, the probability of intent is greater insofar as there are no superior reasons for the observed redaction.* The sources for all relevant passages are uncertain, so no additional support is gained through this test.

Test 7: *If the elements of correspondence that constitute the literary* *device are related to important Lukan themes, the probability of intent is enhanced.* Since Lk. 24:47–49 relates the final words of Jesus to his disciples before his ascension, these themes are important regardless of their frequency or location prior to this point. Nevertheless, each is found in key locations throughout the Gospel and in fair number. Jesus' "name" holds special authoritative weight on several occasions (Lk. 9:48, 49; 10:17; 21:8, 12). Beside Luke 24:47, repentance and forgiveness occur together in this formulaic sense in Luke only at 3:3, another key location – ἄφεσις and μετάνοια (17:3, 4 is the only other passage combining the two; using the verbal forms). Individually, however, the ideas of repentance and forgiveness are well represented. Regarding the universality of the mission "to all nations," the concept is found in the infancy narrative (Lk. 2:31–32), the introduction to John the Baptist (3:6), the account of the healing of the centurion's servant (7:1–10), Jesus' ministry in Samaritan territory (9:46–62), the parable of the good Samaritan (10:30–37), and the story of the ten lepers (17:11–19). As for the centrality of Jerusalem to the Gospel, it is a structural refrain from 9:51 on and is plainly the goal of the plot. The theme of apostolic witness is also inherent to Luke. The terminology is not prevalent – Luke 21:13 is the only instance before 24:48 where the disciples are associated with the act of "witnessing" (in this case it refers to verbal expression of their experience with Jesus); yet, the presence of the disciples with Jesus and their participation in ministry and proclamation is essential to the coherence of the Gospel. Finally, reference to the Spirit is central to the Gospel, as evidenced in the infancy narrative, the temptation, baptism, and Nazareth accounts along with the sending of the seventy-two (Lk. 10:21), and Jesus' teaching (Lk. 11:13 and 12:10, 12). All these themes exhibit Lukan concern and therefore are part of a reasonable pool of themes from which he could have constructed literary parallels. Tannehill's preview is well supported by this test.

Test 8: *Intent is more certain if there is no clear historical or genre expectation for the inclusion of the features in question and their sequence, if parallelism of sequence is observed.* For example, any suggested geographical "chiasm" covering Luke-Acts, like movement toward Jerusalem in Luke, then movement away in Acts, is at risk since this is a reasonable skeletal description of Jesus' historical progress coupled with the spread of the Church. In other words, Luke could rationally have developed these descriptions independently of each other with no underlying literary relationship intended.[80] How does the test apply to the features in the

---

80 Philippe Rolland attempts to prove Lukan intent behind the geographical chiasm centered on Jerusalem by offering a few specific parallels and a somewhat new framework into which the geographical sections fit; "L'organisation du Livre des

present analysis? No particular sequence in the features is required by Tannehill's proposal, so historical expectation is the only issue. Certainly, the beginning of the Church in Jerusalem and the sending of the Holy Spirit are historical facts and would likely be included in a record of this type, so they do not strengthen the case for intent. If however the author of Acts, Luke or otherwise,[81] is assumed to have been dependent on Luke, then the preoccupation of the Gospel with Jerusalem as the city of destiny is a strong foundation for a literary device. Likewise, the role of the Spirit in the ministry of Jesus and in the future ministry of the disciples as expressed in the Gospel also establishes a strong foundation. The nature of the other features as concepts rather than specific events requires that other relevant literature be examined to determine whether this combination of concepts was pervasive and could have been inspired by sources other than the gospel of Luke. The New Testament corpus provides a more than adequate resource.

Throughout the whole of the New Testament, reference to the "name" (ὄνομα[82]) of Jesus is found with little meaningful variation in concentration from book to book. Clearly, Acts has the highest concentration, but the concept sufficiently permeates the New Testament with such frequency that a work which records first century evangelistic preaching would be expected also to exhibit it.[83] No doubt, it was common Christian terminology and originated from typical contemporary figures of speech that communicated authority and representation.

The concept of apostolic witness must be analyzed in the light of genre, authorship and subject matter. Beyond the Gospels and Acts in the canon,

---

Actes et de l'ensemble de Luc," *Bib* 65 (1984) 81–6. His argument is unconvincing because it demands no more than what could occur incidentally as Luke composed his two works. Rudolf Pesch effectively argues against Acts 1:8 being a geographical scheme for the book (and this damages the strength of the Luke-Acts geographical chiasm). He lists several breaks in the geographical flow and demonstrates Jerusalem to be central throughout. Furthermore, he observes that the actual geographical scheme is theological and moves from the Jews to the Gentiles. See his *Die Apostelgeschichte: 1 Teiband Apg 1–12*, Evangelisch-Katholischer Kommentar zum Neuen Testament (Zürich: Benziger, 1986) 38.

81 I believe Luke and Acts to be of common Lukan authorship for cumulative reasons beyond the scope of this work. My argumentation and conclusions, however, are not dependent on this belief.

82 All references Tannehill cites in Luke and Acts use the noun form of ὄνομα, and this word alone provides sufficient data for the study.

83 Luke actually contains fewer instances per ten-thousand words (4.6) than Mt. (6.5), Mk. (7.1) or Jn. (8.3), which may suggests less interest on Luke's part. Yet one could argue the key location of Luke's reference in Lk. 24.

the occurrence of the term "witness" (μάρτυς) and its various forms,[84] used in reference to apostolic activity, drops dramatically. There are only statements by Paul, Peter and John regarding their own witness; but never does the subject matter of these books give much occasion for further concern with the topic. Rather, the Gospels and historical works more naturally incorporate the concept of human representation of Christ's ministry in the Church: preparation of representatives by Jesus in the Gospels, and their actual ministry in Acts. As with the "name" of Jesus, the highest concentration of the concept of apostolic witness is in Acts, where the subject matter demands it.[85] In addition, the terminology of "witness" in connection with the apostles is not prevalent in Luke over the other Gospels. Therefore, apart from the prominent location of the preview in Luke's Gospel, the distribution and frequency of the apostolic witness theme in the New Testament holds no surprises.

Not only does first and second century Church history encompass the geographical extension of the Church to all nations, this extension is also an underlying and explicit theme in all the Gospels, particularly Matthew, and the majority of the Pauline corpus. Indeed the general inclusion of the Gentiles is assumed in virtually all the New Testament books. The historical data would not have demanded Luke's discussion of the beginnings of the Church to include this concept, but it would establish a possible predisposition. Certainly, it was a common idea in New Testament Christianity and a cause of serious contention early on. Consequently, a combination of the literary milieu with the historical creates some expectation that the theme would be included in Acts regardless of whether it is dependent on Luke.

Surprisingly, the explicit formulaic association of repentance (any form of μετάνοια) with forgiveness of sins (expressed using any form of ἄφεσις and/or ἁμαρτία) to summarize salvation is restricted entirely to Mark, Luke and Acts (Mk. 1:4; Lk. 3:3; 24:47; Acts 2:38; 3:19; 5:31). This suggests it was not necessarily a prevalent form of expression for this concept, though the concept itself is actually prevalent throughout the New Testament. This restricted use of terminology offers strong support for Lukan intent, especially in conjunction with the clustering of the themes under discussion within Luke 24:47–49.

According to this test, since all but the repentance formula of the pro-

---

84 As an essential part of his delineation of this preview Tannehill only includes references which explicitly employ this term.
85 Similar to the observations regarding the frequency of Jesus' name, Luke is not special with respect to the presence of the apostolic witness theme (Lk., 3x, 1.5 per 10,000 words; Mt., 2x, 1.1 per 10,000; Mk., 2x, 1.8; Jn., 5x, 3.2 per 10,000; and Acts, 14x, 7.6 per 10,000).

posed features are historically predisposed or literarily common, and would be expected in a work like Acts, only the formula provides individual support for the intentional construction of Luke 24:47–49 as a preview of Acts. If narrative unity is assumed, this evidence is strong due to the prominent position of 24:47–49; but if unity is not assumed, this proposed preview is poor evidence on its own.

Test 9: *If a sequence or grouping of features in parallel is uncommon in other relevant literature, then the likelihood of coincidence due to common expression is diminished.* The discussion above has primarily treated the features individually. This test assumes the equivalent value of all features contained in a passage since they are each constituents of the parallelism. Naturally, the more elements there are, the stronger the case. Based on the analyses provided by the eight tests above, the only other book in the New Testament that contains each feature is Mark, which may be explained by Luke's literary dependence on it. Only Matthew and John clearly exhibit five of the six features. Mark does not cluster all the features into one passage, however. The closest comparison to Luke 24:47–49 is Mark 13:9–11, with Matthew 24:9–14 a close second. This suggests that the Lukan passage is an intentional preview, but this must be tempered by another consideration that results from the closeness of the Markan and Matthean passages. One might find concepts in these sections that are paralleled in Acts, but not in Luke. Then Mark and Matthew could appear stronger than Luke as background for these features in Acts. Nevertheless, the clustering of themes in the prominent position of Luke 24, the link established by Acts 1:1 and numerous parallels Tannehill and others have demonstrated weigh strongly in favor of Luke creating the connection. No doubt, a grouping of six features unparalleled elsewhere but in Acts and Mark establishes it as an uncommon expression; yet, this must not be pushed since only the repentance formula shows meaningful restriction to the relevant books.

Test 10: *If the passages that constitute parallel groupings of passages are contiguous within the groupings, and not distributed broadly throughout the text, then selectivity on the part of the reader is diminished.* This does not mean that Luke could not have created parallels that span large blocks of material with unrelated passages interspersed. He probably did. Still, with the number of pericopes in Luke and in Acts, and the frequent repetition of common themes, an observer looking for parallel patterns will readily find simple, coincidental ones based on general themes. In the instance of the present preview of Acts, one passage is parallel to several others that span five chapters. For judging contiguity, the pericopes of these chapters (Acts 1–5) may be demarcated as follows: 1:1–11; 1:12–26; 2:1–

47; 3:1–26; 4:1–31; 4:32–5:11; 5:12–42.[86] The boundaries take into account complete scenes rather than smaller units that might be labeled "pericopes". Under this scheme, Tannehill's set of parallels is absolutely contiguous (see the table on page 61). Nevertheless, if the references to Jesus' name in 4:7, 10, 12 and to apostolic witness in 1:22 and 4:33 are discounted, since they stand alone without the corroboration of even a second feature, the set loses contiguity. Still, when these scenes are discounted, not much "extraneous" material is interspersed within the set (1:12–26; 4:1–31 and 4:32–5:11), so the loss of contiguity is not devastating. Actually, if the references to repentance (5:31) and apostolic witness (5:32) are discounted as coincidental, the set is reduced to 1:1–3:26 and only 1:12–26 breaks the contiguity of the remaining passages. Naturally, if the pericopes are demarcated in smaller units then contiguity is damaged; but the scenes outlined here are more natural as unit narrative contexts for a device than smaller possible divisions. In summary, this test suggests that subjectivity behind these observations is suitably restricted to favor validity. Weakening the strength of this conclusion, however, is the frequency of most of these features in Acts.

Test 11: *The probability of intent increases as more of the above tests are passed.* If one assumes the literary dependence of Acts on Luke indicated in Acts 1:1, this system of features proposed by Tannehill supports the likelihood that Luke 24 intentionally previews Acts; and this is primarily on the strength of the clustering of features in the prominent position of Luke 24, and the restricted use of the repentance and forgiveness of sins formula. To varying degrees, a slight majority of the tests favored intentional construction of the preview, with one or two casting doubt. Still, if it was not originally intended as a preview, Luke 24:47–49 could have been transformed into one by composing Acts with the necessary connections, thereby producing the same results. If the literary relationship is doubted, though, this proposed preview may not serve as decisive evidence for unity due to the overall commonality and frequency of the features in Acts and other relevant literature. Tannehill presents a potent cumulative case for unity, however, despite occasional weaknesses as revealed in the above discussion.

2.1.2 Review of Luke in Acts

Tannehill also illustrates the narrative unity between Luke and Acts through numerous reviews of the story of Jesus resident in Acts. He observes that speeches are prime locations for this device, noting, "Characters in Acts frequently reflect on Luke through review of the Gospel story, especially

---

86 This is consistent with the table which presents this preview above (page 61).

the death and resurrection of Jesus, in the mission speeches".[87] Many of the reviews that refer to the death and resurrection, however, contain little to nothing more of the Gospel story, which makes it difficult to identify them as reviews particularly of Luke (e.g. the end of Stephen's speech, 7:52–56; Paul's messages at Pisidian Antioch, 13:16–41, Thessalonica, 17:2–3, and Athens, 17:31; his defense before the Sanhedrin, 23:6 [see also 24:21 and 25:19], and his defense before Agrippa 26:22–23). A few reviews appear to be more substantial in their links with Luke, however, the strongest of which will serve as a test case (Acts 10:36–43).

Regarding Acts 10:36–43,[88] a portion of Peter's speech in Cornelius' house, Tannehill states, "If v. 36 refers to Luke's birth narrative, the whole of vv. 36–43 presents a summary of Luke's Gospel in Chronological order, from the birth of Jesus to the commission of the apostles at the end of Luke 24."[89] Before we present the parallel features he discusses, the first one, v. 36 as a reference to the birth narrative, requires some evaluation.[90] The similarities are as follows:

Luke 2:10–11, 14	Acts 10:36
εὐαγγελίζομαι (v. 10)	εὐαγγελίζομαι
παντὶ "**all** the people" (v. 10)	πάντων "Lord of **all**"[91]
Χριστὸς κύριος (v. 11)	**Ἰησοῦ Χριστοῦ**
εἰρήνη "on earth **peace**" (v. 14)	εἰρήνην "**peace**"

| Lk. 2:10–11, 14 "And the angel said **to them,** 'Do not be afraid; for behold, I bring you good news (**εὐαγγελίζομαι**) of a great joy which shall be for **all** the people; for today in the city of David there has been born for you a Savior, who is **Christ** the Lord…Glory to God in the highest, And on earth **peace** among men with whom he is pleased.'" | Acts 10:36 "The word which he sent **to the sons of Israel**,[92] preaching (**εὐαγγελίζομαι**) **peace** through Jesus **Christ** (He is Lord of **all**)…" |

---

87 Tannehill, *Narrative Unity*, 2:6.
88 For Tannehill's discussion of this review, see *Narrative Unity*, 2:140–142.
89 Tannehill, *Narrative Unity*, 2:140.
90 His presentation of this parallel is found in *Narrative Unity*, 2:138–140.
91 Naturally these specify two sets of people, the "all" in the Gospel a subset of the group in Acts: Israel vs. everyone. Tannehill sees this as an indication of Peter's development in understanding; *Narrative Unity*, 2:139.
92 Tannehill reasonably believes that "sons of Israel" refers to the shepherds; *Narrative Unity*, 2:139.

These similarities, in the supportive context of the features below, may reasonably be assumed to establish the first parallel feature.

The full set of parallel features between Acts 10:36–43 and Luke may now be presented:

Acts 10:36–43			Luke
1.	v. 36	This feature is described above.	2:10–14
2.	v. 37	The public event of Jesus' ministry begins with John's baptism and Jesus' Galilean ministry.	3:3
3.	v. 38	Words in Acts recall the Nazareth account: Spirit, anointed, Nazareth.	4:18
4.	v. 38	Jesus' healing ministry is described.	[throughout]
5.	vv. 39–41	The presence of the disciples as witnesses of Jesus' ministry and resurrection is indicated.	[throughout and at end]
6.	v. 41	Reference to the disciples' meal with the resurrected Christ is made.	24:43
7.	v. 42	Next is recorded Jesus' command that the disciples bear witness and preach.	24:46–48
8.	v. 43	Associated with this is the witness of the prophets.	24:46
9.	v. 43	Finally, also associated with the command is forgiveness of sins through the name of Jesus.	24:47

Test 1: *Restriction to passages* – Since each of the features clearly refers to a unique, individual element in the story of Jesus, the restriction of each need not be questioned in the context of the Gospels. The frequency of occurrence in Acts, however, is relevant.

If the four words that establish the first parallel feature, εὐαγγελίζομαι, Χριστὸς, εἰρήνη, and πᾶς, are searched for in the New Testament, Luke 2:10–14 and Acts 10:36 are the only two instances where they all occur within a single pericope (or where the first three occur, for that matter). John's baptism is mentioned five times in Acts (feature 2), but the collocation of the terms in feature 3 is restricted solely to Acts 10:38. Surprisingly, reference to the incarnate healing ministry of Jesus is limited to Acts 10:38 (feature 4). The witness theme is commonly associated with the resurrected Lord, but regarding Christ's incarnate ministry it is confined to Acts 10:39 (feature 5). Furthermore, it appears that only in Acts 10:41 and 42 is there mention of the meal with the resurrected Jesus or the commissioning of the disciples (features 6 and 7). As expected, the concepts of the witness of the prophets about Jesus and forgiveness of sins through his name are frequent in Acts (features 8 and 9). In summary, six of the nine features are highly, if not exclusively, restricted to their locations in Acts.

Test 2: *Number of features* – Tannehill proposes many reasonable parallel features, the parallel passages being regarded as Acts 10:36–43 and the whole gospel of Luke.

Test 3: *Number of panels/passages* – The sequence to the features is central to this "review", and Tannehill demonstrates that it coincides with that of the gospel of Luke. The other Gospels will be examined for this arrangement under test nine. Two panels is, of course, the minimum case.

Test 4: *Attracts attention* – None of the features is trivial. To a disinterested reader they might not be striking, but to one who is familiar with the story of Jesus, each represents an important aspect of that story and of Jesus' identity.

Test 5: *Constructive complexity* – Certainly the gospel of Luke is a complex unit in parallel with Acts 10:36–43. Because the sequence of features is identical, the parallelism is completely constructive.

Test 6: *Redaction criticism* – On the assumption that Acts was based on Luke, redactional adjustment of the Gospel to suit Peter's speech is dubious. Even if one holds that Luke is dependent on Acts, the sources of Acts are unavailable, so redaction criticism is speculative.

Test 7: *Important themes* – As noted above, each feature relates to an important aspect of the story of Jesus and of his identity. Each demonstrably corresponds to a key Lukan theme or account.

Test 8: *Historical/genre expectation* – This test is important since historical facts, as known by early Christians, may have encouraged the adherence of any rough sketch of Jesus' life and significance to a fundamental order. Actually, the features present a most basic historical outline. Therefore, an effective means to ascertain the existence of an expectation of this arrangement is to turn to the other New Testament Gospels. Therefore, test 9 will incorporate this test.

Test 9: *Common expression* – *Matthew* does not conform to this sequence. There is nothing similar to the Lukan angelic announcement of Christ's birth with its proclamation of potential peace to all through him. Nazareth receives a cursory reference prior to the baptism of Jesus, a reversal of features two and three, and there is no reference to anointing or to the Spirit. Certainly, features 4 and 5 are exhibited, but the meal with the resurrected Lord is absent. Finally, the commission in Matthew 28 lacks the witness of the prophets and the explicit terminology of "witness," "preaching," and forgiveness of sins (though, these are implied). The name of Jesus, however, is noted as foundational to the mission. There is little resemblance between Peter's description and Matthew's arrangement; therefore, this Gospel does not suggest an expected generic order to these features.

Mark lacks an angelic announcement and any similar wording to feature 1 at the beginning of the Gospel. Jesus' baptism, apparently public, is present at the outset. Report of the Nazareth event is delayed until after extensive narration of the healing ministry, but this is not a significant problem since much healing follows. Still, the account of his visit to his hometown lacks reference to its name, to Jesus' anointing and to the Spirit. Naturally, the disciples witness the ministry of Jesus (feature 5), but the shorter ending of Mark excludes any indication of apostolic witness of the resurrected Christ. The meal and commission are also missing. If the longer ending is accepted, the meal and commission are included (hence, apostolic witness of the resurrected Jesus), yet the explicit terminology of "witness" and forgiveness of sins in the name of Jesus are still absent. Neither is there mention of the prophets. In either form, Mark does not convincingly match the arrangement suggested by Peter's speech.

Luke, however, matches the required sequence and terminology perfectly, as evident in the last column in the table above (page 69). If the Gospel of John fails to coincide with the sequence, then the odds appear to be against an expected order for these features. Nevertheless, coincidence is not ruled out, since these basic historical events somewhat naturally lend themselves to this arrangement. The exact correspondence, with nothing lacking in Luke, is noteworthy however.

John, like Mark, lacks the angelic announcement and its associated terminology (feature 1). The public baptism of Jesus is alluded to (Jn. 1:29–34) and is followed shortly by a Galilean ministry (Jn. 1:43), but there is no equivalent Nazareth account. Features 4 and 5 naturally follow, this time including apostolic witness of the resurrected Christ, contrary to Mark. There is no subsequent commission to the collective disciples, no explicit use of "witness" or "preaching" terminology, and no mention of prophetic testimony regarding Jesus. Only forgiveness of sins, without reference to the name of Jesus, is found (Jn. 20:23), so features 7 through 9 are not adequately represented.

Therefore, test 9, incorporating test 8, supports Tannehill's proposition that the Lukan Gospel is intentionally reviewed in Acts 10:36. Coincidental correspondence due to historical fact, common presentation, or typical *genre* content has been demonstrated to be inadequate as an explanation for the exact parallelism.

Test 10: *Contiguity* – Contiguity is essentially achieved since the entire Gospel from 2:10 on is summarized by the parallel elements of Acts 10:36–43, especially due to the breadth of features 4 and 5.

Test 11: *Cumulative case* – Every relevant test supports to some degree the probability that Acts 10:36–43 was intended as a review of Luke as a whole. This is one of the strongest literary devices presented by Tannehill in terms of intentionality. Theological statements generated from this literary association will have greater certainty of authorial intent than statements based on devices that do not fare as well when tested.

2.2 Echo and Parallel

Robert Tannehill's literary devices have stood up well under the eleven tests so far, as the majority of his proposals do. The following section will intentionally examined one of the few devices that perform poorly. This will exemplify the analysis of a device that appears less likely to be intentional.

Tannehill presents many parallels between Jesus' ministry and Paul's, which he understands to be an integral part of Luke's purpose in Acts. He proposes that Acts 19:21 echoes Luke 9:51 and that it encourages the anticipation that Paul will encounter suffering in Jerusalem just as did Jesus.[93] The parallel is established through two features: (1) each indicates Jerusalem as a destination in the journey, and (2) there is an element of divine necessity in each. Lk. 9:51 reads, "And it came about, when the days were approaching for His ascension, that He resolutely set His face to go to Jerusalem..." Acts 19:21 reads, "Now after these things were finished, Paul purposed in the spirit to go to Jerusalem after he had passed through Macedonia and Achaia, saying, 'After I have been there, I must [δεῖ] also see Rome.'" The divine necessity of Jesus' arrival in Jerusalem is only indirectly expressed: the time of his ascension appears to be set, presumably by God; Jesus' divine unity with the Father ensures that they share this resolution regarding Jerusalem; and the various other indicators of divine necessity associated with different points in his journey may apply, indicators such as fulfillment of prophecy (e.g., Lk. 18:31 and 24:45–46) and the apparent equation of Jesus' visit with that of the Father's (Lk. 19:41–44).

Apart from the establishment of a system of substantial parallels between Paul and Jesus, this echo proves weak. It gains little support from the tests.

---

93 See Tannehill, *Narrative Unity*, 2:139–40 for his discussion.

If tested as part of such a system, it would probably appear stronger.[94] Nevertheless, a poor showing in these tests does not deny authorial intent. It indicates less certainty.

Test 1: *Restriction to passages* – There are three other instances in Luke where Jesus is said to be going to Jerusalem (13:22; 17:11 and 19:28) and these are not suggested as part of the echo. However, of course there is only one instance in Luke where Jesus' initial determination to travel to Jerusalem is related (9:51), and the same is true for Paul in Acts (19:21). The implication and explication of divine necessity is strewn throughout Luke and Acts, and the possibility of coincidental concurrence is real, but the rarity of the first feature produces a good result under this test.

Test 2: *Number of features* – Tannehill only confidently proposes two features, which is little corroboration between two large and complex narratives. He tentatively adds the sending of representatives as a parallel feature between Luke 9:51–52 and Acts 19:22,[95] which slightly strengthens the device.

Test 3: *Number of panels/passages* – Only two passages are involved in this echo, so no substantial support is gained through numbers.

Test 4: *Attracts attention* – Both the destination of Jerusalem and the theme of divine necessity, if it is actually a clear theme in the Lukan passage, attract the reader's attention, so this test lends moderate support. The sending of representatives, however, is somewhat common (Acts 9:38; 10:5–8; 15:27; 19:22) and therefore indifferent as evidence.

Test 5: *Constructive complexity* – These two passages are not complex, so this test does not apply.

Test 6: *Redaction criticism* – Redaction criticism of Acts is somewhat speculative, so this test is unable to add certainty.

Test 7: *Important themes* – This literary device finds healthy support in the fact that both features are important Lukan themes evident in the Gospel.

Test 8: *Historical/genre expectation* – Luke's choice to cover the ministry of Paul would naturally present him with the option of including the historical fact of the final voyage to Jerusalem. One would expect that such an important event would be narrated. To set the stage for the journey, Luke needed to introduce it, and this is most effectively accomplished by describing the point of decision. Therefore, the recounting of Paul's initial determination to go to Jerusalem is strongly encouraged by the facts. Similarly, insofar as divine necessity may be considered an historical fact

---

94 Radl develops a series of parallels between Paul and Jesus in *Paulus und Jesus*. For similar coverage of such parallels, see Talbert, *Literary Patterns*.
95 Tannehill, *Narrative Unity*, 2:240.

(Luke, as both historian and theologian, would have had this perspective[96]), and considering Luke's concern to communicate God's activity through the apostles, the facts as he knew them probably pressed for some expression of divine initiative. Therefore, history adequately accounts for the inclusion of these features.

Test 9: *Common expression* – Divine necessity to travel to Jerusalem is uncommon in relevant literature outside of the Gospels. This is accounted for, nevertheless, by limitations of subject matter, i.e. the topic of travel to Jerusalem.

Test 10: *Contiguity* – Contiguity is not an issue with single pericopes in parallel.

Test 11: *Cumulative case* – Only three tests, 1, 4 and 7, enhance the probability of conscious construction of this proposed echo. Test 2 may provide weak support.

So, apart from a context of additional strong parallels between Paul and Jesus, little theological weight may be attributed to this particular echo. It may serve, however, as minor evidence toward parallelism between these two main characters. Of course, Luke might have intended this subtle echo, but it has eluded the majority of scholarly attention. Tannehill's thesis, that at this point in the narrative the reader is to anticipate suffering for Paul based on the "echo," is too strong apart from a cumulative case. The tests help to quantify how noticeable a device is and, accordingly, this instance has little effect on the reader.

Tannehill has demonstrated Luke's strong predisposition to compose his Gospel using a wide variety both of correspondences and of their constituents. He reveals the deep level of detail at which the Evangelist worked. Furthermore, he has effectively developed the purposes and functions of these types of correspondences as employed by Luke. Our evaluation using the eleven tests for intentionality has largely confirmed the authorial intent behind Tannehill's observations, though the presentation here has been restricted to a few. This result is important because theological and interpretational statements derived from phenomena that are not clearly intentional are on less firm ground than those derived from what is intentional. Too often we make a tentative assertion and later treat it as established evidence in our reasoning. Tannehill, without an expressed system of criteria for the detection of authorial intent, has largely avoided this problem through exceptional sensitivity to Lukan theology. The problem

---

96 See I. Howard Marshall's insightful defense of the inclusion of theologically informed fact in historical writing, *Luke: Historian and Theologian* (Grand Rapids: Zondervan, 1970) 21–37.

arises when those who are less sensitive apply his methodology without effective controls.

CHAPTER 2

Lukan Correspondences Observed by Charles H. Talbert

In the introduction, a proposal for the structure of Luke was presented in table form (see page 28), which is the heart of this book. This multifold cyclical parallelism consists of numerous detailed parallels forming twelve strata in four cycles. To one unfamiliar with ancient patterned literature or unaware of scholarly work on parallels in Luke-Acts, this may seem an unusual suggestion. In fact, patterned structure was the norm in the ancient world, as will be demonstrated shortly in this chapter and in chapter 3; and scholarly offerings of parallels and structure within Luke and between Luke and Acts abound. If some of these could be proven intentional, especially the structured ones, then that would provide substantial groundwork for our structural proposal. Of all scholars who have discussed this matter, Charles Talbert offers the most numerous, extensive and rigorously supported set of individual and structured parallels for Luke, Luke-Acts and Acts. Much of the work of other scholars is incorporated into his. Therefore, if a thorough application of our eleven tests for intentionality to his work, *Literary Patterns, Theological Themes, and the Genre of Luke-Acts*, demonstrates some parallels and patterns to be of Lukan intent, then this would also give major support to the hypothesis that Luke extensively composed his Gospel in such a fashion. This would support our proposal for the structure of Luke. To be most certain that Luke wrote this way, all of Talbert's proposals for Luke and Luke-Acts will be examined in this chapter. His proposals for Acts are treated in Appendix A because our primary concern is with the structure and composition of the Gospel. A further benefit of this examination is gained from Talbert's heavy investment in redactional support for his correspondences. He studies in great detail redactional evidence for how Luke could have formed each parallel. This meshes well with our interest in the method of composition for the Gospel. Furthermore, the thrust of what Talbert makes of his parallels theologically will be evaluated since we too shall draw theological meaning from our structural proposal.

The literary artistry of the gospel of Luke is not restricted to the literary devices demonstrated by Robert Tannehill. An excellent example of this is the variety of architectonic patterns Talbert propounds within Luke, within Acts, and spanning the two.[1] These patterns, though based on parallelism, as were Tannehill's, are generally more extensive and detailed. They incorporate sufficient amounts of material and are of such a structural nature that the term "architecture" is an accurate description. Since they are based on parallelism, the tests for intentionality implemented in our evaluation of Tannehill's literary devices effectively apply. Actually, because Talbert's patterns involve more features and passages in parallel, the tests are more decisive in casting doubt on their validity. For the majority of Tannehill's devices, parallelism plays the subservient role of merely creating a noticeable phenomenon that establishes an immediate and relatively limited function in the reading process. It does not need to be rigorous to be successful. Talbert's patterns maintain an element of purpose that is generally much more aesthetic and prolonged. Parallelism is now the foundational characteristic and a primary goal. Although the patterns have important functions in the narrative, the aspect of pattern itself takes on artistic importance coordinate to any other function. Therefore, substantial violation of pattern threatens the validity of an observed architectonic scheme. Talbert's caution will be noted, however, that minor violation was expected and, therefore, should not invalidate a proposal. Still, the essential aspect of pattern enhances the value of the tests as indicators of intent or lack of intent.

The relationship between pericopes in Luke evidenced by these patterns (and Tannehill's parallels) demonstrates that Luke read texts in the light of each other. A modern reader who gives little thought to the sources behind the Gospel will be oblivious to this point. Insofar as Luke arranged traditional material to construct architectonic patterns, or any sort of parallels, he treated this material as interrelated. Obviously, parallels that result from complex compilation may have been missed by the compiler, but the concern of our investigation is the determination of that which was intended. When intentional parallels are convincingly identified, one may assume underlying theological and/or literary purposes behind their constructed interrelationship and attempt to identify those purposes. If this aim is satisfactorily achieved, then greater confidence is justified for theological statements flowing from the parallels.

All of Talbert's correspondence patterns will be evaluated using our eleven tests for intentionality in the section below entitled "Evaluation of Talbert's Patterns Using the Tests for Intentionality" (pages 89ff.).[2] Since he begins his study with correspondences between Luke and Acts, this is

---

1   Talbert, *Literary Patterns*.
2   Those entirely within Acts however will be analyzed in Appendix A.

where we will begin our evaluation. This study will develop our broad understanding of how Luke composed his Gospel, as part of a two-volume work. Later we will focus on the Gospel alone and examine his correspondences within Luke. Before we begin, an application of our tests for intentionality to Talbert's patterns however, his foundational arguments for the existence of architectonic patterns in Luke will be summarized and examined first, in the section entitled "Talbert's Theoretical Basis for the Existence of Architectonic Patterns" just below. This is the necessary theory required for an evaluation of the correspondences. It will become evident that Talbert would benefit from more controls being applied to his individual patterns, which highlights the value of our tests. Despite the lack of controls, many of his proposals find support through this analysis. As mentioned in our discussion of Tannehill's work, our tests do not deny the intentionality of patterns that perform poorly. Rather, they determine those in which we may have more confidence.

1 Talbert's Theoretical Basis for the Existence of Architectonic Patterns

Charles Talbert's book, *Literary Patterns, Theological Themes, and the Genre of Luke-Acts*[3] is one of the few works on correspondences and architectonic patterns in Luke-Acts that thoroughly develops the foundation for such phenomena in the ancient Greco-Roman and Near Eastern literary milieu. This foundation is three-pronged: literature, art and "cultural mentality".[4] The purpose behind his discussion of art is to demonstrate that the ancient mentality was highly attuned to the "principal of balance and symmetry" perceived in nature and had the propensity to produce literature that reflected this balance. These three prongs comprise the "external controls" on subjectivity to be employed with each proposal of a pattern of correspondences. In other words, if a pattern is detected in a literary work then, to be believable, it must have its formal counter-part in other contemporary or relevant literature as well as in contemporary visual art and culture. Sufficient corroboration that a document could have evidenced such a pattern is established in this manner. The actual existence of the pattern in that document is verified through "internal controls"[5] that will be discussed later.

---

3   Talbert, *Literary Patterns*.
4   Talbert, *Literary Patterns*, 67–88.
5   Talbert, *Literary Patterns*, 8–9.

1.1 Interplay between Art and Literature

Among Talbert's accumulation of valuable evidence from the realms of ancient art and literature, a statement by Horace likening a poem to a painting is one of the few ancient testimonies that literary forms were intentionally dependent upon forms in art or nature.[6] T.B.L. Webster's *The Interplay of Greek Art and Literature* is cited as demonstration of this dependence.[7] Explicit statements regarding the dependence of literature on art are not frequent in extant documents, but comparisons with art abound.[8] Lucian may be cited, as he likens the arrangement of material in the writing of history to the art of sculpting.[9] Duckworth also cites two instances where Virgil describes his writing in architectural terms.[10] The evidence proffered by Talbert, apart from Webster's contribution, does suggest the likelihood of some subconscious dependence at the very least. Undoubtedly, the many ancient works exhibiting detailed architectonic structure, like the *Aeneid*, are artistic in their very form. Therefore, the interplay between art and literature is demonstrably close.

1.2 Literary Precedent

Chapter five of Talbert's book establishes, through his "external controls," three literary (and artistic) patterns of correspondences that were in common use in Luke's period: "in simplest form either AB:A′B′ or AB:B′A′ or ABCA′".[11] Most of the sets of correspondences he analyzes match one of the three patterns.

Consistent with his expressed methodology, Talbert produces several examples of relevant literature in chapter five that establish precedent for Lukan structural correspondences. Numerous works from "the classical

---

6   For an extended treatment of the subject by Horace, see his *The Art of Poetry* in D.A. Russel and M. Winterbottom (trs.), *Ancient Literary Criticism* (Oxford: Clarendon Press, 1972) 279–291.
7   Talbert, *Literary Patterns*, 68–9; as cited, "(London: H.K. Lewis, 1949) 2."
8   Such ancients as Plato, Aristotle, Horace, Ovid, Dionysius of Halicarnassus, Cicero, Senaca, Plutarch, Quintilian, Pliny, Longinus, Lucian and Philostratus make direct comparison of writing with art, as is revealed in a survey of references under "painting" and "sculpture" in the index of Russel and Winterbottom (trs.), *Ancient Literary Criticism*.
9   Lucian, *How to Write History*, in D.A. Russel and M. Winterbottom (trs.), *Ancient Literary Criticism*, 544–45. George E. Duckworth notes Vergil's comparison of his poetry with architecture, in *Structural Patterns and Proportions in Virgil's Aeneid: A Study in Mathematical Composition* (Ann Arbor: University of Michigan Press, 1962) 1.
10 Duckworth, *Structural Patterns*, 1.
11 Talbert, *Literary Patterns*, 84, n.26.

world," from the Near Eastern world (from OT times to Luke's era) and from early Christianity are listed that lay a strong foundation for the possibility of Luke's use of such patterns. Literature from the classical period is shown to be relevant to Luke through the Roman educational system of the New Testament era. Virgil, Horace and Homer, each of whom constantly employed detailed and layered architecture, were the primary educational models for style and structure.[12] From the Old Testament, an obvious potential influence on Luke's structure, Jonah (among several listed) is demonstrated to have layers of parallelism.[13] Reference is made to several examples from the New Testament and that period to the effect that they exhibit types of parallelism.[14] (We are interested in regular parallelism, which is not the sort Talbert cites from the NT, so chapter 3 will present several NT texts – also OT and Greco-Roman – exhibiting extensive regular parallelism as found in the Third Gospel.) The thrust of the whole of Talbert's chapter five is to impress the reader with the fact that the Lukan literary milieu was dramatically more concerned with balanced architectonic correspondence than we are today.

Talbert's presentation would have been even stronger had he included observations on the manner in which parallels were established within patterns in ancient writing. In other words, were units made parallel primarily through common theme, or through wording, or setting or action? In addition, in which ways could these modes of parallelism be mixed within a single pattern? These are important questions since a random selection of two pericopes in Luke frequently results in some overlap of theme, wording, setting or action. Presumably, the correspondences presented in *Literary Patterns* were considered consistent with contemporary methods of drawing structural parallels. We will investigate this very subject in chapter 3 where relevant literature bearing similar structure to Luke's is reviewed, and in chapter 4 where our proposal for Lukan structure is developed. Talbert's basic approach is upheld, but he may perhaps allow for too great a variety in the types of correspondences within individual sets. This will become clearer as we begin to analyze his correspondence sets shortly.

A frequent question regarding patterns of correspondence is whether in fact the intended readership would have detected the structure. This relates to the larger question of the function of structural correspondences, concerning which Charles Talbert has much to say. The reader's awareness was enhanced by the cultural expectation of architectonic structure, an

---

12 Talbert, *Literary Patterns*, 70.
13 Talbert, *Literary Patterns*, 71–72.
14 Talbert, *Literary Patterns*, 75–76.

expectation much less keen in the modern reader. Yet, precise reader awareness of structural rhythm was apparently not always important to the writer, who sought his readership to *"feel* with the author in this rhythm".[15] "It seems more probable that the architectonic patterns would have been immediately sensed or felt but not consciously and rationally perceived until after reflection."[16] This is consistent with the three functions of patterns that Talbert enumerates, functions that may be found in any combination within the same text: "(a) an assist to the memory of the readers/hearers, that is, a mnemonic device; (b) an assist to the meaning of the whole or of a section; or (c) an abstract architectonic principle, a convention, used solely for aesthetic purposes".[17]

1.3 The Nature of Talbert's Architectonic Correspondences and How He Supports Them

One of the objections levied against some of Talbert's correspondence schemes is that too few elements may establish any one correspondence. For instance, a single word in common between two passages is hardly enough to establish authorial awareness, let alone intent. Actually, Talbert's patterns largely avoid this problem since rarely does any correspondence contain fewer than two associated elements in parallel, usually three or more. Thus, the correspondence is specifically defined. Nevertheless, the Lukan use of type-scenes[18] or typical modes of relating an account may explain likenesses between passages and the occurrence of unintentional or non-structural "correspondences". To overcome this, parallels should be in the context of a set of parallel passages to suggest authorial intent. This will be dealt with in greater depth, shortly, in a discussion of structural intentionality.

Another objection to some proposed patterns is that they are formed through a variety of types of correspondences: one is based on a key word, another on theme and another on action. Bailey's chiastic scheme for the central section of Luke (9:51–19:48), for instance, is subject to this criticism.[19] Such freedom may make it too easy to identify chiasmus where it does not exist. Once again, knowledge of how parallels were actually

---

15 Talbert, *Literary Patterns*, 80–81.
16 Talbert, *Literary Patterns*, 81.
17 Talbert, *Literary Patterns*, 81.
18 For a definition of "type-scene" see Robert C. Tannehill, *Narrative Unity*, 1:18, 170–171.
19 Kenneth E. Bailey, *Poet and Peasant* and *Through Peasant Eyes: A Literary Approach to the Parables of Luke*, Combined Edition (Grand Rapids: Eerdmans, 1976 and 1980 respectively) 79–85 of *Poet and Peasant*.

formed by ancient writers would clarify whether such variety should be expected. Even so, it could be argued that Luke was not strictly bound by convention; but conventional support makes the argument more likely. In fact, key words are largely absent from Talbert's patterns, and this contributes to the consistency of the approach. Seldom does one feel that a convenient word has been selected to substantiate a correlation.

Important to any discussion of correspondences is intentionality. Obviously, the author's message is more surely conveyed through intentional arrangement of material than through an apparent structure that occurred accidentally or subconsciously. Intentionally patterned arrangement sheds light on the meaning and purpose of a work: emphasis is achieved through reiteration and variation from the expected, the genre of the text may be indicated, theology may be reflected, and an interpretative framework may be provided for individual pericopes. Therefore, it is necessary to evaluate Talbert's proposals from the perspective of whether his patterns are incidental or an intentional product of Luke's compositional method.

A survey of Talbert's patterns reveals occasional irregularities in the expected order of corresponding units. To one unfamiliar with the ancient philosophy behind literary structure and the means whereby such structure was imposed on a prose work, irregularities present an apparent stumbling block that suggests subconscious or accidental correlations. *Literary Patterns*, however, includes a discussion of the two interrelated issues of the philosophy and the means behind the construction of patterns. Evidence is provided to the effect that ancient writers strove for symmetry, yet disliked absolute symmetry. The result was that they often structured their works with a high degree of symmetry but virtually always disturbed it in some way.[20] This accounts well for the irregularities in Talbert's patterns but may appear to foster the observation of more patterns than were constructed by Luke. Yet, to require a structure to display *absolute* regularity as a test for intentionality is an unrealistic criterion and may result in unjustified negative conclusions. Consistent with this, he resists the temptation to force material into an unrealistic, perfectly balanced scheme like Heinrich Baarlink's treatment of Luke 9:43b–19:28.[21]

What about the means by which patterns were incorporated into a prose work? Talbert establishes the fact that classical writers who desired detailed pattern would construct an outline that reflected that pattern and compose the work from the outline.[22] Modern writers often employ an outline but rarely match the ancient concern for aesthetic arrangement; therefore, the

---

20 Talbert, *Literary Patterns*, 77–79.
21 Heinrich Baarlink, "Die zyklische Struktur von Lukas 9.43b–19.28," *NTS* 38 (1992) 481–506.
22 Talbert, *Literary Patterns*, 79.

modern reader is much less sensitive to artistic patterns in literature.

Unfortunately, when Talbert treats matters relating to intentionality he rarely discusses specifically the possibility that his proposed patterns are subconscious or accidental occurrences.[23] Rather, his argumentation is positive, highlighting the evidence for Lukan construction of the patterns. Clearly, any useful study of structure that results from subconscious processes would be a book in itself and is more under the domain of structuralism; yet, to my knowledge, no structuralist theory has propounded patterns of Talbert's type.

Two parts comprise Talbert's argument in favor of the intentionality of the patterns in Luke, his "internal controls" that safeguard against subjectivity:

> (1) It should be possible to exhibit a pattern controlling the arrangement of large units throughout an author's work, and in units of all sizes. At least in the classical sources where similar architectural designs are found this is almost always the case. (2) Where possible – e.g., in the Gospels – one should be able to show that the pattern is located in the redactional activity of an author rather than in the tradition.[24]

I would suggest also that a pattern that exists in the tradition could be incorporated or expanded by the redactor into the final form of the pattern. Although not expressed in conjunction with these two "controls," an additional factor is implied by his methodology which tests whether a pattern is intentional: should the pericopes that constitute the correspondences in a particular pattern join to form one or two continuous blocks of material, then the case for intentional construction is strengthened. A minority of Talbert's patterns in Luke-Acts do not form continuous blocks, but it must be remembered that breaks in symmetry should be expected and that ancient writers utilized such techniques as previews, echoes and reviews in a patterned manner without dependence on continuous blocks. Observing contiguity only serves to validate a pattern, not to invalidate it. These three indicators of intentionality must be examined more closely.

1. Redaction Criticism. Appropriately, Charles Talbert depends most heavily on redaction criticism as indication that correspondences were intentionally drawn by the author. The majority of his proposals within the Gospel find redactional support according to his reckoning, though at times he lacks sufficient appraisal of alternative explanations. For example,

---

23 A notable exception to this is his discussion of correspondences between Acts 1–12 and 13–28 where the thrust of his persuasive argumentation would largely apply to his proposed patterns in both Acts and Luke. See *Literary Patterns*, 24–26.

24 Talbert, *Literary Patterns*, 8–9.

Fitzmyer considers that Luke omitted Mark 4:26–29, "the parable of the seed that grows in secret," to avoid duplicate material,[25] a demonstrable concern of Luke's. Talbert's assertion, however, that the Markan pericope would not suit the correspondence pattern, is true and he does allow for multiple factors behind omissions and editing of source material.[26] Additionally, he considers an architectonic pattern one of several motivations behind the "Big Omission," Mark 6:45–8:26.[27] Similarly, he produces several instances where Luke apparently arranges Q and L material to match Markan order. A representative example is the Markan order of a healing story emphasizing faith followed by a revivification account (Lk. 8:43–48 and 8:49–56) matched by a corresponding Q-L sequence (Lk. 7:1–10 and 7:11–17). It would not be surprising if this order was to occur incidentally, but the odds are greatly diminished by the immediate context of other corresponding pericopes.[28]

The success of pattern construction as a viable explanation for Lukan redaction speaks favorably for the existence of architectonic schemes arranged from source material. Although by itself it cannot prove the existence of patterns, it does provide a common motive behind a number of redactional features that previously attracted only a variety of trivial explanations.

2. Continuous blocks of correspondences. One major difficulty for a structural theory that depends on correspondences between *pairs* of panels, is that even random selections of two pericopes sometimes have common elements that might then be labeled "correspondences". To illustrate this, I randomly selected two passages from Luke: 8:4–10 and 12:22–34. Not surprisingly, they have significant overlap. The first describes the different responses of people to the message of the "kingdom," and the second, the benefits received by those who seek the "kingdom". Each also pictures the act of sowing. The majority of random pairings, however, do not produce such a significant "correspondence" as the "kingdom;" so a test for whether apparent blocks of correspondences, such as Talbert's, are intentional is to view them within the proposed continuous block. Are the other correspondences in the context significant or trivial? If all are significant then the odds are heavily in favor of Lukan design, assuming there are several corresponding pairs of pericopes involved. Unfortunately, "significance" and "triviality" are subjective concepts, but the subjectivity is restricted to a degree by the exclusivity of the elements of the correspondence in the context of the whole Gospel and by the centrality of the elements to the

---

25   Fitzmyer, *Luke I-IX*, 93.
26   Talbert, *Literary Patterns*, 40, 33 n.74.
27   Talbert, *Literary Patterns*, 33 n.74.
28   Talbert, *Literary Patterns*, 39–43.

individual pericope. (Exclusivity will be discussed shortly.) Talbert's patterns usually incorporate seven or more corresponding pairs contiguous within their respective blocks, which virtually precludes accidental or subconscious arrangement so long as the correspondences are not padded with divergent passages. His cycle that compares John and Jesus (Lk. 3:1–4:15), however, involves only three points of correspondence and would be dubious on the present grounds alone.[29] Still, it has received broad scholarly recognition[30] in part due to the larger context of parallelism in chapters one and two.

There is a danger when pairs of corresponding passages are not contiguous within their two panels and are distributed throughout structurally unrelated material. Since there are many common aspects permeating Luke, many of them merely previews and echoes with no strict structural function, it is possible that an eye searching for patterns could perceive one not intended by Luke. If the correspondences were not contiguous, then the two panels would need the corroboration of a third panel or more for certainty. C.F. Evans recognizes this danger in his evaluation of Talbert's approach to Luke. He considers the correspondences between Luke 1:1–8:56 and Acts 1:1–12:17 to be contrived for this reason.[31] Perhaps his criticism of this parallelism has some justification with regard to architectonic structure, but he is incorrect in his implication that all of Talbert's patterns fail for the same reason. Actually, a minority of the patterns in *Literary Patterns* would be subject to Evans' criticism, the sole reason he offers for rejecting Talbert's approach. Another pattern that exemplifies this risk is the "loose parallelism" proposed between Acts 1–12 and 13–28.[32] There are large gaps that do not have corresponding material within this pattern: 4:1–6:7; 8:5–9:43; 13:4–15; 14:1–7. Although "only rarely have the correspondences between these two halves of Acts been denied," the gaps suggest that the correspondences might not form an "architectonic pattern".[33] Perhaps these are merely previews or echoes, or perhaps the similarities are coincidental and simply reflect the historical details as they occurred.

History itself may produce similar events that, when recorded, may appear to correspond. Some of the correspondences in Talbert's Acts 1–12 and 13–28 pattern might demonstrate this. The first parallel presented is "a special manifestation of the Spirit" (2:1–4 and 13:1–3), a common phenomenon in Acts. A comparison of these two passages reveals mainly the

---

29 Talbert, *Literary Patterns*, 45–8.
30 See as representative examples, Nolland, *Luke 1–9:20*, 137; C.F. Evans, *Saint Luke*, 228; Tannehill, *Narrative Unity*, 1:51–52.
31 C.F. Evans, *Saint Luke*, 43 n.v.
32 Talbert, *Literary Patterns*, 23–24.
33 See Talbert's discussion of this "pattern;" *Literary Patterns*, 23–26.

difference between them in the light of the frequency of material relating to manifestations of the Spirit. One records the initial outpouring of the Spirit which results in speaking in tongues (Acts 2:1–4). The other recounts the Spirit's revelation to the church at Antioch that Paul and Barnabas were chosen (Acts 13:1–3). The next three parallels form a sequence that could be the coincidental product of history.

"Apostolic preaching results from the special manifestation of the Spirit" (2:14–40 and 13:16–40).

"A mighty work follows. A man, lame from birth, is healed" (3:1–10 and 14:8–13).

"The healing of the lame man is followed by a speech prompted by the response to the healing. It begins, 'Men…why?'" (3:12–26 and 14:15–17).[34]

Preaching is likely to be a direct or indirect consequence of a special manifestation of the Spirit, and a healing will inevitably follow at some point in a work that relates numerous miracles. Similarly, preaching is the expected advantage taken of the occasion. These events may simply have occurred in this sequence. Nevertheless, Talbert argues convincingly for the likelihood that Luke exercised great selectivity in the material incorporated and in the manner it is related, and he thereby tips the balance toward the intentionality of the correspondences.[35] Are the parallels between Acts 1–12 and 13–28 indications of structure, though? Do they divide Acts in two for structural reasons? One wonders whether Luke's selection of material could have been made for other reasons such as typology, continuity, or a non-structural parallel between characters. All of the correspondences listed support a division at the conclusion of chapter twelve, but elsewhere he also proposes many other correspondences that fall within one of the two halves. Yet these others all belong to their own patterns. Without contiguity as discussed above, a decision about the validity of correspondences is confused by the frequency of common elements in Luke's writing and by the possible influence of his perception of salvation-history as a process "structured" by God's consistent will. Perhaps on the grounds of Lukan selectivity the benefit of the doubt should be given to Talbert, and the several other scholars he cites, in favor of the structural nature of the few correspondence patterns that could have an historical explanation.

As mentioned earlier, *Literary Patterns* does not discuss the exclusivity of individual elements of correspondence to their location in the pattern. If the factor that forms a correspondence between two pericopes is common in

---

34 Talbert, *Literary Patterns*, 23.
35 Talbert, *Literary Patterns*, 24–26.

Luke, then contiguity with correspondences formed by rare factors is depended on to support the common one. For instance, repentance is a common theme in Luke (explicitly mentioned in Lk. 3:3, 8; 5:32; 10:13; 11:32; 13:3, 5, 15:7, 10; 16:30; 17:3, 4 and 24:47) yet serves as an element of correspondence in Talbert's chiasm in Luke 10:21–18:30. His case is strengthened by the close or contiguous association of the parallel repentance passages (13:1–5 and 15:1–32) with two exclusive themes, "transcendence of family loyalties" (12:49–53 and 14:25–27) and "prudent action taken ahead of time" (12:54–59 and 14:28–33).[36]

Another way in which Talbert effectively demonstrates the exclusivity of a correspondence that might otherwise appear common is to further qualify the factor that forms the correspondence. In the chiasm just cited, the two Sabbath healings (13:10–17 and 14:1–6) are parallel, but there are three such events in the Gospel (see also 6:6–11). Additional qualification is found in Jesus' reference to an ox and ass only in the parallel accounts. Bailey fails to establish sufficient exclusivity in some categories of his chiastic proposal for the central section of Luke. For example, his correspondence, "people come to Jesus" (9:57–62 and 18:35–43), is weak since it is terribly common, broad and is not strengthened by proximity to other strong correspondences.[37] Talbert's inherent concern for exclusivity makes the form of his chiastic pattern more tenable.

Actually, the correspondences in *Literary Patterns* are at least as exclusive as those that are identified in works like the *Aeneid*[38] and in much of Old Testament poetic parallelism.[39] In fact, the natures of the Lukan patterns and correspondences remarkably resemble those in the *Aeneid*.

3. Pervasiveness of structure. Talbert reminds us that classical sources that employ architectural patterns – several of them used as structural models in Luke's time – nearly always "exhibit a pattern controlling the arrangement of large units throughout an author's work, and in units of all sizes".[40] It should be anticipated, therefore, that if many smaller units in Luke demonstrably adhere to an intentional pattern, then the Gospel as a whole likely does, and vice versa. Undeniably, Luke contains sections that exhibit parallel patterns, such as those frequently acknowledged in Luke 1–4 and in several of the parables.[41] Therefore, it should not be surprising to

---

36 Talbert, *Literary Patterns*, 52.
37 Bailey, *Poet and Peasant*, 80–82.
38 Duckworth, *Structural Patterns*, chapters one and two.
39 For an excellent study of Old Testament poetry, see Robert Alter's *The Art of Biblical Poetry* (New York: Basic Books, 1985).
40 Talbert, *Literary Patterns*, 8.
41 For a detailed presentation of parallel patterns that shape several Lukan parables, see Kenneth E. Bailey's two books, *Poet and Peasant* and *Through Peasant Eyes*.

find additional structure on all levels, even controlling the entire work. Talbert does not fall into the trap, however, that Nils Lund does in his pioneering volume, *Chiasmus in the New Testament*, where he frequently detects pattern where few others would admit it.[42]

Additionally, a pattern finds support in the existence of a similar pattern elsewhere in a structurally corresponding location. Talbert indicates that his chiasm in the center of Acts (18:12–21:26) structurally corresponds to the chiasm in the central section of Luke. The tenability of one is enhanced by the other if it is demonstrable both that Luke and Acts are intentionally parallel in structure to any degree and that one chiasm is intentional.

The manner in which apparently divergent material within a pattern is handled is important to the credibility of the pattern and to the conclusions that can be drawn about its generation. By way of example, Luke 12:1–12 is assigned a variety of parallels in the range of chiasmus proposals for the central section.

1. Baarlink's approach defends a rigid structure with no violations of parallelism in arrangement, with the result that 12:1–12 is parallel to 17:1–4, 7–10 (more broadly, 11:33–12:12 parallel to 17:1–10). The similarities he lists are: a warning against dependence on good works, a summons (*Aufruf*) to response, a reference to forgiveness, and one "*Bildwort*" that expresses a negative idea (a second one, positive in nature, is incorporated in 11:33–36 and 17:5–6).[43] Each of these is common in Luke and there are clear dissimilarities between these two "parallels". Good works is cast in dramatically different light in each. "Summons/*Aufruf*" may be identified in most Lukan pericopes. Direct references to forgiveness permeate the Gospel. Finally, there is more than one *Bildwort* in 12:1–12: e.g., sparrows and hairs. Obviously, since Baarlink does not allow any violation of parallelism, the source of the structure would presumably be Luke.

2. Bailey's approach is more flexible since he demands only that Luke's source be chiastic. Breaks in parallelism occur where redaction supposedly took place. This is a tenable scenario, but it allows any inconsistency to be labeled redaction. In fact, 12:1–12 is described as "extra material" that was inserted into the chiasm and therefore has no corresponding passage.[44] Thus, Bailey avoids forcing the most difficult material for his case into the scheme.

3. Talbert's approach attributes the construction of patterns to Luke, but allows for some variation from identical order. Theoretically, he would also

---

42 Nils W. Lund, *Chiasmus in the New Testament: A Study in the Form and Function of Chiastic Structures* (Peabody, Massachusetts: Hendrickson, 1970; first published in 1942).
43 Baarlink, "zyklische Struktur," 488, 496.
44 Bailey, *Poet and peasant*, 80.

accept unparalleled material, but none of his patterns exhibits this. According to his chiastic proposal for the central section, 12:1–12 corresponds to 16:19–31 and both have the theme, "the threat of hell".[45] Clearly, that is the common theme, but is it important enough within each pericope for Luke to employ it as the element of correspondence? Nolland identifies the primary theme of 12:1–12 as "the need to be ready for the coming judgment," which agrees acceptably with Talbert.[46] Marshall, commenting on 16:19–31, identifies one of the two major themes as "the reversal of fortunes in the next world for the rich and the poor".[47] Again, this reasonably agrees with Talbert. Whether one concurs with his wording or not, clearly Luke could have understood the pericopes to share, as prominent, the concept of the eternal consequences of present life. In Talbert's scheme, however, 12:1–12 is first in a series of three themes that comprise a unit (12:1–48) parallel to another unit of three themes. In this other unit, 16:19–31 lies third rather than first. Such violation of sequence is consistent with patterned composition in the first century and results in a more natural correspondence. Talbert's treatment of 12:1–12 is therefore the most credible of the three.

2 Evaluation of Talbert's Patterns Using the Tests for Intentionality[48]

Now that we have examined Talbert's theoretical basis for his correspondences, a thorough and balanced evaluation of these patterns is possible using the eleven tests for intentionality. For convenience, these tests are reiterated below:

1. The greater the restriction of elements of correspondence to the relevant passages, the greater is the probability of authorial intent.

2. The greater the number of reasonable parallel features between parallel passages, the greater is the probability of intent.

3. Similarly, the greater the number of parallel passages (or panels) that match a proposed pattern or grouping of features, the greater is the case for intent.

4. An element of correspondence that attracts the reader's attention

---

45 Talbert, *Literary Patterns*, 52.
46 Nolland, *Luke 9:21–18:34*, 681.
47 Marshall, *Gospel of Luke*, 632.
48 In this section, all material within tables that present Talbert's patterns is directly quoted from *Literary Patterns*. Quotation marks have been omitted for the sake of clarity. All instances of bold case have been added where helpful to distinguish the elements of parallel assumed for the analysis.

contributes to the probability of intent.

5. Parallelism between complex units, such as combined pericopes, that appears constructive rather than random or coincidental increases the probability of intent.
6. If redaction critical observations yield evidence of Lukan adjustment to include or create the elements that constitute the literary device, the probability of intent is greater insofar as there are no superior reasons for the observed redaction.
7. If the elements of correspondence that constitute the literary device are related to important Lukan themes, the probability of intent is enhanced.
8. Intent is more certain if there is no clear historical or genre expectation for the inclusion of the features in question and their sequence, if parallelism of sequence is observed.
9. If a sequence or grouping of features in parallel is uncommon in other relevant literature, then the likelihood of coincidence due to common expression is diminished.
10. If the passages that constitute parallel groupings of passages are contiguous within the groupings, and not distributed broadly throughout the text, then selectivity on the part of the reader is diminished.
11. The probability of intent increases as more of the above tests are passed.

2.1 General Correspondences between Luke and Acts and Their Analysis

Presenting the application of all the tests to all the correspondences of all Talbert's patterns would occupy a vast amount of space, so primarily in instances where there is difficulty in satisfying a test will comments be made. Accordingly, when no comment is made, one may assume that the element of correspondence finds support in the test. The implication of each test, however, will be evaluated whether or not difficulties had been noted. Be forewarned that Talbert's defense of his individual patterns employs redaction criticism almost exclusively, so citations of his argumentation will necessarily be concentrated in the discussions of test six.

Our work is concerned with intentional correspondences involving the gospel of Luke. Accordingly, analysis of Talbert's correspondences restricted to material in Acts will be covered in an appendix, Appendix A.

Talbert begins his presentation of patterns with correspondences observed between Luke and Acts. The following is his presentation of "the parallelism between the sequence of events in the Third Gospel and Acts".[49] On three occasions, he elaborates on detailed parallel patterns within individual correspondences (parallels 5, 12, and 26). These will be analyzed at the conclusion of the general correspondences between the two volumes.

LUKE		ACTS
1:1–4 A **preface** dedicates the book to **Theophilus**.	1.	1:1–5 A **preface** dedicates the book to **Theophilus**.
3:21 Jesus is **praying** at his **baptism**.	2.	1:14, 24 The disciples are **praying** as they await their **baptism** of the Holy Spirit.
3:22 The **Spirit** descends **after Jesus' prayer** and in a **physical** form.	3.	2:1–13 The **Spirit** fills the disciples **after their prayers** with accompanying **physical** manifestations.
4:16–30 Jesus' **ministry opens with a sermon** which gives the theme for what follows, **fulfillment of prophecy** and **rejection of Jesus**.	4.	2:14–40 The Church's **ministry opens with a sermon** which gives the theme for what follows, **fulfillment of prophecy** and **rejection of Jesus**.
4:31–8:56 The theme of fulfillment mentioned in 4:16–30 is illustrated by examples of **preaching** and **healing**. Conflicts illustrate the note of **rejection**.	5.	2:41–12:17 The theme of fulfillment is illustrated by examples of **prophesying** and **wonders**. **Persecutions** illustrate the note of unbelief.

Talbert continues the general correspondences between Luke and Acts after treating a pattern evident within parallel 5. This pattern will be discussed later (page 104).

---

49 For Talbert's presentation and discussion of these correspondences, see *Literary Patterns*, 16–23.

10:1–12 The **mission** of the seventy which foreshadows the **Gentile** mission of the Church.	**11.** Chs. 13–20 The **missionary journeys** of Paul to the **Gentiles**.
9:51–19:28 Jesus makes a **journey to Jerusalem** which is a **passion journey** (9:31; 9:51; 12:50; 13:33; 18:31–33) under **divine necessity** (13:33) and characterized by the disciples' **lack of understanding** (9:45; 18:34).	**12.** 19:21–21:17 Paul makes a last **journey to Jerusalem** which is a **passion journey** (20:3; 20:22–24; 20:37–38; 21:4; 21:10–11; 21:13) under **divine necessity** (20:22; 21:14) and characterized by his friends' **lack of understanding** (21:4; 21:12–13).

The general parallels are continued by Talbert following a presentation of the detailed pattern of parallel 12. Again, evaluation of this parallel will be postponed (page 108) until the general parallels have been discussed. Regarding the next seven correspondences, Talbert states, "Not only is Jesus' journey to Jerusalem parallel to that of Paul, but also the events that take place when the two men reach the city, and after, are similar".[50] Therefore, in parallels 20–26, an additional feature inherent in each is that the correspondence is between Jesus and Paul.[51]

19:37 Jesus **receives a good reception** and the **people praise God for the works** they have seen.	20. 21:17–20a Paul **receives a good reception** and **God is glorified for the things done** among the Gentiles.
19:45–48 Jesus **goes into the Temple**. He has a **friendly attitude toward it**.	21. 21:26 Paul **goes into the Temple**. He has a **friendly attitude toward it**.

---

50 Talbert, *Literary Patterns*, 17.
51 Radl develops a very similar series of parallels between Paul and Jesus to Talbert's, covering much the same territory; *Paulus und Jesus*. His approach is more general and thematic, however, and his defense of each is often less rigorous than Talbert's. Therefore a detailed evaluation of his correspondences would be very redundant here.

20:27–39 The **Sadducees do not believe in the resurrection**. The **scribes support Jesus**.	22.	23:6–9 The **Sadducees do not believe in the resurrection**. The **scribes support Paul**.	
22:19a At a **meal** Jesus λαβὼν ἄρτον εὐχαριστήσας ἔκλασεν.	23.	27:35 Paul has a **meal** in which he λαβὼν ἄρτον εὐχαριστήσεν...καὶ κλάσας.	
22:54 A **mob** **seizes** Jesus.	24.	21:30 A **mob** **seizes** Paul.	
22:63–64 Jesus is **slapped** by the **priest's assistants**.	25.	23:2 Paul is **slapped** at the **high priest's command**.	
22:26; 23:1; 23:8; 23:13 The **four trials** of Jesus (Sanhedrin; Pilate; Herod; Pilate).	26.	Chs. 23; 24; 25; 26 The **four trials** of Paul (Sanhedrin; Felix; Festus; Herod Agrippa).	

Talbert develops parallel 26 in detail (discussed below, page 111) before he presents this final general correspondence.

Ch. 24 Conclusion. The **ministry of Jesus concludes** on the **positive note of the fulfillment of scripture**.	32.	Ch. 28 Conclusion. The **ministry of Paul concludes** on the **positive note of the fulfillment of scripture**.	

Test 1: *Restriction to passages* – Parallel 2 is formed by the collocation of the act of praying and the involvement of those praying in a form of baptism. Prayer in Acts 1:14, 24 appears however to be unassociated with the baptism; but if the association is granted, then the connection is very loose and may increase the number of passages having this collocation. Actually, in Luke no other passage that fits. However, Acts has two, 2:41–42 and 22:16. Add Acts 8:12–17 and 16:11–15 to these two if those who are praying may be different from those who are baptized. Still, the association of these features is somewhat rare.

Parallel 5 lacks restriction of its features to the specified bounds. Preaching, healing and conflict in Luke (three essential facets of Christ's ministry highlighted in 4:16–30) extend well beyond 8:56. Likewise, prophesying, wonders and persecution reach beyond 12:17 in Acts. The prevalence of these themes argues against their value in establishing this parallel as defined.

Parallel 11 is defined by a mission that is related to the Gentiles. In Luke, the only passage where the preaching of disciples foreshadows the mission to the Gentiles is 10:1–12.[52] If the definition is broadened to include Jesus, then 7:11–19 and 17:1–10 may be added. Nevertheless, this is a small number. Acts contains several missions to Gentiles prior to chapter 13, but these would not apply if Paul were an essential part of the definition. However, even though he is the subject of the two Acts units, the Gospel correspondences are not restricted to a single character since the seventy *and* Jesus are the subjects of the units. This being the case, the missions of Philip (Acts 8:26–39) and Peter (10:1–11:18 and 11:19–21) to the Gentiles should be considered. If Talbert's point is simply that both works incorporate the concept of Gentile mission, he has demonstrated this. Must this imply an intentional literary correspondence rather than a consequence of history and divine plan? Perhaps the distinction is too small. Still, more evidence would be helpful.

Parallel 12 is well established even though Jerusalem is not the location of Paul's execution. No other journey to Jerusalem that shares the other three features exists in either work.

Among *parallels 20–26* and *32*, all parallel units are completely restricted to their locations with one minor exception (assuming *parallel 24* is the final seizure before trial). Luke 2:45–49 is an instance where Jesus enters the Temple with a favorable attitude toward it.

Eleven of the fifteen parallels are absolutely restricted to their defined locations. *Parallels 5* and *11* are weakest. Overall, the pattern finds strong support from this test.

Test 2: *Number of features* – Most of the parallels (9 of 15) contain only two features,[53] admittedly often strong ones. Yet, two is not an altogether impressive number. The collocation of prayer and baptism alone in *parallel 2* is not particularly strong (see test 1 above). In addition, the striking of Jesus (δέρω) and Paul (τύπτω) is tenuously linked by association with a priest (*parallel 25*).

This pattern of passages is reasonably supported by numbers of parallel features. Five of fifteen parallels employ three or more. Yet, the parallels in general are spread noncontiguously throughout Luke-Acts, which weakens the significance of those with merely two features. Coincidence is able to

---

52 See Marshall's discussion of how Lk. 10:1–12 relates to Gentiles, *Gospel of Luke*, 415.

53 The comparison of Jesus and Paul may be considered to form the second feature in parallel 24, but it is preferable to establish parallels without the aid of this comparison since Paul is the subject of so much of Acts and Jesus of virtually all of Luke. Parallel elements must be reasonably restricted for confidence. Another possible feature might be that these are the *final* seizures before trial.

play a greater role. Due to the length of each book, perhaps it is best to conclude that test 2 strongly supports the "pattern" in sections where three or more features form each parallel (the sections formed by *parallels 3–5*, by *parallel 12*, and by *parallel 26*) and mildly supports those with only two (the remainder). In deference to the strength of certain correspondences with two features, their validity apart from a pattern may be judged individually. For instance, *parallels 22* and *23* are striking.

Test 3: *Number of panels/passages* – Intervening material clouds the matter since it increases the possibility of subjectivity in observation. Nevertheless, two parallel panels exhibiting the proper sequence[54] is a minimum case for intent.[55]

Test 4: *Attracts attention* – In *parallel 3*, as noted earlier, the association between the baptism of the Holy Spirit (in Acts 2:1–13) and the disciples' act of praying is indirect at best. The reader would not notice the temporal relationship. Likewise, in Luke 22:63–64 the association of the men guarding Jesus with the priests is not indicated as relevant in the text. Generally, the elements of correspondence are noteworthy, however, so authorial intent is supported by the test.

Test 5: *Constructive complexity* – As Talbert has defined this pattern, it is completely constructive, with the sequence of parallels unbroken apart from an inversion of the Acts passages of *parallels 22* and *23*. This break in sequence of Acts 23:6–9 (parallel 22) and Acts 27:35 (parallel 23) is insignificant in the context of the entire pattern.[56] Conversely, if the demonstrable pattern is believed to be limited to parallels 20 through 26, then the violation is a significant portion of the whole. Based on the entire pattern as defined by Talbert, the probability of Lukan intent is endorsed. Nonetheless, the presence of intervening material weakens the case (see test 10).

Test 6: *Redaction criticism* – Since redaction criticism plays a vital role in Talbert's argumentation, greater attention will be paid to the strength of his evidence. A nagging question throughout his work is how much we should expect Luke to have adjusted his former book to suit the latter.

Parallel 1 is firmly established in Lukan material.[57] Regarding *parallels 2 and 3*, Talbert lists "the reference to Jesus at his baptism at the time when

---

54 Note that the Acts passages of parallels 22 and 23 are inverted. This should not necessarily be viewed as problematical.
55 Unlike Tannehill, all of Talbert's patterns are restricted to two panels of parallel passages.
56 Talbert notes this point, *Literary Patterns*, 30, n.4.
57 Talbert, *Literary Patterns*, 18. See also Roloff's comments on the Lukan nature of Acts 1:1–12, in *Apostelgeschichte*, 17.

the Spirit descended upon him"[58] as one of two supporting Lukan additions to Mark. Yet, it is not manifest that Mark's meaning differs from Luke's. The second addition is the bodily form of the Spirit.[59] Mark may be understood to imply bodily form, which could mean that Luke was merely making the implication explicit. Pesch and Guelich, with the majority of commentators on Mark, read the phrase (ὡς περιστεράν; Mk. 1:10; Lk. 3:22) adjectivally as an object of Jesus' sight.[60] Making the Spirit a physical manifestation here for the sake of the parallel clearly could have been the motivation behind the redaction. However, Fitzmyer calls the redaction a "characteristically Lucan feature,"[61] suggesting general preference rather than the construction of a parallel.

Schürmann considers Luke's Nazareth account (Lk. 4:16–30) to be loosely drawn from Mark 6:1–6 with additions from Q.[62] Klostermann and Schneider see the Markan passage as the primary source.[63] Nevertheless, Talbert rightly argues for *parallel 4*, that regardless of whether or not Luke 4:16–30 is based on Mark 6:1–6, the themes of fulfillment and rejection are positioned by him at this location.[64]

Parallel 5 is treated as a separate pattern by Talbert. His corresponding discussion of Lukan redaction in this section relates to that pattern and is evaluated shortly (page 104).

Parallels 11 and *12* in Luke are in the travel narrative, which is primarily of Lukan construction, so the parallels could have easily been created by the author. This argument is as good as any other proposed, and generally does not contradict alternative explanations of composition and structure.

Certainly, praise is expressed by the people in the synoptic parallels to Luke 19:28–38 in *parallel 20* (cf. Mk. 11:1–10; Mt. 21:1–9), but the Lukan addition of verse 37 indicates God as a recipient, not solely Jesus, establishing a parallel. Additionally, this verse refers to the works seen by the people

---

58   Talbert, *Literary Patterns*, 18.
59   Talbert, *Literary Patterns*, 18.
60   Rudolf Pesch, *Das Markusevangelium: I. Teil: Einleitung und Kommentar zu Kap. 1,1–8,26*, Herders Theologischer Kommentar zum Neuen Testament (Freiburg: Herder, 1977). Robert A. Guelich, *Mark 1–8:26*, Word Biblical Commentary 34a (Dallas: Word Books, 1989) 32–33.
61   Fitzmyer, *Luke I-IX*, 480.
62   Heinz Schürmann, *Das Lukasevangelium: Erster Teil: Kommentar zu Kap. 1,1–9, 50*, Herders Theologischer Kommentar zum Neuen Testament 3/1 (Freiburg/Basel/Vienna: Herder, 1969) 227–28, 241–242.
63   E. Klostermann, *Das Lukasevangelium*, Handbuch zum Neuen Testament 5 (Tübingen: Mohr, 1929, reprinted 1975) 62; Schneider, *Evangelium nach Lukas*, 106–107.
64   Talbert, *Literary Patterns*, 18–19.

as inspiration for the praise.[65] Other scholars point to the specification of locality or of disciples as sole constituents of the crowd as the motivation for the inclusion of verse 37.[66] Indeed, though Luke incorporates Mark's reference to the location (Lk. 19:29; cf. Mk. 11:1), verse 37 places Jesus even nearer to Jerusalem. Specification of locality is a valid point. So also is the idea that only a crowd of disciples would sufficiently understand the identity of Jesus to offer such praise. Just as these two independent concerns could have been coupled within one verse of redaction without contradiction, so might Talbert's proposal be incorporated into the motivation behind including verse 37, especially since the other two concerns do not account for the elements he specifically cites. It would certainly not be too complex procedure.

Talbert considers as an intentional formation of *parallel 21* Luke's removal of the cursing of the fig tree (Mk.11:12–14) and his addition of Jesus continually teaching in the Temple (Lk. 19:47). First, eradication of the fig tree incident removes the concept of rejection and "softens" the passage. Thus, a more favorable disposition toward the Temple is presented. Second, the note of Jesus' continual habit of teaching there implies acceptance of it.[67] There is general agreement that this habit assumes "a friendly attitude toward it".[68] A variety of theories has been posed for the omission of the fig tree account. Nolland believes that the abbreviation was to emphasize the quote about the Temple in Luke 19:46.[69] This effect is achieved, so the motive is quite possible. Liefeld notes the judgmental strength of Luke 19:41–44 and views the omission as avoidance of overkill.[70] The strength of this argument is that it interacts with other redaction in the immediate context. Similarly, Evans suggests that Luke found the story "enigmatic," or "unedifying". He further offers the avoidance of a doublet with Luke 13:6–9 as a motivation, which is a recognized Lukan tendency.[71] Schlatter believes that Luke was avoiding repetition with the fig parable of Luke

---

65 Talbert, *Literary Patterns*, 20–21.
66 Fitzmyer suggests the interest in locality, *Luke X-XXIV*, 1243; and C.F. Evans develops the importance of the identity of the crowd as disciples, *Saint Luke*, 679–680. Darell L. Bock, notes both, *Luke: Volume 2: 9:51–24:53*, Baker Exegetical Commentary on the New Testament 3b (Grand Rapids: Baker, 1996) 1557.
67 Talbert, *Literary Patterns*, 21.
68 See Nolland, *Luke 9:21–18:34*, 940. For the characterization of the Jerusalem ministry as one of teaching, which is compatible with Talbert's proposition, see Marshall, *Gospel of Luke*, 722; and Liefeld, Walter W. *Luke*, Expositor's Bible Commentary 8 (Grand Rapids: Zondervan, 1984) 1012.
69 Nolland, *Luke 9:21-18:34*, 940.
70 Liefeld, *Luke*, 1012.
71 C.F. Evans, *Saint Luke*, 686.

13:6.[72] Talbert's suggestions are possible, but do not appear to be as strong as some of the others. Since, for instance, the cursing of the fig tree was probably an indictment against Israel, not the Temple,[73] this lessens the need for Talbert's explanation. Furthermore, his idea that Luke intended to display a friendly attitude toward the Temple by stressing Jesus' continual presence there is redundant in light of Jesus' fierce defense of it in the cleansing scene. Certainly, intentional redundancy is possible, but the Lukan desire to portray favorable disposition toward the Temple through these redactions has not been demonstrated to be a preferable explanation.

Luke's addition of scribal support for Jesus (Lk. 20:39; cf. Mk. 12:18–27) when questioned by the Sadducees about resurrection is probably intended to establish the parallel with Acts 23:6–9, according to Talbert (*parallel 22*).[74] Despite doubts about the extent to which Luke would edit the Gospel to suit Acts, other explanations are no stronger. Plummer soundly assumes the historicity of their presence;[75] but without further justification, their inclusion is then almost incidental. Evans merely reflects the difficulty of accounting for the addition by calling it "clumsy,"[76] an unhelpful comment in the light of possible, legitimate motivations. Nolland offers that Luke's motive was to authenticate Christianity as the fulfillment of Judaism through rare support from Jewish leaders, in contrast to their general opposition.[77] This is a strong theory, but it does not apparently explain their sudden appearance in the scene if Luke wanted to wield their approval as a theological weapon. Another useful idea, suggested by Fitzmyer, is that Luke merely ties the scene to the preceding context through the references to scribes in Luke 20:1 and 19.[78] This meshes with his frequent development of larger scenes by linking smaller ones together into one larger occasion. Grundmann holds that Luke merely moves to the conclusion of this passage (Lk. 20:39) an altered form of the Markan ending to the passage that he omitted from Mark just following this account (verses 32–34 of Mk. 12:28–34).[79] Ultimately, Talbert's proposal is just as

---

72 Adolf Schlatter, *Das Evangelium des Lukas: Aus seinen Quellen erklärt* (Stuttgart: Calver, 1960²) 117–118.
73 William L. Lane, *The Gospel According to Mark*, NIC (Grand Rapids: Eerdmans, 1974) 399–400. Against a symbolic interpretation of the passage, see Pesche, *Markusevangelium: II. Teil*, 191–192.
74 Talbert, *Literary Patterns*, 21.
75 Alfred Plummer, *A Critical and Exegetical Commentary on the Gospel According to St. Luke*, ICC (Edinburgh: T. & T. Clark, 1922⁵) 471.
76 C.F. Evans, *Saint Luke*, 720.
77 Nolland, *Luke 1-9:20*, 967.
78 Fitzmyer, *Luke X-XXIV*, 1307.
79 Walter Grundmann, *Das Evangelium nach Lukas*, Theologischer Handkommentar zum Neuen Testament (Berlin: Evangelische Verlagsanstalt, 1984) 376.

viable as these are.

We move now to *parallel 23*, which depends on a minor variation in the wording of Luke from Mark.

Mk. 14:22   Καὶ ἐσθιόντων αὐτῶν λαβὼν ἄρτον *εὐλογήσας* ἔκλασεν καὶ ἔδωκεν αὐτοῖς καὶ εἶπεν· λάβετε, τοῦτό ἐστιν τὸ σῶμά μου.

Lk. 22:19a   καὶ λαβὼν ἄρτον *εὐχαριστήσας* ἔκλασεν καὶ ἔδωκεν αὐτοῖς λέγων

Notice the change from εὐλογήσας to εὐχαριστήσας. Talbert notes that Lk. 22:19a reflects the wording in Acts (see the underlined text) and thereby supports the parallel.[80]

Acts 27:35   εἴπας δὲ ταῦτα καὶ λαβὼν ἄρτον *εὐχαρίστησεν* τῷ θεῷ ἐνώπιον πάντων καὶ κλάσας ἤρξατο ἐσθίειν.

There is a potential problem with the claim, however. Four alternatives exist: (1) Luke readjusted the Gospel to match his wording (εὐχαριστέω) in the subsequent volume (Talbert's theory); (2) Luke preferred a synonym of Mark's word and reflected his alteration of Mark in Acts when he constructed the parallel; (3) Luke 22:19a depends on a separate eucharistic tradition (cf. 1 Cor. 11:23b–24a; ἔλαβεν ἄρτον καὶ εὐχαριστήσας ἔκλασεν καὶ εἶπεν); or (4) the similar wording is incidental, with εὐχαριστέω being coincidentally Luke's preferred word in both accounts. The first alternative is anachronistic. Certainly, Luke would not have recorded the Lord's Supper with Mark's εὐλογέω, composed the account of Paul's meal with εὐχαριστέω and then chosen to revise the Lord's Supper to match Paul's meal. The second alternative solves this problem, but Luke shows no general preference for εὐχαριστέω,[81] despite Schlatter's view that the change is consistent with Greek usage.[82] Still, he might have desired it on this occasion. The third alternative accounts for the different wording from Mark in Luke 22:19a, but it provides no reason other than the fourth alternative for the similarity between Luke 22:19a and Acts 27:35, unless

---

80 Talbert, *Literary Patterns*, 21.
81 Of the three instances of a Markan εὐλογέω in a passage used by Luke, only here does he change it to εὐχαριστέω. One instance is an OT quotation, so a change would not be expected. Nevertheless, Luke employs εὐλογέω thirteen times and εὐχαριστέω four times, which suggests no such preference.
82 Schlatter, *Evangelium des Lukas*, 137.

the assumed eucharistic tradition is considered to lie behind the Acts passage also. Then this individual parallel is necessarily intentional. Yet it is very difficult to be decisive about whether or not Acts 27:35 is eucharistic.[83] The fourth alternative must not be ruled out despite the number of similar words. With the exception of Acts 20:11, every first level narrative account in the New Testament of the initiation of a meal involving ἄρτος (nearly all meals)[84] depicts the taking (λαμβάνω) of bread, so "λαβὼν ἄρτον" is not surprising.[85] Nine of these fourteen instances involve breaking (κλάω) of the bread. Fitzmyer notes that κλάω "is used in the NT only in the context of breaking bread at a meal".[86] It must be said that most, if not all, of the fourteen have been linked with the Lord's Supper because of the wording, but we must ask whether the similarity is simply due to common parlance or to conformity with the Last Supper.[87] With respect to Acts 27:35, the latter possibility is strengthened by the presence of εὐχαριστέω. Accordingly, the similarity of wording is more likely intentional than incidental, but not by means of Talbert's scenario.

Talbert states regarding *parallel 24*, "In v. 54 Luke adds συλλαβόντες to Mark 14:53's statement that they ἀγήγαγον Jesus to the high priest. Matthew 26:57 has Jesus seized, but his word is κρατήσαντες. Luke's addition may very well be significant since Acts 21:30 uses the cognate ἐπιλαβόμενοι with reference to Paul's seizure."[88] Perhaps a stronger suggestion is that Luke has merely delayed the actual arrest by transferring Mark's συλλαβεῖν in 14:48 to this new location.[89] The effect is to allow the arrest "only after [Jesus] has, as it were, given permission".[90] Clearly, this substantial explanation takes precedent over the formation of a minor parallel, if indeed the two are mutually exclusive. Talbert would probably respond that the timing of the arrest is not the concern, but rather the word used to describe it. Therefore, alternative explanations do not necessarily nullify Talbert's position.

---

83 Roloff sees little justification in taking it as eucharistic because of the involvement of non-Christians (*Apostelgeschichte*, 364); but F.F. Bruce hesitantly accepts the possibility because of the cluster of eucharistic terms. See *The Acts of the Apostles: The Greek Text with Introduction and Commentary* (Leicester: Apollos, 1990) 525.
84 Mt. 14:19; 15:36; 26:26; Mk. 6:41; 8:6; 14:22; Lk. 6:4; 9:16; 22:19; 24:30; Jn. 6:11; 21:13; Acts 27:35; 1 Cor. 11:23
85 Thirteen of the fourteen such instances display this word order.
86 Fitzmyer, *Luke X-XXIV*, 1399.
87 The LXX provides no evidence of the relevant wording, so it may be ruled out as a source.
88 Talbert, *Literary Patterns*, 21.
89 See Nolland, *Luke 9:21-18:34*, 1089; and Fitzmyer, *Luke X-XXIV*, 1463.
90 Marshall cites Schneider, *Gospel of Luke*, 840.

No editorial work is evident for *parallel 26*. Talbert contends that none was necessary. The parallel, however, is tenuous (see test 2 above) and could have been made clearer by Luke.

Parallel 26 depends on the same compositional improbability as Talbert's proposal for parallel 23. He notes the increase from Mark's three trials to Luke's four, which corresponds to Paul's four.[91] If one of Luke's Gospel sources included a fourth trial, he explains that Luke could have opted for it because of its correspondence with Paul's experience. However, would Luke model the passion of Jesus to match Paul's even if one source accommodated the desire? More likely, Luke would have trimmed a trial off his account of Paul, unless he had great trust in this Gospel source. Regardless of source theories, the mechanism of altering the Gospel to suit Acts is founded on an improbable prioritization and requires weighty evidence for such a major adjustment as this. See the discussion of parallels 27–31 (page 111) for Talbert's additional evidence in the form of parallels between the four trials of Jesus and those of Paul.

The final general correspondence between Luke and Acts, *parallel 32*, consists of the conclusion of each work with "the positive note of the fulfillment of Scripture". As Talbert informs us, only verses 1–11 of Luke 24 could come from Mark, and both Luke 24:13–32 and 33–49 conclude with the theme that Jesus' death and glorification fulfilled Scripture.[92] This adequately corresponds to Paul's bittersweet quotation from Isaiah that speaks of the benefit to the Gentiles of Jewish rejection of the Gospel. Talbert's proposal is strong.

In summary, then, this test does not conclusively support intentional Lukan construction of the architectonic pattern since there are usually other equally valid explanations for the redactional phenomena. The fact that redaction may frequently be interpreted in favor of the pattern does, however, allow the possibility that Talbert is correct; but this dispersion of a number of redactionally possible correspondences throughout the two volumes allows equally that the pattern has been imposed on a range of material under the influence of a few definite parallels. Unfortunately, guessing the mind of an author from complex editorial work is risky business and liable to produce a host of possibilities from any one instance of redaction. Nevertheless, Talbert has demonstrated viable redactional mechanisms behind a majority of the parallels in this "pattern".

Test 7: *Important themes* – Virtually all of the elements of correspondence that constitute this pattern are important or substantial Lukan themes. The probability of intent is greatly enhanced.

---

91 Talbert, *Literary Patterns*, 22.
92 Talbert, *Literary Patterns*, 22.

Test 8: *Historical/genre expectation* – In *parallels 1–5*, if prayer is seen as an incidental parallel because Luke typically includes it in conjunction with significant events, then the sequence of events here appears quite natural. A preface must naturally come first in a book, if one is desired. Obviously, any effort to couple the two books would be served by a dedication to the same person, especially when that person (or those represented by him) is actually the recipient. Regarding *parallels 2* and *3*, the Lukan elements and the sequence are imported from Mark and are apparently an expected component of the genre, evident by its inclusion in all four Gospels. Not surprisingly, baptism and the preparatory arrival of the Holy Spirit precede the commencement of ministry (*parallel 4*), a mere fact of history. Similarly, it would be remiss of Luke to ignore the physically apparent baptism of the Holy Spirit prior to the beginning of the apostles' ministry if he were aware of the event. To this point, it seems as though Luke was confined by history and genre. However, a programmatic sermon and subsequent outworking of the ministry in accordance with the themes of that sermon are neither historically expected nor required by genre. The absence of such a sermon in Mark and John is witness to the fact.

Parallels 11 and *12* appear both historically and generically expected, but not necessarily in the Lukan form. Each Gospel narrates the extension of Jesus' ministry to Gentiles, and Gentile inclusion in the Church was an inescapable fact of the subject matter in Acts. The journeys to Jerusalem, following contact with Gentiles, were compelled by history and genre (indubitably a feature of the New Testament Gospel genre). This is true of Paul's story, but Luke was not required to include him. He was compelled nevertheless by Paul's historical role in the apostolic church, a role that came to prominence after the initial activity of the other apostles.

Interestingly, each Lukan correspondence from *20* to *26* has a reasonable parallel in the other Synoptic Gospels, and in the identical sequence. This implies genre and/or historical expectation. The inclusion of the corresponding events in Acts however, though historical, was not necessary or expected. Indeed, some lack the distinctiveness that would demand attention over other events in Paul's ministry known to Luke that are not recorded in Acts. Therefore, although the events and sequence are natural for the Gospel, they are optional for Acts. Luke's selection of them therefore favors intentional correspondence with the Gospel.

The verdict of this test casts some doubt on the pattern as a whole being an intentional development. The inclusion and sequence of *parallels 1, 2, 3, 5, 11* and *12* may reasonably be expected by virtue of historical fact and genre. Luke's choice to include them may have been driven by necessity rather than the construction of a parallel pattern. Parallel 4 is, however, not required or expected by genre or apparent history. Yet, it may be explained as coincidental on literary grounds. The Acts half of *parallels 20* through *32* is not historically inevitable or required by genre, so these parallels are the strongest portion of the "architectonic pattern" according to this test, and are consequently supported.

Test 9: *Common expression* – Nowhere else in the New Testament are the elements and sequence of *parallels 1* through *5* approximated. Also, the elements and sequence of parallels *20* through *26*, as strictly defined by Talbert, are found nowhere else. This weighs in favor of intent.

Test 10: *Contiguity* – Talbert's pattern finds little support in this test. Notice the number and size of the gaps between the parallel units in Luke (1:5–3:20; 3:23–4:15; 9:1–50; 19:29–36; 19:38–44; 20:1–26; 20:40–22:18; and further gaps in chapters 22 and 23) and in Acts (1:6–13, 15–23, 25–26; 12:18–25; 21:20b–25; 21:27–29; 21:31–22:30; 27:1–34; and 27:35–44). All the material in these gaps is important, yet unrelated to the elements in the pattern. Such an amount of material increases the possibility of the observer finding coincidental similarities. In fairness, Talbert must be given the benefit of the doubt, here, since he proposes overlapping layers of parallel patterns that could only be engineered by Luke through some intermingling of parallel items from different patterns.

Test 11: *Cumulative case* – Overall, this pattern receives marginally greater support than opposition from the tests. For a proposal based on the existence of pattern, this is a poor result. Theological and literary statements founded on it must therefore be treated as tentative without substantial corroboration. There appear to be valid individual correspondences, however, and the block of parallels 12, 21–26 (parallelism between Jesus and Paul) demonstrates the highest probability in the scheme of being an architectonic pattern.

In summary of the general correspondences between Luke and Acts, Talbert has presented particular parallels that confirm the close unity between the two volumes. Indeed, he has demonstrated a high probability that Luke intended them to foster at least some basic comparisons between Jesus and the apostles. The tests moderate the extent to which we may *confidently* accept the proposed architectonic pattern, however. When we analyze his localized patterns, they will generally achieve results that are more positive.

2.2 Focus on Specific General Correspondences between Luke and Acts and Their Analysis

Three of the general parallels in the over-all correspondence scheme between Luke and Acts are observed by Talbert to contain detailed parallelism of their own. Parallels 5, 12, and 26 are developed in like manner to the general parallels.

2.2.1 Development of General Parallel 5

Talbert proposes a deeper pattern within parallel 5 above (page 91).[93] The theme of fulfillment is developed with examples of preaching/prophesying, healing/wonders, and conflicts/persecutions.

LUKE		ACTS
5:17–26 A **lame man** is **healed** by the authority of **Jesus**.	6.	3:1–10 A **lame man** is **healed** by the name of **Jesus** (cf. 9:32–35).
5:29–6:11 **Conflicts** with the **religious leaders**.	7.	4:1–8:3 **Conflicts** with **religious leaders**.
7:1–10 A **centurion**, well-spoken of **by the Jews**, sends **men to Jesus** to ask him to **come to his house**.	8.	Ch. 10 A **centurion**, well-spoken of **by the whole Jewish nation**, sends **men to Peter** to ask him to **come to his house**.
7:11–17 A story involving a **widow** and a **resurrection**. Jesus says, **"Arise"** (ἐγέρθητι). And the dead man **"sat up"** (ἀνεκάθισεν).	9.	9:36–43 A story involving **widows** and a **resurrection**. Peter says, **"Rise"** (ἀνάστηθι). And the woman **"sat up"** (ἀνεκάθισεν).
7:36–50 A **Pharisee criticizes** Jesus for being touched by the **wrong kind of woman**.	10.	11:1–18 The **Pharisaic party criticizes** Peter for his association with **Gentiles**.

Test 1: *Restriction to passages – Parallel 6* is absolutely restricted,[94] but *parallel 7* is not. Effectively all extended accounts of conflict with religious leaders are contained within Acts 4:1–8:3, except perhaps Paul's defense before the Sanhedrin (22:30–23:11). Yet, there is a small amount of

---

93 For Talbert's presentation and discussion of this set of correspondences, see *Literary Patterns*, 16, 19–20.
94 One might argue that Aeneas, the paralytic whom Peter healed by the name of Jesus Christ (Acts 9:34), was lame. Yet, Luke probably distinguished between παραλύτικος and χωλός. This single incidence does not effectively change our analysis. The healing of the lame man in Acts 14:8–13 does not mention the name Jesus.

intervening material not relating to conflict (Acts 4:32–5:11; 6:1–7). This is relatively inconsequential in size, however, and it hardly disrupts the atmosphere of conflict. In contrast, there are several instances of conflict with religious leaders outside of Luke 5:29–6:11. These include Luke 7:36–50; 10:25–37; 11:37–54; 14:1–14; 16:14–31; 19:45–20:8; and 20:19–26.

Parallels 8 and *9* are absolutely restricted, but *parallel 10* is slightly problematical. In Luke, Pharisees criticize Jesus for his association with the wrong kind of people in 5:27–32 and 15:1–32 as well. Nevertheless, this is a small pool from which to draw coincidental parallels. Regarding Acts 11:1–18, the passage does not clearly identify the circumcised Christians with the Pharisees (v. 2), so it is not certain that *parallel 10* is defined properly or whether Acts 11:1–18 really fits. Apart from this passage, Acts 15:5 accurately matches the requirements, even specifying the critics as Pharisees. If the definition is refined to denote only criticism for association with Gentiles, then these two passages alone in Acts conform and the element may be regarded as reasonably restricted (as unlikely inclusions, see Acts 13:48–50 and 21:27–29).

This test only mildly endorses the pattern. Two of the parallels are not substantially restricted, and another could be better defined.

Test 2: *Number of features* – Each parallel has three or more corresponding elements, except *number 7*. This provisionally favors intent. *Parallel 9*, however, has dissimilarities. In Acts, the widow herself is raised, not her son. The terms for "rise" are different, and "sitting up" is not a strong correspondence. Nevertheless, the similarities are sufficient to accept that Luke might have intended the connection.

Test 3: *Number of panels/passages* – As always, Talbert's pattern consists of two panels, a minimum case for intent. However, again, intervening material clouds the evidence.

Test 4: *Attracts attention* – Each of the elements specified would catch the attention of a first century Jewish or Christian reader, excepting the "Pharisaic" aspect of Acts 11:1–18, as noted earlier. Such striking features would likely be utilized if this pattern were intentional.

Test 5: *Constructive complexity* – Talbert has so defined this pattern that it is constructive, with the sequence of parallels intact, apart from the reversal of Acts 9:36–43 and 10:1–48.[95] As discussed earlier, though, ancient writers desired occasional aberrations in their structures, which means this pattern is not invalidated. In sum, this test reasonably supports the probability that it is intentional but, similarly to test 5 above, the presence of intervening material weakens it (see test 10).

Test 6: *Redaction criticism* – Talbert draws a connection between Luke

---

95 Talbert recognizes the matter, *Literary Patterns*, 30, n.4.

5:17 and Acts 3:12-26 (particularly v. 12) for redactional support of *parallel 6*. Luke adds to Mark, "and the power of the Lord was present for Him to perform healing," the referent of "Lord" being God. Peter's explanation of his healing of the beggar implies the divine origin of the power.[96] Is the addition of 5:17 for the sake of the parallel with Acts, or are there other explanations? C.F. Evans notes the introductory nature of this particular healing to Jesus' healing ministry and that it is therefore an appropriate location to define Jesus' power as divine.[97] Nolland and Fitzmyer remind us that Luke has already established the divine origin of Jesus' power in Luke 4:14, and they justifiably see 5:17 as a possible echo of 4:14.[98] Add to this Luke's tendency to insert the word "power" into passages with the healing theme (see Lk. 4:36; 6:19?; 8:46; 9:1; and 19:37) and there is ample justification for the redaction without Talbert's explanation. His interpretation is not nullified, it is simply less weighty.

No changes to the Markan material were required for *parallel 7*, Talbert explains.[99] They are both inherently conflict sections.

Parallel 8, according to Talbert, was probably formed by Luke through his alteration of the source material behind Luke 7:1-10, particularly 3-5. He concludes that this is so, regardless of whether the source is Q or L tradition. Marshall lucidly conveys the complexity behind the issue of Lukan purpose underlying the evident redaction,[100] and it is significant that Talbert's explanation provides a viable solution to the dilemma.

Talbert uses a circular argument to defend *parallel 9*. Luke 7:11-17 is Lukan, so nothing can be said of editorial work. He states, "That such a tradition should occur just here in the sequence and that it would contain such details as a widow, a resurrection, and the near identical words to the one who had died and the similar description of the revived one's response point to the presence of the Lucan hand in creating the parallel."[101] The conclusion that Luke created the parallel is partially founded on the assumption of a Lukan pattern, the very thing this parallel is to support. Certainly, though, the correspondence in details is remarkable and could

---

96 Talbert, *Literary Patterns*, 19.
97 See C.F. Evans, *Saint Luke*, 300. Evans calls this healing account "the first of the individual healings," "...the fever in 4:39 having been treated as a demon, and the leprosy in 5:12-13 requiring a special type of cleansing. It is meant to cover all the healings." His evaluation of the account of the leper is unconvincing, but his conclusion about 5:17 may still be reasonably maintained as the initiation of Jesus' *public* healing ministry. The accounts of the fever and the leper were not specified as public events.
98 Nolland, *Luke 1-9:20*, 234; Fitzmyer, *Luke I-IX*, 582.
99 Talbert, *Literary Patterns*, 19.
100 Marshall, *Gospel of Luke*, 277-278.
101 Talbert, *Literary Patterns*, 19-20.

indicate Lukan activity; but, then, it could be a consequence of historical fact.

Commenting on the uncertainty of the source behind Luke 7:36–50 (*parallel 10*),[102] Talbert says, "Whatever one's judgment about the source of Luke 7:36–50 it seems probable that its present emphasis, that of Pharisaic criticism of Jesus' permissiveness toward a sinful woman, is due to the Lucan hand (cf. Lk. 14:1; 15:1–2; 16:14; 18:9–14)."[103] It appears however that this assertion is based on Luke's propensity to employ the Pharisees in this manner. Yet, what Luke did elsewhere cannot inform us of the likelihood that he did it here. Regardless of changes he clearly made elsewhere, the Pharisaic element could well have been in his source.

In summary of Talbert's discussion of redactional support for this pattern, it is clear that there is substantial editorial work that corresponds with the parallel elements. He has not demonstrated that his explanations are preferable to others, except for *parallel 8*. Still, the fact that redactional data may be rationally explained by his pattern rules out wholesale abandonment of this pattern. The verdict of this test is "uncertain".

Test 7: *Important themes* – Healing, conflict with religious leaders, and Gentile inclusion are all important Lukan themes. Certain individual elements, though, are relatively inconsequential, like "lame man" and "sat up"; but these are coupled with major themes. This test allows for Lukan intent.

Test 8: *Historical/genre expectation* – Similar passages are found in all the other Gospels, yet no one Gospel other than Luke contains five passages that might be considered parallel to the Acts passages in this pattern. Consequently, there does not appear to be genre or historical predisposition for presenting all five. One would imagine that only *parallels 8* and *9* are specific enough not to be common in Jesus' ministry however. So on the strength of these two parallels, this test lends very minor support.

Test 9: *Common expression* – Only *parallel 9* has no reasonably similar passages among the other Gospels. Of course it has its parallels in the Elijah-Elisha cycle (1 Ki. 17:17–24 and 2 Ki. 4:8–37), which is certainly relevant literature; but apart from conflict with religious leaders, this OT cycle lacks the remaining parallels. There is certainly no cause then to call the group of features, or their sequence, "common expression". Still, on compositional grounds, the inclusion of these events is not surprising. If known to Luke, apostolic miracles of healing and revivification would

---

102 See also Schürmann and Darrell L. Bock for useful discussions on this uncertainty; *Lukasevangelium: Erster Teil*, 429, and *Luke: Volume 1: 1:1–9:50*, Baker Exegetical Commentary on the New Testament (Grand Rapids: Baker, 1994) 689–691, respectively.
103 Talbert, *Literary Patterns*, 20.

necessarily have been recorded in a work such as Acts, especially if they were similar to those of Jesus. The similarities may naturally have been highlighted through the form of the accounts. Furthermore, conflict with Pharisees and other religious leaders would also be expected in Acts. Historically speaking, events defined so generally as in *parallels 6, 7,* and *10*, probably occurred regularly (see Acts 5:12 on apostolic healing), so additional burden rests on *parallels 8* and *9*, which are out of sequence. It seems then that only two corresponding parallels are probably created by intentional selection, and there is no strict need for a pattern to explain the presence of all the parallels. Support from this test is generally minimal.

Test 10: *Contiguity* – There is a contiguity problem within *parallel 7*, as noted under test 1. Intervening material breaks its coherency. More importantly, there are gaps between the parallel units of the pattern, namely Luke 6:12–49; 7:18–35; Acts 3:11–26, and 8:3–9:35. Naturally, the pattern is not automatically invalidated since Luke *could* have constructed the system in this fashion, but a greater degree of subjectivity is possible in the observation of such a pattern. Test 10 does not confirm the proposal.

Test 11: *Cumulative case* – Cumulatively, this pattern does not perform well under the tests. Overall, it is not invalidated, but strong support is lacking.

Talbert has noted some individual correspondences that were probably intentional, yet the arrangement of these into a pattern is poorly substantiated. Theological statements based on the pattern, such as the equation of the course of Peter's ministry with that of Jesus', must be posited cautiously. Parallels are drawn, but they may not be as comprehensive as the patterns suggest.

2.2.2 Development of General Parallel 12

The following table presents Talbert's expansion of the patterned correspondences within general parallel 12. He writes, "Careful examination reveals seven references to the journey to Jerusalem in both the passion journey of Jesus in the Third Gospel and that of Paul in Acts."[104]

LUKE		ACTS
9:51, 53 He **set his face** to go to **Jerusalem**.	13.	19:21 Paul **resolved** to go **to Jerusalem**.
13:22 He was journeying toward **Jerusalem**.	14.	20:22 I am going to **Jerusalem**.

---

104 Talbert, *Literary Patterns*, 13. His defense of the pattern is on p. 20.

13:33 I must go on my way for a prophet cannot perish away from **Jerusalem**.		15.	21:4 They told Paul not to go to **Jerusalem**.
17:11 On the way to **Jerusalem** he was passing between Samaria and Galilee.		16.	21:11–12 Agabus told Paul that the Jews at **Jerusalem** would bind him.
18:31 We are going up to **Jerusalem**. [Jesus' **death** is explicit in the context, 18:32]		17.	21:13 Paul replied that he was ready to **die** at **Jerusalem**.
19:11 He was near to **Jerusalem**.		18.	21:15 We made ready to go to **Jerusalem**.
19:28 He went on ahead, going up to **Jerusalem**.		19.	21:17 When they had come to **Jerusalem**.

Test 1: *Restriction to passages* – According to Talbert, from the inception of each journey there are only seven references to the journey to Jerusalem in each volume, so the restriction would be absolute. A potential snag is that he has coupled two references (Lk. 9:51 and 53) as one, yet kept Acts 21:13 separate from 21:11–12. If Acts 21:13 is distinguished from 21:11–12 because of its reference to death, which is parallel to Luke 18:31, then credibility is maintained; but this is an uncertain proposition. Unfortunately, the entire existence of this pattern rests on the number seven since there is little else claimed for it. Nevertheless, based on restriction alone, intent behind this pattern is well supported.

Test 2: *Number of features* – There are additional references to Jerusalem throughout the relevant sections of each book, but those outside the pattern do not refer to the journey. So each parallel is established by at least two elements, a reference to Jerusalem with the additional concept of journey. Two parallels, therefore, have three elements, *parallels 13* and *17*. This is not a strong showing, but it is not problematical. The pattern receives a modest degree of approval from this test.

Test 3: *Number of panels/passages* – Seven parallels is substantial and suggests intent.

Test 4: *Attracts attention* – The city of Jerusalem and the notion of travel are at the heart of each book, so the probability of intent is enhanced.

Test 5: *Constructive complexity* – With such little variation in the details that establish the parallels it is difficult to judge constructiveness. Both passages of *parallel 13* do depict an initial resolve to travel to Jerusalem, and both passages of *parallel 17* include the preview of death, but these two parallels alone are not convincingly constructive. Accordingly, there is very little support from this test.

Test 6: *Redaction criticism* – Moving to redactional corroboration, Talbert writes concerning the Lukan references, "all are editorial and 13:33 comes from L tradition. Only the reference in Luke 18:31 possibly derives from Mark (10:32) and even that has been recast. Moreover, where his Markan source had a reference to entering Jerusalem in 11:11, Luke omits it altogether, saying merely: 'And he entered the temple' (19:45)".[105] Actually, however, the reference in Luke 19:28 is not editorial (cf. Mk. 11:1 and Mt. 21:1), but this is a minor matter. Generally, the argument is persuasive and enhances the probability of intent. Still, it must be tempered by the fact that the bulk of the Lukan material is peculiar to Luke and any aspect of it may perhaps too easily be interpreted as editorial. This makes less remarkable the statement that "all are editorial".

Test 7: *Important themes* – Jerusalem and the journeys to the city are central aspects of each work, so this test adds strength to the claim of authorial intent.

Test 8: *Historical/genre expectation* – One may justifiably conclude that the journeys to Jerusalem were historically expected for both books, and expected by genre for the Gospel. Of course, the number seven is unsolicited by history or genre. Any support from this test is uncertain due to the almost exclusive dependence upon merely two elements for each parallel, Jerusalem and journey.

Test 9: *Common expression* – Travel to Jerusalem as a theme is not common even in biblical literature, but it is prominent in such events as the return of the Israelites from exile (e.g. Ezra, Nehemiah). The other Gospels emphasize the journey far less than the Third. Therefore, the emphasis on travel to Jerusalem is rare enough not to consider it a "common expression". The probability that Luke intended some references to the journeys to Jerusalem as points of correspondence between the two volumes is backed by this test; but not the specific number of references, seven.

Test 10: *Contiguity* – Plainly the references are not contiguous, so the likelihood of selectivity is not abated. No support is gained here.

Test 11: *Cumulative case* – In that this system of parallels is presented as a pattern, it has not performed exceptionally well. This is particularly due to the little variety in the types of parallel elements. If these references to Jerusalem were not proffered as a "pattern," it would be well established as a significant, but singular, parallel theme between the Gospel and Acts.

To summarize, the clear existence of precisely seven references to the

---

105 Talbert, *Literary Patterns*, 20.

journey to Jerusalem in each work is dubious despite its centrality to the pattern. Regrettably, this proposal stands or falls by the correspondence between the numbers of references, since only two elements of parallelism are offered for five of the seven parallels (journey and Jerusalem). Only the suggestion of pattern is threatened, however. Talbert has demonstrated the parallel importance of the theme to each work along with one or two interesting local instances, like parallel 13. Accordingly, the tests do not bolster the probability of an architectonic pattern in this instance.

2.2.3 Development of General Parallel 26

Talbert's expansion of parallel 26 is presented in the table below. The foundational observation is the presence of four trials for both Jesus and Paul. His concern is to demonstrate that certain details correspond in the appropriate sequence, and thereby bind more closely the stories of the two main characters.[106]

LUKE		ACTS
23:4, 14, 22 **Three times** Pilate **declares Jesus innocent**.	27.	23:9; 25:25; 26:31 **Three men**, Lysias, Festus, and Agrippa, **declare Paul innocent**.
23:6–12 **Pilate sends** Jesus to **Herod** for questioning.	28.	25:13–26:32 A **Herod** hears Paul with the **permission of Festus**.
23:16, 22 **Pilate [the one presiding]** says he will **release** (ἀπολύσω) Jesus.	29.	26:32 **Agrippa [the one presiding]** says: "This man could have been **set free**" (ἀπολελύσθαι).
23:18 The **Jews cry**: "Away with this man" (αἶρε τοῦτον).	30.	21:36 **Jews cry**: "Away with him" (αἶρε αὐτόν).
23:47 A **centurion** has a **favorable opinion** of Jesus.	31.	27:3, 43 A **centurion** has a **favorable relation** with Paul.

Test 1: *Restriction to passages* – Only *parallel 31* is not completely restricted to its location as defined by this pattern (see Lk. 7:1–10), but when only the trial portions of each book are considered, then all parallel

---

106 See Talbert, *Literary Patterns*, pp. 17–8 for the table and p. 22 for his analysis.

features are restricted to the passages in the pattern. The proposal therefore finds support.

Test 2: *Number of features* – Each parallel consists of two reasonable elements, which is few but acceptable. The probability of authorial intent is moderately enhanced.

Test 3: *Number of panels/passages* – Two panels constitute this structure, the minimum required by this test of course. Intent is supported marginally.

Test 4: *Attracts attention* – In *parallel 27*, the declaration of innocence is remarkable, but the triple occurrence might not be noticed by the reader. Otherwise, all the remaining elements catch one's attention, so the pattern is more probably a product of Lukan design.

Test 5: *Constructive complexity* – Although the Acts passage of *parallel 30* is out of sequence,[107] a minor issue for ancient patterned writing, the parallelism is constructive and consistent with conscious formation.

Test 6: *Redaction criticism* – Interestingly, *parallels 27* through *30* are Lukan,[108] as Talbert notes. There appear to be three possible reasons for Luke's insertion of the three declarations of Jesus' innocence (*parallel 27*): (1) one of his sources reflected the tradition[109] and he merely deemed it historical and useful; (2) whatever the source, he primarily desired to create an emphasis on the innocence of Jesus;[110] and (3) he wished to form the parallel observed by Talbert. Marshall concurs with the emphasis on innocence, but also correctly points out that Pilate's statement [in Lk. 23:14] "is designed to take the heat out of the situation".[111] Obviously, Talbert's reason is harmonious with the second one and also with Marshall's observation. However, would Luke shape the Gospel after the model of Acts?

Discussions regarding Luke 23:6–12 (*parallel 28*) revolve around its historicity.[112] Rarely, however, is there a comment as to what literary function Luke intended for the pericope, apart from the mere assumption that it is historical. It may be argued that he was striving to be comprehensive, but one would then have to explain the amount of Markan (and

---

107 Talbert notes this point, *Literary Patterns*, 30, n.4.
108 Talbert discusses his redactional observations regarding this pattern on p. 22 of *Literary Patterns*.
109 Nolland posits a source common with John, since the Fourth Gospel contains a triple declaration of innocence with similarity in wording; *Luke 18:35–24:53*, vol. 35c, Word Biblical Commentary (Dallas: Word Books, 1993) 1115.
110 This may be C.F. Evans' perspective; *Saint Luke*, 848.
111 Marshall, *Gospel of Luke*, 861 and 858 respectively.
112 For a convicing defence of the historicity of the event, see Marshall, *Gospel of Luke*, 854–855.

apparently Q) material omitted. Grundmann and Fitzmyer supply the cogent argument that Herod would constitute the second witness required in Deuteronomy 19:15.[113] This is perhaps the strongest suggestion available, but it is an argument from silence with no contextual indication that this concern was on Luke's mind. To Talbert's credit, the formation of this parallel offers another viable motive for its inclusion. Still, would Luke base the trial scenes of Jesus on Paul's?

Comments specifically on the presence of ἀπολύσω in Luke 23:16 and 22 (*parallel 29*) are rare apart from the thought that release is a natural consequence of the verdict of innocence. Liefeld sheds valuable light, however, when he astutely combines the facts that Pilate was a Roman official and that an apparent purpose of the Gospel was "to show that Christianity deserved to be favorably treated in Rome".[114] "Release" would accentuate the kind of treatment that was appropriate. Talbert's proposal does not conflict with other options and is not necessarily inferior. Indeed, perhaps the theme of appropriate treatment of Christians is even paralleled in Acts 26:32 of this parallel.

Regarding *parallel 30*, the verb in the phrase αἶρε τοῦτον is common in all the Gospels.[115] Nevertheless, it is rare in the mouth of a crowd of Jews. Scholars offer no argument for a purposeful inclusion of the phrase that is superior to Talbert's parallel.

His contention that Luke changed the centurion's statement from Mark's "Truly this man was the Son of God" to "Certainly this man was innocent" to establish the correspondence in *parallel 31* is weak. Mark's wording is no less "favorable" toward Jesus than Luke's.

As noted earlier, inherent in Talbert's proposal is the assumption that Luke amended the Gospel to correspond to Acts. He states, "The entire trial sequence in Luke is shaped…in order to parallel the trial sequence of Paul in Acts."[116] Undoubtedly, he would agree that the subsequent work was similarly edited, but there are no extant sources to reveal specific redaction. It is the extent of Gospel readjustment proposed that demands caution. If, however, Talbert were required to explain some of his parallels as created by alteration of Acts, he would have no solid evidence. He is compelled to find Gospel evidence. Consequently, when the data sound uncertain, caution must be exercised. In the instance of this pattern, most of the evidence is convincing, except for example parallel 31. His redaction evidence favors authorial intent behind this pattern.

---

113 Grundmann, *Evangelium nach Lukas*, 423–24; Fitzmyer, *Luke X–XXIV*, 1488.
114 Liefeld, *Luke*, 1041.
115 Fitzmyer makes this point against Tayler, who tries to draw a parallel with John; *Luke X-XXIV*, 1487. With Talbert, he also notes the parallel with Acts 21:36.
116 Talbert, *Literary Patterns*, 22.

Test 7: *Important themes* – The innocence of Jesus and Paul is important to Luke (*parallel 27*), as is "a Herod," mentioned 14 times in the Gospel (*parallel 28*). *Parallel 29* is related, again, to the innocence of the character. *Parallel 30* revolves around Jewish rejection, which is a recognized Lukan theme. Even *parallel 31* appears to reinforce the concept of Roman/Gentile acceptance of Christianity. This test supports the probability of intent.

Test 8: *Historical/genre expectation* – Since so many of the elements of this pattern are unparalleled in the other Gospels, there is clearly no genre predisposition. Historically, the events in Luke only make sense in their order of appearance, and this sequence makes more sense in Acts. Nevertheless, most of the parallel elements, though historical, are largely subject to Luke's personal choice and not the demand of an essential link in the chain of salvation history. Intent is more certain according to this test.

Test 9: *Common expression* – This group of parallel units, as defined by Talbert, does not likely exist anywhere else, even in the other canonical Gospels. The likelihood of coincidence due to common expression is diminished.

Test 10: *Contiguity* – If the parallels of the Gospel panel are allowed to each have a brief context, then there is contiguity, with only the crucifixion intervening (Lk. 23:26–43). Contrarily, there are substantial gaps between the parallels of the Acts panel (Acts 21:37–22:29; and 23:12–25:12). Consideration must be given that the corresponding trial portion of Acts is more protracted than the Gospel's, which would more likely result in gaps. When account is taken that the trials themselves are elements of correspondence (see general *parallel 26*, page 93), then Acts 23:12–25:12 is actually paralleled. Furthermore, we may excuse Paul's initial defense (Acts 21:37–22:29) as an obligatory introduction to his trials. Therefore, the problem of intervening material may justifiably be dismissed. The conclusion of this test accordingly provides sturdy backing for the probability of Lukan design.

Test 11: *Cumulative case* – Every test supports the probability that Luke intended this parallel pattern between the trials of Jesus and Paul. Consequently, it must be treated as highly probable.

This local pattern has performed better than Talbert's others to this point in terms of our certainty that it was a conscious development. The question remains, however, how likely it is that Luke would have restructured the Gospel to suit Acts; but the proportion of Lukan material employed in the Gospel panel is sufficient to allay our concern, since it permits that compositional freedom was exercised throughout this section. Interestingly, on the strength of this present pattern, more credence may be lent to certain earlier individual parallels between Jesus and Paul (parallels 20 through 25 above). Only certain instances of parallels 20–25 were substantiated under our tests, and the pattern proposed for these parallels was considered uncertain. Nevertheless, Talbert has demonstrated in the present structure Luke's keen interest in a detailed comparison between Jesus and Paul, so we should not be surprised to see it elsewhere.

2.3 Correspondence between Luke 9 and Acts 1

Charles Talbert incorporates into his study of Lukan structure three selected correspondences between Luke 9 and Acts 1 from several proposed by J.G. Davies.[117] He considers the remainder of these proposals invalid. The original intent of Davies' correspondences "was to show that for Luke the transfiguration is a prefigurement of the ascension".[118] Although trimmed to three, the same conclusion may be drawn if the parallels are deemed valid.

LUKE 9		ACTS 1
9:28–36 The transfiguration story involving (1) **Jesus and his disciples going up on a mountain** (9:28); (2) a reference to **dazzling white raiment** (9:29); (3) mention of **two men** (9:30, 32); (4) **these men speak of Jesus'** ἔξοδος (9:31); (5) a **cloud** overshadowed them (9:34–35).	1.	1:9–11 The ascension narrative involving (1) **Jesus and his disciples going up on a mountain** (1:12); (2) a reference to **white robes** (1:10); (3) mention of **two men** (1:10); (4) **these men speak of Jesus' going into heaven** (1:11); (5) a **cloud** took him out of their sight (1:9).
9:1–6 The transfiguration is found in the same context with, but **following, Jesus' commission** to the twelve to preach [the] Kingdom of God. **He gave the power and authority.**	2.	1:8 Jesus' ascension **is preceded by his commission** to the apostles to be witnesses. They will be such after **they receive power**.

---

117 J.G. Davies, "Prefigurement," 229–233.
118 Talbert, *Literary Patterns*, 61. See pages 61–62 for his presentation and discussion of these selected correspondences.

9:11–17 A **meal tradition** is preceded by reference to Jesus' speaking of the **Kingdom of God**.	3.	1:3–4 Reference is made to Jesus' speaking with the apostles of the **Kingdom of God**. This is followed by a reference to **his eating with them**.

Sequence is only a concern between parallels 1 and 2, so the set will not be held accountable as a pattern.

Test 1: *Restriction to passages* – The elements of correspondence in *parallel 1* are well restricted to these passages, especially when taken together. Only one other passage is close, the appearance of the angels to the women at the tomb (Lk. 24:1–8). In *parallel 2*, however, much material about Jesus follows the commission to the twelve in Luke 9:1–9. *Parallel 3* is weak because there is frequent reference to meals in Luke, and Jesus frequently spoke about the kingdom. A conjunction of these themes is not surprising.

Test 2: *Number of features* – *Parallel 1* is particularly strong in the number of parallel features evident. *Parallels 2* and *3* are less persuasive, having only two elements each. One wonders whether a comparison of Moses and Elijah with two angels is reasonable, but the description of each is similar.

Test 3: *Number of panels/passages* – Two panels is the minimum case for parallelism.

Test 4: *Attracts attention* – All the elements of correspondence attract the attention of the reader except for the sequence involving the commissions in *parallel 2*. Intent is supported.

Test 5: *Constructive complexity* – The elements of *parallel 1* are constructive in terms of correspondence. Those of *parallels 2* and *3* are less convincing due to the substantial gaps between passages to which they refer. As a set of parallels, there seems to be little cohesion. This test does not favor authorial intent.

Test 6: *Redaction criticism* – Regarding *parallel 1*, Talbert notes the change from Mark's ἀναφέρει (Mk. 9:2) to ἀνέβη in Luke 9:28. He considers this an intentional link to the ascension, and hence Acts 1.[119] A difficulty is that ἀναβαίνω is not used in either of the Lukan ascension accounts, and the verb is fairly common in Luke (9x). There is also a weighty alternative provided by Nolland. He believes that "Luke makes the account much more an experience in the life of Jesus than did the Marcan version" through this verbal change and the introduction of Jesus' intent to

---

119 Talbert, *Literary Patterns*, 61–62.

pray.[120] A further suggestion of Talbert's is that Luke himself calls Elijah and Moses "two men," just as the angels are called in Acts 1:10.[121] Marshall admits the possibility of the intentional parallel, but also maintains the possibility of special source material behind the wording of the account.[122] Finally, for parallel 1, Talbert notes Luke's addition that the two men spoke of Jesus' ἔξοδος. He reasonably believes the similarity of this word to εἴσοδος in Acts 13:24, used of Jesus' incarnation, suggests that ἔξοδος refers to the ascension. The imagery is indeed similar.

Luke adds δύναμιν in Luke 9:1 to Mark's ἐξουσία, as Talbert holds, to correspond to the δύναμιν in Acts 1:8 (*parallel 2*).[123] It is conceivable that the Evangelist composed the opening account in Acts, noticed that Jesus spoke only of power at the ascension, and strengthened his parallel by adding the word to the commission of the twelve. However, if Luke wrote Acts after the Gospel, would he not perhaps have published the Gospel before composing the introduction to the sequel? If so, an alteration to the Gospel would have been more complicated. A more likely scenario is that at Luke 9:1, the Evangelist is concerned about a correspondence with the ascension account in *Luke*, where only power is mentioned (Lk. 24:49), rather than with Acts. The parallel with Acts would then be secondary since Acts 1:8 reviews the promise of power in Luke 24:49. A further factor is Luke's apparent propensity to add the attribution of δύναμις to Jesus in healing accounts where ἐξουσία is already attributed to him in Mark.[124] In all such instances Luke adds δύναμις: Lk. 4:31–37 (4:36 par. Mk. 1:27); 5:17–26 (5:17 par. Mk. 2:2 – "authority" in 5:24 par. Mk. 2:10); and 9:1–6 (9:1 par. Mk. 6:7).[125] Therefore, it is very difficult to claim its addition for the sake of *structural* parallel. Talbert's contention in further support of parallel 2, that Mark 6:45–8:26 was omitted "to locate the transfiguration and the commission to the Twelve in the same context,"[126] is somewhat weakened by the distance between these two accounts (19 verses, 2

---

120 Nolland, *Luke 9:21–18:34*, 497–498.
121 Talbert, *Literary Patterns*, 62.
122 Marshall, *Gospel of Luke*, 343–344.
123 Talbert, *Literary Patterns*, 62.
124 Schürmann seems only to suggest that Luke added "power" because the disciples would need it to perform healings (*Lukasevangelium: Erster Teil*, 500).
125 In the healing of the centurion's servant (Lk. 7:1–10), authority is only indirectly attributed to Jesus through the centurion's admission that he is under authority. Here, Luke does not add "power." Another instance where Luke *may* have contributed δύναμις in a healing context however is in the return of the seventy, an account peculiar to Luke (Lk. 10:17–20). Of course, such addition is pure speculation in this case.
126 Talbert, *Literary Patterns*, 62 and 65 n.31.

accounts).

Luke adds the topic of Jesus' sermon, the kingdom of God, to the introduction to the Feeding of the Five Thousand (Lk. 9:11 par. Mk. 6:34). Talbert believes this intentionally strengthens *parallel 3*.[127] This is possible, but Luke clearly recognizes the topic as central to Jesus' ministry, and even adds it to the first purpose statement, "I must preach the kingdom of God to the other cities also, for I was sent for this purpose" (Lk. 4:43 par. Mk. 1:38). The addition to the Feeding of the Five Thousand may simply reflect this recognition. Schürmann also notes that the addition of "the kingdom of God" shows that the subject of both the disciples' and Jesus' preaching was the same (compare 9:11 and 9:2).[128]

Redaction criticism does not provide persuasive evidence for the intentional construction of this set of correspondences. The data offered could be interpreted as Talbert suggests, but there are often preferable options.

Test 7: *Important themes* – In *parallel 1*, clothing is not directly related to an important Lukan theme, except perhaps if their whiteness suggest divine presence or revelation. The number of people seems insignificant. Certainly, the mountain scene and cloud are more directly linked to divine revelation or presence, and the departure of Jesus is a major theme. *Parallel 2* depends on a sequence that is not significant, but commission and power are obviously important Lukan themes. Both themes in *parallel 3* are generally recognized as of substantial interest to Luke. Test 7 lends moderately strong approval to this correspondence set.

Test 8: *Historical/genre expectation* – *Parallel 1* contains stock (genre) symbols that obscure our certainty of intentional parallelism: mountain scene, dazzling clothes, cloud and possibly the presence of two characters sent by God. There was likely some historical pressure on Luke to include these parallel features, assuming the events happened as described.[129] Any parallelism would then be God's doing. Nevertheless, Luke exercises the author's right of selection, and this must not be discounted. Apart from the role of selection, the actual historical events probably create the features of *parallel 2*. Regarding *parallel 3*, there are no historical or genre expectations for the features. In summary, this test does not make authorial intent for the set more certain.

Test 9: *Common expression* – The elements of *parallels 1* and *2* are all present in Matthew and Mark, except for the additions by Luke discussed above under test 6. This by no means qualifies the grouping of features as a common expression, so coincidence is not a consideration.

---

127 Talbert, *Literary Patterns*, 62.
128 Schürmann, *Lukasevangelium: Erster Teil*, 513.
129 Both Matthew and Mark record the presence of one angel rather than two.

Test 10: *Contiguity* – Contiguity is a major problem for this set of correspondences. The likelihood for the selection of unintentionally similar material is consequently greater.

Test 11: *Cumulative case* – This set of correspondences fares poorly under the tests for intentionality. Thus, no further support is gained from this test.

Little confidence may be placed in the parallelism between Luke 9 and Acts 1. Notwithstanding, the performance of parallel 1 suggests it may stand on its own merits.

2.4 Correspondences between Luke 24 and Acts 1

The following five correspondences have been widely recognized.[130] With one exception, they conform to a sequence, so the set will be treated as a pattern.

LUKE 24		ACTS 1
24:33–34, 36 **The risen Christ appears to Simon and then to the eleven apostles.**	1.	1:3 **The risen Christ appeared to the apostles whom he had chosen.**
24:36–43 Jesus, now risen, **proves that it is he** who has appeared to the eleven by offering to be handled and by eating before them.	2.	1:3 "To them he presented himself alive after his passion by **many proofs**...."
24:49 "And behold, I send the **promise of my Father** upon you; but **stay in the city**, until you are clothed with power from on high."	3.	1:4 "And while staying with them he charged them **not to depart from Jerusalem**, but to wait for the **promise of the Father**...."

---

130 For Talbert's discussion of this set of correspondences see *Literary Patterns*, 58–61.

24:47–48 "…and that repentance and forgiveness of sins should be preached in his name **to all nations**, beginning from **Jerusalem**. **You are witnesses** of these things."	4.	1:8b "…and **you shall be my witnesses** in **Jerusalem** and in all Judea and Samaria and **to the end of the earth.**"
24:51–52 "…**he parted from them**. And **they** returned **to Jerusalem**.…"	5.	1:9, 12 "…as they were looking on, **he was lifted up**, and a cloud took him out of their sight. Then **they returned to Jerusalem**.…"

Test 1: *Restriction to passages* – The restriction of the elements of correspondence to their respective passages is very tight, especially since the context involves the direct reference in Acts back to the same event in the Gospel. This is a strong result.

Test 2: *Number of features* – Each passage fits the description given, and each parallel has at least two elements of correspondence, except numbers 1 and 2. Moderate support is gained from this test.

Test 3: *Number of panels/passages* – Two panels is the minimum case for correspondence, of course.

Test 4: *Attracts attention* – Every element of correspondence attracts the reader's attention, so our confidence in authorial intent is well bolstered.

Test 5: *Constructive complexity* – The sequence and grouping of features is complex and reasonably maintained, which diminishes the possibility of coincidental correspondence. This test favors intent.

Test 6: *Redaction criticism* – Talbert's redaction-critical defense of this set is naturally speculative because essentially all of the Gospel material is peculiar to Luke, and source theory in Acts is often educated guesswork.[131] He correctly considers the Acts half of parallels 1 through 3 (1:3–4) to be of Lukan composition.[132] Furthermore, he believes the Gospel half to be virtually all of Lukan composition. Consequently, he attributes every parallel to the Lukan hand.[133] Marshall convincingly argues that such certainty is impossible and that the content and wording are probably

---

131 See Bruce, *Acts of the Apostles*, 40; and William Neil, *The Acts of the Apostles*, The New Century Bible Commentary (London: Marshall, Morgan & Scott, 1973) 22–25.

132 See also Richard N. Longenecker, *The Acts of the Apostles*, Expositor's Bible Commentary 9 (Grand Rapids: Zondervan, 1981) 233, 252.

133 Talbert, *Literary Patterns*, 60.

derived essentially from Luke's source.[134] The verdict of this test must remain open. In other words, no support is rendered.

Test 7: *Important themes* – All of the elements of correspondence are related to important Lukan themes, especially in light of Acts. The probability of authorial intent is enhanced.

Test 8: *Historical/genre expectation* – No genre expectation is involved, but there certainly could be an historical basis since each panel records the same events. This test does not increase our confidence in the correspondence set, but Luke's right to filter and select material he relates tempers the judgment.

Test 9: *Common expression* – The sequence and grouping of features in this set is not found in the other Gospels or in other relevant literature. The likelihood of coincidence due to common expression is therefore diminished.

Test 10: *Contiguity* – Contiguity is reasonable, with only minor gaps evident. The likelihood of selectivity on Talbert's part is therefore lessened.

Test 11: *Cumulative case* – This set of correspondences achieves a strong result under the above tests. Accordingly, the cumulative case is strong.

The tests for intentionality strongly affirm that Luke intentionally bound his two volumes together using Luke 24 and Acts 1. Theological and exegetical proposals founded on this literary connection are on solid ground.

2.5 Correspondences between Luke 1:57–80 and Luke 2:1–52[135]

Correspondences occur within the gospel of Luke itself, as observed earlier in our coverage of Robert Tannehill's work. Talbert identifies numerous sets of structured parallels within the Gospel, one of them a brief pattern within Luke 1:57–2:52 where the parallelism between John the Baptist and Jesus, begun earlier, is continued.[136]

---

134 Marshall, *Gospel of Luke*, 890–92, 901, 907–908.
135 Correspondences discussed by Talbert within Lk. 1:1–38 are quite similar to those proposed by Tannehill, which are fully evaluated through our eleven tests in the chapter "Lucan Correspondences From the Literary Perspective of Robert C. Tannehill." Therefore the analysis will not be repeated here.
136 Talbert's presentation and discussion of this pattern is found in *Literary Patterns*, 44–45.

JOHN		JESUS
1:57 Now the time came for Elizabeth **to be delivered** and she **gave birth** to a **son**.	**1.**	2:1–7 The time came for Mary **to be delivered** and she **gave birth** to her first-born **son**.
1:58 And her kinsfolk and neighbors **rejoiced** when they heard what the **Lord had done**.	**2.**	2:8–[16] The shepherds **rejoiced**, glorifying and **praising God** for all they had seen and heard.
1:65–66 These verses give a **description of the reaction (fear)** to the events, a **mention of the news** and of the **laying it up in the hearts of those who heard**.	**3.**	2:17–18 These verses give a **description of the reaction (wonder)** to the event, a **mention of the spreading of the news**, and of **Mary's keeping all this in her heart**.
1:59–64 The child is **circumcised** on the eighth day and **named John as the angel had directed**.	**4.**	2:21 The child is **circumcised** at the end of the eight days and **named Jesus as the angel had directed**.
1:67–79 A **prophetic hymn of God's act** and John's **function**.	**5.**	2:22–38 A **prophetic hymn of God's act** and Jesus' **function**.
1:80a The **child grew** and **became strong** in spirit.	**6.**	2:39–40 The **child grew** and **became strong**.
1:80b He was in the wilderness **until**....	**7.**	2:41–52 He went down to Nazareth **until**....

Test 1: *Restriction to passages* – Each element of correspondence is completely restricted to its corresponding passage. The test favors intent.

Test 2: *Number of features* – Most of the correspondences have two or three parallel features. Only moderate approval is gained.

Test 3: *Number of panels/passages* – Two panels is the minimum required for parallelism.

Test 4: *Attracts attention* – Although few of the elements attract much attention, all are of reasonable interest value.

Test 5: *Constructive complexity* – The breaks in sequence for this pattern are relatively minor, so mild support is attained.

Test 6: *Redaction criticism* – Talbert correctly notes the complexity of source determination for this section. He concludes that "most scholars would take a position on the sources of Luke 1–2 which would lead to the conclusion that the parallels are the result of Lucan design".[137] This is true if the parallelism is considered valid. Occasion for the construction of parallelism is reasonably presumed, but the evidence is not compelling.

Test 7: *Important themes* – Each of the parallel elements is directly related to Lukan themes that are demonstrably important throughout the Gospel. Intent is made more probable.

Test 8: *Historical/genre expectation* – No historical expectation or constraint of genre lies behind the inclusion of these elements. Details such as praise, treasuring in one's heart, and prophetic hymns are not historical events that demand inclusion by their very nature. The probability of authorial intent is enhanced.

Test 9: *Common expression* – This sequence of features is not found in the other canonical Gospels. Intent is favored.

Test 10: *Contiguity* – Only very small gaps are evident, so accidental selectivity on the part of Talbert is made substantially more difficult.

Test 11: *Cumulative case* – Authorial intent is approved to varying degrees by nearly all of the tests, but few results are strong. Test 11 affords only moderate support.

Overall, the tests suggest that Talbert's proposed parallelism be accepted with reasonable confidence as intended by Luke. In conjunction with the other correspondences between John and Jesus in Luke 1–3, more confidence may be placed in this set. Perhaps Talbert has closely approximated what Luke actually constructed. His observation deserves very serious consideration.

2.6 Correspondences between Luke 3:1–20 and Luke 3:21–4:15

Talbert identifies further correspondences between John and Jesus in Lk. 3:1–4:15.[138] They are as follows:[139]

JOHN		JESUS
3:1–6 John's **person**. He is the prophet of the eschaton.	**1.**	3:21–38 Jesus' **person**. He is the Son of God.

---

137 Talbert, *Literary Patterns*, 45.
138 Marshall notes this continuation of parallelism in *Gospel of Luke*, 148–149.
139 For Talbert's presentation and discussion of this pattern, see *Literary Patterns*, 45–48.

3:7–17 John's **mission**. It is **eschatological**, ethical, and anticipatory.	**2.**	4:1–13 Jesus' **mission**. It is the **eschatological** recapitulation of Adam's decisions.
3:18–20 **Summary**. The end of John's mission.	**3.**	4:14–15 **Summary**. The beginning of Jesus' ministry.

Test 1: *Restriction to passages* – Within Luke 3:1–4:15 the elements of correspondence are well restricted to their passages with the possible exception of "Jesus' person". This theme clearly continues into the temptation narrative (4:1–13). Talbert cites Feuillet's conclusion however that the temptations of Jesus loosely correspond to those of Adam.[140] Jesus' successful resistance, in contrast to Adam's failure, suggests that "the temptation narrative then functions for Luke as a means of saying that Jesus in his career reversed the decisions of Adam".[141] Thus, there may be some justification for the label "Jesus' mission" for the temptation account. Moderate support is achieved.

Test 2: *Number of features* – There are few features that establish each parallel since the categories are so broad (person, mission, summary). Regarding fit, there are several problems. First, 3:21–38 is not one pericope but two, yet it is parallel to a single one (3:1–6), a minor issue. Second, the word "eschatological" is applied in two different senses, and is dubious as a label for 4:1–13. Third, Talbert's considering the temptation a description of Jesus' mission is heavily dependent on his interpretation rather than on a straightforward reading of the text. Fourth, the summary for Jesus does not conclude a section, as with John's summary, it begins a new one. The probability of intent is certainly not improved here. Only a broad parallelism between 3:1–20 and 3:21–4:15 appears possible.

Test 3: *Number of panels/passages* – Two panels provides the minimum case.

Test 4: *Attracts attention* – The elements of correspondence are at the heart of these main characters and attract attention by weight of their subject matter. Authorial intent is favored.

Test 5: *Constructive complexity* – Three pairs of parallel passages somewhat limits the possibility of coincidental correspondence.

Test 6: *Redaction criticism* – Talbert simply notes that virtually all of the material in *parallel 1* is peculiar to Luke and that the genealogy is not in the birth narrative, as it is in Matthew. Rather it is in this different location

---

140 Talbert cites A. Feuillet's "Le récit Lucanien de la Tentation [Lc. 4:1–13]," *Bib* 40 (1959) 617–31, in *Literary Patterns*, 47.
141 Talbert, *Literary Patterns*, 47.

where it contributes to the theme of Jesus' identity. He has mainly demonstrated Luke's opportunity to construct parallelism and not its probability. No redaction critical evidence is offered specifically in support of *parallel 2*. Talbert admits for *parallel 3* that the relocation of John the Baptist's imprisonment from late in Mark's Gospel[142] may be motivated by a "desire to separate the Baptist section from the Jesus section".[143] Still he prefers the motivation of parallelism. In light of the earlier parallelism, this is reasonable.

Insufficient evidence is available for significant support from test 6. However, this does not speak against its validity.

Test 7: *Important themes* – Identity/person and mission of John and Jesus are substantial themes in Luke. "Summary" is not a theme, but it is certainly a common literary technique of Luke's. The probability of intent is enhanced.

Test 8: *Historical/genre expectation* – Could there be a genre expectation for the sequence of elements employed? Old Testament prophetic books[144] generally begin with the calling of the prophet, as with John in Luke 3:1–2, and that is probably Luke's point. Naturally, the mission of the prophet is developed throughout the course of the narrative. Surprisingly, of the OT prophetic books, only Jeremiah provides closure to the ministry of the prophet, as we find with John the Baptist. In accounts of prophets within broader OT narratives, rarely if ever are both a full introductory formula like "the word of the Lord came to ____ son of ____" and a decisive closure of the prophet's ministry found for any one prophet. Closure in John's case though is forced by the imprisonment. Closure in the instance of Elijah is also forced, namely by his remarkable departure from earth. In terms of genre therefore there appears to be insufficient consistent use of "person," "mission" and "summary" to exert a strong influence on Luke. Certainly, there is nothing unnatural about Luke's format for this brief account. More surprising is the summary at the beginning of Jesus' ministry (Lk. 4:14–15) that corresponds to the closure summary for John. In conclusion, although the format used by Luke is not surprising, there is no reason to believe he was influenced by a standard genre. History may have

---

142 Regardless of whether Luke has rewritten Mk. 6:17–18 here or not, the content is essentially the same and Luke has omitted it from the corresponding location later in his gospel.

143 He cites Hans Conzelmann in support; *The Theology of St. Luke*, Geoffrey Buswell (tr.), (London: Faber and Faber, 1961) 18–22. Marshall comes to a similar conclusion, but for very different reasons; *Gospel of Luke*, 148–149.

144 Old Testament accounts of prophets would be the most likely possible generic background to Luke's presentation of John since his introduction of the Baptist clearly imitates that of prophets in the Old Testament.

defined the structure of the Baptist's description, but this is not the case for the account of Jesus since the summary was unnecessary. Authorial intent behind this set of correspondences is more certain through this test, yet only marginally so because of the small number of parallels involved.

Test 9: *Common expression* – As implied under test 8, the sequence of "person," "mission" and "summary" is a natural way to recount a story. Most ancient biographies could be demarcated similarly. Coincidence due to common expression is therefore possible. Conversely, only a small fraction of Jesus' ministry has been placed in parallel to the bulk of John's. This treatment of Jesus' story is not common to other relevant literature. Test 9 proves uncertain.

Test 10: *Contiguity* – This pattern is precisely contiguous, so Talbert is less able to have been unintentionally selective.

Test 11: *Cumulative case* – Collectively, the above tests allow for some confidence in the parallelism as described by Talbert, but support is not overwhelming. This test suggests moderate support for intent.

As stated above, only a broad parallelism between Luke 3:1–20 and 3:21–4:15 appears possible since the pericopes do not appear necessarily to fit Talbert's descriptions. Furthermore, how Luke portrays John and Jesus in this section may just be a natural way to tell the stories. However, in conjunction with the detailed parallelism between the two characters in Luke 1–2 the case for intentional parallelism here is made stronger. Clearly, if the parallelism was intended, Luke did not desire here the same level of detail that he developed in chapters 1–2.

2.7 Correspondences between Luke 4:16–7:17 and Luke 7:18–8:56

Talbert explains that these two parallel panels begin and end similarly.[145] He does not include the beginnings and conclusions in his table, but they are worthy of placement there for our analysis. The numbered sequence of correspondences below is described as a, b, c, d, e, f: f, e, b, a, c, d.[146] Consequently, this set will be treated as unstructured, yet clearly defined in scope (4:16–8:56).

---

145 Talbert's table for this set is located on p. 40 and his defense occupies pp. 39–43 of *Literary Patterns*.
146 Talbert, *Literary Patterns*, 50, n.34.

LUKE 4:16–7:17		LUKE 7:18–8:56
[4:16–30 **Jesus' healings and preachings are regarded as fulfillments of Isaianic prophecies**. There is mention of **people taking offense** at Jesus. **God's concern for all men** is expressed.]		[7:18–30 **Jesus' healings and preachings are regarded as fulfillments of Isaianic prophecies**. There is mention of **people taking offense** at Jesus. **God's concern for all men** is expressed.]
4:31–41 **Jesus is in conflict with demons**. One cries: "**What have you to do with us, Jesus** of Nazareth? Have you come **to destroy us**? I know who you are, the **Holy One of God**."	1.	8:26–39 **Jesus is in conflict with demons**. They say: "**What have you to do with us, Jesus**, Son of the most high God? I beseech you not **to torment me**."
5:1–11 **Jesus is in a boat with** Simon. A **nature miracle** takes place.	2.	8:22–25 **Jesus is in a boat with** his disciples. A **nature miracle** takes place.
5:17–26 While Jesus is **in the company of some Pharisees** there arises the **question of Jesus' forgiving sins**. Jesus tells the man: "Man, **your sins are forgiven** you."	3.	7:36–50 While Jesus eats **with a Pharisee** the **question of forgiveness of sins** arises. Jesus tells the woman: "**Your sins are forgiven**."
5:27–6:5 Jesus and his **disciples are shown eating and drinking** in contrast to **John's disciples who fast often**.	4.	7:31–35 **John came neither eating nor drinking**. The **Son of man came eating and drinking**.
6:12–16 The **Twelve** are chosen. This **immediately precedes Jesus' teaching within the hearing of the crowds**.	5.	8:1–3 Jesus is with the **Twelve**. This **immediately precedes Jesus' teaching the crowds**.

6:17–49 Jesus **teaches the multitudes**. The **conclusion concerns "hearing"** Jesus' teaching and **"doing"** it.	6.	8:4–8, 16–21 Jesus **teaches the multitudes**. The **conclusion concerns "hearing"** Jesus' teaching and **"doing"** it.
[7:1–17 **Healing story** with **emphasis on faith** followed by a **resurrection story** (widow's **son**).]		[8:43–56 **Healing story** with **emphasis on faith** followed by a **resurrection story** (Jairus' **daughter**).]

Test 1: *Restriction to passages* – Within Luke 4:16–8:56, apparent allusions to Isaiah in reference to the ministry of Jesus are Luke 4:18–19; 5:21; 7:22 and 8:10 (cf. Is. 61:1–2; 43:25; 61:1 and 6:9–10 respectively). Only the instances of Luke 4:18–19 and 7:22 encompass both the healing and teaching aspects of his ministry. People taking offense at Jesus is found at Lk. 5:21, 30; 6:2, 11; 7:30, and 39; quite common. God's concern for all people is discernible throughout the section. Due to the first element, the *opening passages* are well restricted. *Parallels 1* and *2* are completely restricted. Regarding *parallel 3*, Jesus is in the presence of Pharisees in Luke 5:17–26; 29–39; 6:1–11 and 7:36–50; but the question of forgiving sins, the corresponding declaration, and for that matter the word ἁμαρτία, only occur in the locations specified in this pattern. Therefore, this parallel is absolutely restricted, as is *parallel 4*. The Twelve are specifically mentioned only in the respective locations in *parallel 5*, but Jesus is depicted teaching crowds in Luke 5:1–3, 19(?); 6:17–49; 7:24–35 and 8:4–8 (20–21). Restriction is granted on the grounds of the first element, the Twelve. Of these occasions of teaching the crowd, only 6:17–49 and 8:4–8, 16–21 end with the hearing and doing formula,[147] so *parallel 6* is restricted. Although healing accounts with an emphasis on faith occur at Lk. 5:17–26; 7:1–10, 36–50; 8:43–48 and perhaps 8:49–56, the *closing passages* of each panel are well restricted primarily on the basis of the resurrection stories and the ages of those raised (both children).[148] Overall, the restriction factor of this set is very high.

Test 2: *Number of features* – Generally, not many features establish these parallels. Four of the eight boast only two, with just the closing passages reaching four elements. Support is gained from this test, but it is not overwhelming.

Test 3: *Number of panels/passages* – Two panels presents a minimum case. Intent is only cautiously supported by this test.

---

147 Hearing and doing formulae are located at 6:47; 8:21 and 11:28.
148 These are the only two resurrection stories in the Gospel.

Test 4: *Attracts attention* – Most of the elements in this set are striking. The eating and drinking features of *parallel 4* are mainly memorable because of their pointed contexts. In terms of sequence, reference to the twelve prior to Jesus teaching the crowd would probably go unnoticed (*parallel 5*). Likewise, the aspect of sequence in the *closing passages* is unlikely to be noted. Accordingly, this set of correspondences receives a moderate score from the test.

Test 5: *Constructive complexity* – Two panels of eight paired passages is inherently constructive. Only if there were a strict pattern would this set have received greater support from this test.

Test 6: *Redaction criticism* – Briefly, Talbert notes that six pericopes are omitted by Luke in the Markan parallel to this section: Mk. 1:16–20; 3:20–22; 4:26–29, 30–32, 33–34. He writes, "Not one of these six omissions from Luke 4:16–8:56 would have a place in the correspondences of this section. Their omission from the context is most likely explained as in the interest of the correspondences."[149] Yet, he concludes that "Mark 3:20–22 is probably the source for Luke 11:14–16" and "Mark 4:30–32 is probably the source for Luke 13:18–19".[150] This provides competing justification for their absence in this Lukan section, namely that Luke had reason to place them elsewhere. Certainly, however, the content of these Markan passages would have disturbed the contiguity of the correspondences.

About the parallelism between the two *opening passages*, Talbert proposes that "Regardless of how one settles the source question for Luke 4:16–30 [whether it is a rewriting of Mk. 6:1–6 or an L tradition], ...that it corresponds to 7:18–30 is clearly due to the intent of the Evangelist".[151] He bases this conclusion on the fact that, either way, the (re)location of 4:16–30 was a Lukan choice. Additionally, he believes that 7:18–30 comes from Q and that the universalistic thrust is added by Luke (7:29) to parallel Luke 4:16–30.[152] Concerning the relocation of the Nazareth scene, its programmatic flavor in this location is universally accepted as the Lukan motive for its transposition. Clearly, the formation of a minor parallel in a set where a pattern is not maintained is an inferior explanation. In addition, it is not certain that Luke 7:29 was absent from Q, since Matthew may have omitted it.[153] Nevertheless, it is present in Luke and is a suitable parallel. Marshall indicates the preparatory and explanatory nature of Luke 7:29–30 for verses

---

149 Talbert, *Literary Patterns*, 40.
150 Talbert, *Literary Patterns*, 40.
151 Talbert, *Literary Patterns*, 41.
152 Talbert, *Literary Patterns*, 41. Joachim Jeremias considers the reference to "all the people," a term with universalistic thrust, to be redactional; *Sprache*, 165.
153 Marshall, *Gospel of Luke*, 297. Bock well reflects the complexity of source determination here, *Luke 1:1–9:50*, 659

31–35,[154] which in itself is superior justification for its presence than Talbert's suggestion. Indeed, we may not simply deny Talbert's argument on these grounds, knowing Luke's literary skill, but its certainty is diminished.

Five redactional observations are offered in defense of *parallel 1*, all within Luke 4:31–41 since Luke 8:26–39 is considered by Talbert already to have contained the features Luke desired.[155]

> (1) In 4:33 Luke adds to Mark 1:23's, ἐν πνεύματι ἀκαθάρτῳ the term δαιμονίου so that vs. 33 reads "the spirit of an unclean demon," doubtless to correspond to 8:27. (2) In 4:33 Luke adds φωνῇ μεγάλῃ to parallel 8:28. (3) In 4:39 Jesus rebukes the fever in words reminiscent of the rebuking of the demon in 4:35. Mark 1:31 merely has Jesus take the woman by the hand and raise her up. Luke, therefore, seems to regard the fever as a demon and its cure as an exorcism. (4) In 4:41a Luke adds to Mark the confession of the exorcised demons: "You are the Son of God". This parallels 8:28. (5) in 4:41b the Third Evangelist adds the significant word used in the two preceding pericopes, ἐπιτιμῶν (cf. vv. 35, 39). This makes the section a unity. It is a unity created by Luke to parallel 8:26–39.[156]

Regarding the first observation, Nolland cogently suggests that Luke is "establishing here his basic vocabulary for demon possession.... We should read, therefore, 'a spirit, that is, an unclean demon.'"[157] Indeed, this is the first time we encounter the concept in the Gospel, so it is appropriate for the author to provide clarification for "Greek readers for whom πνεῦμα did not have the sense of 'evil' spirit which it could have in Judaism".[158] In the single other Markan context incorporated by Luke where Mark uses πνεῦμα of a demon without the word δαιμόνιον or a related term (Mk. 9:14–29 par. Lk. 9:37–43), he adds δαιμόνιον. This suggests he was concerned about clarification. Yet in material peculiar to Luke, he sometimes does not add δαιμόνιον (Lk. 7:21; 10:20 and 13:11). In balance, both explanations are reasonable, yet not compatible.

Commentators tend to agree with Talbert's second observation that Luke 4:33 is influenced by 8:28. They note, however, that the phrase φωνῇ με-

---

154 Marshall, *Gospel of Luke*, 298–299.
155 Talbert, *Literary Patterns*, 41.
156 Talbert, *Literary Patterns*, 41.
157 Nolland, *Luke 1–9:20*, 206.
158 Marshall, *Gospel of Luke*, 192. So also Schürmann, *Lukasevangelium: Erster Teil*, 247.

γάλη is already present in the Markan context (Mk. 1:26);[159] so it is not strictly an addition. The change of position in the account may be "to associate it with the actual words of the man".[160] Nevertheless, this explanation is compatible with Luke conforming it to Lk. 8:26–37.[161]

The third observation is hardly certain. If Luke considered the fever demonic and was interested in a parallel with the Gerasene demoniac, why would he not confirm its demonic origin?[162] Still, the similarity of the rebukes (ἐπιτιμάω) sufficiently binds this account to the one preceding (and following). We might add to Talbert's argument that the motif of confrontation with demons is sufficiently established through contextual association since it is sandwiched between two such descriptions (Lk. 4:33–37 and 40–41). Talbert's argument, in this modified form, it is not implausible. Alternative suggestions do not conflict, nor do they provide more likely motives.

Luke's addition of the demon's recognition of Jesus as the Son of God, the fourth redactional observation, is a compelling case for the parallel. Competing proposals, such as an amplification of Mark's "because they knew him" (Mk. 1:34)[163] and a borrowing from Mark 3:11–12 ("Son of God" and, interestingly, ἐπιτιμάω),[164] do not provide more plausible motive than Talbert's.

There is general agreement that Talbert's fifth observation is correct, that the addition of ἐπιτιμάω unifies the section. Based on all five observations, then, redaction supports the view that Luke intentionally formed this parallel.

Parallel 2 involves the source question of Luke 5:1–11. Talbert wisely concludes that it is L tradition. He then asks whether the Evangelist selected the story because it was a natural parallel to Luke 8:22–25. If 5:1–11 is considered a transposition of Mark 1:16–20, the parallel elements would need to have been added. Mark 4:35–41 (the synoptic parallel to Lk. 8:22–25) however contains the required elements without modification.[165] Evans provides the most clear alternative explanation for Luke's choice of 5:1–11.

---

159 See for example Schürmann, *Lukasevangelium: Erster Teil*, 247.
160 Marshall, *Gospel of Luke*, 193.
161 See E. Lohmeyer's brief but useful discussion of typical portrayal of demon possession in *Das Evangelium des Markus*, KEK (Göttingen: Vandenhoeck & Ruprecht, 1953) 36.
162 Marshall rightly concludes that "nothing more than the personification of the malady may be present;" *Gospel of Luke*, 195.
163 Fitzmyer, *Luke I-IX*, 554.
164 Nolland, *Luke 1–9:20*, 214. See also Léopold Sabourin, *L'Évangile de Luc: Introduction et Commentaire* (Rome: Gregorian University, 1985) 141–142.
165 See Talbert's discussion, *Literary Patterns*, 41–42.

A bit harsh on Mark, he considers Mark 1:16-20 "so terse, abrupt and without explanatory background as to be barely intelligible".[166] Furthermore, in light of Peter's importance to Luke, the Third Gospel could hardly have employed a calling "where Peter appears only as one person in two pairs of brothers. As Paul is to be given a special call (A. 9[1ff.]), so must Peter be (cf. Matt. 16[17f.]; John 1[40-42])".[167] Actually, James and John were with Peter, but Peter is clearly singled out. This is certainly a rival to Talbert's theory and therefore challenges it.

Luke adds the presence of the Pharisees (Lk. 5:17) to Mark 2:1-12 to form *parallel 3*, Talbert suggests.[168] No substantial alternative reason for this emendation appears to be available.[169] This parallel offers a clear purpose.

Parallel 4 is formed through four modifications to the Markan material, according to Talbert.[170] First, in 5:29 Luke adds ἐποίησεν δοχὴν μεγάλην Λευὶς αὐτῷ to highlight the idea of eating and drinking and thereby strengthen the correspondence. Fitzmyer sees this reference to "feast" rather as a "concrete expression of Levi's 'following.'"[171] Either explanation is possible. Second, καὶ πίνετε is added to ἐσθίετε of Mark 2:16. The resulting phrase (Lk. 5:30) matches that of Lk. 7:34. Either this was to foster the parallel, or it is merely the use of a "standard pair" of verbs, perhaps derived from the OT.[172] Although drinking is paired with eating in twelve of the thirty-two instances of the verb "to eat," Luke apparently adds the act of drinking only in Luke 5:27-39. Third, Talbert's redactional observation, drawn on the same passage, is that eating and drinking (Lk. 5:33) replaces the Markan reference to fasting (Mk. 2:18), which certainly tightens the parallel. Talbert's proposal is therefore quite reasonable for Luke 5:27-39. Fourth, in Luke 6:1b Luke adds the disciples' eating of grain to the Markan version (Mk. 2:23b). This may be to form of a strong tie with David's eating of the consecrated bread in Luke 6:4. Jesus' defense of the disciples' action is then made more explicitly relevant. This is a stronger purpose for the redaction than Talbert's suggestion of introducing the act of

---

166 C.F. Evans, *Saint Luke*, 287.
167 C.F. Evans, *Saint Luke*, 287.
168 Talbert, *Literary Patterns*, 42.
169 Marshall (*Gospel of Luke*, 212) considers the addition justifiable, "since most of the lawyers were members of the Pharisaic party."
170 For his discussion, see Talbert, *Literary Patterns*, 42.
171 Fitzmyer, *Luke I-IX*, 591.
172 Nolland calls the phrase a "standard pair" (*Luke 1-9:20*, 246) and cites other Lukan instances (5:33; 7:33, 34; 10:7; 12:19, etc.). Schürmann offers a similar list but adds Matthean parallels (*Lukasevangelium: Erster Teil*, 290 n.22). Fitzmyer considers it inspired by the OT (*Luke I-IX*, 591).

eating, since eating is already a dominant theme in Luke 5:27–6:5.

The strength of Talbert's redactional observations is mixed for Luke 5:27–6:5, but the case for 5:27–39 is compelling in light of the second and third observations. Probability therefore moderately favors the intentional formation of this parallel.

Parallels 5 and *6* are covered jointly by Talbert since the sequence of themes that spans them is the same: the Twelve, teaching of a crowd, and "hearing" and "doing".[173] Luke's relocation of the selection of the twelve apostles to precede the Sermon on the Plain (Lk. 6:12–16, 17–49) rather than the Beelzebul controversy (Mk. 3:13–19, 20–30) is to create the first part of the sequence, according to Talbert. Fitzmyer finds no clear reason for this relocation.[174] Nolland however considers it structurally linked to the two preceding calling accounts (Lk. 5:1–11, 27–32) and therefore not an introduction to the sermon.[175] Schürmann, closely links the selection of the apostles with the sermon by citing the mountain experiences of Moses in the book of exodus and by noting that the apostolic selection pericope sets a tone of revelation for the sermon.[176] Bock, observing connections with both contexts, considers 6:12–16 a "bridge".[177] Yet in a highly patterned book, a passage can serve two structural functions. Nolland's scheme is more convincing due to the relatedness of the material (callings) while Talbert's lacks concern with how the passages about the twelve relate to what follows.

The corresponding passage on the twelve apostles is created by the free Lukan composition of 8:1–3. One can hardly perceive this piece of narration to have been included purely for the sake of reference to the twelve however, as Talbert implies.[178] Greater attention is paid to Jesus' travel and to the women who accompanied him.[179]

Talbert further suggests for parallels 5 and 6 that Luke 6:17–19 is a rewriting of Mark 3:7–12, which makes it explicit that Jesus was speaking *to* a crowd. If so, Luke is exceedingly subtle (see Lk. 6:20b). The ability of the crowd to hear Jesus, who was speaking specifically to his disciples, is not explicated until 7:1.

At the conclusion of the second panel of parallel 6 (Lk. 8:4–8, 16–21) we

---

173 For Talbert's discussion of these two correspondences, see *Literary Patterns*, 42–43.
174 Fitzmyer, *Luke I-IX*, 613–614.
175 Nolland, *Luke 1–9:20*, 264–265.
176 Schürmann, *Lukasevangelium: Erster Teil*, 311.
177 Bock, *Luke 1:1–9:50*, 537
178 Talbert, *Literary Patterns*, 43.
179 Fitzmyer (*Luke I-IX*, 696) and Nolland (*Luke 1–9:20*, 364) both note that the reference to the twelve in Lk. 8:1–3 is preparation for the more prominent activity of these disciples in the accounts that follow (e.g. 9:1–6, 10, 20).

find a relocated saying of Jesus regarding the hearing and doing of God's word (Lk. 8:19–21, cf. Mk. 3:31–35). That this was obviously intended to form the conclusion to a section on this theme[180] does not contradict Talbert since the parallel saying (6:47) may be seen as the conclusion to a sermon largely on this theme. Still, the formation of a conclusion with such an appropriate saying is perhaps a stronger explanation on its own than the creation of a correspondence.

Support for parallels 5 and 6 is at best moderate. Other substantial explanations for Talbert's redactional observations are available, and not all of his suggestions clearly fit the text.

Regarding the *closing passages* of this set of correspondences, no alternative explanations for Luke's redaction are superior to or conflict with Talbert's.[181]

Test 6 finds occasional support for individual parallels in this set of correspondences, but fails to sustain its entirety. If the set is to stand, other tests must confirm its integrity.

Test 7: *Important themes* – Most of the elements of correspondence that constitute this set are related to important Lukan themes, some may not be. Certainly Jesus' interaction with demons is an important theme (*parallel 1*), but the potential of Jesus to torment or destroy them is not. In *parallel 2*, travel in a boat is not a major motif. Furthermore, although modern scholars distinguish between nature and healing miracles, it is not clear that Luke did. Reclining at table is an often noted theme of Luke's; but specifically eating and drinking, as in *parallel 4*, is not necessarily an important pair (see test 6 on page 132). The themes of *parallel 6*, teaching of crowds and "hearing" and "doing," are clearly present in the Gospel, but the latter is not prominent as an independent theme. As with the distinction between nature and healing miracles above, resurrection miracles (*closing passages*) are not necessarily distinguished from other miracles by Luke. The application of test 7, here, may be harsh since there is some relationship of these themes to those that are important. Yet they are obscure enough to raise some doubt. Due to the number of themes that are of questionable importance, the test offers little support for this correspondence set.

Test 8: *Historical/genre expectation* – There is no decisive historical or genre expectation for the specific grouping of features present in this set, apart from the basic repetition of events and themes in the ministry of Jesus itself and possibly some traditional story forms (consider parallels 1 and 3). Accordingly, the test moderately favors authorial intent.

---

180 Grundmann, *Evangelium nach Lukas*, 178; Marshall, *Gospel of Luke*, 330; Nolland, *Luke 1–9:20*, 395; and Fitzmyer, *Luke I-IX*, 722–723.
181 See Talbert, *Literary Patterns*, 43.

Test 9: *Common expression* – This grouping of parallel features is too complex to be found in other relevant literature. It even varies from the other canonical Gospels. This test supports intent.

Test 10: *Contiguity* – Contiguity poses a slight problem for this set of correspondences. Several passages do not have parallels (4:42–44; 5:12–16; 6:6–11; 8:9–18;[182] and 8:40–42). This amounts to 12% of the verses encompassed by the set. Although a small percentage, this slightly diminishes the certainty of intent behind the set. Nevertheless, imperfection is expected based on common ancient practice, so little damage is done.

Test 11: *Cumulative case* – Few of the tests offer substantial reason to be confident with this set of correspondences. The cumulative case is weak. Therefore, the probability of intent is not enhanced by this test.

Due to its poor performance, little certainty may be attributed to this proposed grouping of parallels. The results of the tests above may indicate that certain individual parallels are intentional, but it is unclear that Luke 4:16–7:17 and 7:18–56 are constructed to correspond as complete units.

2.8 Correspondences between Luke 9:1–48 and Luke 22:7–23:16

This set of correspondences does not conform to a pattern. The significance Talbert attributes to it, though, is that its parallelism of events in Galilee to events in Jerusalem counter-balances his proposed Jewish-Christian/Gentile-Christian parallelism of Acts 1–12 and 13–28[183] (See Appendix A for evaluation of patterns within Acts). Thereby Luke and Acts are demonstrated to be similar, and more likely a literary unity.

LUKE 9:1–48		LUKE 22:7–23:16
9:1–6 Jesus **sends out the Twelve. Regulations are given** for the journey.	1.	22:35–38 There is a **recollection by Jesus of the time he sent out the Twelve. The regulations for the journey are mentioned**.
9:7–9 **Herod hears of Jesus** and **seeks to see him**.	2.	23:6–16 Herod is glad Jesus is sent to him for he **had heard about him** and was **hoping to see some sign**.

---

182 Talbert includes Lk. 8:16–18 within parallel 6, but it is not clearly directed at the crowds, as is required by Talbert's parallel.
183 Talbert, *Literary Patterns*, 26.

9:10–17 **Jesus speaks of the Kingdom** of God in connection with a meal. **He blessed, broke, and gave to the disciples** to distribute.

3. 22:7–19a (19b–20) **Jesus speaks of the Kingdom** of God in connection with a meal. **He gave thanks, broke, and gave to the disciples.**

9:20–22 **Peter makes a confession** immediately **following the meal.**

4. 22:31–34 **Peter makes a confession** immediately **following a meal.**

9:23–27 If any man would come **after me**, let him…take up his **cross** daily.

5. 22:28–30 You…who have continued **with me** in my **trials.**

9:28–36 **Jesus is on a mountain** with **his disciples.** As he **prays**, he has **heavenly visitors appear** to him and speak of his **departure.** The **disciples are sleepy.**

6. 22:39–46 **Jesus is on the Mount of Olives** with **his disciples.** As he **prays** about his **death** a **heavenly visitor appears** to him. The **disciples are sleeping.**

9:37–43a **Immediately upon coming down from the mountain** Jesus **performs a miracle.** There is a sharp **contrast drawn between Jesus and the disciples.**

7. 22:47–53 **Immediately after the mountain scene** Jesus **performs a miracle.** There is a sharp **contrast drawn between Jesus and his disciples.**

9:43b–45 The **Son of man** is to be **delivered** into the hands of men.

8. 22:21–23 The **Son of man** goes as it has been determined, but woe to the man by whom he is **betrayed**.

9:46–48 There is a **dispute over greatness.**

9. 22:24–27 There is a **dispute over greatness.**

Test 1: *Restriction to passages – Parallel 1 –* If Luke 22:35–38 is about the sending of the Twelve, then these two are the only instances in the Third Gospel that refer to that sending and to these regulations. The probability however is that Lk. 22:35–38 refers to the sending of the seventy.[184] *Parallel 2 –* Apart from Luke 13:31, which is not a comfortable

---

184 See page 139 on this.

fit, the restriction of this parallel is complete. There are several other instances of hearing about Jesus and desiring to see him (see test 7 below) but these do not involve Herod. *Parallel 3* – Luke 24:30 approximates the definition of the parallel, but lacks the topic of the Kingdom of God. Therefore, the restriction is absolute as a collection of elements.[185] *Parallel 4* – Peter makes "confessions" in Luke 9:18–21; 18:28 and 22:33; but the middle instance does not follow a meal.[186] Accordingly, the restriction is perfect. *Parallel 5* – It is difficult to identify precisely on what this parallel is founded. We shall assume it is Jesus speaking to his disciples of the association of trials with discipleship. Other such material is found in the accounts of the sending of the seventy (Lk. 10:1–12); the second of the two passages on the cost of discipleship, where the wording is similar to 9:23–27 (14:25–35; and perhaps the first passage, 9:57–62); the warning of persecution to come in the eschatological discourse of 21:12–19; and perhaps the story of Lazarus and the rich man (16:19–31), where identification with Lazarus would imply trials. Therefore, at least four additional passages conform to the definition. However, Talbert specifies the Galilean and Jerusalem ministries, so only Luke 21:12–19 survives as a rogue candidate. Two of three suitable passages is a reasonable result. The indication of this test, nevertheless, is that passages that match the definition are relatively common. Should it then be viewed as an intentional parallel? It is dubious. *Parallel 6* – This combination of features only occurs in these two locations. The collocation of a mountain scene with prayer is found in Luke 6:12; 9:28; 21:37 and 22:39. Elsewhere, the mountain motif is important to the plot in Lk. 9:37; 19:29, 37; and possibly 4:29 and 21:21. The appearance of heavenly visitors and reference to the sleepiness of the disciples, however, are restricted to these two passages.[187] It is on the strength of these two elements that coincidence may be considered unlikely. *Parallel 7* – These are the only two instances of a miracle immediately following a mountain scene. Miracle accounts are Luke 4:31–37; 4:38–39; 5:1–11; 5:12–16, 17–26; 6:6–11; 7:1–10, 11–17; 8:22–25, 26–39, 40–56; 9:12–17, 37–43; 11:14; 13:10–17; 14:1–6; 17:11–19; 18:35–43;

---

185 Relevant passages where Jesus speaks of the Kingdom are common in Luke: 4:43; 6:17–26(49); 7:28; 8:1–15; 9:10–17, 27, 57–62; 10:9–11; 11:2–4, 14–28; 12:22–34(40); 13:18–21, 22–30; 14:15–24; 16:16–17; 17:20–37; 18:15–17, 18–30; 19:11–27; 21:5–37; 22:7–30 and 23:42–43. Meals are also fairly common: 5:27–39; 7:36–50; 9:10–17; 11:37–52; 14:1–24(17:10); 19:1–27 and 22:7–38. This would suggest a high probability of coincidence. It is the connection with the very restricted prayer and distribution formula (9:16; 22:19 and 24:30) that limits the opportunity for coincidence.
186 For the occurrences of a meal, see the note under test 1, parallel 3 above.
187 Scholars are divided about whether Lk. 22:43–44 is original. See page 143 where its Lukan origin is marginally accepted.

22:51. Mountain scenes are Luke 6:12–16; 9:28–36; 19:28–40; 21:37; 22:39–53. Although it not surprising that a miracle account should occasionally follow a mountain scene, the contrast drawn between Jesus and his disciples limits the odds significantly. The restriction is absolute, but will be accepted with caution. *Parallel 8* – Luke 9:22 and 18:31–34 are also passion predictions that employ the title, "Son of Man;" but 9:22 lacks the note of betrayal in Talbert's parallel, and 18:31–34 is not within the Galilean or Jerusalem ministries. As defined, the restriction is perfect, but one wonders whether the definition is too unnatural. *Parallel 9* – Talbert here employs the only two disputes over greatness in the Gospel.

Test 2: *Number of features* – *Parallel 1–4* – Two parallel features is reasonable, but not weighty. *Parallel 5* – If the parallel elements are considered to be discipleship and attendant trials, then a moderate score is achieved. *Parallel 6* – Five or six parallel elements is impressive. *Parallel 7* – Three features yields a good result. *Parallel 8* – Two features is reasonable. *Parallel 9* – Only one parallel element is weak. One could divide the definition into (1) a dispute, and (2) the topic of greatness, but this may be splitting hairs.

Test 3: *Number of panels/passages* – *Parallel 1–9* – As always, Talbert presents two parallel passages, the minimum case.

Test 4: *Attracts attention* – *Parallel 1* – These are notable features. *Parallel 2* – The possibility of an encounter between the hero of the story and a villain sparks the imagination. *Parallel 3* – Each feature in its context is startling, except for the topic of the kingdom of God in Lk. 9:10–17. Yet, this reference to the kingdom introduces the feeding of the five thousand, so it retains that emphasis. *Parallel 4* – Would it register with the reader that Peter's confession of Lk. 9:20–22 follows a meal? Certainly, though, the sequence is important to 22:31–34. The parallel, as Talbert has defined it, is not clearly supported by this test. *Parallel 5* – Most readers interested in discipleship would prick their ears when told of resultant trials. *Parallel 6* – Obviously, these features grasp the attention and are important to the plot of each account. *Parallel 7* – The mountain location of each parallel is closely connected by Luke with the miracle. Miracles are always worthy of attention, and the contrast drawn between Jesus and the disciples in each is pointed. *Parallel 8* – The title, "Son of Man," and passion predictions, have certainly attracted the attention of modern readers, and probably of Luke's target audience also.[188] *Parallel 9* – Contrasted with the respect held by early Christians for the apostles, a dispute over greatness would be

---

[188] Fitzmyer notes that the targumic attestation of the generic "I" or "he" usage of the term is too late to be relevant to New Testament studies, *Luke I-IX*, 208–11. The result is that all remaining options he lists are replete with significance, and therefore striking.

stark. Contextually, the first dispute follows their failure to perform a miracle and the second is couched in Jesus' poignant farewell address of the Last Supper, both of which highlight the selfishness of the disciples.

Test 5: *Constructive complexity – Parallel 1–9* – This set is not constructive as a pattern would be; but since the parallel elements of any one pericope are precisely matched by those of a corresponding one, the set may be considered constructive.

Test 6: *Redaction criticism – Parallel 1* – Talbert observes that Luke has altered the Markan form of the instructions Jesus gave to the twelve (Lk. 9:1–6, par. Mk. 6:6b–13). In Mark, the disciples were to take a staff, whereas in Luke they were not. Luke 22:35–38, probably L tradition, "implies that the disciples were told to take nothing at all," so the parallel was "quite possibly" deliberate.[189] The adjustment in Luke 9:3 does not form the parallel, but it does tighten it. Alternatively, Nolland suggests that the prohibition against proper travel gear may have been intended as "a prophetic sign of eschatological urgency," or an "identification with the poor," or perhaps an expression of "utter dependence on God".[190] Fitzmyer views it as consistent with "the Lucan view of detachment from earthly possessions which is otherwise characteristic of his writings"[191] Grundmann believes Luke formed a balanced four-line poem spoken by Jesus.[192] Schürmann suggests that the alteration was in part to distinguish the twelve from Hellenistic wandering preachers.[193] More pertinent to the parallel, however, and more damaging to any intent behind it, is the probability that Luke 22:35–38 refers to the sending of the seventy (Lk. 10:1–24) rather than the twelve (9:1–6).[194] Notice the closer similarity between the instructions in Luke 22:35 and 10:4.

Lk. 22:35   ὅτε ἀπέστειλα ὑμᾶς ἄτερ βαλλαντίου καὶ πήρας καὶ ὑποδημάτων, μή τινος ὑστερήσατε;

Lk. 10:4   μὴ βαστάζετε βαλλάντιον, μὴ πήραν, μὴ ὑποδήματα, καὶ μηδένα κατὰ τὴν ὁδὸν ἀσπάσησθε.

Lk. 9:3   μηδὲν αἴρετε εἰς τὴν ὁδόν, μήτε ῥάβδον μήτε πήραν μήτε ἄρτον μήτε ἀργύριον μήτε [ἀνὰ] δύο χιτῶνας ἔχειν.

---

189 Talbert, *Literary Patterns*, 27.
190 Nolland, *Luke 1–9:20*, 427. Bock stresses the latter, *Luke 1:1–9:50*, 816.
191 Fitzmyer, *Luke I-IX*, 754.
192 Grundmann, *Evangelium nach Lukas*, 184.
193 Schürmann, *Lukasevangelium: Erster Teil*, 501–502.
194 Fitzmyer concurs with this conclusion; *Luke X-XXIV*, 1429.

Nevertheless, Luke could have edited the instructions of the twelve (prohibition of the staff) to suit Luke 22:35-38, which itself refers most directly to 10:1-24. Equally, all three passages could be affected by the motives offered by Nolland, Fitzmyer, Grundmann or Schürmann without contradiction to Talbert's proposal. This test offers tentative support to intent behind the parallel.

Parallel 2 – No alternatives more persuasive than Talbert's are offered by the commentators for Luke's addition of Herod's desire to see Jesus.[195] He explains,

> Luke 9:9b adds to Mark [6:14-16] that Herod 'sought to see him.' This appears intended to parallel Luke 23:8 where Luke says that Herod had long desired to see Jesus. Luke 23:6-16, Christ before Herod, is found only in Luke and is probably L tradition. Why it was inserted into Luke's passion narrative is in part doubtless due to Luke's desire for this second correspondence.[196]

Parallel 3 – Luke 9:10-17 is a heavily reworked version of Mark 6:30-44 in which Luke specifies the subject of Jesus' teaching as the kingdom of God (Lk. 9:11 par. Mk. 6:34), whereas Mark uses the general subject, "many things". According to Talbert, Luke strengthens the connection of Luke 9:10-17 to 22:7-20 by adding the subject of the kingdom of God.[197] It has been suggested by others, however, that Luke intended simply to associate the miracle with the kingdom[198] or, further, to maintain "continuity with the central motif for this section (see 8:1) and to underline the continuity between Jesus' ministry and that of the Twelve (see 9:2)".[199] Yet, does this negate Talbert's proposal? To the contrary, it highlights Luke's perspective on the centrality of the kingdom to his subject matter. Although the kingdom of God is present in the Markan parallel to Luke 22:7-20 (see Mk. 14:25), it was added to Luke 9:2. Therefore the redaction of Luke 9:11 may not merely be explained as conformity to 9:2. The emphasis of the kingdom theme in this section is clearly Lukan. Talbert's proposal is harmonious with the other explanations, but this is not enough. The

---

195 C.F. Evans (*Saint Luke*, 398-99) and Fitzmyer (*Luke I-IX*, 757) agree that Luke, here, prepares for his insertion of 23:6-16.
196 Talbert, *Literary Patterns*, 27.
197 Talbert, *Literary Patterns*, 27.
198 Fitzmyer represents this view, *Luke I-IX*, 766.
199 Nolland, *Luke 1-9:20*, 441. The association of the miracle with the kingdom is consistent with the maintenance of continuity, so it need not be treated separately. Similar to the idea of continuity with a "central motif," Grundmann notes that preaching the kingdom and healing are recorded throughout what follows (*Evangelium nach Lukas*, 187).

maintenance of thematic continuity stands well on its own without the formation of a parallel, and may even be considered a superior motive. Accordingly, the correspondence is neither denied nor strengthened by the evidence of this test.

Parallel 4 – Lukan activity affecting both Luke 9:20–22 and 22:31–34 is observed by Talbert. First, Mark 6:45–8:26 is omitted, supposedly to join Peter's confession with the meal of the five thousand as a counterpart to his confession at the Lord's Supper. Second, Peter's confession in Luke 22:31–34 is taken from the Markan walk to the Mount of Olives and inserted into the Supper scene, supposedly to solidify the parallel.[200] We must note a logical problem with the second observation, however, before we mention other explanations. The first confession of Peter is a separate scene that immediately follows the meal in Luke (see Lk. 9:18), as was the second confession in Mark (see Mk. 14:26). Hence, the insertion of the confession into the Supper scene does not draw the parallel closer. It actually distinguishes them. This redaction does not argue his case.

Regarding the omission of Mark 6:45–8:26, Talbert enumerates the various explanations and concludes that his architectonic motive "does not preclude other factors as well". Briefly, the enumerated explanations are as follows:

> (1) Luke employed a version of Mark which did not include the passage in question... (2) Luke, as an astute historian, saw the section as repetitious and omitted it... (3) Luke omitted the section because of considerations of space since papyrus rolls were of limited length... (4) Luke did not use this section for theological reasons. For example, Mark 7:1–23 would be of little interest to Gentiles and the story of the Syro-Phoenecian could be taken to show an anti-Gentile bias.[201]

Although his architectonic explanation may not preclude these other possibilities, their existence diminishes the need for Talbert's. Nevertheless, each of the four above is highly speculative and subject to criticism, and should not be considered superior. On this basis, test 6 cautiously bolsters the probability of intent behind parallel 4.

Parallel 5 – Talbert posits the Lukan insertion of "daily" as an additional bond with Luke 22:28–30 through the phrase "continued with me" in 22:28.[202] The connection is perhaps too obscure to be likely.

Parallel 6 – Relevant redaction in Luke 9:28–36 is identified by Talbert as the addition of Jesus praying (Lk. 9:28 par. Mk. 9:2), the specification of

---

200 Talbert, *Literary Patterns*, 27–28.
201 Talbert, *Literary Patterns*, 33, n.74. See his note for adherents to each position.
202 Talbert, *Literary Patterns*, 28.

Jesus' departure as the topic of conversation with Moses and Elijah (Lk. 9:31 par. Mk. 9:4), and the sleepiness of the disciples (Lk. 9:32). In Luke 22:39–46, Luke has changed "Gethsemane" to the "Mount of Olives" (Lk. 22:39) and has, Talbert suggests, incorporated the angel appearance (Lk. 22:43).[203]

Nolland attributes each of these redactions to Lukan formation of the parallel,[204] but Fitzmyer discloses a few other explanations. He admits the possibility that the addition of Jesus praying foreshadows Luke 22:39.[205] Different to Talbert, however, he observes the appropriateness of the term ἔξοδος to the presence of Moses;[206] but this really only explains the term and not the topic. The sleepiness of the disciples is explained as Luke's means of justifying Peter's concern about shelter, perhaps by indicating it was night.[207] Yet, Mark's version provides sufficient justification in Peter's fear (Mk. 9:6). Luke's shift from fear to sleepiness may have reflected an interest in portraying Peter's faith as more mature, but this is no more certain than his interest in constructing the parallel. Commentators generally perceive the alteration from "Gethsemane" to the "Mount of Olives" as consistent with Luke's motif of prayer on mountains.[208] The existence of only two other instances of this motif in the Gospel however (6:12 and 9:28) makes the argument less compelling. Finally, regarding the appearance of the angel, the textual difficulty surrounding Luke 22:43–44 removes any certainty that might have been gained by this element.[209] Marshall, cautiously accepting the Lukan origin of these verses, indicates the appropriateness of the angel for Jesus' state and as an answer to prayer.[210] Such appropriateness is compatible with Talbert's theory and not superior to it. Certainly, if the parallel is established by the other elements, apart from that of the angel, then the Lukan origin of verse 43 is cautiously supported by the parallel. No one argues that the angel is added by a later redactor to conform the Gethsemane scene to the transfiguration, which is wise since it would not explain the accompaniment of the potentially more

---

203 Talbert, *Literary Patterns*, 28–29.
204 Nolland, *Luke 9:21–18:34*, 491.
205 Fitzmyer, *Luke I-IX*, 798.
206 Fitzmyer, *Luke I-IX*, 794–795.
207 Fitzmyer, *Luke I-IX*, 800–801. See also Schürmann, *Lukasevangelium: Erster Teil*, 558–559.
208 Fitzmyer notes this Lukan association, *Luke X-XXIV*, 1441. Bock suggests that Luke typically omits Semitic terms, *Luke 9:51–24:53*, 1756.
209 For well developed arguments that favor the omission of these verses see C.F. Evans, *Saint Luke*, 812–13, and Bruce M. Metzger, *A Textual Commentary on the Greek New Testament* (London: United Bible Societies, 1975) 177.
210 Marshall, *Gospel of Luke*, 832.

troublesome verse 44.[211]

To summarize, Talbert reveals several instances of Lukan redaction that are consistent with the construction of parallel 6. Other explanations for the observations tend not to provide the substantial motivation inherent in his mechanism. Accordingly, the parallel is well supported by this test.

Parallel 7 – Interestingly, Luke tells us that Jesus healed the ear of the High Priest's servant, while Mark lacks this. Talbert believes that this constitutes a parallel to the healing in Luke 9:37–43a, when viewed in the context of the other parallel elements.[212] The implication of this addition, Marshall rightly concludes, is that Jesus' "movement is not based on force".[213] Mark's account (Mk. 14:43–52) could have been misinterpreted as condoning violent support, so the healing does actually suggest a strong underlying motive. This motive is more potent than the formation of a parallel and is therefore superior. Intent behind parallel 7 is made no more certain by test 6.

Parallel 8 – No favorable redaction is presented for this parallel. "The two predictions of his coming death by Jesus were already present in Luke's sources in approximately the positions needed," Talbert writes.[214] Accordingly, no support may be attributed by this test.

Parallel 9 – Regarding Luke 22:24–27 and its peculiarly Lukan location, Talbert asks, "If the material comes from Mark, why is it positioned here? If it is L tradition, again we must ask, why does it come at this point in the passion narrative? The probable answer is that it appears in the passion narrative at this point in order to make possible the parallel with 9:46–48."[215] Still, we must ask whether Luke, contrary to known history, would have inserted such an event into the Supper scene to correspond with the dispute in Luke 9:46–48, which could easily have been omitted. Commentators only note the logical suitability of the material to the immediate context without providing a compelling reason for its incorporation. Therefore, Talbert's theory is not denied by superior explanations.

Test 7: *Important themes – Parallel 1* – Mission and dependence on God during mission are important Lukan themes. *Parallel 2* – Hearing about Jesus and desiring to see him are themes frequently represented in Luke, both explicitly and implicitly (Explicit: Lk. 4:37, 40–44; 5:15; 7:3; 9:7–9; 19:1–4; 23:6–16. Implicit: Lk. 4:14; 5:17; 6:17–18; 7:18–19; 8:4,

---

211 On this basis, and considering the remarkable balance of the textual evidence (which has resulted in extensive debate) I believe the scales are marginally tipped in favor of the Lukan origin of Lk. 22:43–44.
212 Talbert, *Literary Patterns*, 29.
213 Marshall, *Gospel of Luke*, 837. So also Grundmann, *Evangelium nach Lukas*, 414.
214 Talbert, *Literary Patterns*, 29.
215 Talbert, *Literary Patterns*, 29.

40–41; 9:37, 57–62; 11:29a, 37; 12:1; 13:31; 17:11–13; 18:15, 35–38; 20:27). Although they are not necessarily central, this frequency is witness to their importance. *Parallel 3* – These are clearly important themes. *Parallel 4* – These are recognized Lukan themes. *Parallel 5* – The inevitability of trials in discipleship is undoubtedly a Lukan interest. *Parallel 6* – Mountain scenes (see test 1 above), prayer and Christ's death are important Lukan themes. Heavenly visitors, at least in the form of angels, are manifestly significant in the infancy narrative. Sleepiness of the disciples, however, appears to be an insignificant theme on its own. *Parallel 7* – These are clearly important motifs to the Evangelist. *Parallel 8* – Few themes have greater weight than these. *Parallel 9* – Disputes among disciples only occur here in the Third Gospel. Of course, more are encountered in Acts (e.g. 11:3; 15:1–2, 36–40). These incidents, vital to the plot of Acts, demonstrate the probability that the author considered such disputes significant, despite their infrequency. Caution must be exercised when importing this to the Gospel however. It is safest to view the disputes as an indication of the degree of understanding of the disciples, a Lukan concern, though not as pointed as in Mark.

Test 8: *Historical/genre expectation* – *Parallel 1* – The inclusion of Luke 9:1–6 might be historically expected (with no real genre expectation), but 22:35–38 is not, judging by the absence of parallels in the other Gospels. Intent is therefore enhanced. *Parallel 2* – Herod's initial hearing of Jesus and desire to see him is paralleled in Mark and Matthew. Therefore, a degree of historical expectation exists, since Mark was his primary source. The trial before Herod is unparalleled in the other Gospels, so it is not generically expected. Nevertheless, the nature of the event is compelling reason for its inclusion. Accordingly, if of the Evangelists Luke alone had access to a source that recorded this historical event, then it is no surprise that he incorporated it. If the others had knowledge of it, we should ask why they ignored it. This diminishes the probability that its inclusion was solely to establish a parallel. Luke 23:8, which encompasses Herod's hearing about Jesus and desire to see him, however, does suggest that Luke connected the two events. Such hearing and desire are less historically compelling as the fact of the trial itself. Test 8 offers support for the parallel as fully defined. *Parallel 3* – The synoptic parallels to both Luke 9:10–17 (Mk. 6:32–44 and Mt. 14:13–21) and Luke 22:7–20 (Mk. 14:12–17, 22–25 and Mt. 26:17–20, 26–29) contain each feature, except the subject of the Kingdom in the first of Luke's passages. Although John lacks the second account, it should still probably be considered generically expected or likely. In contrast, one can easily imagine a Gospel without record of a miraculous feeding, so the first account is not anticipated by genre. The feeding of the five thousand is so remarkable and the Last Supper so powerful that they should both probably be reckoned historically expected. The insertion of the Kingdom theme in the feeding story is easily accounted for by Luke's strong interest in the theme. Test 8 does not favor intentional Lukan construction of this parallel because Luke may well have been compelled by history and genre to include the parallel elements. *Parallel 4* – The concatenation of Peter's confession in Luke 9:20–22 with the feeding of the five thousand is performed by Luke alone. No historical or genre expectation may be attributed. The connection of the latter confession with the Supper is anticipated by genre and history, as evidenced by Mark, Matthew and John (Mk. 14:29; Mt. 26:33 and Jn. 13:37). By virtue of the unexpectedness of the first collocation, cautious support is afforded by this test. *Parallel 5* – Each of the New Testament Gospels contains such statements on discipleship. Indeed, Jesus probably spoke often on the subject. We should expect this "parallel" on the grounds of genre and history. Authorial intent is not indicated. *Parallel 6* – Both events are paralleled in each of the Synoptic Gospels and are compelling pieces of history, so their inclusion may reasonably be expected for historical reasons. In terms of genre, they might be expected because of their theological import. Yet, the substantial redaction noted in test 6 indicates a selectivity that precludes our expectation of the details found in parallel. This test therefore moderately contends for intentional formation of the parallel. *Parallel 7* – Neither history nor genre provide reason to expect the inclusion of these features as specified. *Parallel 8* – Jesus undoubtedly announced his passion on a number of occasions, typically using the title Son of Man, according to the synoptic accounts (see Lk. 9:22, 44; 18:31–34; 22:22 and synoptic parallels). It is hard to conceive of the New Testament genre lacking passion predictions, so the features of this parallel are anticipated by the genre. No doubt, too, any historian of the ministry of Jesus would be remiss to omit such predictions if they were in his sources. This test does not support the probability that these two predictions, as defined, were intended as parallels. *Parallel 9* – Historically, Luke probably included the first account because of its presence in Mark. Still, the event is not so compelling that he could not have omitted it. In contrast, the dispute at the Last Supper would have impressed itself more on his mind; yet, again, it is not historically anticipated. No reason of genre is evident to expect either account. This lack of expectation favors intentional parallelism.

Test 9: *Common expression – Parallel 1* – Obviously, the Old Testament is filled with accounts of people in authority sending others on some sort of mission. Apparently, a majority of these involve instructions,[216] but rarely do they specify travel gear. The instructions essentially define the mission. It is perhaps best, then, to see the prohibition against provisions as an aspect of the mission,[217] in which case the Lukan sending is accompanied simply by mission instructions, a common formula. Reminiscences of commissions (here, Lk. 22:35–38), however, are too rare to establish a "common expression". Additionally, if Luke employed Mark as a source here, then Luke 9:1–6 is not sufficiently influenced by Luke's perception of commission formulae for this to be a decisive factor. This is evidenced by his faithfulness to the basic Markan formula. Based, therefore, on the rarity of appropriate reminiscences, common expression may not confidently be considered a viable explanation for the parallel. Intent is more likely. *Parallel 2* – Any desire to see someone obviously presumes an awareness of that person. However, it is another matter to state in a narrative that such desire was founded on hearing a report about the person. The only example in the Old Testament I could locate was the Queen of Sheba's comment to King Solomon, "It was a true report which I heard in my own land about your words and your wisdom. Nevertheless, I did not believe the reports, until I came and my eyes had seen it." (1 Ki. 10:6–7a par. 2 Ch. 9:5–6a). Such explication is apparently rare, as one might expect. Naturally, it would be within Luke's repertoire of narrative strategies since it is logical and reflects the way actual events occur. Yet, its infrequency implies that Luke would not have been compelled by any convention to present it in this manner. The likelihood of this parallel being coincidental due to common expression is diminished. *Parallel 3* – This collocation of features is certainly uncommon in relevant literature. *Parallel 4* – Confession of Christ following a meal is certainly not a literary convention or common expression. *Parallel 5* – Obviously, the connection between the themes of trials and discipleship was common, as is evident throughout the New Testament. The likelihood of coincidental correspondence due to common expression is therefore substantial. *Parallel 6* – Talbert's grouping of features is plainly uncommon in relevant literature outside Gospel parallels. *Parallel 7* – No common formula lies behind this collection of features. *Parallel 8* – As noted under test 4, the generic "I" or "he" usage of "Son of Man" was probably too late to be common in New Testament times. In addition, both parallel accounts were taken from Mark with no addition of relevant features, so Luke was not influenced here by common expression. *Parallel 9* – This is not a grouping of features, so test 9 does not adequately

---

216 The same is true of New Testament "sendings." See, for example, Lk. 10:3–12; and 19:30–31 and parallels.

217 E. Earle Ellis, *The Gospel of Luke*, New Century Bible Commentary (London: Marshall, Morgan & Scott, 1974) 137.

apply.

Test 10: *Contiguity – Parallel 1–9* – Contiguity is not a major issue since Luke 22:54–23:5 (23 verses) is the only noteworthy gap. Luke 22:66–23:5 serves to set the scene for the trial before Herod, so Peter's disowning of Jesus and the mocking of the soldiers (Lk. 22:54–65) is the only extraneous portion. Confidence in this set is strengthened.

Test 11: *Cumulative case – Parallel 1* – Overall support for this parallel is strong, especially from tests 1, 4 and 7. There is a high probability that Luke intended this parallel. *Parallel 2* – As with parallel 1, overall support is strong. The weighty tests of 4 and 6 particularly strengthen this highly probable Lukan parallel. *Parallel 3* – It is tempting to view this parallel as necessarily intentional, but the first ten tests advise a degree of caution. *Parallel 4* – As this parallel is defined, only cautious approval is gained from the tests. *Parallel 5* – According to the tests, this parallel is dubious. It is more probably a product of coincidence than specific Lukan intent. *Parallel 6* – Of all the parallels in the set, this has the highest probability of Lukan intent. There is absolute restriction of suitable features to the one parallel. There are several features, each of which is noteworthy. Additionally, redaction favors the construction. *Parallel 7* – Support for this parallel is generally strong. It should be treated with similar confidence as parallels 1 and 2. *Parallel 8* – As with parallel 3, it is tempting to view this one as necessarily intentional. Again, however, the first ten tests recommend a degree of caution. *Parallel 9* – Parallel 9 should be treated with the same confidence as parallels 1 and 2. Despite there being only one feature, the tests indicate a high probability that Luke intended the parallelism.

In summary, the correspondence between the Lukan transfiguration and Gethsemane scenes (parallel 6) is certainly intentional and easily scores the highest of this set under the tests. Parallels 1, 2, 9 and perhaps 7 should be accepted with confidence. Parallels 3, 4 and 8 deserve cautious acceptance. Finally, parallel 5 should not be treated as intentional.

This set has generally performed well, but the degree of correspondence suggested by Talbert is doubtful. He has successfully demonstrated, however, Luke's concern to link in the reader's mind the Galilean and Jerusalem ministries of Jesus by using occasional striking parallels to provide continuity between textually distant sections.

2.9 Chiastic Correspondence between Luke 10:21–13:30 and Luke 14:1–18:30

Apart from the infancy narratives, perhaps the portion of the Gospel that receives the most attention regarding its patterned structure is this "central section".[218] Numerous scholars have proposed various chiastic structures for this section.[219] Talbert also proposes a chiastic pattern for Luke 10:21–18:30, presented below.[220] Each chiasm proposed by scholars varies in some way from the others, and perhaps this works against the pattern's existence here since there is a lack of consensus.[221] Then again, the frequent recognition of such structure perhaps suggests that at least a trace of chiasm is present, or some other form of parallelism.

Under the eleven tests, Talbert's pattern produces representative results for chiastic proposals for the central section and serves well as an example. As with all schemes that I am aware of, some parallels are strong, but many are doubtful.

---

218 Much attention is also given to the purpose of the "central section." Often its overall theme is viewed in terms of Jesus' death and ascension, and typology for the missionary activity of the church. See for example J.H. Davies, "The Purpose of the Central Section of St. Luke's Gospel," in F.L. Cross (ed.), *Studia Evangelica, II*, Texte und Untersuchungen 87 (Berlin: Akademie-Verlag, 1964) 164–69; and Gerhard Sellin, "Komposition, Quellen und Funktion des lukanischen Reiseberichtes (Lk. IX 51–XIX 28)," *NovT* 20 (1978) 100–135. Our proposal, to be presented in a later chapter, accords somewhat with these proposals but pictures the central section in a manner much more integrated into the whole Gospel.

Proposals of related purposes abound. See Wm.C. Robinson, Jr. who sees it as the "authentication and preparation of the apostolic witness" ("The Theological Context for Interpreting Luke's Travel Narrative (9 51 ff.)," *JBL* 79 (1960) 20–31). Against this is the amount of material that does not relate to the apostles. Frank J. Matera notes the alternation between conflict and non-conflict in the central section and postulates the primary motif of conflict with Israel; "Jesus' Journey to Jerusalem (Luke 9.51–19.46): A Conflict with Israel," *JSNT* 51 (1993) 57–77. His observation of alternation is valid and must be related to the plot, but the very presence of substantial sections without conflict relegates his suggestion to one of many important themes in the central section.

219 Among these are Kenneth E. Bailey (*Poet and Peasant*, 79–85); George Ogg ("The Central Section of the Gospel According to St Luke" *NTS* 18 [1971] 39–53); M.D. Goulder ("Chiastic Structure," 195–202 – although he no longer holds the position), and Heinrich Baarlink ("zyklische Struktur," 481–506). Craig Blomberg denies a chiastic structure for the central section, but affirms a chiastic parables source behind it ("Midrash," 217–61).

220 For Talbert's presentation and discussion of this table see *Literary Patterns*, 51–56.

221 François Bovon, in "Studies in Luke-Acts: Retrospect and Prospect," *HTR* 85 (1992) 185, shares this concern in a comparison of Talbert's chiasm with that of Roland Meynet (*Avez-vous lu saint Luc?*, 32–37).

LUKE 10:21–13:33		LUKE 13:34–18:30
10:21–24 The **Kingdom** is revealed to **babes**. Blessed are the **disciples** for they see.	1.	18:15–17 The **Kingdom** must be received as a **child**, the **disciples** are told.
10:25–37 Jesus is confronted with the question: **"What shall I do to inherit eternal life?"** The **response to Jesus' answer elicits teaching** by Jesus.	2.	18:18–30 Jesus is confronted with the question: **"What shall I do to inherit eternal life?"** The **response to Jesus' answer elicits more teaching** from Jesus.
10:38–42 The story of Mary and Martha **de-emphasizes the importance of good works**.	3.	18:9–14 The parable of the Pharisee and the publican **de-emphasizes the importance of good works**.
11:1–13 **God's willingness to answer prayer.**	4.	18:1–8 **God's willingness to answer prayer.**
11:14–36 A **healing** followed by a discussion of the **signs of the Kingdom of God** and a **warning about the Last Judgment.**	5.	17:11–37 A **healing** followed by a discussion of the **signs of the Kingdom of God** and a **warning about the Last Judgment.**
11:37–54 At a **meal** Jesus **rebukes** the Pharisees and lawyers for their sins.	6.	17:1–10 An exhortation to **rebuke** one's brother when he sins, followed by a parable about a **meal**.
12:1–48 Three themes are treated in the order: (1) the **threat of hell** (vss. 1–12), (2) **riches** (vss. 13–34), (3) **faithful stewardship** (vss. 35–48).	7.	ch. 16 Three themes are treated in the order: (1) **unfaithful stewardship** (vss. 1–8), (2) **riches** (vss. 9–15), (3) the **threat of hell** (vss. 19–31).

12:49–13:9 Four themes are present in the order: (1) **transcendence of family loyalties** (12:49–53), (2) **prudent action taken ahead of time** (12:54–59), (3) **repentance** (13:1–5), (4) the fruitless tree is **cut down** (13:6–9).

8. 14:25–15:32 Four themes are present in order: (1) **transcendence of family loyalties** (14:25–27), (2) **prudent action taken ahead of time** (14:28–33), (3) tasteless salt which **is thrown away** (14:34–35), (4) **repentance** (ch. 15).

13:10–17 A woman is **healed on the Sabbath**. Jesus says the **Jews treat an ox and ass better than a person.**

9. 14:1–6 A man is **healed on the Sabbath**. Jesus says the **Jews treat an ox and ass better than a person.**

13:18–30 **Parables of the Kingdom** of God are concluded by the theme of the **exclusion of privileged ones from the Messianic banquet** and the **inclusion of the disadvantaged.**

10. 14:7–24 **Parables relating to the Kingdom** are concluded by the theme of the **exclusion from the Messianic banquet of certain privileged people** and **the inclusion of the disadvantaged**.

13:31–33 A **prophet** cannot **perish** away from **Jerusalem**.

11. 13:34–35 O **Jerusalem**, Jerusalem, **killing** the **prophets** and stoning those who are sent to you.

Test 1: *Restriction to passages* – Our search for the elements of correspondence noted by Talbert must be restricted to the boundaries of the pattern. Nevertheless, it is interesting to note that just preceding Luke 10:21–18:30 is an account that fits *parallel 1* precisely (9:46–50, the argument over who would be the greatest). The theme of the Kingdom is common in this section of the Gospel, but reference to children is rare. In *parallel 2*, both parallel elements occur only at these locations. De-emphasis of the importance of good works (*parallel 3*) is not so restricted. The theme is found also at 11:37–44; 17:7–10 and 18:18–25, which weakens this particular parallel. Interestingly, teaching of Jesus on prayer is present only in the passages of *parallel 4*. *Parallel 5* consists of three themes in succession: healing, signs of the kingdom, and warning about the Last

Judgment. Each in fact is common.[222] This exact sequence is also found in 13:10–30 and 14:1–24(35). The association of a meal with a rebuke (*parallel 6*) is relatively common. For example, Jesus rebukes Martha while a meal is being prepared (10:38–42), Jesus rebukes some guests at a meal (14:1–14) and, if Luke 15:2 implies that a meal is the setting, 16:15 also matches the elements of this parallel. The three individual themes in *parallel 7* occur elsewhere,[223] but never grouped, as they are in this parallel. Therefore its restriction is moderate. Of *parallel 8*, only "transcendence of family loyalties" and "repentance" are present outside the parallel.[224] This result is fairly strong. The elements of *parallels 9* through *11* are all completely confined to their respective parallels.

Only three of Talbert's parallels perform poorly on this test (3, 5 and 6). This lends general support for the pattern.[225]

Test 2: *Number of features* – Parallels *3* and *4* consist of single parallel elements, which is insubstantial evidence for intent. Otherwise, the results are good. Whether the passages actually fit Talbert's proposed themes is a serious question. In *parallel 1* the role of the disciples is considerably different. One may question, regarding *parallel 2*, whether Martha was intent on "good works". With *parallel 6*, it is dubious that whether an *actual* meal *at which* Jesus rebukes someone can correspond to a *parable about* a meal *before which* Jesus exhorts others to rebuke. Parallel *7* has difficulties. Is Luke 12:35–40 about stewardship, or about the same kind of stewardship as in 16:1–8? Overall, this test provides moderately strong support for intent.

Test 3: *Number of panels/passages* – Two panels is the minimum case.

Test 4: *Attracts attention* – All but two elements of correspondence in this pattern attract the reader's attention at least reasonably well. In *parallel 2*, it is less than striking that "the response to Jesus' answer elicits more teaching from Jesus". The same can be said about the meal in *parallel 6*. Regardless, this is a strong result for the pattern.

Test 5: *Constructive complexity* – Two panels in a reasonably chiastic

---

222 Healings are recounted at 11:14; 13:10–17; 14:1–6 and 17:11–19. Warnings about the Last Judgment are recorded in 12:8–10, 16–21, 42–48, 54–59 and 13:22–30. Discussion of the signs of the Kingdom of God are also naturally frequent.

223 Stewardship is found also in 12:13–21 and 16:19–31. The theme of riches appears in 16:19–31 and 18:18–30. Hell is referred to in 12:46; 13:1–5, 22–30 and perhaps 11:29–32.

224 Transcendence of family loyalties is apparent in 18:29–30, and repentance in 11:32; 16:30; 17:3–4.

225 Earnest Best considers the frequency with which the elements that form parallels in a text occur to be a crucial issue. He further suggests that simple chiasm may be a natural product of certain minds. See his book, *Mark: The Gospel as Story* (Edinburgh: T. & T. Clark, 1983) 104–106.

relationship favors authorial intent. The break in chiastic order of *parallel 8* is minor and inconsequential. When the inversions of order between parallels 1 and 2, and between 9 and 10, are added to this, certainty of intent is diminished.

Test 6: *Redaction criticism* – Talbert defends the Lukan intent behind *parallel 1*, noting about Luke 18:5–17 (par. Mk. 10:13–16)

> ...that the Third Evangelist altered Mark's introduction to the pericope from 'And they were bringing children (παιδία) to him,' to 'Now they were bringing even infants (βρέφη) to him...' By this change Luke guaranteed that the subsequent παιδία in vss. 16, 17 would be read as infants rather than as children. This change seems clearly in the interest of the parallel.[226]

It brings the concept more clearly in line with the parallel passage's use of νήπιος (Lk. 10:21–22). Stein suggests however that Luke considered it more appropriate to picture infants being carried rather than small children.[227] Another reason could be the added emphasis of Jesus' interest in the *smallest* of children. These are strong alternatives to Talbert's explanation.

In the interest of *parallel 2*, Talbert proposes that "Luke 10:25–28 is possibly from Mark 12:28–34 and would therefore be transposed from the final week in Jerusalem to become the introduction to the parable of the Good Samaritan. It would thereby provide a match to the question "What shall I do to inherit eternal life" that elicits further teaching in Luke 18:18–30. Marshall convincingly argues that Luke 10:25–28 and Mk. 12:28–34 are probably accounts of separate events, as suggested by the many substantial differences between them. He admits that Luke apparently recognized the similarity to the Markan account and omitted it to avoid repetition with his preferred story.[228] Transposed or drawn from another source, the parallel (whether structural or not) is still created by this addition.

Parallel 3 consists of two L source passages. No redaction criticism is offered by Talbert.

He suggests for *parallel 4* that Luke 11:9–11 (Q material) is conjoined to 11:5–8 (L material) to develop the theme of prayer established by this Q

---

226 Talbert, *Literary Patterns*, 53.
227 Robert H. Stein, *Luke*, New American Commentary 24 (Nashville: Broadman Press, 1992) 543.
228 Marshall, *Gospel of Luke*, 440–41. Similarly Sabourin, *L'Évangile de Luc*, 225–226. Bock also argues against the dependence of Lk. 10:25–28 on Mk. 12:28–34, *Luke 9:51–24:53*, 1018–1020.

material (the motif of God's willingness to answer). This willingness sharpens the parallel with 18:1–8. Indeed it does; but God's willingness to answer prayer is so central to the concept as to be sufficient motivation alone, apart from parallelism, for its presence here, especially when the parable of the Friend at Midnight might suggest some hesitation on God's part. Talbert's theory is not necessary.

The first panel of the *fifth parallel* presents three sequential themes, each in its own Q passage: healing (11:14–23), signs of the kingdom (vv. 24–26), and warning about the last judgment (vv. 29–32). These Q pericopes have the same relative order as in Matthew, so Talbert turns to the second panel (17:11–37) to detect any manipulation of sources that favors the parallel.

> This section is composed of two L traditions (17:11–19 and 17:20–21) followed by a Q passage (17:22–37 = Matt 24:26–28, 37–41) in the same relative order as in Matthew. The healing is from L (vss. 11–19), the beginning of the discussion of signs also from L (vss. 20–21), and the continuation of the signs discussion and the warning about judgment from Q (vss. 22–37). It is significant that it was material with just these three themes that were selected and that they were arranged in exactly the order they were. Definite indications of the Lucan hand at work seem apparent here.[229]

The designation of 17:22–37 as Q material is not certain, and many recent scholars consider it largely Lukan or from sources peculiar to Luke.[230] Regarding Luke 17:20–21, some consider it an integral part of a block of Q material, 17:20–37.[231] The question of source manipulation is very complicated. There is no clear evidence for what Luke actually did.

The relationship between the themes in Luke 17:1–10 is difficult,[232] and Talbert's treatment of *parallel 6* offers a viable explanation. Perhaps the theme of meal (vv. 7–10, L material) is intentionally appended to that of rebuke (vv. 1–6, Q material) to match the combination of these themes in 11:37–54.[233] Perhaps the best alternative however is to postulate adherence to a source.[234]

Talbert defends the intentional formation of *parallel 7* (Lk. 12:1–48 with

---

[229] Talbert, *Literary Patterns*, 54.
[230] Marshall, *Gospel of Luke*, 656–57; C.F. Evans, *Saint Luke*, 626. Schlatter considers verses 20–23, 26–30, and 32 to be from an apocalyptic source peculiar to Luke (*Evangelium des Lukas*, 390–396).
[231] For example, Schneider, *Evangelium nach Lukas*, 354.
[232] Stein, *Luke*, 428; Bock, *Luke 9:51–24:53*, 1380–1383.
[233] Talbert, *Literary Patterns*, 54.
[234] Marshall, *Gospel of Luke*, 643.

16:1–31) by noting that the first panel consists primarily of Q passages in divergent order from Matthew and the second panel consists of L traditions. The implication he draws is that Luke arranged three themes in inverse relationship between the panels: threat of hell, riches, and stewardship.[235] Certainly he has established the opportunity. No contrary explanations other than pattern – the same as Talbert's – appear available since scholars rarely comment about arrangement of themes in such large blocks.

The same can be said about *parallel 8* as for parallel 7. Talbert defends it in much the same fashion since the intermingling of sources is even more complicated than in parallel 7.[236]

Parallel 9 involves only L material.[237] No decisive observations are possible.

Talbert notes that Luke introduces a banquet parable from Q (Lk. 14:16–24 par. Mt. 22:1–10) by referring to the Messianic Banquet (v. 15), thereby making this theme in the parable explicit; and Talbert interprets this as a tightening of *parallel 10*.[238] This is very possible, but it is unclear whether the parable is from Q[239] and therefore whether the explicit reference to the Messianic Banquet was not in Luke's source in the first place. At the least, Lukan selection of the parable favors Talbert.

Regarding *parallel 11*, Talbert observes that an L passage (13:31–33) is followed by a Q tradition (vv. 34–35).[240] Contrary to his suggestion that the L tradition was inserted for the sake of a structural parallel, the themes being nearly identical is sufficient justification for their combination.

Redaction criticism in the central section of Luke is difficult. Nevertheless, Talbert makes numerous observations that he believes indicate intentional formation of his parallels. Most of these have been demonstrated to have stronger alternative explanations. Accordingly, test 6 does not provide support for this pattern.

Test 7: *Important themes* – Numerous themes on which this pattern depends are minor in the gospel of Luke, which diminishes our confidence in its Lukan intent. Themes like children, response to an answer by Jesus eliciting further teaching, de-emphasis of the importance of good works, rebuke, and treatment of an ox better than a person are not likely candidates for the foundation of such a dominant structural principle. Nonetheless, by virtue of the strong themes that are involved, this test offers a small degree of support for authorial intent.

---

235 Talbert, *Literary Patterns*, 55.
236 Talbert, *Literary Patterns*, 55–56.
237 See Talbert's discussion of this parallel, *Literary Patterns*, 56.
238 Talbert, *Literary Patterns*, 56.
239 Bock, *Luke 9:51–24:53*, 1269–1270.
240 Talbert, *Literary Patterns*, 56.

Test 8: *Historical/genre expectation* – There is no clear historical or genre expectation for the sequence of parallel features suggested by Talbert. This test supports intent.

Test 9: *Common expression* – The sequence of features is not common in other literature, so it may not be considered a "common expression". This test also supports intent.

Test 10: *Contiguity* – Contiguity is perfect in this pattern. It would therefore be more difficult for Talbert to exercise selectivity in the observation of structure. Whether the text always matches his descriptions remains a question (see p. 151).

Test 11: *Cumulative case* – Support for the chiasm as presented by Talbert is varied among the tests. Some of the strongest indicators of intent, e.g. tests 6 and 7, fail to uphold the pattern. Overall, only moderate confidence may be placed in it as presented.

Results under the above tests are generally not stellar for this chiasmus, or for other similar scholarly proposals, the evaluations of which yield similar results to those of Talbert's scheme. Yet, some of the observations he proposes are remarkable and broadly accepted as intentional. Perhaps there is a remnant of a chiastic source that underlies the central section and accounts for some such parallelism; or perhaps there is another form of parallelism here, parts of which are being detected.

Many scholars question the validity of a full-blown chiastic structure for the central section.[241] Yet many of the arguments employed by these scholars would deny broadly recognized parallelism like that in Luke 1–2. For example, requiring perfect chiasmus or exact verbal parallel rather than conceptual correspondence[242] ignores common ancient structural mechanisms.

Yet why have so many scholars suspected that there is chiasmus in the central section? Blomberg moves beyond mere criticism of chiastic schemes and identifies a chiastic parables source behind this section of the Gospel.[243] If he is correct, then it may provide the chiastic principle that tempts certain readers to broaden it, forcing additional material into the pattern. Talbert has been concerned about how Luke formed the patterns he observes, including this one. His heavy emphasis on redaction criticism reflects this. We share that interest in Lukan composition, as discussed in the introduction. Chapter 4 will develop our proposal of structure repre-

---

241 See for example François Bovon, "Studies in Luke-Acts," 185); C.F. Evans, *Saint Luke*, 43–4; Best, *Mark*, 105; and Blomberg, "Midrash," 233–240.

242 See Blomberg, "Midrash," 236, for example. Many of his questions regarding proposals of chiasm for the central section are valid, but he is more stringent in his demands on structure than ancient writers apparently were.

243 See Blomberg's presentation of the chiastic parables source, "Midrash," 240–247.

sented in the table in the introduction (see page 28). Part of that development is to explore how Luke might have constructed the proposed cyclical parallelism. The central section of Luke, comprising the majority of cycles 2 and 3 of the four, is therefore of particular concern to us. Chiastic proposals for the central section fail to satisfy, but hopefully our proposal will. The strength of Blomberg's idea must be reckoned with, however, if ours is to stand the test of scrutiny. In other words, does our conception of the central section mesh with his or clash? If it clashes, then is there sufficient ground to reject Blomberg's view in favor of ours? A brief treatment of the matter is in order here since the subject has been raised for us by Talbert's chiasm.

Blomberg's parables source is described as containing fifteen parables. One difficulty with this scheme is that he has a large pool of at least thirty-one parables in the central section from which he finds seven pairs. The parallelism between some of these pairs is not obvious either: 11:11–13 with 17:7–10; and 14:1–6 with 14:28–33. This leaves only five strong parallels. His case is strengthened however (1) because he seeks to include all parables in this section that are peculiar to Luke, and (2) because he requires both parables of each pair to have similar audiences, reflecting either "controversy" or "discipleship".[244] In other words, he dramatically limits the pool, yet still maintains a chiasm. Regarding the first point, it is certainly possible, assuming an underlying source, that Luke inserted additional parables peculiar to his Gospel, which would obscure the identification of that source. On the second point, the parables are paired based on content, with audience as a check. The content of parables, however, directly corresponds with the audience in the vast majority of cases. Therefore, most parables of similar content will have similar audiences in terms of "controversy" or "discipleship". On another matter, Blomberg overlooks one parable that conforms to all his criteria and that requires only a minor adjustment to the scheme (Lk. 13:10–17). It corresponds far more closely to 14:1–6 than does 14:28–33, and a similar audience is retained, a religious leader. Since Luke 14:1–6 is poorly matched with 14:28–33, it may be re-paired with the superior parallel 13:10–17. This drops the misfit 14:28–33 out of the picture. Since Luke 14:7–24 has no parallel and cannot therefore be included with certainty, it too is dropped. The readjustment that results is as follows:

---

244 Blomberg, "Midrash," 246–47.

10:25-37	18:9-14		10:25-37	18:9-14
11:5-8	18:1-8		11:5-8	18:1-8
11:11-13	17:7-10		11:11-13	17:7-10
12:13-21	16:19-31	⇒	12:13-21	16:19-31
12:35-38	16:1-13		12:35-38	16:1-13
13:1-9	15:1-32		13:1-9	15:1-32
14:1-6	*14:28-33*		*13:10-17*	*14:1-6*
	14:7-24			

One effect of this change is to shift the center of the chiasm to an earlier point in the central section, late in chapter 13 rather than the middle of chapter 14. It also makes his pattern fairly consistent with most other proposals of detailed chiasm without the excess baggage of those schemes.

Interestingly, if the above revision of Blomberg's chiastic parables source hypothesis is correct, the two panels of the chiasm would precisely coincide with the two center panels of the four-fold parallel structure for Luke 4:14–24:53 that will be proposed later. Under this scenario, Luke would have recognized and retained the two-part structure in this parables source, and fleshed it out to match his parallel design for the book. This precise meshing of patterns would be consistent with typical ancient writings that employ multilevel structure.

3 Evaluation of Talbert's Understanding of the Significance behind the Correspondences

We have observed throughout our evaluation of Talbert's correspondence sets that several are probably valid, but a few are not very certain. Still, in most sets there are certain striking individual correspondences. How may we account for these residual parallels when a pattern performs poorly under the eleven tests? Certainly some may be intentional, with the tests simply unable to certify the fact, and others may be incidental. Intentional parallels on a smaller scale than Talbert's patterns have been amply demonstrated by Tannehill, many of which are reviewed in chapter 1. Luke links pairs and even groups of pericopes through such literary techniques as preview, review and type-scene. An example of a valid parallel in an improbable set of correspondences is the first in the parallelism between Lk. 9:1–48 and Lk. 22:7–23:16 (see page 135). Here Luke selectively includes an account of Jesus reminding the disciples of when he sent them out on their mission (9:1–6; 22:35–38). Incidental correspondence also accounts for striking parallels in sets that are improbably intentional.

Similarity of theme, subject matter and historical events may produce this along with the frequent recurrence of general themes. Complex literature will always suggest connections that may be drawn by the reader (perhaps forced) yet were unintended by the author. Another cause of incidental correspondence is the consistency of Luke's wording and manner of relating stories. Even the uniform aspects of Jesus' ministry style and the natural repetition inherent in life would predispose occasional parallels. Correspondence between source material of different provenance often reflects this. An example of parallelism that might be due simply to repetition in the ministry of Jesus is parallel 10 between Lk. 10:21–13:30 and Lk. 14:1–18:30 (see page 150). "Parables of the Kingdom of God are concluded by the theme of the exclusion of privileged ones from the Messianic banquet and the inclusion of the disadvantaged." No doubt, this was a common subject in Jesus' preaching. Accordingly, that certain striking parallels would exist within correspondence sets that prove improbable is not surprising.

We have provided explanations for how incidental and intentional correspondences might be formed in Talbert's correspondence sets that are not probably intentional. Yet the majority of his sets are at least of reasonable probability in terms of authorial intent. An evaluation of the significance he attributes to Luke's use of these structures is therefore in order.

Talbert believes that Luke as a Gentile understood Jesus and the apostles through a Gentile frame of reference, that of the wandering philosopher. He interprets his correspondences in this vein.

> In the context of the Lucan appropriation of the Hellenistic image of the philosopher who as a wandering preacher taught a way of life to his pupils by example even more than by precept and often had the truth of his tradition guaranteed by a succession list, the patterns seem to serve more than merely aesthetic ends. We find in Luke-Acts an architectural pattern of correspondences between the career of Jesus and the life of the apostolic church. We know that in the Lucan milieu that stream of thought which furnished him his controlling image for thinking about Jesus and the disciples emphasized the value and necessity of choosing a master who embodied his teachings and making him one's pattern to imitate. We find that the Evangelist definitely wanted to portray the deeds and teachings of Jesus as the pattern for the acts and instructions of the apostolic church. It is, therefore, nearly impossible to avoid the conclusion that these correspondences between Jesus and the church serve the same *imitatio magistri* motif. In terms of the philosophic image, Jesus is the master who is the source of the Christian way of life. The apostolic church is composed of his pupils who have truly learned his way inasmuch as their

subordination to him as teacher results in a unity of life and doctrine.[245]

However, has Talbert succeeded in proving such architecture that incorporates both Luke and Acts? He represents all his correspondence sets in graphical form, reproduced below:[246]

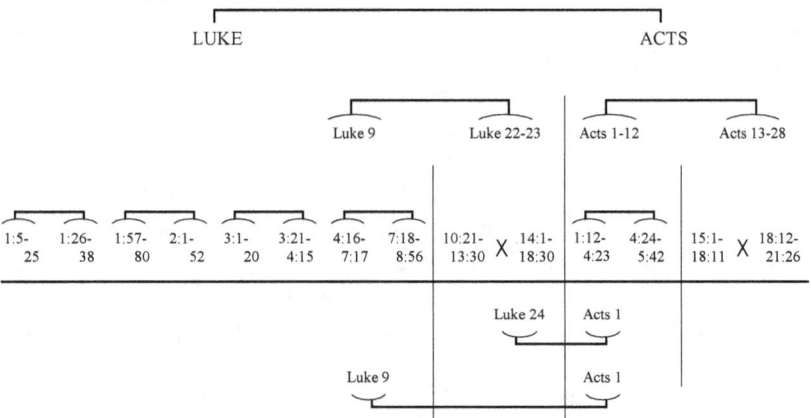

Each horizontal line that connects two texts indicates patterned parallelism between those texts. Therefore, the top line, LUKE ACTS, represents Talbert's patterned parallelism between the whole of Luke and the whole of Acts. Luke 9 Luke 22–23 represents his patterned parallelism between those two texts. When only those correspondence sets that performed well under the tests for intentionality are included in the above chart, and our four-fold parallel structure of Luke 4:14–24:53 is added (this structure will be presented later), the result is as follows:

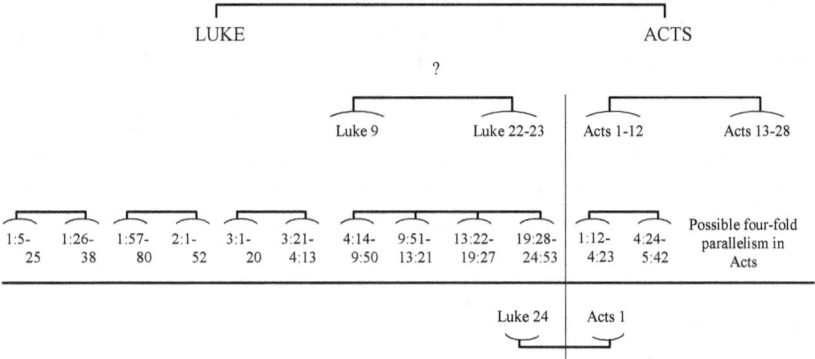

---

245 Talbert, *Literary Patterns*, 98–99.
246 Talbert, *Literary Patterns*, 63.

The top line, LUKE——ACTS, has been kept even though Talbert's pattern of correspondences between the whole of Luke and the whole of Acts performed poorly under the tests (see pages 90–103). This is because a sufficient number of correspondences in this pattern were strong enough to stand as individual parallels linking the two works. Notice that apart from the parallelism between Luke 24 and Acts 1, there are no clearly intentional patterns that span the two books. This weakens Talbert's contention that the patterns "contribute to the overall Lucan appropriation of the Hellenistic image of the philosopher in order to describe the relationships between Jesus and his disciples and between various Christian leaders".[247]

His argument is supported, however, that the parallelism between John the Baptist and Jesus in Luke 1:1–4:15 fosters the themes of Jesus' superiority to his forerunner and the unity between the two. His view that this unity also intentionally communicates a unity of *Heilsgeschichte* from the birth of John onward, contra Conzelmann's more radical disjunction, is likewise sustained.[248] The tests for intentionality encourage confidence in these particular patterns.

According to Talbert, one prominent theological emphasis in the parallelism between Lk. 24 and Acts 1 is the corporeality of the resurrection-exaltation and ascension of Jesus.[249] In both passages, proofs of the physical nature of the events abound. He considers the theme intentional due to the intentionality of the parallelism. Yet corporeality is merely one of many common themes, and to posit a "docetic tendency"[250] based on one emphasis is probably unjustified. His foundation, this intentional parallelism, however, makes the argument at least worthy of careful evaluation. A second prominent theological emphasis derived from this correspondence set is "the continuity between the one who ascends and the one who suffered, died, and was raised".[251] No one would dispute this conclusion if intent behind the parallelism were admitted.

Talbert attempts to further this concept of continuity by appeal to his observed parallelism between Luke 9 and Acts 1.

> This Lucan connection between Jesus' journey to Jerusalem and his ascension means that for the Third Evangelist the journey is the first part of that ascent to heaven which he calls Jesus' ἀνάλημψις [9:51]. To regard the journey as the first stage of the ascension means that in Luke the death

---

247 Talbert, *Literary Patterns*, 99.
248 Talbert, *Literary Patterns*, 103–107.
249 Talbert, *Literary Patterns*, 112–114.
250 Talbert, *Literary Patterns*, 114.
251 Talbert, *Literary Patterns*, 114.

and resurrection of Jesus are viewed in an ascension framework.[252]

The tests for intentionality do not support this correspondence set as a whole; but certainly on the strength of the allusion to the ascension in Lk. 9:51 alone a similar conclusion may be drawn. Without the weight of the full set, however, it is difficult to perceive the journey as the "first part" of the ascension.

Finally, Talbert attempts to establish a parallel between Luke-Acts and Diogenes Laertius' *Lives of Eminent Philosophers* in terms of form and content, and therefore genre.[253] The validity of the parallelism of form is our primary concern, especially as it relates to Lukan correspondences. Basically, the structure of Laertius' Lives is "(a) life of the founder + (b) narrative about disciples and successors + (c) summary of the doctrine of the school".[254] Talbert notes that Luke-Acts contains only two of these, (a) + (b), and demonstrates that this was the case for most of Laertius' sources.[255] He further shows that this two-part structure was common in contemporary and precedent biographies of philosophers, but is not found in relevant Christian and OT literature, which therefore implies literary dependence of Luke on these biographies.[256] The role of the Lukan correspondence patterns in this context is actually only to demonstrate that Luke and Acts comprise a single work.

The tests for intentionality seriously question one of the two correspondence sets that Talbert proposes between the two books, that of Luke 9 with Acts 1, but the parallel between the transfiguration and ascension accounts in this set of three parallels appear intentional. Effectively, the glue that he believes binds the books together is a little less cohesive than assumed. Nevertheless, the introductory verses of Acts establish an important connection. In addition to the proposed joint structure between the Lukan books, Talbert depends heavily on similarity of content between Luke-Acts and the "lives of eminent philosophers," which is crucial to his case because it is doubtful that his correspondences themselves conclusively demonstrate Luke-Acts to be of that genre.

What Talbert has accomplished is the drawing of attention to the highly artistic nature of the Third Gospel's structure and to the theological underpinnings of that structure. He justifiably probes into theology and genre, and observes many intriguing phenomena. The richness of these findings is evident throughout the above analysis of his work. He has

---

252 Talbert, *Literary Patterns*, 115.
253 Talbert, *Literary Patterns*, 125–136.
254 Talbert, *Literary Patterns*, 127.
255 Talbert, *Literary Patterns*, 131.
256 Talbert, *Literary Patterns*, 133–134.

demonstrated conclusively that Luke composed his Gospel using detailed individual and structured parallels.

CHAPTER 3

Analysis of Ancient Literature Relevant to the Structure of Luke

1 Examples of Literature Preceding and Contemporary with Luke and Bearing Similar Structure

Massive amounts of precedent and contemporary literature to Luke exhibit detailed repetitive structures, both in part and covering the whole text. Nils Lund, earlier this century, devoted an entire book to the study of chiasmus in the New Testament alone.[1] Our concern is not with chiasmus, however, but with "regular parallelism": A B C A´ B´ C´. This is the nature of our structural proposal presented and described in the introduction and developed in detail in the next chapter (see page 206). Representative instances from Old Testament, Greco-Roman and New Testament literature will demonstrate that this particular structure was well known and used. Since our proposed cyclical structure for Luke spans many episodes, only examples covering several events (or episodes) in the text will be studied. As a background for an evaluation of our proposal, the types of parallels drawn in the precedent works will be examined, whether between words, themes, actions, characters, or any other concept. Importantly, each of the patterns below will be evaluated to determine its similarity to Luke.

The entirety of the Gospel of Luke concerns one character, Jesus. If our proposed structure is correct, then the cyclical parallelism occurs entirely within the account of this one character. This is different from the repetition of a pattern between separate, parallel characters. In our analysis, therefore, we will observe which of these two types of parallelism occurs.

Before concluding our discussion on precedent literature, however, it is useful to present a viable mechanism for Luke's adoption of a structure from literature with which he was familiar. Thomas L. Brodie has researched a pervasive ancient methodology, *imitatio* (or imitation), that accounts for remarkable and intentional similarity of content and structure between works of different authors. This mechanism adequately explains Luke's apparent dependence on Mark and accounts for our proposed

---

1 Lund, *Chiasmus*.

cyclical parallel structure. Brodie's work will be treated at the end of this chapter.

1.1 Old Testament Precedent Structures

Old Testament literature is a vitally important background to Lukan composition and probably the most influential precedent. His Gospel is steeped in Old Testament terminology, formulae, style and allusions. In the first three chapters, one gets the impression that Luke's target audience was supposed to feel like they were reading Scripture (the OT for them). We have already noted in the analysis of Tannehill's contributions that the Evangelist employs the structured Old Testament "annunciation genre" in Luke 1. No doubt he had a sound grasp of his Scriptures and probably a greater sensitivity to their structure than modern readers did.[2] Based on the analysis of OT citations in Luke, T. Holtz believes that the Evangelist probably only knew the Minor Prophets, Isaiah and the Psalms (of the LXX),[3] but this is correctly disputed by Bock and Kimball.[4] All or most of the OT books were probably available to Luke as literary models. Below is a representative sample of OT texts that are based on regular parallelism.

1.1.1 ELIJAH-ELISHA CYCLES

Robert L. Cohn delineates the three-fold parallel cyclical structure of 1 Kings 17:1–19:21.[5] This is extremely important for our proposal of Lukan structure in the next chapter because demonstrably the Evangelist interacts significantly with this OT block and apparently produces a structure of the identical type, multifold cyclical parallelism.[6]

---

2 Talbert develops this idea at several points in his book, *Literary Patterns*. See, for example, chapter 5, especially pp. 79–81.
3 T. Holtz, *Untersuchung über die altestamentlichen Zitate bei Lukas* (Berlin: Akademie Verlag, 1968) part 1.
4 Darrell L. Bock, *Proclamation from Prophecy and Pattern: Lucan Old Testament Christology*, JSNT Supplement Series 12 (Sheffield: Sheffield Academic Press, 1987) 14–8. Charles A. Kimball demonstrates Luke's possible awareness of a majority of the Old Testament, in *Jesus' Exposition of the Old Testament in Luke's Gospel* (JSNT Supplement Series 94, Sheffield: JSOT Press, 1984); but only probability is established, not certainty.
5 Robert L. Cohn, "The Literary Logic of 1 Kings 17–19," *JBL* 101 (1982) 333–350.
6 The table is from Cohn's "Literary Logic," 343. Burke O. Long, in his impressive study of literary form in 1 Kings, supports Cohn's analysis; *I Kings: With an Introduction to Historical Literature*, vol. 9 of *The Forms of the Old Testament Literature* (Grand Rapids: Eerdmans, 1984) 176–177.

A. Announcement
    by Elijah (17:1)   by God (18:1)   by Jezebel (19:2)

B. Journey [by Elijah]
    from Israel (17:2–5)   to Israel (18:2)   from Israel (19:3–4)

C. Two encounters
    ravens (17:6–7)   Obadiah (18:7–16)   an angel (19:5–6)
    widow (17:8–16)   Ahab (18:17–20)   the angel of the Lord (19:7)

D. Miracle
    resuscitation (17:17–23) fire (18:21–38)   theophany (19:9–18)

E. Conversion
    widow (17:24)   Israel (18:39–40)   Elisha (19:19–21)
                           Ahab (18:41–19:1)

Cohn explains the chart thus:

> Each act in the narrative begins with an announcement (A) which initiates the action and, thereby, precipitates a crisis. The announcement propels Elijah to a new locale (B). In the new setting he has two successive encounters or confrontations (C). The second encounter results in a challenge which requires Yahweh's intervention to resolve (D). Finally, in response to this intervention, individuals are "converted" and declare or exhibit their loyalty to Yahweh (E).[7]

He further explains that there are occasional key words and themes across the three cycles that bind parallel sections together. Additionally, in the "miracle" stratum there is a sequence of elements repeated in all three panels. Each miracle also occurs in a high place. He demonstrates in this stratum in fact that a theme peculiar to that stratum can be developed linearly through the text. In this case, "The intervention of Yahweh becomes progressively more direct."[8] The above structure is formed through parallelism of action, literary form/genre, theme, words, and narrative setting. Note that it is also historical-biographical narrative, as is the Third Gospel. Although the actual history behind 1 Kings 17:1–19:21 forms the basis for its structure, authorial selectivity best accounts for the identical sequence from cycle to cycle. Interestingly, the sequence of several episodes repeated in each cycle here has a subtle logic, as we will also note in our proposal for Lukan structure. All three cycles occur within the account of one character, Elijah. In sum, the essential similarities between the Elijah-Elisha cycles and Luke's apparent cyclical structure are striking.

---

7 Cohn, "Literary Logic," 344.
8 Cohn, "Literary Logic," 346–347.

1.1.2 1 SAMUEL 9–31

Regular parallelism exists within 1 Samuel, covering the life of one character, Saul. The structure is of the same type as the Elijah-Elisha cycle above, multifold cyclical parallelism. The structure is delineated by W. Lee Humphreys:[9]

Introduction: Saul as a man of heroic potential (1 Sam 9:1–2).

> Part I: Saul becomes king over Israel (1 Sam 9–14).
>
>> A. The first encounter with Samuel: announcement of future greatness (1 Sam 9:3–10:16).
>>
>> B. The first constructive phase of his kingship: public acknowledgment and initial success (1 Sam 10:17–11:15).
>>
>> C. The first destructive phase: hints of disintegration (1 Sam 13–14).
>
> Part II: The disintegration of Saul and his kingship (1 Sam 15–27).
>
>> A. The second encounter with Samuel: announcement of divine rejection (1 Sam 15:1–16:13).
>>
>> B. The second constructive phase: David enters Saul's court and fights his wars (1 Sam 16:14–19:10).
>>
>> C. The second destructive phase: Saul's disintegration (1 Sam 19:11–28:2).
>
> Finale: The last days of king Saul (1 Sam 28–31).
>
>> A. The third encounter with Samuel: announcement of defeat and death (1 Sam 28:3–25).
>>
>> B. A merging of destructive and constructive phases: the death and burial of Saul (1 Sam 29–31 and especially ch. 31).

The constructive phase is where "Saul realizes some success," and "in each destructive phase what is gained in the preceding constructive phase is undone".[10] Here a sequence of features is repeated within the historical-biographical account of the one character. These features include encounters with a character, literary form, and thematic trends in the plot. Saul's life no doubt followed the ups and downs indicated by this structure, which

---

9 W. Lee Humphreys, "The Tragedy of King Saul: A Study of the Structure of 1 Samuel 9–31," *JSOT* 6 (1978) 18–19.

10 Humphreys, "Tragedy," 19 and 20 respectively.

suggests the parallelism may be coincidental. However, the constructive-destructive sequence evident in his life is probably the very point of the author. A portrayal that lends itself to such a well-defined analysis probably reflects the author's conscious evaluation of the character's life along the lines of the analysis.

1.1.3 2 SAMUEL 11–20

Shimon Bar-Efrat reveals the parallel narrative structure of 2 Samuel 11–20 constructed from accounts involving David, Amnon, Absalom and Adonijah.[11] As above, it is multifold cyclical parallelism. He observes

---

[11] I propose that there is further use of cyclical parallelism between the Old Testament historical-biographical narratives of 1 Samuel, 2 Samuel and 1 Kings, namely between the Samuel/Saul, David and Solomon cycles.

1 SAMUEL 3–14	2 SAMUEL 2–18	1 KINGS 1–14
3 Call of Samuel	2–5 David becomes king and takes Jerusalem.	1b–4 Solomon made king by David and reign described as wise.
4–6(7) Matters of the Ark	6 Matters of the Ark	5–8 Matters of the Ark and Temple
8 Israel asks for king and God responds.	7 God promises eternal Davidic throne.	9a God's promise to Solomon regarding Davidic throne
9–10 Saul made king.		
11 Consolidation of kingdom	8–10 Consolidation of kingdom	9b–10 Consolidation of kingdom
12 Samuel's farewell		
13 Samuel rebukes Saul and punishment decreed by God on household.	11–12 Nathan rebukes David and punishment decreed by God on household.	11a Solomon sins and punishment decreed by God on household.
14 Events involving Saul's son = punishment	13(–18) Events involving David's sons = punishment	11b–12a Events involving Solomon's son = punishment

Deeper analysis would reveal the extent of the material's conformity to the proposed pattern, but this is beyond the scope of this work.

It is uncertain that Luke would necessarily have noticed these correspondences; but given the greater sensitivity of readers in his day to such pattern, it is entirely possible. Regardless, the existence of this parallelism further establishes the avail-

...that the thematic structure of the narratives is analogous: as with David, so with Amnon and Absalom (and also, to some extent, with Adonijah) sexual transgression gives rise to murder.

David	+ Bathsheba	→The killing of Uriah
Amnon	+ Tamar	→The killing of Amnon
Absalom	+ David's concubines	→The killing of Absalom
(Adonijah	+ Abishag)	→The killing of Adonijah

This analogous structure reflects the view embodied in these narratives and operating as a unifying factor: David is forced to see how the same vices of lust and violence to which he succumbed reemerge in his sons, causing disaster and great suffering. Thus, the principle of measure for measure, or rather, son's measure for father's measure, operates here. David's sons follow in his footsteps, but the punishment imposed on them is presented as being simultaneously their father's.[12]

Here parallelism is created through characters, actions and themes. One or two brief interludes are allowed. This example demonstrates the effective use of multifold cyclical parallelism in historical-biographical narrative probably familiar to and highly respected by Luke. Through reading this text, he may have sensed the value of such a technique. At the very least, it confirms the use of such structures in the Old Testament.

Bar-Efrat's structure appears at first glance to reflect simply major events in the lives of the main characters rather than to communicate a message. He is probably correct however about the author's interest in the measure for measure principle. It is strongly conveyed by the causal relationship presented between sexual transgression and murder. Here the parallelism is between several characters.

1.1.4 2 CHRONICLES 14–35

Less substantial, but nevertheless helpful, is the formulaic structure of the historical-biographical narrative in 2 Chronicles 14–35.

---

ability of the technique to Luke. Here parallelism is between actions, themes, literary forms and characters. Several characters are involved in the parallelism.

12 Shimon Bar-Efrat, *Narrative Art in the Bible*, JSOTSS 70 (Sheffield: Almond Press, 1989) 137.

Asa	Purified the **temple** (ch. 15)
	"did what was…**right** in the eyes of the Lord"
Jehosaphat	"did what was **right** in the eyes of the Lord"
Jehoram	"did *evil* in the eyes of the Lord"
Ahaziah	"did *evil* in the eyes of the Lord"
Joash	Restored the **temple** (ch. 24)
	"did what was **right** in the eyes of the Lord"
Amaziah	"did what was **right** in the eyes of the Lord"
Uzziah	"did what was **right** in the eyes of the Lord"
Jotham	"did what was **right** in the eyes of the Lord"
Ahaz	"did *not* do what was right in the eyes of the Lord"
Hezekiah	Repaired and restored the **temple** (chs. 29–31)
	"did what was **right** in the eyes of the Lord"
Manasseh	"did *evil* in the eyes of the Lord"
Amon	"did *evil* in the eyes of the Lord"
Josiah	Repaired and purified the **temple** (chs. 34–35)
	"did what was **right** in the eyes of the Lord"
Jehoahaz	(No evaluation is given, probably because his reign lasted only three months.)
Jehoiakim	"did *evil* in the eyes of the Lord"
Jehoiakin	"did *evil* in the eyes of the Lord"
Zedekiah	"did *evil* in the eyes of the Lord"

The depiction of the life of most kings also follows a typical pattern, a "regnal resumé". Simon De Vries describes the typical resumé very similarly to the following observation:[13]

1. "[The king] was…years old when he became king, and he reigned…years in Jerusalem."

2. Mother's name

3. Whether he did right or evil in the eyes of the Lord

4. Biography justifying the evaluation

5. Death and burial

---

[13] See the various instances of the "regnal resumé" genre identified throughout 1 and 2 Chronicles by Simon J. De Vries in *1 and 2 Chronicles*, vol. xi of *The Forms of the Old Testament Literature* (Grand Rapids: Eerdmans, 1989).

Therefore, there is parallelism of wording, form, characters, theme, action and setting. Our proposal for Luke does not evidence anything like the obvious formulaic framework of this text. 2 Chronicles only demonstrates the availability of regular parallelism for the composition of historical-biographical narrative.

Certainly, the history of Israel's kings followed the moral pattern elucidated in 2 Chronicles. The formulaic presentation of this pattern however indicates the author's intent behind the structure. He was reflecting historical pattern through literary pattern for the sake of his message. Of course, many characters are involved in the parallelism.

1.1.5 JUDGES

The book of Judges is notable in terms of its structure. Bar-Efrat discloses the parallel pattern of the book. He writes,

> [Judges] is not simply a collection of narratives concerning the various judges, but has a considerable degree of unity and cohesion, primarily because of the outlook which characterizes it. This view, which is stated explicitly in chapter 2, maintains that the Israelites abandoned God and worshipped Baal; as punishment God sent them an enemy in the form of one of the neighboring nations; the Israelites cried to the Lord, who sent them a judge in order to save them from the enemy, and then all over again. The book of Judges is built so that the narratives about the various judges are embedded within this general scheme, illustrating and detailing the stage in the cycle of events at which the judge rescues the Israelites suffering under the enemy's yoke. The chronological system which governs the book of Judges, according to which the land was at peace for forty years (once for eighty years and once for twenty) after each great judge, also contributes to the book's unity.[14]

For clarity, these features, repeated for each judge, may be placed in point form:

1. "The Israelites abandoned God and worshipped Baal"

2. "God sent them an enemy in the form of one of the neighboring nations"

3. "the Israelites cried to the Lord"

4. "He sent them a judge in order to save them from the enemy"

5. "the land was at peace for forty years"

---

14 Bar-Efrat, *Narrative Art*, 139.

Parallels are formed using actions and themes. Although there are not as many parallels in this historical-biographical narrative as in our Lukan proposal, the pattern is central and is rigidly maintained. This regular parallelism would have been noticed by Luke if he had read Judges and would therefore have enhanced any predisposition he had toward the structure. No direct literary dependence is claimed, of course.

Just as the history of Israel's kings followed the moral pattern related in 2 Chronicles, so the spiritual history of Israel followed the pattern revealed in the book of Judges. As in 2 Chronicles, the exposition of this pattern through verbal repetition indicates the author's intent behind the structure. Historical pattern is reflected through literary pattern for the sake of the message. Parallelism is between many characters.

1.1.6 JOB

In terms of volume, Job is primarily poetry and only secondarily prose narrative. Still, the poetry is couched in a narrative setting. Due to the distance of genre from Luke, the value of Job as precedent literature must not be over emphasized. The narrative of the book however is highly structured. There is dual parallelism within the prologue, between the prologue and the epilogue, and within the epilogue. Throughout the body, there is three-fold cyclical parallelism. John Hartley and David Clines propose very similar parallelisms to the following suggestion.[15]

Prologue[16]			Epilogue (42:7–17)
1:6–8	2:1–3	Verbatim repetition of interaction between Satan and God about Job.	
1:9–12a	2:4–6	God puts Job in Satan's hands. Much verbatim repetition.	
1:12b–22		Loss of oxen, donkeys, sheep, camels, and sons and daughters. Job did not sin.	The Lord restores Job's oxen, donkeys, sheep, and camels, and gives him sons and daughters
	2:7–10	Loss of health. Job did not sin.	

---

15 John E. Hartley, *The Book of Job* (Grand Rapids: Eerdmans, 1988) 36–9; and David J.A. Clines, *Job 1–20*, Word Biblical Commentary 17 (Dallas: Word Books, 1989) xxxvi–xxxvii.

16 For a similar treatment of the prologue see Hartley, *Job*, 36.

Discourses[17]

3	12–14	21	Job's speeches
4–5	15	22	Eliphaz's speeches
6–7	16–17	23–24	Job again
8	18	25	Bildad's speeches
9–10	19	26–31	Job again
11	20	32–37*	Zophar's speeches (*Elihu's speech)

Final Cycle[18]

38–39	40b–41	the Lord
40:1–5	42:1–6	Job

There is also a degree of parallelism of content and structure between the corresponding speeches of each cycle.[19] In Job, there is parallelism of theme, action, literary form, character, words and setting.

As with our proposal for the structure of Luke, the cyclical parallelism of Job is largely a literary construction with some degree of apparent historical foundation. The prologue exhibits parallelism between panels with a sequence of several events, as we find in Luke. This parallelism centers on Job, but heavily involves other characters.

1.1.7 DANIEL

Daniel is also shaped by cyclical parallelism. As with Job, it is different in genre from Luke; but it has many characteristics of an historical record. In this sense, a comparison is useful.[20]

2:1–18 Nebuch.	4:1–18 Nebuch.	5:1–12 Belshaz.	Matter arises that requires interpretation.
2:19–49	4:19–27	5:13–29	God provides Daniel with the interpretation.
3	4:28–37	5:30–31	Dream/writing fulfilled (at least partially); Nebuch. repents then praises God.

---

17 For a similar demarcation of cycles, see Clines, *Job 1–20*, xxxvi–xxxvii.
18 See Hartley again for a similar treatment of this section, *Job*, 37.
19 See Hartley, *Job*, 38–39.
20 Gleason L. Archer's analysis of the book reflects this pattern to a degree, especially as he understands chapter 3 to be directly related to and a consequence of the dream in chapter 2. See *Daniel*, Expositor's Bible Commentary 7 (Grand Rapids: Zondervan, 1985) 29, 50.

Analysis of Ancient Literature 173

The Darius section is similar to the Nebuchadnezzar sections:

6:1–15   King creates circumstance for Daniel's involvement.
6:16–24 God acts on behalf of Daniel.
6:25–28 Darius praises God.

The book of Daniel is structured in part on parallelism of theme and action in the portion most resembling historical-biographical narrative. Obviously, Luke would not have based his structure on Daniel, but the concept of such structure is provided for him.

The events behind Daniel clearly exert some control over its repetitive structure; but certainly one of the intended points of the book, emphasized by the pattern, is God's sovereignty. God cryptically reveals what will take place. Only a person of God is capable of interpreting the revelation. What was revealed occurs. Apparently, the author recognized the pattern of events in history with its theological import and reflected this literarily through selective inclusion of only the relevant events.

Talbert notes parallelism in several other Old Testament texts.[21] Beyond these, additional instances of regular parallelism could be produced, but the above suffice to demonstrate an exceptionally strong precedent for Luke to employ cyclical parallelism in his Gospel. His clear effort to make his work sound "scriptural" favors the possibility that he also borrowed from Old Testament structural principles.

1.2 Similar Structure in New Testament Writings

Although regular parallelism in the Old Testament is more likely to have impacted Luke than any in the New Testament, instances in the latter would suggest that the concept was readily available to him. It is apparent that he was acquainted with at least a majority of the LXX,[22] but apart from Mark, there is little certainty of which New Testament texts he knew. Acts, obviously, is a special case. If such parallelism is identifiable there, then parallel structure in Luke would not be surprising.

1.2.1 JOHN 2:1–12:50

Although many commentators note the extreme importance of signs in this Gospel, as Beasley-Murray points out,[23] rarely is an outline produced that

---

21 Talbert, *Literary Patterns*, 70–73.
22 See our discussion and footnote regarding Luke's knowledge of the OT above on page 164.
23 George R. Beasley-Murray, *John*, Word Biblical Commentary 36 (Waco, Texas: Word Books, 1987) xc.

takes suitable account of them. Leon Morris' structure primarily divides the book according to signs and discourses, but is not thoroughly consistent with the structural location of the signs.[24] This is understandable if a consistent pattern involving them is not recognized. Beasley-Murray, however, develops his outline for John 2:1–12:50 with most sections initiated by one or two signs. The repetitive portion is reproduced below (bold type mine):[25]

II. 1:19–12:50   THE PUBLIC MINISTRY OF JESUS

    A. 1:19–51:   *Testimonies to Jesus*
                          The Witness of John the Baptist and the Early Disciples.

    B. 2:1–4:42:   *The Revelation of the New Order in Jesus*
                          Two Signs exhibiting the new order, the water into wine and the cleansing of the temple (chap. 2); the Nicodemus **discourse** answering to the former (chap. 3); the Samaritan **discourse** answering to the latter (chap. 4).

    C. 4:43–5:47:   *Jesus the Mediator of Life and Judgment*
                          Two signs, the healing of the officer's son and the paralytic at Bethesda, with **discourse** elucidating their significance in relation to Jesus' eschatological task.

    D. 6:1–71:   *Jesus the Bread of Life*
                          Two signs, the feeding of the multitude and Jesus' walking on the water, with a **discourse** expounding their significance and revealing Jesus as the fulfillment of the Passover feast.

    E. 7:1–8:59:   *Jesus the Water and Light of Life*
                          Jesus as the fulfillment of the Feast of Tabernacles; the conflict between the representatives of God and the world.

---

24 Leon Morris, *The Gospel According to John*, New International Commentary on the New Testament (London: Marshall, Morgan & Scott, 1971) 65–69.
25 For this outline, see Beasley-Murray, *John*, xci–xcii.

F. 9:1–10:42:   *Jesus the Light and Shepherd of Humankind*
                  The **sign** of the healing of the man born blind, the **discourse** of the Good Shepherd, and Jesus as the fulfillment of the feast of the Dedication of the Temple.

G. 11:1–54:   *Jesus the Resurrection and the Life*
                  The **sign** of the healing of Lazarus and the plot of the high priests against Jesus.

H. 11:55–12:50:   *Jesus the King, Triumphant through Death*
                  Two significant acts, the anointing of Jesus and his entry into Jerusalem, with a **discourse** on his glorification and epilogue to his ministry.

This is indeed a useful approach, but some modifications are possible to reflect more closely John's intent. Notice that John does not consider the cleansing of the temple (Jn. 2:12–25) a "sign" because he designates the healing of the official's son the *second* sign (Jn. 4:54). John employs the term σημεῖον purposefully, such that particular acts narrated in the text are identified as signs at 2:11; 4:54; 6:14; 9:16; 11:47 and 12:18. Accordingly, the Johannine signs would be the changing of the water to wine (2:1–11), the healing of the official's son (4:43–54), the feeding of the five thousand (6:1–15), the healing of the man born blind (9:1–34), and the raising of Lazarus (11:1–44). In each case where Beasley-Murray has indicated "two signs," it is best to view it as one sign with the second event performing a different function. Actually, each second act in his scheme leads to people's disapproval of Jesus, and this may well have been John's intent. This can be taken further. Such an act follows each Johannine sign. The cleansing of the temple clearly results in disapproval (2:18–25). Jewish persecution in 5:16–30 is spurred by the Sabbath healing at the pool (see 5:16). After crossing the lake on foot, the crowds sought Jesus, and when found he drove many of them away with hard teaching on his body and blood (6:25–71) – the feast scene, which follows immediately, is also characterized by conflict with the Jews (7:1–52). Jesus' declaration of his identity and mission to the healed blind man instigates opposition from the Pharisees (9:35–10:21; also, 9:13–34 describes conflict between the Pharisees and the blind man). Finally, the Pharisees' hatred of Jesus intensifies when they hear about the raising of Lazarus (11:45–57), and opposition continues through the anointing at Bethany (12:1–11).

When we bring another major theme of John into play, testimony, this accounts for nearly all of the remainder of the text. The Fourth Evangelist uses only two forms of the root μαρ, namely μαρτυρία and μαρτυρέω, in reference to witness about Jesus (within the "Book of Signs," 1:7; 3:11, 32, 33; 5: 31, 32, 34, 36; 8:13, 14; and 1:7, 8, 15, 32, 34; 3:11, 26, 32; 4:39; 5:31, 32, 33, 36, 37, 39; 8:13, 14, 18; 10:25; 12:17 respectively). If these references adequately represent their contexts – the contexts being 1:6–34; 3:1–4:42; 5:31–47; 8:12–59; 10:22–42; and 12:12–19 – then the following arrangement is confirmed (the letters in the left column are the same as Beasley-Murray's for comparison):

A.	1:6–51	Testimony – John the Baptist, (the first disciples)
B.	2:1–11	**Sign – water to wine**
	2:12–17	Act that leads to opposition – cleansing of the temple
	2:18–25	Opposition
	3:1–4:42	Testimony – Nicodemus, John the Baptist, Samaritan woman
C.	4:43–54	**Sign – healing of the official's son**
	5:1–15	Act that leads to opposition – healing at the pool
	5:16–30	Opposition
	5:31–47	Testimony – John the Baptist, the Father, the Scriptures
D+E.	6:1–15	**Sign – feeding of the five-thousand**
	6:16–24	Act that leads to opposition – walking on the water
	6:25–7:52	Opposition
	8:12–59	Testimony – self, the Father, Abraham
F.	9:1–12	**Sign** that leads to opposition – **healing of blind man**
	9:13–10:21	Opposition
	10:22–42	Testimony – miracles, John the Baptist
G.+H.	11:1–44	**Sign** that leads to opposition – **raising of Lazarus**
	11:45–12:11	Opposition
	12:12–19	Testimony – the great crowd

Whether one prefers Beasley-Murray's outline or the one just above, a reasonably consistent, though simple, repetitive pattern is evident. Of course, it may be simple enough to be a coincidental product of John's way of thinking, but his clustered uses of the terms "witness" and "sign" suggest probable intent.[26] Parallelism is formed through functions of pericopes, key words, type of narrative, motif, and possibly theme.

Although this structure is simpler than our proposal for Luke, it has many similarities. The most important for our present analysis is that it is probably not entirely determined by the order of historical events. John has developed a literary-historical pattern. In addition, parallelism is within the account of one lead character. Accordingly, Luke's apparent method has a close counterpart in John's.

1.2.2 MATTHEW

Davies and Allison support the basic structural proposal of B.W. Bacon for the five-part arrangement of material in the First Gospel; but they rightly reject his belief that it was based on the Pentateuch, since there is insufficient thematic contact with these books. The authors present Bacon's pattern as below.[27]

Preamble or Prologue:
1–2: The birth narrative

Book I: (a) 3.1–4:25: Narrative material

(b) 5.1–7:27: [Discourse] The sermon on the mount

Formula: 7.28–9: '*And when Jesus finished these sayings*, the crowds were astonished at his teaching, for he taught them as one who had authority, and not as their scribes'.

Book II: (a) 8.1–9.35: Narrative material

(b) 9.36–10.42: Discourse on mission and martyrdom

Formula: 11.1: '*And when he had finished instructing his twelve disciples*...'.

---

26 If correct, this pattern argues against some proposals of later church redaction, perhaps by a Johannine school, such as by Siegfried Schulz's in *Das Evangelium nach Johannes*, Neue Testament Deutsch, Band 4 (Göttingen: Vandenhoeck & Ruprecht, 1983) 9–10. A repetitive pattern is more easily formed by the original author than by a later redactor who merely reorders pericopes in the text.

27 W.D. Davies and Dale C. Allison, Jr., *A Critical and Exegetical Commentary on the Gospel According to Saint Matthew*, ICC 1 (Edinburgh: T. & T. Clark, 1988) 59, 61. D.A. Carson holds to an almost identical basic arrangement in *Matthew*, Expositor's Bible Commentary 8 (Grand Rapids: Zondervan, 1984) 50–57. Nevertheless, Davies and Allison later present their own structure incorporating Bacon's arrangement but based on parallel triads between the five "books," 68–9. The scheme occasionally appears contrived.

Book III: (a) 11.2–12.50: Narrative and debate material

(b) 13.1–52: [Discourse-] Teaching on the kingdom of Heaven

Formula: 13.53: '*And when Jesus had finished these parables…*'.

Book IV: (a) 13.54–17.21: Narrative and debate material

(b) 17.22–18.35: Discourse on church administration

Formula: 19.1: '*Now when Jesus had finished these sayings…*'.

Book V: (a) 19.2–22.46: Narrative and debate material

(b) 23.1–25.46: Discourse on eschatology: farewell address

Formula: 26.1: '*When Jesus finished all these sayings*, he said to his disciples…'.

Epilogue: 26.3–28.20: From the last supper to the resurrection

Gundry cautions against any detailed structural proposals, doubting Matthew employed one.[28] Yet, the above outline sufficiently lacks detail that it avoids this warning. It is also founded on demonstrable features. Of course, the parallelism is not as detailed as in our proposal for Luke, but it is a small conceptual step between a simple regular parallelism and a detailed one. Few doubt Matthean intent behind the pattern, though the structural significance of it is sometimes debated.[29] It is founded merely on three features: narrative material, discourses and formulae.[30] Furthermore, the repetitive pattern covers the account of just one character, Jesus.

---

28 R.H. Gundry, *Matthew: A Commentary on His Literary and Theological Art* (Grand Rapids: Eerdmans, 1982) 10.

29 For example, David R. Bauer believes the five discourses are not used by Matthew in a way that indicates structure. He advocates three major sections (1:1–4:16; 4:17–16:20; 16:21–28:20) into which the five discourses are smoothly integrated. His demotion of the discourses from essential features of structure seems motivated by a desire to clear the way for his own proposal, which in itself is not convincing since he has not adequately demonstrated that ancient writers structured texts in the manner he suggests for Matthew. See *Structure of Matthew's Gospel*.

30 J. Smit Sibinga, in an analysis of Matthew's use of syllables, finds systematic numerical groupings. See "Eine literarische Technik im Mattäusevangelium," in M. Didier (ed.), *L'Évangile selon Matthieu: Rédaction et théologie*, Bibliotheca Ephemeridum Theologicarum Lovaniensium XXIX (Gembloux: J. Ducelot, 1972) 99–105. If correct, then the Evangelist's concern for detailed structure is greater than most scholars recognize. Sibinga's study, however, lacks sufficient presentation of data to be conclusive.

Luke's apparent structure is far more detailed in its parallelism than is Matthew's, but they have an important similarity. We mentioned earlier that the proposed pattern for the Third Gospel is primarily literary. Matthew's alternation of narrative and discourse regularly punctuated by a formula is entirely literary. In this sense, Matthew is a significant counterpart to the proposal for Luke.

1.2.3 ACTS

There is good reason to believe, as most scholars do, that Acts follows Luke as, in some sense, the second volume. Whether the two constitute one continuous work of a single genre, or are of separate genres combined for cumulative effect, has not been proven decisively. Clearly, however, the author had the former book in mind when he composed the latter (Acts 1:1). If he had arranged the Gospel material in a parallel fashion, then we might expect the same for Acts. Similarly, if Acts exhibits an overall repetitive regular parallelism, then our confidence in the cyclical structure of Luke may be emboldened. On careful analysis, a repetitive pattern does indeed emerge, as follows.[31]

---

31 M.D. Goulder observed a fourfold structure in Acts that he no longer holds. Its weakness included frequent violations of sequence, selection of four passages per theme from several in Acts that fit, and significant lack of contiguity within the structure. See *Type and History in Acts* (London: SPCK, 1964) 65–97.

Spread of gospel, and God's selection of Matthias for mission (see final stratum)
1:4–8 and 1:9–26

Contention caused by remarkable activity of the Spirit through people filled (πίμπλημι) with the Spirit
2:1–13   6:8–7:1   13:4–12   [19:23–41]

Lengthy sermon that culminates with Christ as fulfillment of prophecy
2:14–40   7:2–53   13:13–41   [20:17–35]

Immediate response to the sermon
2:41 (positive) 7:54–8:1a (negative) 13:42–48 (mixed) [20:36–38]

Summary of broader aftermath to sermon, with emphasis on spread of the gospel
2:42–47   8:1b–4   13:49–52

Summary indicating that miracles provide occasion for and validate witness
(2:42–47)   8:5–8 (summary)   14:1–7 (summary)

Events that exemplify the above parallel
3:1–26	cripple	8:9–25 Simon	14:8–20 cripple
		8:26–40 eunuch	14:21–28 effective
		9:1–31 Saul	ministry during
		9:32–43 Aeneas +	Paul's return to
		Tabitha	Antioch
		10:1–48 Cornelius	

Controversy relating to what precedes
4:1–22   11:1–3   15:1–5

Believers gather to resolve the controversy
4:23–31 request   11:4–18 God saves   15:6–35 Gentiles   [21:1–16]
power and boldness Gentiles   need not be
for witness   circumcised and be
                                           under Mosaic law

Mission in the light of the resolution
4:32–5:16 miraculous 11:19–30 Gentiles at 15:36–16:15 Broad
events and many   Antioch saved and   Gentile mission while
conversions   accepted by   delivering decision
                       Jerusalem; harmony

Official opposition followed by imprisonment, miraculous escape and a related outcome
5:17–6:6   12:1–23   16:16–40   [21:17–28:16]

Further mission in the light of the resolution
                                   17:1–19:19   [28:17–28]

Summary on spread of gospel, and God's selection of people for mission
6:7 ὁ λόγος τοῦ   12:24 Ὁ δὲ λόγος   19:20 τοῦ κυρίου ὁ   [28:30–31]
θεοῦ ηὔξανεν; and τοῦ θεοῦ ηὔξανεν;   λόγος ηὔξανεν; and
6:1–6   and 13:1–3   19:21–22

N.B. Regarding 19:23–28:31, parallels between Paul and Jesus (Luke's 4th cycle) dominate the 4th cycle of Acts, so it is certainly not rigidly parallel to the first three Acts cycles, hence the brackets around the references. Note the geographical progression across the cycles: cycle 1 takes place in Jerusalem; cycle 2 in Judea, Samaria and Syria; cycle 3 extends to Macedonia and Achaia; and cycle 4 extends to Rome.

One might wonder whether this structure is coincidental or is merely a product of Luke's subconscious logic. An application of the tests for intentionality favors conscious construction, however. Very briefly: (1) There is nearly perfect restriction of all features to their strata. (2) There are several elements that define most of the parallels. When these are delineated in greater detail than above, all parallels have several elements. (3) Three, perhaps four, panels are involved. (4) Each element of correspondence attracts attention. (5) The parallelism is completely constructive. (6) Redaction criticism is not possible with confidence. (7) All elements of correspondence are aspects of important Lukan themes. (8) Any historical predisposition to the pattern would still require a high degree of selectivity to achieve this result. Genre certainly does not come into play. (9) It is doubtful that the sequence is frequent enough elsewhere to be a common expression. (10) Contiguity is nearly perfect. (11) All but one or two tests clearly favor authorial intent. Statistically speaking, with a high degree of restriction and strong contiguity, a subconscious three/four-fold repetition of a sequence of at least eleven plot units is quite improbable. In conclusion, the similarity of this structure to that proposed for the Gospel is emphatic support for the Gospel structure, the two being the product of one mind.

A brief word about the summary statements in Acts is in order. Longenecker chooses to base the entire structure of the book on them, with each concluding its own panel (6:7; 9:31; 12:24; 16:5; 19:20; and 28:31).[32] On this foundation, he indicates a very basic regular parallelism of panel 1 to panel 4, panel 2 to panel 5, and panel 3 to panel 6. He also affirms Talbert's further correspondences between the two halves of Acts.[33] Such a pattern, if authorially intentional, would also support a similar structure in the Gospel, such as our proposal. Nevertheless, others consider the summary statements to be nonstructural.[34] The conclusion however must be based on the strength of the argument for any structure that utilizes the summary

---

32 R. Longenecker, *Acts*, 233–35. See also David Gooding, *True to the Faith: A Fresh Approach to the Acts of the Apostles* (London: Hodder & Stoughton, 1990) v.
33 Longenecker, *Acts*, 233–235.
34 See for example I. Howard Marshall, *The Acts of the Apostles: An Introduction and Commentary*, Tyndale New Testament Commentaries (Leicester: Inter-Varsity Press, 1980) 51–4; Bruce, *Acts of the Apostles*, viii–xv; and Gerhard A. Krodel, *Acts*, Augsburg Commentary on the New Testament (Minneapolis: Augsburg Publishing House, 1986) 47–49.

statements. Both Longenecker's and our proposals are convincing, but the latter is perhaps more defensible. Note that the summary statements at 9:31 and 16:5, employed by Longenecker, are of a different character to the others and they mark significantly lesser transitions in the narrative. Furthermore, there are additional summary statements akin in these respects to 9:31 and 16:5 (4:32–35; 5:12–16; 5:42) for which Longenecker does not account. Our proposal considers as structural only those that mark strong narrative transitions and that employ like terminology. Our proposal is also considerably more detailed, and therefore more falsifiable (and more defensible, if correct, using the eleven tests for intentionality).

Not surprisingly, our suggested structure of Acts is nearly as much a literary construction as that of our proposal for Luke. Both place historical episodes into a patterned literary framework that organizes them. Acts perhaps exhibits a closer adherence to the order of history than does the Gospel. This would be achieved by the Evangelist's selective exclusion of material that did not fit his structure for Acts rather than a rearrangement of episodes, as was occasionally his method with the Gospel.

1.2.4 REVELATION

The genre of Revelation is distant from the gospel of Luke, but may be tabled as evidence that multiple parallelism was known in Luke's era. An analysis of the structure of the Apocalypse of John is a complex task, as Richard Bauckham demonstrates in his discussion on the subject.[35] The formulaic parallel pattern underlying each of the letters to the seven churches in chapters two and three is universally recognized, however, and might suggest that there is a structure to the whole book. Beasley-Murray's treatment of the parallelism between the seals, trumpets and bowls is less comprehensive a structure and more conservative than some proposals.[36] He believes they are parallel in that "the three series of judgments...describe under different images a single short period of history, namely, the time of the end which precedes the coming of Christ's kingdom".[37] Interludes are allowed to fall within the first two series without

---

35 Richard Bauckham, *The Climax of Prophecy: Studies in the Book of Revelation* (Edinburgh: T. & T. Clark, 1993) 2–22.
36 For example, Leon Morris additionally highlights the seven-fold nature of the letters (chapters 2–3) and the seven "significant signs" (chapters 12–14) in his structure; *The Revelation of St. John*, Tyndale New Testament Commentaries (London: Tyndale Press, 1969) 43–44.
37 George R. Beasley-Murray, *The Book of Revelation*, New Century Bible Commentary (London: Marshall, Morgan & Scott, 1974) 31. J.P.M. Sweet holds a similar view, but understands the starting point of each successive series of judgments to be closer to the end; *Revelation* (Philadelphia: Westminster Press, 1979) 44.

invalidating the parallelism.[38] It is important to note that he does not draw parallels between the first judgments, the second judgments, and so on. Only the basic period of time and the terminus, the advent of Christ, are parallel. This structure is clearly from our proposal for Luke, but there is some value in its precedent. Beasley-Murray's scheme may be represented as follows:

		"The time of the end"							
6:1–8:5	Seven Seals	1	2	3	4	5	6	Interlude (ch. 7)	7	Advent
8:6–11:19	Seven Trumpets	1	2	3	4	5	6	Interlude (10:1–11:13)	7	Advent
12–14	Interlude									
15–16	Seven Bowl-Cups	1	2	3	4	5	6		7	Advent

Of course, the structure of the book is debated, but some sort of regular parallelism is usually espoused. As Beasley-Murray perceives it, the parallelism is formed through themes and imagery, and is not harmed by interludes. Multiple characters are involved in the parallelism.

Since the events of Revelation primarily depict the future from John's perspective, the evident structure is obviously not determined by history. It is in a significant sense, then, a literary construction.

1.2.5 1 JOHN

Although I. Howard Marshall is probably correct in his conclusion regarding the various outlines proposed for this letter, that "it seems preferable to regard the Epistle as being composed of a series of connected paragraphs whose relation to one another is governed by association of ideas rather than by a logical plan,"[39] many scholars have discerned regular parallelism. There is indeed a lack of consensus among scholars over the book's structure, which is caused by the severely restricted and frequently repeated number of themes in the text. Accordingly, we will only tentatively offer as an example one of the parallel structures proposed, that of Stephen Smalley.[40]

---

38 Beasley-Murray, *Revelation*, 31–32.
39 I. Howard Marshall, *The Epistles of John* (Grand Rapids: Eerdmans, 1978) 26.
40 Stephen Smalley, *1, 2, 3 John*, Word Biblical Commentary 51 (Waco, Texas: Word Books, 1984) xxxiii–xxxiv.

I. Preface (1:1–4) The Word of Life

II. Live in the Light (1:5–2:29)

   (a) God is Light (1:5–7)

   (b) First Condition for Living in the Light: Renounce Sin (1:8–2:2)

   (c) Second Condition: Be Obedient (2:3–11)

   (d) Third Condition: Reject Worldliness (2:12–17)

   (e) Fourth Condition: Keep the Faith (2:18–29)

III. Live As Children of God (3:1–5:13)

   (a) God is Father (3:1–3)

   (b) First Condition for Living as God's Children: Renounce Sin (3:4–9)

   (c) Second Condition: Be Obedient (3:10–24)

   (d) Third Condition: Reject Worldliness (4:1–6)

   (e) Fourth Condition: Be Loving (4:7–5:4)

   (f) Fifth Condition: Keep the Faith (5:5–13)

IV. Conclusion (5:14–21) Christian Confidence

Note that the structure is supported only by themes, making it a weak precedent for the Gospel. The genre is also quite different from Luke as well.

1.3 Precedent Structures from Greco-Roman Literature

A wealth of examples of regular parallelism, and other types of structure, is available in Greco-Roman writings, especially in poetry. Charles Talbert develops this topic thoroughly in *Literary Patterns, Theological Themes, and the Genre of Luke-Acts*,[41] so we will avoid excessive overlap with his evidence. For our purposes, however, most examples will be restricted to historical or biographical works.

The thought of patterned literary structure raises an issue that must be addressed briefly: the modern mind tends to view patterned structuring of historical and biographical texts as a violation of truth, or at least a ma-

---

41 Talbert, *Literary Patterns*, chapters I, V and VIII.

nipulation of it. This was clearly not the perception of the ancient mind.[42] Lucian saw the historian's craft as similar to that of the sculptor, "to superinduce upon events the charm of order, and set them forth in the most lucid fashion he can manage".[43] Even if Lucian is seen as an exception, his contemporary historians and biographers were demonstrably more amenable to it than moderns were.

1.3.1 HERODOTUS' HISTORIES

Herodotus, considered by many to be the first true historian, had a profound influence on literature throughout the following centuries.[44] It is quite possible that Luke was familiar with his style. Herodotus is now known to have utilized multiple complex patterns within individual works. Frequently throughout his masterpiece, the *Histories*, for example, he describes campaigns of various kings according to a consistent pattern. Immerwahr identifies "a fixed order of topics, varied...according to circumstances" employed in this fifth century BC book.[45]

1. Plan of aggressor.

2. His preparations.

3. Section on causation (*aitiê*-section).

4. March of aggressor to place of action.

5. Preparation of defender.

6. March of defender to place of action.

7. Battle.

8. Epilogue: consequences of battle (retreat and pursuit; stories about victors in valor; further pursuit of enemy).

---

[42] See Talbert, *Literary Patterns*, chapter V. This fact is also assumed by other scholars. See for example John M. Carter (ed.), *Suetonius Divus Augustus* (Bristol: Bristol Classical Press, 1982) 8; Alan Wardman, *Plutarch's Lives* (London: Paul Elek, 1974) 147; D.A. Russel, *Plutarch* (London: Gerald Duckworth & Company, 1973) 102–26; Henry R. Immerwahr, *Form and Thought in Herodotus* (Cleveland, Ohio: Western Reserve University Press, 1966) 46–78; H.W. Fowler and F.G. Fowler (trs.), *The Works of Lucian of Samosata*, (Oxford: Clarendon Press, 1905) 2:131.
[43] Lucian of Samosata, *The Way to Write History*, in Fowler and Fowler, *Works of Lucian*, 2:132.
[44] Immerwahr, *Form and Thought*, 1–2.
[45] Immerwahr, *Form and Thought*, 68.

The battle sections (#7) follow a fixed form also:[46]

1. Movement of aggressor into position.
2. Movement of defender into position.
3. Council of defender.
4. (Less commonly) a council for the attacker.
5. Description of action.
6. Epilogue, i.e. No. 8 above.

Among other patterns, Immerwahr observes the "elaborate *pattern of the rise and fall of a ruler*" in the sections on Croesus, Cyrus and Darius.[47]

1. Origin of the ruler (how he was born, or how he came to power).
2. Early reign until full power is achieved. (This is usually brief, and there is a sudden rise to high fortune.)
3. Further reign, told at length, and leading to destruction, or at least to a decline.

In terms of the combination of different types of parallel features, Herodotus' parallels in the *Histories* are simpler than later examples of Greco-Roman historical and biographical literature we will examine. His are founded simply on actions and themes. Naturally, the pattern recurs from one character to the next.

Herodotus' structures as literary constructions are not as complex as Luke's apparent structure. They are a more natural way of recounting the subject matter. Regardless, the choice of a consistent order of presentation shows some degree of concern for parallel structure.

1.3.2 THUCYDIDES' HISTORY OF THE PELOPONNESIAN WAR

Hunter Rawlings observes the following regular parallelism in Thucydides' *History of the Peloponnesian War*.[48]

---

46 Immerwahr, *Form and Thought*, 69.
47 Immerwahr, *Form and Thought*, 76.
48 Hunter Rawlings, *The Structure of Thucydides' History* (Princeton: Princeton University Press, 1981) 5.

I. Introduction
> II. First Years of the War
>> III. Revolt and Revolution
>>> (IV and V)

VI. Introduction
> VII. First Years of the War
>> VIII. Revolt and Revolution
>>> (IX and X)

The parallelism is topical and allows for sections that do not correspond (IV–V with IX–X). This is important to our structural proposal for Luke since it too has some non-corresponding material in parallel positions. Several main characters are covered by the structure.

1.3.3 PLUTARCH'S LIVES

Plutarch, a contemporary of Luke, employs regular parallelism in his historical biographies for comparative reasons. He wanted to enable the reader to evaluate the life of one character against that of another, or the early life of a subject against his later life. In his *Lives*, for each pair of famous people he provides parallel accounts of their lives according to a pattern of character qualities.[49] Furthermore, all of the statesmen are compared through a common structure.[50]

1. Description of non-public life.

2. Description of political life.

3. Description of military life.

4. Depiction of the statesman's death.

If one objects that this is a natural chronological progression and not a literary strategy, realize that Plutarch's discussion of non-public life also includes that which is contemporaneous with the political and military career. In addition, there is temporal overlap between the political and military sections. Therefore, it is not simply a chronological progression from private to public life. His parallelism in this case is a literary construction formed through character traits and broad spheres of personal activity;

---

49 Russel, *Plutarch*, 108–116.
50 See Wardman, *Plutarch's Lives*, 239, 241.

and parallel repetition occurs within an individual "life" and between "lives".

1.3.4 PLUTARCH'S ALCIBIADES

Plutarch's *Alcibiades* is a helpful example of how he occasionally created regular parallelism within the presentation of an individual life. Here he divides the life into the private, younger life and the public, older life and portrays the static character of the individual by treating the same themes in each half, often in the same order.[51] These include such themes as relationships, bravery and self-assurance.

1.3.5 LIVY'S HISTORY

T.J. Luce demonstrates that books 1–45 of Livy's *History* are architectonically developed in pentads and decades with a degree of regular parallelism. The same is posited for the remainder of the work, books 46–142.[52] He believes that this historian from the first century BC first designed the architecture of the whole, then inserted material to suit.[53] Unfortunately, he does not explicate the parallelism he believes is there.

1.3.6 VERGIL'S AENEID

Greco-Roman epic poetry is replete with architectonic structures, many of them based on regular parallelism.[54] Of the epic poets, Vergil and Homer were the most influential. Implying the probable influence of Vergil and other classical poets on Luke, Talbert writes,

> At the beginning of the Christian era...the Roman educational process tended to reinforce and cultivate the classical perspective just as Greek education had done prior to this time. This was true both of what was read and of how it was read. In what was the equivalent of our secondary schools Vergil was the first Latin poet put into the hands of the young and he served as the foundation of the Latin course. Next to him Horace was most read. Homer's works, of course were the basis for the Greek course. It is precisely in these works that the architectonic skills of the classical world are greatest. A system of education which focused on Homer and

---

[51] Russel, *Plutarch*, 118–126.
[52] T.J. Luce, *Livy: The Composition of His History* (Princeton, New Jersey: Princeton University Press, 1977) 3–32.
[53] Luce, *Livy*, 188–93. See also Talbert (*Literary Patterns*, 79), who cites instances where an architectonic outline, a "preliminary sketch," was used by Greco-Roman writers.
[54] William G. Thalmann reveals several instances of regular parallelism, as well as chiasmus, in early Greek epic poetry, in *Conventions of Form and Thought in Early Greek Epic Poetry* (London: Johns Hopkins University Press, 1984) 1–77.

Vergil so that they were the only nourishment of the youthful intellect of necessity early developed a sense of form which became second nature for impressionable minds. After completion of this beginning study of poetry, lads and young men were admitted into the rhetorical schools where they studied prose instead of poetical models. Here speech was valued as an artistic product quite apart from its content or significance. The effect of rhetorical dominance of education was that even prose had a poetical quality.[55]

Therefore, it is likely that Luke was familiar with the regular parallelism in Vergil's poems, especially the *Aeneid*. This, the most famous of his works, exhibits regular parallelisms, chiasms and alternating rhythms of several layers. We are interested in a taste of the regular parallelisms since this is the nature of our structural proposal for Luke in the next chapter.

In his groundbreaking and well-received study of structural patterns in the *Aeneid*, George E. Duckworth first reveals the regular parallelism on the broadest plane.

Vergil has composed his epic in two large parallel panels, with an alternating rise and fall of tension and with each book of the second panel balancing the corresponding book of the first. The twelve books of the *Aeneid* may be presented in the following diagrammatic form:

I Juno and storm
    II DESTRUCTION OF TROY
        III Interlude (of wandering)
            IV TRAGEDY OF LOVE
                V Games (lessening of tension)
                    VI FUTURE REVEALED
VII Juno and war
    VIII BIRTH OF ROME
        IX Interlude (at Trojan camp)
            X TRAGEDY OF WAR
                XI Truce (lessening of tension)
                    XII FUTURE ASSURED[56]

More deeply, each pair of books is paralleled through numerous corre-

---

55 Talbert, *Literary Patterns*, 70. On Vergil's works in the Roman educational system just prior to the beginning of the Christian era and on his influence on early Christianity, see J.W. MacKail, *The Aeneid* (Oxford: Clarendon Press, 1930) lxix–lxxii.
56 Duckworth, *Structural Patterns*, 7–8.

sponding features, each employing regular parallelism. Books two and eight will serve as a typical example:[57]

II	VIII
DESTRUCTION OF TROY	BIRTH OF ROME
Story of Carthage interrupted	Story of Trojan camp interrupted
Laocoon killed by two serpents	Two serpents killed by Hercules
Greeks destroy	Greeks help to found
Trojans suffer from Greeks	Trojans profit from Greeks
Helplessness of aged Priam	Helpfulness of aged Evander
Luxury of Priam's palace	Simplicity of Evander's home
Destruction of Troy	Picture of later Rome
Aeneas center of stage	Aeneas center of stage
Anchises prominent–father of Aeneas	Evander prominent–father of Pillas
Venus as goddess appears to Aeneas	Venus as goddess appears to Aeneas
Gods against Troy	Gods for Rome (at Actium)
Ascanius–fire about head, comet	Augustus–fire about head, comet
At end, Aeneas carries on shoulders his father (symbolic of past)	At end, Aeneas carries on shoulder the shield (picture of future)

Notice in the above example that the parallelism is exact. In two instances of parallel books, however, there is an irregularity in the parallelism. First, two consecutive features of eleven total parallel features are reversed in book XI from the order in book V, not depicted here.[58] Second, depicted below, a greater break in regularity occurs between books I and VII.[59]

---

57 See Duckworth, *Structural Patterns*, 9.
58 See Duckworth, *Structural Patterns*, 10.
59 See Duckworth, *Structural Patterns*, 8.

Analysis of Ancient Literature 191

I	VII
Juno and storm	Juno and war
Invocation of Muse	Invocation of Muse
Trojans *laeti*	Trojans and Aeneas *laeti*
Juno laments lack of power	
Juno arouses storm on sea with aid of Aeolus and forces of nature	
Arrival in strange land	Arrival in strange land
Banquet on shore	Banquet on shore
Prophecy of Roman greatness (Jupiter to Venus)	Prophecy of Roman greatness (Faunus to Latinus)
Venus in disguise meets Aeneas– reveals identity	
Trojans already known	Trojans already known
Pictures of Trojan past	Statues of Latin past
Dido receives Trojans	Latinus receives Trojans
Ilioneus speaks for Aeneas	Ilioneus speaks for Aeneas
Friendship and gifts offered	Friendship and gifts offered
	Juno laments lack of power
	Juno arouses war on land with aid of Allecto and human forces
	Allecto in disguise visits Turnus– reveals identity
Venus prevails over Juno	Juno prevails over Venus
Closing of Gates of War (in Jupiter's prophecy)	Opening of Gates of War
Effect of Cupid on Dido	Effect of serpent on Amata
Movement of book–misery to happiness	Movement of book–happiness to misery

Vergil creates his parallelisms through themes, actions, settings, forms, functions of units in the plot, contrasting features, and even books. As demonstrated by slight variation in the positioning of correspondences, he is not slavishly bound by perfect balance. Further testimony to this is that corresponding sections and books differ in length to varying degrees.[60] Although Luke's Gospel is not poetry, the likely familiarity of the Evangelist with Vergil would ensure that regular parallelism was a part of his compositional repertoire. Since such parallelism is amply attested in major precedent cases of historical and biographical narrative, the influence that the *Aeneid* had on the Evangelist could certainly have been to increase his

---

60 Vergil, *The Aeneid*, C.H. Sisson (tr.), (Manchester: Carcanet Press and Northumberland: Northumberland Arts Group, 1986).

disposition to use the pattern.

Vergil was happy enough to adjust the order of historical events to suit his architecture. From this standpoint, history did not overwhelmingly restrict his pattern development. We do not claim this extent of freedom for Luke. Interestingly, the Evangelist apparently practiced significant freedom only with units of source material that had few if any chronological tags.

In conclusion, nearly all of the above structures receive scholarly support and each provides precedent evidence for the type of structure we propose for Luke. Cumulatively they confirm that multifold cyclical parallelism was familiar to writers of the Evangelist's period and earlier. Numerous other patterned parallel structures were in frequent use, like chiasmus, but even a representative sampling of these would require too much space for our purposes. Were our examples intended by their authors, or are they merely the byproduct of natural repetition in history? Some structures discussed are facilitated by the historical events behind them, but the author actually constructs the pattern through the selection and rearrangement of material. Other structures, it may be claimed, are solely the product of the overwhelming similarity between the events recorded, similarity that governs the author. Yet under scrutiny, authorial selectivity is the best explanation for most, perhaps all, of the above patterns. If common literary form is credited for the parallelism, then still some degree of parallelism is intended by the author, that of basic form. Clearly several of the patterns are purely literary with no historical basis that defines them. The collection of examples above therefore firmly establishes the precedent for Luke to use multifold cyclical parallelism and the likelihood that he was familiar with it. Several of them also demonstrate that a patterned literary construction can be a valid framework for historical material. Our proposal for Luke's handling of the Gospel material is therefore affirmed.

2 Basis for Structural Correspondence:
An Analysis of the Above Precedent and Contemporary Cases

In order to determine whether our structural proposal for Luke is reasonable in terms of the conventions of the day, the means by which regular parallelism was created in the precedent literature must be examined. This will enable the determination of whether our proposal exhibits the same types and combinations of correspondences found in writings that were available to the Evangelist. We should expect that if he intended his structure to have an impact, it would be formed through conventional means understood by his readers. In addition, our proposal contains three of sixty-two pericopes that may be considered by some not to fit their parallels, and three gaps where parallel material might have been expected. The above precedent literature exhibits the same phenomena, demonstrating that it is indeed not abnormal. As mentioned before, Talbert concludes after exhaustive study of architectonic structures in the ancient world that "imperfections of form are the rule," and he cites statements of classical authors to that effect.[61] For example, he cites the statement of Longinus, who lived around the time of Luke, regarding the process of structured writing, "Perfect precision runs the risk of triviality, whereas in great writing as in great wealth there must needs be something overlooked."[62] This is borne out by our examples:

First, a look at the types of correspondences utilized reveals a wide variety even from the most ancient times. Available to Luke from the Old Testament would be parallelism using theme, literary form, action, characters, setting, wording and formulae, among others, with allowance for interludes that lack correspondence. From the Greco-Roman world we may add such features as character traits, broad spheres of personal activity, function of unit texts in the plot, contrast, and numerical pattern, again with allowance for interludes of unparalleled material. Even apart from Luke, most of these are employed in the New Testament examples: theme, literary form, action, characters, wording, formulae, function of unit texts in the plot, and minor numerical patterning. Interludes of unparalleled material are also accepted. Interestingly, the methods of forming correspondences within epic poetry and within prose of all sorts are essentially the same. The main differences are the amount of detail in correspondence and the number of layers of pattern. Certainly, broad architectonic structure based on parallelism is more common in epic poetry, but there is obviously no dearth even in historical-biographical literature.

Second, the combination of various types of correspondences to form a structure is evident from the oldest of Old Testament and Greco-Roman writings up to the New Testament texts and their contemporary Greco-Roman works. Interestingly, the Old Testament may generally exhibit a greater variety of combinations than Greco-Roman literature. Early Greek epic poetry, however, probably marks the beginning of highly structured work with multiple layers of patterns.

The point has been made that imperfections in structure were expected in patterned writing. In several instances in the above literature, there are certain passages that do not conform to the defined parallels. These may perhaps be interpreted as "interludes". The proportion of the text occupied by this material is often substantial, for example: 1 Samuel 9–31, about 4% by pericope; 2 Samuel 11–20, at least 45% by pericope; Revelation 6–16, about 53% by number of lines; 1 John, about 18% by number of lines;

---

61 Talbert, *Literary Patterns*, 77–79.
62 Talbert, *Literary Patterns*, 78.

Thucydides' *History of the Peloponnesian War*, about 40% by book. If Luke occasionally employs material that does not apparently conform to our proposal, this should not be considered problematical or we are demanding more of him than is realistic.

Omission of parallel material, leaving "gaps," is common in our precedent literature and obviously not considered defective. A few examples will suffice. Omission is found in 2 Chronicles 14–35, where occasionally elements of the regnal resumé of a king are omitted, even the biographical section (as with Jehoiachin). Similarly, in Judges, various elements of the standard format for each Judge are occasionally missing. In Job, we find a phenomenon similar to that in our Lukan proposal, where an expected parallel is omitted and replaced with slightly divergent material. For example, the expected speech of Zophar at the end of the third cycle is replaced by one from Elihu. Apparently, the change is to highlight the new material. Even in John, two "signs" or acts that lead to opposition are lacking. Such omissions were common practice for Herodotus, Thucydides and Plutarch. Aside from poetry, the message and plot are always allowed to override the structure when desired. Any "gaps" in a Lukan structure, if few, should be accepted as reasonable, especially if the plot affords a reasonable explanation.

Therefore, whether Luke was more dependent on the structural influence of his Scriptures or that of the Greco-Roman literary milieu, there is ample precedent for instilling architectonic pattern into works of similar genres to his Gospel. The above examples are only a taste of all that was available to him. Therefore, it should be no surprise to find similar structure in the Third Gospel.

3 Thomas L. Brodie's Greco-Roman *Imitatio* as a Possible Lukan Compositional Mechanism

Merely to demonstrate that architectonic patterns were common in literature preceding and contemporary with Luke stops short of providing clear motivation and mechanism for its incorporation in the Gospel. Thomas Brodie fills this gap most effectively through his study of Greco-Roman *imitatio*, or imitation.[63] He reveals a compositional technique that was

---

63 Thomas L. Brodie has written extensively on the subject: "A New Temple and a New Law," *JSNT* 5 (1979) 21–45; "Greco-Roman Imitation of Texts as a Partial Guide to Luke's Use of Sources," in Charles H. Talbert (ed.), *Luke-Acts, New Perspectives From the Society of Biblical Literature Seminar* (New York: Crossroad, 1984) 17–46; "Towards Unraveling Luke's Use of the Old Testament: Luke 7.11–17 as an *Imitatio* of 1 Kings 17.17–24," *NTS* 32 (1986) 247–67; *Luke the Literary Interpreter: Luke-Acts as a Systematic Rewriting and Updating of the Elijah-Elisha*

pervasive in the ancient world and that would encourage the Evangelist's use of literary structures found in literature that he respected, such as Scripture. It involved the imitation of virtually any facet of a prior piece of literature, from its content to its skeletal structure (e.g. the mere pattern A B C A´ B´ C´ without concern for imitation of content).

The pervasiveness of the technique strengthens the likelihood that Luke was influenced by it. Certainly, Brodie has established a compelling case, represented by his summary of the evidence he has amassed.[64]

> In order to understand the origin of most of the literature of the Greco-Roman world it is necessary to understand imitation. Unlike modern writers, who tend to emphasize originality, ancient writers generally put the emphasis on imitation, on the adapting of existing texts. It was a practice which was central until the latter part of the eighteenth century – until the development, that is, of individual-centered romanticism, and until the publication, in 1759, of Edward Young's "Conjectures on Original Composition.[65]

His examples of ancient authors using imitation in virtually all genres is impressive, such authors as Horace, Vergil, Juvenal, Ennius, Ovid, Seneca, Lucrecius, Livy, Homer, Herodotus, Plutarch, Thucydides, and Tacitus.[66] He states, "The list of indebtedness is almost monotonous, but it acts as a corrective to the widespread modern presupposition that literary originality and excellence largely exclude indebtedness."[67] As to whether the practice was prevalent in Luke's day he writes,

> By the time one gets to the general period in which the gospels were written, during the era of Quintilian, imitation has a central role, and among modern scholars of antiquity it is taken for granted that much of Latin

---

Narrative in 1 and 2 Kings (Rome: Pontifical University of St. Thomas Aquinas, 1988); "The Departure for Jerusalem (Luke 9,51–56) as a Rhetorical Imitation of Elijah's Departure for the Jordan (2 Kings 1,1–2,6)," *Bib* 70 (1989) 96–109; "Luke 9:57–62: A Systematic Adaptation of the Divine Challenge to Elijah (1 Kings 19)," in David J. Lull (ed.) *SBL Seminar Papers* 28 (Atlanta: Scholars Press, 1989) 237–245; "Not Q but Elijah: The Saving of the Centurion's Servant (Luke 7:1–10) as an Internalization of the Saving of the Widow and Her Child (1 Kings 17:1–16)," *IBS* 14 (1992) 54–71; and "Re-Opening the Quest for Proto-Luke: The Systematic Use of Judges 6–12 in Luke 16:1–18:8," *Journal of Higher Criticism* 2 (1995) 68–101.

64 See especially Brodie, *Literary Interpreter*, 5–70; "Greco-Roman," 22–32; and "Towards Unraveling," 247–249.
65 Brodie, "Departure," 97.
66 Brodie, "Greco-Roman," 22–32.
67 Brodie, "Greco-Roman," 23.

writing consists of a reworking of ancient Greek writing.[68]

It has been well established that imitation was pervasive in the ancient world, including Luke's time. But what of the methodology of *imitatio*? Specifically, could it involve the incorporation of patterned structure? Brodie best describes the technique, so he will be allowed to speak at some length.

> Imitation involved not only *form* but also content. And it was not slavish. In imitating a text, one of the basic purposes was to go beyond it to produce something better – so much so that eventually imitation became synonymous with emulation or rivalry (Gk., *zēlos*; Lat., *emulatio*).
>
> Among the many techniques employed in the process of imitation the most basic were modernization, abbreviation, elaboration, division and fusion. Modernization, abbreviation, and elaboration seem self-explanatory. Division consisted of taking a text, breaking it into segments, and then using the various segments as starting-points for the construction of diverse passages. Fusion consisted of blending passages that were originally distinct. These basic techniques, and many others, were used in a wide variety of ways. *Ultimately there was no clear limit on what the imitator could and could not do in reworking a text.*
>
> Imitation was not something specialized. Just as rhetoric was pervasive in the Greco-Roman literary world, so also was imitation. It was one of the first rules of literary composition and is found in every genre.[69] (italics mine)

Furthermore, imitation regularly spans different genres. For instance, ancient historiography often shows dependence on poetry, rhetoric and drama.[70] Obviously, the imitation of structure could be practiced as part of *imitatio*, so theoretically Luke could have decided to deploy any architectonic structure he knew of, such as from the precedent literature discussed above. Most of Brodie's discussions of Luke's use of the technique actually demonstrate that the imitation of structure is foundational, from the level of plot in a single pericope[71] even to the framework of multi-episode narra-

---

68 Brodie, "Departure," 98. In support of this same point, he notes the agreement of George A. Kennedy, a prominent scholar of ancient rhetoric (*The Art of Persuasion in Greece* [Princeton: Princeton University, 1963] 332–33) in "Towards Unraveling," 249.
69 Brodie, "Departure," 98.
70 Brodie, "Greco-Roman," 26–28.
71 See for example Brodie's "Towards Unraveling," 247–67; "Not Q but Elijah," 54–71; or *Literary Interpreter*, 128–366, and especially 367–368.

tives.[72] Thomas Green concurs, citing Grube, that imitation involved "all external matters of form".[73]

The majority of the attention in Brodie's writings is focused on Luke's imitation of the Elijah-Elisha narrative of 1 and 2 Kings and of particular events within it. He constructs his case on three pillars: (1) that Luke imitates the LXX, a conclusion commonly accepted by scholars today;[74] (2) that he consciously depends to some extent on the Elijah-Elisha narrative, again commonly accepted, and evidenced in part by his redaction of Luke 4:16–30;[75] and (3) that numerous Gospel pericopes bear significant resemblance to Elijah/Elisha accounts in structure and content.[76]

His precision in the identification of imitative literary dependence in Luke on the Elijah-Elisha narrative probably should not be accepted without reservations however. Regarding larger narrative structure, some of his proposals seem to be forced. It is doubtful for example that "the essential plan of Luke-Acts – two balancing parts centered on an assumption (Acts 1:2) – is the same as that of the Elijah-Elisha narrative"[77] by Luke's design. History would suggest this format if Luke wanted to trace the ministries of Jesus and the apostles and show their connectedness. The lack of ascension accounts in the other canonical Gospels does argue somewhat in his favor however. An extract from his comparison between 1 and 2 Chronicles and Luke 1:1–2:52[78] further illustrates the weaknesses of some of his broad structures:

---

[72] Good examples are discussed in Brodie's "Departure," 98–100; "New Temple," 21–45; and *Literary Interpreter*, 367–368.

[73] Thomas M. Green, *The Light in Troy: Imitation and Discovery in Renaissance Poetry* (London: Yale University Press, 1982).

[74] Nolland offers a brief but insightful evaluation of the evidence for and against Lukan Septuagintal imitation in his comments on Lk. 1:5–25, siding in favor of some imitation; *Luke 1–9:20*, 21–22. See also A.T. Robertson, *A Grammar of the Greek New Testament in the Light of Historical Research* (New York: Hodder & Stoughton, 1923) 121, and Nigel Turner, *A Grammar of New Testament Greek, Vol. IV: Style* (Edinburgh: T. & T. Clark, 1976) 46–50. Our discussion of "type-scene" in the chapter on Tannehill also provides useful evidence for Lukan Septuagintal imitation.

[75] See for example Craig A. Evans, "Luke's Use of the Elijah/Elisha Narratives and the Ethics of Election," *JBL* 106 (1987) 75–83. Furthermore, a survey of references to Elijah and/or Elisha in any thorough commentary on Luke yields ample evidence that Luke was conscious of this OT narrative during his composition of the Gospel.

[76] Brodie, "Not Q but Elijah," 55–57.

[77] Brodie, "Not Q but Elijah," 56.

[78] Brodie, "New Temple," 24.

1 and 2 Chronicles	**Luke 1:1–2:52**
Preparation for David's reign (chs 1–10)	Preparation for Jesus' Davidic reign (1:1–25)
Nathan announces David's reign (11–12; 17)	Gabriel announces Jesus' reign (1:26–38)
The ark in the hills (ch 13)	Mary in the hill-country (1:39–45, 56)
God gives David victory (14; 18–20)	Mary's victorious *Magnificat* (1:46–55)
Priestly service, sons and song (15–16)	Zechariah, his son and his song (1:57–80)
The census and the origin of the Temple (21–22)	The census and the birth of Jesus (2:1–20)
The people and piety of the Temple (23–29)	People and piety around Jesus (2:21–38)
The building of the Temple (2 Chr 1:1–5:1)	Jesus grows up (2:39–40)
The Lord takes possession of his Temple (5:2–ch 9)	Jesus in the Temple (2:41–52)
Life and decline of the Temple (chs 10–36)	....

The hills are hardly important to 1 Chronicles 13, or Luke 1:39–45 for that matter, and "victory" between the fourth parallel is contrived. Similar objections clearly apply elsewhere in the scheme. Brodie would probably appeal to the complexity of the imitative process[79] and the right of the author to do as he pleases,[80] but the results must still be reasonable, assuming Luke is reasonable. This particular scheme simply fails. Nevertheless, problems in some of Brodie's proposals for broad structural imitation do not in any way diminish the likelihood that Luke employed the methodology less specifically. In other words, he could have borrowed the basic architecture of a text without creating any correspondence in *content* between his Gospel and that text.

On the level of the individual pericope, his study of the imitative structural dependence of Luke 7:11–17 (the raising of the widow's son at Nain) on 1 Kings 17:17–24 (the raising of the widow's son at Zarephath) is

---

79 Brodie, "Greco-Roman," 35–36.
80 Brodie, "Departure," 98.

instructive.[81] Although we may have similar objections here as to the above scheme, there are verbal similarities that significantly strengthen his case.[82]

1 Kings 17:17–24	Luke 7:11–17
'It happened after this...' (17a)	'It happened afterwards...' (11a)
[17.10: At the gate of Sarepta Elijah met a widow.]	At the gate of Nain Jesus meets...a widow (11b, 12a, c)
The son of the widow died. (17b)	The widow's son was dead. (12b)
The widow's sense of her sinfulness. (18)	[7.10: The centurion professes unworthiness.]
Elijah carries the boy upstairs, sadly asks the Lord if he cares, and breathes into the boy. (19–21a)	The Lord felt compassion, and touched the bier, and the bearers stood still. (13–14a)
Elijah prays to the Lord for the return of the soul of the child. (21b)	The Lord commands the boy to rise. (14b)
'And it was so and the child cried out.' (22)	'And the dead person sat up, and began to talk.' (15a)
And he led him down 'and gave him to his mother.' (23)	'And he gave him to his mother.' (15b)
The woman acknowledges the man of God and the word in his mouth. (24)	All the people recognize that a great prophet of God has come, and this word went forth. (16–17)

Only one or two of the correspondences seems questionable in this instance. Yet as Brodie has segmented these accounts for the sake of comparison, the essential outline appears to be as one might naturally tell a revivification story. This implies an accidental relationship. He assures us however that "among available resuscitation stories of antiquity no such general pattern existed". Additionally, he notes that no consistent pattern exists within the NT.[83] (Interestingly, the plot of the healing of Jairus' daughter bears somewhat less resemblance to the OT account.) Chance could still account for the similarity, but he has indeed reduced the likelihood. Add a few verbal similarities and the case is more compelling, but not entirely proven. Imitation seems clearly involved, but the structural relationship lies just beyond definitive proof. Brodie produces further

---

81 Brodie, "Towards Unraveling," 249–259.
82 See Brodie's table of verbal similarities in "Towards Unraveling," 252–253.
83 Brodie, "Towards Unraveling," 262.

confirmation that Luke was actually practicing *imitatio* however. It is apparent "even through a brief examination of some leading Greco-Roman writers, that there is considerable similarity of detail between the adaptive methods of Luke and those of the writers of his general era".[84] He cites Vergil's "Romanizing" of Homer, a detailed and thoroughgoing rework, and draws a parallel to Luke's Christianizing of an OT text.[85] Among other similar processes to Vergil, he notes the occasional inclusion of an entire sentence from the source, as between 1 Kings 17:23 and Luke 7:15b. Further, Seneca and Livy are revealed to have imitatively worked their sources similarly to Luke. The evidence drives Brodie correctly to the belief that through "not only Luke's general affinity with rhetoric and the spirit of imitation, but also his more detailed resemblances to the imitative practices of particular Greco-Roman authors – it seems reasonable to conclude that his work should be classified as an *imitatio*, or at least should be regarded as involving imitative techniques".[86]

Excursus: The Deuteronomy Hypothesis

Other proposals of a similar extensive imitative dependence have been proffered, namely a dependence of Luke's central section on Deuteronomy. The major proponents are C.F. Evans[87] and David P. Moessner.[88] An initial caution is issued by Adrian Hastings for this theory, that there is a "danger of reading into slight similarities of order much more than is in fact there".[89] Evans' approach is more compact and straightforward, so it will serve for a brief evaluation of possible literary dependence.

Craig L. Blomberg offers an insightful assessment of Evans' proposal,[90] and for clarity of discussion, he summarizes the list of parallels as follows:

---

84 Brodie, "Towards Unraveling," 260.
85 Brodie, "Towards Unraveling," 259–262.
86 Brodie, "Towards Unraveling," 262.
87 C.F. Evans, "The Central Section of St. Luke's Gospel," in D.E. Nineham (ed.), *Studies in the Gospels: Essays in Memory of R.H. Lightfoot* (Oxford: Blackwell, 1955) 37–53; and *Saint Luke*, 34–36.
88 David P. Moessner, *Lord of the Banquet: The Literary and Theological Significance of the Lukan Travel Narrative* (Minneapolis: Fortress Press, 1989).
89 Adrian Hastings, *Prophet and Witness in Jerusalem: A Study of the Teaching of Saint Luke* (London: Longmans, Green & Co., 1958) 69.
90 See his "Midrash," 217–61, especially 221–228.

Analysis of Ancient Literature 201

Luke	Deuteronomy	
10:1–3, 17–20	1:1–46	sending forerunners
10:4–16	2:1–3:22	inhospitable kings and cities
10:21–24	3:23–4:40	special revelation
10:25–27	5:1–6:25	the summary of the Law
10:29–37	7:1–26	relations with foreigners
10:38–42	8:1–3	spiritual food
11:1–13	8:4–20	no privation
11:14–26	9:1–10:11	casting out wicked people and demons
11:27–36	10:12–11:32	keeping God's word, light, and frontlets
11:37–12:12	12:1–16	clean and unclean
12:13–34	12:17–32	richness towards God
12:35–53	13:1–11	reward/punishment for faithfulness/unfaithfulness
12:54–13:5	13:12–18	communal judgment and repentance
13:6–9	14:28	bearing fruit
13:10–21	15:1–18	Sabbath release from debt, slavery, disease
13:22–35	16:1–17:7	feasting in Jerusalem
14:1–14	17:8–18:22	food for Levites/banquet parables
14:15–35	20:1–20	excuses from battle and banquet
15:1–32	21:15–22:4	father and son, restoration of the lost
16:1–18	23:15–24:4	slaves, usury, and divorce
16:19–18:8	24:6–25:3	fair treatment of poor and oppressed
18:9–14	26:1–19	obeying the Law.

After noting the wholesale acceptance of the scheme by a few prominent scholars, Blomberg poses three important questions to Evans. "What parallels in ancient literature exist to the approach which he views Luke as employing? How close in fact are the parallels which he has identified? To what extent do these parallels exclude other equally suggestive parallels that might be drawn between Luke and Deuteronomy but which would destroy his orderly sequence?"[91] In response to the first question, Blomberg correctly demonstrates that Jewish Midrash does not provide a convincing parallel,[92]

---

91 Blomberg, "Midrash," 223.
92 Blomberg, "Midrash," 223–225.

but he misses the many parallels in the Greco-Roman literary realm,[93] to which Brodie amply testifies. His third question would deny virtually any lengthy text that was in fact intentionally constructed in the manner Evans suggests, so it is not particularly helpful. Such a work that contains a reasonably complex web of repeated themes and terminology will inevitably allow random correspondences to be found that were not deliberate, despite the intentional literary dependence. It is Blomberg's second question that topples Evans' scheme. He proceeds to expose the vagueness and generality of most of the parallels.[94] Craig A. Evans and James A. Sanders, who maintain the Deuteronomy Hypothesis, attempt a defense against this question. In reference to it they state, "Blomberg…is certainly correct in his observation that many of the alleged parallels are vague and sometimes found outside the Deuteronomy sequence, and that some extended sections of Deuteronomy are unparalleled altogether."[95] Unfortunately, they only explain why portions of Deuteronomy are unparalleled: that there would not be sufficient dominical material to parallel all of Deuteronomy. They fail adequately to handle the problem of vagueness, generality and lack of fit between parallel passages.[96] Indeed, the methodology espoused throughout fails to avoid adequately the problem of subjectivity.[97] Accordingly, the Deuteronomy Hypothesis should be considered untenable.

It is reasonable to believe that Luke practiced the prevalent literary technique of *imitatio*, a process that could involve the borrowing merely of an architectonic pattern from a respected source. Therefore it is also reasonable to believe that he could have been inspired by precedent or contemporary texts, such as those reviewed earlier in this chapter, to structure his Gospel according to a detailed parallel pattern. Possibly the multi-fold parallel cyclical structure of the Elijah-Elisha cycles (1 Kings 17:1–19:21),

---

93 Craig A. Evans and James A. Sanders, in their defense of the Deuteronomy Hypothesis, agree with Blomberg that midrash is not a legitimate parallel, but they successfully identify the parallel in Greco-Roman writing; *Luke and Scripture: The Function of Sacred Tradition in Luke-Acts* (Minneapolis: Fortress Press, 1993) 123–124.
94 Blomberg, "Midrash," 225–228.
95 Evans and Sanders, *Luke and Scripture*, 125.
96 Evans and Sanders, *Luke and Scripture*, 125–126.
97 Evans and Sanders, *Luke and Scripture*, 121–139.

to which he refers so regularly throughout the Gospel, is his structural model. Of course, Luke provides no decisive indication.[98]

---

98 It is an interesting question whether καθεξῆς in Lk. 1:3 could refer to *imitatio*. Indeed, *imitatio* is an organizing principle. But there is a difficulty. The Evangelist appears to be placing the entire book under the umbrella of καθεξῆς. If imitation is no more extensive than what Brodie has decisively demonstrated in Luke, then it could hardly describe the entire work. It is however conceivable that it refers to the imitation of a patterned structural principal that Luke uses to govern the whole. Nevertheless, there is insufficient data, both contextual and lexical, regarding καθεξῆς to draw any firm conclusion on this matter. See Appendix A for a detailed discussion of the possible meanings for this word in the context of Luke's Gospel.

CHAPTER 4

A New Proposal for the Structure and Composition of Luke 4:14–24:53

1 The Cyclical Narrative Structure of Luke 4:14–24:53

Many have observed the highly structured nature of the gospel of Luke. Proposals of pattern have been made for many individual pericopes and for several larger sections, like the travel narrative. Nevertheless, Luke's design for the book as a whole has eluded scholarly detection. This chapter explains and defends the four-fold cyclical narrative pattern for Luke 4:14–24:53 presented briefly in the introduction, covering the entire ministry of Jesus. Coupled with the well-attested parallelism between Jesus and John the Baptist in Luke 1–3, the structure of the whole Gospel becomes apparent (see the table below). Since our earlier analysis (chapters 1 and 2) has found a number of proposals of correspondence wanting, this new proposal must be subjected to the same if not more rigorous evaluation.

1.1 Presentation of the Narrative Structure

The observed pattern behind Luke 4:14–24:53 is based on narrative features of the text involving such phenomena as conflict accounts, teaching of the crowds, Jesus' warning of the disciples against religious leaders, verbalizations of faith and commitment toward Christ by Peter, and passion predictions including the resurrection (see the list of features below). Each feature is further defined by a number of parallel elements, sub-units of the feature also held in common by the parallel passages. When the passages exhibiting each feature are distributed in table form, parallel strata emerge that run across four cycles.

The table below presents the passages of Luke by chapter and verse in their respective location in the pattern. Next to each passage, in the shaded columns, numerical representations of the features inherent in each of these passages are provided, with their corresponding descriptions in the narrative feature list following the table. Note the bands, or strata, that constitute the four cycles. Each cycle progresses sequentially by pericope. The beginning of cycle 2 immediately follows the end of cycle 1 in Luke, and so on. Each passage defined represents a complete narrative unit, usually the equivalent of a unit of tradition. The parallels (designated in the first column), which will usually be called "strata," are established by pericopes that are characterized by common narrative features. Every instance of each feature in Luke 4:14–24:53 is represented in the table below, so the degree of restriction to its stratum is observable for each. A basic discussion of the table follows it.

	1:1–4	
	John the Baptist	Jesus
	1:5–25	1:26–38
	1:39–56	
	1:57–66	2:1–21
	1:67–80	2:22–40
	2:41–52	
	3:1–20	3:21–4:13

	Cycle 1		Cycle 2		Cycle 3		Cycle 4	
	passage	feature	passage	feature	passage	feature	passage	feature
Stratum 1	4:14–15	to Galilee	9:51	1	13:22	1	19:28	1
Stratum 2	4:16–30	2	9:52–56	2	13:23–30	2	19:29–40	2
			9:57–62	2	13:31–35	2	19:41–44	2
Stratum 3	4:31–37	3a, b	10:1–24	3a, b	14:1–14	3a, f	19:45–20:8	3b, e
	4:38–39	3a						
	4:40–44	3a						
	5:1–11	3c						
	5:12–16	3a						
	5:17–26	3a, b, d	10:25–37	~3f				
	5:27–32	3c	10:38–42	3g				
	5:33–39	3e	11:1–13	3e				
	6:1–5	3f						
	6:6–11	3a, f						
	6:12–16	3c						
	6:17–49	3a, g	11:14–26	3a				
	7:1–10	3a,b						
	7:11–17	3a						
	7:18–35	3e; 4a						
	7:36–50	3d						
Stratum 4	8:1–21	4a, b	11:27–36	4a, b	14:15–24	4b	20:9–18	4a, b
					14:25–35	4a, b		
Stratum 5			11:37–54	5	15:1–16:31	5	20:19–44	5
Stratum 6			12:1–21	6	17:1–4	6	20:45–47	6
Stratum 7	8:22–25	7	12:22–34	7	17:5–10	7	21:1–4	7
					17:11–19	7; 3a		
Stratum 8	8:26–39	~8; 3a	12:35–40	8	17:20–37	8	21:5–38	8
	8:40–56	~8; 3a			18:1–8	8		
Stratum 9	9:1–17	9; 3a, b	12:41–48	9	18:9–17	9	22:1–30	9
Stratum 10	9:18–21	10			18:18–28	10	22:31–34	10; 3a
Stratum 11	9:22–27	11	12:49–53	11	18:29–34	11	22:35–24:53	11
Stratum 12[1]	9:28–36	–*	12:54–59	4a*	18:35–43	3a		
	9:37–45	3a	13:1–9	–*	19:1–10	–		
	9:46–50	–	13:10–17	3a	19:11–27	3b		
			13:18–21	–*				

Reference Table Indicating Cycles and Parallel Strata Along with Corresponding Features[2]

---

1 Stratum 12 is considered an interlude in the structure. See the first paragraph of the section "Discussion of the Narrative Strata Across the Four Cycles" below, p. 210.
2 For a discussion of how the passages in a stratum fit that stratum, see the pages in columns A and B for that stratum in the table below. For why certain passages outside a stratum do not fit that stratum, see the page in column C for that stratum.

Explanation of the table: In the table above, the numbers in the shaded area correspond to the narrative features in the list below. Each row of numbers within an individual cell represents one pericope that exhibits the feature(s) indicated by the number(s). For example, cycle 3, stratum 4 contains two rows. The first row shows that Luke 14:15–24 exhibits feature 4b, and the second row shows that Lk. 14:25–35 exhibits two features, 4a and 4b. A dash (–) indicates a pericope in that location that bears none of the specific narrative features in the list. Pericopes with an asterisk (*) are those in the final three strata that clearly relate to the presence or delay of the Kingdom. A tilde (~) notes a passage that exhibits the feature in modified form.

1.1.1 Parallel Narrative Features that Establish the Strata

The narrative features that form the strata in the above structure are presented below with their numerical designations.

Stratum 1:

Feature #1: The key phrase, "to Jerusalem" (εἰς Ἱεροσόλυμα or εἰς Ἱερουσαλήμ), is found in an introductory section to a pericope (narrator's voice) where the context highlights this destination as the driving purpose of Jesus' journey.

Stratum 2:

Feature #2: The prophetic status of Jesus is conveyed, involving direct reference and/or allusion to the Elijah-Elisha cycle in 1 and 2 Kings, and is accompanied by the theme of divine rejection of those who reject Jesus/God. This immediately follows a reference to the journey to Jerusalem.

Stratum 3:

Feature #3a: An account or summary of healing is related (validation of authority).

Feature #3b: Ἐξουσία is attributed to Jesus.

Stratum	A	B	C	Stratum	A	B	C
1	215	234	228	7	220	250	232
2	216	235	231	8	221	251	232
3	216	240	230	9	223	255	232
4	217	244	231	10	225	259	232
5	218	246	231	11	225	260	232
6	219	249	231				

Feature #3c: Jesus chooses disciples or designates apostles (exercise of authority).

Feature #3d: Jesus forgives sins (expression of authority).

Feature #3e: The ministry of Jesus is likened to or related to that of John the Baptist (a recognized authority), but not equated.

Feature #3f: Jesus asks, "Is it lawful?" (assertion of authority to interpret the law).

Feature #3g: The priority of hearing (ἀκούω) the word (λόγος) of Jesus.

Stratum 4:

Feature #4a: Jesus directly teaches a crowd (ὄχλος or λαός) of non-disciples (content of teaching included).

Feature #4b: A parable representing Jesus as bearer of a message from God is related, concluding with parables that convey the importance of responding to Jesus' message.

Stratum 5:

Feature #5:   Jesus personally confronts Jewish leaders, exposing their typical spiritual, moral and religious depravity and therefore implying a lost state.

Stratum 6:

Feature #6:   Jesus warns (προσέχετε) the disciples or others against being like the religious leaders.

Stratum 7:

Feature #7:   Jesus encourages the disciples to have greater faith.

Stratum 8:

Feature #8:   Jesus delivers an eschatological discourse to his disciples.

Stratum 9:

Feature #9:   Jesus addresses the twelve regarding their role.

Stratum 10:

Feature #10:   Peter verbalizes faith and commitment toward Christ.

Stratum 11:

Feature #11:   Jesus predicts his passion (and resurrection) in the context of the cost of discipleship.

Stratum 12:

Apparently, no well-restricted features link these passages. The timing of the Kingdom seems to be a common thread, however, and the reappearance of feature 3a, a healing account, establishes tentative parallelism.

The strata that cut across the cycles in Luke are formed by narrative features held in common by the relevant pericopes. Shimon Bar-Efrat's lucid and thorough exploration of the nature of parallel structural elements in OT literature will help to define what is meant here by "narrative features".[3] He describes the types of features placed in parallel within valid biblical structures, categorizing them into four levels: (1) verbal – verbatim repetition of words and phrases;[4] (2) narrative technique – involving "variations in narrative method, such as narrator's account as opposed to character's speech (dialogue), scenic presentation versus summary, narration as against description, explanation, comment, etc.;"[5] (3) narrative world/content – including characters and events;[6] and (4) conceptual content – themes and ideas.[7] Our term "narrative feature" overlaps primarily with Bar-Efrat's "narrative world" where characters, actions and events, qualified slightly by subject matter, are placed in parallel. For example, in stratum 9 of Luke's structure, Jesus (character) addresses the twelve (action) regarding their role (qualification). "Narrative feature" is a little broader however. It includes some verbal repetition in the narrative (such as the recurrence of "to Jerusalem" in stratum 1 of the cycles), with a dash of "narrative technique" (such as *allusion* to the Elijah-Elisha cycle in stratum 2) and conceptual content (such as "authority" in certain passages of stratum 3). Therefore, generally, "narrative feature" equates with Bar-Efrat's "narrative world".

It is evident from Bar-Efrat's analysis, and is borne out in our proposal for Lukan structure, that features of correspondence need not be *the* central thrust of the pericopes in which they lie. However, they should generally be strongly related to it. Sixteen exceptionally well-restricted features have been identified, along with one of less restriction but demonstrable value (feature #3a below). Each is closely related to or identical with the central thrust of the pericopes in which they appear. As with all of the precedent literature reviewed in the previous chapter, the exact relationship of the

---

3   Shimon, "Some Observations on the in Biblical Narrative," *VT* 30 (1980) 154–173.
4   Bar-Efrat, "Observations," 157–158.
5   Bar-Efrat, "Observations," 158–161.
6   Bar-Efrat, "Observations," 161–168.
7   Bar-Efrat, "Observations," 168–170.

features of correspondence to the central thrust of their respective passages naturally varies with the author's desire. Therefore, a single definition cannot be formulated here. A basic development of these relationships for the Third Gospel is provided however in the section "Domain and Size of the Units That Comprise the Narrative Strata" below (page 214). A more thorough picture is developed throughout the remainder of this chapter. Certainly, it is reasonable to view Luke's structure as his "outline" for the Gospel, with the cycles roughly equivalent to chapters. If this was his intent, then each pericope should be read in light of the features that define the stratum in which it is located. The interpretation of passages should not be hijacked by the structure though, because the structure cannot contain all valid interpretations. Units of tradition have valid meaning apart from the structural context. A valid central thrust of a pericope viewed apart from its structural context may be different from its valid central thrust within the structure. The structure demonstrates Luke's train of thought. In other words, our proposal does not automatically invalidate the interpretations of scholars that differ from our conclusions.

1.1.2 Discussion of the Narrative Strata across the Four Cycles

For the present purposes, material in each cycle that lies below stratum 11 will be disregarded because it appears to be of a more diverse nature than the rest of the material. I have not observed any consistent correspondences between these sections, though they may have been there in Luke's mind. To be cautious, stratum 12 should probably be considered an interlude, or a section where the Evangelist placed accounts that he wanted included but that did not fit his pattern. This sort of phenomenon was observed in the precedent literature reviewed in the previous chapter.

A cursory glance at the correspondence table reveals strata formed by the occurrence of specific and important narrative features. There is obviously flexibility in the number of occurrences of a specific feature, yet there is little flexibility in the relative location of a feature in relation to the others (with the exception of healing accounts, as would be expected). Such a phenomenon involving eighteen narrative features[8] forming strata in identical order must be intentional, especially when each is corroborated by Lukan redaction.[9]

---

8 Eighteen is of course not a magic number. Luke may have employed additional elements in his parallels, but these have escaped my observation.
9 Luke provides no statement that he has structured the Gospel in such a fashion as proposed. To do so was not standard practice for patterned works of the period. As usual for such works, only the pattern itself demonstrates its existence. A study of καθεξῆς in the preface to the Gospel is suggestive but inconclusive (see Appendix B).

Analysis of the correspondence chart in conjunction with the synoptic relationship between Luke and Mark suggests that cycle 4 is the primary of the four and served as the pattern for the other three (see the table on page 264 where Markan passages are placed in their corresponding Lukan strata). Note that cycles 1 and 4 are based on Markan material and that, generally, cycle 4 has fewer omissions and additions of pericopes than cycle 1 (more on this later). Cycles 2 and 3 are Lukan with the exception of some material in strata 9 through 13 of cycle 3. Also note both that, apart from features 3a-g (features that convey authority), all of the remaining narrative features occur singularly and in sequence within cycle 4, and that each stratum is represented by a single passage. Cycle 3, however, contains two passages relating to the crowds and the message Jesus had for them (stratum 4), two passages where the disciples faith is at issue (stratum 7), and two "eschatological" pericopes (stratum 8; these two could however be understood as a single passage). Cycle 2 increases the number of pericopes with the authority features of cycle 4. It omits an expression of faith and commitment toward Christ by Peter, yet Peter does *speak* in the corresponding location. Cycle 1, largely Markan, omits the "to Jerusalem" indicator and adds several more pericopes with the authority features of cycle 4 or with additional features directly linked with ἐξουσία in their extended context. It omits the sections where Jesus personally confronts the religious leaders (stratum 5) and where Jesus warns the disciples or others against being like these leaders (stratum 6). Cycle 1 also matches the "eschatological" discourse with healing accounts, and omits two large blocks of Markan material that lack the appropriate narrative correspondences for their location in relation to cycle 4. Accordingly, it appears that cycle 1 was tailored from Markan blocks to resemble cycle 4, whereas cycles 2 and 3 were constructed with smaller units (mostly non-Markan) to match cycle 4 more closely.

The relationship of the four cycles to one another is more obvious in a feature-by-feature discussion. At the beginning of cycles 2–4 (stratum 1), in material introductory to a pericope, we find in narrator's voice the phrase "to Jerusalem" as an expression of purpose behind the movement of Jesus. This phrase and context only occurs elsewhere at 17:11 and is more incidental there. Also, initiating all four cycles (stratum 2) is material conveying the prophetic status of Jesus (always involving direct reference and/or allusion to the Elijah-Elisha cycle in 1 and 2 Kings), and perhaps formulated by means of *imitatio*.[10] It seems that the crowd's expression of

---

10 See Thomas Brodie's *Literary Interpreter*; "Departure," 96–109; and "Luke 9:57–62: A Systematic Adaptation of the Divine Challenge to Elijah (1 Kings 19)," in David J. Lull (ed.), *SBL Seminar Papers* 28 (Atlanta: Scholars Press, 1989) 237–245.

homage in the triumphal entry scene (Mk. 11:8 par. Lk. 19:36) reminded Luke of 2 Kings 9:13,[11] and the donkey and exultation of the crowd (Lk. 19:35–38) reminded him of 1 Kings 1:32–48.[12] Accordingly, he selected material based on 1 and 2 Kings to insert at the corresponding locations in the first three cycles. This will be discussed in detail later.

Stratum 3 (Lk. 4:31–7:50; 10:1–11:28; 14:1–14; 19:45–20:8) is more directly defined by its narrative characteristics. The passage in the fourth cycle (Lk. 19:45–20:8) contains two primary indicators of authority that are then reflected in detail in cycles 1 and 2. (1) The ministry of Jesus is likened to or related to that of John the Baptist, but not equated, and (2) ἐξ-ουσία is attributed to Jesus. In cycle 2, one of the above features is found in three of the corresponding five passages, and five of the corresponding fifteen passages in cycle 1. A well-defined stratum begins to emerge. Outside of these ranges, only Luke 9:1–11 and 19:11–27 exhibit any one of these three features, namely the attribution of authority (ἐξουσία) to Jesus.

Further definition of this band on authority is obtained when passages that relate Jesus forgiving sins (feature #3d), appointing disciples or apostles (feature #3c), declaring something lawful in contradiction of religious authorities (feature #3f), or pressing the priority of hearing his word (feature #3g) are considered. These only occur within the authority section of cycles 1 and 3. Clearly, forgiveness of sins may only be accomplished with divine *authority*. The question, "Who can forgive sins, but God alone?" is answered by Jesus, "in order that you may know that the Son of Man has *authority* on earth to forgive sins…" *Authority* over the lives of people underlies the designation of them as disciples or apostles. Furthermore, *authority* as the ultimate interpreter of the law is exercised when Jesus corrects the interpretation of the legal experts "to their faces". Finally, the priority of hearing the word of Jesus rests on its *authority*.

All of the remaining passages within this stratum across the four cycles are healings. They are included under the concept "authority" through the direct attribution of authority to Jesus' healing ministry in the opening pericope of this stratum in cycle 1 (Lk. 4:31–37). As the first healing account, it establishes an interpretative framework for the rest. "What is this message? For with *authority* and power He commands the unclean spirits and they come out" (4:36b, italics mine). The few accounts of healing external to this stratum tend to perform relatively different functions.

In consideration of the high frequency of these "authority" features within the one stratum and only two features (#3a and b) understandably

---

11 Fitzmyer (*Luke X–XXIV*, 1250) and Marshall (*Gospel of Luke*, 714) suggest this allusion.
12 See also Marshall, *Gospel of Luke*, 714.

found as exceptions, the passages within stratum 3 (Luke 4:31–7:50, 10:1–11:28, 14:1–14, and 19:45–20:8) may be considered exclusively unified as parallels. The terminus of this stratum is corroborated by the next two narrative features.

Surprisingly, with the sole exception of Luke 12:54–59, all explicit accounts of Jesus directly teaching a crowd of non-disciples (feature #4a) occur in Luke 8:1–21, 11:29–36, 14:25–35 and 20:9–18 (stratum 4).[13] Congruous with this new emphasis on non-disciples, Jesus exclusively in this band relates parables representing himself as bearer of a message from God (feature #4b).

The next clearly defined stratum (stratum 5) is formed by Jesus' personal confrontation of the religious leaders, exposing their typical spiritual, moral and religious depravity and therefore implying a lost state (feature #5). These occur purely within this band but only in cycles 2–4. Suitably, all occasions where the disciples or others are warned against being like the religious leaders (feature #6) appear immediately following feature #5 exposé accounts.

Cycle 1 rejoins the other three cycles at the next narrative feature, an expression of need for greater faith (feature #7), found only in stratum 7. This feature in cycles 2 and 3 probably was inspired more by its presence in the Markan material of cycle 1 (Lk. 8:22–25, the calming of the storm) than the corresponding passage of cycle 4 (Lk. 21:1–4, the widow's offering) in which the need for greater faith is implied, not literally stated. Nevertheless, the striking clarity of this feature in the first three cycles ("Where is your faith?" [8:25], "O men of little faith!" [12:28], "Increase our faith!" [17:5]) strongly establishes this stratum.

Scholars ponder the existence of *three* "eschatological" discourses in Luke, more in number than the other Synoptic Gospels. Each discourse is located in cycles 2–4 of stratum 8, (feature #8). Healing accounts form the parallel section in cycle 1 (more on these later).

When Jesus addresses the twelve regarding their role (feature #9), all four instances constitute the next band (stratum 9). Following this, in cycles 1, 3 and 4, Peter verbalizes faith and commitment toward Christ in response to the preceding address (stratum 10 and feature #10).

Finally, all four passion predictions that include the concept of resurrection in the context of the cost of discipleship occur in the last clearly defined stratum (stratum 11 and feature 11). The remaining portions of each cycle are related to each other thematically, but lack obvious narrative clues that join them, as mentioned above.

---

13 For a discussion of why Lk. 5:3; 20:1, and certain other passages outside this stratum, do not fit the stratum, see under stratum 4, test 1 below, page 231.

Several particularly remarkable correspondences between pairs of cycles exist (such as 13:34–35 and 19:38, 41–44) and will be drawn out in the course of our evaluation of the cyclical structure of the Third Gospel. These further buttress our proposal that Luke intended four parallel cycles tied by prominent narrative features.

1.2 Domain and Size of the Units that Comprise the Narrative Strata

Domain, which refers to the boundaries of each stratum and the conformity of the material to its defining features, is an important consideration for the validity of the proposed parallel structure. Does the material within each parallel actually conform to the narrative definition of that parallel? For instance, the vast majority, if not all, of the passages within Luke 4:31–7:50 should relate directly to the authority of Jesus. Is there any excessive overlap between strata within each cycle? If in fact Luke created these parallels, one would expect a clear initiation of each stratum and a reasonably obvious transition from one type of material to the next. For example, each account where Jesus personally confronts religious leaders, exposing their typical spiritual, moral and religious depravity, ends decisively (parallel 5). Then Jesus clearly turns to his disciples to warn them or others against being like the leaders (parallel 6). There is no overlap.[14] On rare occasions, however, pericopes are found between strata that contribute to each. This is simply for the sake of smooth transition. It is good writing technique. Preferably, also, there should be few if any significant blocks of material falling between sections and not matching one of the two adjacent strata. Contiguity would then be a concern. Another issue, the relative size of parallel sections in each stratum and of the strata themselves, must be treated. For example, is it problematic that stratum 3 of cycle 1 is considerably longer than its counterparts in the stratum are, or for that matter longer than any other section in the Gospel? Strata 1, 6, 7 and 11 are quite brief compared to the others. Is this a difficulty?

Regarding the relative size of parallel sections, this is not actually a significant issue. In the last chapter, it was clear that accepted parallel structures in precedent and contemporary literature to the Third Gospel exhibit variations of the same sort. In the chapter where Talbert's correspondences were evaluated, those patterns that proved to be most certainly of Lukan intent also display variations in proportion. He demonstrates "that while symmetry is dominant in Greek and Roman literature from the

---

14 The precedent literature analyzed in the last chapter does not suggest that verbal indications of structure or parallelism should be expected, even at the boundaries of the strata.

arrangement of a whole to the organization of the parts, it was considered poor form to have a too perfect symmetry. There must be asymmetrical elements present".[15] And one of these asymmetrical elements is the length of units.[16] For Luke this variation does not seem to be without purpose since the length of a section may be related to its function in the plot. Take, for example, the authority stratum of cycle 1. It is thoroughly appropriate that the authority of Jesus be emphasized most strongly at the inception of his public ministry. Another reason we should not be particularly concerned about "mismatched" lengths of parallel sections is that length is obviously influenced by the size of the underlying tradition. Some parables in Luke's sources were longer than others. In some instances, there might have been a lack of suitable source material, which might be the cause behind the "missing" expression of faith by Peter in cycle 2 of stratum 10. Another influence on length is the formal nature of the material. Obviously, passion predictions are shorter than conflict accounts. Finally, Luke had the freedom of choice to base his parallels on whatever features he deemed reasonable. If this resulted in slight imbalance, then that was his choice. It is clear from the broadly accepted patterns in the Gospel that Luke is by no means a slave to the principle of balance.

It will be confirmed next and below under test 10 that there is possibly only one extraneous pericope within strata 1 through 11, Luke 8:1–3. Yet, this passage may simply serve to set the scene for what follows. If we consider stratum 12 a grouping of material that Luke wanted to incorporate, but that had no suitable position in the strata, then there is no extraneous material in the whole structure besides possibly 8:1–3.

For the sake of clarity, the domain of each stratum will be considered individually. The questions asked will be whether the boundaries of the sections displaying the parallel features reasonably coincide with the boundaries of the stratum, and whether all the material within the stratum conforms to its definition. Any passages that require explanation will be covered here.

Stratum 1 – Cycles 2 through 4 exhibit the phrase "to Jerusalem," and cycle 1, "to Galilee". This latter phrase satisfies the feature as defined except for the place name. Naturally, it would have been strange to portray Jesus on a journey to Jerusalem before beginning his Galilean ministry, so we should not demand the "to Jerusalem" phrase at this early point. It is indeed conceivable, and justifiable, that Luke chose not to use this feature in cycle 1. Whatever the conclusion, each instance lays within the stratum,

---

15 Talbert, *Literary Patterns*, 78.
16 See Talbert, *Literary Patterns*, 77–9, for his discussion of asymmetry in ancient literature that is characterized by balance.

with no overlap into the next. For additional discussion, see under tests 6 (page 234) and 1 (page 228) below.

Stratum 2 – All of the material within this stratum conforms to the feature that establishes it. This is thoroughly discussed below under tests 6 (page 235) and 1 (page 229). A brief note on Luke 13:23–30 and 19:41–44 would be helpful at this point. Recall the definition of this stratum: "the prophetic status of Jesus is conveyed, involving direct reference and/or allusion to the Elijah-Elisha cycle in 1and 2 Kings, and is accompanied by the theme of divine rejection of those who reject Jesus/God." The parable of the narrow door (13:23–30) vividly portrays the exclusion from the kingdom (divine rejection) of those who reject discipleship (vv. 26–27). The prophetic lament over Jerusalem (19:41–44) both depicts Jesus prophesying and proclaiming that the divine destruction (rejection) of the city is a consequence of their rejection of God's visitation. Never are the passages immediately following this stratum considered to be related to the prophetic status of Jesus or the Elijah-Elisha cycle. Therefore, the boundaries are distinct, with no overlap.

Stratum 3 – A few passages in this stratum should be discussed briefly. Luke 6:17–49 of cycle 1, the sermon on the plain, begins as a healing account and summary that validates Jesus' authority to preach. The divine authority of Jesus is foundational to the sermon as evidenced by Jesus, at the climactic conclusion, stressing the priority of hearing his word (Lk. 6:46–49), feature 3g. Naturally, the reference in the conclusion to "hearing his word" points back to the whole sermon, with his audience being called "those who hear" (v. 27). Furthermore, within the sermon Jesus speaks on behalf of the Father, revealing the divine will, and in the conclusion he accepts the title "Lord" and commands obedience to his word, "Why do you call me 'Lord, Lord,' and do not do what I say?" (Lk. 6:46). In fact, the authority validated in the healing summary is that exercised in the sermon; so the healing summary and sermon are essentially a thematic unit. Turning to Luke 10:25–37 (the parable of the Good Samaritan), it does not precisely exhibit any of features 3a-g. Nevertheless, it uses a means of communicating the authority of Jesus identical to several other passages in this stratum. A Jewish leader, in this instance a teacher of the law, is shown to be of lesser authority on legal matters than Jesus is. In this sense, it is akin to feature 3f. On Luke 10:38–42 of cycle 2, at the home of Mary and Martha, feature 3g is displayed as Jesus affirms the priority of Mary's hearing his word (v. 39) to Martha's socially expected preparations. I. Howard Marshall goes straight to the point, however, when he summarizes the thrust of this pericope as "the duty of listening to Jesus as the teacher of the word of

God".[17] Understood in this manner, authority is a central issue. Regarding Luke 19:45–48 of cycle 4, the clearing of the temple, if it were considered to be a separate passage to 20:1–8, the questioning of Jesus' authority, then it would not contain any of the identified features for this stratum. How is joining them justified? Quite simply, along with the teaching in 20:1, Luke 19:45–48 is employed by Luke as a referent to ταῦτα in the religious leaders' question. Fitzmyer expresses some doubt however, suggesting that Luke has temporally distanced the challenge from the clearing of the temple, believing that Mark places it "the next day" (11:12) while Luke considers it "on one of the days".[18] He fails to see the passing of yet another day or more in Mark. Note that Mark 11:19 describes Jesus and the disciples leaving the city that evening, Καὶ ὅταν ὀψὲ ἐγένετο, ἐξεπορεύοντο ἔξω τῆς πόλεως, and returning in the morning. Lane explains that "the particle ὅταν in Mark usually means 'when' and not 'whenever.'"[19] However, Luke often uses it with the sense "whenever". It is doubtful that he did a word study of Mark, so he may well have understood it as reading, "whenever evening came, they went out of the city". This could suggest to Luke, "on one of the days". Furthermore, Marshall rightly stresses the active nature of ποιεῖς (Lk. 20:2), which more likely includes the cleansing along with the teaching. The setting of the temple also connects the two passages. Therefore, Luke 19:45–48 comfortably joins 20:1–8 as a unit.

None of the identified features of this stratum spill over into the next. Accordingly, the boundary is well defined across the stratum. See also the discussion under tests 6 (page 240) and 1 (page 230) below.

Stratum 4 – Three pericopes will be discussed regarding their conformity to this stratum. First, Luke 8:1–3 of cycle 1 tells of Jesus traveling about with the twelve and some women who were supporting them. None of the features of stratum 3 or 4 is evident. It is not clearly about authority, nor is Jesus telling a parable or speaking to the crowds. Generally, scholars view it as an introduction to a new section of itinerant ministry. For this reason, it has been placed with stratum 4. Perhaps Luke intended it to stand out by its violation of the pattern, but this effect is not achieved because the reader can only perceive the pattern after the first cycle. On later readings it would be more noticeable. Even without awareness of Luke's cyclical structure commentators have noted the peculiarity of this text and the resultant emphasis on the role of the women.[20] We should probably view it as an introduction (only three verses) integral to the following material and

---

17 Marshall, *Gospel of Luke*, 450.
18 Fitzmyer, *Luke X–XXIV*, 1273.
19 Lane, *Mark*, 403, n.34.
20 Liefeld is representative, *Luke*, 905.

therefore not separately subject to the requirements of a stratum. Second, Luke 8:18–21 of cycle 1 appears to break the address to the crowd when Jesus is told that his family wants to see him. Nevertheless, his equation of his word with that of God is a perfect closure to this section on that very topic. No feature binds it to the stratum, but its theme certainly does. In fact, it should be seen as the close of the previous scene and not as a separate entity. Third, Luke 11:27–28 of cycle 2 relates an interjection from a woman in the crowd. Again, Jesus equates his word with that of God. In this case, it functions not as a closure but as an introduction to this topic. Immediately Luke presents Jesus telling the crowd a parable teaching that his message is from God. It lacks the observed features for the stratum, but it is intimately bound to it in theme and should not be seen as independent of what follows.

There is a major change of scene at the end of this stratum in each cycle. No longer does Jesus speak to the crowds and no longer does the theme of the stratum continue. The boundary is crystal clear. For additional discussion of this stratum, see under test 6 below (page 244).

Stratum 5 – Two passages in this stratum should be mentioned. First, Luke 15:1–32 of cycle 3 is accepted so strongly by scholars as a parables chapter that the setting is often overlooked. The Lukan setting places the Pharisees and teachers of the law in Jesus' presence and directs the parables at them (Lk. 15:1–2). Their reaction, confirming the confrontation, is revealed at Luke 16:14. This reaction aids our understanding of the function of the second passage, Luke 16:1–13, the parable of the shrewd manager.[21] Although Jesus speaks to his disciples, the Pharisees take offense. There is no reason to assume that the Lord's parabolic evaluation of the religious leaders has ceased at the close of chapter 15.[22] He continues the exposé in their hearing, but also as a lesson to his disciples. Indeed, the parable appears to be a comment on Pharisaic practice. This stratum suggests that according to Luke the shrewd manager symbolizes the Pharisees and not the disciples, which solves the problem posed by the commendation toward the end.[23] We may see the action commended to be the manager's removal

---

21 Walther Bindemann recognizes the parable's role as a confrontation or provocation ("Ungerechte als Vorbilder: Gottesreich und Gottesrecht in den Gleichnissen vom 'ungerechten Verwalter' und 'ungerechten Richter,'" *TLZ* 120 (11, 1995) 955–70; see especially 959–961).
22 Contra Green, *Gospel of Luke*, 589.
23 H. Binder considers this a parable against the Pharisees and scribes in light of 15:1–2, but he incorrectly equates the steward with Jesus ("Missdeutbar oder eindeutig? – Gedanken zu einem Gleichnis Jesu," *TZ* 51 (1995) 41–9). C.S. Mann attempts to equate the steward with the Essenes by an emendation of ἀδικία to ἀνικία, but has insufficient textual warrant; "Unjust Steward or Prudent Manager?," *ExpTim* 102 (1991) 234–35. R.G. Lunt adequately demonstrates that the steward stands for the

of his self-serving excess demand on the debtors, which has its parallel in the careers of the Pharisees. The other details fit this scheme also. The manager (Pharisees) was accused of wasting the possessions of the rich man, presumably God (Lk. 16:1). This could imply that the Pharisees were mismanaging cultic finances (favored by v. 9) or, more metaphorically, any divinely ordained religious responsibilities under their domain. The rich man in response had removed him from his managerial position (v. 2). In other words, the Pharisees were no longer legitimate leaders in God's kingdom. To gain the respect of those under his influence, soon to be peers, the manager lessens their debt burden (vv. 3–7). Those under his influence appear to be the people of God in this parable since their homes in verse 4 parallel eternal dwellings in verse 9. Precisely what these debts refer to in real life and whether the manager's original mismanagement involved increasing the size of each debt for his own profit is never made clear, but seems likely. The commendation (v. 8–9) however is for the easing of burdens, which in some way relates to their acceptance into the kingdom (v. 9). Accordingly, the Pharisees are probably encouraged here to use their waning authority to ease (cultic? financial?) burdens that oppress the people, probably to reflect God's actual demands. Such action hopefully would reflect the type of heart necessary for entrance into the kingdom. This accords with the expressed desire of the manager in verse 4 to be an accepted part of the community (of God), which possibly here refers to the Church. Jesus' statement about the incompatibility between the love of God and the love of money (v. 13) may reflect this apparent focus in the parable on the correct heart that disavows financial profit. The statement seems to imply that love for God is the assumed motivation in the parable.

Stratum 6 – Although 12:13–21 may be seen to have similarities to what follows (12:22–34, stratum 7) in that the parable of the rich fool may be understood to encourage faith, it is still a warning against imitation of the religious leaders' greed and therefore fits stratum 6. Since it is not spoken to the disciples and since it is more a warning against a Pharisaic attitude than an encouragement to faith, it does not fit stratum 7. For a discussion of Luke 17:1–4, see the redaction-critical study of "stratum 6" under test 6

Pharisees, in "Expounding the Parables: III. The Parable of the Unjust Steward (Luke 16 $^{1-15}$)" *ExpTim* 77 (1965–66) 132–36, an expansion of his earlier article "Towards an Interpretation of the Parable of the Unjust Steward (Luke xvi. 1–18)," *ExpTim* 66 (1955) 335–37. See also Ehrhard Kamlah, "Die Parabel vom ungerechten Verwalter (Luk. 16, 1ff.) im Rahmen der Knechtsgleichnisse," in O. Betz (*et. al.*), *Abraham unser Vater, für O. Michel* (Leiden: E.J. Brill, 1963) 276–94. Thomas Hoeren's suggestion is unpersuasive, that a Sabbatical year law under Hillel is a background to this passage, placing religious law over secular law, "Das Gleichnis vom ungerechten Verwalter (Lukas 16.1–8a) – zugleich ein Beitrag zur Geschichte der Restschuldbefreiung," *NTS* 41 (4, 1995) 620–629.

below, page 249.

At the end of this stratum in cycles 2 through 4, the scene does not change but the tone of Jesus' teaching does. He moves from warning to encouragement, from detrimental influences to the positive response. This transition occurs precisely at the boundary of the stratum. Consistent with this, cycle 1 resumes at this point with a new scene (Lk. 8:22–25, calming of the storm).

Stratum 7 – Regarding Jesus' healing of the ten lepers in cycle 3 (Lk. 17:11–19), the one problem for our proposal is that it is not a lesson directed at the disciples, though Luke probably understood them to be present. It is however commonly regarded as thematically linked to the preceding account where the disciples ask Jesus to increase their faith.[24] In this sense, it serves to introduce the theme and to exemplify the power of faith. Admittedly, this is the most difficult passage for our proposed structure. The options are either to consider it an instance where Luke's interpretation differs from what most would conclude about the passage, or to assume that Luke only intended it to fit loosely into the Gospel's structure. Since defense of such a vast and detailed structure as Luke's is necessarily a cumulative case, rejection of Luke 17:11–19 must be seen in this light. Even if it is rejected, the case is hardly diminished. See the discussion in the conclusion of this section, page 225. In cycle 4, encouragement of the disciples to have greater faith is not as explicit in Luke 21:1–4 as in the parallel passages. This account of a widow's offering lacks the term πίστις, but that does not mean the concept is not there, and Lukan parallels clearly do not require verbal repetition. It appears that the widow is used by Jesus as an object lesson on faith for the disciples, which is essentially encouragement to have greater faith.[25] Certainly a main point of the passage is that "the true measure of a gift is not how much is given but how much remains behind, or the percentage of one's means (the cost to the giver)," as Fitzmyer states.[26] However, he may go too far in rejecting all views that consider the motive of the woman. He argues that "nothing is said about the inner 'spirit' of the widow".[27] Indeed, nothing is explicitly said. It may certainly be implied however. Fitzmyer (and possibly all commentators) readily admits that the widow is favorably compared to the teachers of the law described in Luke 20:45–47. Yet he determines that the teachers' flaw here is in improper motive that reveals itself in actions.[28] If

---

24 See for example Nolland, *Luke 9:21–18:34*, 844.
25 See Bock's helpful discussion, *Luke 9:51–24:53*, 1633, 1644–1648.
26 Fitzmyer chooses this view of the five that he presents. See the various scholars that hold to each view, in *Luke X–XXIV*, 1320–1321.
27 Fitzmyer, *Luke X–XXIV*, 1321.
28 Fitzmyer, *Luke X–XXIV*, 1317.

there is actually a comparison, then it is reasonable that not only the widow's action is an element but also her motive. Marshall, Geldenhuys and Danker, among others, appropriately consider the widow's faith to be a main point of the passage.[29] As Marshall writes, "the incident fits in with Luke's emphasis on the way in which true religion affects a person's attitude to wealth…; in the present case the widow gave all that she had and thereby expressed her faith in God to provide for her needs."[30] The phrase "all that she had to live on" may legitimately imply an act of faith because she has placed herself willingly at risk. Nevertheless, if this passage is considered a poor fit with this stratum, it still meshes neatly with the preceding material as a comment on the negative example of the scribes. So it could be seen as part of stratum 6, leaving a vacancy in stratum 7. Such a gap is demonstrably acceptable in ancient patterned literature (see the previous chapter) and it does no damage to the overall strength of our proposal.

In cycles 1, 3 and 4, the termination of this stratum is accomplished by a change in scene. With the second cycle, a clear change of topic occurs. The boundary is therefore well defined for this stratum. For a redaction-critical analysis, see under test 6 below (page 250).

Stratum 8 – For our discussion of Luke 8:26–56 below, it would be helpful first to establish two points: (1) that Luke was familiar with the concept of Jesus' involvement in judgment at the general resurrection and even of his effecting it; and (2) that he shows some structural interest in the subject such that it might color Luke 8:26–56 through parallelism. First, Synoptic evidence that Jesus will be involved in last day judgment (which occurs at the general resurrection) abounds, some passages more direct than others. See Luke 12:35–40 (par. Mt. 24:43–44); Lk. 12:42–46[31] (par. Mt. 24:45–51); Lk. 17:26–38;[32] 19:12–27; 21:34–36;[33] Mk. 13:26–27 (par. Mt. 24:30–31); <u>Mt. 13:24–30</u>, <u>36–43</u>; 25:14–30, and <u>31–46</u>. Though less relevant, evidence in the Gospel of John is readily available. See John <u>5:28–29</u>; <u>6:44</u>, <u>54</u>; <u>11:25–26</u>; and <u>14:2–3</u>. The underlined passages go beyond presenting his involvement in judgment at the general resurrection.

---

29 Marshall, *Gospel of Luke*, 750; Norval Geldenhuys, *Commentary on the Gospel of Luke* (London: Marshall, Morgan & Scott, 1950) 520–21; Frederick W. Danker, *Jesus and the New Age: According to Luke. A Commentary on the Third Gospel* (St. Louis: Layton, 1972) 327–328.
30 Marshall, *Gospel of Luke*, 750.
31 Marshall correctly understands this passage to refer to judgment at the parousia; *Gospel of Luke*, 532–545.
32 That this passage refers to the final judgment, see Marshall, *Gospel of Luke*, 656–669.
33 Marshall notes that the phrase "stand before the Son of Man" pictures Jesus as judge; *Gospel of Luke*, 783.

They describe him as in some sense effecting the resurrection. No doubt the idea was known to Luke.[34] Second, it is interesting that three of the five Lukan passages above lie in stratum 8 (12:35–40; 17:26–38; 21:34–36), the same as the accounts of the Gerasene demoniac and Jairus' daughter. Luke 12:42–46 immediately follows in stratum 9. Marshall correctly understands each of these passages to refer to final judgment (see the notes to the passages above). This background prepares us for a discussion of Luke's stratum 8 material in cycle 1.

The two passages of cycle 1 may appear not to conform to the eschatological feature #8: the Gerasene demoniac (Lk. 8:26–39), and the complex of the healings of Jairus' daughter and the woman with the hemorrhage (Lk. 8:40–56). These Markan accounts are not discourses, but Luke chose to keep them in parallel with three later eschatological discourses. Consequently, the stratum will still be described by the term "eschatological discourse" even though "eschatology" alone might be sufficient. Do the two accounts in question touch on any eschatological themes? Indeed they do. Luke introduces such a theme into the Gerasene account through reference to the Abyss. See the discussion of this under test 6 below (page 251).

The revivification account within 8:40–56 should also be considered "eschatological". Both Harris and Liefeld cite καθεύδω (Lk. 8:52) as a metaphorical allusion to the general resurrection (cf. 1 Thes. 4:13–14; 5:10; Jn. 11:11),[35] a parousia event. The thrust of their argument is that "sleep" in reference to death brings to mind a point of "awakening," a common metaphor in New Testament discussions of the resurrection; and they understand this to be an intentional, dominant thematic element in the present pericope. Even if καθεύδω itself did not direct Luke's mind to the eschatological resurrection, and this may be the case, any account of revivification would probably do so. The passage would therefore draw a close comparison between Jesus' ability to raise the dead during his incarnate ministry and his ability to effect the general resurrection.

In his study of revivification accounts in the Gospels, Harris delineates five christological themes illustrated by them: (1) "They pointed to the Messiahship of Jesus," (2) "They demonstrated the power of Jesus," (3) "They illustrated the compassion of Jesus," (4) "They pictured the conquest of Jesus over death," (5) "They prefigured the resurrection of

---

34 See also Murray J. Harris' discussion of the general resurrection in *Raised Immortal: Resurrection and Immortality in the New Testament* (Grand Rapids: Eerdmans, 1983) 172–185.

35 Liefeld, *Luke*, 917; Murray J. Harris, "'The Dead are Restored to Life': Miracles of Revivification in the Gospels," in vol. 6 of David Wenham and Craig Blomberg (eds.), *Gospel Perspectives, The Miracles of Jesus*, (Sheffield: JSOT Press, 1986) 306.

Jesus and of all people." Of the five, the themes that primarily distinguish this pericope from others are four and five, both of which are fully realized only in the eschaton. He develops the fifth theme in part as follows:

> How are the 'raisings' linked to 'resurrection'? In the Synoptics the link is forged by the ambiguity of the verbs ἐγείρειν and ἀνιστάναι, which may mean 'get up' from a reclining or lying position, or 'arise' from the dead. So when Jesus addresses the young man at Nain with the word ἐγέρθητι (Lk 7:14) and Jairus's daughter with the word ἔγειρε (Mk 5:41), both forms meaning 'Up you get!,' the Christian reader thinks of the coming resurrection day when the same command will be issued, 'Arise!' (cf. Eph 5:14). When, in response to the command of Jesus, it is said that the little girl 'got up' (ἠγέρθη, Mt 9:25; Mk 5:42; Lk 8:55), the reader would have recalled that exactly the same forms were traditionally used of the resurrection of Jesus (e.g., Mk 16:6 and 1 Thess 4:14, respectively) and the same verbs of the resurrection of Christians (e.g., 1 Cor 15:52 and Mt 12:41, respectively).[36]

Therefore, it is reasonable to assume that Luke employed for structural purposes in this pericope the prefiguration of the general resurrection effected by Christ in conjunction with his return, especially in light of his addition of the Abyss in the preceding passage. Further discussion of Luke 8:40–56 is located under test 6 below (page 254).

In summary, there is substantial reason to believe that Luke discerned the common thread of these pericopes to be eschatological. These manifestations of divine power disclose the ability and authority Jesus possesses to function as final Judge, even of demons, and as the instrument through whom the dead will be raised. Various redactional and pre-Lukan features, as well as corroboration from Matthew, focus the broad themes in the texts onto their relationship with the return of Christ and its associated events. For a redaction critical look at this stratum, see under test 6 below (page 251).

The transition from stratum 8 to 9 in cycle 1 is accomplished through a change in scene (9:1). In cycle 2, Luke signals the focus on the twelve with a question from Peter, "Lord, are you telling this parable to us, or to everyone" (12:41) a rather blatant indication to the reader. The transition is not as clear for cycle 3, and this will be treated next under stratum 9. Finally, the transition in cycle 4 is a change in scene. Therefore, apart from cycle 3, the boundary between stratum 8 and 9 is clear.

Stratum 9 – Episodic narrative of the type throughout Jesus' public ministry ends at this stratum in cycle 4 (22:1). Now events flow into one

---

36 Harris, "Dead are Restored," 318–320.

another more causally, and perhaps temporally,[37] and Luke begins to select simply representative features. After all, he now has to match episodic material (cycles 1–3) with this more continuous material (cycle 4).

Jesus addresses the twelve regarding their role in stratum 9. How should we view Luke 22:1–6, Judas' betrayal, in conjunction with 22:7–30 of cycle 4, the last supper? The arrest of Jesus was soon to occur, as foreshadowed in Luke 22:1–6 by another reference to the hatred of the religious leaders and by Judas' betrayal. In this light, the Lord arranged for private fellowship with the "apostles" to display his love for them through a portrayal of his impending sacrifice, the Last Supper. Luke omits the anointing at Bethany contained in Mark, thus maintaining the heightened tension and concentration on the twelve.

In the midst of this meaningful, intimate scene, Luke amazingly inserts a dispute among the disciples about who was greatest. Neither Mark nor Matthew include this selfishly inappropriate behavior on the part of the twelve here. Such conduct displays a serious misunderstanding of ministry, which Jesus corrects with the statement, "…the greatest among you should be like the youngest, and the one who rules like the one who serves" (22:26). This dispute conveys that the disciples still had much to learn. Interestingly, each of the parallel sections in the other cycles relates directly to the disciples learning about their ministry.

Luke prefaces the blessing of the children, in cycle 3, with the parable of the Pharisee and the tax collector from L tradition (18:9–14). As a preview, it identifies the error of the disciples in 18:15–17. Jesus' saying on humility, "for everyone who exalts himself shall be humbled, but he who humbles himself shall be exalted" (v. 14) concludes the parable and sets the next passage in stark contrast, where the pride of the disciples is exhibited when they rebuke those bringing children. Marshall notes this strong connection through the theme of humility.[38] (Interestingly, if Bock is correct that verse 14 is eschatological,[39] then the preceding parable should be taken as the conclusion to the "eschatological discourse," as far as our structure is concerned.) Naturally the latter passage is about who may enter the kingdom. This is universally recognized. However, it is also about the role of the disciples in the presence of Jesus. He addresses *them*, and corrects *them*. They should not be "blocking entrance to the Kingdom;"[40] rather, they should be fostering it. Clearly, they had not learned the lesson of the previous parable, which may be understood as part of the disciples' instruction; and this is what the stratum suggests. Commentators frequently

---

37 C.F. Evans observes this transition, in *Saint Luke*, 765.
38 Marshall, *Gospel of Luke*, 677, 681.
39 Bock, *Luke 9:51–24:53*, 1465.
40 See Danker, *Jesus and the New Age*, 298–299.

suggest that the audience expands at Luke 18:9 from just disciples to include "certain ones who trusted in themselves that they were righteous," like Pharisees.[41] The disciples are still necessarily present. However, τις in reference to people, in the sense of "some" or "certain," often continues the focus on those who are already central in the immediate context, unless of course a qualifier obviously changes the subject (e.g. "of the Pharisees").[42] In other words, "some" in Luke 18:9 may indeed refer to an immature subset of the disciples, who are already central in the immediate context (18:1). Certainly, the mere presence of a Pharisee in a parable does not demand that the parable is directed to Pharisees. Either way, the disciples are present and the parable functions as an interpretative backdrop or setting for the disciples' lesson in Luke 18:15–17.

For cycles 1, 3 and 4, the stratum is cleanly terminated by Peter's verbalizations of faith and commitment. Cycle 2 ends distinctly as Jesus predicts his passion, a completely different subject to the role of the disciples.

Stratum 10 – All three of Peter's expressions of faith and commitment reside in this stratum. Obviously, the boundary between these and the following passion predictions is precise.

Stratum 11 – Three times in Luke, Jesus predicts his passion and resurrection in the context of the cost of discipleship (9:22–27; 12:49–53; 18:29–34). These, along with the actual passion and resurrection, constitute stratum 11. Resurrection is a subordinate feature that is explicit in cycles 1 and 3, but implied by the term "baptism" in cycle 3 (12:49–53).[43] The passion prediction of 9:44 may very indirectly imply the resurrection if it is seen as a review of 9:22. Yet this is considerably more subtle than the typical Lukan parallel. The lack of a cost of discipleship context disqualifies it however. Similar arguments apply to Luke 17:25.[44]

Stratum 12 – The pericopes in this stratum appear to deal with the presence or delay of the kingdom. Unfortunately, "the kingdom" is such a common and pervasive theme in the Gospel that no confidence can be maintained that Luke had this alone in mind. It is best to err on the side of caution.

Conclusion: We have found that few passages appear to have any difficulty with conformity to the feature that defines their strata. They amount to

---

41 Fitzmyer, *Luke X–XXIV*, 1185–86; Nolland, *Luke 9:21–18:34*, 875.
42 Some examples are Mk. 14:4; Lk. 21:5; Rom. 3:3; 2 Cor. 2:2 and 10:2 (both having the same grammatical construction as Lk. 18:9); Phil. 1:15; Heb. 4:6 and 10:25.
43 For a discussion of how the baptism that Jesus refers to in Lk. 12:50 might imply the resurrection and why this is not an artificial distinction, see p. 260f.
44 See note 170 on page 261 for a more detailed discussion of why Lk. 17:25 does not fit the definition of this stratum.

a small fraction of the total number in the Gospel. If the healings of the Gerasene demoniac (Lk. 8:26–39), Jairus' daughter in conjunction with the woman with the hemorrhage (8:40–56), and the ten lepers (17:11–19) are not accepted as in conformity with their strata, then only 3 of 68 pericopes (4%) throughout strata 1–11 are "misfits". Such lack of conformity is seen in similar to much greater proportions in some of the well accepted patterned works in our analysis of precedent literature in the last chapter: 1 Samuel 9–31, about 5% by pericope; 2 Samuel 11–20, at least 45% by pericope; Revelation 6–16, about 55% by number of lines; 1 John, about 20% by number of lines; Thucydides' *History of the Peloponnesian War*, about 40% by book. Indeed, if Luke 1:5–2:52 is considered primarily a comparison between John the Baptist and Jesus, and if Fitzmyer's analysis of it is basically correct, then about 25% (by number of lines) does not clearly conform. The 4% for our structure is quite impressive. Furthermore, if the first cycle of Luke is ignored, only 1 of 39 pericopes (2.5%) has any trouble with conformity. When it is remembered that ancient writers generally considered it best to violate their patterned structures (discussed in chapter 2), the three slightly difficult passages in Luke's structure are not problematic.

At this point, it is useful to examine precedence for Luke's omission of parallel units in his structure, namely strata 5 and 6 of cycle 1, and stratum 10 of cycle 2. Regarding the latter, it may be that Luke simply did not have available a fourth verbalization of faith and commitment toward Christ by Peter, as suggested at the beginning of this discussion of domain. The two gaps in the first cycle are probably related to plot, just as is the length of the authority section in that cycle. It is appropriate for Luke to highlight the authority of Jesus at the beginning of his public ministry. Likewise, he may appropriately have wanted to avoid portraying Jesus as an aggressor, or as in conflict, this early on. The precedent cases presented in the last chapter demonstrate that omissions of parallels were common and not considered defective. They are found in 2 Chronicles 14–35, Judges, Job and John. In Job, just as in Luke, for dramatic effect an expected parallel is omitted and material apparently slightly divergent is inserted in its place. Furthermore, omissions were common practice for Herodotus, Thucydides and Plutarch. Aside from poetry, message and plot are always allowed to override the structure when desired.

The boundaries of each stratum are clearly defined and the contiguity of relevant material is perfect throughout strata 1 through 11. Variation in the relative lengths of sections (e.g. cycle 2, stratum 4 or cycle 4, stratum 10) is natural in patterned writing of that era and demonstrates that Luke was not a slave to the principle of balance. Additional analysis is possible to test the validity of the four-fold cyclical structure of Luke. First, we will determine whether the strata are founded on types of features commonly used in precedent and contemporary patterned literature to the Third Gospel. Second, the tests for authorial intent applied to Talbert's and Tannehill's correspondences will be applied to our structure.

1.3 Reasonableness of the Narrative Bases for the Correspondences

Since our analysis of precedent literature needed to be brief and therefore sketchy, we will only make some general observations about how the fourfold repetitive structure of Luke conforms to the precedent. Clearly, it is thoroughly consistent with the structures examined in the previous chapter. Within this literature – throughout the time span represented and across the three categories of OT, NT and Greco-Roman – the types of features used to form regular parallel patterns encompass those employed by the Evangelist. He uses themes, literary forms, formulae, actions/events, wording, function of unit texts in the plot, and characters to construct his overall pattern. Interestingly, of the literature surveyed, most of the observed parallel features peculiar to Greco-Roman works of around Luke's day are not represented in his pattern: character traits, broad spheres of personal activity, contrast (opposites in parallel), and numerical pattern. This suggests that the more ancient literature had a stronger structural influence on him. Yet the combination, types and number of features in the narrative structure of the Gospel coincide most closely with the Old Testament examples, especially the Elijah-Elisha cycles. There is also strong similarity in this regard with the parallelism in 1 and 2 Samuel and 1 Kings as well as that in 2 Chronicles 14–35. Therefore, it is reasonable to conclude that his structural concept for the Gospel was dependent to some degree on Old Testament patterns, whether consciously or subconsciously.

Our precedent literature also answers the concern over stratum 12, which does not clearly contain the types of correspondences discerned in the other strata. "Interludes" of this sort exist in several of the precedent cases: the Elijah-Elisha cycles, 1 and 2 Samuel with 1 Kings, 2 Samuel 11–20, Revelation, and Thucydides. Such breaks should not be viewed as problematical, but as evidence that the author was bound more by his concern for communication, or other interests, than by pattern. The pattern is a tool, just as are interludes.

Based on the literary conventions familiar to Luke and his readers, as evidenced in the precedent literature, the observed features that form the strata of the Third Gospel are eminently reasonable. If the Lukan audience were sensitive to the common structural cues utilized by their contemporary authors, then recognition of the Gospel structure to some degree would be probable, especially if the expectation was there. Modern readers are neither familiar with these cues nor expecting such patterns, which we consider "artificial". Although the modern trend is demonstrably appropriate, to interpret the Gospels as story (not implying fiction) rather than a mere collection of traditional units,[45] it is still possible for them to exhibit detailed parallel structure. The Old Testament historical-biographical texts examined in the previous chapter are fine examples. They were written as factual stories, yet the facts were selected and shaped to be conveyed in repetitive form. Accordingly, our proposal for the structure of the Lukan Gospel is entirely reasonable.

1.4 Application of the Tests for Intentionality to the Cyclical Narrative Structure of Luke 4:14–24:53

As demonstrated in the analysis of Charles Talbert's literary patterns, the tests for intentionality are particularly useful in the evaluation of structured parallelism for authorial intent. Such phenomena produce strong results under tests 8 and 9 and especially test 5. In order confidently to consider as intentional the proposed structure of Luke 4:14–24:53, its performance under the tests must generally be strong. In the introduction, the tests were themselves evaluated against the universally recognized parallelism between John the Baptist and Jesus in the infancy narratives. Ten of the eleven tests correctly indicated Lukan intent. Test 6 did not apply because redaction criticism is not confidently possible in this section. Correspondingly, if the proposed structure of Luke 4:14–24:53 approximates the strength of this result, it too must be confidently accepted as a product of Lukan design, or at least a close approximation of what Luke intended.

Test 1: *The greater the restriction of elements of correspondence to the relevant passages, the greater is the probability of authorial intent.*

Stratum 1 – The elements of this parallel are (1) the words εἰς Ἱεροσόλυμα or εἰς Ἱερουσαλήμ, (2) in a context that highlights the destination as the driving purpose of Jesus' journey, and (3) in an introductory section to a pericope (narrator's voice). Only in Luke 9:51–56; 13:22–30; 19:28–40 and 17:11 are the words εἰς Ἱεροσόλυμα or εἰς Ἱερουσαλήμ located in an introductory portion, but the latter has a distinctly more incidental flavor than the other three. Reference to Jerusalem here appears more to explain Jesus' presence in the border region of Samaria and Galilee.

---

45 See, for example, Ernest Best, *Mark*; and Bas van Iersel, *Reading Mark*, W.H. Bisscheroux (tr.), (Collegeville, Minnesota: Liturgical Press, 1988).

Lk. 9:51 Ἐγένετο δὲ ἐν τῷ συμπληροῦσθαι τὰς ἡμέρας τῆς ἀναλήμψεως αὐτοῦ καὶ αὐτὸς τὸ πρόσωπον ἐστήρισεν τοῦ πορεύεσθαι εἰς Ἰερουσαλήμ.

Lk. 13:22 Καὶ διεπορεύετο κατὰ πόλεις καὶ κώμας διδάσκων καὶ πορείαν ποιούμενος εἰς Ἰεροσόλυμα.

Lk. 19:28 Καὶ εἰπὼν ταῦτα ἐπορεύετο ἔμπροσθεν ἀναβαίνων εἰς Ἰεροσόλυμα.

Lk. 17:11 Καὶ ἐγένετο ἐν τῷ πορεύεσθαι εἰς Ἰερουσαλὴμ καὶ αὐτὸς διήρχετο διὰ μέσον Σαμαρείας καὶ Γαλιλαίας.

So the context of Luke 17:11 does not highlight this destination as the driving purpose of Jesus' journey, as the parallelism demands by Luke's choice. Certainly "to Jerusalem" in Luke 17:11 may function as an intentional parallel of a non-structural variety. However, its purpose must be pursued on other grounds than the cyclical structure. The phrase "to Jerusalem" also occurs at Luke 18:31, but it is not in the narrator's voice. This is important since the beginning of an entirely new section is more clearly indicated for the reader by the narrator than by the words of a character, especially in Luke since the other indications of new sections are in the narrator's voice. Consequently, the restriction is perfect. If the exclusion of Luke 17:11 is denied, then the restriction (3 of 4) is still remarkable in a work so dominated by the journey.

It should be noted at this point that Luke 4:14–15 conforms to the requirements of this parallel if "to Galilee" is allowed to replace "to Jerusalem". Obviously, the Galilean ministry could not easily have been characterized as part of the journey to Jerusalem. Nevertheless, this phrase is found in an introductory section to a pericope (narrator's voice) where the context highlights this destination as under the divine purpose of the Holy Spirit. "To Galilee" in parallel with "to Jerusalem" is not essential to the structure, so it will not be pushed; but there is reason to accept the possibility of intent.

Stratum 2 – Restriction of direct reference or allusion to the Elijah-Elisha cycle of the material in this stratum (Lk. 4:16–30; 9:52–56, 57–62; 13:23–30, 31–35; 19:29–40 and 41–44) is not the best, due to their frequency in the Gospel. A reasonable list of commonly cited passages related to this OT text within Luke 4:15–24:53 would include Luke 4:16–30; 5:12–16; 7:11–17; 9:7–9, 10–17, 18–27, 28–36, 52–56, 57–62; 13:23–30, 31–35; 17:11–19; 19:29–40, 41–44.[46] For a discussion of the passages of stratum 2 and

---

46 See any thorough commentary that has strong interaction with the Old Testament.

how they conform to the parallelism, see the redaction critical analysis below, which begins on page 235. The theme of divine rejection of those who reject Jesus/God is even more frequent: Lk. 4:16–30; 9:5, 9:23–26, 57–62; 10:10–16; 11:29–32, 42–52; 12:9–10; 12:13–21(?), 42–46(?), 54–59; 13:1–9, 22–30, 34–35; 14:15–24, 25–35(?); 16:19–31; 19:11–27, 41–44 and 20:9–18. The likelihood of some collocations of these two elements of feature 2 is significant. Collocations actually occur in Luke 4:16–30; 9:1–9, 18–27, 51–62; 13:22–35 and 19:29–44. Four of these six are immediately preceded by "to Jerusalem" or "to Galilee" phrases, those of stratum 2.[47] As defined, the parallelism is absolutely restricted. If it is objected that requiring the connection with "to Jerusalem/Galilee" "stacks the deck," four of six is still fairly strong, especially since 9:1–9 and 9:18–27 are close together, providing less opportunity for coincidental parallelism.

Stratum 3 – The incident with the synagogue ruler in Luke 13:10–17, which lies outside the stratum, is a healing account, so it displays feature #3a. Accordingly, it could have been placed in stratum 3, but for some reason Luke chose otherwise. It is difficult to say why since it now lies in the interlude stratum (12), which manifests no consistent parallelism. There are two other healing accounts in the interlude and five others dispersed throughout the structure. This by far the least restricted feature of all and, given the place of healing in Jesus' ministry and its varied significances, this should not be surprising. (In fact, apart from passages bearing this feature, only 2 of the 76 passages in the structure are outside their expected strata!) Notice that all healing accounts outside both stratum 3 and the interlude have an additional feature that ties them most appropriately to another stratum, so they are certainly not rogue passages, just perhaps "dual purpose". In stratum 3, the authority of Jesus is also presented through a likening of the ministry of Jesus to that of John the Baptist, whose authority was previously established and perhaps more generally accepted (feature 3e). These instances are also found only in this stratum. Attribution of authority (ἐξουσία) to Jesus is an additional feature (#3b) of this stratum and is obviously a direct expression of the common thread throughout. Five of the seven instances of this feature within Luke 4:14–24:53 are confined to the stratum (Lk. 9:1–17 and 19:11–27 are the exceptions; see the structure table on page 206). Jesus' exercise of the authority to choose disciples or designate apostles (feature 3c), his expression of the authority to forgive sins (feature 3d), and his assertion of ultimate authority to interpret the law, initiated by the question "Is it lawful?" (feature 3f) are

---

[47] Furthermore, the pericopes of stratum 2 constitute four of the seven Elijah-Elisha passages that convey the prophetic status of Jesus (Lk. *4:16–30*; 7:11–17; 9:7–9, 18–27, *51–62*; *13:31–35* and *19:29–44*).

each absolutely restricted to pericopes of this stratum, as is the theme of the priority of "hearing" Jesus' "word" (feature 3g).

The "divine authority of Jesus" is by far the most broad stratum definition, and some might object that this blurs the boundaries. To the contrary, the restriction of the above key indicators to a single band across the four cycles indicates authorial preoccupation with the theme in these four sections of his book. Furthermore, the boundaries are crystallized by strata 2 and 4. Additional features could be presented to manifest authority as the intended common thread throughout parallel 3, but those demonstrated above more than adequately prove this thread for the stratum. Appropriately, Luke chose to emphasize Jesus' authority most at the beginning of the ministry through a lengthier section in cycle 1.

Stratum 4 – This parallel is characterized by two features. Number 4a, Jesus directly teaching a crowd of non-disciples, is remarkably only found in two locations outside this stratum: Lk. 7:18–35 and 12:54–59.[48] Luke 5:3 and 20:1 do not fit this stratum because the content of Jesus' teaching is not related. Occurrences of a parable representing Jesus as bearer of a message from God (feature 4b) are completely contained within this stratum. Furthermore, each is qualified further by concluding parables that convey the importance of responding to Jesus' message. Collocation of the two features is appropriate since non-disciples needed most to understand the origin of Jesus' message.

Stratum 5 – All three instances where Jesus personally confronts Jewish leaders, exposing their typical spiritual, moral and religious depravity and therefore implying a lost state are located in this stratum. Luke chose not to include corresponding material in cycle 1, perhaps to restrain the conflict motif early in the ministry. Luke 14:7–14, Jesus at the Pharisee's house, may at first glance appear to fit this stratum. However, Jesus' words are not clearly directed to a group of Jewish leaders, but to guests of the Pharisee, unless these may be inferred to be leaders. Furthermore, the passage does not appear to suggest their spiritual depravity or lost state.[49]

Stratum 6 – Jesus warns (προσέχετε) the disciples or others against

---

48 Jesus does possibly address the crowd in Lk. 12:15–21, but this is quite indirectly conveyed, which indicates that the feature is not intended to be prominent at this location. Actually, the feature does not strictly exist here because the crowd is not explicitly stated as the audience when Jesus speaks to "them," as is indeed the case with the parallel passages (ὄχλος or λαός). Furthermore, it is not altogether certain that the two brothers are not the addressees of Lk. 12:15–21, or even the disciples, as Charles H. Talbert contends in *Reading Luke: A Literary and Theological Commentary on the Third Gospel* (New York: Crossroads, 1989) 140. This latter suggestion is unlikely however since Jesus turns to his disciples in Lk. 12:22.

49 See Nolland, *Luke 9:21–18:34*, 748–751.

being like the religious leaders only in this stratum. Since this warning is closely linked to his personal confrontation of the religious leaders, which is lacking in cycle 1, Luke again chose not to include corresponding warning material in that cycle.

Stratum 7 – Jesus specifically encourages his disciples to have greater faith only in this parallel.[50]

Stratum 8 – The three "eschatological" discourses of the Third Gospel were placed in cycles 2 through 4 of this stratum.[51] In cycle 1, the corresponding material consists of two healing accounts. For a discussion of their suitability for this parallel, see the section on "domain," which begins on page 214.

Stratum 9 – All instances where Jesus addresses the Twelve regarding their role occur here.

Stratum 10 – Each of Peter's verbalizations of faith and commitment toward Christ falls within this parallel.[52]

Stratum 11 – Passion predictions including the resurrection in the context of the cost of discipleship are absolutely restricted to this stratum.

"Stratum" 12 – There appear to be no features that form valid strata in these sections. The three healing accounts do not have any evident interrelationship, but for the sake of interest they have been distinguished in the structure table (page 206). It is noteworthy, however, that there is a high concentration of pericopes on the presence or delay of the parousia and on the kingdom.

The high degree of restriction of the parallel features to their respective locations in the structure argues well for Lukan intent. If the pattern had been read into the text, most parallel features would necessarily be found violating the defined strata. This is clearly not the case.

Test 2: *The greater the number of reasonable parallel features between parallel passages, the greater is the probability of intent.*

The parallelism is primarily between narrative features of four extensive cycles, not strictly individual pericopes. Therefore, each cycle may be treated as a passage according to this test. Eighteen features is an exceed-

---

50 For a discussion of the account of the widow's offering in Lk. 21:1–4 (cycle 4 of this stratum), see the section on "domain," page 214.
51 John T. Carrol in his book *Response to the End of History: Eschatology and Situation in Luke-Acts* (Atlanta, Georgia: Scholars Press, 1988) 37–118, also treats Lk. 19:11–27 as "eschatological" since it specifies when the eschaton will occur. It is not however delivered to the disciples.
52 There is sufficient similarity between Lk. 5:8; 18:28 and 22:33 to consider these literary parallels of the sort typically identified by Tannehill, e.g. echo. They do not however contribute to the cyclical structure of the Gospel. Luke 5:8 does not fit this stratum because Peter does not verbally express commitment to Jesus; nor does he yet understand him to be Christ. See Nolland, *Luke 9:21–18:34*, 452–453.

ingly strong result, so support for authorial intent is weighty. On the level of individual passages, the large majority of features have a bare minimum of three discernable components to them. Even on this level the result is strong.

Test 3: *The greater the number of parallel passages (or panels) that match a proposed pattern or grouping of features, the greater is the case for intent.*

The existence of four panels is exceptionally strong and makes coincidental or subjective parallelism extremely unlikely.

Test 4: *An element of correspondence that attracts the reader's attention contributes to the probability of intent.*

Stratum 1 – Universally, the motif of the journey to Jerusalem is recognized as prominent in Luke (feature #1).[53] It has captured the interest of modern readers. No doubt the same is true of Luke's intended audience. *Stratum 2* – The prophetic status of Jesus and divine rejection are potent issues, but what about the Elijah-Elisha cycle? Elijah plays a relatively prominent role in the Gospel, and we may assume therefore that he was considered noteworthy by the Evangelist. *Stratum 3* – Each parallel feature of this stratum represents an important aspect of the characterization of Jesus. Furthermore, each is pointedly conveyed in its context. *Stratum 4* – The distinction between disciple and non-disciple audiences is clearly maintained by Luke. Although not a striking feature (#4a), a careful reader will observe when Jesus directly teaches a crowd that does not believe as opposed to one that generally does. When Jesus claims the divine origin of his Message (feature #4b), who could not notice? *Stratum 5* – Confrontation of respected religious leaders would arouse any interested reader (feature #5). *Stratum 6* – Similarly, a warning against these respected leaders would be striking (#6). *Stratum 7* – Readers of Luke are intended to identify with the disciples. In Luke's day they would have been highly regarded for their faith; so, an encouragement by Jesus for them to have greater faith could not go unnoticed (#7). *Stratum 8* – What will happen in the future, especially when there is persecution and judgment, grips the attention (#8). *Stratum 9* – To Luke's readers, even more familiar with the prominent role of the apostles in the ancient Church than we are, training of the Twelve for this role would be intriguing (#9). *Stratum 10* – Need anything be said of Peter's verbalizations of faith and commitment toward Christ (#10)? *Stratum 11* – Passion predictions are powerful features of each Gospel. The cost of discipleship is also a topic that would catch the

---

53 See for example Sabourin who observes that the prominent references to travel toward Jerusalem are artificial in a context that lacks further travel development and that this therefore demonstrates Luke's particular interest in the destination; *L'Évangile de Luc*, 17.

reader's attention, especially in the context of a passion prediction. Naturally, Jesus' predictions of his own resurrection would be remarkable to the first century reader contemplating Christian claims, let alone predictions of his own death.

Each parallel feature catches the attention, and has throughout history. If Luke intended to impact his readers in some way through this pattern, he would have constructed it with notable building blocks. This is clearly the case here.

Test 5: *Parallelism between complex units, such as combined pericopes, that appears constructive rather than random or coincidental increases the probability of intent.*

The order of appearance of strata 1 through 11 is identical over the four cycles, excepting the two gaps in cycle 1 (strata 5 and 6) and the one in cycle 2 (stratum 10). Therefore, the parallelism is completely constructive since none appears out of order. Support for Lukan intent from this test is very great.

Test 6: *If redaction critical observations yield evidence of Lukan adjustment to include or create the elements that constitute the literary device, the probability of intent is greater insofar as there are no superior reasons for the observed redaction.*

It has been proposed that Luke developed cycles 1 through 3 based on the sequence of narrative features in cycle 4. This sequence of features existed in the parallel Markan material and was taken over intact by Luke. For this reason, it is appropriate in our coverage of relevant redaction to move from cycle 4 to cycle 1 respectively to highlight most effectively the Markan nature of cycle 4.

Much of the actual redaction in the travel narrative, apart from pericopes with clear Q and Markan parallels, is difficult to discern, and commentators rarely offer Lukan motivation with any confidence.[54] By their nature, structural proposals generally offer the strongest Lukan motivation for the arrangement of pericopes in the central section. Proposals of chiasm tend to be the strongest alternative explanations of redaction, but these are not superior in principle to the present thesis since both are structural. They may even coexist. Chiastic proposals have been evaluated in chapter 2 and, for the sake of brevity, will not be reiterated here.

Stratum 1 – In *cycle 4*, Luke adds purpose to the Markan introduction: Καὶ ὅτε ἐγγίζουσιν εἰς Ἱεροσόλυμα (Mk. 11:1) becomes Καὶ εἰπὼν ταῦτα ἐπορεύετο ἔμπροσθεν ἀναβαίνων εἰς Ἱεροσόλυμα (Lk. 19:28).

---

54 Joachim Jeremias perhaps provides the most thorough redactional analysis of the central section, in *Sprache*. Generally, however, he does not deal with Lukan motivation.

The εἰς Ἱεροσόλυμα is retained, but made more emphatic. This reference to Jerusalem perhaps forms an inclusio with that of 19:11 around the parable of the ten minas,[55] but this does not explain the intensification of the second reference. It appears that the addition of purpose was to highlight this aspect of the journey motif. Regardless of the source behind Luke 13:23–30 (*cycle 3*), the introductory setting, verse 22, is probably Lukan.[56] Therefore, the destination, Jerusalem, as the driving force behind the journey is likely an added theme at this point. The verse both signals the beginning of a new section[57] and "keeps the journey motif alive".[58] This is consistent with its function in the pattern. No superior or conflicting explanations are proposed. *Cycle 2* begins with Luke 9:51, commonly held as the beginning of the travel narrative and as a Lukan introductory composition. Jerusalem again is presented as the driving purpose behind the journey. Of course, at the inception of *cycle 1* the phrase "to Jerusalem" is not to be found, and rightly so. Jesus could not begin the journey until he had at least begun his Galilean ministry. If a correspondence with "to Jerusalem" is desired, Lk. 4:14a (εἰς τὴν Γαλιλαίαν; from Mk. 1:14a) may be appropriate. Purpose would be contributed by the Lukan addition, "returned…in the power of the Spirit," but this correspondence need not be pressed.

Interestingly there is one Markan verse (Mk. 10:32) that contains this "to Jerusalem" feature as we have defined it, and it is removed by Luke. The key phrase, "to Jerusalem" (εἰς Ἱεροσόλυμα), is found in an introductory section to a pericope (narrator's voice) where the context highlights this destination as the driving purpose of Jesus' journey. Although the introduction is deleted, he includes the pericope it introduces (Mk. 10:32–34 par. Lk. 18:31–34).[59] To leave it in would have confused the function of the other instances with which Luke initiates his cycles.

In summary for stratum 1, the basic feature was present in the Markan material behind cycle 4 (and cycle 1?). The corresponding texts of cycles 2 and 3 are Lukan formulations.

Stratum 2 – Immediately following Mark's "to Jerusalem" introduction of Mark 11:1 is the triumphal entry (Mk. 11:1–11). Luke retains this sequence in *cycle 4*. There are three features of the Markan entry account

---

55 John Nolland, *Luke 18:35–24:53*, Word Biblical Commentary 35c (Dallas: Word Books, 1993) 917.
56 Marshall, *Gospel of Luke*, 563. See also Schlatter's argument from style that 13:22–27 is Lukan; *Evangelium des Lukas*, 328–329.
57 Marshall, *Gospel of Luke*, 562.
58 Nolland, *Luke 9:21–18:34*, 733.
59 For an explanation of why the phrase "to Jerusalem" in Lk. 18:31 does not fit this stratum, see test 1, stratum 1 on page 228.

that could well have reminded Luke of the Elijah-Elisha cycle. These, included in his story, are (1) the spreading of garments in Luke 19:36, (2) the quote of Psalm 118:26 in Luke 19:38, and (3) the colt, which may have been reminiscent of an earlier passage in 1 Kings (of course, the primary referent would still be Zc. 9:9). First, the spreading of garments (ἱμάτιον) occurs within the Elijah-Elisha cycle at the anointing of Jehu as king of Israel (verse 13 of 2 Ki. 9:1–13). This is almost universally cited as the allusion.[60] Note, also, that the Markan spreading of branches, not a feature of the Jehu narrative, is omitted by Luke (Lk. 19:36, cf. Mk. 11:8). This draws the similarity to the OT narrative even closer. Second, Ellis argues that Psalm 118:26 was recited at the ancient Jewish "throne of Elijah" ceremony and that, therefore, the people of Luke 19:38 likely had Elijah in mind.[61] Third, although Zechariah 9:9 is the primary referent to the use of a colt, Nolland and Sabourin believe 1 Kings 1:33 may have been in Luke's thought, Solomon riding David's donkey to his coronation.[62] Certainly, it is impossible to prove precisely what Luke was thinking, but it is reasonable to assume that he was aware of the relationship of this material to the Elijah-Elisha cycle. Luke's addition of ὁ βασιλεὺς to the otherwise exact quotation of Psalm 118:26 adds further confirmation. This could well echo the crowd's proclamation, "Jehu is king," ἐβασίλευσεν Ἰού, in 2 Kings 9:13, the verse alluded to by the spreading of garments (see the first point above). Again, the primary referent is probably Zechariah 9:9, but Luke's obvious familiarity with and employment of the stories of Elijah and Elisha favors this conscious association. No compelling reasons have been proposed for the insertion of "the King". Fitzmyer's observation that this is the final development of the "throne of David" theme foreshadowed in Luke 1:32 and 18:38–39[63] may be correct, yet the theme is not strong in the Gospel. Bock considers that the combination of eschatological overtones here with the reference to Jesus as king creates a "messianic claim," a probable option that meshes with our own since the messianic theme is present in other passages of this stratum.[64] Of course, it could be another allusion to Zech. 9:9.

Just as important as the prophetic status of Jesus in this stratum, however, is the concept of divine rejection in response to rejecting Jesus. This

---

60 See for example Walter Grundmann, *Evangelium nach Lukas*, 366–67; Marshall, *Gospel of Luke*, 714; Fitzmyer, *Luke X–XXIV*, 1250; Nolland, *Luke 18:35–24:53*, 922; C.F. Evans, *Saint Luke*, 679; Ellis, *Gospel of Luke*, 225; D.A. Carson, *Matthew*, 438.
61 Ellis, *Gospel of Luke*, 78, 191, 225.
62 Nolland, *Luke 18:35–24:53*, 925; Sabourin, *L'Évangile de Luc*, 315.
63 Fitzmyer, *Luke X–XXIV*, 1251.
64 Bock, *Luke 9:51–24:53*, 1558.

motif is conveyed through Luke 19:41–44. The destruction of the city, ultimately by God, is conditioned on the lack of recognition of "the time of your visitation," in other words, the divine visitation in the person of Jesus. Luke probably considered this pericope to be a clearer, more appropriate substitute for Mark's cursing of the fig tree, which also carries the rejection theme.

Few proposals for Lukan motive behind the insertion of this Lukan pericope are available. Fitzmyer believes that the lament "may well go back to Jesus in some form, but that the reformulation of it in the pre-Lukan tradition was affected both by the destruction of the city itself in AD 70 and by allusions to that under Nebuchadnezzar in the OT".[65] So the motivation would primarily be compelling historical fact. It is by no means certain, however, that the Gospel was composed after the destruction of Jerusalem. Marshall reminds us of "the complete lack of interest in the fall of Jerusalem in Acts and the way in which that book ends its story before the death of Paul". He therefore rightly contends for a date prior to the destruction.[66] If so, the inclusion of the passage demands a motive other than the impact of the actual event on Luke. Aside from positing that he knew of the tradition and simply wanted to convey the information to his readers, our structure provides a strong motive.

Moving to *cycle 3*, the relevant text has no parallel in Mark (Lk. 13:23–35, the parable of the narrow door, and the second lament over Jerusalem). The strongest case for a dependence on Q is for 13:34–35, but no apparent modifications of such material enhance the parallelism in Luke's scheme. Luke 13:23–30 clearly teaches the divine exclusion from the kingdom of those who do not favorably respond to the teaching of Jesus (v. 26). The expression of Jesus' prophetic status and any contact with 1 and 2 Kings are concentrated in Luke 13:31–35 (containing the prophetic lament over Jerusalem) where the theme of divine rejection conditioned on rejection of Jesus is also continued.

Before we continue, notice its remarkable similarity to Luke 19:37–44 (its parallel in cycle 4):

Lk. 13:31–35	Lk. 19:38–44
31–33 The Pharisees speak to Jesus and he responds.	38–40 The Pharisees speak to Jesus and he responds.

---

65 Fitzmyer, *Luke X–XXIV*, 1255. So also Sabourin (*L'Évangile de Luc*, 317).
66 Marshall, *Gospel of Luke*, 35.

34 "O Jerusalem, Jerusalem, the city that kills the prophets and stones those sent to her! How often I wanted to gather your children together, just as a hen gathers her brood under her wings, and you would not have it!	41 And when He approached, He saw the city and wept over it,
	42 saying, "If you had known in this day, even you, the things which make for peace! But now they have been hidden from your eyes.
35 "Behold, your house is left to you desolate; and I say to you, you shall not see Me until the time comes when you say,	43 "For the days shall come upon you when your enemies will throw up a bank before you, and surround you, and hem you in on every side,
	44 "and will level you to the ground and your children within you, and they will not leave in you one stone upon another, because you did not recognize the time of your visitation."
35b 'Blessed is He who comes in the name of the Lord!'"	**38a "Blessed is the King who comes in the name of the Lord."**

Only Luke 19:38 is derived from Mark, so any broad parallelism would probably be from Luke's hand, at the very least by his selection of the tradition.

Jesus' prophetic status is explicit in the prophetic lament of Luke 13:31–35 (verses 34–35 par. Mt. 23:37–39), "it cannot be that a prophet should perish outside of Jerusalem" (v. 33). It also contains contacts with the Elijah-Elisha cycle of 1 and 2 Kings and its broader context. Fitzmyer notes Jezebel's killing of many prophets (1 Ki. 18:4, 13; 19:10, 14) as a general backdrop to verse 33.[67] Nolland links verse 35 to Elijah, stating that it "is probably right to appeal to Jewish traditions of figures translated to heaven in preparation for a future eschatological role (beginning from 2 Kings 2:11–12 and the OT anticipation of a future role for Elijah; cf. esp. 2 Esd 6:26)".[68]

The parallel pericopes in *cycle 2* are Luke 9:52–56 (rejection by the

---

67 Fitzmyer, *Luke X–XXIV*, 1532.
68 Nolland, *Luke 9:21–18:34*, 742.

Samaritans – L tradition) and 57–62 (three potential disciples – parallel to Mt. 8:18–22 through verse 60a). Interestingly, there is early textual evidence for the explicit association with Elijah of the disciples' desire to perform the prophetic act of calling down fire (including A C D and W). This is probably a gloss, since the evidence for omission is stronger (including ℵ B L Ξ and vg). Nevertheless, the gloss appears early enough to suggest that the interpretation could have existed in Luke's day and that Luke may have been aware of it, admittedly a speculative argument. Much stronger is the similar language between Lk. 9:54 and 2 Kings 1:10, 12 and 14[69] about calling fire down (see also 1 Ki. 18:36–38 which may be the primary referent). Along with the Elijah motif that highlights the prophetic nature of Jesus' ministry, we find a mild form of the rejection theme.[70] The Samaritans do not receive him, so he passes them by. Luke's incorporation of the Q pericope (Lk. 9:57–62[71] par. Mt. 8:18–22) again imports the Elijah and rejection motifs. Both the second and third encounters are distinctly reminiscent of the call of Elisha.[72] In the cases of these three individuals, their rejection of the stringent demands of following Jesus results in rejection from the kingdom, "No one, after putting his hand to the plow and looking back, is fit for the kingdom of God" (v. 62).

It has been demonstrated that feature 2 was established in cycles 2 and 3 through Lukan redaction. The same is true for *cycle 1* (Lk. 4:16–30). First, the rejection in Nazareth is transposed from a later position in Mark to the very first account of the public ministry of Jesus. Luke probably noticed the self-identification of Jesus with the prophets in Mark 6:4, which he retains in Luke 4:24, and amplified it through the addition of the Elijah-Elisha references (Lk. 4:25–27) to match the allusions in cycle 4 and his development of the themes in cycles 2 and 3.[73] Therefore, the prophetic status of Jesus is inherent in the Markan account, but the themes of the divine rejection of those who reject Jesus and of Elijah/Elisha are contributed by

---

69 See also the discussions of Marshall (*Gospel of Luke*, 407) and Grundmann (*Evangelium nach Lukas*, 202). Tannehill develops the connection as well, *Narrative Unity*, 1:230.
70 This aspect of rejection is an important element in Craig A. Evans' argument for a judgmental tone; see "'He Set His Face': On the Meaning of Luke 9:51," in Craig A. Evans and James A. Sanders, *Luke and Scripture: The Function of Sacred Tradition in Luke-Acts* (Minneapolis: Fortress Press, 1993) 103.
71 Marshall successfully argues for the origin of verses 61–62 in the Q pericope partially quoted by Matthew (8:18–22), *Gospel of Luke*, 408. Schlatter (*Evangelium des Lukas*, 271–73) and Grundmann (*Evangelium nach Lukas*, 203–204), however, consider verses 61 and 62 to be Lukan.
72 Marshall (*Gospel of Luke*, 411–2), Sabourin (*L'Évangile de Luc*, 216–17), and Grundmann (*Evangelium nach Lukas*, 205–206) concur.
73 Schürmann, *Lukasevangelium: Erster Teil*, 227–28, 241–242.

the redactor.

It would strengthen our case if it were evident that Luke removed explicit references to Elijah or Elisha from source material he used and that he did not add such references in locations outside the parallel. Extraneous references would cloud the parallelism, so one would expect these to be eradicated. In fact, no additions are made outside parallel 2. Furthermore, some references are removed from source material incorporated into Luke. Mark's transfiguration account includes reference to the rejected eschatological Elijah (Mk. 9:11–13), but Luke omits it; and references to Elijah at the death of Jesus are also removed (Lk. 23:44–48 par. Mk. 15:33–39).

To summarize, feature 2 was present in cycle 4 and was clarified only slightly by Luke. Naturally, the parallels in cycles 2 and 3 were generated by him. In cycle 1, the parallel existed in the Markan material through expression of the prophetic status of Jesus; but the first passage, the Nazareth account, was relocated to suit the structure and was developed further to tighten the correspondence.

Stratum 3 – Jesus' cleansing of the temple followed by the question about his authority (Lk. 19:45–20:8) constitute the parallel unit of *cycle 4*. Luke joins the cleansing closely with the questioning through his omission of the second part of the fig tree account, the whole of which is replaced by the clearer lament over Jerusalem. Admittedly, the cursing of the fig tree is a demonstration of authority in a sense, so its omission was probably on non-structural grounds. Nolland believes the abbreviation is to emphasize the OT quotation in Luke 19:46,[74] an effect that is certainly achieved. Schlatter sees it as an avoidance of repetition with the fig tree parable at Luke 13:6.[75] Whatever the reasons for his adjustments, it is demonstrable that cycles 1 through 3 match the authoritative atmosphere of cycle 4. Two features define this section of the fourth cycle: (1) the ministry of Jesus is related to that of John the Baptist, one popularly recognized as authoritative (feature 3e); and (2) authority (ἐξουσία) is attributed to Jesus (feature 3b). Each of these features is present in the Markan version, which as we have seen is the basic pattern for the other cycles.

The healing of the man with dropsy at the Pharisee's house is imported by Luke from L tradition[76] (*cycle 3*; Lk. 14:1–14), and two of his parallel features are imported with it. First, it is a healing account, which validates Jesus' authority. Second, Jesus asks the Pharisees, "Is it lawful?," a question that introduces his superior authority as interpreter of the law.

In cycle 2, Luke 10:1–24 (the sending of the seventy-two) involves heal-

---

74 Nolland, *Luke 18:35–24:53*, 935.
75 Schlatter, *Evangelium des Lukas*, 117–118.
76 See Schlatter, *Evangelium des Lukas*, 333–340.

ing summaries (vv. 9, 17–20) and the attribution of ἐξουσία to Jesus ("Behold, I have given you authority," Lk. 10:19), as found in cycle 4. There is frequent similarity with Matthew apart from verses 1 and 17–20, but regardless of whether or not Luke 10:17–20 is Q material,[77] the explication of authority was a direct or indirect consequence of Lukan choice. Was its inclusion, however, for the sake of this ascription of authority? Fitzmyer believes that "it gives to the passage about the praise of the Father a better psychological background, following not immediately on the instruction to the disciples, but on the report of their success. This passage then builds up to the authority of the Son"[78] conveyed in verses 21–22. Actually, the concept of Jesus' divine authority permeates the whole account. Luke 11:1–13, instructions about prayer, repeats the John the Baptist feature found in cycle 4. Just as the authoritative Baptist had taught his disciples to pray, so Jesus' disciples request their teacher to instruct them. There is no Markan parallel, and the passage seems to join two Q texts (parallel to Mt. 6:9–13 and 7:7–11)[79] with a Lukan parable sandwiched in between (Lk. 11:5–8). John is introduced in the first verse of the scene and is lacking in the Matthean parallel. Regardless of whether this verse is from a Lukan source[80] or is his own composition,[81] selectivity was exercised in its inclusion. If it is his creation, Marshall's observation that "the reference to John's disciples…adds nothing to the scene"[82] must be answered. Evans views it as a reflection of "Luke's interest in John and his relation to Jesus,"[83] a motive consistent with the formation of this stratum. Certainly, the present stratum is an adequate explanation. If on the other hand it is from a source, the presence of the entire passage must be explained. Again, the present stratum suffices as an explanation. Marshall places the passage in a section of teaching on "the characteristics of disciples,"[84] and this would account for its presence. Still, however, this section fits within the stratum and suits its theme. Grundmann considers the passage to be an example of the main point in the Mary and Martha account

---

77 Marshall presents good reasons to believe it is from Q, *Gospel of Luke*, 427–428.
78 Fitzmyer, *Luke X–XXIV*, 859.
79 Joachim Gnilka affirms the Q origin of the Matthean passages, in *Das Matthäusevangelium: I. Teil: Kommentar zu Kap. 1,1–13,58*, Herders Theologischer Kommentar zum Neuen Testament (Freiburg: Herder, 1988) 214, 261.
80 Marshall, *Gospel of Luke*, 456. Here, he correctly favors the setting as historical. This would imply that most or all of the pericope was imported to form the parallel, if indeed John the Baptist was the key element inherent in the source material.
81 Fitzmyer, *Luke X–XXIV*, 897–98. Schlatter is undecided (*Evangelium des Lukas*, 295).
82 Marshall, *Gospel of Luke*, 456.
83 C.F. Evans, *Saint Luke*, 477–478.
84 Marshall, *Gospel of Luke*, 454.

just preceding it, the importance of the word of Jesus.[85] This view suits the stratum well. We move now to the final passage in the authority stratum of cycle 2, Luke 11:14–26, the Beelzebub controversy.[86] It is a healing account, as in the cycle 3 parallel (Lk. 14:1–14). Commentators broadly conclude that Luke depends here on Q. Few persuasive arguments however are offered for its location in the Third Gospel. Grundmann presents one of the strongest suggestions. He supposes that the Beelzebub controversy (Lk. 11:14–26) develops the contrast between the rule of Satan and the rule of God, the latter of which is highlighted in 11:1–13. He also, less convincingly, understands it to interpret the second request in the Lord's Prayer and to provide an object for the instruction to "ask and it shall be given to you..." (11:9ff.).[87] Indeed, Luke 11:20 explicitly relates the rule of God, expressed by His authority to drive out demons, to Jesus' ministry of exorcism. Naturally, then, as an expression of the divine authority of Jesus, 11:14–26 supports the stratum. Bock, also taking a thematic approach, offers a similarly strong alternative. The Beelzebub passage, affirming that God is at work through Jesus, provides the authoritative grounds both for sitting at Jesus' feet as Mary did, and for adopting the prayer perspective taught in the Lord's Prayer.[88] This view would also support our proposed theme of authority.

Cycle 1 particularly emphasizes the divine authority of Jesus through the sheer volume and number of passages in stratum 3. The three accounts in Luke 4:31–44 are drawn closely from Mark 1:21–39, and all the parallel features evident were present in Mark (three healing accounts and an attribution of ἐξουσία to Jesus). Importantly, in the first pericope authority is directly ascribed to both the teaching of Jesus (Lk. 4:32) and to his healing (Lk. 4:36). This sets the interpretative stage for the greatest collection of healing accounts in the Gospel, found in this section.

Next in cycle 1, Luke inserts from his special material the calling of his first disciples (Lk. 5:1–11), which implies his authority over the entirety of their lives. The precise placement of this "equivalent for Mark 1:16–20"[89] in the authority stratum of cycle 1 is not important at this point.[90] Its new

---

85 Grundmann, *Evangelium nach Lukas*, 228.
86 Marshall identifies the theme as the authority of Jesus, *Gospel of Luke*, 470.
87 Grundmann, *Evangelium nach Lukas*, 236.
88 Bock, *Luke 9:51–24:53*, 1067.
89 Nolland, *Luke 1–9:20*, Word Biblical Commentary 35a (Dallas: Word Books, 1989) 219. See also Tim Schramm, *Der Markus-Stoff bei Lukas: eine literarkritische und redaktionsgeschichtliche Untersuchung* (Cambridge: Cambridge University Press, 1971) 37–38.
90 Joseph A. Fitzmyer is probably right that "by transposing the scene from its Marcan setting, Luke has eliminated the oft-noted implausibility of the Marcan story about the call of the four disciples – the first thing that Jesus does in that Gospel after his

location remains within the same stratum. Both the Markan and Lukan accounts display the authority of Jesus, but Luke's contributes the divine element through the miraculous catch of fish. "The miracle-story (vv. 4–9a) which has been associated with the call of Simon enhances the promise made to him,"[91] presumably by displaying its divine foundation. Schürmann notes that the sovereignty of Jesus expressed in 5:1–3 through his portrayal as the Messianic bearer of God's word is the same sovereignty displayed in the miracle (vv. 4–9a).[92] So alternative suggestions do not conflict with the proposition that Luke 5:1–11 contributes to the attribution of divine authority to Jesus throughout this stratum of cycle 1.

Continuing in cycle 1, Lk. 5:12–6:11 parallels a Markan block (Mk. 1:40–3:6) that contains all the parallel features employed by Luke here. At Lk. 6:11, Luke transposes Mk. 3:7–12 to a later position within the authority section (Lk. 6:17–19), the reason for which is unimportant for our purposes since it remains within the same stratum.

The Markan parallel to Luke 6:12–49 (the choosing of the twelve from among his disciples, followed by his teaching them in the Sermon on the Mount; Mk. 3:13–19) contains each parallel feature displayed in the Lukan text. Luke's sermon (Lk. 6:20–49), not paralleled in Mark, concludes with the authoritative note, "why do you call Me 'Lord, Lord,' and do not do what I say? Everyone who comes to Me, and hears My words, and acts upon them, I will show you whom he is like..." (Lk. 6:46–47).

Jesus' encounter with the centurion from Capernaum (Lk. 7:1–10) is a healing account with direct attribution of ἐξουσία to Jesus. It is parallel to Mt. 8:5–13, which possesses both features. No redaction was apparently necessary beyond its incorporation into the text. The same is true for Luke 7:18–35 (par. Mt. 11:2–19); the ministry of Jesus is related to John the Baptist in Luke's source. The passage in between, a healing account, is peculiar to Luke and obviously needed no redaction.

Luke 7:36–50, the woman with the ointment, repeats feature (#3d). The Evangelist apparently follows an independent tradition here,[93] lengthening the section with this expression of Jesus' divine authority to forgive sins, a theme repeated from Luke 5:17–26. If it is based on Mark 14:3–9 or Q (par. Mt. 26:6–13), both the Pharisaic opposition and the forgiving of sins are added by Luke.

---

baptism and desert sojourn. In the Lucan context, Jesus has been seen preaching and healing, and Simon (at least) has witnessed one of his mighty deeds (4:38–39);" *Luke I–I X*, 560.
91 Fitzmyer, *Luke I–I X*, 563.
92 Schürmann, *Lukasevangelium: Erster Teil*, 265–266
93 Schramm however does see some influence of Mk. 14:3–9 on the account (*Markus-Stoff bei Lukas*, 43–44).

In summary, each of the parallel features utilized by Luke to express authority throughout this stratum is present in the equivalent sections of Mark for cycles 4 and 1. Therefore, they constitute the background pattern. The parallel material in cycles 2 and 3 is entirely due to Lukan redaction. In addition, pericopes unparalleled in Mark that exhibit these very features are appended to the Markan authority block behind cycle 1, and one is inserted within Luke 19:45–20:8 of cycle 4. Clearly, the cyclical structure of the Gospel accounts for a large amount of Lukan redaction.

Stratum 4 – Two features establish this stratum: Jesus directly teaching a crowd of non-disciples, and a parable representing Jesus as bearer of a message from God. The parable exists in this location within the Markan material parallel to *cycle 4* (Lk. 20:9–18 par. Mk. 12:1–11, the parable of the tenants). Luke, however, changes the audience from the chief priests, scribes and elders (Mk. 11:27) to the people, apparently to match the audience in cycle 1. The commentators offer no substantial motive for this interesting alteration. Schramm merely suggests that Luke was specifying the audience again, which does not address the change in audience from Mark's account.[94] Note the short parable at the end that conveys the importance of responding to Jesus' message (Lk. 20:17–18). Parables with this function will conclude each section of this stratum. In *cycle 3*, the Lukan parable (Lk. 14:15–24, parable of the great supper, Q material) precedes the reference to the crowd (Lk. 14:25, Lukan). The people in this crowd, who are now the recipients of Jesus' teaching, are clearly not disciples (vv. 26, 27, 33). The parables of Luke 14:25–35, namely the conditions of discipleship (L) and the parable of the salt (par. Mk. 9:50a and Mt. 5:13), convey the importance of responding to Jesus' message. Luke 11:27–36 of *cycle 2*, a compilation of Q and L material, was apparently reworked to suit the stratum. A comparison of this Jonah parable with its Matthean parallel (Mt. 12:38–42) reveals that Luke added the reference to the crowds (Lk. 11:29), probably to clarify the audience after his insertion of a woman's interjection (Lk. 11:27–28; L tradition).[95] This clarification obviously favors our parallel, which requires the audience to be a crowd. He also transforms the focus of the parable from the sign of his three days "in the heart of the earth" to the sign of his preaching, which is necessary for the stratum's focus on the message borne by Jesus. The reference to the sign of his death is removed so that the wisdom of Solomon and the preaching of Jonah, now placed in the emphatic final position,

---

94 Schramm, *Markus-Stoff bei Lukas*, 154.
95 See also Marshall, *Gospel of Luke*, 482.

imply the type of sign manifest in Jesus, his message.[96] In sum, the parable has been made to fit the stratum more closely.

The interjection mentioned above (Lk. 11:27–28; L tradition) also favors our parallel. It corresponds to the account where Jesus' mother and brothers try to see him (Lk. 8:19–21 of cycle 1). Notice the similarity between Jesus' declarations in the latter parallel:

Lk. 8:21   "My mothers and My brothers are *these who here the word of God* and *do it*."

Lk. 11:28   "On the contrary, blessed are *those who hear the word of God*, and *observe it*."

So the instance in cycle 2 was inserted to correspond with that of cycle 1. Fitzmyer's comment, "it is hard to say why Luke put this episode here,"[97] reflects scholarly opinion and highlights the value of this correspondence as an explanation.

Once again, following the pattern of cycle 4, the section concludes with parables that convey the importance of responding to Jesus' message: the parables of the lamp (Lk. 11:33 par. Mk. 4:21 and Mt. 5:15) and of the eye (11:34–36 par. Mt. 6:22–23). The lamp parable is verbally very similar to the corresponding passage in cycle 1 (Lk. 8:16), and was probably conformed to it:[98]

Lk. 11:33   Οὐδεὶς λύχνον ἅψας εἰς κρύπτην τίθησιν [οὐδὲ ὑπὸ τὸν μόδιον] ἀλλ' ἐπὶ τὴν λυχνίαν, ἵνα οἱ εἰσπορευόμενοι τὸ φῶς βλέπωσιν.

Lk. 8:16   Οὐδεὶς δὲ λύχνον ἅψας καλύπτει αὐτὸν σκεύει ἢ ὑποκάτω κλίνης τίθησιν, ἀλλ' ἐπὶ λυχνίας τίθησιν, ἵνα οἱ εἰσπορευόμενοι βλέπωσιν τὸ φῶς.

Most commentators postulate a thematic connection between the lamp

---

96 For an argument in favor of the resurrection as central to the sign here, see M.-J. Lagrange, *Évangile selon Saint Luc*, Études Bibliques (Paris: Gabalda, 1948[7]) 337–338.
97 Fitzmyer, *Luke X–XXIV*, 926.
98 Luke 8:16 (par. Mk. 4:21–25) has been edited by Luke, but this is not a problem. The end result is a strong correspondence. Generally, the Markan material of cycles 1 and 4 are the pattern for the middle cycles, so the likelihood is that Lk.11:33 was tailored after 8:16. Another option is that Luke preferred this form of the parable from an independent source and incorporated it into both locations. Still, this yields the same conclusion, a conscious similarity.

parable and the preceding context as the motive behind its inclusion.[99] This is equally the case in both cycles 4 and 1, so Luke has simply maintained his pattern.

Moving to *cycle 1*, each parallel feature is present in the Markan material behind this section (Lk. 8:4–18 par. Mk. 4:1–25; Lk. 8:19–21 par. Mk. 3:31–35). Luke enhances its similarity to the parallel material in cycle 4 by specifying the divine origin of Jesus' message in the explanation of the parable of the sower ("the seed is the word of God," Lk. 8:11 par. "the sower sows the word," Mk. 4:14).[100] Furthermore, he changes Mark's "For whoever *does the will* of God..." (Mk. 3:35) to "these who *hear the word* of God and do it" in Luke 8:21, thus more closely identifying Jesus' message with the Father.[101] There is general consensus on this explanation.

There is evidence that Luke removed references to crowds from source material employed outside this stratum to enhance the clarity of the parallelism. Luke employs three Markan passages where his source had Jesus directly teaching a crowd of non-disciples, Mk. 4:1–9; possibly 8:34–9:1; and 12:37b–40. He uses the first in this stratum (Lk. 8:4–8). Since Luke locates the second in stratum 11 of cycle 1, the Markan crowd is removed, leaving only disciples. Likewise, the third passage forms stratum 6 of cycle 4, so he changes the direct address to the "great crowd" of Mark to the indirect "while all the people were listening, He said *to His disciples*..." (italics mine).

In summary regarding redaction criticism of stratum 4, evidence of the Lukan hand favors the parallel features in all four cycles. The passages of the middle two cycles are adjusted the most to follow the first and last cycles. Luke slightly modifies the material of cycles 1 and 4 to clarify the parallelism or to intensify the presence of a particular parallel feature. He also removes references to Jesus directly teaching crowds that are not employed in stratum 4; thus, he avoids clouding the parallelism.

Stratum 5 – On three occasions in the Third Gospel Jesus personally confronts Jewish leaders, exposing their typical spiritual, moral and

---

99 See Marshall, *Gospel of Luke*, 487; Fitzmyer, *Luke X–XXIV*, 939; and Nolland, *Luke 9:21–18:34*, 656, for example.

100 Notice that Mk. 3:31–35 is relocated from what would have been the beginning of its section in cycle 1, a position more suitable to the parallel with cycle 2, to the end of the section. Each one of the interruptions (Lk. 8:19–21 from cycle 1 and 11:27–28 from cycle 2) is more aesthetic and sensible in its present location, so obviously the Evangelist felt free to reposition a section's material for clarity's sake as long as it remained within the stratum. In the instance of cycle 1, positioning Lk. 8:19–21 after 8:18 is based on the key verb "to hear": "take care how you listen" (Lk. 8:18; Mark uses "what" you hear) leads to, "these who hear the word of God and do it" (Lk. 8:21).

101 See also Marshall, *Gospel of Luke*, 332.

religious depravity and therefore implying a lost state: Lk. 11:37–54; 15:1–16:31; and 20:19–44 (cycles 2 through 4 respectively). In *cycle 4*, 20:19 is taken directly from Mark and is probably the feature Luke wished to develop, "And the scribes and the chief priests tried to lay hands on Him that very hour, and they feared the people; *for they understood that He spoke this parable against them*" (italics mine). Apparently, the Evangelist wanted to highlight the tension in this section initiated by Jesus' parable against the leaders, because he omits from within Luke 20:19–44 Mark's account of the scribe who sincerely asks Jesus about the primary commandment (Mk. 12:28–34).[102] Fitzmyer believes that Luke here avoids a doublet with Luke 10:25–28.[103] Of course, this is possible since Luke exhibits such a tendency, but it is not certain. The number of existing doublets in the Gospel is similar to the number of instances of avoidance, as listed by Fitzmyer.[104] The Lukan avoidance of doublets is not a "rule". In addition, the two accounts are significantly different. For instance, one presents a scribe, the other a lawyer, but this distinction may not be significant (see 11:52–53); one relates a question about commandments, the other about eternal life; and one includes a substantial response to Jesus, the other does not. Fitzmyer's suggestion is not invalid, it is simply not the final word.[105] With the omission, Luke 20:41–44 (Christ as David's son) now immediately follows the efforts of the Sadducees to trap Jesus. It is addressed not to the people in the temple, as in Mark, but it continues Jesus' address to the Sadducees.[106] Therefore, the peaceful instruction of the crowd is converted into a continuation of Jesus' exposé of Sadducaic legal misinterpretation. Clearly, Luke removes or adjusts material that would otherwise tone down the atmosphere of tension.

Moving to *cycle 3*, Luke 15:1–16:31, Luke presents a series of parables with no Markan parallel other than Mk. 10:11–12 (par. Lk. 16:18).[107] Importantly, he constructs his own introduction to them (15:1–3)[108] that establishes the presence of the Pharisees and scribes. He further constructs

---

102 As noted earlier, he employs a similar account in cycle 2, stratum 3 where the lawyer's intent was hostile, Lk. 10:25–28.
103 Fitzmyer, *Luke X–XXIV*, 1309. So also Grundmann, *Evangelium nach Lukas*, 376.
104 Fitzmyer, *Luke I–IX*, 81–82.
105 Schramm notes the differences between Mk. 12:28–34 and Lk. 10:25–28, but accepts the idea that the Markan account had a degree of influence on Luke's (*Markus-Stoff bei Lukas*, 47–49).
106 Marshall also notes this in *Gospel of Luke*, 747.
107 Luke 15:4–7 is parallel to Mt. 18:12–14; Lk. 16:13 to Mt. 6:24; Lk. 16:16–17 to Mt. 11:12–13 with 5:18; and Lk. 16:18 is parallel to Mt. 19:9 and Mk. 10:11–12.
108 Fitzmyer, *Luke X–XXIV*, 1072; Marshall, *Gospel of Luke*, 598–99. Contrary to this, Grundmann believes that this introduction originally initiated the parable of the Prodigal Son; but he offers insufficient ground (*Evangelium nach Lukas*, 304).

the statement on reaction of the Pharisees to the parables at Luke 16:14–15,[109] which functions as the transition between Jesus' incitement of opposition in Luke 15:1–16:13 and the direct confrontation in 16:16–31 (one-sided in Jesus' favor). Actual motivation behind the inclusion of the Pharisees and scribes is lacking in the commentaries. Bailey assumes the historicity of the audience, that Jesus was speaking to them as though they were lowly shepherds in order to shock them.[110] This may well have been the case, but there is little evidence that this audience was in Luke's sources. The explanation is possible, but not conclusive. Regarding the response of the Pharisees in Luke 16:14–15, Nolland correctly identifies its function of linking 16:1–31 with 15:1–32 through 15:1 (same audience),[111] a function entirely consistent with our proposal. No other substantial alternatives are available.

Luke apparently reworks the setting of the woes against the Pharisees and lawyers in *cycle 2*, a section constructed probably from Q material (Lk. 11:37–54).[112] In the setting, the Pharisee marvels (θαυμάζω) that Jesus did not wash his hands before the meal (v. 38). "The context determines whether [θαυμάζω is used] in a good or bad sense,"[113] and here, although it is a negative reaction, it does not demand a sense of conflict, merely surprise. Plummer astutely concludes that the Pharisee's "surprise" indicates that he was not trying to find fault in Jesus, otherwise he would not have been surprised.[114] Therefore, Jesus' list of woes stands out more strongly as an intentional confrontation since it is not simply a reaction to an attempt to provoke Jesus.

Luke incorporates all instances of this feature in Mark into this stratum. Therefore, lack of source material may be the reason for the "missing" parallel in cycle 1.

In summary, the Markan background material of stratum 5, cycle 4, contained the confrontation of the Jewish leaders by Jesus, but this feature was strengthened and highlighted by Luke. Cycles 2 and 3 show substantial redaction that is consistent with the formation of this stratum. Alternative

---

109 "It is normally taken as a Lukan construction," writes Nolland, *Luke 9:21–18:34*, 809.
110 Kenneth E. Bailey, *Poet and Peasant*, 147.
111 Nolland, *Luke 9:21–18:34*, 809.
112 Marshall, *Gospel of Luke*, 491–93. Schlatter attributes 11:37–41, 44, 45, 52–54 to Luke (*Evangelium des Lukas*, 303–308).
113 See θαυμάζω in Walter Bauer, William. F. Arndt, F. Wilbur Gingrich, Frederick W. Danker, *A Greek-English Lexicon of the New Testament and Other Early Christian Literature*, Rev. and trans. from Walter Bauer's 5th ed. of *Griechisch-Deutsches Wörterbuch* (Chicago: University of Chicago Press, 1979) 352.
114 Plummer, *St. Luke*, 309.

explanations either mesh with our argument or are far from certain.

Stratum 6 – In this stratum Jesus warns his disciples or others against being like the religious leaders: Lk. 12:1–21; 17:1–4; 20:45–47 (cycles 2 through 4 respectively). Usually Luke draws the features he employs from the Markan material behind cycle 4. Here, he largely generates it himself. He changes the primary audience of Jesus' warning against the scribes from the crowd in Mark to the disciples in cycle 4 (Lk. 20:45 par. Mk. 12:37b). In the next verse, the first word of warning becomes προσέχετε from βλέπετε, and he will use it in all three cycles. Nolland believes the word came from a source in common with Matthew,[115] which would not affect our proposal. Marshall, however, understands it possibly to be taken from Luke's source behind Luke 12:1.[116] This, of course, would support the stratum since it acknowledges the parallel with 12:1–21 of cycle 2. The motivation behind the change of audience eludes the concern of the commentators and is only important here because it indicates Lukan attention.

The audience of the corresponding passage in *cycle 3*, Luke 17:1–4 (on sin, faith and duty), is designated by Luke as the disciples (v. 1). He also adds the word of warning from cycle 4, προσέχετε, as the final caution (v. 3).[117] Marshall sees the insertion of προσέχετε ἑαυτοῖς as a link between the preceding and following verses,[118] which well suits our structure. Commentators usually disjoin Luke 17:1–4 from the subject of its preceding context, the greedy Pharisees (16:14), because of the change in audience. It is better to picture Jesus' exposé of Pharisaic hypocrisy as continued here, the Pharisee as typical of "him through whom [stumbling blocks] come" (17:1).[119] Then, 17:3–4 would enjoin the disciples not to follow their bad example. This certainly unifies the section with its context more than viewing it as a change of topic. The Pharisees as the subject are not found in the Markan and Matthean contexts of the parallels to Luke 17:1–3 (Mk. 9:42 and Mt. 18:6–7), so it is probably a Lukan contribution.

In *cycle 2*, the corresponding section (Lk. 12:1–21) is a complex of Q and L material where Jesus first warns his disciples against being like the hypocritical Pharisees and encourages them not to fear them, and then issues a brief general warning to the crowd against the dangerous influence

---

115 See Nolland, *Luke 18:35–24:53*, 976.
116 Marshall, *Gospel of Luke*, 749.
117 This warning is commonly considered a Lukan addition. See Jeremias, *Sprache*, 262; Marshall, *Gospel of Luke*, 642; and Fitzmyer, *Luke X–XXIV*, 1137.
118 Marshall, *Gospel of Luke*, 642.
119 Danker draws the same conclusion here, *Jesus and the New Age*, 386. Grundmann suggests that the introduction was originally directed at the Pharisees (*Evangelium nach Lukas*, 331).

of greed.[120] Luke specifically designates the disciples as the addressees of Jesus' warnings and then specifies the Pharisees as the particular danger by incorporating the saying, "Beware (προσέχετε) of the leaven of the Pharisees, which is hypocrisy" (v. 1). The source behind the saying is irrelevant since its inclusion was highly selective. Nolland correctly considers it to function as a transition between the preceeding conflict with the Pharisees and lawyers and the following warnings,[121] a function consistent with the typical transition between strata 5 and 6.

Both Markan accounts that qualify under the definition of this stratum (Mk. 8:14–21 and 12:38–40) are used by Luke in the formation of the stratum, and the word προσέχω is introduced by Luke. The second of the two passages constitutes stratum 6 in cycle 4 and the saying within the first passage begins stratum 6 of cycle 2, though the Markan context is omitted.

To summarize, Luke significantly altered the equivalent Markan pericope behind cycle 4 to suit his purposes. A key word was introduced and the audience was changed specifically to the disciples. Cycles 2 and 3 were then conformed to this pattern. No extraneous Markan material matching this pattern elsewhere in Mark needed to be removed for the sake of clarity.

Stratum 7 – In this stratum Jesus encourages his disciples to have greater faith: Lk. 8:22–25; 12:22–34; 17:5–10 and 21:1–4 (cycles 1 through 4 respectively). It appears that the Markan pericope behind *cycle 1* was the basis for the parallelism, so we will begin there. The parallel feature is already present in the Markan account of the stilling of the storm, "How is it that you have no faith?" (par. Lk. 8:25), though Luke appears to emphasize the issue of faith, isolating it by omitting the question, "Why are you so timid?" (Mk. 4:40).

Moving to *cycle 2*, we find Luke 12:22–34 composed of Q material parallel to Matthew 6:25–34 and 6:19–21.[122] In all the cycles, these encouragements not to be anxious, to trust the Father and to give sacrificially as an expression of faith are a counterbalance to the preceding negative warnings about the religious leaders. Luke introduces the disciples as the audience for this teaching (12:22) that explicitly encourages greater faith, "O men of little faith! (v. 28). Proposals for why Luke placed this teaching material here agree that it is in essence "a commentary on the parable of the rich fool".[123] Therefore, it comments on material in the preceding stratum. Since the parallel accounts in cycles 3 and 4 play the same role in their contexts, that of commenting on material in the preceding

---

120 Note that greed and Pharisaic hypocrisy are common major motifs in this stratum of each cycle.
121 Nolland, *Luke 9:21–18:34*, 677.
122 See Grundmann, *Evangelium nach Lukas*, 259.
123 Fitzmyer, *Luke X–XXIV*, 976.

stratum, then the stratum is supported by that relationship.[124] In *cycle 3*, Luke presents the "apostles" exclaiming, "Increase our faith!" in response to Jesus' stern warning (Lk. 17:5–10, see v. 5). This section on the mustard seed and the unprofitable servants (stratum 7 of cycle 2) is Lukan[125] and serves as comment on how the disciples may have sufficient faith to rebuke a brother who sins and to continually forgive him. Likewise, the story of the widow's offering (Lk. 21:1–4, *cycle 4*) exemplifies how not to be like the Pharisees, who are proud, greedy, and "who devour widows' houses" (20:47). The disciples were to follow her example of risk-taking faith in that "she out of her poverty put in all that she had to live on," whereas the others gave "out of their surplus" (21:4).[126] Luke kept this story in its Markan position and no redaction was required for the correspondence.

The one Markan pericope that matches this feature and is not incorporated by Luke into the stratum is omitted entirely, Mark 11:22–26. Jesus says in v. 22, "Have faith in God," in response to the disciples surprise at the withered fig tree. Even if its absence was primarily on other grounds, the clarity of stratum 7 may have been a contributing factor.

In summary, Mark exhibited the feature in question in this location of cycle 4. Correspondingly, after the omission of Mark 4:26–34, the stilling of the storm was in the appropriate position in cycle 1. Cycles 2 and 3 were constructed following this pattern, as redaction criticism supports.

Stratum 8 – Luke, in contrast to the other Gospels, chose to present three "eschatological" discourses: Lk. 12:35–40; 17:20–18:8 and 21:5–38 (cycles 2 through 4 respectively).[127] In each case, it is delivered to the disciples. *Cycle 4* is present in Mark at this location in the plot (Mk. 13:1–37). Any Lukan redaction is for other reasons. This stratum of *cycle 3* is formulated from Q, L and Mk. 13 material (Lk. 17:20–18:8). Commentators generally do not venture to suggest why the Evangelist has included this section, but Danker's supposition that it is linked to the account of the ten lepers (Lk. 17:11–19) through the misunderstanding of both the lepers and the Pharisees regarding the true identity of Jesus[128] is possible. However, then the question of location is simply passed to the healing of the lepers. The creation of stratum 8 provides a firm answer. An evaluation of Luke 12:35–

---

124 For a discussion of why Lk. 12:13–21 best fits stratum 6, see page 219.
125 See Marshall's analysis of the origin of Luke's mustard seed saying in *Gospel of Luke*, 643–644.
126 See the discussion on page 220f.
127 Probably the most thorough treatment of these discourses is Josef Zmijewski's *Die Eschatologiereden des Lukas-Evangeliums: Eine traditions- und redaktionsgeschichtliche Untersuchung zu Lk 21,5–36 und Lk 17,30–37* (Bonn: Peter Hanstein Verlag, 1972).
128 Danker, *Jesus and the New Age*, 181.

40, the parable on watchfulness (*cycle 2*), reveals that verses 35–38 are unparalleled in Mark or Matthew but they could be from Q,[129] as verses 39–40 definitely are. The thematic suitability of the passage to its context is evident – and is the most common explanation for Luke's use of it[130] – but is not a decisive justification for its selection. Other suitable material could have been accepted if it were available. Again, the stratum poses a viable solution.

The corresponding portion, stratum 8 of *cycle 1*, is different in nature from the other cycles. Three healing accounts (the Gerasene demoniac, Lk. 8:26–39; Jairus' daughter and the woman with the hemorrhage, 8:40–56), rather than an eschatological discourse, are retained by Luke in the Markan sequence of events at this location. Here he encountered material that had potential to match his stratum 8, but adjustments would have to be made. His choices were to strengthen the correspondence, to remove the accounts and leave a structural gap, or to replace them with more suitable material – all reasonable options for ancient writers. Luke apparently chose simply to strengthen the correspondence that was already subtly present. Schramm's redaction-critical evaluation of the section suits this suggestion, seeing it as drawn from the Markan parallel with somewhat free revision of it.[131]

Luke's faithful rendition of Mark's account of the Gerasene demoniac contains one striking redactional feature that suggests this pericope may have been understood by the early church to attribute to Jesus the final judgment of demons. Rather than begging not to be sent out of the country, as in Mark, Legion requests not to be sent εἰς τὴν ἄβυσσον. "Abyss," not challenged textually, has some scriptural association with the parousia (Rev. 20:1). Bock recognizes the eschatological implications of the term: "A cosmic sneak preview takes place in this event."[132] Rienecker and Schlatter note the connection of the Abyss with the final judgment,[133] and Fitzmyer in his analysis of the word, though not specifying a link with the parousia, does interpret "abyss" as the "final prison" of demons.[134] Lagrange takes a similar position.[135] If correct, the passage indicates that Jesus has authority to consign demons to this prison. Since this alteration to the Markan account is so radical and distinguishes it from all other Lukan

---

129 Marshall, *Gospel of Luke*, 533.
130 See, for example, C.F. Evans in *Saint Luke*, 532–33. See also Grundmann, *Evangelium nach Lukas*, 264.
131 Schramm, *Markus-Stoff bei Lukas*, 126.
132 Bock, *Luke 1:1–9:50*, 775.
133 Fritz Rienecker, *Das Evangelium des Lukas*, Wuppertaler Studienbibel (Wuppertal: R. Brockhaus, 1966) 221.
134 Fitzmyer, *Luke I–IX*, 739.
135 Lagrange, *Évangile selon Saint Luc*, 249.

healing stories, the change must play a central role in the determination of the pericope's function. Clearly Lukan healing accounts serve to attribute authority to the healer and assume this authority to be from God, but such authority is further qualified in the present case to include final judgment of demons. The essential question that remains is when this judgment expected by Legion will actually take place. In other words, does this healing account make a statement about the "eschatological" role of Christ, as do the other texts in this stratum?

Matthew's parallel account (Mt. 8:28–34) supports the proposition that this judgment was yet future and was to be carried out at the "appointed time" (καιρός, Mt. 8:29).[136] It is probable that Matthew and Luke express in different ways the common belief that Jesus would be the final judge of demons at the consummation of the kingdom of God. Such is D.A. Carson's interpretation of Matthew 8:29. He states, "…there will be a time for demonic hosts to be tortured and rejected forever (cf. Jude 6; Rev 20:10; cf. 1 Enoch 16:1; Jub 10:8–9; T Levi 18:12; 1QS 3:24–25; 4:18–20). As the question is phrased, it recognizes that Jesus is the one who will discharge that judicial function at 'the appointed time'…".[137] In Luke the consummation of the kingdom of God is contemporary with the return of Christ (Lk. 21:27–31), perhaps identical, so it is fair to understand Luke's reference to the "abyss" as an allusion to a parousia event (cf. 2 Thess. 2:1–8).[138] This argument is even more emphatic if one assumes Markan priority, since both Matthew and Luke similarly alter Mark at this point, which suggests like concern. Matthew places his referent most probably at the day of judgment.

Some scholars consider ἄβυσσος here to refer to the abode or origin of demons contemporaneous with Jesus,[139] a view that excludes allusion to the parousia. The inherent difficulty in this is that it does not adequately explain the urgency of Legion's plea (παρεκάλουν αὐτόν, Lk. 8:31) and the association with torment (βασανίζω, 8:28), nor is it consistent with Matthew's reference to "the appointed time". It is more likely that the demon recognized Jesus as the final Judge, realized that he stood con-

---

136 Gnilka observes that the demons recognize that they have a period of grace (*Matthäusevangelium: I. Teil*, 321). Adolf Schlatter observes the connection with the final judgment; *Der Evangelist Matthäus: Seine Sprache, sein Ziel, seine Selbständigkeit* (Stuttgart: Calwer, 1959) 293.
137 Carson, *Matthew*, 218.
138 Ernst Lohmeyer, however, considers the demons in Matthew to be mistaken because he sees the "time" as already fulfilled in Christ's arrival; *Das Evangelium des Matthäus*, Kritisch-exegetischer Kommentar über das Neue Testament (Göttingen: Vanderhoeck & Ruprecht, 1962).
139 See Luke Timothy Johnson, *The Gospel of Luke*, Sacra Pagina (Collegeville, Minnesota: The Liturgical Press, 1991) 137.

demned and feared the possibility of the initiation of final punishment immediately.

Luke's redaction of the healings of Jairus' daughter and the woman with the hemorrhage (Lk. 8:40–56) makes no appreciable adjustment to the Markan version beyond certain minor clarifications of detail. Yet, one particular clarification is essential to the thrust of the passage. Luke makes explicit the fact of the girl's death, a fact that is ambiguous in Mark. This is exemplified by the addition of καὶ ἐπέστρεψεν το πνεῦμα αὐτῆς (cf. 1 Ki. 17:21, LXX). Therefore, the account undoubtedly is of revivification.[140]

Debate has surrounded the purpose behind nesting two healing stories one within the other. Whether this is a pre-Markan form or not has little effect on the apparent purpose. Johnson does suggest that Mark has a propensity to such arrangement, but this does not contribute to ascertaining a thematic reason. He does however concur with Stock that the existence of basic similarities between the two stories provides the impetus behind their association. As a result, Johnson and Stock place equal emphasis on both accounts.[141] Nevertheless, the relevant question at present is not Mark's purpose, but rather the importance attributed by Luke to each event.

Marshall rightly concludes that regardless of whether or not the order of events occurred as described in the final form, or is a Markan or pre-Markan intercalation, undoubtedly the record of the woman with the hemorrhage is intended to provide the interval of time in which the girl dies.[142] This subordinate role is consistent with the comparison between the natures of the two miracles. Naturally, a revivification is more striking and memorable than the healing of a hemorrhage. Consequently, Luke must have utilized primarily if not solely a theme inherent in the account of Jairus' daughter with respect to any arrangement of material he might have pursued; nevertheless, the hemorrhage pericope is clearly complimentary in theme.

Important to discerning Luke's perception of this theme is the interpretative context created for revivification at Luke 7:22. There, Jesus' response to John the Baptist concerning his identity consists entirely of Isaianic allusions, all of which are Messianic in their own OT contexts. Carson notes this fact and observes that each also has the immediate context of final judgment.[143] The resurrection of the dead referred to by Jesus (Is.

---

140 Murray J. Harris enumerates the various Matthean and Lukan redactions which certify the death of the girl, "Dead are Restored," 306–307.
141 Johnson, *Gospel of Luke*, 143; Augustine Stock, *The Method and Message of Mark* (Wilmington, Delaware: Michael Glazier, 1989) 173.
142 Marshall, *Gospel of Luke*, 341.
143 Carson, *Matthew*, 262.

26:19[144]) occurs, according to Isaiah, at the coming of the Lord when final judgment takes place (Is. 26:21). No doubt Luke was aware of these facts and could have included the revivification account of Jairus' daughter here based on the final judgment and the parousia motifs. His clarification of the fact of her death indicates sufficient interest. We need not be overly concerned however for these healing accounts to fit the stratum. Literary patterns in ancient writing were usually expected to be imperfect. Nevertheless, there is strong reason to believe that these conform to the primary eschatological thrust of the stratum.

Evidently, in summary, this section of cycle 4 served as the pattern for the others. Cycles 2 and 3 display redaction consistent with the formation of the stratum, with no compelling alternative explanations. The Markan background to this stratum in cycle 1, though not an "eschatological discourse," appears to have been considered by the Evangelist to communicate a similar message. He, like Matthew, highlights the eschatological nature of Christ's activity in these two pericopes. There are no Markan discourses of this type other than those used by Luke, so no omissions were necessary for the clarity of the stratum.

Stratum 9 – The feature that establishes this stratum is Jesus addressing the twelve regarding their role, Luke 9:1–17; 12:41–49; 18:9–17 and 22:1–30 (cycles 1 through 4 respectively). Luke alters the Markan block behind *cycle 4* of this stratum. He deletes a pericope and inserts one of his own to concentrate Luke 22:1–30 on his chosen feature.[145] Specifically, the anointing at Bethany (Mk. 14:3–9) has nothing to do with the role of the disciples and it delays the Supper scene, so it is omitted. Most scholars maintain that the similarity with the anointing in Luke 7:36–50 is the motivation behind this omission,[146] but there are sufficient differences to deny certainty.[147] The wording is substantially different. The host and location are different. The part of Jesus' body that is anointed differs. The complaint is radically different, as is Jesus' response. Several commentators

---

144 Isaiah 26:19 is also cited by Marshall in *Gospel of Luke*, 292.
145 Marion L. Soards determines after exhaustive analysis of Lk. 22, with regard to dependence on sources, that Luke adapted his material primarily on theological grounds and not because he was forced by the content of available material. This accords with our discussion of parallels 9 through 11 of cycle 4. Although one may differ with many of his judgments about what source lies behind which words, his general argument is sound and convincing. See *The Passion According to Luke: The Special Material of Luke 22*, JSNT Supplement Series 14 (Sheffield: JSOT Press, 1987).
146 See, for example, Nolland, *Luke 18:35–24:53*, 1029; Marshall, *Gospel of Luke*, 787; Schramm, *Markus-Stoff bei Lukas*, 182 n.5; Fitzmyer, *Luke X–XXIV*, 1373; and C.F. Evans, *Saint Luke*, 774.
147 Grundmann also makes this point (*Evangelium nach Lukas*, 388–389).

add that the removal of the Markan passage closely links the desire of the religious leaders to kill Jesus (Lk. 22:1–2) with the betrayal by Judas (vv. 3–6), which were probably originally a unit.[148] This is the stronger argument, given Luke's tendency to clarify confusing or rough details in Mark. Since cycle 4 is probably the pattern for the others, the actual reason behind the present form is not crucial. Of course, the Lukan desire to transform the section into more purely a scene of Jesus with his disciples is favorable to our proposal and is a tenable explanation. Although not directly associated with the role of the disciples, the betrayal by Judas is essential to the plot and could not be removed. Nevertheless, Judas provides an interesting backdrop to the attitudes of the disciples exhibited in their dispute.

Luke's addition to the Markan Last Supper is much more striking. In the midst of this poignant scene, we find a dispute among the disciples over who would be the greatest! Neither Mark nor Matthew has a parallel to Luke 22:24–30 at the Supper. With the further addition of Luke 22:15–18 (L), a simple chiasm is formed that places the dispute and Jesus' lesson at the emphatic center:

A   Eating and drinking in association with the kingdom (15–20)

   B   Betrayal by one of the disciples (21–23)

      C   Dispute over greatness and resultant lesson (24–27)

   B´ "You are those who have stood by me in my trials" (28)

A´ Eating and drinking in association with the kingdom (29)

Thus, the role of the disciples as servant-leaders who have been assigned a kingdom is a major motif, created by Luke for this section.

Two motives are offered by the commentators for the insertion of Luke 22:15–18. First, Nolland believes it may be to cast the Passover as a meal like the Lord's Supper because Luke "wants to present the Lord's Supper as now eclipsing the old Passover".[149] Second, Evans poses the complementary view that the Evangelist considered the Markan account too brief for such a weighty liturgical institution in his church.[150] Both proposals are

---

148 Nolland, *Luke 18:35–24:53*, 1029; and Fitzmyer, *Luke X–XXIV*, 1373 are representative. Marshall suggests that perhaps Luke was "acquainted with a form of the tradition in which the anointing story was not included at this point," *Gospel of Luke*, 787, which provides a viable mechanism but not the motive behind Luke's selection of tradition.

149 Nolland, *Luke 18:35–24:53*, 1044. Sabourin offers the related idea that Luke was showing the Lord's to be a Passover meal (*L'Évangile de Luc*, 341).

150 C.F. Evans, *Saint Luke*, 780.

A New Proposal

excellent because they are theologically founded and eminently reasonable. Regarding the addition of Luke 22:24–30, again two motives are worthy of consideration. Fitzmyer writes, "It manifests some of Luke's concern to have a discourse at the Last Supper; and the collocation of the material at this point in it may be explained by the relation of the strife and Jesus' comments on it to the immediately preceding announcements of the betrayal of Jesus by one of his own. If that is the nadir to which a chosen and called disciple can sink, then who is the greatest."[151] The logic of this "relation" is not so manifest in the text as to be compelling, though it is possible. However, his point about concern for a discourse is well taken and is supported by Grundmann.[152] Evans takes a different tack. He supposes that Luke conforms to the "farewell speech of a dying man" genre in 22:21–30, which involves (1) the leader having a meal with his own, (2) warnings and commands, (3) prayer for those left behind, and (4) the establishment of a successor.[153] However, in this instance the commands are not planned by Jesus, except for one, but they follow in response to the disciples' spontaneous error. Furthermore, the prayer is not actually related, nor is the appointment of a successor clearly evident. The fit is not sufficiently close to be convincing. Still, if correct, the emphasis on the disciples as being prepared to be successors is consistent with this stratum.

We may summarize the viable alternative explanations for Luke's redaction thus: Luke desires to expand with theologically valued material a section that is important to him and his church and that is unsatisfactorily brief in Mark. This is actually compatible with the requirement of this stratum because all that is necessary is the thesis that Luke here focuses on the instruction of the disciples as leaders. If the portion on the bread and cup is perceived as the institution of the Lord's Supper to the future leaders of the church, then the existence of this stratum is supported.

In *cycle 3*, Luke 18:9–17, Luke resumes his dependence on Mark with the account of the blessing of the children (Lk. 18:15–17). The narrative feature of this stratum is inherent in the Markan passage.[154]

For *cycle 2*, Luke has taken a block from Q to span strata 8 and 9, Luke 12:39–46 par. Matthew 24:43–51, the parable of the unexpected thief followed by that of the faithful steward. We are interested in the second parable, Luke 12:41–48 par. Matthew 24:45–51 for this stratum. Interestingly, the Matthean version does not direct this parable specifically at the

---

151 Fitzmyer, *Luke X–XXIV*, 1412.
152 Grundmann, *Evangelium nach Lukas*, 400.
153 C.F. Evans, *Saint Luke*, 792.
154 For a discussion of how Lk. 18:9–15 fits this stratum, see pages 224f.

twelve,[155] although it is spoken to Jesus' disciples (see Mt. 24:1). Luke's version dedicates it to the twelve either by retaining Peter's question in verse 41 from his source or by its insertion, "Lord, are You addressing this parable to us, or to everyone else as well?" Peter's question is probably Lukan,[156] so Jesus' instruction on leadership here is thereby altered in a manner that suits the stratum. Most who comment on the reason for Luke's redaction suggest the insertion was to provide a referent to ἄρα in the Q account (v. 42).[157] However, Luke could more easily have removed this word, so the explanation is not decisive. Nolland does not believe the question restricts the parable beyond "those who are already disciples," but he gives no reason for the conclusion.[158] Since Jesus is already speaking to disciples (12:22), any further qualification, especially when requested by Peter, must focus on the twelve. The concept of leadership is also stronger here than in Mark, with the shift from δοῦλος to οἰκονόμος in verse 42 and the subordination of the other servants in verse 45.[159] Universally, the emphasis on leadership is accepted, and this favors the stratum.

Luke 9:1–17 of *cycle 1* (the mission of the twelve and the feeding of the five thousand) is parallel to Mark 6:7–44 with the omission of Mark 6:17–29 (the death of John the Baptist). The emphasis on the role of the disciples is intrinsic to the Markan material preserved by Luke, but not to the narration of John the Baptist's murder. Luke is satisfied simply to mention the execution at this point (Lk. 9:9). Interestingly, he portrays Herod as confident of John's demise, contrary to Mark (9:9). Marshall reflects the scholarly uncertainty regarding Luke's motive for the deletion.[160] If, however, the role of the twelve is to reflect the ministry of Christ, then their success at this is more evident if Herod equates their preaching activity with Jesus rather than with John. More importantly, Luke passes over the execution of the Baptist, probably because the execution breaks the concentration on the powerful role of the twelve. I. Howard Marshall argues convincingly that the story "was an obvious candidate for sacrifice" because it "cast a shadow over the destiny of Jesus" and "does not deal directly with [him]".[161] All that we really for our case here is the develop-

---

155 Alan Hugh McNeile, *The Gospel According to St. Matthew* (Grand Rapids: Baker, 1980 reprint of 1915 edition) 358; and Carson, *Matthew*, 510.
156 Marshall lucidly clarifies the quagmire of opinions on source in *Gospel of Luke*, 539–40. See also C.F. Evans, *Saint Luke*, 536; and Grundmann, *Evangelium nach Lukas*, 266.
157 See for example Marshall, *Gospel of Luke*, 540; C.F. Evans, *Saint Luke*, 536
158 Nolland, *Luke 9:21–18:34*, 702.
159 See also C.F. Evans, *Saint Luke*, 536.
160 Marshall, *Gospel of Luke*, 357.
161 Marshall, *Gospel of Luke*, 355.

A New Proposal 259

ment of the disciples' mission by Jesus, which is so characteristic of this section.

Mark's narrative on the request of the sons of Zebedee to sit at the right and left of Jesus in his glory (Mk. 10:35–45) would have fit this stratum since Jesus calls all twelve together (Mk. 10:41–42) and instructs them on authority and servanthood. Yet Luke removes it from what would have been stratum 11 or 12, and possibly transposes a portion of it to this stratum in cycle 4 (see Lk. 22:25–26 par? Mk. 10:42–43). If it is actually a transposition (the texts are similar, but far from identical), then Luke apparently did it to strengthen the already existing parallelism in stratum 9. Regardless of the source, the same effect is achieved.

In summary, Luke concentrates the Last Supper more on the disciples and their role than the Markan account. This feature is already present in the right location of the Markan parallel to cycle 3, the blessing of the children, but the Evangelist strengthens it by adding a parable on humility. In cycle 2, he specifies the twelve as the referent of a Q parable and proceeds to strengthen its statement on leadership. Finally, he removes the distraction of the death of John the Baptist to produce a continuous unit on the mission of the twelve. This scenario rationally accounts for the observed redactions.

Stratum 10 – Peter verbalizes faith and commitment toward Christ in cycles 1, 3 and 4 of this stratum (Lk. 9:18–21; 18:18–28 and 22:31–34 respectively). Luke finds such an incident in this position in the Markan material behind *cycle 4* (Lk. 22:33 par. Mk. 14:29, 31). The focus on Peter is sharpened by his addition of Jesus' prayerful defense of Peter against Satan's wishes, vv. 31–32. Consistent with this, Fitzmyer believes both that the addition was intended to "soften the following prediction of Peter's denial of Jesus" and that through the overall redaction of this pericope, "Simon Peter is clearly being singled out by the Lucan Jesus".[162] So Peter and his expressions of faith are made to stand out much more visibly than in Mark, which intensifies our proposed parallelism.

The Markan parallel to Luke 18:18–28 of *cycle 3* is Mark 10:17–28 (the rich ruler), which is in the proper location of the Markan narrative for Luke's purpose and contains Peter's expression of his (and the disciples') devotion to Jesus in response to the ruler's failure to commit. No editorial work was required for the correspondence.

Cycle 2 does not contain a verbalization of faith and commitment toward Christ by Peter. The closest occasion to stratum 10 of cycle 2 where he does

---

162 Fitzmyer, *Luke X–XXIV*, 1422. See also Marshall, *Gospel of Luke*, 820.

speak, and he rarely speaks in the Gospel,[163] is Luke 12:41 (stratum 9). Yet this is hardly an expression of faith and commitment. It is probably best to assume that the author had no instance of another such verbalization in his sources and did not want to create one.

For *cycle 1*, Luke retains the Markan verbalization of faith and commitment by Peter found at this location (Lk. 9:18–21 par. Mk. 8:27–30). No redaction was necessary.

We have seen that Luke observed the three Markan verbalizations of faith and commitment by Peter in three of the desired locations for this stratum. He singled out Peter and his expression of faith and commitment in cycle 4, which highlights the overall parallelism.

Stratum 11 – Here, Jesus predicts his passion and resurrection in the context of the cost of discipleship, and in cycle 4 he experiences the actual passion and resurrection, Luke 9:22–27; 12:49–53; 18:29–34 and 22:35–24:46 (cycles 1 through 4 respectively). Obviously, no changes to Mark were required for *cycle 4*. Similarly, the prediction in *cycle 3* is in Mark at this location and needed no alteration. *Cycle 2*, however, introduces a pericope unparalleled in the other Gospels about the baptism Jesus had to undergo, Luke 12:49–53. Certainly this implies his death.[164] Just as this is implicit rather than explicit, the concept of resurrection is not explicit but is implicit. It may reside in the symbolism of baptism, as is the reception of new life (see Rom. 6:3–4; 1 Pet. 3:21–22). Most discussions of the meaning of βαπτίζω in Luke 12:50 focus on the sense of overwhelming catastrophe found in relevant Greek literature, which is certainly present here.[165] However, it is possible that the "Lukan community" also associated Jesus' statement with Christian baptism, as C.F. Evans notes.[166] In the light of Matthew 28:19, Jesus himself could have combined the sense of overwhelming circumstances with the sense of Christian baptism, which at least later had resurrection connotations. Consistent with this, the resurrection is also closely associated with Christ's death in Acts (2:31–32; 17:31; 26:23), a Lukan book where the resurrection itself is broadly emphasized. The concept of resurrection may also reside in the phrase πῶς συνέχομαι

---

163 Peter speaks briefly at Lk. 5:8; 8:45; 9:20, 33; 12:41; 18:28; 22:33, 57, 58 and 60. Other than Jesus, Peter probably speaks in more instances than any other character. Yet this is still quite infrequent for a narrative as long as Luke which contains much dialog.

164 K.H. Rengstorf, *Das Evangelium nach Lukas*, Neue Testament Deutsch 3 (Göttingen: Vandenhoeck und Ruprecht, 1962⁹) 166; Nolland, *Luke 9:21–18:34*, 708; Stein, *Luke*, 364–365.

165 See for example William Manson, *The Gospel of Luke* (London: Hodder and Stoughton, 1955) 160; Stein, *Luke*, 364–365.

166 C.F. Evans, *Saint Luke*, 540–541.

ἕως ὅτου τελεσθῇ (Lk. 12:50). Most commentators correctly see in this a link between the death of Jesus and the division described in Luke 12:51–53.[167] Some understand Jesus' focus to be on his role in the events following his death.[168] This is consistent with the preceding context, and it presumes the resurrection. Evans sees more in the phrase however. He observes the temporary nature of Jesus' constraint. It is a constraint that ends at the accomplishment of his "baptism".[169] The resurrection is a natural point at which his constraint/preoccupation would end. H.F. Bayer, in his study of passion predictions that include the resurrection, recognizes Luke 12:49–50 to be a vindication/resurrection prediction, though implicit.[170] Even if the modern reader finds the connection with the resurrection indirect, it has been demonstrated that Luke could reasonably have interpreted 12:49–50 in this fashion. If we view the development of this stratum as Luke's motivation for including Luke 12:49–53, then the valid problem noted by Marshall, that "the connection of thought between the preceding section and this section is not at all clear,"[171] is answered. There need not be a connection. Even if the passage is viewed as part of a "section on preparing for the coming judgment (12:1–13:9),"[172] the question remains open, why this pericope and why here? Turning to *cycle 1* we find that Luke continues to follow Mark (Lk. 9:22–27 par. Mk. 8:31–9:1). Jesus' announcement of his death and resurrection was already there, so no adjustment was required for the stratum.

Mark has a passion prediction including the resurrection in 9:30–32. This naturally falls into stratum 12 of cycle 1, where Luke retains it (Lk. 9:43b–45). Interestingly, he extracts from it the reference to the resurrection apparently because if it remained, stratum 11 would be blurred by this extraneous instance of feature 11.

In summary, the stratum was established in the Markan material at the appropriate locations for cycles 1, 3 and 4, with no redaction necessary. Cycle 2, on the other hand, was formed by Luke. No other predictions

---

167 For example Rengstorf, *Evangelium nach Lukas*, 166; and Marshall, *Gospel of Luke*, 547. Each describes the baptism as a pre-condition for what follows.
168 Nolland, *Luke 9:21–18:34*, 708; C.F. Evans, *Saint Luke*, 541.
169 C.F. Evans, *Saint Luke*, 541.
170 H.F. Bayer, "Predictions of Jesus' Passion and Resurrection," in Joel B. Green, Scot McKnight, and I. Howard Marshall (eds.), *Dictionary of Jesus and the Gospels* (Leicester: IVP, 1992) 630–633.
   Luke 17:25 may appear at first to be a passion-resurrection prediction of similar clarity to Lk. 12:49–50. It is actually a passion-parousia prediction according to H.F. Bayer. He demonstrates that the two were clearly distinct entities in the sayings of Jesus ("Predictions," 632–633).
171 Marshall, *Gospel of Luke*, 545.
172 Nolland, *Luke 9:21–18:34*, 707.

involving the resurrection were available in Mark and perhaps in his other sources, so a metaphorical substitute was employed.

Stratum 12 – This stratum does not appear to be clearly formed. It may consist of stories important to Luke but that did not find a place in the narrative structure. Since no obvious basis for parallelism has been identified, redaction criticism yields no returns.

Conclusion to Test 6: This test has revealed a vast amount of editorial work that is thoroughly consistent with the intentional formation of strata 1 through 11. Although several instances have adequate alternative explanations, few if any are not complementary to or assumed by those afforded by our proposal. Importantly, some instances with no satisfactory solution are explained by the strata. Particularly in the travel narrative, where the reason behind the arrangement of material has eluded so many scholars, the four-fold cyclical structure of the Gospel provides a clear authorial rationale. Therefore, this test strongly supports Lukan intent behind the pattern.

The success of this pattern, along with many of Talbert's patterns, in generating reasonable explanations for redactional phenomena adds weight to his contention that "redaction critical work cannot be done in a satisfactory way without attention to the formal patterns that make up the architecture of a writing".[173] Indeed, if a pattern is proven, account must be taken for it in redaction criticism of the text.

An important conclusion from the redactional observations made throughout this section is that Luke based the sequence of material in cycles 1 through 3 on that in the Markan material behind the fourth cycle. The Markan material behind cycle 1 served as a subordinate guide in the formation of the middle two cycles and occasionally for the introduction of details in the final cycle.[174] Several implications of this will be developed in the next chapter, which is devoted to the implications of the narrative structure as a whole.

Test 7: *If the elements of correspondence that constitute the literary device are related to important Lukan themes, the probability of intent is enhanced.*

The journey to Jerusalem, identification of Jesus with Elijah and Elisha, the divine authority of Jesus, his divine message to unbelievers, conflict with religious leaders, faith, eschatology, the role of the Twelve, Peter's recognition of the identity of Jesus, passion predictions and resurrection, these are all important Lukan themes in their own right. Luke would not have structured his whole book around themes he considered unimportant.

---

173 Talbert, *Literary Patterns*, 5.
174 Talbert finds considerable reason to believe that Luke could have composed from a "preliminary plan," *Literary Patterns*, 79. This would probably have involved his procedure for the use of Mark and other sources.

A New Proposal 263

This pattern passes the test admirably.

Test 8: *Intent is more certain if there is no clear historical or genre expectation for the inclusion of the features in question and their sequence, if parallelism of sequence is observed.*

Only Mark evidences anything like the same sequence of features identified in each cycle of the Third Gospel, and this is because of Luke's literary dependence on Mark. The complete set of features is exhibited in Mk. 11:1–16:8, most of it is resident in Mk. 1:14–9:40, and some of it in Mk. 10:13–52. See the following table where the Markan material is positioned in its corresponding strata in the Lukan narrative structure.

264   *Lukan Theology in the Light of the Gospel's Literary Structure*

Strat.	Cycle 1 Luke	Cycle 1 Mark	Cycle 2 Luke	Cycle 2 Mark	Cycle 3 Luke	Cycle 3 Mark	Cycle 4 Luke	Cycle 4 Mark
1	4:14–15	1:14–15	9:51		13:22		19:28	11:1a
2	4:16–30	(6:1–6a)	9:52–56 9:57–62		13:23–30 13:31–35		19:29–40 19:41–44	11:1b–10
3	4:31–37 4:38–39 4:40–44 5:1–11 5:12–16 5:17–26 5:27–32 5:33–39 6:1–5 6:6–11 6:12–16 6:17–49 7:1–10 7:11–17 7:18–35 7:36–50	1:21–28 1:29–31 1:32–39 (~1:16–20) 1:40–45 2:1–12 2:13–17 2:18–22 2:23–28 3:1–6 3:13–19 (3:7–12)	10:1–24 10:25–37 10:38–42 11:1–13 11:14–26	(3:20-30)	14:1–14		19:45-20:8	11:11–33
4	8:1–21	3:31-4:25	11:27–36		14:15–24 14:25–35		20:9–18	12:1–11
5			11:37–54		15:1-16:31		20:19–44	12:12–37a
6			12:1–21		17:1–4		20:45–47	12:37b–40
7	8:22–25	4:35–41	12:22–34		17:5–10 17:11–19		21:1–4	12:41–44
8	8:26–39 8:40–56	5:1–20 5:21–43	12:35–40		17:20–37 18:1–8		21:5–38	13:1–37
9	9:1–17	6:6b–16, 30–44	12:41–48		18:9–17	10:13-16	22:1–30	14:1–25
10	9:18–21	8:27–32			18:18–28	10:17-28	22:31–34	
11	9:22–27	8:33–9:1	12:49–53		18:29–34	10:29–34	22:35–24:53	14:26–16:8
12	9:28–36 9:37–45 9:46–50	9:2–8 9:14–32 9:33–41	12:54–59 13:1–9 13:10–17 13:18–21		18:35–43 19:1–10 19:11–27	10:46-52		

Explanation of above table: Shaded Lukan passages have been taken from Mark. Darker shading indicates little redaction, while lighter shading indicates substantial redaction. Parentheses designate a transposed Markan passage. Dotted lines indicate a significant omission of Markan material.

There is obviously no historical expectation for these features and their sequence in cycles 1 through 3. Luke freely alters the Markan order in cycle 1, and the sequence and nature of the events in cycles 2 and 3 are chosen by

A New Proposal

him. There is no apparent genre expectation either, since the other Gospels, Matthew and John, are radically different. This test strongly favors Lukan intent.

Test 9: *If a sequence or grouping of features in parallel is uncommon in other relevant literature, then the likelihood of coincidence due to common expression is diminished.*

No other work than Mark exhibits the sequence of features repeated in each cycle. No series of pericopes even in Matthew or John exhibits nearly the same sequence. Consequently, there is no likelihood of common expression causing the four-fold repetition. The likelihood of authorial intent is enhanced by this test.

Test 10: *If the passages in parallel groupings of passages are contiguous within the groupings, and not distributed broadly throughout the text, then selectivity on the part of the reader is diminished.*

Apart from stratum 12, which may exhibit loose parallelism anyway, there is absolute contiguity. Redaction criticism reveals that Markan material that would have been situated between strata, and that would not fit either one, was removed or transposed to a suitable location. This was probably to maintain contiguity. These instances will now be examined.

Mark 4:26–29, 30–34 – These kingdom parables about the growing seed and the mustard seed are omitted by Luke. If they had not been extracted, they would have been located in cycle 1 within stratum 4, 5, 6 or 7. Remember, the themes of these strata are: "Jesus directly teaches a crowd of non-disciples" and relates "a parable representing himself as bearer of a message from God," "Jesus personally confronts Jewish leaders, exposing their typical spiritual, moral and religious depravity and therefore implying a lost state," "Jesus warns the disciples or others against being like the religious leaders," and "Jesus encourages the disciples to have greater faith". Obviously, these two parables do not match any of these themes. Fitzmyer wonders why Luke omits the two parables yet retains the parable of the sower just before them in Mark.[175] Marshall discerns correctly that Mark 4:26–34 "was not relevant to his present purpose of presenting Jesus' teaching on the importance of hearing the word of God aright".[176] Since in the parable of the sower Jesus is in fact the one bearing this "word of God," Marshall's explanation matches that required by our strata.

Mark 6:1–6a – Mark's rejection of Jesus at Nazareth would have fallen in cycle 1, either in the "eschatological" stratum or the one where Jesus addresses the twelve regarding their role. Luke's motive in transposing the account is clear, with commentators universally recognizing its program-

---

175 Fitzmyer, *Luke I–IX*, 716.
176 Marshall, *Gospel of Luke*, 330.

matic function in the new setting at the beginning of Jesus' public ministry (Lk. 4:16–30). It is also interesting to note that it would not have fit the Lukan structural context in which it originally lay.

Mark 6:45–8:26 – Luke's "Big Omission" occurs in cycle 1 between the stratum on the role of the twelve and that of Peter's verbalizations of faith and commitment. This Markan block is essentially a collection of miracle stories with two scenes included where Jesus is confronted by the Pharisees and then takes the opportunity to caution people about these Jewish leaders. None of the accounts relates to the role of the twelve, nor do they contain a verbalization of faith and commitment by Peter. Fitzmyer evaluates the five most common explanations for the omission:

> (a) Luke sensed a need to curtail because of his own inserts.... This is a possible reason, but not very convincing, since he still retains so much Marcan material. (b) Luke omits a block of episodes that begin and end at Bethsaida, outside of Galilee (Mark 6:45; 8:22); it is a sort of omission by homoeoteleuton.... This is, however, a rather tenuous reason, because Luke has substituted Bethsaida for the Marcan phrase, "deserted place," of 6:32...; and then suppresses the mention of Caesarea Philippi as the location of Peter's confession. (c) If...there are two series of similar episodes in Mark 6:30–7:37 and 8:1–26, both beginning with a multiplication of loaves and fish, then Luke's tendency to avoid doublets may be a factor in the omission of Marcan material. That does not wholly explain the matter, because he has no parallel at all to some of the "duplicated" material. (d) Luke is at pains to limit Jesus' ministry to Galilee in this part of the Gospel; hence he omits the Marcan material in which Jesus goes to the areas of Tyre and Sidon in Phoenicia. This is important to his geographical perspective. The omission is therefore to be understood in terms of Luke's composition.[177]

The fifth explanation he does not consider a "reason," though in fact it is. He writes,

> The reasons for the omission of the Marcan material are not nearly as important as the resultant shape of this part of the Lucan Gospel. It gives to chap. 9, along with the insertion of the travel account at 9:51, a crucial

---

[177] Fitzmyer, *Luke I–IX*, 770–71. Elsewhere he suggests that the "Big Omission" was to remove geographical references that did not conform strictly to movement from Galilee to Jerusalem (*Luke I–IX*, 166). Of course this is possible, but in the same paragraph he lists the identical number of instances where Markan episodes that do not geographically conform are incorporated by Luke after he extracts a reference to location. It is therefore not a foregone conclusion that the Big Omission solved a geographical problem for the author.

form. Immediately it brings the confession of Peter into close proximity, not only with the feeding of the five thousand, but also with the question posed by Herod in 9:9.[178]

This is indeed a "reason" if Luke had a shape toward which he was working. Based on the narrative strata of the Gospel, if he wanted to retain this confession of Peter, it needed to follow the feeding of the five thousand or some inserted pericope treating the role of the twelve.

Mark 10:2–12 – The Pharisees' testing of Jesus on divorce and celibacy would have been situated in cycle 3 within the "eschatological" stratum or the one on the role of the twelve. It clearly suits neither. Indeed, Mark 10:11–12 is paralleled earlier, in Luke 16:18, so the omission is probably due to the avoidance of a doublet.[179] However, this does not explain why the saying was inserted earlier, thereby ruling out the use of the entire pericope later. Apparently, it was schematically out of place in its Markan location, so it was removed. Once extracted, it was available for use elsewhere without risk of a doublet. If this is so, Mark 10:2–12 was not removed to avoid repetition, but to accommodate his strata; the avoidance of repetition, then, came later. This scenario both accepts the Lukan avoidance of doublets and accounts for the relocation. The difference between these views is that the first assumes linear composition, where Luke starts from the beginning and, if he draws material from later in a source, will not use it a second time when he reaches that later point in his source. The latter view proposes that Luke planned the whole Gospel first, removed the Markan material that did not conform to his outline, and made it available for incorporation elsewhere as suitable.

Test 10 strongly rules out selectivity in the observation of the Gospel strata. There is no extraneous material within strata 1 through 11.

Test 11: *The probability of intent increases as more of the above tests are passed.*

Every test emphatically supports authorial intent behind the four-fold cyclical narrative structure of Luke. This is a superior result to that of the parallelism in Luke 1:5–38, evaluated in the chapter covering Tannehill's work.

Conclusion to the Application of the Tests: According to the tests, the proposed narrative structure of Luke 4:14–24:53 should be accepted confidently as of Lukan design. Its performance exceeds even that of the structure in Luke 1:5–38, which is universally accepted as intentional. Specifically, in tests 1, 5, 7, 9 and 10, the results for the two structures are

---

178 Fitzmyer, *Luke I–IX*, 771.
179 Fitzmyer, *Luke X–XXIV*, 1191; and Marshall, *Gospel of Luke*, 400.

quite similar; but in the remaining tests, ours is superior. By way of review, under *test 2*, Luke 1:5–38 exhibits ten parallel features whereas Luke 4:14–24:53 exhibits eighteen. Only two parallel panels are observed under *test 3* for the infancy narratives, while four are evident in our proposal. A higher percentage of the parallel features in the larger structure attract the attention of the reader than in the smaller (*test 4*). As mentioned above, the infancy narratives lack the support of redaction criticism, but the four-fold structure is amply supported (*test 6*). Finally, *test 8* reveals an annunciation genre underlying the pattern in Luke 1:5–38, but the overall Gospel structure has no hint of genre expectation. Accordingly, theological, interpretational and compositional arguments validly derived from the proposed narrative structure should be given considerable weight.

A COMMENT ON STRATUM 12

Some brief comments are in order for stratum 12. It has been mentioned earlier that it incorporates material on the delay or presence of the kingdom of God. Luke 9:27–50 of cycle 1 is initiated by the concept of the kingdom, "But I tell you truly, there are some of those standing here who shall not taste death until they see the kingdom of God," and the transfiguration scene following is probably to be interpreted in this light. As Liefeld puts it, "the vision of Jesus' glory in the transfiguration is a vision of Jesus as he will be when, through resurrection and exaltation, he begins his messianic reign. Since Jesus' reign is closely connected with God's reign, the transfiguration seems to provide a first fulfillment of the promise in 9:27 that some of Jesus' acquaintances will see God's reign."[180] Both of the following accounts, the healing of the boy and the argument about greatness, are closely linked in the narrative to the transfiguration scene and consequently may conceivably fall under the influence of the kingdom theme also. This, however, is far from certain. Luke's parable of the fig tree in cycle 2, Luke 13:6–9, seems to teach the delay of the kingdom. In the same cycle, the parables of the mustard seed and the yeast follow so abruptly the healing of the crippled woman (13:10–17) that they possibly attribute the kingdom theme to this healing. The parable of the ten minas in cycle 3, Luke 19:11–27, is probably partly intended to establish an interval of time before the consummation of the kingdom. If the above sketch is accurate, that the kingdom is the primary common motif intended by Luke in this stratum, we might conclude, then, that it was inspired by the passage on the delay of the kingdom caused by the mission of preaching repentance

---

180 Walter W. Liefeld, "Theological Motifs in the Transfiguration Narrative" in Richard N. Longenecker and Merrill C. Tenney (eds.), *New Dimensions in New Testament Studies* (Grand Rapids: Zondervan, 1974) 179.

and forgiveness of sins to all nations, in cycle 4 (Lk. 24:47). This final cycle, we have established, serves as his primary pattern. Still, the ties within this stratum appear to be less tight and convincing than within the other strata.

2 Lukan Introductions to Episodes: An Argument for Markan Priority in Lukan Composition

Thus far in the present chapter, we have only presented and evaluated our proposal for the Gospel's structure, and Luke's composition of the structure has mainly been studied through redactional analysis (see test 6, pages 234–262), which presumes Markan priority. To complete our picture of how Luke appears to have composed the structure, we must now discuss the likelihood of his dependence on Mark as a compositional mechanism. Although the establishment of Markan priority is irrelevant to the validity of the four-fold cyclical structure of Luke, it is harmonious with the proposition that the first three cycles were modeled to varying degrees after the fourth, which most strictly adheres to the basic order of episodes in the parallel Markan section[181] and contains the entire climax of the Gospel. Still, this modeling could have been achieved without possession of Mark. One could say that Luke's cyclical structure was constructed from other sources and that Mark drew from the Third Gospel, unaware of or indifferent to its structure. Unfortunately, most every argument for literary dependence is somewhat circular in that each is considerably more persuasive under the assumption of whatever priority they espouse than when viewed from the reverse dependence. In fact, most arguments may be reversed to argue the opposite case. The phenomena presented below maintain their value as evidence for Markan priority regardless of the compositional methodology assumed.[182]

---

[181] The passion narrative is continuous narrative in that the events are more causally, and perhaps temporally, related to each other than in the rest of the Gospel, which is episodic narrative. Luke only selects three features from this continuous narrative to parallel in the other cycles, and the Markan order of these features is retained. Despite Streeter's arguments that Luke's passion narrative is not based on Mark, evidenced by the small amount of verbal similarity and the alterations in the order of events (Bernett Hillman Streeter's *The Four Gospels: A Study of Origins, Treating of the Manuscript Tradition, Sources, Authorship, and Dates* [London: Macmillan, 1924] 202–203) the features Luke employs are nevertheless present in the Markan parallels. If the Lukan passion narrative is viewed as drawn from a different source, our ultimate conclusion is the same, that cycles one through three follow cycle four.

[182] For a classic presentation of the arguments for Markan priority, see Streeter's *Four Gospels*.

2.1 The Need for Another Argument

For years, the Synoptic Problem has been debated and numerous arguments have been proposed for Markan, Matthean and Lukan priority. Our present interest purely regards the literary dependence between Mark and Luke. Obviously, arguments for the priority of each have been tabled. Nevertheless, these suffer from a common weakness. The data on which they depend may reasonably be reversed to argue the opposite conclusion.[183] A brief discussion of the most common arguments is in order.[184]

First, based on the large amount of shared material between the two Gospels (about half of Mark is found in Luke), some believe that Mark would not have omitted much of the Lukan material lacking in his book.[185] The basic problem with this line is that Mark was free to do as he pleased, and it is notoriously difficult to guess the mind of an author on such matters.[186] If we imagine that he used Luke and Matthew and wanted to produce a shorter work, then his selection of pericopes is reasonable. Are those "omitted" necessarily better for his purpose? In addition, if Markan priority is assumed, Luke's big and little omissions exemplify the same problematic phenomenon. The supposed general tendency to expand documents would suggest that Mark's relative brevity compared to the other Synoptics means that it is the earlier. Nevertheless, Mark could reasonably have abridged Matthew and Luke. Stein objects that although Mark is shortest in overall length, many of the pericopes that it shares with the others are actually longer.[187] This, however, denies Mark the sophistica-

---

183 Harold Riley notes certain arguments that may be reversed to support alternative conclusions on literary dependence, and then proposes his own argument for Mark's dependence on Matthew and Luke which he believes is irreversible; *Preface to Luke*, Macon (Georgia: Mercer University Press, 1993) 14–17. His argument, based on "double phrases" in Mark, at first appears convincing. Its major weaknesses, however, is his combination of statistical theory on randomness and the preferences of Matthew, Mark and Luke. Riley treats the redactional activity of the Evangelists as random events, which they are obviously not. He also depends on a terribly small statistical base of twenty-three data, which is insufficient for statistical proof. Nevertheless, he has earned a hearing.
184 For a summary of the arguments, see Fitzmyer, *Luke I–IX*, 66–71.
185 See Fitzmyer, *Luke I–IX*, 66; and W.R. Farmer, "Modern Developments of Griesbach's Hypothesis," *NTS* 23 (1976–1977) 283–289.
186 Fitzmyer's five point attempt to tip the scales toward Markan priority, based on whether Mark *would* have wanted to rework Luke and Matthew as required by the final form of his Gospel, is not entirely convincing. He must conclude that "it might even be admitted that no one of these reasons is in itself cogent or sufficient to prove the priority of Mark"; *To Advance the Gospel: New Testament Studies* (New York: Crossroad Publishing Company, 1981) 6–7.
187 Robert H. Stein, *The Synoptic Problem: An Introduction* (Grand Rapids: Baker Book House, 1987) 49–51.

tion of being able to trim the length of a work while also livening it with details that he appreciated. He also objects to the abridgment theory because Mark would have had to omit a great deal of teaching material while frequently inserting statements about Jesus' teaching ministry.[188] However, if Mark chose to remove teaching material for the sake of brevity, might he not compensate with short descriptions of Jesus as a teacher?

Second, the similar or identical wording between portions of the two Gospels is offered by many as evidence for Markan priority. Fitzmyer admits that "abstractly stated, this identity would not argue to Marcan priority," yet adds,

> but that conclusion is unavoidable after concrete comparison of the texts in a *Synopticon* such as that of W.G. Rushbrooke or W.R. Farmer, both of which use various colors to highlight the agreements between the various Gospels. When the Marcan material is examined in either Matthew or Luke [in the Triple Tradition], only one conclusion is possible; nothing, furthermore, suggests in such an examination that Mark has borrowed from or abridged Matthew and Luke. All the probabilities lie in the other direction.[189]

Farmer, however, is able to examine the same material and conclude Lukan priority to Mark.[190] Comparison of this material in a synopsis, however, mainly reveals which words are the same and not how they got that way. Unfortunately, Fitzmyer does not justify his statement that "only one conclusion is possible". Personal stylistic preferences may account for most differences from either perspective of priority. Stein's redactional evidence in his book *The Synoptic Problem* is persuasive, but is not the final solution.[191] He does not account adequately for authorial preference and for personal stylistic differences between episodic and non-episodic narrative (material after Lk. 22:1).[192]

Third, Fitzmyer clearly states the argument for Markan priority from sequence of episodes:

> The sequence of episodes in the Third Gospel closely follows that of Mark, even when Luke otherwise adds or omits something. The relatively same order of pericopes is even more crucially apparent when one consid-

---

188 Stein, *Synoptic Problem*, 51–52.
189 Fitzmyer, *Luke I–IX*, 69.
190 William R. Farmer, *The Synoptic Problem: A Critical Analysis* (London: Collier-Macmillan Limited, 1964) 233–283.
191 Stein, *Synoptic Problem*, 76–83.
192 C.F. Evans notes the transition from episodic to non-episodic narrative at 22:1, in *Saint Luke*, 765.

ers the sequence of episodes in the Triple Tradition. The episodes which Matthew and Luke have in common with Mark generally agree with the Marcan sequence; when Matthew and Luke depart from this sequence, each differs from the other as well, pursuing an independent course.... The best illustration of the use of this relative Marcan order is seen in what both Matthew and Luke do with the "Q" material that they insert into it; no portion of "Q" ever appears in the same place (after the temptation scenes).[193]

The assumption of a simple Markan methodology, however, accounts for this phenomenon in all its detail. If Mark merely chose to follow the order of episodes when Matthew and Luke coincide, but to omit instances where they differ on the same pericope, believing this to achieve the more accurate historical order, then the sequence of episodes in the Triple Tradition and the lack of the "Q" pericopes in Mark is reasonably explained.

Four, the argument based on grammar, which interprets "colloquialisms and incorrect grammar," "Aramaic expressions" and "redundancy" in Mark as indications of priority since Matthew and Luke exhibit higher literary quality,[194] has been attacked by David Alan Black. He cautions that this higher literary standard of Greek does not preclude the possibility that Mark made his Gospel colloquial for the benefit of his readers. Indeed, Mark could reasonably choose to incorporate these poorer quality features.[195] Fitzmyer writes only that these "*may* suggest primitiveness, but that is as far as one can conclude".[196]

Five, Mark's theology is generally considered more primitive than the other Synoptic Gospels, which suggests priority.[197] If, however, early dates are accepted for Matthew and Luke, the time lapse from the writing of Mark would be too short for dramatic theological development. Furthermore, if Mark chose to reflect the theology of Jesus' day, a more primitive expression might be expected in his Gospel.

The various arguments are often packaged as a cumulative case, but when most or all of the constituent arguments may be reversed, the resulting case is still not decisive. There is room for evidence that cannot reasonably be reversed to argue Lukan priority to Mark, the implications of which do not change under different assumptions of authorial stylistic or theological preference. Such evidence is available in the Lukan introduc-

---

193 Fitzmyer, *Luke I–IX*, 66.
194 Stein, *Synoptic Problem*, 52–62.
195 David Alan Black, Katharine Barnwell and Stephen Levinsohn, eds. *Linguistics and New Testament Interpretation: Essays on Discourse Analysis* (Nashville: Broadman Press, 1992) 90–98.
196 Fitzmyer, *Luke I–IX*, 69.
197 Stein, *Synoptic Problem*, 84–86.

tions to episodes.

2.2 A New and Irreversible Argument

If Luke's language were to provide any indication of changes from one source to another, conscious or not, it would more likely appear in his introductions to episodes. These are nearly all heavily Lukan and presented him with the greatest opportunity for grammatical or verbal formulae that might correlate with his handling of sources. Certain formulae in fact are present in these introductions, specifically in those that indicate a change in scene. Remarkably, there is strong correlation between these formulae and the relationship of Luke to the Markan order of episodes. This correlation, it will be shown, demands the priority of Mark for a satisfactory explanation. Apparently, at changes of scene, Luke used the formulae below as transitions when moving to or from the Markan order of episodes, or when joining material from different sources. He was not bound by this technique, but employed it most of the time (about 74%). The irreversibility of this procedure is evident. Assuming Markan dependence on Luke, a high degree of correlation between the formulae and Lukan transitions to or from the Markan order of episodes would require Mark to have based the locations his redaction of Luke primarily at these seemingly innocuous formulae. Markan omissions or insertions are found both before and after the sites of these formulae in the Lukan text, but Mark exhibits no awareness of or concern about them. Virtually all are removed, still assuming Lukan priority. Apart from dramatic coincidence, there is no reason why Mark should choose such a method. That is the strength of this argument for Markan priority, it makes sense only from the perspective of Luke's dependence on Mark. Analysis and discussion of the evidence below will follow.

2.3 Introductions to Episodes with a Change of Scene[198]

The following system will be used to highlight the relevant aspects of the data:

---

198 All introductory formulae occur here, except for at 11:27 and 19:41 where there is no substantial scene change.

Formulae:

( )   ἐγένετο ἐν τῷ + infinitive
[ ]   ἐγένετο ἐν τῷ + non-infinitive
{ }   ἐγένετο ἐν + **article** + form of ἡμέρα
< >   initial καί of apparent Lukan origin[199]

Key:

bold ch:vs   indicates change to or from the Markan order of episodes, regardless of source.

no underline   signifies words in formulae unique to Luke.*

_____   denotes words in formulae with Markan parallel alone.*

=======   specifies words in formulae with Markan and Matthean parallels.*

_ _ _ _ _ _   highlights words in formulae with Matthean parallel alone.*

| marks a continuous block of Markan material.

* All instances of initial καί are evaluated.

Data:

1:1	Ἐπειδήπερ πολλοὶ ἐπεχείρησαν ἀνατάξασθαι
1:5	{Ἐγένετο ἐν ταῖς ἡμέραις}
1:8	(Ἐγένετο δὲ ἐν τῷ ἱερατεύειν)
1:26	Ἐν δὲ τῷ μηνὶ τῷ ἕκτῳ ἀπεστάλη ὁ ἄγγελος Γαβριὴλ
1:39	Ἀναστᾶσα δὲ Μαριὰμ ἐν ταῖς ἡμέραις ταύταις
1:59	{<Καὶ> ἐγένετο ἐν τῇ ἡμέρᾳ}
2:1	{Ἐγένετο δὲ ἐν ταῖς ἡμέραις}
2:8	<Καὶ> ποιμένες ἦσαν ἐν τῇ χώρᾳ τῇ αὐτῇ.

---

199 Stein, *Synoptic Problem*, 144–61. Randall Buth demonstrates a purposeful pattern in the use of καί, δέ, and οὖν in the Gospel of John in his chapter "Οὖν, Δέ, Καί and Asyndeton in John's Gospel." Accordingly, it is no surprise that Luke uses καί in the purposeful manner of an initial formula.

A New Proposal

	2:21	<Καὶ> ὅτε ἐπλήσθησαν ἡμέραι ὀκτὼ
	2:22	<Καὶ> ὅτε ἐπλήσθησαν αἱ ἡμέραι
	2:41	<Καὶ> ἐπορεύοντο οἱ γονεῖς αὐτοῦ.

Markan section 1	3:1	Ἐν ἔτει δὲ πεντεκαιδεκάτῳ
Begin verbal dependence on Mk after Q and L. Mk ⇨ Q/L	3:21	(Ἐγένετο δὲ ἐν τῷ βαπτισθῆναι)
	3:23	<Καὶ> αὐτὸς ἦν Ἰησοῦς ἀρχόμενος ὡσεὶ ἐτῶν τριάκοντα,
	4:1	Ἰησοῦς δὲ πλήρης πνεύματος ἁγίου ὑπέστρεψεν
Q ⇨ Mk/L	4:14	<Καὶ> ὑπέστρεψεν ὁ Ἰησοῦς ἐν τῇ δυνάμει τοῦ πνεύματος
L ⇨ Mk	4:31	Καὶ κατῆλθεν εἰς Καφαρναοὺμ
	4:38	Ἀναστὰς δὲ ἀπὸ τῆς συναγωγῆς εἰσῆλθεν
	4:40	Δύνοντος δὲ τοῦ ἡλίου
	4:42	Γενομένης δὲ ἡμέρας ἐξελθὼν ἐπορεύθη εἰς ἔρημον τόπον·
Mk ⇨ L	5:1	(Ἐγένετο δὲ ἐν τῷ τὸν ὄχλον ἐπικεῖσθαι)
L ⇨ Mk	5:12	(<Καὶ> ἐγένετο ἐν τῷ εἶναι) αὐτὸν ἐν μιᾷ τῶν πόλεων
	5:17	{Καὶ ἐγένετο ἐν μιᾷ τῶν ἡμερῶν}
	5:27	Καὶ μετὰ ταῦτα ἐξῆλθεν
	6:1	Ἐγένετο δὲ ἐν σαββάτῳ
	6:6	Ἐγένετο δὲ ἐν ἑτέρῳ σαββάτῳ
Resume Mk after brief omission.	6:12	{Ἐγένετο δὲ ἐν ταῖς ἡμέραις}

Q ⇨ Q	7:1	Ἐπειδὴ ἐπλήρωσεν πάντα τὰ ῥήματα αὐτοῦ
Q ⇨ L	7:11	[<Καὶ> ἐγένετο ἐν τῷ] ἑξῆς
L ⇨ Q	7:18	<Καὶ> ἀπήγγειλαν Ἰωάννῃ οἱ μαθηταὶ αὐτοῦ
Q ⇨ L	7:36	Ἠρώτα δέ τις αὐτὸν τῶν Φαρισαίων

Markan section 2 Lk ⇨ Mk after "small insertion."	8:1	[Καὶ ἐγένετο ἐν τῷ] καθεξῆς
Resume Markan order after insertion of relocated Mk pericope.	8:22	{Ἐγένετο δὲ ἐν μιᾷ τῶν ἡμερῶν}
	8:26	Καὶ κατέπλευσαν εἰς τὴν χώραν τῶν Γερασηνῶν,
	8:40	Ἐν δὲ τῷ ὑποστρέφειν τὸν Ἰησοῦν
Resume Mk after relocation of 6 verses.	9:1	Συγκαλεσάμενος δὲ τοὺς δώδεκα
	9:12	Ἡ δὲ ἡμέρα ἤρξατο κλίνειν·
Resume Mk after "big omission."	9:18	(<Καὶ> ἐγένετο ἐν τῷ εἶναι) αὐτὸν προσευχόμενον
	9:28	Ἐγένετο δὲ μετὰ τοὺς λόγους τούτους
	9:37	Ἐγένετο δὲ τῇ ἑξῆς ἡμέρᾳ
	9:46	Εἰσῆλθεν δὲ διαλογισμὸς ἐν αὐτοῖς,

Mk ⇨ L	9:51	(Ἐγένετο δὲ ἐν τῷ συμπληροῦσθαι) τὰς ἡμέρας τῆς ἀναλήμψεως αὐτοῦ
L ⇨ Q	9:57	<Καὶ> πορευομένων αὐτῶν ἐν τῇ ὁδῷ
Q ⇨ Q	10:1	Μετὰ δὲ ταῦτα ἀνέδειξεν ὁ κύριος ἑτέρους ἑβδομήκοντα δύο
Q ⇨ Q/Mk	10:25	Καὶ ἰδοὺ νομικός τις ἀνέστη
L ⇨ L	10:38	Ἐν δὲ τῷ πορεύεσθαι αὐτοὺς

L ⇨ Q	11:1	(<Καὶ> ἐγένετο ἐν τῷ εἶναι) αὐτὸν ἐν τόπῳ τινὶ προσευχόμενον,
Q ⇨ Q	11:14	<Καὶ> ἦν ἐκβάλλων δαιμόνιον
Q ⇨ Q	11:37	Ἐν δὲ τῷ λαλῆσαι ἐρωτᾷ αὐτὸν Φαρισαῖος
Q ⇨ Q	12:1	Ἐν οἷς ἐπισυναχθεισῶν τῶν μυριάδων τοῦ ὄχλου,
Q/L ⇨ L	13:1	Παρῆσαν δέ τινες ἐν αὐτῷ τῷ καιρῷ
L ⇨ L	13:10	Ἦν δὲ διδάσκων ἐν μιᾷ τῶν συναγωγῶν ἐν τοῖς σάββασιν.
Q ⇨ L	13:22	<Καὶ> διεπορεύετο κατὰ πόλεις καὶ κώμας διδάσκων
L ⇨ L	13:31	Ἐν αὐτῇ τῇ ὥρᾳ προσῆλθάν τινες Φαρισαῖοι
Q ⇨ L	14:1	(<Καὶ> ἐγένετο ἐν τῷ ἐλθεῖν) αὐτὸν εἰς οἶκόν
Q/L ⇨ L	17:11	(<Καὶ> ἐγένετο ἐν τῷ πορεύεσθαι) εἰς Ἰερουσαλὴμ
L ⇨ L/Q	17:20	Ἐπερωτηθεὶς δὲ ὑπὸ τῶν Φαρισαίων

Markan section 3	18:31	Παραλαβὼν δὲ τοὺς δώδεκα εἶπεν πρὸς αὐτούς·
Resume Mk after relocated Markan pericope.	18:35	(Ἐγένετο δὲ ἐν τῷ ἐγγίζειν) αὐτὸν εἰς Ἰεριχὼ
Mk ⇨ L	19:1	<Καὶ> εἰσελθὼν διήρχετο τὴν Ἰεριχώ.
L ⇨ Mk	19:28	<u>Καὶ</u> εἰπὼν ταῦτα
Resume Mk after insertion of L and omission of Mk.	19:45	<u>Καὶ</u> εἰσελθὼν εἰς τὸ ἱερὸν
Resume Mk after brief omission.	20:1	{<u>Καὶ</u> ἐγένετο ἐν μιᾷ τῶν ἡμερῶν}
	20:19	<u>Καὶ</u> ἐζήτησαν οἱ γραμματεῖς καὶ οἱ ἀρχιερεῖς ἐπιβαλεῖν ἐπ' αὐτὸν τὰς χεῖρας
	20:20	<u>Καὶ</u> παρατηρήσαντες ἀπέστειλαν ἐγκαθέτους ὑποκρινομένους ἑαυτοὺς δικαίους εἶναι,
	20:27	Προσελθόντες δέ τινες τῶν Σαδδουκαίων,

Begin non-episodic narrative.	22:1	Ἤγγιζεν δὲ ἡ ἑορτὴ τῶν ἀζύμων ἡ λεγομένη πάσχα.
	22:7	Ἦλθεν δὲ ἡ ἡμέρα τῶν ἀζύμων,
	22:14	<u>Καὶ</u> ὅτε ἐγένετο ἡ ὥρα,
	22:39	<u>Καὶ</u> ἐξελθὼν ἐπορεύθη κατὰ τὸ ἔθος εἰς τὸ ὄρος τῶν ἐλαιῶν,
	22:66	<u>Καὶ</u> ὡς ἐγένετο ἡμέρα,
	23:1	<u>Καὶ</u> ἀναστὰν ἅπαν τὸ πλῆθος αὐτῶν
	23:26	<u>Καὶ</u> ὡς ἀπήγαγον αὐτόν,
	23:32	Ἤγοντο δὲ καὶ ἕτεροι κακοῦργοι δύο σὺν αὐτῷ ἀναιρεθῆναι.
	23:50	<u>Καὶ</u> ἰδοὺ ἀνὴρ ὀνόματι Ἰωσὴφ
	24:1	Τῇ δὲ μιᾷ τῶν σαββάτων ὄρθρου βαθέως

Leave Markan dependence for L.	**24:13**	<Καὶ> ἰδοὺ δύο ἐξ αὐτῶν
	24:36	Ταῦτα δὲ αὐτῶν λαλούντων αὐτὸς ἔστη ἐν μέσῳ αὐτῶν
	24:50	Ἐξήγαγεν δὲ αὐτοὺς ἔξω ἕως πρὸς Βηθανίαν,

2.4 Introductions with Minimal Change in Scene

1:57 Τῇ δὲ Ἐλισάβετ ἐπλήσθη ὁ χρόνος

6:17 Καὶ καταβὰς μετ' αὐτῶν

8:19 Παρεγένετο δὲ πρὸς αὐτὸν ἡ μήτηρ

11:27 Ἐγένετο δὲ ἐν τῷ λέγειν αὐτὸν ταῦτα

11:29 Τῶν δὲ ὄχλων ἐπαθροιζομένων

12:13 Εἶπεν δέ τις ἐκ τοῦ ὄχλου αὐτῷ·

12:41 Εἶπεν δὲ ὁ Πέτρος· κύριε,

14:15 Ἀκούσας δέ τις τῶν συνανακειμένων ταῦτα

14:25 Συνεπορεύοντο δὲ αὐτῷ ὄχλοι πολλοί,

15:1	Ἦσαν δὲ αὐτῷ ἐγγίζοντες πάντες οἱ τελῶναι καὶ οἱ ἁμαρτωλοὶ ἀκούειν αὐτοῦ.
16:14	Ἤκουον δὲ ταῦτα πάντα οἱ Φαρισαῖοι
18:1	Ἔλεγεν δὲ παραβολὴν αὐτοῖς
18:9	Εἶπεν δὲ καὶ πρός τινας τοὺς πεποιθότας ἐφ' ἑαυτοῖς
18:15	Προσέφερον δὲ αὐτῷ καὶ τὰ βρέφη ἵνα αὐτῶν ἅπτηται·
18:18	Καὶ ἐπηρώτησέν τις αὐτὸν ἄρχων
19:11	Ἀκουόντων δὲ αὐτῶν ταῦτα
19:37	ἐγγίζοντος δὲ αὐτοῦ
19:41	Καὶ ὡς ἤγγισεν ἰδὼν τὴν πόλιν ἔκλαυσεν ἐπ' αὐτὴν
21:1	Ἀναβλέψας δὲ εἶδεν
21:5	Καί τινων λεγόντων περὶ τοῦ ἱεροῦ
22:24	Ἐγένετο δὲ καὶ φιλονεικία ἐν αὐτοῖς, τὸ τίς αὐτῶν δοκεῖ εἶναι μείζων.
22:47	Ἔτι αὐτοῦ λαλοῦντος
22:54	Συλλαβόντες δὲ αὐτὸν

2.5 Analysis of Introductions in Markan Sections of Luke

Markan Section 1 (incorporating introductions 3:1–6:12):

Changes of scene with attendant change to or from the Markan order of episodes	9
Those accounted for by the formulae	6

Markan Section 2 (incorporating introductions 8:1–9:51):

Changes of scene with attendant change to or from the Markan order of episodes	5
Those accounted for by the formulae	4

Markan Section 3 (incorporating introductions 18:31–24:13):

Changes of scene with attendant change to or from the Markan order of episodes	6
Those accounted for by the formulae	4

Notice that 14 of 19 changes of scene with attendant change to or from the Markan order of episodes (74%) are accounted for by formulae, out of 46 introductions with a change of scene. Naturally, only a strong tendency to employ the formulae is claimed, not perfect adherence.

Correlation of individual formulae with change to or from the Markan order of episodes:[200]

ἐγένετο ἐν τῷ + infinitive	6 of 6 occurrences
initial καὶ of apparent Lukan origin	6 of 6
ἐγένετο ἐν τῷ + non-infinitive	1 of 1
ἐγένετο ἐν + article + form of ἡμέρα	3 of 4

Clearly, the formulae have a near perfect rate of correlation with source changes from the perspective of the Four Source Theory. This obviously accords well with the presumption of Markan priority; but the possibility of a Markan methodology producing this result has not yet been ruled out.

When examined from the perspective of Luke as a Markan source, the formulae are troublesome because, although they are inconsequential to the Lukan narrative,[201] they are inexplicably the primary sites for Markan redaction. For the purpose of analysis, Markan dependence on Luke will be

---

200 The formulae appear to correspond highly with transitions between Q and L, but no certainty is possible regarding major source manipulation behind them.

Correlation of individual formulae with apparent change between Q and L in non-Markan sections:

ἐγένετο ἐν τῷ + infinitive	3 of 3 occurrences
initial καὶ of apparent Lukan origin	7 of 8
ἐγένετο ἐν τῷ + non-infinitive	1 of 1
ἐγένετο ἐν + article + form of ἡμέρα	0 of 0

201 Adelbert Denaux rightly criticizes Frans Neirynck's interpretation of the καὶ ἐγένετο formula as an independent structural indicator. See Denaux, "The Delineation of the Lukan Travel Narrative Within the Overall Structure of the Gospel of Luke," in Camille Focant (ed.), *The Synoptic Gospels: Source Criticism and the New Literary Criticism*, Bibliotheca Ephemeridum Theologicarum Lovaniensium cx (Leuven: Leuven University Press, 1993) 377–82; and Neirynck (ed.), *L'Évangile de Luc, The Gospel of Luke* (Leuven: Leuven University Press, 1989) 64–66.

assumed in the following section.

2.6 Markan Redaction of Lukan Episodic Order, Assuming Lukan Priority[202]

(References in Luke are to the initial verse of episodes removed or altered in juxtaposition by Mark. **Bold** references indicate a clear change of Lukan scene. An asterisk (*) indicates that the formula was deleted or radically altered in Markan redaction.)

Formulae:

1. ἐγένετο ἐν τῷ + infinitive
2. ἐγένετο ἐν τῷ + non-infinitive
3. ἐγένετο ἐν + **article** + form of ἡμέρα
4. initial καί of apparent Lukan origin

All Markan "Redaction" of Episodic Order	Luke	Mark	Formula	
Begin basic adherence to Lukan order of episodes	3:1			
Begin verbal dependence on Lk	3:21	1:9	1, *?	ἐγένετο ἐν τῷ + infinitive
Omit genealogy	3:23		4 *	initial καί
Resume Lukan episodic order	4:1	1:12		
Transpose Nazareth account and insert a pericope after this introduction	4:14	1:14	4 *	initial καί
Resume Lukan episodic order	4:31	1:21	4	initial καί
Omit Lukan episode	**5:1**		1 *	ἐγένετο ἐν τῷ + infinitive
Resume Lukan episodic order after omission of episode	5:12	1:40	1 4 *	initial καί + ἐγένετο ἐν τῷ + infinitive
Resume Lukan episodic order after omission of episode	6:12	3:13	3 *	ἐγένετο ἐν + article + ἡμέρα

---

202 For this analysis, Lukan episodes are equated with scenes defined by Lukan changes of scene. The analysis was performed with the aid of *Synopsis of the Four Gospels*, Kurt Aland (ed.), (New York: UBS, 1983[6]).

Omit **part** of episode (sermon)	6:17			
Resume Lukan episodic order after omission of 4 episodes	**8:1**		2 4 *	initial καὶ + ἐγένετο ἐν τῷ + non-infinitive
Resume Lukan episodic order after insertion of parables	8:22	4:35	3 *?	ἐγένετο ἐν + article + ἡμέρα
Resume Lukan episodic order after transposed episode	9:1	6:7		
Expansion of Lukan episode	19:10	6:30		
Resume Lukan episodic order after insertion of episodes	9:18	8:27	1 4 *	initial καὶ + ἐγένετο ἐν τῷ + infinitive
Omit 16 episodes	**9:51**		1 *	ἐγένετο ἐν τῷ + infinitive
Resume Lukan episodic order after insertion and omission of 16 episodes	18:15	10:13		
Resume Lukan episodic order after insertion of episode	**18:35**	10:46	1 *	ἐγένετο ἐν τῷ + infinitive
Omit Lukan episode	**19:1**		4 *	initial καὶ
Resume Lukan episodic order after omission of episode	**19:28**	11:1	4	initial καὶ
Resume Lukan episodic order after omission of part of an episode and insertion of part of an episode	**19:45**	11:15	4	initial καὶ
Resume Lukan episodic order after insertion of episode	**20:1**	11:27	3 4 *	initial καὶ + ἐγένετο ἐν + article + ἡμέρα
Resume Lukan episodic order after replacement of episode	20:41	12:35		
Replace **part** of episode	21:34			
Begin non-episodic narrative at 22:1	___	___		
End Markan Gospel (shorter)	**24:13**		4 *	initial καὶ

Note that 17 of 20 (85%) changes to the basic Lukan order of episodes with attendant change of Lukan scene occur at formulae. There are 23 changes to this Lukan order in total.[203] Interestingly, each instance of an ἐγένετο formula in Luke (where there are Markan parallels) is a site for Markan redaction. If Mark edited Luke, the above data means that he heavily favored sites with these formulae present for omissions, insertions and translocations of Lukan episodes (85% of the time). At first glance, however, it may appear as though there were few other locations for such redaction (locations lacking the formulae) and that we should expect this result. But a study of the 66 Lukan introductions to episodes with a change of scene in Luke's episodic narrative, material prior to Luke 22:1,[204] shows otherwise (see pages 274 to 278). There are 28 out of these 66 without formulae (15 out of 36 in the Markan blocks alone) that are possible sites for Markan redaction of Lukan episodic order. Only three of these correspond to such supposed activity, Luke 3:1; 4:1 (par. Mk. 1:12); 9:1 (par. Mk. 6:7).[205] Mark therefore did not at all prefer changes of scene as sites for source changes. Indeed, the assumption of Markan redaction of Luke inevitably means that Mark was heavily predisposed to alter Lukan order of episodes at the formulae.

Would Mark have chosen to base his method (and it must be called a method) on Lukan formulae? He certainly could have. If so, one would expect that the formulae so important to him would be preserved or paralleled in some form in the Markan text. This is not the case. Only 2 of the 10 Lukan ἐγένετο formulae show even a minor trace in Mark (Lk. 3:21 and 8:22), and only 5 of 11 initial καὶs are preserved in the whole of Mark's Gospel. No parallel formulae exist in Mark. Perhaps he considered the formulae appropriate locations at which to insert or omit material, due to their temporal/introductory flavor. This approach would restrict disruption of the chronological and logical flow in his foundational source, Luke. Indeed, eight of the ten Lukan ἐγένετο formulae actually coincide with the

---

203 Three instances are listed above where only a portion of an episode is effected (at Lk. 6:17; 9:10a and 21:34). These are included because the associated omissions, insertions or transpositions are large enough to be mistaken as entire episodes. Only seven other instances of supposed Markan omissions, insertions or transpositions that are treated as text units in Aland's *Synopsis* are not listed in the table above, Lk. 3:7–9, 10–14, 19–20; 19:19–20; Mk. 9:11–13; 11:11–14 and 13:21–23. Clearly, these are only small portions of the scenes in which they lie.

Due to the subjectivity in judgment concerning redactional activity, disagreement may occur over the number of changes to the order of episodes and the significance and location of the terminus of the episodic narrative. Nevertheless, the resultant changes would be so insignificant as to have no impact on our conclusions.

204 See C.F. Evans, *Saint Luke*, 765.

205 Initial καί, from Mark's perspective as a hypothetical reader of Luke, would include all such instances rather than those unique to Luke.

resumption of Lukan order of episodes after supposed Markan insertion and/or omission of material (the significance of the initial καὶ coincidence is complicated by the frequency with which Mark's uses it), but nearly all may be accounted for with thematic explanations. For example, the redaction may establish thematic unity (e.g. the "insertion" of a parables section, Mark 4:26–34, after the parable material of Mark 4:1–25 and prior to Lk. 8:22). It would then depend on coincidence that Mark had thematically similar texts to insert only after material just preceding formulae. In other words, if Mark inserted passages where they suited the context, why do so almost solely at Lukan formulae?

Most satisfying and consistent with the data is the conclusion that Luke consciously or subconsciously employed the formulae to maintain continuity after the majority of shifts to or from the order of episodes in Mark, and perhaps in his other source material. The temporal and continuative natures of the formulae naturally suit this function. The above study supports our contention that Luke modeled his initial three cycles after the climactic fourth, which was founded on the climax of Mark's Gospel.

CHAPTER 5

Literary and Theological Purposes and Implications of the Proposed Narrative Structure of Luke

Very often literary purposes are closely allied with theological purposes.[1] A literary effect may serve to communicate or highlight the author's theological interest. This is usually the case with observations regarding Luke's cyclical structure. Therefore, it is perhaps a bit artificial to separate this section into two parts, literary and theological. Nevertheless, in certain instances the evident purposes are considerably more theological than literary. Drawing a distinction then becomes useful for clarifying what theology is more central to his message. The structure reflects Luke's interpretation of Gospel accounts and is a direct expression of his conscious theological purposes. Consequently, it aids in the distinction between theology that Luke intended to communicate and that which was not intended yet is a valid construal of the text. This is not to say that the Evangelist would not have noticed or approved of the unintended theology. It is simply to say that his specific intent would not have encompassed all theology validly derivable from the text. On a more subtle level, we gain insight through his structure into Luke's theological purposes in the Gospel that he apparently did not *consciously* communicate. Just as certain redaction-critical observations reveal the writer's theological presuppositions that he did not intend to communicate explicitly in the text, so does Luke's structure. This subtle level will also be explored along with more general implications of the structure.

---

1 See Joel B. Green's narrative approach to the theology of Luke; *The Theology of the Gospel of Luke*, New Testament Theology (Cambridge: Cambridge University Press, 1995).

1 Literary Purposes and Implications of the Structure

1.1 Reader Oriented Purposes

The purposes behind repetitive parallelism in ancient writing were several, some of which apply to Luke and contribute to our understanding of his purpose.[2] One of the most common reasons for repetitive parallelism is to foster memory.[3] Not only does repetition reinforce concepts, but also when these concepts are placed in parallel sequences it also provides a framework in which details are more easily remembered. No doubt with the ancient emphasis on memory and the importance attributed to the life and words of Jesus by the early church, repetition should be of no surprise.

Another purpose for repetitive parallelism is to provide a meaningful framework for material.[4] This may be applied to the Third Gospel. If loose Q and L material is assumed to have been added to a Markan base, the pattern or framework provided by this base is more suitable for Luke's orderly work than a haphazard arrangement. Such a framework also enables the author to exercise greater control over more plot constituents than otherwise possible, as will be demonstrated in the next section. Actually, since cycles 1 through 3 of Luke are structured on the pattern of cycle 4 (the Jerusalem ministry, crucifixion and resurrection), it may be that Luke intended to characterize the entire public ministry of Christ as a series of events leading naturally and directly to the passion. Such was obviously the case for the sequence of events in cycle 4.

More helpful for determining Luke's purpose is his use of repetitive parallelism to emphasize trends in plot. For example, the basic trend in each cycle is as follows: the establishment or reiteration of Jesus' authority (strata 2–3), appeal to the uncommitted crowds based on that authority (stratum 4), exposé of the religious leaders who mislead the people (stratum 5), warning of disciples about these leaders (stratum 6), encouragement of disciples to greater faith (stratum 7), instruction of disciples regarding things to come (stratum 8), instruction of disciples regarding their role (stratum 9) and, finally, preparation of disciples for the passion and resurrection (strata 10–11). Manifestly, each cycle moves from an emphasis on public ministry to concentration on the disciples as the passion/passion

---

2 Janice Capel Anderson studies verbal repetition in Matthew and links its functions to the aural nature of ancient literature, *Matthew's Narrative Web: Over, and Over, and Over Again*, JSNT Supplement Series 91 (Sheffield: Sheffield Academic Press, 1994). Unfortunately for our purposes, this type of repetition is only one of several relevant to Lukan structure.
3 See Talbert, *Literary Patterns*, 81.
4 Talbert, *Literary Patterns*, 81.

prediction draws near. Additionally, the healing aspect of Jesus' ministry is progressively diminished through each cycle and from one cycle to the next. More evident through the observation of these cycles is Jesus' destiny: not simply the cross, but also the resurrection. It must be remembered however that the background to this flow through each cycle is largely that of the Markan Jerusalem ministry underlying Luke's fourth cycle. Therefore, we may only say that the Third Evangelist approved of the basic plot sufficiently to retain it. His personal contribution to the overall plot is better demonstrated through the development of material from one cycle to the next within each stratum. We will treat this shortly.

Repetitive parallelism also builds a sense of expectation and anticipation the further the reader progresses in the story.[5] A subtle familiarity with an event due to its similarity to previous events, and their outcomes, encourages subconscious and conscious expectations concerning the outcome of the present event.[6] This is similar to anticipating the next song on a familiar album or CD. Such a phenomenon also highlights any breaks from what is expected. When Luke constructed his Gospel, his interpretation of the constituent traditions allowed for his associations between pericopes to be developed into strata. Therefore, the relationship of the pericopes within a stratum and across all four cycles reflects Lukan plot development.

Accordingly, an important function of the strata is to enhance the development of the plot through the associations created by the parallels. Trends are evident moving from cycle 1 to cycle 4 that would not be noticed without knowledge of the Lukan structure. They would certainly wield a subconscious influence on the reader, but the deeper understanding of the author's intent engendered by awareness of his reading of the pericopes would be missing.[7] Overall, the trends across the strata combine to create a

---

5 E.K. Brown examines various types of repetition and their function in a novel. He does not cover repetition in parallel patterned structure, however, and his focus is on modern writing. Nevertheless, his conclusions are insightful and have some bearing on the function of Lukan repetition. See *Rhythm in the Novel* (Lincoln, Nebraska: University of Nebraska Press, 1978).
6 This is one of Robert Tannehill's main contentions in *Narrative Unity*, 1.
7 Did Luke intend his structure to be noticed by his readers? Certainly modern readers are less attuned to pattern than the ancients, so our performance is little indication. As evident from the examples in chapter 3, the Evangelist provides all the clues that are employed in other relevant literature of similar pattern. I am unaware of any explicit statements from ancient literary critics to the effect that readers were supposed to detect patterned structure, but it would be surprising if ancient writers exercised such artistry with no expectation that it would be appreciated. At the very least we may assume that Luke deployed the structure for the advantage of exceptional control over plot development. With the justifiable assumption that ancient readers were sensitive to pattern, we should probably conclude that Luke expected it to be detected to some degree.

multifaceted, ever increasing intensity as we move successively from cycle 1 to cycle 4. Observations not strictly related to structure corroborate this development in the plot. For example, clearly, tension in the Gospel increases as Jesus moves closer in time to his death, with its climax at the crucifixion/resurrection scenes. David Moessner's "audience criticism" of the Gospel suggests an interesting window into this trend in the plot. He tabulates Jesus' audiences under the terms "crowds," "disciples" and "Pharisees" as they appear sequentially in the text and notes certain developments, including tension; however, he restricts his view to the central section and is insufficiently specific about the nature of the audience, whether hostile or benign.[8] We may use his audience criticism to our benefit. If the audiences within each episode from Luke 4:14 up to the passion narrative (Lk. 22:1ff.) are assessed as hostile or benign, an interesting phenomenon is manifest that moves beyond Moessner's observations. In cycle 1, about five benign episodes separate/buffer episodes involving hostile audiences. In cycle 2, the buffer is on average three benign episodes. This is further reduced to one in cycle 3, and in cycle 4 we find that all episodes include a hostile audience or character. A step change in intensity of opposition occurs from one cycle to the next. Moessner also observes an increase in tension across the meal scenes in the central section: Lk. 10:38–42; 11:37–54; 14:1–24 and 19:1–10.[9]

More directly related to the cyclical structure of Luke are the trends within individual strata. As would be expected, the references in *stratum 1* to Jesus' journey depict geographical progress toward Jerusalem. In cycle 1 he begins his Galilean ministry, far from the city. At Luke 9:51 he determines to go to Jerusalem, "And it came about, when the days were approaching for His ascension, that He resolutely set His face to go to Jerusalem." Naturally, in Luke 13:22 he is portrayed as traveling, "And He was passing through from one city and village to another, teaching, and proceeding on His way to Jerusalem." Finally, in Luke 19:28 he arrives at his destination, "He was going on ahead, ascending to Jerusalem." References to other locations are few in Luke and progress toward the city is maintained. Thus Luke uses the goal of the cross and ascension as a subtle but definite backdrop to the whole journey ministry.[10] He chose to begin each cycle with this motif; but not only does he begin each cycle on this note, in *stratum 11* he concludes his parallel material with passion predictions that include the resurrection (in the fourth cycle, the actual events are

---

8 Moessner, *Banquet*, 212–216.
9 Moessner, *Banquet*, 221–222.
10 Léopold Sabourin also notes that we must view the references to Jesus' travel to Jerusalem in the light of the passion that would take place there; *L'Évangile de Luc*, 17–18.

related). So the passion backdrop is reconfirmed at the conclusion of each cycle.

The material in *stratum 2* also shows progression and heightening tension. In Luke 4:16–30 (cycle 1) Jesus quotes a passage from Isaiah that speaks metaphorically of divine physical aid that he now offers as fulfillment of the prophecy. Rejection by his hometown would result in the withholding of that aid, as happened in the ministries of Elijah and Elisha where the prophets went not to Israelites, but to Gentiles, to provide food and healing. Notice that only physical well-being is explicitly at issue, though the spiritual is clearly implied. Cycle 2, however, emphasizes the more important spiritual sphere over the physical. Although the Samaritans reject Jesus, the threat of physical destruction by fire is removed (Lk. 9:52–56); but the spiritual peril of rejecting Jesus comes to the fore. The consequence is unfitness for the kingdom of God (Lk. 9:57–62). In cycle 3, the matter is intensified further as spiritual and physical peril are combined. The parable of the narrow door teaches exclusion from the kingdom of those who are not known by Jesus (Lk. 13:23–30), and the following lament over Jerusalem implies the physical threat of divine abandonment to its enemies (Lk. 13:31–35). Apparently, this threat could potentially be averted before Jesus' triumphal entry, if the people were willing (v. 35).[11] The final tone is struck in cycle 4 with Luke 19:29–44. Jerusalem's persistent rejection of Jesus, indicative of spiritual blindness,[12] has drawn the sentence of absolute divine destruction.

Further plot development is achieved in *stratum 3*. Appropriately, Luke chooses to emphasize the authority of Jesus early in his ministry with an extensive exposition on the motif in cycle 1 (Lk. 4:31–50, 16 pericopes). With his authority established in the first cycle, the subject requires less treatment thereafter. Accordingly, cycle 2 contains only 5 pericopes, cycle 3 only 14 verses, and cycle 4 only 12 verses. This trend also suits the progressive heightening of tension in the plot since affirmation of Jesus' authority tends to ease the tension. Appropriately, to Luke's plot, emphasis on the authority of Jesus diminishes with each cycle as opposition mounts.

Luke creates a growing intensity across the cycles of *stratum 4*, similar to stratum 2. In the first cycle, the parable that presents Jesus as bearer of a message from God of cycle 1 (Lk. 8:1–17; the parable of the sower) is a somewhat gentle challenge to respond. Immediately following, the parable of the lamp explains that one's decision will be disclosed (Lk. 8:16–18), and the consequence will be that "whoever has, to him shall more be given; and whoever does not have, even what he thinks he has shall be taken away

---

11 So Marshall, *Gospel of Luke*, 576; and Fitzmyer, *Luke X–XXIV*, 1037.
12 Nolland, *Luke 18:35–24:53*, 930–933.

from him" (v. 18). The corresponding parables of cycle 2 (Jonah, the Queen of the South and Solomon at Luke 11:29–32; and *another* lamp parable at 11:33–36) intensify the matters of response to Jesus' message and its consequence. Response is the more active repentance, and the consequence of rejection is condemnation at the judgment. This second lamp parable here adds the risk of darkness, not present in the first. As expected, these matters are intensified further in cycle 3. If one declines Jesus' invitation, he is excluded from the kingdom of God (Lk. 14:16–24). This alone is no more severe than the condemnation in cycle 2, but the next set of parables on discipleship adds a new stringent dimension to the here and now. To be a disciple and avoid exclusion from the kingdom one must effectively give up everything in this present life (Lk. 14:25–33). Furthermore, even destruction is hinted at in the following parable, of the salt that is thrown out (Lk. 14:34–35). The climax of intensity in this stratum is achieved at cycle 4, as expected. In the first parable (Lk. 20:9–16), Jesus is depicted as coming to receive what was due the Father. Reaching full force now, the response is described as violent rejection of Jesus, obviously foreshadowing the crucifixion. The consequence of rejection is now defined as destruction, "What, therefore, will the owner of the vineyard do to them? He will come and destroy these vine-growers and will give the vineyard to others" (vv. 15–16). Destruction is re-emphasized in the following parable of the capstone (Lk. 20:17–18), "Everyone who falls on that stone will be broken to pieces; but on whomever it falls, it will scatter him like dust" (v. 18). The issues of response to Jesus and the consequences of that response have been shaped by Luke for the benefit of his plot using stratum 4. He intensifies the demand for a positive response with each successive cycle. Clearly, this contributes to the overall development of the climax by the crucifixion and resurrection in cycle 4.

As noted earlier, Luke apparently chose to keep the relative level of conflict low in cycle 1, and this is reflected in *stratum 5*. Here he presents no account of Jesus personally confronts Jewish leaders, exposing their typical spiritual, moral and religious depravity and therefore implying a lost state. A possible trend is evident across the remaining cycles however. Although Jesus' invective against the religious leaders does not change, their reaction does. In Luke 11:37–54 (cycle 2) the Pharisees and teachers of the law still react as though he were an unknown quantity. Their opposition has become fierce by now and they try to catch him in error (v. 53), but there appears to be a remnant of respect for him as an opponent since they only resort to asking questions. By cycle 3, their respect has vanished as they grumble and scoff at him (15:2; 16:14). Finally in cycle 4 they try to arrest him immediately (a new dimension) by using various legal traps (vv. 19–20 of Lk. 20:19–44). Of course, this growth in resentment is developed throughout the course of the Gospel and not merely in this stratum, but it is made more evident through the comparison encouraged by the parallelism.

Moving to *stratum 6*, there is no warning of the disciples against religious leaders in cycle 1 since there is no personal confrontation by Jesus to provide the context. The three instances in cycles 2 through 4 show no apparent development, but each speaks of divine punishment for behavior that is like that of the Jewish leaders (Luke 12:1–21; 17:1–4 and 20:45–47).

Apparently, no obvious enhancement of plot development is intended by *stratum 7*. Various aspects of faith are explored, but there is no clear progression.

Potent intensification of tension is created however through the eschatological discourses of *stratum 8*. Christ's return is only hinted at in the Gerasene demoniac account of cycle 1 and the following healing and revivification (Lk. 8:26–56; see the redaction-critical discussion on this passage in the previous chapter under test 6). Then, in cycle 2 (6 verses), the audience is explicitly enjoined to be ready for the return of the Son of Man and told of the attendant reward for readiness. Greater tension results in cycle 3 (32 verses) when the return of the Lord is ever so briefly described but the preceding horrific events are driven home: the passion and a time of remarkable human wickedness (Lk. 17:20–37). Immediately following this (18:1–14), disciples are encouraged to persevere in humility through this period. Finally, the crescendo reaches its culmination in cycle 4 (34 verses). The pre-parousia period of tribulation including false Christs, international turmoil, persecution, pending desolation of Jerusalem and heavenly signs is vividly portrayed and is designated "days of vengeance". Note that in stratum 8 not only is the length devoted to each eschatological section progressively greater, so is the intensity of horror. Once again, Luke gradually builds the intensity of emotive material, cycle by cycle, to achieve his powerfully climactic fourth cycle.

Stratum 9 achieves a partial development, but in terms of the time period in which the disciples' role is depicted. In cycle 1, the sending of the twelve and the feeding of the five thousand dwell solely on their ministry during the incarnation (Lk. 9:1–17). The corresponding passage of cycle 2 (Lk. 12:41–48) is a parable that depicts the disciples as stewards given responsibility over others during Jesus' absence, presumably the "Church age". There is no progression with cycle 3, which merely emphasizes the quality of humility to be exhibited in their ministry (Lk. 18:9–17). However, the final definition of the disciples' role, cycle 4, is the most temporally broad and extends even into the eschaton (Lk. 22:29–30).[13] This trend is only tentatively proposed because cycle 3 fails to contribute to it. If it is intentional, the temporal build-up (salvation-historical) suits the general increase in tension throughout the whole Gospel.

Peter's verbalizations of faith and commitment exhibit intensification across *stratum 10*. Initially he merely expresses his belief in the identity of Jesus, that he is "The Christ of God" (Lk. 9:20 of cycle 1). At the next occurrence he measures his own faith in Christ, and that of the other eleven, by their denial of all standard comforts (Lk. 18:28 of cycle 3). This moves beyond the acknowledgment of identity to a sacrificial commitment to the Lord's mission. In the end, Peter is willing to exceed even these bounds and "go both to prison and to death" for Jesus (Lk. 22:33 of cycle 4).[14] His developing expressions of commitment match the increasing level of opposition and threat against his master as Luke progressively prepares the reader for the climactic events in the life of Christ.

Interestingly, the three passion predictions that include the concept of resurrection maintain a gripping potency right through to the actual fulfillment (*stratum 11*). The trend is not in the description of the passion but in the following context, the implications for the disciple of bearing one's cross. In cycle 1 (Lk. 9:22–27) the very salvation of the follower is in the balance: "whoever wishes to save his life shall lose it, but whoever loses his life for my sake, he is the one who will save it" (9:24). Next, the severity of the implications decreases (Lk. 12:49–53 of cycle 2). Here only family unity will be disrupted when one becomes a disciple. Cycle 3 is devoid of implications for the disciples and thus highlights more greatly the passion prediction. The more the emphasis is placed on ramifications of discipleship for disciples, the more the focus on the passion prediction itself is diffused. Therefore, although the predictions themselves display no intensification, their following contexts increasingly leave the reader's attention on the crucifixion and resurrection, an appropriate contribution to the overall plot of the book.

Stratum 12 is an interlude without certain parallelism, so in turn we may not be certain regarding trends within its material. One might expect Lukan plot development, but authorial intent behind any observations would be difficult to establish.

---

13 See Nolland, *Luke 18:35–24:53*, 1066–68. M.-J. Lagrange understands the judging of the twelve tribes of Israel to refer either to the final judgment or, symbolically, to a presiding over the new Israel; *Évangile selon Saint Luc*, 551–552.

14 Peter's denial of the Lord in the high priest's courtyard adds potent irony to this last expression of commitment to Jesus. The intensification across this stratum therefore lies not in a stable progression in Peter's faith and understanding, but in the expressions of commitment themselves.

In conclusion, Luke has constructed the strata to contribute individually to the increasing tension in the plot of the whole Gospel. Sometimes this is accomplished through progressively briefer treatment of comfortable themes or distracting subjects, but usually through the arrangement of the relevant material by strengthening intensity. When we perceive the structure employed by Luke, it enables our cognizance of these plot constituents, which would otherwise go unnoticed. But this is not all. His use of such parallelism provides a remarkably controlled mechanism for plot development. Without it, fewer strands could be intentionally woven by him with such precision through the course of the book. With it, he could ensure that many more features were actually progressing harmoniously toward the climax, regardless of whether they would be perceived consciously or subconsciously by the reader.

1.2 Lukan Interpretation of Passages

Since our correspondences have been demonstrated to be intentional in the previous chapter, each feature would serve to indicate the Lukan function or meaning of the associated pericopes, which might vary to a degree from their independent function or meaning. For example, "The Pharisee and the Publican" (18:9–14) appears to have been placed just prior to "The Blessing of the Infants" (18:15–17) to contrast the pride of the disciples with the humility of the publican.[15] This emphasis on the disciples is suggested by the fact that the second half of this pericope complex is one of the only four passages where Jesus addresses the twelve regarding their role, all four being parallel to each other. This is not to say that the theme of how to enter the kingdom is not possibly the primary concern of the second pericope by itself; it does mean that on top of this Luke has applied the theme of humility from the first pericope to the disciples in the second. In other words, without destroying the traditional meaning, Luke transforms the disciples into startling negative examples of that which the infants are positive examples. In like manner, the other narrative correspondences defined by the strata provide interpretative cues for determining how Luke's reading of pericopes may be richer, broader, than their independent traditional meanings. His apparent interpretation of numerous other

---

15 Stephen H. Levinsohn's principle, that "the absence of a marked form of encoding [of subject] at the apparent beginning of a narrative unit implies that the writer perceived an overall theme which united the passages concerned," also applies here since the subject is merely implied by the verb. See his article, "Participant Reference in Koine Greek Narrative," in David Allan Black with Katharine Barnwell and Stephen Levinsohn, eds., *Linguistics and New Testament Interpretation: Essays on Discourse Analysis* (Nashville: Broadman Press, 1992) 43.

individual pericopes is presented in the section entitled "Domain and Size of the Units That Comprise the Narrative Strata" in the previous chapter.

1.3 Contribution to Redaction Criticism

Redaction criticism is very much a literary discipline. Yet it is also theological since it seeks to determine the theology that motivated specific redaction. For numerous examples where the Lukan adherence to his planned structure best accounts for certain redactional observations, see the previous chapter under test 6 in the section entitled "Application of the Tests for Intentionality to the Cyclical Narrative Structure of Luke 4:14–24:53." We shall not rehearse these again. Nevertheless, some brief comments are in order here. It has been demonstrated that the two substantial omissions of Markan material, Mark 6:45–8:26 and 9:42–10:12, occurred primarily because these blocks did not conform to the definitions of the strata under which they would have fallen.[16] Scholars sometimes resort too easily to the "avoidance of doublets" argument for these omissions.

Regarding proposed avoidances of doublets elsewhere in Luke, some are better accounted for by Luke's adherence to his planned architecture. Fitzmyer's list of "instances where Luke has omitted Marcan material because he has used something similar at an earlier occasion in the Gospel"[17] provides a strong analytical base:

1. Mark 4:23 (ears to hear)   see after Luke 8:17; cf. Luke 8:8b ("Mk")

2. Mark 4:24b (measure)   see after Luke 8:18; cf. Luke 6:38 ("Q")

3. *Mark 8:1–9* (feeding of four thousand)   see Luke's Big Omission; cf. Luke 9:12–17 ("Mk")

4. Mark 10:31 (last will be first)   see after Luke 18:30; cf. Luke 13:30 ("L")

5. *Mark 12:28–34* (great commandment)   see after Luke 20:40; cf. Luke 10:25–28 ("L")

---

16 As noted earlier, Joseph A. Fitzmyer suggests that the "Big Omission" was to remove geographical references that did not conform strictly to movement from Galilee to Jerusalem (*Luke I–IX*, 166). Of course this is possible, but in the same paragraph he lists the identical number of instances where Markan episodes that do not geographically conform are incorporated by Luke after he extracts a reference to location. It is therefore not a foregone conclusion that the Big Omission solved a geographical problem for the author.

17 For the quotation and table see Fitzmyer, *Luke I–IX*, 82.

6. Mark 13:15–16 (person on the roof at the endtime)	see after Luke 21:21–22; cf. Luke 17:31 ("L," or is it simply "Mk" transposed earlier?)
7. Mark 13:21–23 (culmination of troubles)	see after Luke 21:24; cf. Luke 17:23–24 ("Q")
8. Mark 13:33–36 (end of eschatological discourse)	see after Luke 21:33; cf. Luke 12:35–40 ("Q")
9. *Mark 14:3–9* (anointing in Bethany)	see after Luke 22:2; cf. Luke 7:36–50 ("L")

Each of the above three instances where an entire event is omitted by Luke (shown in italics), rather than a mere saying, is accounted for by the formation of the Gospel's structure. They simply do not fit the Lukan stratum in which they would lie, so they are extracted. This reduces the number of confident doublet avoidances to six brief sayings, according to this list. Even though Luke does not intentionally create doublets, he may not avoid them as rigorously as is often assumed, especially when the *six* remaining avoidances are compared with the *twelve* existing doublets in Luke that are listed by Fitzmyer.[18]

The implication of the above analysis is that redaction criticism must take stock of structure in addition to theology and style for explanations of editorial activity. Of course, this new consideration does not simplify matters; rather, it increases the complexity of the decisions. Still, an awareness of the detailed pattern of the Gospel supplies a glimpse into authorial intent that is unmatched in the redaction-critical discipline. If the proposed structure is accepted, it warrants major consideration in all instances where omissions, transpositions or insertions favor the formation of the strata.

1.4 The Composition of the Gospel of Luke and the Proto-Luke Hypothesis

Markan priority to Luke is held by a majority of scholars today, but it is not a necessary presupposition to our proposed cyclical structure. Theoretically, the Third Gospel could have been created with all its artistry and later become a major source for Mark. The structure does not preclude this. Markan priority however is a viable mechanism for the pattern's construction. We have seen that the sequence of features in the first three cycles of the Gospel is the same as that in the fourth, and that this sequence is

---

18 See Fitzmyer, *Luke I–IX*, 81.

inherent in the parallel Markan material behind the latter cycle and largely evident in such material behind the first cycle.

The affinity of the present proposal with the Proto-Luke hypothesis lies primarily in the acceptance of Markan priority. However, as explained in the previous paragraph, Luke's dependence on Mark is not a *requirement* for our structure, even though it accounts well for the pattern's formation. It is a requirement for Proto-Luke where Q and L material are thought to have been combined first into a single finished text and Markan material added later to form our present Gospel. The primary difference between Proto-Luke and my suggestion for the role of Mark is that I favor the Second Gospel as the provider of the sequence of features that guided most of Luke's placement of Q and L (or Proto-Luke) material. The use of Mark is prior to or contemporary with that of Q and L.

If Markan priority is assumed, a number of redactional observations (noted below) provide further clues to Luke's use of sources. Several of these observations in fact motivated the formation of the Proto-Luke Hypothesis.[19] (1) The Third Gospel exhibits alternating blocks of Markan and non-Markan material, and if the Markan sections are removed, the remainder is a basically coherent narrative. It is also claimed that the Markan blocks are topical groups bearing no connection with each other.[20] Along with this, (2) Q material is found nearly always in the context of L material and rarely in a Markan context.[21] (3) Luke's passion is dissimilar in wording and order to Mark's, and removal of the Markan material leaves a relatively continuous narrative.[22] Finally, (4) over a third of the Second Gospel is omitted in Luke.[23] Interestingly, Taylor recognizes that these and other observations in favor of Proto-Luke may have other explanations and he cautions, "Their force is *cumulative*".[24] In other words, the strength of the theory is not that it explains particular phenomena conclusively, but that it accounts for or accepts the whole group of important redactional observations enlisted by its proponents. Indeed, criticisms and viable alternative

---

19 For a concise summary of the most commonly noted observations, see Donald Guthrie's *New Testament Introduction* (Downers Grove: Inter Varsity Press, 1970³) 176–79. Streeter provides the first full development of the hypothesis in *Four Gospels*, 199–222. Additionally, Vincent Taylor ably defends it in *Behind the Third Gospel* (Oxford: 1926), *Formation*, 191–201, and *The Gospels, A Short Introduction* (London: Epworth Press, 1960) 36–43.
20 See for example Streeter, *Four Gospels*, 201; and Taylor, *The Gospels*, 39.
21 For example Taylor, *The Gospels*, 38.
22 For instance Streeter, *Four Gospels*, 202–203; and Taylor, *The Gospels*, 38–39.
23 See for instance Taylor, *The Gospels*, 39–40.
24 See for example Taylor, *The Gospels*, 38.

explanations have been tendered for each of these observations,[25] but they have not been successfully packaged as a consistent or simple methodological theory. The basic approach of Proto-Luke itself however is questioned by Robert M. Grant who contends, "The theory carries as much, and as little, conviction as any similar theory essentially based on the removal of part of a book to see what the remainder looks like". He further considers that "almost all analysis of this sort ultimately fails because it neglects the extent to which the evangelists were involved in the transmission of the Christian tradition as well as the extent to which they were free to arrange and rewrite their materials in ways which seems meaningful to them and to the communities of which they were members".[26] The caution is helpful but overstated. If we remove Markan material, which we can usually identify accurately, then we actually learn something about Luke's other sources. His use of sources allows such an approach. Grant's concern is true where the sources of a book are unknown, and it would be more justified for Luke if we did not have access to Mark. Nevertheless, his point about the freedom of an author is correct, as Guthrie concurs.[27] Luke was free to rewrite and rearrange his sources as extensively as he pleased, but he was also free to follow the mechanism of the Proto-Luke Hypothesis. Grant's contention is inconclusive.

Just as the Proto-Luke Hypothesis successfully explains or accepts the various redactional observations listed above, so does the mechanism implied by the four-fold cyclical structure of Luke.[28] First, the alternating blocks of Markan and non-Markan material are a natural product of Luke's construction of parallel strata based primarily on the Markan order of episodes (see the redaction critical study in the previous chapter under test 6 in the section entitled "Application of the Tests for Intentionality to the Cyclical Narrative Structure of Luke 4:14–24:53"), and a product of plot development. When blocks of Markan material are inherently parallel and in the correct location for Luke's structure, they are retained intact in Lukan strata. Otherwise, Q and L material fills out the structure. Streeter's analysis of Markan and non-Markan ("Luke's disuse of Mark") blocks is as fol-

---

25 For example, see Joseph A. Fitzmyer, *Luke I–IX*, 90–91; Werner Georg Kümmel, *Introduction to the New Testament*, Howard Clark Kee (tr.), (Nashville: Abingdon, 1975) 132–37; and Guthrie, *Introduction*, 179–182.
26 Robert M. Grant, *A Historical Introduction to the New Testament* (London: Collins, 1963) 118.
27 Guthrie, *Introduction*, 182, where he concludes that if Luke is considered a free editor of Mark then Proto-Luke is unnecessary. This is true, but it does not deny the possibility of the theory's mechanism.
28 At this point the two theories appear to be rivals. It will be demonstrated later that they may actually work together with slight modification to Proto-Luke.

lows:[29]

non-Markan	Markan	non-Markan	Markan	non-Markan	Markan
3:1–4:30	4:31–6:19	*6:20–8:3*	8:4–9:50	*9:51–18:14*	18:15–43
(68 verses)	(72)	(83)	(103)	(351)	(29)
(5 episodes)	(11)	(5)	(10)	(16)	(3)

19:1–27	19:28–22:13	*22:14–24:53*
(27)	(119)	*(167)*
(1)	(3)	*(11?)*

Based on his analysis, only Luke 6:20–8:3(7:50) breaks a block of Markan material inherently parallel to other Markan material in Luke's structure. In this instance it merely develops further the theme of Jesus' authority.

The claim is essentially true that if the Markan sections are removed the remainder is a basically coherent narrative and that the incorporated Markan material in isolation is occasionally rough. However, the coherence of this Markan material is irrelevant if Luke was primarily trying to match the sequence of features in the final cycle and was willing to omit portions as necessary. He would not have been concerned about its coherence. The numerous omissions, transpositions and substitutions of Markan material to construct the strata ensure a less coherent narrative when Proto-Lukan blocks are removed. Actually, if any important Markan pericopes are substituted, like perhaps Luke 4:16–30 for Mark 6:1–6a as proposed by Streeter, then the coherence of the Markan material is sacrificed and that of the non-Markan material is enhanced. Coherence of the non-Markan material is also accounted for by the proportion of the Gospel it occupies (about three fifths) and by the fact that a number of transitions between non-Markan blocks according to Streeter's analysis occur at major transitions in the Gospel's plot, such as Luke 8:1–3; 9:50–51 and 19:27–28. Therefore, it includes important transitional statements and pericopes necessary for coherence. Some scholars even question the coherence of this non-Markan material however.[30] In summary, the methodology behind the proposed structure for Luke expects the alternating blocks and the differing levels of coherence based on the proportions of the material employed.

Second, our proposal accounts for the phenomenon that Q material is found nearly always in the context of L material and rarely in a Markan

---

29 Streeter, *Four Gospels*, 199. See also Schramm, *Markus-Stoff bei Lukas*, 4–9.
30 Kümmel believes that the coherence of the non-Markan material is not obvious (*Introduction*, 133–34), as does Guthrie who notes some incoherent transitions (*Introduction*, 179–182).

context. If Mark was the primary source, with Q and L as supplementary material to fill out and expand the structure, then it should be expected that Q material and combinations of Q and L would be located in the structure where Markan material left gaps. This is precisely what is observed with the large majority of the material. It fills the gap of strata 1 through 9 in cycle 3 and forms the entirety of cycle 2. Virtually all of the remainder expands the authority stratum of cycle 1. To demand of our proposal that Q material be more finely interspersed within the Markan sections is no different from demanding of Proto-Luke that Markan material be more finely interspersed within Q (+L) sections; so neither theory has the advantage in this regard. What of the L material? The designation (L) is generally considered to encompass a greater number and diversity of sources than Q. L material was therefore more likely to be used to support both Markan and Q passages. Consistent with this, a broader distribution of it is observed in the Gospel.

Third, it is observed that Luke's passion is dissimilar in wording and order to Mark's and that removal of the Markan material leaves a relatively continuous narrative. This is irrelevant to the formation of the Gospel's cyclical structure and for that matter to the Evangelist's use of sources before Luke 22:1. There is no guarantee that his passion source is the same as any other he utilized. Only three features are employed by our structure from the passion narrative, and these lie in the same order in Mark as they do in Luke's final form. No matter what source is behind his passion account, only the sequence of three features must be explained for the Gospel's structure.

Fourth, construction of the parallel cyclical structure from a source that is not rigorously parallel (Mark) demands that large portions of material be omitted or transposed. Over a third of the Second Gospel is omitted in Luke precisely for this reason. It is unnecessary to suppose that Mark was inserted into an earlier work, though this is not an argument against that possibility.

Both the Proto-Luke Hypothesis and the formation of the cyclical narrative structure of Luke account for the observations that inspired the former theory. Yet the two need not be mutually exclusive. It is possible that Luke assembled Q and L material into a "Proto-Luke" and then upon acquisition of Mark rearranged his first document to match the sequence of features identified in the Jerusalem ministry and passion block of his new source. This suggests that he favored Mark, at least up to the passion account where he may have used a different source. There is obvious reason why he would favor Mark to Q. The nature of Q material suggests that it was a sayings source,³¹ so Markan material with its narrative context would have been attractive in comparison. Yet "L," which includes Lukan composition of transitional material, could have provided an adequate narrative context for the sayings in Proto-Luke. Therefore, if the Evangelist desired a basis for a parallel structure, the choice was apparently between his own narrative framework and Mark's. If he deemed the Markan framework more historically trustworthy or theologically meaningful than his own, he likely would have opted for the Markan sequence of episodes and rearranged the Q-L document. It is reasonable to assume that a published fluid narrative that he considered trustworthy enough to be a major source would possibly have been thought a more accurate arrangement than his own.

Any theory of composition, whether Proto-Luke or cyclical parallelism, must account for the correspondence pattern between Luke 13:22–18:8 and 19:28–21:38. Apart from some minor insertions and omissions in the eschatological discourse, the latter block is taken almost verbatim from Mark 11:1–13:37; and the former block matches it. Here the sequence of a Q+L block is precisely parallel to the sequence of a Markan block. Only the Q+L block could have been composed after the pattern of its matching block.³²

LUKE 13:22–18:8	LUKE 19:28–21:38
13:22 "To Jerusalem"	19:28 "To Jerusalem"
13:23–30 Entrance into the kingdom of God denied for some Jews	19:29–40 Entrance of King into Jerusalem ("Blessed is He who comes in the name of the Lord!")
13:31–35 Jesus laments over Jerusalem. ("Blessed is He who comes in the name of the Lord!")	19:41–44 Jesus laments over Jerusalem

---

31 See Fitzmyer, *Luke I–IX*, 75–81.
32 The source work behind 22:1–24:53 is much more complex, with the wording often varying greatly from Mark. So the parallelism between 22:1–24:53 and 18:9–34 does not contribute to this argument. Furthermore, Luke's dependence on Mark resumes at 18:15, thus terminating the Q+L block. Accordingly, strata 9 through 12 of the Lukan structure are irrelevant to our argument.

14:1–14 Without provocation, religious leaders try to find fault in Jesus (healing of man with dropsy) – Jesus' authority confirmed.	19:45–20:8 Without provocation, religious leaders try to find fault in Jesus – Jesus' authority questioned in temple.
14:15–24 Parable representing Jesus as bearer of a message from God – parable of the great banquet	20:9–16 Parable representing Jesus as bearer of a message from God – parable of the tenants
14:25–15:32 Parables dealing with response to Jesus	20:17–18 Parable dealing with response to Jesus
16:1–18 Teaching on stewardship – against religious leaders, who take offense	20:19–26 Teaching on stewardship – against religious leaders, who take offense
16:19–31 Teaching on life after death and resurrection – with reference to Abraham, Moses and the Old Testament	20:27–44 Teaching on life after death and resurrection – with reference to Abraham, Moses and the Old Testament
17:1–4 Jesus warns the disciples against religious leaders.	20:45–47 Jesus warns the disciples against religious leaders.
17:5–19 The disciples need for greater faith is expressed.	21:1–4 The disciples need for greater faith is expressed.
17:20–18:8 Jesus delivers an eschatological discourse.	21:5–38 Jesus delivers an eschatological discourse.

Naturally, our cyclical structure accounts for this correspondence. Proto-Luke may also explain it if one accepts that its material was rearranged when combined with Mark. It is reasonable to assume that he reworked that document at least as much as he did Mark.

In the section of the previous chapter entitled "Lukan Introductions to Episodes: An Argument for Markan Priority," the formulae used by Luke to introduce pericopes are analyzed, and their distribution suggests as much redactional activity in the central section (Proto-Lukan section) as in the Markan blocks. This establishes sufficient grounds to believe that Luke might have rearranged this material to match the pattern of the fourth cycle. Of course, the redaction indicated by the formulae may be from the original combination of Q and L; but the formulae, their usage and frequency are so similar to that in the Markan blocks that they suggest concurrent composition. Although this argument for the rearrangement of Proto-Luke is circumstantial, the strengths of that Hypothesis are maintained and the above correspondence pattern does not invalidate it. The argument for Luke's narrative structure is not circumstantial however, so if one accepts the Proto-Luke Hypothesis, the rearrangement of that document must be accepted.

2 Theological Purposes and Implications of the Structure

Ancient writers usually employed architectonic structures for literary and not simply artistic purposes. Often meaning was also intended to be conveyed through them. Plutarch is a good example. Typifying the belief of his period, he demonstrates that a man's character remains static throughout life. In his biography of *Alcibiades*, the subject's life is divided into the private/younger life and the public/older life and the themes covered in the first half are repeated in essentially the same order in the second. The reader is led to observe that the man's character is virtually unchanged from childhood to manhood.[33] Vergil, as another example, enhances the message of the individual books that form his epics by placing them in a parallel structure, thereby fostering comparison and contrast between pairs.[34] Luke himself architectonically compares and contrasts John the Baptist with Jesus in the first three chapters of his Gospel. In biblical studies, such meaning conveyed through structure is often highly theological, as in the case of the gospel of Luke.

Any theologizing founded on arrangement of pericopes is obviously at some risk of speculation. Under this caution, a few noteworthy points may be drawn confidently from our structure of Luke. This confidence is warranted because the theology is founded on redactional activity proven intentional and is consistent with Lukan theology commonly proposed by scholars. It is however not simply a restatement of what others have said. Indeed, the narrative structure has much to contribute toward our understanding of the Gospel's theology. We will now explore some of the theology communicated by Luke through his narrative features and strata.

2.1 Christology Communicated through the Structure (Strata 1–3 and 11)

As would be expected, most of the theology that motivated the construction of the Gospel's structure, and that which was intended to be communicated through it, revolves around Christ. His authority and mission are particu-

---

[33] Russel, *Plutarch*, 118–126.
[34] Duckworth, *Structural Patterns*, 1–2.

Literary and Theological Purposes and Implications 303

larly developed. Obviously, for Luke's intended audience exploring Christianity for the first time or as relatively new converts, such emphases would be eminently rational.

2.1.1 DEATH AND RESURRECTION AS THE GOAL OF
JESUS' INCARNATE MINISTRY (STRATA 1 AND 11)

At the inception of each of the last three cycles, Luke explicates the geographical goal of the Lord's journey, Jerusalem (stratum 1). His readers would have known that the crucifixion occurred there. Having positioned these references to the city, the passion predictions that include the resurrection (stratum 11) then create a frame around the cycles. The destination and the events to take place there function as a backdrop to all the events in the public ministry of Jesus.[35] This is not to say that the Evangelist intends his audience to interpret every episode as dominated by that theme. Rather, the underlying anticipation and tension created is probably meant to add a sense of urgency throughout, an urgency that forces into bold relief each of Jesus' conflicts with the religious leaders, who would soon bring about his execution. The same urgency, however, accentuates his concern for the lost, the poor and the outcast as he takes precious time to meet their needs. Furthermore, the importance of the disciples' preparation to perpetuate his ministry is more pressing under the constraint of this goal. In effect, through his structure Luke has inextricably linked the ministry of Jesus as a whole to the passion.

Consistent with our identification of the resurrection of Christ as an emphasis in Luke's structure, scholars have noted the general importance of the resurrection, ascension and vindication in both Luke and Acts.[36] It even plays an integral role in the Evangelist's treatment of divine necessity (see Lk. 9:22; 24:7, 26).[37]

2.1.2 PROPHETIC STATUS OF JESUS (STRATUM 2)

Luke begins each cycle with a section that depicts Jesus as a rejected prophet.[38] In three (perhaps four) of these instances some comparison is

---

35 This meshes well with Luke's theological focus on the divine plan of "salvation-history." Scholars have noted other indications of necessity and sovereignty including Luke's use of δεῖ and βουλή. See further Stein, *Luke*, 45–6; I. Howard Marshall, *Luke: Historian and Theologian* (Grand Rapids: Zondervan, 1970) 103–111; Conzelmann, *Theology*, 149–54; Fitzmyer, *Luke I–IX*, 179–81; and C.A. Evans, "'He Set His Face,'" 545–548.
36 So Liefeld, *Luke*, 811.
37 See Marshall's helpful discussion in *Historian and Theologian*, 106–111.
38 John Navone states, "Matthew presents Jesus as the new Moses, the legislator of the new law. Jesus appears as the Son of God in the Fourth Gospel. Luke, however,

made between the Lord and Elijah (or possibly Elisha also), not equating the two, but manifesting the prophetic character of Christ through comparison with a well-known and accepted prophet. Perhaps the stratum behind this theological theme (stratum 2) should be understood as the initiation of or basis for the authority stratum (#3), since prophetic status implies divine authority and sometimes power, as seen in the Old Testament accounts of Elijah. We may be confident that Luke intended this as an important statement because the stratum itself is probably almost entirely the result of redaction.[39]

In cycle 1, Luke inserts references to Elijah and Elisha immediately after he retains the Markan implication by Jesus that he was a prophet ("no prophet is welcome in his home town," Luke 4:24 par. Mark 6:4), and probably the eschatological prophet.[40] These references (Lk. 4:25–27) programmatically liken his divine mission to that of the Old Testament "men of God". Just as God sent Elijah and Elisha only to non-Israelites because the Israelites had rejected Him, so He would restrict the ministry of Jesus from those who reject him. Within the sphere of this prophetic ministry are not only the words of God but also miraculous deeds,[41] which both begin immediately in the next pericope. After teaching and healing a man, the people exclaim, "What is this *message*? For with authority and power He commands the unclean spirits, and *they come out*" (Lk. 4:36, italics mine). Denial of Jesus' ministry (and ultimately of entrance into the kingdom) from those who reject him is also communicated in cycle 2, Luke 9:52–62. The Samaritan village that did not receive him was not the recipient of his ministry, and the would-be disciples who lack sufficient commitment are not fit for the kingdom of God. In cycle 3, the parable of the narrow door and the prophetic lament over Jerusalem (Lk. 13:23–35) continue to bear this theme with the added dimension of judgment. The triumphal entry itself does not portray Jesus as a prophet (Lk. 19:29–40), but the following prophetic lament over Jerusalem obviously does (Lk. 19:41–44). He pronounces divine judgment on the city because it did not

> recognize the time of [its] visitation" (ἐπισκοπή). Marshall clarifies that this is "the coming of God whether for good...or for judgment.... Here the visitation is intended to be the occasion of salvation as proclaimed by

---

depicts Jesus especially as a prophet." See *Themes of St. Luke* (Rome: Gregorian University, 1970) 132.

39 See the redaction-critical discussion of this stratum under test 6 in the previous chapter.

40 Marshall has a fine discussion of this Lukan identification in Lk. 4:16–30 (*Historian and Theologian*, 125–128).

41 See further C.F. Evans, *Saint Luke*, 70–71.

Jesus; unrecognized as such, the same visitation becomes the basis for a judgment yet to follow.[42]

The sense that God has visited in Jesus acts as a summary of the force behind Jesus' characterization as a prophet. Now the initiation of each cycle with the prophetic status motif is amplified in significance. Rejection of Jesus is tantamount to rejection of the Father. This is why rejection of Jesus draws the consequence of exclusion from the kingdom (salvation) as described in this stratum. Luke's placement of this material – which ultimately equates Christ's words and deeds with the Father's – at the beginning of each cycle explicates the authority over the reader's life wielded by the teaching of Jesus recorded by the Evangelist in each cycle. In essence, if one chooses to reject it (or Jesus) then exclusion from the kingdom is the consequence.

2.1.3 AUTHORITY (STRATUM 3)

Emphasis on the prophetic status of Jesus naturally flows into the theme of divine authority in stratum 3. Luke does not produce a static analysis of Christ's authority but develops it through a variety of means. Whether Luke intended it or not, the early establishment of Jesus' authority in the Gospel and in each stratum is an effective strategy to persuade his readers to become disciples if they are not already.

2.1.3.1 Authority Displayed through Conflict

Luke employs several conflict accounts to demonstrate the supremacy of Jesus' authority over that of the Jewish leaders (Lk. 5:17–26; 6:1–5, 6–11; 7:36–50; 10:25–37; 14:1–14; 19:45–20:8). In each case the leaders try to find fault in Jesus regarding his obedience to or interpretation of the law, but the tables are inevitably turned in their encounters with the ultimate legal authority. This is the counterpart to Luke's emphasis on the reversal of fortune for the outcast.[43] The last shall be first and the first shall be last.

In the account of the healing of the paralytic (Lk. 5:17–26) Luke indicates at the outset that Jesus' ability to heal was derived from God (v. 17).[44] The Jewish leaders consider Jesus' pronouncement of forgiveness for the

---

42 Marshall, *Gospel of Luke*, 719.
43 Stein provides a brief but helpful summary of the Lukan concept of reversal for the outcast in *Luke*, 49–50. He does not however cover the counterpart. For a thorough treatment of numerous types of "bi-polar" reversal in Luke see John O. York's *The Last Shall be First: The Rhetoric of Reversal in Luke*, JSNTSS 46 (Sheffield: JSOT Press, 1991). He convincingly demonstrates that the technique of reversal is so prevalent and often explicit that it may rightly be considered a major theme of the Evangelist.
44 The anarthrous κύριος refers to God. See Marshall, *Gospel of Luke*, 212.

invalid to be blasphemous since God alone has authority to forgive sins, a fact of Scripture. This is the point, however, as revealed in the statement, "the Son of Man has authority on earth to forgive sins" (v. 24). Hence, this account stresses the authority of Christ.[45]

Sabbath law becomes the issue in Luke 6:1–5 and 6:6–11. When accused of reaping on the Sabbath, an act contrary to Old Testament law, Jesus notes an exceptional instance where David himself was justified in doing what was "illegal" for the sake of sustenance. In other words, the Jewish leaders' interpretation of one passage did not adequately account for other passages. Jesus, being the superior interpreter of the law, is more aware of the relevant passages and demonstrates greater interpretative ability and correctness, if not authority. Clearly, authority is central to the account since Jesus declares himself "Lord of the Sabbath" (v. 5). Another Sabbath controversy follows immediately. Here, when about to heal a man's shriveled hand, the Lord of the Sabbath asks, "...is it lawful on the Sabbath to do good or to do evil, to save a life, or to destroy it?" (v. 9). Note that the question does not allow the response, "neither". The silence of the Pharisees and teachers of the law suggests that they could not successfully refute the challenge and that they were bested.

Simon, when Jesus is at his home, questions both his prophetic knowledge and his adherence to the law (Lk. 7:36–50).[46] Jesus should know that the woman touching him is a sinner and according to the law he should not permit such contact. The response is not a reference to legal interpretation but recognition that the woman is no longer a sinner because her sins have been forgiven.[47]

> V 48 cannot be read as a fresh forgiveness of the woman, but it can and should be read as a confirmation of the woman's forgiveness, on the basis of Jesus' own authority. In the pericope already the connection is drawn between the woman's forgiveness and Jesus and his coming. Now this connection becomes explicit by means of Jesus' authoritative word: it is Jesus who brings the eschatological forgiveness of God (in 5:20 for the first time, here as confirmation and in the form of a deeper entry into the restored relationship with God implicit therein).[48]

When the expert in the law tests Jesus about how to gain eternal life, the

---

[45] Marshall also draws this conclusion in *Gospel of Luke*, 210.
[46] Roland Meynet correctly concludes that Simon is the main character in the story, not the woman ("'Celui à qui est remis peu, aime un peu...' (Lc 7,36-50)," *Greg* 75 (2, 1994) 267–280.
[47] This is the force of the perfect tense. See Plummer, *St. Luke*, 214; and Nolland, *Luke 1–9:20*, 359.
[48] Nolland, *Luke 1–9:20*, 359.

tables are turned once again (Lk. 10:25–37). The true expert in the law, Jesus, points out that complete obedience is not selective. We may not choose whom to love and how much. A proper understanding of the law must involve wholesale acceptance of its demands. As Marshall explains, the emphasis on the two commandments "was obviously regarded as a key element in the teaching of Jesus, one which expressed his basic agreement with the fundamental teaching of the OT and brought out the continuity between the law, rightly understood, and his own teaching".[49] The irony of this story must be highlighted. An expert in the law who assumed he knew how to gain eternal life, and really should have known, is corrected by someone that he considered less of an expert. Thereby the superior authority of Jesus as interpreter of the law is demonstrated.

Sabbath controversy and instruction of those who should not have needed such instruction are combined in Luke 14:1–14, where Jesus dines at a Pharisee's house. The Lord clarifies Sabbath law for these Jewish experts and proceeds to teach them on humility, both actions of superior authority.

In the final conflict account through which Luke emphasizes the Lord's authority, Luke 19:45–20:8, Jesus assumes the right to clear the temple on God's behalf. When questioned by the chief priests, teachers of the law and elders about his authority to behave in such a manner and to teach, he frustrates them with their own excessive concern for public acceptance (20:5–6). By this point in the narrative, the reader understands that his divine authority is implicitly communicated in this passage even though Jesus avoids a direct statement.

Clearly, the message to Luke's readership through these passages is that Christianity now bears divine authority rather than the Judaism represented by these Jewish leaders. Luke does not decisively break Jesus and his disciples from Judaism, but rather he demonstrates the divine authority behind this new movement and thereby legitimates it. Notice further that the compassion behind Jesus' expressions of authority has been consistently highlighted through contrast with the Jewish leaders. This strengthens the persuasiveness of the Lukan argument for his Lord and for Christianity. Not only is there solid legal legitimacy, but the reader is warmed by the much greater compassion shown by Jesus than by his Jewish counterparts.

2.1.3.2 Authority Displayed through Healing

The very first, and programmatic, healing account (Lk. 4:30–37) elicits the response from the crowd, "What is this message? For with *authority* and power He commands the unclean spirits, and they come out" (v. 36, italics

---

[49] Marshall, *Gospel of Luke*, 440.

mine). Later, demons acknowledge his authoritative identity as Son of God and Christ when cast out by him (Lk. 4:41), and his authority to forgive sins is affirmed in the healing of a paralytic (Lk. 5:17–26, discussed above). Luke uses Sabbath healings to demonstrate his authority, as treated above. Further on, authority is at the center of the account where Jesus heals the centurion's servant (Lk. 7:1–10) as demonstrated when the centurion considers Jesus' healing ability to be a matter of authority, just as he has authority to command others. When the Lord raises a widow's son (Lk. 7:11–17) his authoritative status as "a great prophet" is declared and the people exclaim, "God has visited His people". Even the ability of the seventy (two) to cast out demons is attributed to his authority (v. 19 of Lk. 10:1–24). Finally, in a moment of great tension, when accused of casting out demons by Beelzebub Jesus counters with the implication that it is actually by the "finger of God" (v. 20 of Lk. 11:14–26), a statement that divine authority undergirds his healing of those with demons.

In none of these instances is Jesus' authority pictured as derived from human authority structures. His ability to heal is consistently founded on the authority and power of God. In a work designed to strengthen or instill faith in Christ, it makes sense to explain the significance of these events. Luke's purpose of linking Jesus (and therefore Christianity) with the Father would not be served if the reader were allowed to draw the conclusion that this wonder worker possessed his own independent authority or that he occasionally overstepped the bounds of his authority in confrontation with the Jewish leaders.

2.1.3.3 Authority Displayed over Disciples

To any of Luke's intended audience considering the Christ event (Lk. 1:4), the absolute authority of Jesus over a person's life is best illustrated through the experience of the disciples. In the two callings of disciples in the Third Gospel (Lk. 5:1–11 and 27–32) those called "left *everything* and followed Him" (italics mine). This first account is Lukan, but the second is taken from Mark. Importantly, Luke adds the detail that Levi left everything, probably to echo the statement in the first account. Furthermore, the rigorous demands of the sermon on the plain, which touch on virtually all aspects of life, are delivered to his disciples (Lk. 6:20–49). The readers are impressed not simply with the need to effectively "leave everything" to be a disciple, but also with the corresponding authority of Jesus over them.

There are other means by which Luke displays the authority of Jesus, but these are considerably less significant theologically than those discussed above, or they have been touched on already. Surprisingly, this theme has not been broadly recognized in Lukan studies. As a single emphasis, it occupies more of the structure than any other occupies and is a logically

Literary and Theological Purposes and Implications 309

vital element in a persuasive argument for discipleship. Christ's authority is demonstrated to originate from the Father and to have domain over one's entire life. It is based on having established this authority that Luke depicts Jesus turning to the crowds of non-disciple to appeal for their lives (stratum 4).

2.2 Salvation and the Crowds/People (Stratum 4)

At this transition to non-disciples, we most clearly see Luke's perception of Jesus' teaching on the decision necessary for salvation. In each cycle, Jesus challenges the crowd to make a black-and-white decision about him. This is particularly clear in the brief concluding parables of each section. In Luke 8:16, the person's lamp is either lit or not. This concept is repeated in 11:33, but is developed further:

> The lamp of your body is your eye; when your eye is clear, your whole body is also full of light; but when it is bad, your body also is full of darkness. Then watch out that the light in you may not be darkness. If therefore your whole body is full of light, with no dark part in it, it shall be wholly illuminated, as when the lamp illuminates you with its rays. (Lk. 11:34–36)

Salt in Luke 14:34–35 represents the stark difference the decision makes. Here, sea salt is either salty or the salt has been leached away leaving worthless grit. Finally, in Luke 20:17–18 everyone who rejects Jesus will be destroyed. Presumably, all who accept him are safe in this regard.

The appeal of Jesus, and consequently Luke, is not to a gradual slide into salvation but to a radical change.[50] This has implications not only at the judgment but also for present life.[51] We saw earlier that in Luke's structure the decision for or against Jesus is soundly grounded on Christ's authority.

2.3 Discipleship (Strata 6–9)

As we should expect, the Gospel's structure has one of its focal points on

---

50 Brian E. Beck shows that Luke's concept of conversion was of a radical change. See *Christian Character in the Gospel of Luke* (London: Epworth, 1989) 71–92.
51 Eric Franklin considers Luke's primary purpose to be "to bring about a response in the present;" *Christ the Lord: A Study in the Purpose and Theology of Luke-Acts* (Philadelphia: Westminster, 1975) 174. He appropriately entitles the last chapter of this book "Luke the Evangelist."

discipleship (strata 6–9).[52] According to the features employed by the Evangelist in these strata, Luke had at least four particular aspects especially in mind: (1) threat from misguided religious leaders, (2) challenge to grow in faith in light of this threat, (3) the return of Christ as motivation for greater faith and ministry, and (4) the role of the disciples as apprentices and perpetuators of Christ's ministry.

2.3.1 Threat against Disciples from Misguided Religious Leaders (Stratum 6)

In stratum 6, Jesus warns his disciples against the misguided religious leaders whom he has just confronted. In each case the assumption is that their behavior and attitudes could be negatively affected.[53] A disciple is not immune to such influence. In cycle 2, Jesus begins his discourse (Lk. 12:1–21) saying, "Beware of the leaven of the Pharisees, which is hypocrisy" (v. 1). He explains that God is not fooled. A disjunction is too often drawn between 12:3 and 4 where he moves from direct reference to Pharisaic hypocrisy to the statement, "And I say to you, My friends, do not be afraid of those who kill the body, and after that have no more that they can do." It would be strange for Jesus briefly to warn his disciples against the hypocrisy of the Pharisees and then launch into a separate topic. Probably, in light of his impending execution at the hands of Jewish leaders, he was still referring to the Pharisees. Strikingly, this expands their threat to the disciples beyond mere behavioral influence to that of being murdered by them. Notice that Jesus does not promise the removal or alleviation of these threats, but only encourages faith and trust in the God who cares about them.

In cycle 3, Luke 17:1–2 is usually considered separate from the preceding discourse of Jesus against the Jewish leaders. As Fitzmyer writes, "Luke now continues his travel account with further sayings of Jesus, which are completely unrelated to the foregoing chapter or parable."[54] However, Luke places them in the same episode. In response to the sneering of the greedy Pharisees (Lk. 16:14), Jesus has just told a parable about the spiritual and eternal consequences of greed, that of the rich man and Lazarus (Lk. 16:19–31). Naturally, the next statement, "It is inevitable that stumbling blocks should come, but woe to him through whom they come" (Lk. 17:1) may be

---

52 Discipleship is commonly noted as an important theme in Luke. See for example Fitzmyer, *Luke I–IX*, 235–57; Beck, *Christian Character*, 93–104; Liefeld, *Luke*, 814.

53 The Pharisees are typically understood by Luke as a threat to the behavior of disciples according to Beck (*Christian Character*, 130–44). He tends however to be harder on the Pharisees than Luke may have been.

54 Fitzmyer, *Luke X–XXIV*, 1136.

read as a continuation of comment about the Pharisees, especially since they are still in his presence. The disciples should avoid emulating the Pharisees, who foster sin in others, because punishment will be severe.

As in the two previous cases in this stratum, in cycle 4 Jesus warns his disciples against the leaders he has just opposed (Lk. 20:45–47), "Beware of the Scribes." Followers of Christ are not to imitate their ostentation because of God's disfavor with such behavior.

The Jewish leaders, as examples for their religious community, modeled hypocrisy, greed and pride. Human nature is to emulate people in positions of respect, and the disciples were not immune to such influence. Luke's readership may still have respected the non-Christian Jewish leaders of their day, which would subject them to the same threat. To be sure, such negative influence would be wielded even by misguided Christian leaders. Through Jesus' warnings, specific behaviors and their underlying motivations are displayed as abhorrent to God and dangerous therefore to the disciple.

2.3.2 CHALLENGE TO GROW IN FAITH (STRATUM 7)

In stratum 7, Luke presents Jesus challenging his disciples to increase their faith.[55] In cycles 2 through 4, the preceding context is the danger of ungodly behavior and the following context is an eschatological discourse. Particularly in cycles 2 and 3, the need for faith is directly linked to the preceding contextual theme as a necessary response. At Luke 12:22 (cycle 2) Jesus continues from his parable against greed (the rich fool) saying, "For this reason…" (Διὰ τοῦτο). The point he then makes is that trust in the Father for physical necessities is the proper response to the threat of greed. Immediately following this section on faith in the Father's care (Lk. 12:22–34), without a transition by the narrator, Jesus speaks about preparedness for the parousia. Although it is not explicit, the implication is that faith in the Father is a foundation for preparedness for the parousia. As Marshall puts it,

> Freed from worldly cares through trust in the fatherly care of God and hope in the coming of the kingdom, the disciples are not to let themselves be enticed by the temptations of the world to laziness, self-indulgence and self-assertion, but are to spend their time profitably and in readiness to serve the Son of Man when he appears.[56]

A similar phenomenon occurs in cycle 3. In response to the risk of ungodly behavior, the disciples exclaim, "Increase our faith!" (Lk. 17:5). Faith

---

55 Faith is of course an important theme in the Gospel. See for example Navone, *Themes*, 47–50.
56 Marshall, *Gospel of Luke*, 532.

is what is needed to avoid behavior abhorrent to God (Lk. 17:5–19). In this case, the eschatological discourse does not flow within the same episode directly from Luke's treatment of faith as it does in cycle 2. However, faith as the foundation for preparedness for the parousia is still an essential concept. At the emphatic position of the conclusion to the eschatological discourse, we find the question, "However, when the Son of Man comes, will he find faith on the earth?" The identical interdependence of these sections in cycles 2 and 3 is not repeated fully in the corresponding Markan based material of cycle 4 (Lk. 20:45–21:6 par. Mk. 12:37b–13:2).[57] There, rather than the widow's faith being a response to the risk of ungodly behavior, her humble faith is contrasted with the arrogant faithlessness of the scribes. Rather than the widow's faith being presented explicitly as a model foundation for preparedness for the parousia, Jesus' observation of the widow probably actually preceded his comment about the destruction of the temple.[58] Narratively, however, the connection is implicit.

Lukan discipleship therefore involves the response of faith against the threat of negative influence on behavior by misguided religious leaders. Additionally, faith is the groundwork of readiness for the parousia. This latter association has implications for the Lukan function of the eschatological discourses of stratum 8.

2.3.3 RETURN OF CHRIST AS MOTIVATION FOR GREATER FAITH AND MINISTRY (STRATA 7 AND 8)

Faith as the groundwork of readiness for the parousia is not evident in the connection between stratum 7 (faith) and the stratum 8 (parousia) in cycle 4. Luke does not make the thematic association any greater than was present in his Markan source. He appears to have interpreted the relationship in this manner however, because the parallel material in cycles 2 and 3 (and perhaps 1) picture the return of Christ and events related to it as motivation for greater faith.[59] In cycle 2, faith in the caring Father (Lk.

---

57 In the Markan parallel material of cycle 4 the connections are established partly through key words. In their pride the Pharisees "devour *widows'* houses" (Lk. 20:47, italics mine), a *widow* places all she has in the *temple* treasury (21:1–4), and the *temple* will be destroyed (21:5–6). This is not the whole story however, as William L. Lane demonstrates in *Mark*, 442. A contrast is intended between the Pharisees and the widow, and Jesus' observation of the widow at the temple probably actually elicited his statement about the building's destruction.

58 Lane, *Mark*, 442.

59 Regarding the passages of stratum 7, Beck concurs that faith is a response to the eschatological events in the following contexts, but he speaks more in terms of persistence in faith rather than growth. The distinction may be minor, but Luke challenges the disciples not merely to persevere, but to develop in faith. See *Christian Character*, 85–90.

12:22–34) frees one for readiness for the parousia (12:35–40) and is an aspect of that readiness. Furthermore, the imminent return serves as motivation for readiness, for faith: "You too, be ready; for the Son of Man is coming at an hour that you do not expect" (12:40).

In cycle 3, the eschatological discourse (Lk. 17:20–18:8) ends with the question, "However, when the Son of Man comes, will He find faith on the earth?" This startling question reminds the reader of the disciples' earlier entreaty, "Increase our faith!" (Lk. 17:5). The days before the parousia will be so difficult for the disciples (17:22; 18:7) that faith itself will be a precious commodity. But in a sense it is faith that is required to survive this time, "Whoever seeks to keep his life shall lose it, and whoever loses his life shall preserve it alive" (17:33). Therefore, eschatological distress before the parousia is motivation for greater faith.

Cycle 1 appears to convey the same idea, but implicitly, as in cycle 4. Luke does not make it any more explicit than in his Markan source, which lies behind stratum 7 (Lk. 8:22–25 par. Mk. 4:35–41, the calming of the sea) and stratum 8 (Lk. 8:26–56 par. Mk. 5:1–43, the Gerasene demoniac with the dead girl and sick woman). Talbert correctly identifies the four miracles of Luke 8:22–56 as a unit with the sending of the twelve, Luke 9:1–6.[60] He concludes, "the location of the four miracles just prior to the sending of the Twelve seems to say that...the third evangelist aimed to demonstrate the authority Jesus possessed before telling us he gave this power and authority to the Twelve".[61] If, on the other hand, we concentrate on the readiness of the disciples to be sent, a quality made dubious by their behavior in the storm (Lk. 8:22–25), then their faith in Jesus' authority and power has opportunity to be strengthened by the intervening miracles. In this sense, these healings with eschatological flavor[62] motivate greater faith in the disciples. This conclusion for cycle 1 must be tentative, however, because of the implicit nature of the thematic association and the relative weakness of the eschatological character of the healing accounts.

In addition to the parousia being a motivation for greater faith, it serves as a motivational backdrop for Luke's treatment of the ministerial role of the disciples (stratum 9). When Jesus sends out the twelve (Lk. 9:1–6 of cycle 1, par. Mk. 6:6b–13), Luke adds the authority "to heal diseases" (9:1) to the Markan conferral of authority to the disciples "over the unclean spirits" (Mk. 6:7). He may have been influenced by Q at this point (cf. Mt.

---

60 See Talbert's several reasons in *Reading Luke*, 95. His dependence on certain key words is not entirely convincing, but the overall argument is strong.
61 Talbert, *Reading Luke*, 96.
62 See our discussions of the eschatological nature of the healings in Lk. 8:26–56 under the tests for intentionality in the previous chapter.

10:1),⁶³ but the result is a closer connection to the preceding miracles. Jesus exhibited authority over demons in the account of the Gerasene demoniac and demonstrated authority over disease in the accounts of the dead girl and the woman with the hemorrhage; now the disciples have authority to do the same in their first taste of ministry.⁶⁴ Without the knowledge that their Lord had authority to perform such ministry, the disciples would naturally doubt their own ability even after the commission. The healings in a sense provide additional motivation to the disciples to make an attempt. Of course, these same passages provide the reader with a greater understanding of Jesus' power, authority and right to commission disciples for such ministry, but when read in conjunction with the corresponding material in the other cycles it appears that the Lukan stress was on the preparation of the twelve.

This is certainly the thrust in cycle 2. Preparedness of disciples in general for the return of the Son of Man (Lk. 12:35–40) has special significance for the disciples who would be placed in positions of responsibility over others. Peter's question, "Lord, are you addressing this parable to us, or to everyone else as well" (Lk. 12:41), is answered with the parable of the faithful steward (12:42–48) where the parousia is pictured as a time when unfaithful leadership/service will be punished. Thus, the Lord's return serves as motivation for the twelve to fulfill their ministerial role faithfully.

We find the same connection established in cycle 3. After delivering an eschatological discourse (Lk. 17:20–18:8), Jesus turns to people "who trusted in themselves that they were righteous" and might not have been worried by his last question, "when the Son of Man comes, will He find faith on the earth?" (Lk. 18:8–9). Through the parable of the Pharisee and the tax collector, the point is made that "everyone who exalts himself shall be humbled, but he who humbles himself shall be exalted" (18:14). Evans is unsure of "how far…the eschatological force of *will be* is preserved – i.e. will be abased by God, or exalted by him, in the final judgment;"⁶⁵ but the almost verbatim wording with Luke 14:11, which is in an eschatological context (see 14:14), strengthens the probability that Luke employed this force. Humility before God, therefore, is to be motivated by the prospect of judgment. Startlingly, the next event, still within the same episode, exposes the disciples complete misunderstanding of the principle (Lk. 18:15–17). We may presume that they had heard the parable, yet they proceed to repel infants, the epitome of humility, from Jesus. Though the return of Christ is to motivate humility before God, the role that the disciples choose to play ignores this very principle. Their proper ministry is quickly redefined by

---

63 Fitzmyer concurs, *Luke I–IX*, 751.
64 See also Nolland, *Luke 1–9:20*, 425.
65 C.F. Evans, *Saint Luke*, 645.

Jesus: "Permit the children to come to Me, and stop hindering them, for the kingdom of God belongs to such as these" (Lk. 18:16).

After Jesus' eschatological discourse in the fourth cycle (Lk. 21:5–38), we find the betrayal by Judas, the preparations for the Passover and the institution of the Lord's Supper. After these events, Luke relates the disciple's dispute over greatness, which results in Jesus' teaching on the proper attitude toward their role. Thus, the concept of the parousia back in the eschatological discourse appears rather distant. Regardless of the primary source behind the Lukan Last Supper account, whether Mark, a Proto-Lukan text or an independent passion tradition, the Evangelist has chosen to present a dispute amongst the disciples over greatness that is followed by an allusion to Christ's return (Lk. 22:24–30),[66] perhaps an echo of the eschatological discourse a few verses earlier. Accordingly, although Jesus' teaching on the disciples' role is separate from the eschatological discourse, the concept of the parousia is refreshed by the author. Furthermore, the parallelism between Jesus and the disciples in this teaching establishes the disciples' eschatological role as motivation for humble service in the present. They were to model themselves after Jesus – "The kings of the Gentiles lord it over them; and those who have authority over them are called 'Benefactors.' But not so with you...But I am among you as one who serves" (Lk. 22:25–27) – and this modeling of leadership applies from the present on into the eschaton (vv. 29–30). The seriousness of "judging the twelve tribes of Israel" motivates responsible leadership.

Each cycle presents the return of Christ as motivation for the disciples toward both greater faith and more suitable service for the kingdom. This is especially the case in the first three cycles. When viewed in this light it is evident why Luke has included three eschatological discourses (and a corresponding healings section in cycle 1 with apparent eschatological flavor), more than the other Synoptic Gospels. In terms of the function of these eschatological sections in the Gospel's structure, Luke's concern was not to account for the delay of the parousia for Christians who had expected it immediately, as Conzelmann's proposal would lead us to anticipate.[67] Rather, the function is to demonstrate to the reader the necessity of faith in light of the imminent return of the Son of Man and to provide motivation for responsible service.

---

66 The association of verses 28–30 with the parousia is probable since this is the context of the Matthean form of the saying in Mt. 19:28. This future time frame does not preclude reference to the role of the disciples as leaders of the church. See Marshall, *Gospel of Luke*, 814–815.

67 See Conzelmann's *Theology*.

2.3.4 ROLE OF THE DISCIPLES AS APPRENTICES AND PERPETUATORS OF CHRIST'S MINISTRY (STRATUM 9)

Whenever Jesus instructs his disciples regarding their role, the circumstance behind it is always a degree of misunderstanding by the disciples (stratum 9). In cycle 1, the disciples had doubted Jesus' authority over the sea shortly before they were sent on a mission (Lk. 8:22–25 and 9:1–6). After this miraculous mission under Jesus' authority (9:1–2, 6–10) they fail to obey his command to miraculously feed the five thousand. Peter in cycle 2 is unsure of whether a parable applies to the twelve specifically or to all listening (Lk. 12:41), admittedly a minor misunderstanding. In contrast, the misunderstanding in cycle 3 is substantial. After a parable on humility is directed to some of them, the disciples repel parents from bringing humble children to Jesus (Lk. 18:9–17). Finally, in cycle 4 the disciples have the gall to discuss their greatness at the Last Supper while Jesus expresses his incomparable humility (Lk. 22:24–27). This consistent background sets the stage for lessons on modeling Christ's ministry.

When Jesus sends the twelve in cycle 1, he gives them authority and power to do precisely what he had been doing in his ministry: "And He called the twelve together, and gave them power and authority over all the demons, and to heal diseases. And He sent them out to proclaim the kingdom of God, and to perform healing" (Lk. 9:1–2; cf. 4:36, 40, 43). In addition, just as Jesus went from one village to another preaching, with the disciples in his presence (8:1), so the disciples went from one village to another preaching (9:6).[68] Interestingly, although it is the disciples' (plural) activity, Herod and the people who have heard by word of mouth wonder what *individual* has created such a stir, John the Baptist, Elijah, or another OT prophet; and he tries to see *him* (Lk. 9:7–9). The disciples must have been attributing their activity to Jesus and preaching about him in order for rumor to spread about an individual. Luke must intend to suggest some identification of the disciples' ministry with that of Jesus here. In the next scene the disciples are instructed to feed the five thousand (Lk. 9:10–17), a nature miracle that one might think only the Lord could perform. In the light of their previous miraculous activity, however, we now have no reason to believe that the disciples could not miraculously comply. In fact, the disciples fail here. Jesus' command coupled with his performance of the miracle makes the disciples appear like apprentices "learning the trade," learning to perpetuate his ministry.

Similarly, the parable of the wise steward in cycle 2 pictures the disciples

---

68 Nolland correctly concludes that "we have here something of a dress rehearsal for the post-Pentecost role of the Twelve" (*Luke 1–9:20*, 428). François Bovon relates it also more broadly to the missionary practice of the early church, in *Evangelium*, 455.

as perpetuators of the master's activity (Lk. 12:41–48).[69] He is responsible for the timely distribution of rations to the servants, but in his absence the faithful steward is given that very responsibility. In other words, aspects of Jesus' ministry are placed under the disciples' responsibility between his ascension and return, a perpetuation of his ministry.

In cycle 3, the disciples learn to accept under their ministry the type of person Jesus accepts (Lk. 18:15–17), the humble person who receives the kingdom like a child. Unlike in the feeding of the five thousand, here the disciples are rebuked for their misunderstanding. Finally, at the Last Supper, (cycle 4) in response to their argument over greatness Jesus instructs the disciples to model their ministry after his in the quality of humility (Lk. 22:24–27).

Luke's structural emphasis on Jesus' instruction of the twelve regarding their role pictures them as apprentices and perpetuators of Christ's ministry. Naturally, this foreshadows the first half of Acts. The Evangelist strives to demonstrate that apostolic leadership was planned and commissioned by Jesus, and that those chosen were specifically equipped for the task. This counters any claim that the disciples began a movement of their own accord and distinct from that which Jesus initiated. It also counters the distinction drawn by Conzelmann between the disciples in the period of Jesus' ministry and those in the period of the church.[70] If the reader accepts the authority of Jesus, he must now accept the authority of the church's apostolic foundation.

2.4 Ecclesiology

At the end of each of the four cycles, Jesus concentrates on the disciples to prepare them to perpetuate his ministry. In the light of Acts, this preparation translates readily to the needs of the Church in its infancy. Notice first that cycle 1 emphasizes mission through the sending of the twelve and the feeding of the five thousand (Lk. 9:1–17), and with the twin themes that the kingdom of God is to be preached and physical needs are to be met. In the first passage, the particular physical need is sickness and in the second it is hunger. Second, in cycle 2 care for the believing community is highlighted in the parable of the faithful steward (Lk. 12:42–48).[71] Third, in cycle 3

---

69 See also Marshall's thorough discussion in *Gospel of Luke*, 532–535.
70 Conzelmann, *Theology*, 215–218.
71 See also E. Earle Ellis, *Gospel of Luke*, 181. Nolland opposes the restricted identification of the steward with Christian leaders; *Luke 9:21–18:34*, Word Biblical Commentary 35b (Dallas: Word Books, 1993) 703, but he may not adequately account for Luke's redactional emphasis on the steward's status in relation to the

mission is repeated but the stress is now on who can be saved and the attitude of the disciples toward such people (Lk. 18:15–17). Finally, in cycle 4, care for the believing community is repeated with an emphasis on servanthood (Lk. 22:24–27).

Luke balances his treatment of mission with pastoral care.[72] The church is not simply an organism occupied solely with growth, but one that must also maintain its internal health. Accordingly, Jesus prepares his disciples not merely as missionaries but also as pastors. In order to fulfill its purpose, therefore, the church must maintain a similar balance. This is exemplified in Acts where church expansion is intermingled with internal maintenance. Acts 2:42–47 is a representative cross section. Internal health is maintained in verses 42–47a and expansion occurs in verse 47b. Through such an approach, the church will more closely approximate the balance in the ministry of Jesus and thereby perpetuate it, as was intended by the Lord.

3 Conclusion

When the theology expressed through Luke's structure is examined with a view toward the central theological theme of the Gospel, I. Howard Marshall's proposal of "salvation" is confirmed.[73] The Evangelist frames his cycles with references to Jerusalem and the crucifixion/resurrection. This elevates the saving work of Christ's death to a most prominent position.[74] When Jesus' prophetic status is developed in the structure, the significance is that his message of salvation is divinely authorized. Furthermore, Luke's emphasis on authority focuses on the validation of the Lord's saving message and deeds. Through successful conflict with Jewish legal experts, Jesus' message is confirmed. Through healing accounts, his divine right to heal/save/forgive is proven. Through his authority to call disciples, he establishes a missionary team who would fish for people. Stratum 4 is dedicated to the divine message of salvation brought by him. Luke's treatment of discipleship also hinges on salvation. The threat of

---

other servants and the likelihood that these servants represent Christians. See Marshall's treatment of the passage in *Gospel of Luke*, 533, 540–544.

72 Such balance between these two themes is also evident in the approach of scholars to Lukan ecclesiology, as François Bovon indicates in *Luke the Theologian: Thirty-three Years of Research (1950–1983)*, trans. by Ken McKinney (Allison Park, Pennsylvania: Pickwick Publications, 1987) 309–311.

73 See Marshall, *Historian and Theologian*, 92–222.

74 Although Luke's theology of the atoning significance of Christ's death is not explicit and certain redactional observations suggest the removal of the concept from his sources, Robert Stein demonstrates that it is by no means absent. He demonstrates that commonly cited instances of redaction may be explained for other reasons. See *Luke*, 54–56.

ungodly behavioral influence on the disciple is a matter of spiritual life and death. Progressive growth in faith is the proper response to this threat, and faith is the ground of salvation. The parousia is a motivation to the disciple because it is the time of judgment when one's spiritual condition is manifested. Salvation is also central to the role of disciples as apprentices and perpetuators of Christ's ministry since Jesus says, "I must preach the kingdom of God...for I was sent for this purpose" (Lk. 4:43) and "the Son of Man has come to seek and to save that which was lost" (19:10). This purpose is transferred not simply to the twelve but to the church. Therefore, not only is salvation the central motif of the Gospel's content, it is also the thrust of its structure.[75] Actually, the combination of these two facts justifies the description of Luke as patently and unabashedly evangelistic.

---

75 The flow of thought along each cycle, as described in this chapter, is similar to what I have termed "narrative argument," an authorially intended sequence of propositional statements communicated by a sequence of respective narrative events, and where the sequence of propositional statements drawn from the narrative events forms a coherent argument. Such argument is typically not syllogistic or structured according to strict principles of "logical argument". Rather, it is comparatively free flowing. This, in fact, is a phenomenon quite common in biblical and ancient extrabiblical narrative. My hope is to publish some examples in the near future.

Chapter 6

Conclusion

Several needs in Lukan studies are presented in the introduction that map out a course for our discussion. As with any investigation, many more discoveries and contributions are made than can be outlined in a brief prologue. The same is true for this concluding statement. My intention at this stage therefore is merely to highlight the more important contributions and to sketch out how these integrate into a cohesive body that suggests further exploration and benefit to Lukan scholarship beyond the scope of this work.

Also discussed in the introduction and demonstrated throughout the book is that Luke may be viewed as a reader who saw relationships between units of tradition in his sources. He positioned them in his narrative, transformed some and established literary connections between others in such a way as to communicate these relationships to the reader, more than could be explicitly stated. At times, our focus is purely on the final form of the text, without regard for sources or author. Yet at other times the author Luke is a focal point, for instance in the analysis of his compositional methodology. Accepting both the validity of seeking authorial intent and the value of reading selected texts in the light of each other without necessary concern about source dependence or author provides benefits from both worlds, benefits that are found to integrate easily.

Our first investigation studies the approach to Luke-Acts of Robert Tannehill[1] (chapter 1). He reveals a variety of means whereby Luke directs the reader's attention from the passage being read to other passages so that they may be interpreted in conjunction with each other. Previews, reviews, echoes, type-scenes and other literary techniques employed by the Evangelist are demonstrated. Tannehill has sometimes been accused of finding more than was actually intended, but often these accusations have lacked objectivity or a basis in actual ancient literary practice. A method of rigorous evaluation was needed to test his proposals (and those of Talbert

---

1 Tannehill, *Narrative Unity*, vol. 1; and *Narrative Unity*, vol. 2.

and this book) and enable judgments that are more objective. We developed eleven tests for the probability of authorial intent in consultation with actual ancient compositional practice. These are tested in the introduction against overwhelmingly accepted instances of parallelism and the tests perform perfectly. This establishes them as valuable tools for scholarly study of narrative. They are applied to many of Tannehill's examples with the result that many are established as highly probable but several are objectively deemed uncertain. Theology that he derives from the more probably intentional interrelationships is accordingly on firmer ground than otherwise.

Tannehill's work provides three areas of groundwork for our proposal. First, he demonstrates the large variety of types of correspondences and their constituents employed by Luke. Our structure is formed of correspondences within the range of these types and constituents. Second, he demonstrates Luke's strong predisposition to interconnect passages in various ways even to the level of fine detail. Certainly, our structure reflects such a predisposition. Third, he examines the purposes and functions of previews, reviews, echoes, parallels, and type-scenes in Luke-Acts, and their theological and literary implications for interpretation. Our task in chapter 5 is to discern the apparent purposes and functions of the many correspondences defined by our structure.

Charles Talbert approaches Luke-Acts more from the perspective of literary structure.[2] Drawing on a wealth of past proposals of correspondence patterns within the Third Gospel and between Luke and Acts, and contributing many of his own, he explores the structural architecture of the whole. He thereby attempts to connect the two-volume work to the same genre as Diogenes Laertius' *Lives of Eminent Philosophers*, "wandering philosopher". Our eleven tests for authorial intent are applied to his correspondences with the result that many are recognized as being probable to certain while several are deemed uncertain (chapter 2). On the strength of this outcome, he succeeds in demonstrating the intentional literary connection between Luke and Acts. His argument for genre however must depend primarily on content rather than structure since he does not demonstrate with much certainty that Luke exhibits the same architectonic features as works of the proposed genre. Talbert proves decisively the extensive use of architectonic parallel patterns by Luke.

The groundwork Talbert provides for our work is substantial. He demonstrates that patterned structure was the norm in ancient composition and that Luke indeed employed it in his Gospel. He also explores through redaction-criticism how Luke might have formed many of the parallels. This meshes

---

2 Talbert, *Literary Patterns*.

well with our interest in Lukan composition. Further, Talbert derives theology from his correspondences, which provides background for chapter 5.

Related to the endeavors of Tannehill and Talbert in Luke-Acts is the long-standing question over the structure of Luke 4:14–24:53, and especially the logic behind the arrangement of material in the "central section" of the Gospel. A four-fold cyclical structure that covers Luke 4:14–24:53 – and resembles the parallelism between Jesus and John the Baptist in the infancy and preparation narratives (1:5–4:13) – is proposed and empirically tested using the eleven tests that were applied to the observations of Tannehill and Talbert (chapter 4). Its performance is as impressive as that for the universally accepted parallelism between Jesus and John in Luke 1–2. Therefore, the entire Gospel (apart from the prologue) is covered by our structural proposal when coupled with the parallelism of 1:5–4:13. Hence, an additional benefit is that the question regarding the arrangement of material in the central section is provided a viable response, where chiasmus had failed.

In support of whether the Evangelist had reasonable precedent to create such a literary design, numerous examples of relevant literature, precedent and contemporary to Luke, are presented that exhibit similar patterns (chapter 3). Examples from the whole range of his cultural milieu are marshaled. Clearly, as was argued, he had been thoroughly exposed to this prevalent literary technique.

Exposure is one thing, but would Luke have had a viable mechanism by which to incorporate traditional material into a prearranged scheme. Indeed he did. The compositional technique *imitatio* (imitation) that was all pervasive by Luke's day provides just such a mechanism. Thomas Brodie's study of imitation in the Third Gospel is reviewed to demonstrate the fact (chapter 3).[3]

With literary precedent and mechanism established, we explore Luke's probable compositional methodology as suggested by his structure. Each of the first three cycles is apparently designed to match sequentially important narrative features he selected in the climactic Jerusalem ministry, the fourth cycle. This decision naturally provided the organizing principle for the central section. Rather than constructing a chiasm or incorporating wholesale a chiastic document, he built two cycles patterned after the climax of Jesus' ministry. Therefore, he chose to imitate one of the types of parallel structures he was familiar with, perhaps one from the OT, and sought to incorporate various units of source material into this prearranged pattern. The ancient use of an outline in the composition of history and biographies

---

[3] For a comprehensive listing of his works on the subject, consult chapter 3.

was noted. How then was the sequence of narrative features for the fourth cycle determined? They are virtually all present in the identical order in the Markan account of the Jerusalem ministry and passion, so he possibly founded the structure on this portion of Mark. Of course, Markan priority is not required since Luke could have developed the sequence on his own or found it in another source, with Mark then depending on Luke. However, Markan priority is defended in a discussion on the Synoptic Problem. A new argument is presented that avoids a major weakness inherent in most literary dependence arguments (chapter 4). The weakness is that the evidence can be reversed to support an opposing conclusion. For instance, if it is claimed that one evangelist used another evangelist's gospel and tended to condense the accounts, someone else could claim the reverse dependence and a tendency to expand accounts. Our proposal cannot be rationally reversed, so, with the reinforcement of evidence amassed by others, Markan priority is accepted into our proposal for Luke's compositional methodology.

Luke's structural parallelism has major implications when it is realized that his interpretation of pericopes is reflected through their structural relationships. We gain significant clues to how Luke, an early Christian, interpreted gospel material, clues not necessarily noticeable through any other approach. Additionally, his intended plot is further clarified through awareness of the Gospel's structure. When we know that two or more pericopes are placed in parallelism with each other because they share common features, then we know that to the author's mind these features are considered reasonably important to the thrust of each passage. The interpretation is not hijacked by the parallelism however. However, often fresh significance intended by the author, yet not highlighted in any other way, is gained. One example is where Jesus says, "I have a baptism to undergo, and how distressed I am until it is accomplished" (Lk. 12:50). According to Luke's interpretation, as evidenced by the structure, this passage shares the concepts of death and resurrection with the others in this location within the structure (9:22–27; 18:31–34; 22:35–24:53). Our structure also serves to clarify plot. For example, several of the strata intensify from one cycle to the next. Across stratum 4, Jesus' call to discipleship becomes more and more urgent and the consequences of denial more and more devastating. This is one means whereby Luke builds to the climax, which would not be noticed without an awareness of the structure. A general "feel" might be developed, but nothing more definitive. When the cycles are scanned from top to bottom, other facets of Luke's plot become evident. A transition takes place in each cycle at stratum 6, for example. Attention moves suddenly, and for virtually the remainder of each cycle, specifically to the twelve; and their preparation for future ministry takes a central role, which culminates in Acts. Luke demonstrates that a transition of ministry from Jesus to the twelve/church was to occur. With all this in mind, it is evident that through various harmonious progressions across the strata and down each cycle, Luke is able to achieve a well-controlled two-dimensional development of plot. The specific means by which he accomplishes this (narrative features, themes, and the like) emerge from what Luke consciously considered very important to the significance of Jesus and his ministry. An awareness of the structure informs us of these aspects of Luke's message often more explicitly than any other cue. The interrelationships advised by Luke through his parallels are obviously of tremendous value for modern readers. Indeed, a great deal more may be said along these lines than was possible within the scope of this book. Luke has created the framework of associations, and we have the context of the entire Gospel against which to check our conclusions for authorial interest. Couple this with the vast supply of exegetical work already available and the possibilities are enticing.

Various points of theology may be deduced with confidence from Luke's chosen interrelationships between passages. Several are discussed in the book (chapter 5). His initiation of the cycles with references to Jerusalem and conclusion of each with the themes of Jesus' death and resurrection, to illustrate, probably reflects a desire to portray his entire ministry against the backdrop of the passion. In addition, at the beginning of each cycle Luke establishes the prophetic status of Jesus, which he then employs as the foundation for demonstrations of his divine authority. Consequently, these must have been considered by Luke as important to knowledge of and faith in Jesus. Although theological statements drawn directly from the structure itself are bound to be rather limited, the interpretative interaction of the parallelism with individual passages is fertile ground for further growth in our understanding of Lukan theology.

An integral part of testing our proposed structure is the identification of any redaction that favors the formation of the observed parallels (chapter 4). Many instances are discussed. Part of the analysis involves interaction with scholarly explanations for the observed editorial work. Often the structure provides a solution for a particular instance of redaction that remains inadequately explained. Luke's "great omission" of Markan material (Mk. 6:45–8:26), for example, justifiably receives a great amount of scholarly attention; but explanations are rarely put forward with confidence, due to the speculation involved. Those who suppose that the material did not suit the theme of the section he was developing depend heavily on their interpretation of the relevant context, and often other scholars divide and interpret the text differently around the location of the omission. The problem is that we do not have an explicit statement from Luke, or a single widely recognized theme that spans a broad swath of material before and after the omission against which to compare the Markan material. Luke's structure provides a more objective and external check, and as close to an explicit statement from him as will ever be available. Indeed, the Markan material he omits does not match the parallel material in the other *three* cycles, so the basic explanation offered by some scholars is correct (mismatch) but not for the right reason. Redaction criticism would benefit substantially from a greater appreciation of Luke's structural interests because frequently redaction is actually explained by the Evangelist's formation of the parallels. The heart of redaction-criticism is the theology that may be discerned, so structural matters are usually of lesser interest to redaction-critics. Nevertheless, we have shown that structure is not a theological desert and that redaction-criticism coupled with an awareness of Luke's structure is a lush field of opportunity.

Recently, renewed attention has been focused on how correctly to decipher theology from narrative. Usually, and appropriately, the concern is to identify the *author's* theological intention first and then perhaps his theological presuppositions (which is inherently riskier business). The determination of intention behind story however poses special difficulties in comparison with propositional texts, and naturally the circumstances are not helped by the two-thousand year gap between our time and the writing of the Gospel. Fortunately, Luke has provided additional help.

APPENDIX A

Evaluation of Talbert's Correspondences within Acts

The concern of this work has been Lukan interrelationships between pericopes primarily within the gospel of Luke and secondarily between the Gospel and other literature. It is useful for our purposes, however, to study proposed correspondences within Acts to determine whether the same structural techniques uncovered in the Gospel exist also in "volume two". Talbert depends on this phenomenon to join the two works closely into one genre.[1]

1 Correspondences between Acts 1–12 and 13–28

Talbert notes that Acts may be divided into halves that correspond to each other, the first covering Jewish Christianity and the second, Gentile Christianity.[2] He observes regarding the correspondences between Acts 1–12 and 13–28 that "only rarely have the correspondences between these two halves of Acts been denied," and that they are "the most widely recognized aspect of Lucan architecture".[3] Characterizing them he writes, "The correspondences...include a loose parallelism of content and sequence along with certain similarities that do not occur in any specific order. We mention first the list of parallels which involve both content and sequence."[4] Our discussion of this pattern will be shorter than that for the patterns in the body of this work since specific redaction is neither available nor presented as evidence by Talbert.

---

1 For a thorough discussion of the parallels between Paul and the other apostles, see Andrew C. Clark, *Parallel Lives: The Relation of Paul to the Apostles in the Lukan Perspective* (Carlisle, Cumbria, UK: Paternoster, 2001).
2 Talbert, *Literary Patterns*, 26.
3 Talbert, *Literary Patterns*, 23.
4 Talbert, *Literary Patterns*, 23. His table and defense are found on pages 23–6.

ACTS 1–12		ACTS 13–28
2:1–4 A **special manifestation** of the **Spirit**.	1.	13:1–3 A **special manifestation** of the **Spirit**.
2:14–40 **Apostolic preaching results** from the special **manifestation of the Spirit.**	2.	13:16–40 **Apostolic preaching results** from the special **manifestation of the Spirit.**
3:1–10 A mighty work follows. A **man, lame from birth,** is **healed**.	3.[5]	14:8–13 A mighty work follows. A **man, lame from birth**, is **healed**.
3:12–26 The healing of the lame man is **followed by a speech prompted by the response** to the healing. It **begins, "Men…why?"**	4.	14:15–17 The healing of the lame man is **followed by a speech prompted by the response** to the healing. It **begins, "Men…why?"**
6:8–8:4 Stephen is **stoned** to death at the **instigation of Jews from** Asia and elsewhere **after a speech**. The **result of the persecution is the spread of the preaching in a widening circle.**	5.	14:19–23 Paul is **stoned** at the **instigation of Jews from** Antioch and Iconium **after a speech** so that he is supposed dead. The **result of the persecution is further preaching in a wider context**.
Chs. 10–11 Peter has a **mission to the Gentiles** (cf. 15:7–11). **Divine guidance** leads Peter in a **direction other than that planned** by him. In 10:9–16 Peter objects three times but the Spirit guides him through a **vision**. Peter then **has to justify his actions in Jerusalem.**	6.	Chs. 13–21 Paul has a **mission to the Gentiles. Divine guidance** leads Paul in a **direction other than that planned** by him. In 16:6–10 Paul, through a **vision**, is led to Macedonia. Both in ch. 15 and ch. 21 Paul **has to justify his actions in Jerusalem.**

---

5 Augustin George presents this parallel in slightly more detail than Talbert in *Études*, 55.

Ch. 12 The first **half of Acts ends with the imprisonment of Peter** (12:4) **at an important Jewish feast** (12:4). Peter's imprisonment is **associated with Herod** (12:5–6, 11); involves **escape from the hands of the Jews** (12:3–4, 6–11); **concludes abruptly with no information about the fate** of Peter (12:17); but Acts does make a **statement about the success of the Word of God** (12:24).	7.	Chs. 21–28 The second **half of Acts ends with the imprisonment** of Paul, beginning **at an important Jewish feast** ([20]:16). Paul's imprisonment in Palestine has a loose **relation to a Herod** (25:13, 23–24); involves **escape from death at the hands of the Jews** (23:12–35); **concludes rather abruptly with no information about the fate** of Paul (28:30–31); but Acts does give a **statement about the success of the Word of God** (28:30–31).

Test 1: *Restriction to passages* – Luke 2:1–4 refers to the manifestation of tongues of fire and speaking in tongues, while Acts 13:1–3 indicates a verbal message from the Spirit during corporate worship. The latter manifestation is the less remarkable of the two and may serve as a minimum definition for a "special manifestation". Certainly there are several occasions where people receive the Spirit, or are filled with the Spirit in a fashion that would have been viewed as "special manifestations" at the time. Even if these are excluded as not special, there are still a number of other occasions where "special" manifestations occur (Acts 8:29, 39; 10:19, 46; 11:28; 13:9–11; 16:6–7; 19:6; 20:22–23 and 21:4–11). Thus, *parallel 1* is not well restricted.

Nevertheless, only the manifestations specified in *parallel 1* are followed by apostolic preaching as a consequence. *Parallels 1* and *2* are best combined for the sake of restriction. In fact, Talbert's wording of *parallel 2* incorporates *parallel 1*; so, for the purpose of this test, the weakness of *parallel 1* might be ignored.

Parallel 3 contains the only accounts of the healing of men χωλὸς ἐκ κοιλίας μητὸρς. The wording is noteworthy.

Regarding *parallel 4*, only three speeches begin with, "Men...why?" Acts 1:11; 3:12 and 14:15. This already reasonable restriction is made absolute when coupled with the other elements, a speech / prompted by response to a healing, since these are the only two passages in Acts that exhibit these features.

Parallel 5 is completely restricted by the single criterion of a stoning. The other elements certify the parallel. Similarly, the elements of parallelism listed in *parallel* 6 are unique (though the substantial length of the parallel passages may make it easy to find unique parallel elements).

Parallel 7 looks like a pattern of correspondences in its own right. Certain elements, however, are quite weak. For example, the abrupt conclusion of Peter's prison account with no information about his fate is dubious since he appears later in the book, so his fate is clearly implied, contrary to Paul's. Regarding "Herod," Paul had an audience with the *son* of the Herod associated with Peter. However, perhaps this is too particular a complaint. Another weakness is the "statement about the success of the Word of God". Acts 28:30–31 says nothing of its success, only that Paul was free to preach. Yet, even if these weak elements are set aside, the remainder produces an absolutely restricted pair.

Each phenomenon, as defined, is limited solely to the correspondences represented by the pattern, with the exception of the first parallel. This is a strong result.

Test 2: *Number of features* – This test heartily enhances the probability of intent with five of the seven parallels established by three or more elements (*parallels 5* through *6* with five or more).

Test 3: *Number of panels/passages* – As always with Talbert, the minimum of two complete panels is presented.

Test 4: *Attracts attention* – For the entire structure, all but perhaps the "Herod" and "abrupt conclusion" elements (*parallel 7*) are attention grabbing. Considering the number of parallel elements proposed, this is impressive.

Test 5: *Constructive complexity* – There is no break in sequence in this pattern, so it is strictly constructive parallelism.[6] Authorial intent is indicated.

Test 6: *Redaction criticism* – Talbert discusses the source theories proposed for Acts and rightly concludes that any tenable theory implies that the parallels in this structure either are impossible coincidences or they necessitate a great deal of selectivity on the part of the author to engineer them.[7] Selectivity is obviously the more probable mechanism.

Test 7: *Important themes* – Virtually all of the elements may be considered closely related to important aspects of Acts. As in test 4, this is impressive considering the number of elements proposed.

Test 8: *Historical/generic expectation* – Talbert defends his proposal

---

6 Talbert appeals to the sequence maintained by both panels as evidence of conscious repetition, *Literary Patterns*, 25.
7 Talbert, *Literary Patterns*, 25.

against Rackham's belief that "'the parallelism arises out of the facts'" by appealing to the selectivity required by the author to achieve the identical sequence of events, and the verbal similarities between the parallel passages. Certainly, any selection of a large number of events that happen to correspond so precisely, coupled with an accidental or unconscious arrangement of them in identical order, is highly improbable.[8] Intentional construction is indicated.

Test 9: *Common expression* – Talbert has defined the parallels so specifically that even the Gospel has nothing similar in sequence.

Test 10: *Contiguity* – Meaningful breaks in the first panel are: Acts 2:5–13 (which is closely tied to 2:1–4 and probably should have been incorporated into the first parallel); 2:40–47; 4:1–6:7; and 8:5–9:43; 11:19–30 (which is unrelated to the definition of *parallel 7*). In the second panel no gaps seem to be allowed because *parallels 6* and *7* span the entire text of panel (13:4–15; 13:41–14:7; 14:14, 18 are missing from parallels 1 through 5). The two large gaps in the first panel are disturbing but not devastating. These sections may have had a different purpose, for instance the introduction of Paul through his conversion (9:1–31). This test offers cautious approval.

Test 11: *Cumulative case* – Overall, the parallelism between Acts 1–12 and 13–28 is well supported by the tests. Only test 6 does not favorably apply. Test 10 alone is cautious in its support.

Although Talbert's broad parallel pattern between Luke and Acts was not well substantiated under the tests, this broad pattern is. The implication is that the evangelist was more concerned about literary structure and structural coherence within each volume than between them.

2 Additional Correspondences between Acts 1–12 and 13–28

The following table presents correspondences between Acts 1–12 and 13–28 "which occur in no apparent systematic order".[9] Consequently, each parallel will be treated more individually than in the pattern above. A not on contiguity (test 10) is necessary however before we begin. Since Talbert is noting correspondences that are scattered throughout the text, test 10 cannot apply. This certainly does not invalidate his proposal, it merely denies him any support from the test.

---

8 Talbert, *Literary Patterns*, 25.
9 Talbert, *Literary Patterns*, 24. His table is on the same page.

ACTS 1–12		ACTS 13–28
8:9–24 **Peter and John** confront a **magician**, Simon, who **draws Peter's curse.**	1.	13:6–12 **Barnabas and Saul** confront a **magician**, Elymas, who **draws Paul's curse.**
9:36–43 Peter **raises Dorcas from the dead.**	2.	20:9–12 Paul **raises Eutychus from the dead.**
10:25–26 Peter **restrains the Gentile Cornelius from worshipping him** with the words, "Stand up; **I too am a man.**"	3.	14:13–15 Barnabas and Paul **restrain the Gentiles at Lystra from worshipping them** with the words, "**We also are men**, of like nature with you."
12:6–11 Peter is **miraculously delivered from prison.**	4.	16:24–26 Paul and Silas are **miraculously delivered from prison.**
8:14–17 **The Spirit is given** by the **laying on of hands** of the Jerusalem apostles.	5.	19:1–6 **The Spirit is given** by the **laying on of hands** of Paul.
6:1–6 The Jerusalem apostles **appoint** the seven **with prayer** and the laying on of hands.	6.	14:23 Barnabas and Paul **appoint** elders **with prayer** and fasting.
5:34–39 A **Pharisee defends** the Jerusalem apostles **in the Sanhedrin.**	7.	23:9 **Pharisees defend** Paul **in the Sanhedrin.**
6:13–14 Stephen is **accused of acts against the law**, the **temple**, and the **customs of Moses.**	8.	21:20–21; 25:8 Paul is **accused of acts against the law**, the **temple**, and **customs of Moses.**
1:21–22 The Jerusalem apostles are **designated witnesses** by the **risen Christ.**	9.	23:11; 26:16 Paul is **designated a witness** by the **risen Christ.**

Parallel 1: *Test 1* – Magicians are only encountered in the passages of

this parallel,[10] and each time by a pair of missionaries, one of whom curses the magician. *Test 2* – Three features is a good result. *Test 3* – The minimum of two passages are present. *Test 4* – These are striking features. *Test 5* – This test is not applicable since the passages are not complex (the set is not a pattern). *Test 6* – Adequate redaction criticism is not possible. *Test 7* – Opposition is a key theme in both Acts and Luke. *Test 8* – Although not historically expected, the novelty of these events is compelling reason to include them. Novelty, however, favors authorial awareness of the correspondence. In terms of genre, there is no predisposition. The parallel is supported. *Test 9* – Encounters with sorcerers are not common in relevant extant literature. *Test 10* – Contiguity is not applicable, so this test does not apply. *Test 11* – Collectively, the tests fortify Talbert's contention that Luke planned this parallel.

Parallel 2: *Test 1* – These are the only two revivifications in Acts. *Test 2* – A single parallel element is unconvincing. *Test 3* – Two passages, the minimum, are presented. *Test 4* – Readers would remember a revivification. *Test 5* – This test is not applicable since the passages are not complex (the set is not a pattern). *Test 6* – Adequate redaction criticism is not possible. *Test 7* – Healing is prominent in both volumes. *Test 8* – What was said under test 8 for parallel 1 may be repeated here. Novelty would encourage inclusion, but suggests awareness of the correspondence. This test promotes the probability of intent. *Test 9*[11] – A single element does not permit an evaluation of common expression. Revivification stories were not unheard of; but no degree of influence may be ascertained regarding the basis of Talbert's definition of the parallel. *Test 10* – Contiguity is not applicable, so this test does not apply. *Test 11* – Only cautious approval is awarded to this parallel by the body of tests.

Parallel 3: *Test 1* – This type of event is only found in these locations of Acts. *Test 2* – Two parallel elements is a minimal case. *Test 3* – The minimum of two passages are present. *Test 4* – Worship of an apostle seizes the attention. *Test 5* – This test is not applicable since the passages are not complex (the set is not a pattern). *Test 6* – Adequate redaction criticism is not possible. *Test 7* – It is difficult to see what central Lukan theme underlies these stories. One might draw a contrast with Luke's

---

10 μαγεύω in Acts 8:9; μαγία in 8:11; and μάγος in 13:6, 8.

11 F.F. Bruce indicates that Luke employed traditional forms of presentation "in the kerygmatic outlines of the sermons, in the healing miracles, in the escapes from prison, and in the story of the voyage and shipwreck in ch. 27." See *Acts of the Apostles*, 45. Only parallels 2 and 4 fall into these categories. For these parallels Talbert has required no specific form, merely a single parallel element each, so a judgment as to whether a correspondence set is due to common expression is not possible.

christological portrayal of Christ's willingness and worthiness to accept praise (e.g., Lk. 19:28-40), but this is indirect. Additionally, Luke's anthropological distinction between the impotent human instrument and the potent divine implementation of the instrument may be invoked. This is more defensible, but the Lystra account lacks explication of the distinction. The healing is never explicitly attributed to God, whereas God's orchestration of Peter's visit with Cornelius is plain. In caution, support from this test must be withheld. *Test 8* – See test 8 of parallels 1 and 2. *Test 9* – I am unable to find any precedent for these two elements: a human restraining others from worshipping him, and appealing to his mere humanity. To my knowledge it is too infrequent to achieve the status of "common expression". *Test 10* – Contiguity is not applicable, so this test does not apply. *Test 11* – Some support for intent is gained by collective evaluation.

Parallel 4: *Test 1* – Aside from these accounts, the apostles are miraculously delivered from prison in 5:17-21. Still, two of three is acceptable. *Test 2* – A single parallel element is weak. *Test 3* – Two passages are required to form a parallel, and two are provided. *Test 4* – A miraculous escape from prison captures the imagination. God's intervention always takes prominence. *Test 5* – This test is not applicable since the passages are not complex (the set is not a pattern). *Test 6* – Adequate redaction criticism is not possible. *Test 7* – Each of the three miraculous deliveries is essential to the plot of Acts (see also Acts 28:1-6 where Paul miraculously suffers no ill effects from snakebite). They may even be foreshadowed by Luke 21:12-19 and 12:11-12. Divine delivery/vindication is certainly evident elsewhere in Luke's Gospel (Lk. 4:28-30; 8:22-25; 9:24; and 13:10-16), but these bear little similarity to the accounts in Acts. This test provides support. *Test 8* – Perhaps this is a subjective evaluation, but the prison events are nuclear aspects of church beginnings that could hardly be omitted. Accordingly, less than hearty approval is gained from this test. *Test 9* – Again (see parallel 2, test 9), a single element does not permit an evaluation of common expression. F.F. Bruce notes, "Richard Reitzenstein traces in various literatures a similar common framework for stories of escape from prison,"[12] which suggests literary precedent, but Talbert's parallelism does not depend on any common form. *Test 10* – Contiguity is not applicable, so this test does not apply. *Test 11* – The conclusions of the tests are mixed, so only tentative support is afforded.

Parallel 5: *Test 1* – Reception of the Spirit upon the laying on of hands occurs only in these two locations. Laying on of hands is found in Acts 6:6; 8:17; 9:17; 13:3; 19:6; and 28:8. The Spirit is received in Acts 2:4; 8:15-17; 10:44-45; and 19:1-7. If these two types of events were not causally

---

12 Bruce, *Acts of the Apostles*, 45.

linked in the passages of parallel 5 and very brief in their description, their frequency of occurrence would raise the possibility of coincidence. *Test 2* – Two elements is a minimal case. *Test 3* – Talbert observes the minimum of two parallel passages. *Test 4* – A link between human action and provision of the Holy Spirit was probably even in Luke's day considered infrequent, and Simon the sorcerer's reaction would be understood. Mild approval is gained. *Test 5* – This test is not applicable since the passages are not complex (the set is not a pattern). *Test 6* – Adequate redaction criticism is not possible. *Test 7* – Reception of the Spirit is universally accepted as central to Acts. *Test 8* – This period of church history demands some coverage of the various receptions of the Spirit, regardless of the mode. If the apostles typically employed this mode, then we might expect mention of it. No confidence is contributed by this test. *Test 9* – Luke's description of mode must be attributed to actual practice and not to literary influence. Although the act was known in both the Old Testament (Gn. 48:14; Nu. 27:16–18; and hands placed on animals, Lv. 1:4; 3:2, etc.) and in admission to the Sanhedrin,[13] it is insufficiently frequent in relevant literature to suggest that Luke's references originated from common expression rather than from apostolic practice. In further support, the Spirit is associated with the symbol elsewhere in the New Testament only in 1 Timothy 4:14 and 2 Timothy 1:6.[14] Gospel references conjoin it only with healing and blessing.[15] Therefore, Luke's association of the Holy Spirit with the laying on of hands is more likely derived from actual practice than from a typical literary form of expression. The parallel is therefore less probably a coincidental consequence of typical expression. *Test 10* – Contiguity is not applicable, so this test does not apply. *Test 11* – Collectively, any enhancement of our certainty that Luke intended this as a parallel as defined by Talbert is minor.

Parallel 6: *Test 1* – There are two other instances of appointment accompanied by prayer, Acts 1:24 (Matthias) and 13:3 (Barnabas and Saul). This result is not strong. *Test 2* – Only two parallel elements may be allowed, which is a minimal case. *Test 3* – The minimum of two passages is established. *Test 4* – The appointment of leaders by a body of believers is of interest to any church, but the accompaniment of prayer might go unnoticed. This slightly weakens the support from this test. *Test 5* – This test is not applicable since the passages are not complex (the set is not a pattern). *Test 6* – Adequate redaction criticism is not possible. *Test 7* –

---

13 Bruce, *Acts of the Apostles*, 184–185.
14 Each refers to Timothy's spiritual gifts. All other references to reception or indwelling of the Spirit in the New Testament lack mention of the laying on of hands.
15 Healing – Mt. 9:18; Mk. 5:23; 6:5; 7:32; 8:23, 25; 16:18 Lk. 4:40; 13:13; Blessing – Mt. 19:13, 15.

Although apostolic leadership and the concept of authority are significant in Acts, appointment to an office other than apostle does not rate as an important theme, even though it is perhaps ecclesiastically significant. No enhancement of probability is attained through this test. *Test 8* – Considering the ecclesiological nature of the content, we should perhaps expect an etiology of church offices such as deacon and elder. Lukan intent behind the parallel is uncertain according to this test, especially since prayer is typically coupled with such solemn occasions in Acts. *Test 9* – Prayer in accompaniment of appointment to an office is common in the Old Testament. Consecration of priests was performed before the Lord, the sacrifices being a type of prayer (Ex. 29:1–28). The Lord appointed Joshua Moses' successor while Moses prayed (Nu. 27:12–23). Saul was selected as king during Samuel's prayer (1 Sa. 8:1–22), as was David (1 Sa. 16:1–3). David took his oath "before the Lord" at his coronation (2 Sa. 5:3). When Solomon was made king a blessing was said (1 Ki. 1:36–7). The Lord designated Elisha successor to Elijah during prayer (1 Ki. 19:9–18). It is reasonable to assume that first century Christians familiar with the Old Testament, like Luke, would naturally associate prayer with appointment to a spiritual office. Regardless of whether or not he knew that prayer was said on the occasions in the parallel, it was a rational supposition that it was. This is evidently confirmed by Luke's addition of Jesus' prayer in Luke 6:12–16 prior to his designation of the apostles. Rather than a conscious construction of parallel passages, prayer in conjunction with these appointments could well have arisen from a common association. Accordingly, the certainty of intent behind this parallel is not aided by this test. *Test 10* – Contiguity is not applicable, so this test does not apply. *Test 11* – This parallel performs poorly across the battery of tests. Parallel 6 should not be held with confidence.

Parallel 7: *Test 1* – Only these two accounts depict a Pharisee defending a Christian in the Sanhedrin. Indeed, these are the only two instances of a Pharisaic defense of anything. The Sanhedrin, however, is central to Acts 4:1–22; 5:21–41; 6:12–7:60; 22:30–23:30 and 24:20. Nevertheless, the specific reference to the Pharisees in the Sanhedrin abates the likelihood of coincidental collocation of the motifs in this parallel. *Test 2* – Two parallel elements is a minimal argument. *Test 3* – The minimum of two passages are present. *Test 4* – These accounts are remarkable, especially in contrast to the portrayal of Pharisees in the Gospel. *Test 5* – This test is not applicable since the passages are not complex (the set is not a pattern). *Test 6* – Adequate redaction criticism is not possible. *Test 7* – Support from religious leaders is rare in Lukan writings (in Luke, see 20:39). Perhaps Luke understood this as a fulfillment of Jesus' promised protection at trials (Lk. 21:12–19). Clearly the Lord's encouragement of Paul (Acts 23:11) corroborates this. If to this indirect connection with important Lukan themes we add the role of the Sanhedrin in the trials of Jesus and Paul, then the performance of this parallel under test 7 is improved. It may be attributed minor approval. *Test 8* – Although this is a novel occurrence, it is not on the level of a revivification or encounter with a sorcerer. Neither history nor genre solicit selection of the Pharisees' defenses in the Sanhedrin. Consequently, it is more certain that Luke intended this parallel, according to this test. *Test 9* – Pharisaic defense of a Christian before the Sanhedrin is unparalleled in relevant literature. *Test 10* – Contiguity is not applicable, so this test does not apply. *Test 11* – A fair degree of certainty may be attributed to this parallel for its successful results.

Parallel 8: *Test 1* – Stephen is accused of all three crimes within one scene. Talbert must stretch between Acts 21:20–21 (law and Moses) and 25:8 (law and temple) to encompass all three accusations against Paul. Admittedly, these are the only two characters so accused, but the parallel seems tenuous. *Test 2* – Three parallel elements is reasonably effective. *Test 3* – Two passages, the minimum, are presented. *Test 4* – Since Jewish/Christian issues were still relevant to Luke's audience, and since Paul and martyrs (perhaps Stephen himself) were highly esteemed in the church, such accusations would impose themselves as ridiculous, especially in light of the text's portrayal of their godliness. *Test 5* – This test is not applicable since the passages are not complex (the set is not a pattern). *Test 6* – Adequate redaction criticism is not possible. *Test 7* – Generally, opposition is an important theme, as is innocence. Therefore, such accusations are related to important themes. *Test 8* – No doubt any biographical presentation that captures the more important matters in the lives of Paul and Stephen would include similar Jewish accusations. Luke's purpose behind the selection of Stephen for his plot is a separate matter to the correspondence of the accusations, so the parallel is probably a product of history. Law, temple and the customs of Moses are such common Jewish themes that they hardly strengthen confidence in the parallelism. No greater certainty results from this test. *Test 9* – It is common knowledge that Jewish (and Gentile) Christians were accused of violating Jewish traditions, so it was a readily available theme for Luke. Our conclusion on this test may rest on our presumption of whether Luke would create such facts or not. Objectivity drives us to an inconclusive result on probability. *Test 10* – Contiguity is not applicable, so this test does not apply. *Test 11* – Lukan intent behind this parallel remains uncertain because of its unconvincing performance under the collection of tests.

Parallel 9: *Test 1* – The restriction is total, but perhaps 1:8 should be listed rather than 1:21–22. *Test 2* – A minimal case is established by two features. *Test 3* – As always with Talbert, the minimum of two passages is demonstrated, despite the reference to Acts 26:16, which is a recounting of 23:11. *Test 4* – Any activity on the part of the risen Christ would hold special interest. *Test 5* – This test is not applicable since the passages are not complex (the set is not a pattern). *Test 6* – Adequate redaction criticism is not possible. *Test 7* – Naturally, the risen Christ and the theme of witness are crucial to the story. *Test 8* – Assuming the witness theme was inevitable due to the nature of apostolic preaching, the designation of the Jerusalem apostles and Paul as witnesses may be reckoned historically and generically expected. Probability of intent is not substantiated by this test. *Test 9* – The designation by the risen Christ of the apostles and Paul as witnesses is explicit and implicit throughout the entire New Testament. It is risky to assert that Luke's purpose was to establish a parallel when a coincidental parallel was virtually inescapable for him. This is not to say that he could not have been aware of or intended it. Our confidence, however, is challenged. *Test 10* – Contiguity is not applicable, so this test does not apply. *Test 11* – The tests offer a mixed response. Although one's inclination is to view this as an intentional parallel, there is good reason to be cautious.

Based on the tests for intentionality, parallels 1, 3 and 7 assert themselves above the rest as engineered by Luke. Often the reader may find between various passages similarities that were not conscious constructions, and therefore not necessarily contributory to the intended meaning of the work. No doubt, the individual passages above that lie in unconvincing parallels play important roles in their immediate contexts, but additional evidence is required to substantiate the extensive bridging proposed by Talbert in this set of correspondences.

3 Correspondences between Acts 1:12–4:23 and 4:24–5:42

Talbert produces a set of correspondences within Acts that maintain a sequence.[16] Since he has defined the relevant text as 1:12–5:42, it will be treated autonomously for the purpose of this analysis.

ACTS 1:12–4:23		ACTS 4:24–5:42
1:12–26 **Gathered together, the church is at prayer.**	**1.**	4:24–31a **Gathered together, the church is at prayer.**
2:1–13 They were **all filled with the Holy Spirit.**	**2.**	4:31b They were **all filled with the Holy Spirit.**

---

16 See Talbert, *Literary Patterns*, 35–9 for his presentation of these correspondences and their defense.

Appendix A

	2:14–41 Peter **preaches**.	**3.**	4:31c They **spoke the word** of God with boldness.
	2:42–47 The **communal life of the church is portrayed**.	**4.**	4:32–35 The **communal life of the church is portrayed**. It is illustrated by examples in 4:36–37 and 5:1–10.
	2:43a **Fear comes upon every soul**.	**5.**	5:5b, 11 **Fear comes upon the whole church and all who heard**.
	2:43b **Wonders and signs** are done **by the apostles**.	**6.**	5:12a **Signs and wonders** are done **by the apostles**.
	3:1–11 A lame man is **healed by Peter** and John.	**7.**	5:13–16 **Healings by Peter**.
	3:12–26 Peter delivers a speech in **Solomon's Portico**.	**8.**	5:12b They are all together in **Solomon's Portico**.
	4:1–7 The **apostles are arrested by the Sadducees**. They are **kept in custody until the morrow**. Then they are **brought before the council**.	**9.**	5:17–28 The **apostles are arrested by the Sadducees**. They are **kept in custody over night**. Then they are **brought before the council**.
	4:8–12, 19–20 **Peter's defense**.	**10.**	5:30–32 **Peter's defense**.
	4:13–17 The **council deliberates**.	**11.**	5:33–39 **The council deliberates**.
	4:18, 21–23 The **apostles are released**.	**12.**	5:40–42 The **apostles are released**.

Test 1: *Restriction to passages* – The elements of *parallels 1* and *2* are restricted to their parallels within Acts 1:12–5:42. Regarding *parallel 3*, Peter preaches also in 3:11–26 and 4:8–17, and a summery similar to 4:31c is found at 5:42. The restriction of this parallel is therefore not the best. Each element of *parallels 4* through *12* are found only in their respective parallels. Talbert's pattern is strongly supported by test 1.

Test 2: *Number of features* – Individually, only *parallel 9* has the weight of more than two features. As a pattern, however, twelve parallels is impressive.

Test 3: *Number of panels/passages* – Two panels is only the minimum required for parallelism, of course.

Test 4: *Attracts attention* – None of the features fails to attract attention.

Test 5: *Constructive complexity* – With the exception of Acts 5:12b (*parallel 8*) being out of sequence, and 2:43a and 43b (parallels 5 and 6) being drawn from within 2:42–47, the parallelism is totally constructive. These variations are minor.

Test 6: *Redaction criticism* – Talbert deals with the question of sources and concludes that multiple sources lie behind 1:12–5:42.[17] Regardless, no confident redactional observations are possible, so this test does not apply.

Test 7: *Important themes* – Each feature is directly related to important Lukan themes, except perhaps Solomon's Portico. This is certainly excusable.

Test 8: *Historical/generic expectation* – Talbert dialogs with Jeremias over whether the basis for the parallelism is "the two stages of proper Jewish legal process". He musters Reicke and Haenchen in his contention that the Lukan accounts do not correspond to this process.[18] No proposal, though, whether historical or generic, accounts for a majority of the parallels presented, so this test indicates authorial intent.

Test 9: *Common expression* – Certainly, this sequence of twelve units is uncommon in relevant literature.

Test 10: *Contiguity* – Only Acts 4:36–5:4 (six verses); 5:6–10 and 5:29 break the contiguity. This is minor for such a length of text.

Test 11: *Cumulative case* – This test enhances the probability that Luke intended the parallelism in this section since each applicable test favorably agrees.

Although some degree of parallelism in 1:12–5:42 is universally recognized, it is not always attributed to authorial intent. Even if Luke, here, employed a single source for the entire section, the tests indicate that the pattern is intentionally designed by someone.

---

17 Talbert, *Literary Patterns*, 36–38.
18 Talbert, *Literary Patterns*, 38–39.

APPENDIX B

The Preface to Luke as a Possible Indication of the Gospel's Structural Nature

Does Luke provide any indication at the beginning of the Gospel to indicate that he has employed a detailed structure? Such indication is by no means standard practice for patterned works of his time, but if available it would establish firmer ground for our own proposal later on. An examination of Luke's preface is in order.

Many have written on the importance of the preface to the Third Gospel for an understanding of its purpose, and most of these discussions appropriately place great weight on the term καθεξῆς as some indication of Luke's structural intent for the book.[1] Scholars generally agree that the essential meaning of the word is "sequence" and/or "order," with possible related nuances. A few maintain that it has the weaker sense of "as follows" or "the

---

1 The following are representative: Fearghus Ó Fearghail, *The Introduction to Luke-Acts: A Study of the Role of Lk 1,1–4,44 in the Composition of Luke's Two-Volume Work* (Rome: Editrice Pontificio Instituto Biblico, 1991); Martin Völkel, "Exegetische Erwägungen zum Verständnis des Begriffs ΚΑΘΕΞΗΣ im lukanischen Prolog," *NTS* 20 (1974) 289–99; Loveday Alexander, *The Preface to Luke's Gospel: Literary Convention and Social Context in Luke 1:1–4 and Acts 1:1* (Cambridge: Cambridge University Press, 1993); Gerhard Schneider, "Zur Bedeutung von καθεξῆς im lukanischen Doppelwerk," *ZNW* 68 (1977) 128–31; Franz Mussner, "Καθεξῆς im Lukasprolog," in E.E. Ellis and E. Grässer (eds.), *Jesus und Paulus: Festschrift für W.G. Kümmel*, (Göttingen: Vandenhoeck & Ruprecht, 1975) 253–55; Raymond E. Brown, "Luke's Method in the Annunciation Narrative of Chapter One," in Charles H. Talbert (ed.) *Perspectives on Luke-Acts*, (Edinburgh: T. & T. Clark, 1978) 126–38; Richard J. Dillon, "Previewing Luke's Project from His Prologue (Luke 1:1–4)," *CBQ* 43 (1981) 205–23; Günter Klein, "Lukas 1,1–4 als theologisches Programm," in E. Dinkler (ed.), *Zeit und Geschichte: Für Rudolf Bultmann* (Tübingen: J.C.B. Mohr, 1964) 193–216; and I.I. du Plessis, "Once More: The Purpose of Luke's Prologue (Lk. 1:1–4)," *NovT* 16 (1974) 259–271.

Loveday Alexander offers a comprehensive comparison of Luke's preface with several types of ancient literary prefaces, but he says relatively little on καθεξῆς; *Preface*, 131–132.

following,"[2] but this is often because they draw too close a connection with ἑξῆς, which may exhibit this weaker sense. Surveying the studies available, the sense of καθεξῆς may manifest itself in temporal, geographical or logical spheres,[3] and these suit Luke's uses of the word. In which sphere any particular instance resides, of course, depends on the context. With so few instances of καθεξῆς,[4] it remains debatable as to whether the sense of the word itself differs substantially from one sphere to the next or whether the context alone supplies the temporal, geographical or logical nuance.

It is instructive to examine briefly the four Lukan contexts of καθεξῆς other than Luke 1:3 (Lk. 8:1; Acts 3:24; 11:4; and 18:23). In Luke 8:1, the sphere is apparently temporal; Καὶ ἐγένετο ἐν τῷ καθεξῆς, "And it came about soon afterwards...." Dillon considers the geographical sphere possible here because of the travel summary immediately following the word. In Acts 3:24, the sphere again seems to be temporal; πάντες δὲ οἱ προφῆται ἀπὸ Σαμουὴλ καὶ τῶν καθεξῆς, "all the prophets who have spoken, from Samuel and [his] successors onward...." The sphere of Acts 18:23 clearly has a geographical flavor; ἐξῆλθεν διερχόμενος καθεξῆς τὴν Γαλατικὴν χώραν καὶ Φρυγίαν, "he departed and passed successively through the Galatian region and Phrygia...."

We will examine Acts 11:4 in greater depth because of the similarity of the context to that of Luke 1:3, in contrast to the instances just covered. Peter describes an oral account he is about to deliver in confirmation of the conversion of Cornelius, a Gentile. In Luke 1:3, the Evangelist describes a written account he is about to deliver in confirmation of what Theophilus had been taught about Jesus. At first glance the sphere appears to be temporal; ἀρξάμενος δὲ Πέτρος ἐξετίθετο αὐτοῖς καθεξῆς λέγων, "But Peter began [speaking] and [proceeded] to explain to them in orderly sequence, saying...." What becomes evident is that he significantly varies the chronological order of the events from that previously presented in Acts. As Dillon notes, among other examples, earlier in the text the Gentiles receive the Spirit after Peter preaches (Acts 10:44), but in Peter's

---

[2] See for example du Plessis, "Once More," 259–71; Schuyler Brown, "The Role of the Prologues in Determining the Purpose of Luke-Acts," in Charles H. Talbert (ed.), *Perspectives on Luke-Acts* (Edinburgh: T. & T. Clark, 1978) 99–111; and J. Kurzinger, "Lk 1,3:...ἀκριβῶς καθεξῆς σοι γράψαι," *BZ* 18 (1974) 249–255.

  Further against the meaning "as follows," Alexander observes that καθεξῆς "seems too far from the end of the preface for this sense;" *Preface*, 132.

[3] Dillon bases his evaluation of meaning on these three spheres; "Previewing," 219.

[4] In the Greek NT: Lk. 1:3; 8:1; Acts 3:24; 11:4 and 18:23. Völkel, who examines the most extra-biblical instances of the word, cites only eight, "Erwägungen," 295–298.

review this happened as he began to speak (11:15).⁵ Furthermore, Ó Fearghail highlights the incompleteness of the apostle's account and its obvious design as a logical/rhetorical defense.⁶ Its persuasive purpose, and the desire to communicate through events the message that God was behind those events, were best facilitated through alteration of the chronology and selectivity of material (in a manner that was not misleading). Similarly, the Gospel itself demonstrates intentional variance from Mark's chronology⁷ (e.g. Lk. 4:16–30) and a high degree of selectivity (e.g. big omission). It is also a communication of a message through events. Clearly, the contextual similarity of the Gospel to Peter's speech is significant and far greater than to the other Lukan accounts containing καθεξῆς.

Turning to Luke 1:3, Völkel, after a thorough analysis of the Lukan instances and several extra-biblical occurrences, adheres to the above distinction: καθεξῆς referring to the attempt to communicate through events, versus καθεξῆς referring merely to recording them. He concludes that καθεξῆς does not refer to the accurate chronology or completeness of the record of events, but to the portrayal of the proper understanding of those events.⁸ Mussner counters Völkel with the suggestion that καθεξῆς is the counterpart to πᾶσιν in the same verse. Luke would therefore mean that he included all the traditions that he considered accurate from the sources available to him.⁹ This does not accord however with the quantity of Markan material that Luke passes over.¹⁰ Similar to Völkel, and appropriately influenced by the Acts 11 passage, Dillon opts for the meaning "logical or idea-sequence".¹¹ Indeed, since Luke does diverge from the chronology of his sources, he probably does not claim chronological sequence in καθεξῆς. Furthermore, although many have considered the Third Gospel to follow a basic geographical outline (the term "travel narrative" is a prime example) there are far fewer geographical references than would be expected if Luke intended to sequence the material in such

---

5 Dillon, "Previewing," 219–220.
6 Ó Fearghail, *Introduction to Luke-Acts*, 105–107.
7 Several scholars observe this comparison between Peter's speech and the Gospel. See for example Robert J. Karris, *Luke: Artist and Theologian: Luke's Passion Account as Literature* (New York: Paulist Press, 1985) 9; Dillon, "Previewing," 220; and Green, *Gospel of Luke*, 43–44, who uses the term "persuasive order".
8 Völkel, "Erwägungen," 294.
9 Mussner, "Καθεξῆς," 253–255.
10 Schneider, "Bedeutung von καθεξῆς," 129. But his contention that καθεξῆς refers to the frequently occurring "promise-fulfillment" theme fails because his observation of the theme in each Lukan context of the word is often forced.
11 Günter Klein also rejects the "order of material" sense, but unconvincingly argues for a broader chronological structure: the history of Jesus followed by the time of the early church ("Lukas 1,1–4," 210–211).

fashion. Some sort of logical/rhetorical structure remains as the sphere for καθεξῆς. In perhaps the most balanced evaluation of the evidence, Ó Fearghail defines the semantic range of possible senses, and reflects the difficulty of the decision by withholding a final choice. He includes continuity of the narrative, "good order" (logical/rhetorical sphere), demonstration of "the presence of a divine guiding hand in the course of events narrated as in Acts 11:4–18" (logical sphere), and adherence to a traditional arrangement of material.[12] It is probably best to emulate his caution, especially since Luke may have intended more than one of these concepts.

For our purposes, it is sufficient to recognize that the Evangelist *could* have been referring to a logical/rhetorical or "idea-sequenced" format around which he arranged his material.[13] The patterns observed in the precedent literature above often fall into this category. While it would be pleasing to decisively define καθεξῆς for Luke 1:3, Luke provides insufficient contextual boundaries in the preface for such certainty. Nevertheless, the contexts following Acts 11:4 and Luke 1:1–4 are similar and suggest a reasonable preference. In Acts 11:4, καθεξῆς refers to Peter's rhetorical/"idea-sequenced" speech. In Luke 1:1–4, the reference is obviously to the whole Gospel, and perhaps to Luke-Acts.[14] It was demonstrated in chapter 4 ("A New Proposal for the Structure and Composition of Luke 4:14–24:53") that, like Peter's speech and the precedent literature above, the entire Gospel is structured in a rhetorical/"idea-sequenced" fashion, just as has already been demonstrated for Luke 1–2. Perhaps this is Luke's primary referent for καθεξῆς.

---

12 Ó Fearghail, *Introduction to Luke-Acts*, 108–110.
13 See Joel B. Green's insightful discussion, *Theology*, 16–21.
14 L.C.A. Alexander develops evidence that Lk. 1:1–4 is the preface to Luke-Acts, "Luke's Preface in the Context of Greek Preface Writing," *NovT* 28 (1986) 28–74.

APPENDIX C

The Relationship between Intertextuality and the Theory Espoused in This Book

Modern literary theory has many facets and many distinct disciplines. Much of it of course may be applied to biblical studies with fruitful results. Intertextuality is a modern literary theory regarding the interrelationship between texts that has recently found its way into biblical research. Since this book is a study of the interrelatedness of Lukan pericopes, intertextuality naturally relates. An excerpt from the book *Intertextuality: Theories and Practices* by Judith Still and Michael Worton will serve at this point as a provisional definition for this theory.

> The theory of intertextuality insists that a text...cannot exist as a hermetic or self-sufficient whole, and so does not function as a closed system. This is for two reasons. Firstly, the writer is a reader of texts...before s/he is a creator of texts, and therefore the work of art is inevitably shot through with references, quotations and influences of every kind....This repetition of past or of contemporary texts can range from the most conscious and sophisticated elaboration of other poets' work, to a scholarly use of sources, or the quotation (with or without the use of quotation marks) of snatches of conversation typical of a certain social milieu at a certain historical moment....
>
> Secondly, a text is available only through some process of reading; what is produced at the moment of reading is due to the cross-fertilization of the packaged textual material (say, a book) by all the texts which the reader brings to it. A delicate allusion to a work unknown to the reader, which therefore goes unnoticed, will have a dormant existence in that reading. On the other hand, the reader's experience of some practice or theory unknown to the author may lead to a fresh interpretation.[1]

Our discussion works on the level of the first reason in the above quotation, viewing Luke as a reader of texts. The relevant details of intertextuality and

---

1 Judith Still and Michael Worton, *Intertextuality: Theories and Practices* (Manchester: Manchester University Press, 1990) 1–2.

precisely how we have employed the theory in our discussion are clarified below. Although literary theories are often esoteric and faddish, it will be evident that this particular form of intertextuality is extremely practicable and ever relevant to Lukan scholarship. Our analysis of the interconnections between pericopes in Luke is consistent with the process of intertextuality as practiced by certain intertextualists. See for example Huub Welzen's chapter, "Loosening and Binding: Luke 13.10–21 as Programme and Antiprogramme of the Gospel of Luke," in *Intertextuality in Biblical Writings: Essays in Honor of Bas van Iersel*.[2]

1 The Problem of the Author in the Theory of Intertextuality

Two distinct levels of approach are taken in this book. We consider Luke's act of composition, including his use of sources. This is an author-based approach. We also take a text-based approach where interpretation concentrates specifically on the structured interrelatedness between passages in the final form without reference to how the form came to be. The second approach is appropriate since Luke did not indicate what his sources were and when he was moving from one to another. Through an intertextual study, how the Evangelist interpreted the material incorporated in his Gospel becomes more evident through the comparison of passages placed in parallel with each other. Intertextuality may be a text- *and/or* reader-based theory concentrating on the final form of a text and/or what the reader makes of that text.

1.1 The Intertextualists' Tendency to Deny the Author's Importance

Literary theorists in the field of intertextuality frequently disavow the importance of the author of a text.[3] The reasons for this disavowal will be explained shortly. Nevertheless, not all find this presupposition necessary. For instance, James W. Voelz in his discussion on "Elements of Intertextuality" demonstrates concern for what is implied about the author by a text.[4]

---

2 Sipke Draisma (ed.), (Kampen: Uitgeversmaatschappij J.H. Kok, 1989) 175–187.
3 A useful discussion of this is found in Howard Felperin's *Beyond Deconstruction: The Uses and Abuses of Literary Theory* (Oxford: Clarendon, 1985) 28–40, 200–211. Also see Roland Barthes' "The Death of the Author," which is often considered the classic expression of this perspective; *Image, Music, Text*, Stephen Heath (ed.), (New York: Hill and Wang, 1977) 142–148.
4 James W. Voelz, "Multiple Signs and Double Texts: Elements of Intertextuality," in Sipke Draisma (ed.), *Intertextuality in Biblical Writings: Essays in Honor of Bas van Iersel* (Kampen: Uitgeversmaatschappij J.H. Kok, 1989) 29.

Additionally, Willem S. Vorster believes that *Redaktionsgeschichte*, with its reference to a compiler/author, has its place in the analysis of a text.[5] The fruit of redaction-criticism is justification enough. Yet, the authorship of Luke's sources is obviously not significant since he did not even provide this information to his readers. His composition was designed to communicate through its final form without any indication of sources and source manipulation.

The theory of intertextuality itself usually claims that authorship is of little to no importance to interpretation. This is the consequence of the intertextualist's view of what a text actually is. In the often-quoted words of Roland Barthes who spurns the concept of author ("Author-God" below is derogatory),

> We know that a text is not a line of words releasing a single 'theological' meaning (the 'message' of the Author-God) but a multi-dimensional space in which a variety of writings, *none of them original*, blend and clash. *The text is a tissue of quotations drawn from the innumerable centres of culture.* Similar to Bouvard and Pécuchet, those eternal copyists, at once sublime and comic and whose profound ridiculousness indicates precisely the truth of writing, the writer can only imitate a gesture that is always anterior, never original. *His only power is to mix writings*, to counter the ones with the others, in such a way as never to rest on any one of them.[6] (italics mine)

With each text being reduced to merely a complex "network of references to other texts (intertexts)"[7] and the author to "never more than the instance of writing,"[8] the vast interconnection of prior "authors" whose voices are heard within each text apparently diminishes the importance of the person writing by making him simply one in an innumerable chorus. This view, though there is some strength to it, is overly disparaging in its denial of originality. Nevertheless, we may still legitimately look at interpretational interplay between intertexts – standard pericopes for our purposes – without concern about literary priority or authorship of each unit, and simply analyze the intertextuality of the final form without regard for how it got that way. For completeness however, we have done this in conjunction with a study of the Gospel's formation.

---

5 Willem S. Vorster, "Intertextuality and Redaktionsgeschichte," in Sipke Draisma (ed.), *Intertextuality in Biblical Writings: Essays in Honor of Bas van Iersel* (Kampen: Uitgeversmaatschappij J.H. Kok, 1989) 15–26.
6 Barthes, *Image*, 146.
7 Vorster, "Intertextuality," 21.
8 Barthes, *Image*, 145.

1.2 The Debate among Literary Theorists: Arguments in Favor of the Author's Importance

Text- and reader-based theories that deny the author to varying degrees should not be glossed over without some presentation of the debate among literary theorists over the validity of the concept of "author". This is valuable to our study because we frequently refer to the composer of the Third Gospel (assumed to be Luke). Most literary theorists it seems have jumped on the bandwagon which is given classical expression by Roland Barthes in his essay "The Death of the Author"[9] where he argues against any value of the author for the reader's interpretation. W.K. Wimsatt and Monroe C. Beardsley actually offered essentially the identical arguments several years in advance of Barthes (though with different perspectives on text and reader).[10] Add to these the perspective of Julia Kristeva,[11] another highly regarded proponent, and the arsenal is mighty against the importance of the author for interpretation. Their arguments include the following. (1) How are we to determine whether an author successfully communicated what he/she wanted? All we have is the text.[12] (2) The author implied by the text is different from the actual writer, and is the only truly important and meaningful "author".[13] (3) Once something is said or written, it is disconnected from its source; and the language speaks, not the author.[14] (4) The writer is "born simultaneously with the text, is in no way equipped with a being preceding or exceeding the writing, is not the subject with the book as predicate; there is no other time than that of the enunciation and every text is eternally written here and now".[15] In other words, the author is in a state of flux culturally, emotionally, intellectually and in many other

---

9 Barthes, *Image*, 142–148.
10 W.K. Wimsatt and Monroe C. Beardsley, "The Intentional Fallacy," in David Newton-de Molina (comp.), *On Literary Intention*, (Edinburgh: Edinburgh University Press, 1976) 1–13.
11 Julia Kristeva, *Desire in Language: A Semiotic Approach to Literature and Art*, Leon S. Roudiez (ed.), Thomas Gorda, Alice Jardine, and Leon S. Roudiez (trs.), (Columbia, N.Y.: Columbia University Press, 1980).
12 Wimsatt and Beardsley, "The Intentional Fallacy," 1–2.
13 Wimsatt and Beardsley, "The Intentional Fallacy," 2. This line is also adopted as the opening point in Louise M. Rosenblatt's book *The Reader, the Text, the Poem: The Transactional Theory of the Literary Work* (Carbondale, Illinois: Southern Illinois University Press, 1978), which is a good example of a thoroughly reader-based approach to text. Although theories in the literary-critical world are subject to rapid transformations and transitions, reader-based theories still hold pride of place after several decades. An example is the recent book edited by Gary A. Olson, *Philosophy, Rhetoric, Literary Criticism: (Inter)views* (Carbondale, Illinois: Southern Illinois University Press, 1994).
14 Barthes, *Image*, 142–143.
15 Barthes, *Image*, 145.

ways, so that the precise person who wrote ceases to exist after the writing. (5) A writer merely rewrites previous "texts,"[16] which may be written texts, life experiences, history[17] or even culture.[18] (6) The reader is where meaning is resident, not in the writer.[19] Such arguments have indeed persuaded many.

Foucault, among others, has resisted the extent of this denial of the author however. In his essay, "What is an Author," he salvages at least an "author-function".[20] He writes, "The function of an author is to characterize the existence, circulation, and operation of certain discourses within a society."[21] Regarding those who completely deny the author, he observes the incongruity between this denial and their reference to writings as "works". Hence his question, "What…is the strange unit designated by the term, work? What is necessary to its composition, if a work is not something written by an 'author'?"[22] Furthermore, certain elements in a text can only be explained by the existence of an author with individuality. For instance, the author is a responsible explanation for unity evident in a text.[23] Still, to Foucault the author-function "does not refer, purely and simply, to an actual individual insofar as it simultaneously gives rise to a variety of egos and to a series of subjective positions that individuals of any class may come to occupy".[24] This view is a step closer to acceptance of an actual person behind each text who conveys his intentions through rules of language and communication, but there are literary critics who move even further.

Not surprisingly, there is a powerful reaction among some literary theorists against the denial of the importance of the author. A superb book devoted purely to the subject is *On Literary Intention*.[25] In it, several international scholars respond to the essay by W.K. Wimsatt and Monroe C.

---

16 Barthes, *Image*, 146; and Vorster, "Intertextuality," 20.
17 Voelz, "Multiple Signs," 31.
18 Kristeva, *Desire*, 36.
19 Barthes, *Image*, 148; and Voelz, "Multiple Signs," 27.
20 See Michel Foucault, *Language, Counter-Memory, Practice: Selected Essays and Interviews*, Donald F. Bouchard (ed.), Donald F. Bouchard and Sherry Simon (tr.), (Ithaca, N.Y.: Cornell University Press, 1977) 113–38. Foucault's interest in the *power* of discourse, noted by Raman Selden in *A Reader's Guide to Contemporary Literary Theory* (Lexington, Kentucky: University Press of Kentucky, 1985) 98–100, is intimately connected with this author-function.
21 Foucault, *Language*, 124.
22 Foucault, *Language*, 118.
23 Foucault, *Language*, 128.
24 Foucault, *Language*, 130–131.
25 David Newton-de Molina, compiler, *On Literary Intention* (Edinburgh: Edinburgh University Press, 1976).

Beardsley entitled "The Intentional Fallacy" which, as suggested earlier, is representative of the classic denial of the author.[26] E.D. Hirsch in particular constructs an impressive attack that raises crucial problems with the theory.[27] It is useful to mention some of these.

Hirsch observes the contradiction of claiming that a text cannot represent an author's meaning. "The text had to represent *somebody's* meaning – if not the author's then the critic's,"[28] if the critic's, then the critic effectively becomes the author of the meaning. "Whenever meaning is attached to a sequence of words it is impossible to escape an author."[29] This argument merely establishes the validity of the author concept.

In response to the proposition that "it does not matter what an author means – only what his text says," Hirsch acknowledges the existence of imaginative interpretation, but draws a clear distinction between that and valid interpretation. Just because a reader may construe a variety of meanings from the words of a text does not necessarily exclude the existence of the author's meaning or its value. Additionally, if a variety of interpretations are valid then the text has no particular meaning,[30] and this diminishes the value of any such interpretation.[31]

To the charge that "since we are all different from the author, we cannot reproduce his intended meaning in ourselves, and even if by some accident we could, we still would not be certain that we had done so,"[32] Hirsch admits that we cannot be *certain* of an author's meaning. However, he explains, "It is a logical mistake to confuse the impossibility of certainty in understanding with the impossibility of understanding".[33] He correctly prefers to speak in terms of probability that the author intended a particular meaning, and probability is a reasonable approach (one which is taken in this book). Certainly if an author *intended* to convey everything in his/her mind through the written word, it would be impossible for the reader to apprehend all of it simply because it would be impossible for the writer to succeed in placing it all in the text. However, authors are more realistic than this. Their intentions are usually sensible and this sensibility is gained through a realization, developed by the experience of *successful communi-*

---

26 Wimsatt and Beardsley, "The Intentional Fallacy," 1–13.
27 E.D. Hirsch, Jr., "In Defense of the Author," 87–103, and "Objective Interpretation," in David Newton-de Molina (comp.), *On Literary Intention* (Edinburgh: Edinburgh University Press, 1976) 26–54.
28 Hirsch, "Defense," 89.
29 Hirsch, "Defense," 89–90.
30 Hirsch, "Defense," 93–96.
31 This argument does not deter those who reject the author because, for example, Still and Worton even consider a misreading of a text to be of value (*Intertextuality*, 29).
32 Hirsch, "Defense," 96.
33 Hirsch, "Defense," 98.

cation, of how fully readers understand from what is written.[34] Furthermore, the probability that a reader's interpretation is close to that intended may realistically be established by a process of verification that Hirsch describes, which includes standard principles of hermeneutics like reading from the perspective of the author's known and probable outlook.[35]

There are a couple of other crucial problems with abandoning the author, apparently not discussed in the book *On Literary Intention*. First, the logic of the argument, that what is spoken becomes disconnected from its source and thereby makes the author irrelevant, is shown to be absurd when generalized. People would be irrelevant to our relationships since all that they communicate verbally and physically becomes disconnected from them and may not be attributed to their intent. Second, it is untrue that we may never know certainly anything of what an author intended, because there are aspects of texts that can only exist by intention. If a work is published, then clearly the author intends it to communicate something. If a patterned structure with detail overwhelmingly beyond what could be incidental is manifestly evident, then it must be intentional. If a work is dominated by joyous language then a positive response is probably intended, even if it is to be dashed by a tragic ending or the reader is to realize a devastating irony. The positive response is necessary and intended in such communication. Furthermore, we may know with reasonable certainty other aspects of what an author intended. If a text is of a particular genre then it is likely that the author intended to take advantage of communication that is typical for that genre. For example, science fiction is typically written at least in part to entertain, so we may infer that any work of science fiction is *probably* intended to some degree as entertainment. Other similar arguments could be mustered, but the point has been adequately established.

Throughout *On Literary Intention*, and in the above paragraph, serious questions are raised about any theory that has no place, or even a diminished place, for the importance of the actual author in the process of interpretation, especially when text is considered communication. Those who hold only to text- and/or reader-based theories, such as Barthes, Kristeva and perhaps Foucault, have not adequately answered most of these questions.[36] The burden of proof remains with them. Therefore it is reasonable and within the theoretical bounds of intertextuality, for us to study the compositional process behind the gospel of Luke and to speak of the

---

34 Hirsch, "Defense," 98–99.
35 Hirsch, "Objective Interpretation," 47–54.
36 Not all literary critics who adhere to text- and reader-based theories totally reject author-based theories. Ellen van Wolde is an example; "Trendy Intertextuality," in Sipke Draisma (ed.), *Intertextuality in Biblical Writings: Essays in Honor of Bas van Iersel* (Kampen: Uitgeversmaatschappij J.H. Kok, 1989) 45–47.

author's intent.

2 The Form of Intertextuality Exhibited in this Book

Having demonstrated that the actual author of a text is an important concept despite those who argue to the contrary, we might be disposed to reject the theory of intertextuality as an ineffective approach. Although most intertextualists appear to jettison the author, the theory itself operates effectively without such a presupposition. A description of the theory will make this apparent.

Intertextuality, in reference to a text that is assimilated into another, understands it to have only the significance attributed to it by the newer text.[37] The author of the assimilated text is ignored – and I believe sometimes unjustifiably so – but the author of the newer text has an identifiable function. Although he/she is a writer, the author is also a reader of the texts being assimilated. One expression of the theory of intertextuality considers

> that a writer should neither be regarded as a completely autonomous and conscious authority, nor as a reproducer of previous texts, but as a reader, 'digester' and re-arranger of texts and experiences. In addition to this he is part of the intertextual universe of his own time, which is determined by codes, conventions and logical rules. He uses these codes and rules to express his experiences with. On the other hand he is, as a reader, in continuous interaction with other texts which, for him, function as synchronic texts. These texts, too, he assimilates with the help of the codes of his time. The text produced by a writer is thus a processing of other (con)texts and also a reply to other (con)texts, with which the writer is maintaining a living dialogue.[38]

The interpreter must maintain an attentiveness to and awareness of these assimilated texts, but also, according to intertextuality, of external texts that bear resemblance to any part of the text being read.

> In producing sentences the maker of any text creates a fabric which points to many other prior texts. However, the texts that really matter are those intertexts which have been used in comparable contexts. Birth stories, for example, point to other birth stories and so do apocalyptic texts. 'Birth story' is the intertext within which other texts of similar content function and point to. The text type presupposes a particular context of utterance to

---

37 Wolde, "Trendy Intertextuality," 45–46.
38 Wolde, "Trendy Intertextuality," 46.

Appendix C

which the utterance is related.[39]

Voelz describes this procedure of reading texts in the light of other similar texts, the essence of intertextuality, as "matrixing".[40] This involves in the process of interpretation the interconnecting (between texts) of any type of sign that points toward meaning.[41] The process is quite fluid and undefined despite the detailed description Voelz provides. The procedural role of the reader's whims contributes to this fluidity. For example, Jean Delorme considers the motif of motion a useful intertextual link between the narratives of Abraham, Jacob, Ruth, Paul and several parables.[42] Comparisons and contrasts are then observed between these texts along the lines of motion. Another reader may never have reason to think of such connections. John Frow, an intertextualist, demonstrates that the method places the reader's interpretation above the text when he explains that even the selection of an intertext (required at the outset for a careful intertextual reading) is in itself "an act of interpretation".[43] Since the actual procedure varies substantially from practitioner to practitioner, no decisive methodology will be offered here. It is the philosophy behind intertextual reading and the general approach that is important for us, not a specific procedure.

This book practices "matrixing" by looking at texts interconnected by Luke and interpreting them in the light of each other. The whim of the reader, the problem mentioned above, is limited in our case because the interconnections are determined by Luke, not the reader.

Importantly, both the philosophy and general methodology of intertextuality are not actually crippled by the concept of author for the newer text, despite protests from certain theorists. Intertextualists who maintain the concept are not hard to find.

Although "...proponents of intertextuality focus on texts as networks pointing to other texts, not to the intentions of the author,"[44] we may justifiably speak of Luke as an author who has performed certain composi-

---

39 Vorster, "Intertextuality," 21–22.
40 Voelz, "Multiple Signs," 30–32.
41 Jacob Neusner chooses to identify intertexts among Jewish literature using similarity between such signs as community, scripture, logic and rhetoric, topic and proposition; *Canon and Connection: Intertextuality in Judaism* (London: University Press of America, 1987).
42 Jean Delorme, "Intertextualities About Mark," in Sipke Draisma (ed.), *Intertextuality in Biblical Writings: Essays in Honor of Bas van Iersel* (Kampen: Uitgeversmaatschappij J.H. Kok, 1989) 35–42.
43 John Frow, "Intertextuality and Ontology," in Judith Still and Michael Worton, *Intertextuality: Theories and Practices* (Manchester: Manchester University Press, 1990) 45–55.
44 Vorster, "Intertextuality," 22.

tional actions for his various reasons. However, intertextuality is a diverse theory[45] that logically can incorporate the author concept. Accordingly, our approach to Luke is an "intertextual study" guided by authorial intent. It is not limited by the non-importance of the author and it bears legitimate concern about how final form came to be. The discussion encompasses the process of composition. Our approach to intertextuality in the Gospel highlights *Luke's* reading and use of pericopes, his probable intentions, not merely the final form of the text. It seeks *probable* interpretations for what Luke *the author* has done. It demonstrates that authorial intent may be discerned. So in effect our approach is a composite of author-, text-, and reader-based theories that avoids some of the inherent limitations of each:[46] author-based because Luke's authorial intent is sought; text-based because frequently the final form of the Gospel is examined in its own right without any reference to the author; and reader-based because Luke the Evangelist is treated as a reader of the texts he incorporates. This type of reader-base is somewhat atypical since the common intertextual perspective is not employed, that meaning only occurs in the reading process. Rather, the meaning that Luke as reader found in his units of tradition is our concern, not what the wording means to us apart from an awareness of the author and his life-situation. It may be suggested that the study of interrelationships between passages within a single text, such as Luke, is closer to the discipline of *intra*textuality (within the text). This theory however "concerns the life (and life-giving force) of a **[finished]** text". The text acts as a "medium of interpretation," "a relatively autonomous structure that makes sense of the reader, and which provides that reader with the 'grammar' to

---

45 Vorster also makes the observation that intertextuality is a diverse theory, in "Intertextuality," 18.
46 Some of the limitations of the strict theory of intertextuality in biblical interpretation are evident in the following essays where the interpretation produces nothing new, exhibits primarily the imagination of the reader rather than communication from God, or seems hardly worth mentioning: Vorster, "Intertextuality," 22–6; Delorme, "Intertextualities," 35–42; Huub Welzen, "Loosing and Binding," in Sipke Draisma (ed.), *Intertextuality in Biblical Writings: Essays in Honor of Bas van Iersel* (Kampen: Uitgeversmaatschappij J.H. Kok, 1989) 175–87; and W.J.C. Weren, "Psalm 2 in Luke-Acts: an Intertextual Study," in Sipke Draisma (ed.), *Intertextuality in Biblical Writings: Essays in Honor of Bas van Iersel* (Kampen: Uitgeversmaatschappij J.H. Kok, 1989) 189–203.

Communication from God through the Bible is logically incompatible with intertextuality that denies the importance of authorial intent. Maintaining that meaning is only resident in the text or experienced in the process of reading, and not related at all to the author, conflicts with the concept of biblical inspiration where ultimate (divine) truth is believed to be contained in the text. David L. Miller for example embraces this conflict with inspiration because of his adherence to this form of intertextuality ("The Question of the Book," *Semeia* 40 [1987] 57–58).

Appendix C

interpret all subsequent texts".⁴⁷ Our goal of discerning how Luke read passages and linked them through literary techniques is too enmeshed with interest in his compositional methods to be *intra*textual. Furthermore, the essential concern of *intra*textuality for how the text *impacts* life today, and "makes sense of the reader," plays a minor part in our approach.

---

47 For the full wording of this representative definition of intratextuality see Danna Nolan Fewell (ed.), *Reading Between Texts: Intertextuality and the Hebrew Bible* (Louisville, Kentucky: Westminster/John Knox, 1992) 23.

Bibliography

Achtemeier, Paul J., "The Lukan Perspective on the Miracles of Jesus: A Preliminary Sketch," in Charles H. Talbert (ed.), *Perspectives on Luke-Acts*, (Edinburgh: T. & T. Clark, 1978) 153–167.
Aland, Kurt (ed.), *Synopsis of the Four Gospels* (New York: UBS, 1983⁶).
Alexander, Loveday, *The Preface to Luke's Gospel: Literary Convention and Social Context in Luke 1:1–4 and Acts 1:1* (Cambridge: Cambridge University Press, 1993).
Alexander, L.C.A., "Luke's Preface in the Context of Greek Preface Writing," *Novum Testamentum* 28 (1986) 28–74.
Alter, Robert, *The Art of Biblical Narrative* (New York: Basic Books, 1981).
– *The Art of Biblical Poetry* (New York: Basic Books, 1985).
– and Frank Kermode (eds.), *The Literary Guide to the Bible* (Cambridge, Mass.: Harvard University Press, 1987).
– *The World of Biblical Literature* (London: SPCK, 1992).
Anderson, Janice Capel, *Matthew's Narrative Web: Over, and Over, and Over Again*, JSNT Supplement Series 91 (Sheffield: Sheffield Academic Press, 1994).
Archer, Gleason L., Jr., *Daniel*, Expositor's Bible Commentary 7 (Grand Rapids: Zondervan, 1985).
Aune, David E., *The New Testament in Its Literary Environment*, Library of Early Christianity (Philadelphia: Westminster Press, 1987).
– *Greco-Roman Literature and the New Testament* (Atlanta: Scholars Press, 1988).
Baarlink, Heinrich, "Die zyklische Struktur von Lukas 9.43b–19.28," *New Testament Studies* 38 (1992) 481–506.
Bailey, Kenneth E., *Poet and Peasant* and *Through Peasants Eyes: A Literary Approach to the Parables of Luke,* Combined Edition (Grand Rapids: Eerdmans, 1976 and 1980 respectively).
Bar-Efrat, Shimon, "Some Observations on the Analysis of Structure in Biblical Narrative," *Vetus Testamentum* 30 (1980) 154–173.
– *Narrative Art in the Bible*, JSOTSS 70 (Sheffield: Almond Press, 1989).
Barthes, Roland, "The Struggle with the Angel; Textual Analysis of Genesis 32:23–33," in R. Barthes, F. Bovon, F.-J. Leenhardt, R. Martin-Archard, and J. Starobinski, *Structural Analysis and Biblical Exegesis: Interpretational Essays* (Pittsburgh, Pickwick Press, 1974) 21–33.
– *Image, Music, Text*, Stephen Heath (comp. and ed.), (New York: Hill and Wang, 1977).
Barthes, R., F. Bovon, F.-J. Leenhardt, R. Martin-Archard, and J. Starobinski, *Structural Analysis and Biblical Exegesis: Interpretational Essays* (Pittsburgh, Pickwick Press, 1974).
Bauckham, Richard, *The Climax of Prophecy: Studies in the Book of Revelation* (Edinburgh: T. & T. Clark, 1993).
Bauer, B., *Die Apostelgeschichte des Paulinismus und des Judentums innerhalb der christlichen Kirche* (Berlin: Hempel, 1850).
Bauer, David R., *The Structure of Matthew's Gospel: A Study in Literary Design*, JSNT Supplement Series 31 (Sheffield: Sheffield Academic Press, 1988).
Bauer, Walter, William. F. Arndt, F. Wilbur Gingrich, and Frederick W. Danker, *A*

Bibliography

Greek-English Lexicon of the New Testament and Other Early Christial Literature, rev. and tr. from Walter Bauer's 5th ed. of *Griechisch-Deutsches Wörterbuch* (Chicago: University of Chicago Press, 1979).

Baur, F.C., *Paulus, der Apostel Jesu Christi: Sein Leben und Wirken, seine Briefe und seine Lehre: Ein Beitrag zu einer kritischen Geschichte des Urchristentums*, (Leipzig: Fues, 1866).

– *Paul: the Apostle of Jesus Christ* (London: Williams & Norgate, 1875).

Bayer, H.F., "Predictions of Jesus' Passion and Resurrection," in Joel B. Green, Scot McKnight, and I. Howard Marshall (eds.), *Dictionary of Jesus and the Gospels* (Leicester: IVP, 1992) 630–633.

Beasley-Murray, George R., *The Book of Revelation*, New Century Bible Commentary (London: Marshall, Morgan & Scott, 1974).

– *John*, Word Biblical Commentary 36 (Waco, Texas: Word Books, 1987).

Beck, Brian E., *Christian Character in the Gospel of Luke* (London: Epworth, 1989).

Best, Ernest, *Mark: The Gospel as Story* (Edinburgh: T. & T. Clark, 1983).

Betz O. (*et. al.*), *Abraham unser Vater, für O. Michel* (Leiden: E.J. Brill, 1963).

Bietenhard, H., "Hell, Abyss, Hades, Gehenna, Lower Regions (ἄβυσσος)," in Colin Brown (ed.), vol. 2 of *New International Dictionary of New Testament Theology* (Grand Rapids: Zondervan, 1971) 205–210.

Binder, H., "Missdeutbar oder eindeutig? – Gedanken zu einem Gleichnis Jesu," *Theologische Zeitschrift* 51 (1995) 41–49.

Bindemann, Walther, "Ungerechte als Vorbilder: Gottesreich und Gottesrecht in den Gleichnissen vom 'ungerechten Verwalter' und 'ungerechten Richter'," *Theologische Literaturzeitung* 120 (11, 1995) 955–970.

Blass, F., and A. Debrunner, *A Greek Grammar of the New Testament and Other Early Christian Literature*, trans. and revised by Robert W. Funk (Chicago: University of Chicago Press, 1961).

Blomberg, Craig L., "Midrash, Chiasmus, and the Outline of Luke's Central Section," in R.T. France and David Wenham (eds.), vol. 3 of *Gospel Perspectives, Studies in Midrash and Historiography* (Sheffield: JSOT Press, 1983) 217–261.

– "When is a Parallel Really a Parallel? A Test Case: The Lucan Parables," *Westminster Theological Journal* 46 (1984) 78–103.

Bock, Darrell L., *Proclamation from Prophecy and Pattern: Lucan Old Testament Christology*, JSNT Supplement Series 12 (Sheffield: Sheffield Academic Press, 1987).

– *Luke: Volume 1: 1:1–9:50*, Baker Exegetical Commentary on the New Testament 3a (Grand Rapids: Baker, 1994).

– *Luke: Volume 2: 9:51–24:53*, Baker Exegetical Commentary on the New Testament 3b (Grand Rapids: Baker, 1996).

Bovon, François, *Luke the Theologian: Thirty-three Years of Research (1950–1983)*, Ken McKinney (tr.) (Allison Park, Pennsylvania: Pickwick Publications, 1987).

– *Das Evangelium nach Lukas (Lk 1,1–9,50)*, EKK (Zürich: Benziger Verlag, 1989).

– "Studies in Luke-Acts: Retrospect and Prospect," *Harvard Theological Review* 85 (1992) 175–196.

Brawley, Robert L., *Luke-Acts and the Jews: Conflict, Apology and Conciliation*, SBLMS (Atlanta: Scholars Press, 1987).

Brodie, Thomas L., "A New Temple and a New Law," *Journal for the Study of the New Testament* 5 (1979) 21–45.

– "Luke the Literary Interpreter: Luke-Acts as a Systematic Rewriting and Updating of the Elijah-Elisha Narrative in 1 and 2 Kings," Ph.D. diss. (Rome: Pontifical Univer-

sity of St. Thomas Aquinas, 1981).
- "Greco-Roman Imitation of Texts as a Partial Guide to Luke's Use of Sources," in Charles H. Talbert (ed.), *Luke-Acts, New Perspectives From the Society of Biblical Literature Seminar* (New York: Crossroad, 1984) 17–46.
- "Towards Unravelling Luke's Use of the Old Testament: Luke 7.11–17 as an *Imitatio* of 1 Kings 17.17–24," *New Testament Studies* 32 (1986) 247–267.
- *Luke the Literary Interpreter: Luke-Acts as a Systematic Rewriting and Updating of the Elijah-Elisha Narrative in 1 and 2 Kings* (Rome: Pontifical University of St. Thomas Aquinas, 1988).
- "The Departure for Jerusalem (Luke 9,51–56) as a Rhetorical Imitation of Elijah's Departure for the Jordan (2 Kings 1,1–2,6)," *Biblica* 70 (1989) 96–109.
- "Luke 9:57–62: A Systematic Adaptation of the Divine Challenge to Elijah (1 Kings 19)," in David J. Lull (ed.), *SBL Seminar Papers* 28 (Atlanta: Scholars Press, 1989) 237–245.
- "Not Q but Elijah: The Saving of the Centurion's Servant (Luke 7:1–10) as an Internalization of the Saving of the Widow and Her Child (1 Kings 17:1–16)," *Irish Biblical Studies* 14 (1992) 54–71.
- *The Gospel According to John: A Literary and Theological Commentary*, (Oxford: Oxford University Press, 1993).
- "Re-Opening the Quest for Proto-Luke: The Systematic Use of Judges 6–12 in Luke 16:1–18:8," *Journal of Higher Criticism* 2 (1995) 68–101.

Brown, E.K., *Rhythm in the Novel* (Lincoln, Nebraska: University of Nebraska Press, 1978).

Brown, Raymond E., "Luke's Method in the Annunciation Narrative of Chapter One," in Charles H. Talbert (ed.), *Perspectives on Luke-Acts* (Edinburgh: T. & T. Clark, 1978) 126–138.
- *The Birth of the Messiah: A Commentary on the Infancy Narratives in the Gospels of Matthew and Luke* (London: Geoffrey Chapman, 1993).

Brown, Schuyler, "The Role of the Prologues in Determining the Purpose of Luke-Acts," in Charles H. Talbert (ed.), *Perspectives on Luke-Acts* (Edinburgh: T. & T. Clark, 1978) 99–111.

Bruce, F.F., *The Acts of the Apostles: The Greek Text with Introduction and Commentary* (Leicester: Apollos, 1990).

Bultmann, Rudolf, *The History of the Synoptic Tradition*, John Marsh (tr.), (Oxford: Basil Blackwell, 1968).

Carrol, John T., *Response to the End of History: Eschatology and Situation in Luke-Acts* (Atlanta, Georgia: Scholars Press, 1988).

Carson, D.A., *Matthew*, Expositor's Bible Commentary 8 (Grand Rapids: Zondervan, 1984).
- *The Gospel According to John* (Leicester: Inter-Varsity Press, 1991).

Carter, John M. (ed.), *Suetonius Divus Augustus* (Bristol: Bristol Classical Press, 1982).

Carter, Warren, "Kernels and Narrative Blocks: The Structure of Matthew's Gospel," *Catholic Biblical Quarterly* 54 (1992) 463–481.

Clark, Andrew C., *Parallel Lives: The Relation of Paul to the Apostles in the Lukan Perspective*, Paternoster Biblical and Theological Monographs (Carlisle, Cumbria, UK: Paternoster, 2001).

Clines, David J.A., *Job 1–20*, Word Biblical Commentary 17 (Dallas: Word Books, 1989).

Coats, George W., *Genesis: With an Introduction to Narrative Literature*, vol. 1 of *The Forms of the Old Testament Literature* (Grand Rapids: Eerdmans, 1983).

Coggins, R.J., and J.L. Houlden (eds.), *A Dictionary of Biblical Interpretation* (London: SCM Press, 1990).
Cohn, Robert L., "The Literary Logic of 1 Kings 17–19," *Journal of Biblical Literature* 101 (1982) 333–350.
Coleridge, Mark, *The Birth of the Lukan Narrative: Narrative as Christology in Luke 1–2* (Sheffield: JSOT Press, 1993).
Colson, F.H. (tr.), *Philo*, LCL 6 (London: William Heinmann Ltd, 1935).
Conzelmann, Hans, *The Theology of St. Luke*, Geoffrey Buswell (tr.), (London: Faber and Faber, 1961).
Crehan, J.H., "The Purpose of Luke in Acts," in F.L. Cross (ed.), *Studia Evangelica, II*, Texte und Untersuchungen 87 (Berlin: Akademie-Verlag, 1964) 354–368.
Cross, F.L. (ed.), *Studia Evangelica, II*. Texte und Untersuchungen, 87 (Berlin: Akademie-Verlag, 1964).
Dalton, J.F., *Roman Literary Theory and Criticism: A Study in Tendencies* (London: Longmans, Green and Co., 1931).
Danker, Frederick W., *Jesus and the New Age: According to Luke. A Commentary on the Third Gospel* (St. Louis: Layton, 1972).
Davies, J.G., "The Prefigurement of the Ascension in the Third Gospel," *Journal of Theological Studies* n.s., 6 (1955) 229–233.
Davies, J.H., "The Purpose of the Central Section of St. Luke's Gospel," in F.L. Cross (ed.), *Studia Evangelica, II*, Texte und Untersuchungen 87 (Berlin: Akademie-Verlag, 1964) 164–169.
Davies, W.D., and Dale C. Allison, Jr., *A Critical and Exegetical Commentary on the Gospel According to Saint Matthew*, ICC 1 (Edinburgh: T. & T. Clark, 1988).
Delling, G., "λαμβάνω (ἀνάλημψις)," in Gerhard Kittel (ed.), Geoffrey W. Bromily (tr.), vol. iv of *Theological Dictionary of the New Testament* (Grand Rapids: Eerdmans, 1964) 7–9.
Delorme, Jean, "Intertextualities About Mark," in Sipke Draisma (ed.), *Intertextuality in Biblical Writings: Essays in Honor of Bas van Iersel* (Kampen: Uitgeversmaatschappij J.H. Kok, 1989) 35–42.
Denaux, Adelbert, "The Delineation of the Lukan Travel Narrative Within the Overall Structure of the Gospel of Luke," in Camille Focant (ed.), *The Synoptic Gospels: Source Criticism and the New Literary Criticism*, Bibliotheca Ephemeridum Theologicarum Lovaniensium cx (Leuven: Leuven University Press, 1993) 357–392.
Dewey, Joanna, "Mark as Interwoven Tapestry: Forecasts and Echoes for a Listening Audience," *Catholic Biblical Quarterly* 53 (1991) 221–236.
Didier, M. (ed.), *L'Évangile selon Matthieu: Rédaction et théologie*, Bibliotheca Ephemeridum Theologicarum Lovaniensium XXIX (Gembloux: J. Ducelot, 1972).
Dillon, Richard J., "Previewing Luke's Project from His Prologue (Luke 1:1–4)," *Catholic Biblical Quarterly* 43 (1981) 205–223.
Dinkler, E., *Zeit und Geschichte: Für Rudolf Bultmann* (Tübingen: J.C.B. Mohr, 1964).
Dodd, C.H., *The Apostolic Preaching and Its Developments* (London: Hodder and Stoughton, 1963).
Draisma, Sipke (ed.), *Intertextuality in Biblical Writings: Essays in Honor of Bas van Iersel* (Kampen: Uitgeversmaatschappij J.H. Kok, 1989).
Duckworth, George E., *Structural Patterns and Proportions in Vergil's Aeneid, A Study in Mathematical Composition* 9Ann Arbor, Michigan: University of Michigan Press, 1962).
Ellis, E. Earle, *The Gospel of Luke*, New Century Bible Commentary (London: Marshall, Morgan & Scott, 1974).

- and E. Grässer (eds.), *Jesus und Paulus: Festschrift für W.G. Kümmel* (Göttingen: Vandenhoeck & Ruprecht, 1975).
Evans, C.F., "The Central Section of St. Luke's Gospel," in D.E. Nineham (ed.), *Studies in the Gospels: Essays in Memory of R.H. Lightfoot* (Oxford: Blackwell, 1955) 37–53).
- *Saint Luke*, TPI New Testament Commentaries (London: SCM, 1990).
Evans, Craig A., "'He Set His Face': A Note on Luke 9,51," *Biblica* 63 (1982) 545–548.
- "Luke's Use of the Elijah/Elisha Narratives and the Ethics of Election," *Journal of Biblical Literature* 106 (1987) 75–83.
- and James A. Sanders, *Luke and Scripture: The Function of Sacred Tradition in Luke-Acts* (Minneapolis: Fortress Press, 1993).
William R. Farmer, *The Synoptic Problem: A Critical Analysis* (London: Collier-Macmillan Limited, 1964).
- "Modern Developments of Griesbach's Hypothesis," *New Testament Studies* 23 (1976–1977) 283–289.
Felperin, Howard, *Beyond Deconstruction: The Uses and Abuses of Literary Theory* (Oxford: Clarendon, 1985).
Feuillet, A., "Le récit Lucanien de la Tentation (Lc. 4:1–13)," *Biblica* 40 (1959) 617–631.
Fewell, Danna Nolan (ed.), *Reading Between Texts: Intertextuality and the Hebrew Bible* (Louisville, Kentucky: Westminster/John Knox, 1992).
Fitzmyer, Joseph A., *To Advance the Gospel: New Testament Studies* (New York: Crossroad Publishing Company, 1981).
- *The Gospel According to Luke I–IX*, Anchor Bible 28 (Garden City, New York: Doubleday, 1981).
- *The Gospel According to Luke X–XXIV*, Anchor Bible 28A (Garden City, N.Y.: Doubleday, 1985).
Flender, Helmut, *St. Luke: Theologian of Redemptive History* (Philadelphia: Fortress, 1967).
Focant, Camille (ed.), *The Synoptic Gospels: Source Criticism and the New Literary Criticism*, Bibliotheca Ephemeridum Theologicarum Lovaniensium cx (Leuven: Leuven University Press, 1993).
Foucault, Michel, *Language, Counter-Memory, Practice: Selected Essays and Interviews*, Donald F. Bouchard (ed.), Donald F. Bouchard and Sherry Simon (trs.), (Ithaca, N.Y.: Cornell University Press, 1977).
Fowler, H.W., and F.G. Fowler (trs.), *The Works of Lucian of Samosata*, vol. 2 (Oxford: Clarendon Press, 1905).
France, R.T., and David Wenham (eds.), *Gospel Perspectives, Studies in Midrash and Historiography*, vol. 3 (Sheffield: JSOT Press, 1983).
Franklin, Eric, *Christ the Lord: A Study in the Purpose and Theology of Luke-Acts* (Philadelphia: Westminster, 1975).
Frow, John, "Intertextuality and Ontology," in Judith Still and Michael Worton (eds.), *Intertextuality: Theories and Practices* (Manchester: Manchester University Press, 1990) 45–55.
Galland, Corina, "An Introduction to the Method of A.J. Greimas," in Alfred M. Johnson, Jr. (ed. and tr.), *The New Testament and Structuralism* (Pittsburgh: Pickwick Press, 1976) ch. 1.
Geldenhuys, Norval, *Commentary on the Gospel of Luke* (London: Marshall, Morgan & Scott, 1950).
George, Augustin, *Études sur l'oeuvre de Luc*, Sources Bibliques (Paris: Gabalda,

1978).
Gnilka, Joachim, *Das Matthäusevangelium: I. Teil: Kommentar zu Kap. 1,1–13,58*, Herders Theologischer Kommentar zum Neuen Testament (Freiburg: Herder, 1988).
Gooding, David, *True to the Faith: A Fresh Approach to the Acts of the Apostles* (London: Hodder & Stoughton, 1990).
Goulder, M.D., "The Chiastic Structure of the Lucan Journey," in F.L. Cross (ed.) *Studia Evangelica, II*. Texte und Untersuchungen 87 (Berlin: Akademie-Verlag, 1964) 195–202.
– *Type and History in Acts* (London: SPCK, 1964).
– *The Evangelists' Calendar: A Lectionary Explanation of the Development of Scripture* (London: SPCK, 1978).
– *Luke: A New Paradigm*, 2 vols. (Sheffield: Sheffield Academic Press, 1989).
Grant, Robert M., *A Historical Introduction to the New Testament* (London: Collins, 1963).
Green, Joel B., Scot McKnight, and I. Howard Marshall (eds.), *Dictionary of Jesus and the Gospels* (Leicester: IVP, 1992).
Green, Joel B., *The Theology of the Gospel of Luke*, New Testament Theology (Cambridge: Cambridge University Press, 1995)
– *The Gospel of Luke*, New International Commentary on the New Testament (Grand Rapids: Eerdmans, 1997)
Green, Thomas M., *The Light in Troy: Imitation and Discovery in Renaissance Poetry* (London: Yale University Press, 1982).
Grube, G.M.A., *The Greek and Roman Critics* (London: Methuen & Co., 1965).
Grundmann, Walter, *Das Evangelium nach Lukas*, Theologischer Handkommentar zum Neuen Testament (Berlin: Evangelische Verlagsanstalt, 1984).
Gundry, R.H., *Matthew: A Commentary on His Literary and Theological Art* (Grand Rapids: Eerdmans, 1982).
Guthrie, Donald, *New Testament Introduction* (Downers Grove: Inter Varsity Press, 1970³).
Guelich, Robert A., *Mark 1–8:26*, Word Biblical Commentary 34a (Dallas: Word Books, 1989).
Harris, Murray J., *Raised Immortal: Resurrection and Immortality in the New Testament* (Grand Rapids: Eerdmans, 1983).
– "'The Dead are Restored to Life': Miracles of Revivification in the Gospels," in David Wenham and Craig Blomberg (eds.), vol. 6 of *Gospel Perspectives, The Miracles of Jesus* (Sheffield: JSOT Press, 1986).
Hartley, John E., *The Book of Job* (Grand Rapids: Eerdmans, 1988).
Hastings, Adrian, *Prophet and Witness in Jerusalem: A Study of the Teaching of Saint Luke* (London: Longmans, Green & Co., 1958).
Hays, Richard B., *Echoes of Scripture in the Letters of Paul* (London: Yale University Press, 1989).
Heil, John Paul, "The Progressive Narrative Pattern of Mark 14,53–16,8," *Biblica* 73 (1992) 331–358.
Hirsch, E.D., Jr., "In Defense of the Author," in David Newton-de Molina (comp.), *On Literary Intention* (Edinburgh: Edinburgh University Press, 1976) 87–103.
– "Objective Interpretation," in David Newton-de Molina (comp.), *On Literary Intention* (Edinburgh: Edinburgh University Press, 1976) 26–54.
Hoeren, Thomas, "Das Gleichnis vom ungerechten Verwalter (Lukas 16.1–8a) – zugleich ein Beitrag zur Geschichte der Restschuldbefreiung," *New Testament Studies* 41 (4, 1995) 620–629.

Holtz, T., *Untersuchung über die altestamentlichen Zitate bei Lukas* (Berlin: Akademie Verlag, 1968).
Humphreys, W. Lee, "The Tragedy of King Saul: A Study of the Structure of 1 Samuel 9–31," *Journal for the Study of the Old Testament* 6 (1978) 18–27.
Iersel, Bas van, *Reading Mark*, W.H. Bisscheroux (tr.), (Collegeville, Minnesota: Liturgical Press, 1988).
Immerwahr, Henry R., *Form and Thought in Herodotus* (Cleveland, Ohio: Western Reserve University Press, 1966).
Jeremias, Joachim, "ἄβυσσος," in Geoffrey W. Bromily (ed. and tr.), vol. 1 of *Theological Dictionary of the New Testament* (Grand Rapids: Eerdmans, 1964) 9–10.
– *Die Sprache des Lukasevangeliums: Redaktion und Tradition im Nicht-Markusstoff des dritten Evangeliums*, Kritisch-exegetischer Kommentar über das Neue Testament (Göttingen: Vandenhoeck & Ruprecht, 1980).
Johnson, Alfred M., Jr. (ed. and tr.), *The New Testament and Structuralism* (Pittsburgh: Pickwick Press, 1976).
Johnson, Luke Timothy, *The Literary Function of Possessions in Luke-Acts*, SBL Dissertation Series 39, Howard C. Kee and Douglas A. Knight (eds.), (Atlanta: Scholars Press, 1977).
– *The Gospel of Luke*, Sacra Pagina 3 (Collegeville, Minnesota: Liturgical Press, 1991).
Kamlah, Ehrhard, "Die Parabel vom ungerechten Verwalter (Luk. 16, 1ff.) im Rahmen der Knechtsgleichnisse," in O. Betz (et al.), *Abraham unser Vater*, für O. Michel (Leiden: E.J. Brill, 1963) 276–294.
Karris, Robert J., *Luke: Artist and Theologian: Luke's Passion Account as Literature* (New York: Paulist Press, 1985).
Kennedy, George A., *The Art of Persuasion in Greece* (Princeton: Princeton University, 1963).
– *New Testament Interpretation Through Rhetorical Criticism* (London: University of North Carolina Press, 1984).
Kilgallen, John J., "The Purpose of Luke's Divorce Text," *Biblica* 76 (1995) 229–238.
Kimball, Charles A., *Jesus' Exposition of the Old Testament in Luke's Gospel*, JSNT Supplement Series 94 (Sheffield: JSOT Press, 1984).
Klein, Günter, "Lukas 1, 1–4 als theologisches Programm," in E. Dinkler (ed.), *Zeit und Geschichte: Für Rudolf Bultmann* (Tübingen: J.C.B. Mohr, 1964) 193–216.
Klostermann, E., *Das Lukasevangelium*, Handbuch zum Neuen Testament 5 (Tübingen: Mohr, 1929, reprinted 1975).
Kristeva, Julia, *Desire in Language: A Semiotic Approach to Literature and Art*, Leon S. Roudiez (ed.), Thomas Gorda, Alice Jardine, and Leon S. Roudiez (trs.), (Columbia, N.Y.: Columbia University Press, 1980).
Krodel, Gerhard A., *Acts*, Augsburg Commentary on the New Testament (Minneapolis: Augsburg Publishing House, 1986).
Kümmel, Werner Georg, *Introduction to the New Testament*, Howard Clark Kee (tr.), (Nashville: Abingdon, 1975).
Kurz, William S., *Reading Luke-Acts* (Louisville, Kentucky: Westminster/John Knox Press, 1993).
Kurzinger, J., "Lk 1,3:…ἀκριβῶς καθεξῆς σοι γράψαι," *Biblische Zeitschrift* 18 (1974) 249–255.
Lagrange, M.-J., *Évangile selon Saint Luc*, Études Bibliques (Paris: Gabalda, 1948[7]).
Lane, William L., *The Gospel According to Mark*, NIC (Grand Rapids: Eerdmans, 1974).

Laurentin, Reni, *Structure et théologie de Luc I–II*, E. Bib. (Paris: Gabalda, 1964).
Lenski, R.C.H., *The Interpretation of Luke* (Mineapolis, Minnesota: Augsburg Publishing House, 1946).
Liefeld, Walter W., "Theological Motifs in the Transfiguration Narrative," in Richard N. Longenecker and Merrill C. Tenney (eds.), *New Dimensions in New Testament Studies* (Grand Rapids: Zondervan, 1974).
– *Luke*, Expositor's Bible Commentary 8 (Grand Rapids: Zondervan, 1984).
Lohmeyer, E., *Das Evangelium des Markus*, KEK (Göttingen: Vandenhoeck & Ruprecht, 1953).
– *Das Evangelium des Matthäus*, Kritisch-exegetischer Kommentar über das Neue Testament (Göttingen: Vanderhoeck & Ruprecht, 1962).
Long, Burke O., *I Kings: With an Introduction to Historical Literature*, vol. 9 of *The Forms of the Old Testament Literature* (Grand Rapids: Eerdmans, 1984).
Long, V. Philips, *The Art of Biblical History*, vol. 5 of *Foundations of Contemporary Interpretation* (Grand Rapids: Zondervan, 1994).
Longenecker, Richard N., *The Acts of the Apostles*, Expositor's Bible Commentary 9 (Grand Rapids: Zondervan, 1981).
Luce, T.J., *Livy: The Composition of His History* (Princeton, New Jersey: Princeton University Press, 1977).
Lull, David J. (ed.), *SBL Seminar Papers* 28 (Atlanta: Scholars Press, 1989).
Lund, Nils W., *Chiasmus in the New Testament: A Study in the Form and Function of Chiastic Structures* (Peabody, Massachusetts: Hendrickson, 1942, renewed 1970 by Mrs. N.W. Lund).
Lunt, R.G., "Towards an Interpretation of the Parable of the Unjust Steward (Luke xvi. 1–18)," *Expository Times* 66 (1955) 335–337.
– "Expounding the Parables: III. The Parable of the Unjust Steward (Luke 16 $^{1-15}$)," *Expository Times* 77 (1965–66) 132–136.
MacKail, J.W., *The Aeneid* (Oxford: Clarendon Press, 1930).
Muhlack, G., *Die Parallelen von Lukas-Evangelium und Apostelgeschichte*, Teologie und Wirklichkeit 8 (Frankfurt: Lang, 1979).
Mann, C.S., "Unjust Steward or Prudent Manager?," *Expository Times* 102 (1991) 234–235.
Manson, William, *The Gospel of Luke* (London: Hodder and Stoughton, 1955).
Marshall, I. Howard, *Luke: Historian and Theologian* (Grand Rapids: Zondervan, 1970).
– *The Epistles of John* (Grand Rapids: Eerdmans, 1978).
– *The Gospel of Luke: A Commentary on the Greek Text*, The New International Greek Testament Commentary (Exeter: Paternoster Press, 1978).
– *The Acts of the Apostles: An Introduction and Commentary*, Tyndale New Testament Commentaries (Leicester: Inter-Varsity Press, 1980).
Matera, Frank J., "Jesus' Journey to Jerusalem (Luke 9.51–19.46): A Conflict with Israel," *Journal for the Study of the New Testament* 51 (1993) 57–77.
Mattil, A.J., Jr., "The Jesus-Paul Parallels and the Purpose of Luke-Acts: H.H. Evans Reconsidered," *Novum Testamentum* 17 (1975) 15–46.
McNeile, Alan Hugh, *The Gospel According to St. Matthew* (Grand Rapids: Baker, 1980 reprint of 1915 edition).
Metzger, Bruce M., *A Textual Commentary on the Greek New Testament* (London: United Bible Societies, 1975).
Meynet, Roland, "'Celui à qui est remis peu, aime un peu...' (Lc 7,36–50)," *Gregorianum* 75 (2, 1994) 267–280.
Miesner, Donald R., "The Missionary Journeys Narrative: Patterns and Implications," in

Charles H. Talbert (ed.), *Perspectives on Luke-Acts* (Edinburgh: T. & T. Clark, 1978) 199–214.
Miller, David L., "The Question of the Book," *Semeia* 40 (1987) 53–64.
Minear, Paul S., "Luke's Use of the Birth Stories," in L.E. Keck and J.L. Martyn (eds.), *Studies in Luke-Acts* (Nashville: Abingdon, 1966) 111–130.
– "Jesus' Audiences, According to Luke," *Novum Testamentum* 16 (1974) 81–109.
Moessner, David P., *Lord of the Banquet: The Literary and Theological Significance of the Lukan Travel Narrative* (Minneapolis: Fortress Press, 1989).
Moore, Stephen D., "Are the Gospels Unified Narratives?," in Kent Harold Richards (ed.), *SBL Seminar Papers* 26 (Atlanta: Scholars Press, 1987) 443–458.
Morgenthaler, R., *Die lukanische Geschichtsschreibung als Zeugnis: Gestalt und Gehalt der Kunst des Lukas*, ATANT 14, vol. 1 (Zurich: Zwingli, 1949).
Morris, Leon, *The Revelation of St. John*, Tyndale New Testament Commentaries (London: Tyndale Press, 1969).
– *The Gospel According to John*, New International Commentary on the New Testament (London: Marshall, Morgan & Scott, 1971).
– "The Gospels and Jewish Lectionaries," in R.T. France and David Wenham (eds.), vol 3 of *Gospel Perspectives, Studies in Midrash and Historiography* (Sheffield: JSOT Press, 1983) 129–156.
Muhlack, G., *Die Parallelen von Lukas-Evangelium und Apostelgeschichte*, Theologie und Wirklichkeit 8 (Frankfurt: Lang, 1979).
Mussner, Franz, "Καθεξῆς im Lukasprolog," in E.E. Ellis and E. Grässer (eds.), *Jesus und Paulus: Festschrift für W.G. Kümmel* (Göttingen: Vandenhoeck & Ruprecht, 1975) 253–255.
Navone, John, *Themes of St. Luke* (Rome: Gregorian University, 1970).
Neil, William, *The Acts of the Apostles*, New Century Bible Commentary (London: Marshall, Morgan & Scott, 1973).
Neirynck, F. (ed.), *L'Évangile de Luc, The Gospel of Luke* (Leuven: Leuven University Press, 1989).
Neusner, Jacob, *Cannon and Connection: Intertextuality in Judaism* (London: University Press of America, 1987).
Newton-de Molina, David (comp.), *On Literary Intention* (Edinburgh: Edinburgh University Press, 1976).
Neyrey, Jerome, *The Passion According to Luke: A Redaction Study of Luke's Soteriology* (New York: Paulist Press, 1985).
Nineham, D.E. (ed.), *Studies in the Gospels: Essays in Memory of R.H. Lightfoot* (Oxford: Blackwell, 1955).
Nola, Mike F., *Towards a Positive Understanding of the Structure of Luke-Acts*, Ph.D. diss. (Aberdeen, Scotland: University of Aberdeen, 1987).
Nolland, John, *Luke 1–9:20*, Word Biblical Commentary 35a (Dallas: Word Books, 1989).
– *Luke 9:21–18:34*, Word Biblical Commentary 35b (Dallas: Word Books, 1993).
– *Luke 18:35–24:53*, Word Biblical Commentary 35c (Dallas: Word Books, 1993).
Ó Fearghail, Fearghus, *The Introduction to Luke-Acts: A Study of the Role of Lk 1,1–4,44 in the Composition of Luke's Two-Volume Work* (Rome: Editrice Pontificio Instituto Biblico, 1991).
Ogg, George, "The Central Section of the Gospel According to St Luke," *New Testament Studies* 18 (1971) 39–53.
Olson, Gary A., *Philosophy, Rhetoric, Literary Criticism: (Inter)views* (Carbondale, Illinois: Southern Illinois University Press, 1994).

O'Toole, R.F., "Parallels Between Jesus and His Disciples in Luke-Acts: A Further Study," *Biblische Zeitschrift* 27 (1983) 195–212.
Parsons, Mikeal C., "Reading Talbert: New Perspectives on Luke-Acts," in Kent Harold Richards (ed.), *SBL Seminar Papers* 26 (Atlanta: Scholars Press, 1987) 687–717.
– and Richard I. Pervo, *Rethinking the Unity of Luke and Acts* (Minneapolis: Fortress Press, 1993).
Patte, Daniel, *What is Structural Exegesis?* (Philadelphia: Fortress Press, 1976).
– and Aline Patte, *Structural Exegesis: From Theory to Practice* (Philadelphia: Fortress Press, 1978).
Pesch, Rudolf, *Das Markusevangelium: I. Teil: Einleitung und Kommentar zu Kap. 1,1– 8,26*, Herders Theologischer Kommentar zum Neuen Testament (Freiburg: Herder, 1977).
– *Das Markusevangelium: II. Teil: Einleitung und Kommentar zu Kap. 8,27–16,20*, Herders Theologischer Kommentar zum Neuen Testament (Freiburg: Herder, 1977).
– *Die Apostelgeschichte: 1 Teiband Apg 1–12*, Evangelisch-Katholischer Kommentar zum Neuen Testament (Zürich: Benziger, 1986).
Plessis, I.I. du, "Once More: The Purpose of Luke's Prologue (Lk. 1:1–4)," *Novum Testamentum* 16 (1974) 259–271.
Plümacher, Eckhard, *Lukas als hellenistischer Schriftsteller* (Göttingen: Vandenhoeck & Ruprecht, 1972).
Plummer, Alfred, *A Critical and Exegetical Commentary on the Gospel According to St. Luke*, ICC (Edinburgh: T. & T. Clark, 1922[5]).
Praeder, Susan Marie, "Jesus-Paul, Peter-Paul, and Jesus-Peter Parallelisms in Luke-Acts: A History of Reader Response," in Kent Harold Richards (ed.), *SBL Seminar Papers* 23 (Chico: Scholars Press, 1984) 23–39.
Radl, Walter, *Paulus und Jesus im lukanischen Doppelwerk: Untersuchungen zu Parallelmotiven im Lukasevangelium und in der Apostelgeschichte*, Europäische Hochschulschriften (Bern: Herbert Lang, 1975).
Rawlings, Hunter, *The Structure of Thucydides' History* (Princeton: Princeton University Press, 1981).
Reicke, Bo, *The Gospel of Luke*, Ross Mackenzie (tr.), (London: SPCK, 1965).
Rengstorf, K.H., *Das Evangelium nach Lukas*, Das Neue Testament Deutsch 3 (Göttingen: Vandenhoeck und Ruprecht, 1962[9]).
Rhoads, David, and Donald Michie, *Mark as Story: An Introduction to the Narrative of a Gospel* (Philadelphia: Fortress Press, 1982).
Richards, Kent Harold (ed.), *SBL Seminar Papers* 23 (Chico: Scholars Press, 1984).
– (ed.), *SBL Seminar Papers* 26 (Atlanta: Scholars Press, 1987).
Rienecker, Fritz, *Das Evangelium des Lukas*, Wuppertaler Studienbibel (Wuppertal: R. Brockhaus, 1966).
Riley, Harold, *Preface to Luke* (Macon, Georgia: Mercer University Press, 1993).
Robertson, A.T., *A Grammar of the Greek New Testament in the Light of Historical Research* (New York: Hodder & Stoughton, 1923).
Robinson, Wm.C., Jr., "The Theological Context for Interpreting Luke's Travel Narrative (9 51 ff.)," *Journal of Biblical Literature* 79 (1960) 20–31.
Rolland, Philippe, "L'organisation du Livre des Actes et de l'ensemble de Luc," *Biblica* 65 (1984) 81–86.
Roloff, Jürgen, *Die Apostelgeschichte*, Das Neue Testament Deutsch 5 (Göttingen: Vandenhoeck und Ruprecht, 1981).
Rosenblatt, Louise M., *The Reader, the Text, the Poem: The Transactional Theory of the Literary Work* (Carbondale, Illinois: Southern Illinois University Press, 1978).

Russel, D.A., and M. Winterbottom, *Ancient Literary Criticism: The Principal Texts in New Translation* (Oxford: Clarendon Press, 1972).
Russel, D.A., *Plutarch* (London: Gerald Duckworth & Company, 1973).
Sabourin, Léopold, *L'Évangile de Luc: Introduction et Commentaire* (Rome: Gregorian University, 1985).
Schlatter, Adolf, *Der Evangelist Matthäus: Seine Sprache, sein Ziel, seine Selbständigkeit* (Stuttgart: Calwer, 1959).
– *Das Evangelium des Lukas: Aus seinen Quellen erklärt* (Stuttgart: Calver, 1960²).
Schneckenburger, Matthias, *Über den Zweck der Apostelgeschichte: Zugleich eine Ergänzung der neueren Commentare* (Bern: Christian Fischer, 1841).
Schneider, Gerhard, *Das Evangelium nach Lukas*, Ökumenischer Taschenbuchkommentar zum Neuen Testament 3/1, 2 (Würzburg: Echter, 1977).
– "Zur Bedeutung von καθεξῆς im lukanischen Doppelwerk," *Zeitschrift für die neutestamentliche Wissenschaft* 68 (1977) 128–131.
Schramm, Tim, *Der Markus-Stoff bei Lukas: eine literarkritische und redaktionsgeschichtliche Untersuchung* (Cambridge: Cambridge University Press, 1971).
Schulz, Siegfried, *Das Evangelium nach Johannes*, Das Neue Testament Deutsch 4 (Göttingen: Vandenhoeck & Ruprecht, 1983).
Schürmann, Heinz, *Das Lukasevangelium: Erster Teil: Kommentar zu Kap. 1,1–9, 50*, Herders Theologischer Kommentar zum Neuen Testament 3/1 (Freiburg/Basel/Vienna: Herder, 1969).
– *Das Lukasevangelium: Zweiter Teil: Erste Folge: Kommentar zu Kap. 9,51–11, 54*, Herders Theologischer Kommentar zum Neuen Testament, 3/1 (Freiburg/Basel/Vienna: Herder, 1994).
Schwegler, A., *Das nachapostolische Zeitalter in den Hauptmomenten seiner Entwicklung*, 2 vols. (Tübingen: Fues, 1846).
Scott, Bernard Brandon, "A Master's Praise: Luke 16, 1–8a," *Biblica* 64 (1983) 173–188.
Selden, Raman, *A Reader's Guide to Contemporary Literary Theory* (Lexington, Kentucky: University Press of Kentucky, 1985).
Sellin, Gerhard, "Komposition, Quellen und Funktion des lukanischen Reiseberichtes (Lk. IX 51–XIX 28)," *Novum Testamentum* 20 (1978) 100–135.
Shirock, Robert J., "The Growth of the Kingdom in Light of Israel's Rejection of Jesus: Structure and Theology in Luke 13:1–35," *Novum Testamentum* 35 (1993) 15–29.
Sibinga, J. Smit, "Eine literarische Technik im Mattäusevangelium," in M. Didier (ed.), *L'Évangile selon Matthieu: Rédaction et théologie*, Bibliotheca Ephemeridum Theologicarum Lovaniensium XXIX (Gembloux: J. Ducelot, 1972) 99–105.
Siede, B., "Take (λαμβάνω)," in Colin Brown (ed.), vol. 3 of *New International Dictionary of New Testament Theology* (Grand Rapids: Zondervan, 1971) 747–751.
Sisson, C.H. (tr.), *The Aeneid* (Manchester: Carcanet Press and Northumberland: Northumberland Arts Group, 1986).
Smalley, Stephen, *1, 2, 3 John*, Word Biblical Commentary 51 (Waco, Texas: Word Books, 1984).
Soards, Marion L., *The Passion According to Luke: The Special Material of Luke 22*, JSNT Supplement Series 14 (Sheffield: JSOT Press, 1987).
Stanton, G.N., *A Gospel for a New People: Studies in Matthew* (Edinburgh: T. & T. Clark, 1992).
Stein, Robert H., *The Synoptic Problem: An Introduction* (Grand Rapids: Baker Book House, 1987).
– *Luke*, New American Commentary 24 (Nashville: Broadman Press, 1992).

Sterling, Gregory E., *Historiography and Self-Definition: Josephus, Luke-Acts and Apostolic Historiography* (Leiden: E.J. Brill, 1992).
Still, Judith, and Michael Worton, *Intertextuality: Theories and Practices* (Manchester: Manchester University Press, 1990).
Stock, Augustine, *The Method and Message of Mark* (Wilmington, Delaware: Michael Glazier, 1989).
Streeter, Bernett Hillman, *The Four Gospels: A Study of Origins, Treating of Manuscript Tradition, Sources, Authorship, and Dates* (London: Macmillan, 1924).
Stuhlmacher, Paul (ed.), *The Gospel and the Gospels* (Grand Rapids: Eerdmans, 1991).
Sweet, J.P.M., *Revelation* (Philadelphia: Westminster Press, 1979).
Sylva, Dennis D., "Ierousalém and Hierosoluma in Luke-Acts," *Zeitschrift für die neutestamentliche Wissenschaft* 74 (1983) 207–221.
Talbert, Charles H., *Literary Patterns, Theological Themes and the Genre of Luke-Acts*, (Missoula: Scholars Press, 1974).
– *What is a Gospel? The Genre of the Canonical Gospels* (London: SPCK, 1978).
– (ed.), *Perspectives on Luke-Acts* (Edinburgh: T. & T. Clark, 1978).
– (ed.), *Luke-Acts, New Perspectives From the Society of Biblical Literature Seminar* (New York: Crossroad, 1984).
– *Reading Luke: A Literary and Theological Commentary on the Third Gospel* (New York: Crossroads, 1989).
Tannehill, Robert C., *The Narrative Unity of Luke-Acts: A Literary Interpretation. Vol. 1: The Gospel According to Luke* (Philadelphia: Fortress Press, 1986).
– *The Narrative Unity of Luke-Acts: A Literary Interpretation. Vol. 2: The Acts of the Apostles* (Philadelphia: Fortress Press, 1990).
Taylor, Vincent, *Behind the Third Gospel* (Oxford: Oxford University Press, 1926).
– *The Formation of the Gospel Tradition* (London: Macmillan, 1949).
– *The Gospels, A Short Introduction* (London: Epworth Press, 1960).
Thalmann, William G., *Conventions of Form and Thought in Early Greek Epic Poetry* (London: Johns Hopkins University Press, 1984).
Tiede, David L., *Prophecy and History in Luke-Acts* (Philadelphia: Fortress Press, 1980).
Turner, Nigel, *A Grammar of New Testament Greek, Vol. IV: Style* (Edinburgh: T. & T. Clark, 1976).
Tyson, Joseph B., "Source Criticism of the Gospel of Luke," in Charles H. Talbert (ed.), *Perspectives on Luke-Acts* (Edinburgh: T. & T. Clark, 1978) 24–39.
Unnik, W.C. van., "Éléments artistique dans l'Évangile de Luc," *Ephemerides theologicae lovanienses* 46 (1970) 401–412.
Vries, de, Simon J., *1 and 2 Chronicles*, vol. 11 of *The Forms of the Old Testament Literature* (Grand Rapids: Eerdmans, 1989).
Voelz, James W., "Multiple Signs and Double Texts: Elements of Intertextuality," in Sipke Draisma (ed.), *Intertextuality in Biblical Writings: Essays in Honor of Bas van Iersel* (Kampen: Uitgeversmaatschappij J.H. Kok, 1989) 27–34.
Völkel, Martin, "Exegetische Erwägungen zum Verständnis des Begriffs ΚΑΘΕΞΗΣ im lukanischen Prolog," *New Testament Studies* 20 (1974) 289–299.
Vorster, Willem S., "Intertextuality and Redaktionsgeschichte," in Sipke Draisma (ed.), *Intertextuality in Biblical Writings: Essays in Honor of Bas van Iersel* (Kampen: Uitgeversmaatschappij J.H. Kok, 1989) 15–26.
Wardman, Alan, *Plutarch's Lives* (London: Paul Elek, 1974).
Welzen, Huub, "Loosing and Binding: Luke 13.10–21 as Programme and Antiprogramme of the Gospel of Luke," in Sipke Draisma (ed.), *Intertextuality in Biblical*

Writings: Essays in Honor of Bas van Iersel (Kampen: Uitgeversmaatschappij J.H. Kok, 1989) 175–187.

Weren, W.J.C., "Psalm 2 in Luke-Acts: an Intertextual Study," in Sipke Draisma (ed.), *Intertextuality in Biblical Writings: Essays in Honor of Bas van Iersel* (Kampen: Uitgeversmaatschappij J.H. Kok, 1989) 189–203.

Wessel, Walter L., *Mark*, Expositor's Bible Commentary 8 (Grand Rapids: Zondervan, 1984).

Wilcock, Michael, *The Message of Luke: The Saviour of the World*, Bible Speaks Today (Leicester: Inter-Varsity, 1979).

Wilkens, Wilhelm, "Die theologische Struktur der Komposition des Lukasevangeliums," *Theologische Zeitschrift* 34 (1978) 1–13.

Wimsatt, W.K., and Monroe C. Beardsley, "The Intentional Fallacy," in David Newton-de Molina (comp.), *On Literary Intention* (Edinburgh: Edinburgh University Press, 1976) 1–13.

Wolde, Ellen van, "Trendy Intertextuality," in Sipke Draisma (ed.), *Intertextuality in Biblical Writings: Essays in Honor of Bas van Iersel* (Kampen: Uitgeversmaatschappij J.H. Kok, 1989) 43–49.

Wright, N.T., *The New Testament and the People of God* (London: SPCK, 1992).

York, John O., *The Last Shall be First: The Rhetoric of Reversal in Luke*, JSNTSS 46 (Sheffield: JSOT Press, 1991).

Zeller, E., *Die Apostelgeschichte nach ihrem Inhalt und Ursprung kritisch untersucht* (Stuttgard: Mäcken, 1854).

Zerwick, M., *Biblical Greek Illustrated by Examples*, trans. from Latin 4th ed. by Joseph Smith (Rome: Scripta Pontificii Instituti Biblici, 1963).

Zmijewski, Josef, *Die Eschatologiereden des Lukas-Evangeliums: Eine traditions- und redaktionsgeschichtliche Untersuchung zu Lk 21,5–36 und Lk 17,30–37* (Bonn: Peter Hanstein Verlag, 1972).

Index of Scripture and Ancient Texts

Genesis
16:1–8 *18*
16:1–13 *18*
16:9–11 *18*
16:11 *18*
16:12 *18*
16:13 *19*
17:1–3 *18*
17:15–16 *18*
17:15–21 *18*
17:16 *18*
17:17 *19*
17:19 *18*
17:21 *18*
18:1–2 *18, 19*
18:10 *19*
18:10–15 *18, 19*
18:14 *19*
32:23–33 *21*
48:14 *335*

Exodus
29:1–28 *336*

Leviticus
1:4 *335*
3:2 *335*

Numbers
27:12–23 *336*
27:16–18 *335*

Deuteronomy
1:1–46 *201*
19:15 *113*

Judges
2 *170*
6–12 *195*
13:2–3 *18*
13:2–23 *18*
13:3 *19*
13:3–5 *18*
13:5 *18*
13:15–23 *19*

1 Samuel
167
3 *167*
4–6 *167*
4–7 *167*
8 *167*
8:1–22 *336*
9–10 *167*
9–14 *166*
9–31 *166, 193, 226*
9:1–2 *166*
9:3–10:16 *166*
10:17–11:15 *166*
11 *167*
12 *167*
13–14 *166*
14 *167*
15:1–16:13 *166*
15–27 *166*
16:1–3 *336*
16:14–19:10 *166*
19:11–28:2 *166*
28–31 *166*
28:3–25 *166*
29 *7*
29–31 *166*
29:1–2 *7*
29:3–5 *7*
29:6–10 *7*
29:11 *7*

2 Samuel
2–5 *167*
2–18 *167*
5:3 *336*
6 *167*
7 *167*
8–10 *167*
11–12 *167*
11–20 *167, 193, 226, 227*
13 *7, 167*
13–18 *167*
13:3–5 *7*
13:6 *7*
13:7 *7*
13:8–16 *7*
13:17 *7*
13:18 *7*
13:19–20 *7*

1 Kings
1b–4 *167*
1–14 *167*
1:32–48 *212*
1:33 *236*
1:36–7 *336*
5–8 *167*
9a *167*
9b–10 *167*
10:6–7 *146*
11a *167*
11b–12a *167*
17–19 *164*
17:1 *165*
17:1–16 *195*
17:1–19:21 *164, 165, 202*
17:2–5 *165*
17:6–7 *165*
17:8–16 *165*
17:10 *199*
17:17 *199*
17:17–23 *165*
17:17–24 *48, 107, 194, 198, 199*
17:18 *199*
17:19–21 *199*
17:21 *199, 254*
17:22 *199*
17:23 *199, 200*
17:24 *165, 199*
18:1 *165*
18:2 *165*
18:4 *238*

18:7–16 *165*
18:13 *238*
18:17–20 *165*
18:21–38 *165*
18:36–38 *239*
18:39–40 *165*
18:41–19:1 *165*
19 *195, 211*
19:2 *165*
19:3–4 *165*
19:5–6 *165*
19:7 *165*
19:9–18 *165, 336*
19:10 *238*
19:14 *238*
19:19–21 *165*

2 Kings
1:1–2:6 *195*
1:10 *239*
1:12 *239*
1:14 *239*
2:11–12 *238*
4:8–37 *107*
4:18–37 *48*
9:1–13 *236*
9:13 *212, 236*

1 Chronicles
1–10 *198*
11–12 *198*
13 *198*
14 *198*
15–16 *198*
17 *198*
18–20 *198*
21–22 *198*
23–29 *198*

2 Chronicles
1:1–5:1 *198*
5–9 *198*
9:5–6 *146*
10–36 *198*
14–35 *168, 194, 226, 227*
15 *169*
24 *169*
29–31 *169*

34–35 *169*

Job
1:6–8 *171*
1:9–12 *171*
1:12–22 *171*
2:1–3 *171*
2:4–6 *171*
2:7–10 *171*
3 *172*
4–5 *172*
6–7 *172*
8 *172*
9–10 *172*
11 *172*
12–14 *172*
15 *172*
16–17 *172*
18 *172*
19 *172*
20 *172*
21 *172*
22 *172*
23–24 *172*
25 *172*
26–31 *172*
32–37 *172*
38–39 *172*
40–41 *172*
40:1–5 *172*
42:1–6 *172*
42:7–17 *171*

Psalms
2 *354*
118:26 *236*

Isaiah
6:9–10 *128*
26:19 *255*
26:21 *255*
43:25 *128*
61 *46*
61:1 *128*
61:1–2 *41, 46, 128*

Daniel
2 *172*
2:1–18 *172*

2:19–49 *172*
3 *172*
4:1–18 *172*
4:19–27 *172*
4:28–37 *172*
5:1–12 *172*
5:13–29 *172*
5:30–31 *172*
6:1–15 *173*
6:16–24 *173*
6:25–28 *173*

Zechariah
9:9 *236*

Matthew
1–2 *177*
1:1–4:16 *178*
3:1–4:25 *177*
3:7–10 *45*
4:17–16:20 *178*
5:1–7:27 *177*
5:13 *244*
5:15 *245*
5:18 *247*
6:9–13 *241*
6:19–21 *250*
6:22–23 *245*
6:24 *247*
6:25–34 *250*
7:7–11 *241*
7:28–9 *177*
8:1–9:35 *177*
8:5–13 *243*
8:18–22 *239*
8:28–34 *253*
8:29 *253*
9:18 *335*
9:25 *223*
9:36–10:42 *177*
10:1 *314*
11:1 *177*
11:2–19 *243*
11:2–12:50 *178*
11:12–13 *247*
12:10 *57*
12:38–42 *244*
12:41 *223*
13:1–52 *178*

Index of Scripture and Ancient Texts 371

13:24–30 *221*
13:36–43 *221*
13:53 *178*
13:54–17:21 *178*
14:13–21 *144*
14:19 *100*
15:36 *100*
16:17f. *132*
16:21–28:20 *178*
17:22–18:35 *178*
18:6–7 *249*
18:12–14 *247*
19:1 *178*
19:2–22:46 *178*
19:9 *247*
19:13 *335*
19:15 *335*
19:28 *315*
21:1 *110*
21:1–9 *96*
22:1–10 *154*
23:1–25:46 *178*
23:37–39 *238*
24:1 *258*
24:9–14 *66*
24:26–28 *153*
24:30–31 *221*
24:37–41 *153*
24:43–44 *221*
24:43–51 *257*
24:45–51 *221, 257*
25:14–30 *221*
25:31–46 *221*
26:1 *178*
26:3–28:20 *178*
26:6–13 *243*
26:17–20 *144*
26:26 *100*
26:26–29 *144*
26:33 *145*
26:57 *100*
28 *71*
28:6 *38*
28:19 *260*

Mark
1:4 *65*
1:9 *281*
1:10 *96*
1:12 *281, 283*

1:14 *235, 281*
1:14–15 *264*
1:14–9:40 *263*
1:16–20 *129, 131, 132, 242, 264*
1:21 *281*
1:21–28 *264*
1:21–39 *242*
1:23 *130*
1:26 *131*
1:27 *117*
1:29–31 *264*
1:31 *130*
1:32–39 *264*
1:34 *131*
1:38 *118*
1:40 *281*
1:40–45 *264*
1:40–3:6 *243*
2:1–12 *132, 264*
2:2 *117*
2:10 *117*
2:13–17 *264*
2:16 *132*
2:18 *132*
2:18–22 *264*
2:23 *132*
2:23–28 *264*
3:1–6 *264*
3:2 *57*
3:7–12 *133, 243, 264*
3:11–12 *131*
3:13 *281*
3:13–19 *133, 243, 264*
3:20–22 *129*
3:20–30 *133, 264*
3:31–35 *134, 246*
3:31–4:25 *264*
3:35, *246*
4:1–9 *246*
4:1–25 *246, 284*
4:14 *246*
4:21 *245*
4:21–25 *245*
4:23 *294*
4:24 *294*
4:26–29 *84, 129, 265*
4:26–34 *251, 265, 284*
4:30–32 *129*
4:30–34 *265*

4:33–34 *129*
4:35 *282*
4:35–41 *131, 264, 313*
4:40 *250*
5:1–20 *264*
5:1–43 *313*
5:21–43 *264*
5:23 *335*
5:41 *223*
5:42 *223*
6:1–6 *48, 96, 129, 264, 265, 298*
6:4 *239, 304*
6:5 *335*
6:6–13 *139, 313*
6:6–16 *264*
6:7 *117, 282, 283, 313*
6:7–44 *258*
6:14–16 *140*
6:17–18 *125*
6:17–29 *258*
6:30 *282*
6:30–44 *140, 264*
6:30–7:37 *266*
6:32 *266*
6:32–44 *144*
6:34 *118, 140*
6:41 *100*
6:45 *266*
6:45–8:26 *84, 117, 141, 266, 294, 324*
7:1–23 *141*
7:32 *335*
8:1–9 *294*
8:1–26 *266*
8:6 *100*
8:14–21 *250*
8:22 *266*
8:23 *335*
8:25 *335*
8:27 *282*
8:27–30 *260*
8:27–32 *264*
8:31–9:1 *261*
8:33–9:1 *264*
8:34–9:1 *246*
9:2 *116, 141*
9:2–8 *264*
9:4 *142*
9:6 *142*

9:9 *258*
9:11–13 *240, 283*
9:14–29 *130*
9:14–32 *264*
9:30–32 *261*
9:33–41 *264*
9:42 *249*
9:42–10:12 *294*
9:50 *244*
10:2–12 *267*
10:11–12 *247, 267*
10:13 *282*
10:13–16 *152, 264*
10:13–52 *263*
10:17 *57*
10:17–28 *259, 264*
10:29–34 *264*
10:31 *294*
10:32 *110, 235*
10:32–34 *235*
10:35–45 *259*
10:41–42 *259*
10:42–43 *259*
10:46 *282*
10:46–52 *264*
11:1 *97, 110, 234, 235, 264, 282*
11:1–10 *96, 264*
11:1–11 *235*
11:1–13:37 *300*
11:1–16:8 *263*
11:8 *212, 236*
11:11 *110*
11:11–14 *283*
11:11–33 *264*
11:12 *217*
11:12–14 *97*
11:15 *282*
11:19 *217*
11:22 *251*
11:22–26 *251*
11:27 *244, 282*
12:1–11 *244, 264*
12:12–37 *264*
12:18–27 *98*
12:28–34 *57, 98, 152, 247, 294*
12:32–34 *98*
12:35 *282*
12:37 *249*

12:37–13:2 *312*
12:37–40 *246, 264*
12:38–40 *250*
12:41–44 *264*
13 *251*
13:1–37 *251, 264*
13:9–11 *66*
13:15–16 *295*
13:21–23 *283, 295*
13:26–27 *221*
13:33–36 *295*
14:1–25 *264*
14:3–9 *243, 255, 295*
14:4 *225*
14:12–17 *144*
14:22 *99, 100*
14:22–25 *144*
14:25 *140*
14:26 *141*
14:26–16:8 *264*
14:29 *145, 259*
14:31 *259*
14:31–32 *259*
14:43–52 *143*
14:48 *100*
14:53 *100*
14:53–16:8 *2*
15:33–39 *240*
16:6 *223*
16:18 *335*

Luke
1 *20, 164*
1–2 *14, 33, 47, 123, 126, 155, 322, 344*
1–3 *123, 204*
1–4 *87*
1:1 *274*
1:1–4 *28, 91, 206, 341, 344*
1:1–25 *198*
1:1–38 *121*
1:1–2:52 *197, 198*
1:1–4:13 *2*
1:1–4:15 *160*
1:1–4:44 *341*
1:1–8:56 *85*
1:3 *203, 342, 343, 344*
1:4 *308*
1:5 *25, 274*

1:5–7 *15*
1:5–10 *16*
1:5–11 *18*
1:5–23 *15*
1:5–25 *14, 15, 16, 17, 18, 19, 22, 24, 28, 197, 206*
1:5–38 *14, 22, 23, 24, 26, 27, 267, 268*
1:5–56 *16*
1:5–2:40 *26, 27*
1:5–2:52 *14, 226*
1:5–3:20 *103*
1:5–4:13 *322*
1:8 *274*
1:8–11 *15*
1:11 *16*
1:12 *15, 16, 18*
1:13 *16, 18, 20*
1:13–17 *15, 18*
1:14–15 *18*
1:15 *16, 18*
1:16–17 *18*
1:18 *15, 16, 19*
1:18–22 *19*
1:19 *16, 19, 20*
1:19–23 *15*
1:20 *16*
1:22 *16*
1:23 *16, 20*
1:24–25 *15*
1:26 *19, 274*
1:26–27 *15, 16*
1:26–28 *18*
1:26–38 *14, 15, 16, 17, 18, 19, 22, 24, 28, 198, 206*
1:27 *25*
1:28 *15, 16*
1:29 *15, 16, 18*
1:30 *16, 18, 20*
1:30–33 *15*
1:30–35 *18*
1:31 *16, 18*
1:32 *16, 18, 54, 236*
1:32–33 *18*
1:34 *15, 16, 19*
1:34–38 *19*
1:35 *16, 18, 20*
1:35–37 *15*

Index of Scripture and Ancient Texts 373

1:35–38 *19*
1:36 *16*
1:38 *15, 16, 20*
1:39 *274*
1:39–45 *15, 16, 198*
1:39–56 *15, 26, 28, 206*
1:39–4:13 *27*
1:46–55 *15, 16, 198*
1:56 *15, 16, 198*
1:57 *15, 17, 122, 278*
1:57–58 *15, 17*
1:57–66 *15, 28, 206*
1:57–80 *14, 15, 22, 25, 121, 198*
1:57–2:52 *17, 121*
1:58 *15, 17, 122*
1:59 *274*
1:59–64 *15, 17, 122*
1:59–80 *17*
1:65–66 *15, 17, 122*
1:67–79 *15, 45, 122*
1:67–80 *15, 28, 206*
1:68 *45*
1:68–79 *17, 40*
1:71 *45*
1:74 *45*
1:76 *54*
1:77 *45*
1:78 *45*
1:79 *45*
1:80 *15, 17, 122*
2:1 *274*
2:1–4 *329*
2:1–7 *15, 122*
2:1–12 *17*
2:1–20 *15, 17, 198*
2:1–21 *15, 28, 206*
2:1–27 *15*
2:1–40 *14, 22*
2:1–52 *25, 121*
2:8 *274*
2:8–16 *15, 122*
2:8–20 *15*
2:10 *20*
2:10–11 *68*
2:10–14 *69*
2:12 *20*
2:13–14 *17*
2:14 *45, 47, 68*
2:15–18 *17*

2:17–18 *15, 122*
2:19 *17*
2:20 *17*
2:21 *15, 17, 122, 275*
2:21–38 *198*
2:21–40 *15, 17*
2:22 *275*
2:22–38 *15, 122*
2:22–40 *15, 28, 206*
2:25–38 *17*
2:28–33 *15*
2:29–32 *17*
2:31–32 *63*
2:34–39 *15*
2:39 *17*
2:39–40 *15, 122, 198*
2:40 *15, 17*
2:41 *275*
2:41–52 *15, 17, 28, 122, 198, 206*
2:45–49 *94*
2:51 *17*
2:52 *17*
3:1 *275, 281, 283*
3:1–2 *125*
3:1–6 *123, 124*
3:1–20 *28, 123, 124, 126, 206*
3:1–4:15 *85, 123, 124*
3:1–4:30 *298*
3:1–6:12 *279*
3:3 *42, 63, 65, 69, 87*
3:6 *63*
3:7–9 *283*
3:7–14 *42, 45*
3:7–17 *124*
3:8 *87*
3:10–14 *45, 283*
3:11 *45*
3:18–20 *124*
3:19–20 *283*
3:21 *28, 91, 206, 275, 281, 283*
3:21–38 *123, 124*
3:21–4:15 *123, 124, 126*
3:22 *91, 96*
3:23 *275, 281*
3:23–4:15 *103*
4:1 *275, 281, 283*
4:1–13 *124*

4:13 *28, 206*
4:14 *106, 143, 235, 275, 281, 288*
4:14–15 *28, 124, 125, 206, 229, 264*
4:14–30 *46, 48*
4:14–24:53 *2, 6, 27, 29, 31, 157, 159, 204, 205, 228, 230, 267, 268, 294, 297, 322, 344*
4:15–24:53 *229*
4:16–30 *28, 41, 91, 93, 96, 127, 129, 197, 206, 229, 230, 239, 264, 266, 289, 298, 304, 343*
4:16–7:17 *126, 127, 135*
4:16–8:56 *126, 128, 129*
4:18 *69*
4:18–19 *41, 128*
4:24 *239, 304*
4:25–27 *48, 239, 304*
4:28–30 *334*
4:29 *137*
4:30–37 *307*
4:31 *275, 281*
4:31–37 *28, 117, 137, 206, 212, 264*
4:31–41 *127, 130*
4:31–44 *242*
4:31–50 *289*
4:31–6:19 *298*
4:31–7:50 *212, 213, 214*
4:31–8:56 *91*
4:32 *242*
4:33 *130*
4:33–37 *131*
4:34 *35, 36*
4:35 *130*
4:36 *106, 117, 242, 304, 307, 316*
4:37 *143*
4:38 *275*
4:38–39 *28, 137, 206, 243, 264*
4:39 *106, 130*
4:40 *275, 316, 335*
4:40–41 *131*

4:40–44 *28, 143, 206, 264*
4:41 *130, 308*
4:42 *275*
4:43 *118, 137, 316, 319*
5:1 *275, 281*
5:1–3 *128, 243*
5:1–32 *105*
5:1–11 *28, 39, 42, 127, 131, 133, 137, 206, 242, 243, 264, 308*
5:3 *213, 231*
5:4–9 *243*
5:8 *232, 260*
5:10 *42, 43*
5:12 *275, 281*
5:12–13 *106*
5:12–16 *28, 137, 206, 229, 264*
5:12–6:11 *243*
5:15 *143*
5:17 *49, 106, 117, 132, 143, 275, 305*
5:17–26 *28, 60, 104, 117, 127, 128, 137, 206, 243, 264, 305, 308*
5:17–32 *49, 50, 51, 52, 53*
5:19 *128*
5:20 *306*
5:20–21 *51*
5:21 *128*
5:24 *51, 117, 306*
5:27 *275*
5:27–32 *28, 105, 206, 264, 308*
5:27–33 *133*
5:27–39 *132, 133, 137*
5:27–6:5 *127, 133*
5:29 *132*
5:29–32 *51*
5:29–39 *128*
5:29–6:11 *104, 105*
5:30 *51, 128, 132*
5:32 *51, 87*
5:33 *132*
5:33–39 *28, 206, 264*
6:1 *132, 275*

6:1–5 *28, 57, 206, 264, 305, 306*
6:1–11 *128*
6:2 *128*
6:4 *100, 132*
6:5 *306*
6:6 *275*
6:6–11 *28, 56, 87, 137, 206, 264, 305, 306*
6:7 *57*
6:9 *306*
6:11 *128*
6:12 *137, 142, 275, 281*
6:12–16 *28, 127, 133, 138, 206, 264, 336*
6:12–19 *53*
6:12–49 *108, 243*
6:17 *278, 282, 283*
6:17–18 *143*
6:17–19 *133, 243*
6:17–26 *137*
6:17–49 *28, 128, 133, 137, 206, 216, 264*
6:19 *106*
6:20 *133*
6:20–49 *243, 308*
6:20–7:50 *298*
6:20–8:3 *298*
6:27 *216*
6:30 *45*
6:38 *294*
6:46 *216*
6:46–47 *243*
6:46–49 *216*
6:47 *128, 134*
7:1 *133, 276*
7:1–10 *28, 63, 84, 104, 106, 111, 117, 128, 137, 195, 206, 243, 264, 308*
7:1–17 *128*
7:2–23 *46, 48*
7:3 *143*
7:3–5 *106*
7:10 *199*
7:11 *199, 276*
7:11–17 *28, 48, 84, 104, 106, 137, 194, 198, 206, 229, 230, 264, 308*

7:11–19 *94*
7:12 *199*
7:13–14 *199*
7:14 *199, 223*
7:15 *199, 200*
7:16 *45, 48*
7:16–17 *199*
7:18 *276*
7:18–19 *143*
7:18–30 *127, 129*
7:18–35 *28, 108, 206, 231, 243, 264*
7:18–56 *135*
7:18–8:56 *126, 127*
7:21 *130*
7:22 *41, 128, 254*
7:24–35 *128*
7:28 *137*
7:29 *129*
7:29–30 *129*
7:30 *128*
7:31–35 *127, 130*
7:31–50 *49, 50, 51, 52*
7:33 *132*
7:34 *51, 132*
7:36 *276*
7:36–50 *28, 104, 105, 107, 127, 128, 137, 206, 243, 255, 264, 295, 305, 306*
7:39 *128*
7:48 *306*
7:48–50 *51*
8:1 *140, 276, 282, 316, 342*
8:1–3 *127, 133, 215, 217, 298*
8:1–15 *137*
8:1–17 *289*
8:1–21 *28, 206, 213, 264*
8:1–9:51 *279*
8:4 *143*
8:4–8 *128, 133, 246*
8:4–10 *84*
8:4–18 *246*
8:4–9:50 *298*
8:8 *294*
8:10 *128*
8:11 *246*
8:16 *245, 309*

8:16–18 *135, 289*
8:16–21 *128, 133*
8:17 *294*
8:18 *246, 290, 294*
8:18–21 *218*
8:19 *278*
8:19–21 *134, 245, 246*
8:20–21 *128*
8:21 *128, 245, 246*
8:22 *276, 282, 283, 284*
8:22–25 *28, 127, 131, 137, 206, 213, 220, 250, 264, 313, 316, 334*
8:22–56 *313*
8:25 *213, 250*
8:26 *276*
8:26–37 *131*
8:26–39 *28, 127, 130, 137, 206, 222, 226, 252, 264*
8:26–56 *221, 291, 313*
8:27 *130*
8:28 *35, 36, 130, 253*
8:28–39 *130*
8:31 *253*
8:40 *276*
8:40–41 *144*
8:40–56 *28, 137, 206, 222, 223, 226, 252, 254, 264*
8:43–48 *84, 128*
8:43–56 *128*
8:45 *260*
8:46 *106*
8:49–56 *84, 128*
8:52 *222*
8:55 *223*
8:56 *93*
9 *115, 119, 159, 160, 161, 266*
9:1 *106, 117, 223, 276, 282, 283, 313*
9:1–2 *316*
9:1–6 *115, 117, 133, 135, 139, 144, 146, 157, 313, 316*
9:1–9 *116, 230*
9:1–11 *212*

9:1–17 *28, 206, 230, 255, 258, 264, 291, 317*
9:1–48 *135, 157*
9:1–50 *103*
9:2 *118, 140*
9:3 *139*
9:5 *230*
9:6 *316*
9:6–10 *316*
9:7–9 *135, 143, 229, 230, 316*
9:9 *140, 258, 267*
9:10 *133, 283*
9:10–17 *136, 137, 138, 140, 144, 229, 316*
9:11 *118, 140*
9:11–17 *116*
9:11–27 *230*
9:12 *276*
9:12–17 *137, 294*
9:16 *100, 137*
9:18 *141, 276, 282*
9:18–21 *28, 137, 206, 259, 260, 264*
9:18–27 *229, 230*
9:20 *133, 260, 292*
9:20–22 *136, 138, 141, 145*
9:22 *38, 39, 138, 145, 225, 303*
9:22–27 *28, 206, 225, 260, 261, 264, 292, 323*
9:23–26 *230*
9:23–27 *136, 137*
9:24 *292, 334*
9:27 *137, 268*
9:27–28 *298*
9:27–50 *268*
9:28 *116, 137, 141, 142, 276*
9:28–36 *28, 115, 136, 138, 141, 206, 229, 264*
9:28–37 *53*
9:31 *39, 43, 142*
9:32 *142*
9:33 *260*
9:37 *137, 144, 276*

9:37–43 *130, 136, 137, 143*
9:37–45 *28, 206, 264*
9:43–45 *136, 261*
9:43–19:28 *82*
9:44 *38, 145, 225*
9:46 *276*
9:46–48 *136, 143*
9:46–50 *28, 150, 206, 264*
9:46–62 *63*
9:50–51 *298*
9:51 *28, 63, 72, 73, 108, 109, 160, 161, 206, 229, 235, 264, 266, 276, 282, 288*
9:51ff. *148*
9:51–52 *73*
9:51–56 *195, 228*
9:51–62 *230*
9:51–18:14 *298*
9:51–19:28 *92, 148*
9:51–19:46 *148*
9:51–19:48 *81*
9:52–56 *28, 206, 229, 238, 264, 289*
9:52–62 *304*
9:53 *108, 109*
9:54 *239*
9:57 *43, 276*
9:57–62 *28, 43, 87, 137, 144, 195, 206, 229, 230, 239, 264, 289*
9:61–62 *239*
9:62 *239*
10:1 *241, 276*
10:1–3 *201*
10:1–12 *92, 94, 137*
10:1–24 *28, 139, 140, 206, 240, 264, 308*
10:1–11:28 *212, 213*
10:3–12 *146*
10:4 *139*
10:4–16 *201*
10:7 *132*
10:9 *241*
10:9–11 *137*
10:10–16 *230*
10:13 *87*
10:17–20 *117, 201, 241*

10:19 *241, 308*
10:20 *130*
10:21 *63*
10:21–22 *152, 241*
10:21–24 *149, 201*
10:21–13:30 *147, 158*
10:21–13:33 *149*
10:21–18:30 *87, 148, 150*
10:25 *276*
10:25–27 *201*
10:25–28 *152, 247, 294*
10:25–37 *28, 57, 105, 149, 157, 206, 216, 264, 305, 307*
10:30–37 *63*
10:38 *276*
10:38–42 *28, 149, 151, 201, 206, 216, 264, 288*
10:39 *216*
11:1 *277*
11:1–2 *256*
11:1–13 *28, 149, 201, 206, 241, 242, 264*
11:1–30 *255*
11:2–4 *137*
11:5–8 *152, 157, 241*
11:9–11 *152*
11:9ff. *242*
11:11–13 *156, 157*
11:13 *63*
11:14 *137, 151, 277*
11:14–16 *129*
11:14–23 *153*
11:14–26 *28, 201, 206, 242, 264, 308*
11:14–28 *137*
11:14–36 *149*
11:20 *242, 308*
11:24–26 *153*
11:27 *273, 278*
11:27–28 *218, 244, 245, 246*
11:27–36 *28, 201, 206, 244, 264*
11:28 *128, 245*
11:29 *144, 244, 278*
11:29–32 *151, 153, 230, 290*

11:29–36 *213*
11:32 *87, 151*
11:33 *245, 309*
11:33–36 *88, 290*
11:33–12:12 *88*
11:34–36 *309*
11:37 *144, 277*
11:37–41 *248*
11:37–44 *57, 150*
11:37–52 *137*
11:37–54 *28, 105, 149, 153, 206, 247, 248, 264, 288, 290*
11:37–12:12 *201*
11:38 *248*
11:42–52 *230*
11:44 *248*
11:45 *248*
11:45–52 *57*
11:52–53 *247*
11:52–54 *248*
11:53 *290*
12:1 *144, 249, 250, 277, 310*
12:1–12 *88, 89*
12:1–21 *28, 206, 249, 264, 291, 310*
12:1–48 *89, 149, 153*
12:1–13:9 *261*
12:3 *310*
12:4 *310*
12:5–38 *251*
12:8–10 *151*
12:9–10 *230*
12:10 *63*
12:11–12 *334*
12:12 *63*
12:13 *278*
12:13–21 *151, 157, 219, 230, 251*
12:13–34 *201*
12:15–21 *231*
12:16–21 *151*
12:19 *132*
12:22 *231, 250, 258, 311*
12:22–34 *28, 84, 137, 206, 219, 250, 264, 311, 313*
12:22–40 *137*
12:28 *213, 250*

12:33 *45*
12:35–38 *157, 252*
12:35–40 *28, 151, 206, 221, 222, 252, 264, 295, 313, 314*
12:35–53 *201*
12:39–40 *252*
12:39–46 *257*
12:40 *313*
12:41 *223, 258, 260, 278, 314, 316*
12:41–48 *28, 206, 257, 264, 291, 317*
12:41–49 *255*
12:42 *258*
12:42–46 *221, 222, 230*
12:42–48 *151, 314, 317*
12:45 *258*
12:46 *151*
12:49–50 *261*
12:49–53 *28, 87, 206, 225, 260, 261, 264, 292*
12:49–13:9 *150*
12:50 *225, 260, 261, 323*
12:51–53 *47, 261*
12:54–59 *28, 87, 151, 206, 213, 230, 231, 264*
12:54–13:5 *201*
13 *157*
13:1 *277*
13:1–5 *87, 151*
13:1–9 *28, 157, 206, 230, 264*
13:3 *87*
13:5 *87*
13:6 *98, 240*
13:6–9 *97, 201, 268*
13:10 *277*
13:10–16 *334*
13:10–17 *28, 56, 87, 137, 150, 151, 156, 157, 206, 230, 264, 268*
13:10–21 *201, 346*
13:10–30 *151*
13:11 *130*
13:13 *335*
13:18–19 *129*

Index of Scripture and Ancient Texts

13:18–21 *28, 137, 206, 264*
13:18–30 *150*
13:22 *28, 73, 108, 206, 229, 235, 264, 277, 288, 300*
13:22–27 *235*
13:22–30 *137, 151, 228, 230*
13:22–35 *201, 230*
13:22–18:8 *300*
13:23–30 *28, 206, 216, 229, 235, 237, 264, 289, 300*
13:23–35 *237, 304*
13:25 *289*
13:26 *237*
13:26–27 *216*
13:30 *294*
13:31 *136, 144, 277*
13:31–33 *150, 154, 237*
13:31–35 *28, 206, 229, 230, 237, 238, 264, 289, 300*
13:33 *109, 110, 238*
13:34 *238*
13:34–35 *150, 154, 214, 230, 237, 238*
13:34–18:30 *149*
13:35 *238*
14 *157*
14:1 *107, 277*
14:1–6 *56, 87, 137, 150, 151, 156, 157*
14:1–14 *28, 57, 105, 151, 201, 206, 212, 213, 240, 242, 264, 301, 305, 307*
14:1–24 *137, 151, 288*
14:1–35 *151*
14:1–17:10 *137*
14:1–18:30 *147, 158*
14:7–14 *231*
14:7–24 *150, 156, 157*
14:11 *314*
14:12–14 *45*
14:14 *314*
14:15 *154, 278*

14:15–24 *28, 137, 206, 207, 230, 244, 264, 301*
14:15–35 *201*
14:16–24 *154, 290*
14:25 *244, 278*
14:25–27 *87*
14:25–33 *290*
14:25–35 *28, 137, 206, 207, 213, 230, 244, 264*
14:25–15:32 *150, 301*
14:26 *244*
14:26–27 *43*
14:27 *244*
14:28–33 *87, 156, 157*
14:33 *43, 244*
14:34–35 *290, 309*
15 *53, 218*
15:1 *248, 279*
15:1–2 *107, 218*
15:1–3 *247*
15:1–32 *49, 50, 51, 52, 53, 87, 157, 201, 218, 248*
15:1–16:13 *248*
15:1–16:31 *28, 206, 247, 264*
15:2 *151, 290*
15:4–7 *53, 247*
15:7 *51, 87*
15:10 *51, 87*
16 *149*
16:1 *219*
16:1–8 *151, 219*
16:1–13 *157, 218*
16:1–18 *201, 219, 301*
16:1–31 *154, 248*
16:1–18:8 *195*
16:1ff. *219*
16:2 *219*
16:3–7 *219*
16:4 *219*
16:8–9 *219*
16:9 *45, 219*
16:13 *219, 247*
16:14 *107, 218, 249, 279, 290, 310*
16:14–15 *248*
16:14–18 *57*

16:14–31 *105*
16:15 *151*
16:16–17 *137, 247*
16:16–31 *248*
16:18 *247, 267*
16:19–31 *89, 137, 151, 157, 230, 301, 310*
16:19–18:8 *201*
16:30 *87, 151*
17:1 *249, 310*
17:1–2 *310*
17:1–3 *249*
17:1–4 *28, 88, 206, 219, 249, 264, 291, 301*
17:1–6 *153*
17:1–10 *88, 94, 149, 153*
17:3 *87, 249*
17:3–4 *63, 151, 249*
17:4 *87*
17:5 *213, 251, 311, 313*
17:5–6 *88*
17:5–10 *28, 206, 250, 251, 264*
17:5–19 *301, 312*
17:7–10 *88, 150, 153, 156, 157*
17:11 *73, 109, 211, 228, 229, 277*
17:11–13 *144*
17:11–19 *28, 63, 137, 151, 153, 206, 220, 226, 229, 251, 264*
17:11–37 *149, 153*
17:20 *277*
17:20–21 *153*
17:20–23 *153*
17:20–37 *28, 137, 153, 206, 264, 291*
17:20–18:8 *251, 301, 313, 314*
17:22 *313*
17:22–37 *153*
17:23–24 *295*
17:25 *225, 261*
17:26–30 *153*
17:26–38 *221, 222*
17:30–37 *251*
17:31 *295*
17:32 *153*
17:33 *313*

18:1 *225, 279*
18:1–8 *28, 149, 153, 157, 206, 264*
18:1–14 *291*
18:5–17 *152*
18:7 *313*
18:8–9 *314*
18:9 *225, 279*
18:9–14 *49, 107, 149, 157, 201, 224, 293*
18:9–17 *28, 206, 255, 257, 264, 291, 316*
18:9–34 *300*
18:14 *224, 314*
18:15 *144, 279, 282*
18:15–17 *137, 149, 224, 225, 257, 293, 314, 317, 318*
18:15–43 *298*
18:16 *315*
18:16–17 *152*
18:18 *279*
18:18–23 *57*
18:18–25 *150*
18:18–28 *28, 206, 259, 264*
18:18–30 *137, 149, 151, 152*
18:22 *45*
18:25–28 *152*
18:28 *137, 232, 260, 292*
18:29–30 *151*
18:29–34 *28, 206, 225, 260, 264*
18:30 *294*
18:31 *72, 109, 110, 229, 235, 277*
18:31–34 *138, 145, 235, 323*
18:31–24:13 *280*
18:35 *277, 282*
18:35–38 *144*
18:35–43 *28, 87, 137, 206, 264*
18:38–39 *236*
19:1 *277, 282*
19:1–4 *143*
19:1–10 *28, 49, 50, 51, 52, 53, 206, 264, 288*
19:1–27 *137, 298*

19:9 *51*
19:10 *51, 282, 319*
19:11 *109, 235, 279*
19:11–27 *28, 39, 40, 137, 206, 212, 230, 232, 264, 268*
19:12 *40*
19:12–27 *221*
19:19–20 *283*
19:28 *28, 73, 109, 110, 206, 229, 234, 264, 277, 282, 288, 300*
19:28–38 *96*
19:28–40 *138, 228, 334*
19:28–21:38 *300*
19:28–22:13 *298*
19:29 *97, 137*
19:29–36 *103*
19:29–40 *28, 206, 229, 264, 300, 304*
19:29–44 *230, 289*
19:30–31 *146*
19:35–38 *212*
19:36 *212, 236*
19:37 *92, 96, 97, 106, 137, 279*
19:37–44 *237*
19:38 *40, 45, 47, 214, 236, 238*
19:38–40 *237*
19:38–44 *103, 237*
19:40–44 *45*
19:41 *238, 273, 279*
19:41–44 *28, 39, 40, 42, 72, 97, 206, 214, 216, 229, 230, 237, 264, 300, 304*
19:42 *45, 238*
19:43 *45, 238*
19:44 *45, 238*
19:45 *110, 277, 282*
19:45–48 *92, 217*
19:45–20:8 *28, 105, 206, 212, 213, 240, 244, 264, 301, 305, 307*
19:46 *97, 240*
19:47 *97*
20:1 *98, 213, 217, 231, 277, 282*
20:1–8 *217*

20:1–19 *47*
20:1–26 *103*
20:2 *217*
20:5–6 *307*
20:9–16 *290, 301*
20:9–18 *28, 206, 213, 230, 244, 264*
20:9–19 *39, 40, 42, 43*
20:15–16 *290*
20:16 *40*
20:17–18 *244, 290, 301, 309*
20:18 *290*
20:19 *40, 98, 247, 277*
20:19–20 *290*
20:19–26 *105, 301*
20:19–44 *28, 206, 247, 264, 290*
20:20 *277*
20:27 *144, 277*
20:27–39 *93*
20:27–44 *57, 301*
20:39 *98, 336*
20:40 *294*
20:40–22:18 *103*
20:41 *282*
20:41–44 *247*
20:45 *249*
20:45–47 *28, 206, 220, 249, 264, 291, 301, 311*
20:45–21:6 *312*
20:47 *251, 312*
21:1 *279*
21:1–4 *28, 206, 213, 220, 232, 250, 251, 264, 301, 312*
21:1–30 *255*
21:4 *251*
21:5 *225, 279*
21:5–6 *312*
21:5–36 *251*
21:5–37 *137*
21:5–38 *28, 29, 206, 251, 264, 301, 315*
21:12–19 *137, 334, 336*
21:13 *63*
21:21 *137*
21:21–22 *295*
21:24 *295*

21:27–31 *253*
21:33 *295*
21:34 *282, 283*
21:34–36 *221, 222*
21:37 *137, 138*
22 *103, 255*
22–23 *159*
22:1 *223, 271, 278, 282, 283, 299*
22:1–2 *256*
22:1–6 *224*
22:1–30 *28, 206, 264*
22:1–24:53 *300*
22:1ff. *288*
22:2 *295*
22:3–6 *256*
22:7 *278*
22:7–19 *136*
22:7–20 *140, 144*
22:7–30 *137, 224*
22:7–38 *137*
22:7–23:16 *135, 157*
22:14 *278*
22:14–24:53 *298*
22:15–18 *256*
22:15–20 *256*
22:19 *93, 99, 100, 137*
22:19–20 *136*
22:21–23 *136, 256*
22:21–30 *257*
22:22 *145*
22:24 *279*
22:24–27 *136, 143, 256, 316, 317, 318*
22:24–30 *256, 257, 315*
22:25–26 *259*
22:25–27 *315*
22:26 *93, 224*
22:28 *141, 256*
22:28–30 *136, 141, 315*
22:29 *256*
22:29–30 *292, 315*
22:31–34 *28, 136, 138, 141, 206, 259, 264*
22:32–34 *141*
22:33 *137, 232, 259, 260, 292*
22:35 *139*
22:35–38 *135, 136, 139, 140, 144, 146, 157*
22:35–24:53 *28, 206, 260, 264, 323*
22:39 *137, 142, 278*
22:39–46 *136, 142*
22:39–53 *138*
22:43 *137, 142*
22:43–44 *137, 142, 143*
22:44 *143*
22:47 *279*
22:47–53 *136*
22:51 *138*
22:54 *93, 100, 279*
22:54–65 *147*
22:54–23:5 *147*
22:57 *260*
22:58 *260*
22:60 *260*
22:63–64 *93, 95*
22:66 *278*
22:66–23:5 *147*
23 *103*
23:1 *93, 278*
23:2 *40*
23:4 *111*
23:6–12 *111, 112*
23:6–16 *135, 140, 143*
23:8 *93, 140, 144*
23:13 *93*
23:14 *111, 112*
23:16 *111, 113*
23:18 *111*
23:22 *111, 113*
23:26 *278*
23:26–43 *114*
23:32 *278*
23:37 *40*
23:42–43 *137*
23:44–48 *240*
23:47 *111*
23:50 *278*
24 *38, 62, 64, 66, 67, 68, 93, 119, 121, 160*
24:1 *278*
24:1–8 *116*
24:1–11 *101*
24:6 *38*
24:6–7 *38*
24:7 *303*
24:13 *278, 282*
24:13–32 *101*
24:25–26 *38*
24:26 *303*
24:30 *100, 137*
24:33–34 *119*
24:33–49 *101*
24:33–53 *60*
24:36 *119, 278*
24:36–43 *119*
24:38 *19*
24:43 *69*
24:44 *38*
24:44–46 *38*
24:44–49 *39*
24:45–46 *72*
24:45–49 *60*
24:46 *38, 69*
24:46–48 *69*
24:47 *60, 63, 65, 69, 87, 269*
24:47–48 *120*
24:47–49 *60, 61, 63, 65, 66, 67*
24:48 *60, 63*
24:49 *60, 117, 119*
24:50 *278*
24:51–52 *120*

John
1:6–34 *176*
1:6–51 *176*
1:7 *176*
1:8 *176*
1:15 *176*
1:19–51 *174*
1:29–34 *71*
1:32 *176*
1:34 *176*
1:43 *71*
2 *174*
2:1–11 *175, 176*
2:1–4:42 *174*
2:1–12:50 *173, 174*
2:11 *175*
2:12–17 *176*
2:12–25 *175*
2:18–25 *175, 176*
3 *174*
3:1–4:42 *176*
3:11 *176*
3:26 *176*

3:32 *176*
3:33 *176*
4 *174*
4:39 *176*
4:43–54 *175, 176*
4:43–5:47 *174*
4:54 *175*
5:1–15 *176*
5:16 *175*
5:16–30 *175, 176*
5:28–29 *221*
5:31 *176*
5:31–47 *176*
5:32 *176*
5:33 *176*
5:34 *176*
5:36 *176*
5:37 *176*
5:39 *176*
6:1–15 *175, 176*
6:1–71 *174*
6:11 *100*
6:14 *175*
6:16–24 *176*
6:25–71 *175*
6:25–7:52 *176*
6:44 *221*
6:54 *221*
7:1–52 *175*
7:1–8:59 *174*
8:3 *176*
8:12–59 *176*
8:13 *176*
8:14 *176*
8:18 *176*
9:1–12 *176*
9:1–34 *175*
9:1–10:42 *175*
9:13–34 *175*
9:13–10:21 *176*
9:16 *175*
9:35–10:21 *175*
10:22–42 *176*
10:25 *176*
11:1–44 *175, 176*
11:1–54 *175*
11:1–12:50 *175*
11:11 *222*
11:25–26 *222*
11:45–57 *175*

11:45–12:11 *176*
11:47 *175*
12:1–11 *175*
12:12–19 *176*
12:17 *176*
12:18 *175*
13:37 *145*
14:2–3 *221*
20:23 *71*
21:13 *100*

Acts
1 *115, 116, 119, 121, 160, 161*
1–5 *60, 61, 62, 66*
1–12 *83, 85, 86, 135, 327, 328, 331, 332*
1:1 *66, 67, 179, 341*
1:1–5 *91*
1:1–11 *61, 66*
1:1–12 *60, 95*
1:1–3:26 *67*
1:1–12:17 *85*
1:2 *197*
1:3 *119*
1:3–4 *116, 120*
1:4 *60, 61, 119*
1:4–5 *60*
1:4–8 *180*
1:6–13 *103*
1:8 *60, 61, 115, 117, 120, 337*
1:9 *120*
1:9–11 *115*
1:9–26 *180*
1:10 *117*
1:11 *329*
1:12 *120*
1:12–26 *66, 67, 338*
1:12–4:23 *338*
1:12–5:42 *338, 339, 340*
1:14 *91, 93*
1:15–23 *103*
1:21–22 *332, 337*
1:22 *60, 61, 67*
1:24 *91, 93, 335*
1:25–26 *103*
1:29–36 *40*
2 *39*
2:1–4 *85, 86, 328, 331*

2:1–13 *91, 95, 180, 338*
2:1–47 *67*
2:3 *61*
2:4 *334*
2:5–13 *331*
2:8 *61*
2:14–40 *86, 91, 180, 328*
2:14–41 *339*
2:21 *60, 61*
2:23 *60, 61*
2:31–32 *260*
2:32 *60, 61*
2:38 *60, 61, 65*
2:40–47 *331*
2:41 *180*
2:41–42 *93*
2:41–12:17 *91*
2:42–47 *180, 318, 339, 340*
2:43 *339, 340*
2:47 *318*
3:1–10 *60, 86, 104, 328*
3:1–11 *339*
3:1–26 *67, 180*
3:6 *60, 61*
3:11–26 *108, 339*
3:12 *106, 329*
3:12–26 *86, 106, 328, 339*
3:15 *60, 61*
3:16 *60, 61*
3:19 *60, 61, 65*
3:24 *342*
4:1–7 *339*
4:1–22 *180, 336*
4:1–31 *67*
4:1–6:7 *85, 331*
4:1–8:3 *104*
4:7 *60, 61, 67*
4:8–12 *339*
4:8–17 *339*
4:10 *60, 61, 67*
4:12 *60, 61, 67*
4:13–17 *339*
4:18 *339*
4:19–20 *339*
4:21–23 *339*
4:23–31 *180*
4:24–31 *338*
4:24–5:42 *338*

4:31 *338, 339*
4:32–35 *182, 339*
4:32–5:11 *67, 105*
4:32–5:16 *180*
4:33 *60, 61, 67*
4:36–37 *339*
4:36–5:4 *340*
5:1–10 *339*
5:5 *339*
5:6–10 *340*
5:11 *339*
5:12 *108, 339, 340*
5:12–16 *182*
5:12–42 *67*
5:13–16 *339*
5:17–21 *334*
5:17–28 *339*
5:17–6:6 *180*
5:21–41 *336*
5:29 *340*
5:30–32 *339*
5:31 *60, 61, 65, 67*
5:31–32 *62*
5:32 *60, 61, 67*
5:33–39 *339*
5:34–39 *332*
5:40–42 *339*
5:42 *182, 339*
6:1–6 *180, 332*
6:1–7 *105*
6:6 *334*
6:7 *180, 181*
6:8–7:1 *180*
6:8–8:4 *328*
6:12–7:60 *336*
6:13–14 *332*
7:2–53 *180*
7:52–56 *68*
7:54–8:1 *180*
8:1–4 *180*
8:3–9:35 *108*
8:5–8 *180*
8:5–9:43 *85, 331*
8:9 *333*
8:9–24 *332*
8:9–25 *180*
8:11 *333*
8:12–17 *93*
8:14–17 *332*
8:15–17 *334*

8:17 *334*
8:26–39 *94*
8:26–40 *180*
8:29 *329*
8:39 *329*
9:1–31 *180, 331*
9:1ff. *132*
9:17 *334*
9:20 *181*
9:31 *181, 182*
9:32–43 *180*
9:34 *104*
9:36–43 *104, 105, 332*
9:38 *73*
10 *104*
10–11 *328*
10:1–48 *105, 180*
10:1–11:18 *94*
10:5–8 *73*
10:9–16 *328*
10:19 *329*
10:25–26 *332*
10:36 *68, 69, 71*
10:36–43 *68, 69, 70, 72*
10:37 *69*
10:38 *69, 70*
10:39 *70*
10:39–41 *69*
10:41 *69, 70*
10:42 *69, 70*
10:43 *69*
10:44 *342*
10:44–45 *334*
10:46 *329*
11 *343*
11:1–3 *180*
11:1–18 *104, 105*
11:3 *144*
11:4 *342, 344*
11:4–18 *180, 344*
11:15 *343*
11:19–21 *94*
11:19–30 *180, 331*
11:28 *329*
12 *329*
12:1–23 *180*
12:3–4 *329*
12:4 *329*
12:5–6 *329*
12:6–11 *329, 332*

12:11 *329*
12:17 *93, 329*
12:18–25 *103*
12:24 *180, 181, 329*
13 *94*
13–20 *92*
13–21 *328*
13–28 *83, 85, 86, 135, 327, 328, 331, 332*
13:1–3 *85, 86, 180, 328, 329*
13:1–12 *180*
13:3 *334, 335*
13:4–15 *85, 331*
13:6 *333*
13:6–12 *332*
13:8 *333*
13:9–11 *329*
13:12–35 *329*
13:13–41 *180*
13:16–40 *86, 328*
13:16–41 *68*
13:24 *117*
13:41–14:7 *331*
13:42–48 *180*
13:48–50 *105*
13:49–52 *180*
14:1–7 *85, 180*
14:8–13 *86, 104, 328*
14:8–20 *180*
14:13–15 *332*
14:14 *331*
14:15 *329*
14:15–17 *86, 328*
14:18 *331*
14:19–23 *328*
14:21–28 *180*
14:23 *332*
15 *328*
15:1–2 *144*
15:1–5 *180*
15:5 *105*
15:6–35 *180*
15:7–11 *328*
15:27 *73*
15:36–40 *144*
15:36–16:15 *180*
16:5 *181, 182*
16:6–7 *329*
16:6–10 *328*

16:11–15 *93*
16:16–40 *180*
16:24–26 *332*
17:1–9 *180*
17:2–3 *68*
17:10–15 *180*
17:16–34 *180*
17:31 *68, 260*
18:1–17 *180*
18:12–21:26 *88*
18:18–28 *180*
18:23 *342*
19:1–6 *332*
19:1–7 *334*
19:1–19 *180*
19:6 *329, 334*
19:20 *180*
19:21 *72, 73, 108*
19:21–22 *180*
19:21–21:17 *92*
19:22 *73*
19:23–41 *180*
20:9–12 *332*
20:11 *100*
20:16 *329*
20:17–35 *180*
20:22 *108*
20:22–23 *329*
20:36–38 *180*
21 *328*
21–28 *329*
21:1–16 *180*
21:4 *109*
21:4–11 *329*
21:11–12 *109*
21:13 *109*
21:15 *109*
21:17 *109*
21:17–20 *92*
21:17–28:16 *180*
21:20–21 *332, 337*
21:20–25 *103*
21:26 *92*
21:27–29 *103, 105*
21:30 *93, 100*
21:31–22:30 *103*
21:36 *111, 113*
21:37–22:29 *114*
22:16 *93*
22:30–23:11 *104*

22:30–23:30 *336*
23 *93*
23:2 *93*
23:6 *68*
23:6–9 *93, 95, 98*
23:9 *111, 332*
23:11 *332, 336, 338*
23:12–25:12 *114*
24 *93*
24:20 *336*
24:21 *68*
25 *93*
25:8 *332, 337*
25:13 *329*
25:13–26:32 *111*
25:19 *68*
25:23–24 *329*
25:25 *111*
26 *93*
26:16 *332, 338*
26:22–23 *68*
26:23 *260*
26:31 *111*
26:32 *111, 113*
27 *333*
27:1–34 *103*
27:3 *111*
27:35 *93, 95, 99, 100*
27:35–44 *103*
27:43 *111*
28 *93*
28:1–6 *334*
28:8 *334*
28:17–28 *180*
28:30–31 *180, 329, 330*
28:31 *181*

Romans
3:3 *225*
6:3–4 *260*

1 Corinthians
11:23 *100*
11:23–24 *99*
15:52 *223*

2 Corinthians
10:2 *225*
2:2 *225*

Ephesians
5:14 *223*

Philippians
1:15 *225*

1 Thessalonians
4:13–14 *222*
4:14 *223*
5:10 *222*

2 Thessalonians
2:1–8 *253*

1 Timothy
4:14 *335*

2 Timothy
1:6 *335*

Hebrews
4:6 *225*
10:25 *225*

1 Peter
3:21–22 *260*

1 John
1:1–4 *184*
1:5–7 *184*
1:5–2:29 *184*
1:8–2:2 *184*
2:3–11 *184*
2:12–17 *184*
2:18–29 *184*
3:1–3 *184*
3:1–5:13 *184*
3:4–9 *184*
3:10–24 *184*
4:1–6 *184*
4:7–5:4 *184*
5:5–13 *184*
5:14–21 *184*

Jude
6 *253*

Revelation
2–3 *182*
6–16 *193, 226*
6:1–8:5 *183*
8:6–11:19 *183*
12–14 *182, 183*
15–16 *183*
20:1 *252*
20:10 *253*

1QS
3:24–25 *253*
4:18–20 *253*

1 Enoch
16:1 *253*

2 Esdras
6:26 *238*

Jubilees
10:8–9 *253*

Testament of Levi
18:12 *253*

Livy, *History*
1–45 *188*
46–142 *188*

Thucydides, *History of the Peloponnesian War*
1 *187*
2 *187*
3 *187*
4–5 *187*
6 *187*
7 *187*
8 *187*
9–10 *187*

Vergil, *Aeneid*
1 *189, 190, 191*
2 *189, 190*
3 *189*
4 *189*
5 *189, 190*
6 *189*
7 *189, 190, 191*
8 *189, 190*
9 *189*
10 *189*
11 *189, 190*
12 *189*

Author Index

Aland, K. 281, 283
Alexander, L. 341, 342
Alexander, L.C.A. 344
Allison, D.C. 177, 318
Alter, R. 56, 87
Anderson, J.C. 286
Archer, G.L. 172
Baarlink, H. 82, 88, 148
Bailey, K.E. 81, 87, 88, 148, 248
Bar-Efrat, S. 6, 7, 8, 31, 167, 168, 170, 209
Barthes, R. 21, 346, 347, 348, 349, 351
Bauckham, R. 182
Bauer, B. 10, 11
Bauer, D.R. 2, 178
Bauer, W. 248
Baur, F.C. 3, 10, 11
Bayer, H.F. 261
Beardsley, M.C. 348, 350
Beasley-Murray, G.R. 173, 174, 175, 176, 182, 183
Beck, B.E. 309, 310, 312
Best, E. 151, 155, 228
Betz, O. 219
Bindemann, W. 218
Binder, H. 218
Blomberg, C.L. 9, 148, 155, 156, 157, 200, 201, 202, 222
Bock, D.L. 97, 107, 129, 133, 139, 142, 152, 153, 154, 164, 220, 224, 236, 242, 252
Bovon, F. 15, 21, 22, 26, 148, 155, 316, 318
Brodie, T.L. 163, 194, 195, 196, 197, 198, 199, 200, 202, 203, 211, 322
Brown, E.K. 287
Brown, R.E. 14, 15, 341
Brown, S. 342
Bruce, F.F. 100, 120, 181, 333, 334, 335
Bultmann, R. 21
Carrol, J.T. 232
Carson, D.A. 177, 236, 253, 254, 258

Carter, J.M. 185
Carter, W. 2
Clines, D.J.A. 171, 172
Coats, G.W. 24, 25
Cohn, R.L. 164, 165
Conzelmann, H. 125, 303, 315, 317
Cross, F.L. 3, 148
Danker, F.W. 221, 224, 249, 251
Davies, J.G. 4, 10, 11, 115
Davies, J.H. 148
Davies, W.D. 177
Delorme, J. 353, 354
Denaux, A. 280
Dewey, J. 2
Didier, M. 178
Dillon, R.J. 341, 342, 343
Dinkler, E. 341
Draisma, S. 346, 347, 351, 353, 354
Duckworth, G.E. 79, 87, 185, 189, 190, 302
Ellis, E.E. 146, 236, 317, 341
Evans, C.F. 49, 85, 97, 98, 106, 112, 131, 132, 140, 142, 153, 155, 200, 224, 236, 241, 252, 255, 256, 257, 258, 260, 261, 271, 283, 304, 314
Evans, CA. 197, 201, 202, 239, 303
Farmer, W.R. 270, 271
Felperin, H. 346
Feuillet, A. 124
Fewell, D.N. 355
Fitzmyer, J.A. 16, 17, 20, 22, 26, 49, 57, 58, 84, 96, 97, 98, 100, 106, 113, 131, 132, 133, 134, 138, 139, 140, 142, 212, 217, 220, 225, 226, 236, 237, 238, 241, 242, 243, 245, 246, 247, 249, 250, 252, 255, 256, 257, 259, 265, 266, 267, 270, 271, 272, 289, 294, 295, 297, 300, 303, 310, 314
Flender, H. 4, 10, 11
Focant, C. 280
Foucault, M. 349, 351
Fowler, F.G. 185
Fowler, H.W. 185

France, R.T. 9
Franklin, E. 309
Frow, J. 353
Galland, C. 21
Geldenhuys, N. 221
George, A. 14, 328
Gingrich, F.W. 248
Gnilka, J. 241, 253
Gooding, D. 181
Goulder, M.D. 3, 10, 11, 148, 179
Grant, R.M. 297
Grässer, E. 341
Green, J.B. 15, 218, 261, 285, 343, 344
Green, T.M. 197
Grube, G.M.A. 197
Grundmann, W. 98, 113, 134, 139, 140, 143, 236, 239, 241, 242, 247, 249, 250, 252, 255, 257, 258
Guelich, R.A. 96
Gundry, R.H. 178
Guthrie, D. 296, 297, 298
Harris, M.J. 222, 223, 254
Hartley, J.E. 171, 172
Hastings, A. 200
Heil, J.P. 2
Herodotus 185, 186, 194, 195, 226
Hirsch, E.D. 350, 351
Hoeren, T. 219
Holtz, T. 164
Humphreys, W.L. 166
Iersel, B. van 228, 346, 347, 351, 353, 354
Immerwahr, H.R. 185, 186
Jeremias, J. 45, 129, 234, 249, 340
Johnson, A.M. 21
Johnson, L.T. 45, 253, 254
Kamlah, E. 219
Karris, R.J. 343
Kennedy, G.A. 196
Kimball, A. 164
Klein, G. 341, 343
Klostermann, E. 96
Kristeva, J. 348, 349, 351
Krodel, G.A. 181
Kümmel, W.G. 297, 298, 341
Kurzinger, J. 342
Lagrange, M.-J. 245, 252, 292
Lane, W.L. 98, 217, 312
Laurentin, R. 3, 10, 11, 15

Leenhardt, F.-J. 21
Liefeld, W.W. 97, 113, 217, 222, 268, 303, 310
Livy 188, 195, 200
Lohmeyer, E. 131, 253
Long, B.O. 164
Longenecker, R.N. 120, 181, 268
Luce, T.J. 188
Lucian 79, 185
Lull, D.J. 195, 211
Lund, N.W. 88, 163
Lunt, R.G. 218
MacKail, J.W. 189
Mann, C.S. 218
Manson, W. 58, 260
Marshall, I.H. 40, 48, 49, 57, 58, 74, 89, 94, 97, 100, 106, 112, 117, 121, 123, 125, 129, 130, 131, 132, 134, 142, 143, 152, 153, 181, 183, 212, 216, 217, 221, 222, 224, 235, 236, 237, 239, 241, 242, 244, 246, 247, 248, 249, 251, 252, 254, 255, 256, 258, 259, 261, 265, 267, 289, 303, 304, 305, 306, 307, 311, 315, 317, 318
Martin-Archard, R. 21
Matera, F.J. 148
Mattil, A.J. 10, 11
McNeile, A.H. 258
Metzger, B.M. 142
Meynet, R. 148, 306
Michie, D. 2
Miller, D.L. 354
Minear, P.S. 4
Moessner, D.P. 200, 288
Moore, S.D. 33
Morgenthaler, R. 4, 10, 11
Morris, L. 174, 182
Muhlack, G. 10, 11
Mussner, F. 341, 343
Navone, J. 303, 311
Neil, W. 120
Neirynck, F. 280
Neusner, J. 353
Newton-de Molina, D. 348, 349, 350
Nineham, D.E. 200
Nolland, J., 15, 17, 22, 26, 31, 41, 57, 85, 89, 97, 98, 100, 106, 112, 116, 117, 130, 131, 132, 133, 134, 139, 140, 142, 197, 220, 225, 231, 232,

235, 236, 238, 240, 242, 246, 248,
249, 250, 255, 256, 258, 260, 261,
289, 292, 306, 314, 316, 317
Ó Fearghail, F. 341, 343, 344
Ogg, G. 148
Olson, G.A. 348
Patte, A. 21
Patte, D. 21
Pesch, R. 64, 96
Plessis, I.I. du 341, 342
Plümacher, E. 4
Plummer, A. 98, 248, 306
Plutarch 79, 185, 187, 188, 194, 195, 226, 302
Praeder, S.M. 10, 11, 19, 22, 26
Radl, W. 10, 11, 73, 92
Rawlings, H. 186
Reicke, B. 340
Rengstorf, K.H. 260, 261
Rhoads, D. 2
Richards, K.H. 10, 33
Rienecker, F. 252
Riley, H. 270
Robertson, A.T. 197
Robinson, W.C. 148
Rolland, P. 63
Roloff, J. 60, 95, 100
Rosenblatt, L.M. 348
Russel, D.A. 79, 185, 187, 188, 302
Sabourin, L. 131, 152, 233, 236, 237, 239, 256, 288
Sanders, J.A. 202, 239
Schlatter, A. 97, 98, 99, 153, 235, 239, 240, 241, 248, 252, 253
Schneckenburger, M. 3, 10, 11
Schneider, G., 58, 96, 100, 153, 341, 343
Schramm, T. 242, 243, 244, 247, 252, 255, 298
Schulz, S. 177
Schürmann, H. 45, 96, 107, 117, 118, 130, 131, 132, 133, 139, 140, 142, 239, 243
Schwegler, A. 10, 11
Selden, R. 349
Sellin, G. 148
Sibinga, J. 178
Sisson, C.H. 191
Smalley, S. 183
Soards, M.L. 255

Stanton, G.N. 5
Starobinski, J. 21
Stein, R.H. 152, 153, 260, 270, 271, 272, 274, 303, 305, 318
Still, J. 345, 350, 353
Stock, A. 254
Streeter, B.H. 269, 296, 297, 298
Suetonius 185
Sweet, J.P.M. 182
Talbert, C.H. 2, 3, 4, 5, 6, 8, 10, 11,
14, 15, 22, 26, 73, 76, 77, 78, 79,
80, 81, 82, 83, 84, 85, 86, 87, 88,
89, 90, 91, 92, 93, 94, 95, 96, 97,
98, 99, 100, 101, 103, 104, 105,
106, 107, 108, 109, 110, 111, 112,
113, 114, 115, 116, 117, 118, 119,
120, 121, 123, 124, 126, 129, 130,
131, 132, 133, 134, 135, 137, 138,
139, 140, 141, 142, 143, 146, 147,
148, 150, 151, 152, 153, 154, 155,
157, 158, 159, 160, 161, 164, 173,
181, 184, 185, 188, 189, 193, 194,
214, 215, 227, 228, 231, 262, 286,
313, 320, 321, 322, 327, 328, 329,
330, 331, 333, 334, 335, 337, 338,
339, 340, 341, 342
Tannehill, R.C. 2, 3, 4, 5, 6, 8, 9, 10,
11, 12, 14, 17, 18, 20, 26, 33, 34,
35, 36, 37, 38, 39, 40, 41, 42, 43,
44, 45, 46, 47, 48, 49, 50, 51, 52,
53, 54, 55, 56, 57, 58, 59, 60, 61,
63, 64, 65, 66, 67, 68, 70, 71, 72,
73, 74, 76, 77, 78, 81, 85, 95, 121,
157, 164, 197, 227, 232, 239, 267,
287, 320, 321, 322
Taylor, V. 21, 296
Thalmann, W.G. 188
Thucydides 186, 194, 195, 226, 227
Turner, N. 197
Unnik, W.C. van 4
Vergil 79, 80, 188, 189, 191, 192, 195, 200, 302
Voelz, J.W. 346, 349, 353
Völkel, M. 341, 342, 343
Vorster, W.S. 347, 349, 353, 354
Vries, S.J. de 169
Wardman, A. 185, 187
Welzen, H. 346, 354
Wenham, D. 9, 222
Weren, W.J.C. 354

Wilkens, W. 5, 31
Wimsatt, W.K. 348, 349, 350
Winterbottom, M. 79
Wolde, E. van, 351 352
Worton, M. 345, 350, 353

Wright, N.T. 21
York, J.O. 305
Zeller, E. 10, 11
Zmijewski, J. 251

Paternoster Biblical Monographs

(All titles uniform with this volume)
Dates in bold are of projected publication

Joseph Abraham
Eve: Accused or Acquitted?
A Reconsideration of Feminist Readings of the Creation Narrative Texts in Genesis 1–3
Two contrary views dominate contemporary feminist biblical scholarship. One finds in the Bible an unequivocal equality between the sexes from the very creation of humanity, whilst the other sees the biblical text as irredeemably patriarchal and androcentric. Dr Abraham enters into dialogue with both camps as well as introducing his own method of approach. An invaluable tool for any one who is interested in this contemporary debate.
2002 / 0-85364-971-5 / xxiv + 272pp

Octavian D. Baban
Mimesis and Luke's On the Road Encounters in Luke-Acts
Luke's Theology of the Way and its Literary Representation
The book argues on theological and literary (mimetic) grounds that Luke's on-the-road encounters, especially those belonging to the post-Easter period, are part of his complex theology of the Way. Jesus' teaching and that of the apostles is presented by Luke as a challenging answer to the Hellenistic reader's thirst for adventure, good literature, and existential paradigms.
2005 / 1-84227253-5 / approx. 374pp

Paul Barker
The Triumph of Grace in Deuteronomy
This book is a textual and theological analysis of the interaction between the sin and faithlessness of Israel and the grace of Yahweh in response, looking especially at Deuteronomy chapters 1–3, 8–10 and 29–30. The author argues that the grace of Yahweh is determinative for the ongoing relationship between Yahweh and Israel and that Deuteronomy anticipates and fully expects Israel to be faithless.
2004 / 1-84227-226-8 / xxii + 270pp

Jonathan F. Bayes
The Weakness of the Law
God's Law and the Christian in New Testament Perspective
A study of the four New Testament books which refer to the law as weak (Acts, Romans, Galatians, Hebrews) leads to a defence of the third use in the Reformed debate about the law in the life of the believer.
2000 / 0-85364-957-X / xii + 244pp

November 2004

Mark Bonnington
The Antioch Episode of Galatians 2:11-14 in Historical and Cultural Context

The Galatians 2 'incident' in Antioch over table-fellowship suggests significant disagreement between the leading apostles. This book analyses the background to the disagreement by locating the incident within the dynamics of social interaction between Jews and Gentiles. It proposes a new way of understanding the relationship between the individuals and issues involved.

2005 / 1-84227-050-8 / approx. 350pp

David Bostock
A Portrayal of Trust
The Theme of Faith in the Hezekiah Narratives

This study provides detailed and sensitive readings of the Hezekiah narratives (2 Kings 18–20 and Isaiah 36–39) from a theological perspective. It concentrates on the theme of faith, using narrative criticism as its methodology. Attention is paid especially to setting, plot, point of view and characterization within the narratives. A largely positive portrayal of Hezekiah emerges that underlines the importance and relevance of scripture.

2005 / 1-84227-314-0 / approx. 300pp

Mark Bredin
Jesus, Revolutionary of Peace
A Non-violent Christology in the Book of Revelation

This book aims to demonstrate that the figure of Jesus in the Book of Revelation can best be understood as an active non-violent revolutionary.

2003 / 1-84227-153-9 / xviii + 262pp

Robinson Butarbutar
Resolving a Dispute, Past and Present
An Exegetical Study of Paul's Apostolic Paradigm in 1 Corinthians 9

The author sees the apostolic paradigm in 1 Corinthians 9 as part of Paul's unified arguments in 1 Corinthians 8–10 in which he seeks to mediate in the dispute over the issue of food offered to idols. The book also sees its relevance for dispute-resolution today, taking the conflict within the author's church as an example.

2005 / 1-84227315-9 / approx. 280pp

Daniel J-S Chae
Paul as Apostle to the Gentiles
His Apostolic Self-awareness and its Influence on the Soteriological Argument in Romans
Opposing 'the post-Holocaust interpretation of Romans', Daniel Chae competently demonstrates that Paul argues for the equality of Jew and Gentile in Romans. Chae's fresh exegetical interpretation is academically outstanding and spiritually encouraging.
1997 / 0-85364-829-8 / xiv + 378pp

Luke L. Cheung
The Genre, Composition and Hermeneutics of the Epistle of James
The present work examines the employment of the wisdom genre with a certain compositional structure and the interpretation of the law through the Jesus tradition of the double love command by the author of the Epistle of James to serve his purpose in promoting perfection and warning against doubleness among the eschatologically renewed people of God in the Diaspora.
2003 / 1-84227-062-1 / xvi + 372pp

Youngmo Cho
Spirit and Kingdom in the Writings of Luke and Paul
The relationship between Spirit and Kingdom is a relatively unexplored area in Lukan and Pauline studies. This book offers a fresh perspective of two biblical writers on the subject. It explores the difference between Luke's and Paul's understanding of the Spirit by examining the specific question of the relationship of the concept of the Spirit to the concept of the Kingdom of God in each writer.
2005 / 1-84227-316-7 / approx. 270pp

Andrew C. Clark
Parallel Lives
The Relation of Paul to the Apostles in the Lucan Perspective
This study of the Peter-Paul parallels in Acts argues that their purpose was to emphasize the themes of continuity in salvation history and the unity of the Jewish and Gentile missions. New light is shed on Luke's literary techniques, partly through a comparison with Plutarch.
2001 / 1-84227-035-4 / xviii + 386pp

November 2004

Andrew D. Clarke
Secular and Christian Leadership in Corinth
A Socio-Historical and Exegetical Study of 1 Corinthians 1–6

This volume is an investigation into the leadership structures and dynamics of first-century Roman Corinth. These are compared with the practice of leadership in the Corinthian Christian community which are reflected in 1 Corinthians 1–6, and contrasted with Paul's own principles of Christian leadership

2005 / 1-84227-229-2 / 200pp

Stephen Finamore
God, Order and Chaos
René Girard and the Apocalypse

Readers are often disturbed by the images of destruction in the book of Revelation and unsure why they are unleashed after the exaltation of Jesus. This book examines past approaches to these texts and uses René Girard's theories to revive some old ideas and propose some new ones.

2005 / 1-84227-197-0 / approx. 344pp

Scott J. Hafemann
Suffering and Ministry in the Spirit
Paul's Defence of His Ministry in II Corinthians 2:14–3:3

Shedding new light on the way Paul defended his apostleship, the author offers a careful, detailed study of 2 Corinthians 2:14–3:3 linked with other key passages throughout 1 and 2 Corinthians. Demonstrating the unity and coherence of Paul's argument in this passage, the author shows that Paul's suffering served as the vehicle for revealing God's power and glory through the Spirit.

2000 / 0-85364-967-7 / xiv + 262pp

Scott J. Hafemann
Paul, Moses and the History of Israel
The Letter/Spirit Contrast and the Argument from Scripture in 2 Corinthians 3

An exegetical study of the call of Moses, the second giving of the Law (Exodus 32–34), the new covenant, and the prophetic understanding of the history of Israel in 2 Corinthians 3. Hafemann's work demonstrates Paul's contextual use of the Old Testament and the essential unity between the Law and the Gospel within the context of the distinctive ministries of Moses and Paul.

2005 / 1-84227-317-5 / 498pp

November 2004

Douglas S. McComiskey
Lukan Theology in the Light of the Gospel's Literary Structure
Luke's Gospel was purposefully written with theology embedded in its patterned literary structure. A critical analysis of this cyclical structure provides new windows into Luke's interpretation of the individual pericopes comprising the Gospel and illuminates several of his theological interests.
2004 / 1-84227-148-2 / approx. 400pp

Stephen Motyer
Your Father the Devil?
A New Approach to John and 'The Jews'
Who are 'the Jews' in John's Gospel? Defending John against the charge of antisemitism, Motyer argues that, far from demonising the Jews, the Gospel seeks to present Jesus as 'Good News for Jews' in a late first century setting.
1997 / 0-85364-832-8 / xiv + 260pp

Esther Ng
Reconstructing Christian Origins?
The Feminist Theology of Elizabeth Schüssler Fiorenza: An Evaluation
In a detailed evaluation, the author challenges Elizabeth Schüssler Fiorenza's reconstruction of early Christian origins and her underlying presuppositions. The author also presents her own views on women's roles both then and now.
2002 / 1-84227-055-9 / xxiv + 468pp

Robin Parry
Old Testament Story and Christian Ethics
The Rape of Dinah as a Case Study
What is the role of story in ethics and, more particularly, what is the role of Old Testament story in Christian ethics? This book, drawing on the work of contemporary philosophers, argues that narrative is crucial in the ethical shaping of people and, drawing on the work of contemporary Old Testament scholars, that story plays a key role in Old Testament ethics. Parry then argues that when situated in canonical context Old Testament stories can be reappropriated by Christian readers in their own ethical formation. The shocking story of the rape of Dinah and the massacre of the Shechemites provides a fascinating case study for exploring the parameters within which Christian ethical appropriations of Old Testament stories can live.
2004 / 1-84227-210-1 / xx + 350pp

Ian Paul
Power to See the World Anew
The Value of Paul Ricoeur's Hermeneutic of Metaphor in Interpreting the Symbolism of Revelation 12 and 13

This book is a study of the hermeneutics of metaphor of Paul Ricoeur, one of the most important writers on hermeneutics and metaphor of the last century. It sets out the key points of his theory, important criticisms of his work, and how his approach, modified in the light of these criticisms, offers a methodological framework for reading apocalyptic texts.

2005 / 1-84227-056-7 / approx. 350pp

Robert L. Plummer
Paul's Understanding of the Church's Mission
Did the Apostle Paul Expect the Early Christian Communities to Evangelize?

This book engages in a careful study of Paul's letters to determine if the apostle expected the communities to which he wrote to engage in missionary activity. It helpfully summarizes the discussion on this debated issue, judiciously handling contested texts, and provides a way forward in addressing this critical question. While admitting that Paul rarely explicitly commands the communities he founded to evangelize, Plummer amasses significant incidental data to provide a convincing case that Paul did indeed expect his churches to engage in mission activity. Throughout the study, Plummer progressively builds a theological basis for the church's mission that is both distinctively Pauline and compelling.

2005 / 0-85364-333-7 / approx. 324pp

David Powys
'Hell': A Hard Look at a Hard Question
The Fate of the Unrighteous in New Testament Thought

This comprehensive treatment seeks to unlock the original meaning of terms and phrases long thought to support the traditional doctrine of hell. It concludes that there is an alternative—one which is more biblical, and which can positively revive the rationale for Christian mission.

1997 / 0-85364-831-X / xxii + 478pp

Sorin Sabou
Between Horror and Hope
Paul's Metaphorical Language of Death in Romans 6.1-11

This book argues that Paul's metaphorical language of death in Romans 6.1-11 conveys two aspects: horror and hope. The 'horror' aspect is conveyed by the 'crucifixion' language, and the 'hope' aspect by 'burial' language. The life of the Christian believer is understood, as relationship with sin is concerned ('death to sin'), between these two realities: horror and hope.

2005 / 1-84227-322-1 / approx. 224pp

November 2004

Rosalind Selby
The Comical Doctrine
Mark and Hermeneutics
This book argues that the gospel breaks through postmodernity's critique of truth and the referential possibilities of textuality with its gift of grace. With a rigorous, philosophical challenge to modernist and postmodernist assumptions, Selby offers an alternative epistemology to all who would still read with faith *and* with academic credibility.
2005 / 1-84227-212-8 / approx. 350pp

Kevin Walton
Thou Traveller Unknown
The Presence and Absence of God in the Jacob Narrative
The author offers a fresh reading of the story of Jacob in the book of Genesis through the paradox of divine presence and absence. The work also seeks to make a contribution to Pentateuchal studies by bringing together a close reading of the final text with historical critical insights, doing justice to the text's historical depth, final form and canonical status.
2003 / 1-84227-059-1 / xvi + 238pp

George M. Wieland
The Significance of Salvation
A Study of Salvation Language in the Pastoral Epistles
The language and ideas of salvation pervade the three Pastoral Epistles. This study offers a close examination of their soteriological statements. In all three letters the idea of salvation is found to play a vital paraenetic role, but each also exhibits distinctive soteriological emphases. The results challenge common assumptions about the Pastoral Epistles as a corpus.
2005 / 1-84227257-8 / approx. 324pp

Alistair Wilson
When Will These Things Happen?
A Study of Jesus as Judge in Matthew 21–25
This study seeks to allow Matthew's carefully constructed presentation of Jesus to be given full weight in the modern evaluation of Jesus' eschatology. Careful analysis of the text of Matthew 21–25 reveals Jesus to be standing firmly in the Jewish prophetic and wisdom traditions as he proclaims and enacts imminent judgement on the Jewish authorities then boldly claims the central role in the final and universal judgement.
2004 / 1-84227-146-6 / xxii + 272pp

Lindsay Wilson
Joseph Wise and Otherwise
The Intersection of Covenant and Wisdom in Genesis 37–50
This book offers a careful literary reading of Genesis 37–50 that argues that the Joseph story contains both strong covenant themes and many wisdom-like elements. The connections between the two helps to explore how covenant and wisdom might intersect in an integrated biblical theology.
2004 / 1-84227-140-7 / xvi + 340pp

Stephen I. Wright
The Voice of Jesus
Studies in the Interpretation of Six Gospel Parables
This literary study considers how the 'voice' of Jesus has been heard in different periods of parable interpretation, and how the categories of figure and trope may help us towards a sensitive reading of the parables today.
2000 / 0-85364-975-8 / xiv + 280pp

Paternoster
PO Box 300,
Carlisle,
Cumbria CA3 0QS,
United Kingdom
Web: www.authenticmedia.co.uk/paternoster

November 2004

Paternoster Theological Monographs
(All titles uniform with this volume)
Dates in bold are of projected publication

Emil Bartos
Deification in Eastern Orthodox Theology
An Evaluation and Critique of the Theology of Dumitru Staniloae
Bartos studies a fundamental yet neglected aspect of Orthodox theology: deification. By examining the doctrines of anthropology, christology, soteriology and ecclesiology as they relate to deification, he provides an important contribution to contemporary dialogue between Eastern and Western theologians.
1999 / 0-85364-956-1 / xii + 370pp

Iain D. Campbell
Fixing the Indemnity
The Life and Work of George Adam Smith
When Old Testament scholar George Adam Smith (1856–1942) delivered the Lyman Beecher lectures at Yale University in 1899, he confidently declared that 'modern criticism has won its war against traditional theories. It only remains to fix the amount of the indemnity.' In this biography, Iain D. Campbell assesses Smith's critical approach to the Old Testament and evaluates its consequences, showing that Smith's life and work still raises questions about the relationship between biblical scholarship and evangelical faith.
2004 / 1-84227-228-4 / xx + 256pp

Tim Chester
Mission and the Coming of God
Eschatology, the Trinity and Mission in the Theology of Jürgen Moltmann
This book explores the theology and missiology of the influential contemporary theologian, Jürgen Moltmann. It highlights the important contribution Moltmann has made while offering a critique of his thought from an evangelical perspective. In so doing, it touches on pertinent issues for evangelical missiology. The conclusion takes Calvin as a starting point, proposing 'an eschatology of the cross' which offers a critique of the over-realised eschatologies in liberation theology and certain forms of evangelicalism.
2005 / 1-84227-320-5 / approx. 224pp

Sylvia Wilkey Collinson
Making Disciples
The Significance of Jesus' Educational Strategy for Today's Church
This study examines the biblical practice of discipling, formulates a definition, and makes comparisons with modern models of education. A recommendation is made for greater attention to its practice today.

2004 / 1-84227-116-4 / xiv + 278pp

Darrell Cosden
A Theology of Work
Work and the New Creation
Through dialogue with Moltmann, Pope John Paul II and others, this book develops a genitive 'theology of work', presenting a theological definition of work and a model for a theological ethics of work that shows work's nature, value and meaning now and eschatologically. Work is shown to be a transformative activity consisting of three dynamically inter-related dimensions: the instrumental, relational and ontological.

2004 / 1-84227-332-9 / xvi + 208pp

Stephen M. Dunning
The Crisis and the Quest
A Kierkegaardian Reading of Charles Williams
Employing Kierkegaardian categories and analysis, this study investigates both the central crisis in Charles Williams's authorship between hermetism and Christianity (Kierkegaard's Religions A and B), and the quest to resolve this crisis, a quest that ultimately presses the bounds of orthodoxy.

2000 / 0-85364-985-5 / xxiv + 254pp

Keith Ferdinando
The Triumph of Christ in African Perspective
A Study of Demonology and Redemption in the African Context
The book explores the implications of the gospel for traditional African fears of occult aggression. It analyses such traditional approaches to suffering and biblical responses to fears of demonic evil, concluding with an evaluation of African beliefs from the perspective of the gospel.

1999 / 0-85364-830-1 / xviii + 450pp

Andrew Goddard
Living the Word, Resisting the World
The Life and Thought of Jacques Ellul
This work offers a definitive study of both the life and thought of the French Reformed thinker Jacques Ellul (1912-1994). It will prove an indispensable resource for those interested in this influential theologian and sociologist and for Christian ethics and political thought generally.
2002 / 1-84227-053-2 / xxiv + 378pp

David Hilborn
The Words of our Lips
Language-Use in Free Church Worship
Studies of liturgical language have tended to focus on the written canons of Roman Catholic and Anglican communities. By contrast, David Hilborn analyses the more extemporary approach of English Nonconformity. Drawing on recent developments in linguistic pragmatics, he explores similarities and differences between 'fixed' and 'free' worship, and argues for the interdependence of each.
2005 / 0-85364-977-4

Roger Hitching
The Church and Deaf People
A Study of Identity, Communication and Relationships with Special Reference to the Ecclesiology of Jürgen Moltmann
In *The Church and Deaf People* Roger Hitching sensitively examines the history and present experience of deaf people and finds similarities between aspects of sign language and Moltmann's theological method that 'open up' new ways of understanding theological concepts.
2003 / 1-84227-222-5 / xxii + 236pp

John G. Kelly
One God, One People
The Differentiated Unity of the People of God in the Theology of Jürgen Moltmann
The author expounds and critiques Moltmann's doctrine of God and highlights the systematic connections between it and Moltmann's influential discussion of Israel. He then proposes a fresh approach to Jewish-Christian relations building on Moltmann's work using insights from Habermas and Rawls.
2005 / 0-85346-969-3 / approx. 350pp

Mark F.W. Lovatt
Confronting the Will-to-Power
A Reconsideration of the Theology of Reinhold Niebuhr
Confronting the Will-to-Power is an analysis of the theology of Reinhold Niebuhr, arguing that his work is an attempt to identify, and provide a practical theological answer to, the existence and nature of human evil.

2001 / 1-84227-054-0 / xviii + 216pp

Neil B. MacDonald
Karl Barth and the Strange New World within the Bible
Barth, Wittgenstein, and the Metadilemmas of the Enlightenment
Barth's discovery of the strange new world within the Bible is examined in the context of Kant, Hume, Overbeck, and, most importantly, Wittgenstein. MacDonald covers some fundamental issues in theology today: epistemology, the final form of the text and biblical truth-claims.

2000 / 0-85364-970-7 / xxvi + 374pp

Keith Mascord
No Challenge Unfaced
Alvin Plantinga's Contribution to Christian Apologetics
This book draws together the contributions of the philosopher, Alvin Plantinga, to the major contemporary challenges to Christian belief, highlighting in particular his ground-breaking work in epistemology and the problem of evil. Plantinga's theory that both theistic and Christian belief is warrantedly basic is explored and critiqued, and an assessment offered as to the significance of his work for apologetic theory and practice.

2005 / 1-84227-256-X / approx. 304pp

Gillian McCulloch
The Deconstruction of Dualism in Theology
With Reference to Ecofeminist Theology and New Age Spirituality
This book challenges eco-theological anti-dualism in Christian theology, arguing that dualism has a twofold function in Christian religious discourse. Firstly, it enables us to express the discontinuities and divisions that are part of the process of reality. Secondly, dualistic language allows us to express the mysteries of divine transcendence/immanence and the survival of the soul without collapsing into monism and materialism, both of which are problematic for Christian epistemology.

2002 / 1-84227-044-3 / xii + 282pp

November 2004

Leslie McCurdy
Attributes and Atonement
The Holy Love of God in the Theology of P.T. Forsyth
Attributes and Atonement is an intriguing full-length study of P.T. Forsyth's doctrine of the cross as it relates particularly to God's holy love. It includes an unparalleled bibliography of both primary and secondary material relating to Forsyth.
1999 / 0-85364-833-6 / xiv + 328pp

Nozomu Miyahira
Towards a Theology of the Concord of God
A Japanese Perspective on the Trinity
This book introduces a new Japanese theology and a unique Trinitarian formula based on the Japanese intellectual climate: three betweennesses and one concord. It also presents a new interpretation of the Trinity, a co-subordinationism, which is in line with orthodox Trinitarianism; each single person of the Trinity is eternally and equally subordinate (or serviceable) to the other persons, so that they retain the mutual dynamic equality.
2000 / 0-85364-863-8 / xiv + 256pp

Eddy José Muskus
The Origins and Early Development of Liberation Theology in Latin America
With Particular Reference to Gustavo Gutiérrez
This work challenges the fundamental premise of Liberation Theology, 'opting for the poor', and its claim that Christ is found in them. It also argues that Liberation Theology emerged as a direct result of the failure of the Roman Catholic Church in Latin America.
2002 / 0-85364-974-X / xiv + 296pp

Jim Purves
The Triune God and the Charismatic Movement
A Critical Appraisal from a Scottish Perspective
All emotion and no theology? Or a fundamental challenge to reappraise and realign our trinitarian theology in the light of Christian experience? This study of charismatic renewal as it found expression within Scotland at the end of the twentieth century evaluates the use of Patristic, Reformed and contemporary models of the Trinity in explaining the workings of the Holy Spirit.
2004 / 1-84227-321-3 / xxiv + 246pp

November 2004

Anna Robbins
Methods in the Madness
Diversity in Twentieth-Century Christian Social Ethics
The author compares the ethical methods of Walter Rauschenbusch, Reinhold Niebuhr and others. She argues that unless Christians are clear about the ways that theology and philosophy are expressed practically they may lose the ability to discuss social ethics across contexts, let alone reach effective agreements.
2004 / 1-84227-211-X / xx + 294pp

Ed Rybarczyk
Beyond Salvation
Eastern Orthodoxy and Classical Pentecostalism on becoming like Christ
At first glance eastern Orthodoxy and classical Pentecostalism seem quite distinct. This ground-breaking study shows they share much in common, especially as it concerns the experiential elements of following Christ. Both traditions assert that authentic Christianity transcends the wooden categories of modernism.
2004 / 1-84227-144-X / xii + 356pp

Signe Sandsmark
Is World View Neutral Education Possible and Desirable?
A Christian Response to Liberal Arguments
(Published jointly with The Stapleford Centre)
This book discusses reasons for belief in world view neutrality, and argues that 'neutral' education will have a hidden, but strong world view influence. It discusses the place for Christian education in the common school.
2000 / 0-85364-973-1 / xiv + 182pp

Hazel Sherman
Reading Zechariah
The Allegorical Tradition of Biblical Interpretation through the Commentary of Didymus the Blind and Theodore of Mopsuestia
A close reading of the commentary on Zechariah by Didymus the Blind alongside that of Theodore of Mopsuestia suggests that popular categorising of Antiochene and Alexandrian biblical exegesis as 'historical' or 'allegorical' is inadequate and misleading.
2005 / 1-84227-213-6 / approx. 280pp

Andrew Sloane
On Being a Christian in the Academy
Nicholas Wolterstorff and the Practice of Christian Scholarship
An exposition and critical appraisal of Nicholas Wolterstorff's epistemology in the light of the philosophy of science, and an application of his thought to the practice of Christian scholarship.
2003 / 1-84227-058-3 / xvi + 274pp

Damon So
Jesus' Revelation of His Father
A Narrative-Conceptual Study of the Trinity with Special Reference to Karl Barth
This book explores the trinitarian dynamics in the context of Jesus' revelation of his Father in his earthly ministry with references to key passages in Matthew's Gospel. It develops from the exegeses of these passages a non-linear concept of revelation which links Jesus' communion with his Father to his revelatory words and actions through a nuanced understanding of the Holy Spirit, with references to K. Barth, G.W.H. Lampe, J.D.G. Dunn and E. Irving.
2005 / 1-84227-323-X / approx. 380pp

Daniel Strange
The Possibility of Salvation Among the Unevangelised
An Analysis of Inclusivism in Recent Evangelical Theology
For evangelical theologians the 'fate of the unevangelised' impinges upon fundamental tenets of evangelical identity. The position known as 'inclusivism', defined by the belief that the unevangelised can be ontologically saved by Christ whilst being epistemologically unaware of him, has been defended most vigorously by the Canadian evangelical Clark H. Pinnock. Through a detailed analysis and critique of Pinnock's work, this book examines a cluster of issues surrounding the unevangelised and its implications for christology, soteriology and the doctrine of revelation.
2002 / 1-84227-047-8 / xviii + 362pp

Scott Swain
God according to the Gospel
Biblical Narrative and the Identity of God in the Theology of Robert W. Jenson
Robert W. Jenson is one of the leading voices in contemporary Trinitarian theology. His boldest contribution in this area concerns his use of biblical narrative both to ground and explicate the Christian doctrine of God. *God according to the Gospel* critically examines Jenson's proposal and suggests an alternative way of reading the biblical portrayal of the triune God.
2006 / 1-84227-258-7 / approx. 180pp

Graham Tomlin
The Power of the Cross
Theology and the Death of Christ in Paul, Luther and Pascal
This book explores the theology of the cross in St Paul, Luther and Pascal. It offers new perspectives on the theology of each, and some implications for the nature of power, apologetics, theology and church life in a postmodern context.
1999 / 0-85364-984-7 / xiv + 344pp

Graham J. Watts
Revelation and the Spirit
A Comparative Study of the Relationship between the Doctrine of Revelation and Pneumatology in the Theology of Eberhard Jüngel and of Wolfhart Pannenberg
The relationship between Revelation and pneumatology is relatively unexplored. This approach offers a fresh angle on two important twentieth century theologians and raises pneumatological questions which are theologically crucial and relevant to mission in a postmodern culture.
2005 / 1-84227-104-0 / xxii + 232pp

Nigel G. Wright
Disavowing Constantine
Mission, Church and the Social Order in the Theologies of John Howard Yoder and Jürgen Moltmann
This book is a timely restatement of a radical theology of church and state in the Anabaptist and Baptist tradition. Dr Wright constructs his argument in dialogue and debate with Yoder and Moltmann, major contributors to a free church perspective.
2000 / 0-85364-978-2 / xvi + 252pp

Paternoster
PO Box 300,
Carlisle,
Cumbria CA3 0QS,
United Kingdom
Web: www.authenticmedia.co.uk/paternoster

November 2004

www.ingramcontent.com/pod-product-compliance
Lightning Source LLC
Chambersburg PA
CBHW071140300426
44113CB00009B/1037